President without a Party

THE LIFE OF JOHN TYLER

Christopher J. Leahy

LOUISIANA STATE UNIVERSITY PRESS

BATON ROUGE

Published with the assistance of the V. Ray Cardozier Fund

Published by Louisiana State University Press
lsupress.org

Third printing, 2023

DESIGNER: Mandy McDonald Scallan
TYPEFACE: Whitman
PRINTER AND BINDER: Sheridan Books

Library of Congress Cataloging-in-Publication Data
Names: Leahy, Christopher J., author.
Title: President without a Party : The Life of John Tyler / Christopher J.
  Leahy.
Description: Baton Rouge : Louisiana State University Press, [2020] |
  Includes bibliographical references and index.
Identifiers: LCCN 2019041356 (print) | LCCN 2019041357 (ebook) | ISBN
  978-0-8071-7254-4 (cloth) | ISBN 978-0-8071-7355-8 (pdf) | ISBN 978-0-8071-7354-1
  (epub)
Subjects: LCSH: Tyler, John, 1790–1862. | Presidents—United
  States—Biography. | United States—Politics and government—1841–1845.
Classification: LCC E397 .L43 2020 (print) | LCC E397 (ebook) | DDC
  973.5/8092 [B]—dc23
LC record available at https://lccn.loc.gov/2019041356
LC ebook record available at https://lccn.loc.gov/2019041357

To Sharon

and to the memories of

Patricia A. Leahy and

David R. Williams

Contents

Acknowledgments

Completing this work has taken far longer than I anticipated at the outset. During the course of my research and writing, I have benefited from the help of many people, and I am pleased at long last to be able to thank them for their assistance. I apologize in advance for anyone I inadvertently fail to mention. Any errors of fact or interpretation that may have remained in the book are entirely my own.

I spent weeks and months at various archives throughout the United States immersing myself in manuscript collections essential to understanding the life of John Tyler. At the Earl Gregg Swem Library at the College of William and Mary, Margaret Cook welcomed me at the very start of the project and alerted me to collections that proved crucial to my research. Her vast knowledge and good cheer made working at Swem Library one of the very best experiences of my career as a historian. I would also like to thank Susan Riggs, who often went above and beyond the call of duty to help me track down an obscure document. Susan also contacted me whenever William and Mary purchased another John Tyler letter.

The staff of the Virginia Historical Society in Richmond aided my research and writing in many ways. I would especially like to thank Nelson D. Lankford, whose support of my work was instrumental in me being awarded two Mellon Fellowships that allowed me to spend concentrated periods of time in the VHS collections. John McClure, director of library and research at the VHS, and Senior Archivist Eileen Parris helped with tying up loose ends as I completed the project. I thank Graham T. Dozier, Managing Editor of Publications and Virginius Dabney editor of the *Virginia Magazine of History and Biography,* for permission to reprint portions of two articles I published with the journal.

Reference librarians at the Library of Virginia in Richmond helped me navigate through pertinent collections and state documents located there. Brent Tarter encouraged me as I began the project, and his unsurpassed knowledge of Virginia's rich history helped me a great deal. Similarly, the staff at the Albert and Shirley Small Special Collections Library at the University of Virginia in Charlottesville was both welcoming and helpful. My research at the David M. Rubenstein Rare Book and Manuscript Library at Duke University yielded unexpected treasures that (I hope) greatly enhanced the book. I am grateful to the staff there and would like to especially thank Elizabeth Dunn. The Wilson Library at the University of North Carolina at Chapel Hill and UNC's Southern Historical Collection also proved important to my work. I thank the staff who helped me during my time in Chapel Hill. I would also like to thank the staff who aided me at the W. S. Hoole Special Collections Library at the University of Alabama in Tuscaloosa.

I was able to complete most of the research in the John Tyler Papers of the Library of Congress by using microfilm. When I did find it necessary to travel to Washington, DC, to work through Tyler papers not collected on microfilm, or when I wanted to look through other collections relevant to my project, I received a great deal of help and expertise from the staff at the Library of Congress. By chance one day, while working in the Madison Building, I also met and talked with Caspar Weinberger, secretary of defense under President Ronald Reagan, which was a welcome diversion from the seemingly endless William Cabell Rives Papers.

At Yale University's Sterling Memorial Library in New Haven, Connecticut, Michael Frost and Jessica Becker were especially helpful as I braved the massive collection of Gardiner-Tyler Family Papers. I requested hundreds of pages of photocopies of letters while I was at Yale, which the staff members cheerfully and expeditiously fulfilled to my great gratitude.

Archivists at libraries I did not visit personally also graciously provided me with photocopies of letters relevant to my project. I would like to thank the Albany Institute of History and Art, Albany, New York; Julie Koven of the American Jewish Historical Society, New York City; Maggie Heran of the Cincinnati Historical Society, Cincinnati, Ohio; Brian Moeller of the Huntington Library, Huntington, California; Kay Vander Meulen of Seymour Library, Knox College, Galesburg, Illinois; Elisabeth Proffen of the Maryland Historical Society, Baltimore; the Fales Library and Special Collections, Elmer Holmes Bobst Library, New York University, New York City; Sigrid P. Perry of the Charles Deering McCormick Library of Special Collections, Northwestern University, Evanston, Illinois; Dr. Edwin Frank of the Ned R. McWherter Library, University of Memphis, Memphis, Tennessee; and the Archives and Special Collections Department at Rensselaer Polytechnic Institute, Troy, New York.

Judith Ledbetter of Charles City County, Virginia, kindly shared her work on John Tyler's possible African American descendants with me.

Meghan Townes and Mark Fagerburg of the Library of Virginia facilitated the process whereby I secured permission to use the wonderful portrait from the library for the cover of the book.

A number of my former professors and colleagues encouraged me and provided feedback on my work on John Tyler over the years. They include Larry Shumsky at Virginia Tech University; Court Carney, John Rodrigue, Charles Royster, John Sacher, and Chad Vanderford at Louisiana State University; Jeffrey Bell, Sam Hyde, Michael Kurtz, Harry Laver, Peter Petrakis, and William Robison at Southeastern Louisiana University; and Sander Diamond and David Leon at Keuka College. My thanks to them all.

Bertram Wyatt-Brown offered words of wisdom as I began to revise my dissertation into this book and encouraged me to pursue publication with LSU Press. On a research trip to Duke University, I was fortunate to meet Robert Durden, who took an interest in my work and offered sound advice over lunch at the Duke Faculty Club.

A number of people read portions of this work, either as conference papers or after I completed a first draft, and offered valuable feedback. I would especially like to thank Fred Bailey, Fergus Bordewich, Andrew Burstein, Phillip Hamilton, John Lauritz Larson, and Harry L. Watson. Erik Chaput and Russ DeSimone read the chapter on the Dorr Rebellion and offered helpful suggestions. Christopher Childers read the book's early chapters and challenged me to sharpen the thematic aspect of the work. Robert Gudmestad took on the chore of reading the chapters covering Tyler's presidency and impressed upon me the importance of tightening the narrative. He also persuaded me that it is okay to leave some things on the cutting-room floor. I would also like to thank an anonymous reviewer of the manuscript for LSU Press.

The two institutional homes where I have climbed the ranks from assistant professor to full professor have greatly aided me in the completion of this work. At Southeastern Louisiana University my department head, William Robison, helped facilitate a University Faculty Grant that allowed me to spend a portion of one summer in Richmond and New Haven completing research. At Keuka College I want to thank the Faculty Development Committee, as well as President Jorge Diaz-Herrera and Vice President for Academic Affairs Anne Weed, for awarding me a sabbatical in the spring of 2015, when I completed a significant portion of the writing. My Division Chair at Keuka, Tom Tremer, has steadfastly supported my scholarly work. The interlibrary-loan staffs at both Southeastern and Keuka never failed to secure for me obscure journal articles and hard-to-find books. I thank especially Kimberly Fenton, Judith

Jones, Hilda Mannato, and Linda Park at Keuka for their help. I also want to take the opportunity to thank the students in my methods class at Keuka, who (somewhat) enthusiastically embraced the theme of John Tyler in the fall semester 2014. One of the students in that class, Richard Matrassi, deserves special mention for his perceptive reading of Tyler's "Ann Eliza" letter. Four other Keuka students—Kraig Connor, Daniel Esworthy, Matthew McFetridge, and Dillon Springer—never tired of asking me about Tyler and professed to have faith that I would complete the biography in due time.

My greatest intellectual debt is to my dissertation director, William J. Cooper. Through his impeccable scholarship, his towering reputation in the fields of southern history and antebellum politics, his masterly teaching, and his commitment to his graduate students, Bill has set a high standard for what it means to be an academic historian. I went to LSU with a single-minded purpose to work under his direction after having read two of his seminal books as an undergraduate, and he proved to be an outstanding, tough, and fair adviser. His influence permeates this biography, and I hope that he feels I have learned well at least some of the lessons he imparted. Bill played an instrumental role in launching my career, and his expectation that I would eventually finish this book, and his encouragement to keep going, buoyed me during some very low times. He also put me in touch with Christopher Childers. I cannot thank him enough.

I was fortunate to meet John Tyler's grandsons Lyon Tyler and Harrison Tyler during the course of my work on this book. Harrison graciously invited my wife and me to join the Tyler family for the US Army's ceremony at Richmond's Hollywood Cemetery commemorating President Tyler's birthday on March 29, 2004. He and his wife, Payne, also invited us to Thanksgiving dinner at Sherwood Forest in 2008, an experience we will never forget. We are grateful for their friendship and kindness and miss Payne, who died in February 2019. I also want to thank Harrison's son, William Tyler, and his wife, Kay, for their hospitality and interest in my work over the years.

At LSU Press I want to thank Editor in Chief Rand Dotson for his support and patience. I also want to thank Senior Editor Neal Novak; the book's designer, Mandy Scallan; and the marketing staff, especially Kate Barton, for their roles in bringing the book to life. Kevin Brock is a superb copyeditor and was a pleasure to work with.

My wife's family supported my work by providing lodging and by their interest in what I was doing. My mother-in-law, Marie Williams, deserves special thanks, as does my wife's aunt, Norma Williams. My brother-in-law, David R.

Williams, III, offered helpful editorial advice. I regret that my father-in-law, David R. Williams, Jr., did not live to see the publication of this book.

Finally, the most important acknowledgment. My wife, Sharon, never doubted that I could produce a biography of President Tyler, and if she doubted that I *would* produce it, she never let on. Sharon has been my biggest supporter, a tough and perceptive critic, and a source of unending comfort over the years it took to finish the book. She also has an uncanny ability to make me laugh when I need to most. A talented historian in her own right, she transcribed many of Julia Tyler's letters, has a fine ear for language and wields a wicked red pen; her favorite word as an editor is "condense." Thankfully, I am smart enough to take her advice most of the time. Dedicating the book to her seems a small and inadequate repayment for all that she has done for me along the way. I never could have done it without her. So, it is with much love that I offer the dedication and thank her for keeping the faith and for the indispensable role she played in ensuring that I completed what I set out to do.

President without a Party

Decision at Harrisburg

Nobody wanted the vice-presidential nomination. The party leaders tried to get Senator Benjamin Watkins Leigh of Virginia to take it, but he flatly refused their offer. Next, they tried former senator John M. Clayton of Delaware. He expected they might ask and prepared a written statement declining. Senator Nathaniel P. Tallmadge of New York also said no. So, too, did New Jersey senator Samuel L. Southard. At least two other men reportedly begged off. The man whom Pennsylvania Whigs wanted, Daniel Webster, was at that moment crossing the stormy Atlantic after completing a European tour and had not indicated his desire for the nomination.

The members of the General Committee of the Whig Party were understandably in a panic. They were having a difficult time completing the 1840 ticket so as to launch their campaign to unseat the incumbent president, Democrat Martin Van Buren. The Whigs had formed into a coalition opposed to Van Buren's predecessor, Andrew Jackson, in 1834 and offered voters a set of regional candidates for president in 1836. But it was not until the first week of December 1839 that they met in a national convention, this at the newly rebuilt Zion Lutheran Church in Harrisburg, Pennsylvania. There, delegates from twenty-two of the Union's twenty-six states nominated William Henry Harrison for president. Henry Clay had at one time been the frontrunner for the nomination, but his opponents at the convention maneuvered to deny him the prize and secure the top spot for the hero of the Battle of Tippecanoe. Now several prominent Whigs rebuffed attempts to enlist them as Harrison's running mate.[1]

Their refusal was understandable. John Adams, the nation's first vice president, had deemed the office insignificant and spent his two terms in George Washington's administration in virtual obscurity. Adams, of course, ended up winning the presidency in 1796. John C. Calhoun, on the other hand, twice accepted the vice presidency with the thought it would bolster his chances to capture the brass ring. He failed to reach the White House. The vice presidency was not usually a stepping stone to the presidency. In fact, only three of the nine men who served as vice president in the eight administrations before

1840 had been elected president. Surely, the men who refused the offer to join Harrison's ticket recognized this historical pattern.

John Tyler, however, had no qualms about the constitutionally undistinguished position. In fact, he was relatively confident the Whigs would prevail in 1840, so he saw his nomination for the post as a way to continue his national political career, which had ended with his resignation from the US Senate in 1836. The forty-nine-year-old Whig delegate from the Williamsburg district of Virginia eagerly accepted when party leaders approached him about joining the ticket. Striking the pose of disinterestedness honed by the politicians of an earlier time, but which had largely disappeared in an era of unabashed partisanship, he claimed later that his nomination "was up to the moment of its being made, wholly unanticipated by me." The Virginian claimed that he had "never reached forth [his] hand for any office." This was typical Tyler posturing and was not true. He had shrewdly advertised his availability by being named a convention delegate and showing up in Harrisburg. He had all but jumped up and down and begged the convention to choose him. Easy to pick out in a crowd, Tyler was tall—roughly six feet, one inch in height—and thin, with blue-gray eyes, receding sandy-colored hair, a high forehead, and a prominent nose. He worked the spacious second-floor sanctuary of the church where the proceedings were held with the smooth assurance of a consummate politician. Catching up with men he already knew or introducing himself to men he did not, he was in his element. And in the end, of the 231 votes cast for vice president at the conclave, John Tyler received every last one of them. Whig chieftains breathed a sigh of relief.[2]

The difficulty the Whigs faced in coming up with a vice-presidential nominee demonstrated that their party lacked cohesiveness and coherence. They seemed to be in disarray. What prompted the General Committee to settle on Tyler was not merely desperation, though it surely seemed like that on the surface. In fact, his nomination made sense for a number of reasons. For one thing, he was a Clay delegate and had come to Harrisburg to vote for the former secretary of state and Speaker of the House—and current senator—from Kentucky. He fulfilled his duty. A story circulated at the convention that Tyler had "shed tears" when Harrison surrogates had wrested the presidential nomination from the man generally regarded as the heart and soul of the Whig Party. Tyler had not wept, but Clay had been the presumptive nominee. Now the party sought to mollify Clay—if indeed that could be done—by placing one of his avowed supporters on the ticket with Harrison. "It was an attempt of the triumphant Harrisonites to heal the wounds of Mr. Clay's devoted friends," wrote one observer. The irony of that effort would become apparent later.[3]

Tyler brought other benefits to the nomination. He boasted an impressive political resume, having served in the Virginia legislature, as the Old Dominion's governor, and as a congressman and senator. He was a southerner who would balance Harrison—by this time a resident of Ohio—on the ticket. He had also run for vice president as a regional Whig candidate in the campaign of 1836 and had instant name recognition, especially south of the Mason-Dixon Line. The *Washington Daily National Intelligencer,* the Whig Party's newspaper in the capital, confidently pointed out that "all intelligent citizens are acquainted with [Tyler's] character and abilities, both of which qualify him to discharge with ability and honor the trust which he is invited to accept."[4]

But if Tyler's nomination had clear merit, in other respects his selection was a curious one. Along with that name recognition came clear indications of where he stood on the vital issues of the day—and throughout his long career as a champion of Old Republican, states' rights ideology, he had demonstrated positions that were decidedly not within the mainstream of the Whig Party. For example, he had long opposed a national bank. President Jackson had killed the Second Bank of the United States in 1836. Whigs looked to create a third bank if they could win control of Congress and the White House in 1840, believing their efforts could return the county to economic prosperity after the bleak years that followed the Panic of 1837. The party also favored higher tariffs to stimulate and protect American industry. Yet as a supporter of free trade, Tyler had reflexively favored low duties and made that position clear many times. In addition, he had also once been a Jacksonian Democrat. Did any of this matter? The Whigs apparently thought not.

So out of the Harrisburg convention emerged the Harrison-Tyler ticket, and what is surely the most recognizable presidential campaign slogan of all time—"Tippecanoe and Tyler, Too." The Whig diarist Philip Hone would later write that "there was rhyme but no reason in it," suggesting that perhaps the Whigs should have given more thought to whether Tyler could reconcile his longstanding political views with the principles of the party.[5]

But nobody thought to ask.

INTRODUCTION

John Tyler advanced to the pinnacle of American politics on April 4, 1841, because the man who preceded him in office—William Henry Harrison—died just thirty-two days into his term as president. Tyler's political opponents, who quickly dubbed him "His Accidency," never tired of reminding him how he had ended up in the White House as the nation's tenth chief executive. Many—if not most—of these men regarded Tyler as a mediocrity, as someone not fit for the high station in which he found himself.

This was more than just sour grapes. It is true that when placed alongside the leading politicians of his era, Tyler comes up short. He had neither the intellectual ability of John C. Calhoun nor the organizational genius of Martin Van Buren. He could not match the beguiling charisma of Henry Clay or the inspired oratory of Daniel Webster. In fact, he often seemed to be a mere bit player while these other men starred on the stage of national politics. Yet Tyler's career surpassed them all, with the exception of Van Buren, the eighth president of the United States—and Tyler's tenure in the White House was much more consequential than Van Buren's. He confounded them all. Why?

The answer can be found in the three main themes of Tyler's life and career. First, he was a southerner. When the Whig Party nominated him for the vice presidency as Harrison's running mate, geography clinched the deal. Where he came from mattered. Fate took over from there. Tyler was very much a southern man. His attachment to the South and the strong sense of place that came with it shaped every aspect of his life. It defined his politics. As a public figure, Tyler unapologetically defended the South against external threats by using the region's primary political principles—states' rights and a strict construction of the Constitution—as rhetorical weapons. Before his presidency, he took on a hostile US Supreme Court, flayed an increasingly nationalistic agenda in Congress, fought what he argued was President Andrew Jackson's abuse of power, and skewered a growing abolitionist movement. Once he occupied the White House, he tended to champion more moderate policies and usually acted in the best interests of the entire nation, though he never lost sight of his goal to ensure the safety of the South. His attitude toward the institution of slavery reflected the ambivalence found in so many of his fellow southerners. Like his idol Thomas Jefferson, he hoped for slavery's end but (also like Jefferson) did nothing to ensure its ultimate demise. In fact, his pursuit of the annexation of Texas while he served as president reignited the vexing question of slavery's spread into the territories and exacerbated the sectional conflict between North and South. Tyler's role in this should not be minimized. Nor should we forget or absolve him from his support for and participation in the slave system that promoted white supremacy and ultimately brought about the Civil War.

Tyler's southern identity was foundational to his private life. The South's honor culture drove his social world and provided him with the ballast he needed to negotiate through life's difficulties. He did his best to adhere to its dictates but often fell short of the mark. Indeed, his poor handling of money and the unceasing cycle of debt that seemed to define him often placed him at the mercy of other men and undermined his independence. Living in a society that prized a man's mastery over everything and everyone in his life, Tyler found this an especially bitter pill to swallow, all the more so because the good opinion of others mattered to him. He also struggled with poor health for most of his life and was acutely aware of how southern society tended to associate physical prowess with what historian Bertram Wyatt-Brown calls "inner merit." Despite his personal failings, and despite his deviations from some of the tenets of the culture of honor, Tyler's life is a case study in how the southern master class developed and how its culture influenced politics.[1]

As a corollary to his southern identity, John Tyler was a proud Virginian—a Tidewater Virginian at that. In the political arena he often conflated the interests of Virginia with the interests of the South, and for his entire life, he clung to the belief that his native state served as the bellwether for the entire region, even when faced with evidence to the contrary. His love of the Old Dominion reflected his pride in his family's status as one of the First Families of Virginia, in the stature of Virginia as the wellspring of the ideas of the Founding Fathers, and in the primacy of Virginia in shaping the politics of the early American republic. From his father, himself a minor figure in the Revolution and the founding of the country, Tyler inherited a belief in the virtue of public life and the guiding principles he employed in service to the South and his home state.

Yet his devotion to the South and to Virginia often handicapped him by closing his mind to possibilities that other, more worldly men could imagine for the country and for themselves. He often acted as if the whole world revolved around the place where he had been born. For most of his life, the extent of his travel was the well-worn route between Virginia and Washington, DC. His second wife, in fact, was much more cosmopolitan than he, having spent a year abroad as a young woman. In politics Tyler often betrayed his provincialism and played the part of a reactionary. He could be inflexible and self-righteous as he defended his principles. To his credit, when placed into positions of executive authority—first as governor of Virginia and later as president of the United States—he overcame this shortcoming, exhibiting an innovation that surprised the political commentators who often portrayed him as an unbending ideologue who lacked vision. Historians and biographers have long argued that Tyler's ideology hampered him as president and forestalled compromise. My account of his presidency shows that it did not.

Tyler also displayed an independent streak as a politician. In fact, at times he seemed to have no use for formal party affiliations. He was an Old Republican who pledged fealty to the states' rights bible of the Virginia and Kentucky Resolutions, but beyond that it was difficult to pin him down. He became a Jacksonian Democrat but consistently opposed President Jackson. He became a Whig but usually opposed the party's nationalistic agenda. When he did so in the White House, party members banished him, making him a president without a party. Charges of partisan disloyalty never troubled Tyler. In fact, he seemed to enjoy his reputation as a political renegade.

More broadly, Tyler was a member of the generation that oversaw the destruction of the Union that the Revolution had created—American history's ultimate example of political failure. An examination of his life in politics reveals the fundamental tension that existed between his identity as a southerner and Virginian and his genuine love for that Union. When forced in April 1861 to decide whether to remain true to the country or to his home state and region, he chose Virginia and the South and essentially renounced his US citizenship, thereby tarnishing his reputation forever and affixing himself with the appellation "traitor president." In fact, Tyler played a significant role in ensuring Virginia's secession from the Union.

He could not help himself. At big political moments, Tyler wanted to be in on the action, a fact that highlights the second theme of his life: his addiction to politics. From his childhood, his father groomed him for public life.

His upbringing, his education, and his training as a lawyer prepared him for a political career. Tyler honed the gentility that he believed should define a man who aspires to public life. And it was in the national arena that he intended to make his mark. National politics became the means by which he satisfied an overweening ambition and overcame his chronic ill health. Tyler measured his self-worth primarily through his national political career. His status as a national politician became the dominant strand of his identity. He reveled in the political life and sought a measure of fame that would solidify his historical reputation.

That meant, of course, that Tyler devoted himself to a political career at the expense of his family life. His first wife and children suffered from his long-term absences from home as he spent six months out of every year away from Virginia while serving in Congress or as a US senator. The role of absentee father Tyler crafted was not adequate to the task of sustaining a happy marriage or raising well-adjusted children. While it is certainly important to remember that he was a product of his era and that many southern politicians spent long periods of time away from the people they loved, it is still a fair assessment that Tyler largely failed his first family. He seemed to be able to only apply himself for sustained periods to politics. Politics consumed him. He selfishly allowed that to happen. His second wife and second set of children benefited from his constant presence in their lives; their experience with him was markedly different from that of his first family. Yet, in the end, he reentered politics. That he did so as a member of the Confederate government had enormously negative repercussions for his second wife and for his historical reputation. He should have stayed out of it.

Tyler's disastrous last foray into politics, however, proved to be the only time that his masterful sense of timing—the third theme of this book—failed him. His national political career owed a lot to timing and his ability to capitalize on it. Tyler found ways to put himself in the best possible position to succeed and advance his career at just the right time. He had an uncanny knack for doing so. Luck was often involved, but as Tyler realized, if he wanted a long career in politics, he had to make his own luck. He won election to Congress for the first time after a highly popular incumbent died, opening up the office for him. He took advantage of the erratic behavior of John Randolph to win a seat in the US Senate. Clearly, the Virginian was in the right place at the right time when William Henry Harrison died. We see further evidence of this remarkable sense of timing in how Tyler acted once he was elected to office. He could be calculating, sizing up whether taking a highly publicized stand on a particular issue would provide him enough traction with his constituents to win the next election. For example, when he entered the House of Representatives for his first session in Congress, his colleagues began debate on whether to repeal the highly controversial Compensation Act, a measure that granted lawmakers a sizeable pay raise. Tyler jumped right in and staked out a position that put him squarely on the side of the people. The repeal of the hated law allowed him to claim a victory. All of this behavior belies the standard interpretation of Tyler as a dilatory and vacillating politician who could never make up his mind. It is true that as president he sometimes employed a methodical approach to solving problems that frustrated his supporters. But it is just as true that in some matters—deciding to assert his presidential authority as soon as he entered office after Harrison's death (the so-called "Tyler precedent") or his pursuit of American interests in Hawaii—he seized the initiative quickly and did not second-guess himself. He demonstrated an admirable self-confidence.

Taken together, the three themes of this work situate John Tyler into the larger context of southern society and national politics from the early republic to the Civil War. They also establish the framework to explain what made him a successful politician who enjoyed an impressive career in which he held every elected national office available. Overall, his views and positions on the important matters of the day paint him as a fairly typical southern politician. His life and career are thus mostly representative of the antebellum South. Tyler's accession to the presidency, of course, set him apart from most southern politicians. More importantly, his success at reaching the highest level of American politics attests to his significance. Despite the grumblings (and worse) of his enemies, he had not gotten to the White House solely through an accident of fate. He got there because he had prepared himself to take advantage of the opportunity. He was ready for that opportunity when it came.

It is time for a fresh look at John Tyler's entire life and political career. My purpose is not to rehabilitate the reputation of one of America's most poorly regarded presidents. I make no apologies for his failures, and I believe that as a slaveholder and, ultimately, a secessionist, he placed himself on the wrong side of history. But in doing so, he unwittingly gave the men and women who have chronicled his life and career permission to caricature him. Historians have largely followed the lead of the Whigs who banished him from the ranks of their party in September 1841. It is my hope that the portrayal that follows strips away the misconceptions and offers a more complete rendering of the president without a party.

Chapter 1

A VIRGINIA INHERITANCE

The fist seemed to come out of nowhere. Thomas Macon barely had time to cringe as a red-faced John Tyler landed a punch to the side of his face. Macon staggered and nearly fell down but recovered himself and struck back, battering his foe about the upper body with a small riding crop he had been holding. A determined Tyler wrested the weapon away and began using it to rain more blows upon his overmatched adversary.

This violent encounter began in the New Kent County, Virginia, courthouse on a muggy June afternoon in 1822. Tyler, a thirty-two-year-old attorney, had spent the past hour defending the county in a lawsuit brought against it by a Colonel Macon. During the course of the trial, Macon's son Thomas, twenty-five and an aspiring planter, was called as a witness. Visibly displeased with having to appear in court, the younger Macon offered testimony that strayed far from the point of the proceedings. Tyler attempted to nudge him back to the particulars of the case. When Macon continued his incoherent rambling, the increasingly irritated lawyer demanded that the witness "say all you know about the *matter before* the court."

After finishing for the day, Tyler walked outside the courthouse to find Macon waiting for him. "Mr. Tyler," he declared, as he stalked toward him, "you have taken with me a very unjustifiable liberty." The attorney replied that he did not know what Macon was talking about. He turned to walk away, having tried to downplay what had happened in court, but he could not quite resist telling Macon what he thought of his performance in the witness chair. Flushed with anger, Macon blurted out, "you have not acted the part of a gentleman sir." Wheeling around quickly at this insult, Tyler lost his temper, and what had been a verbal spat quickly became a physical altercation. In recounting the incident later to his brother-in-law, Tyler proudly reported that he had sustained no injury. Apparently, Macon was not so lucky. The blow to his face had been hard enough to leave a bruise that, Tyler wrote with some satisfaction days later, "if I do not mistake, his appearance even now gives evidence of."

John Tyler's run-in with Thomas Macon was more than a fight between two young hotheads on a summer day. Indeed, the entire incident is emblematic of the southern culture of honor into which both men had been born. Macon had questioned Tyler's status as a "gentleman," a serious insult in the antebellum South that could not be ignored. Like most men of his birth, upbringing, education, and professional achievement, Tyler believed he embodied gentility. Not a man prone to outbursts of temper or one for whom fisticuffs came easily, he nevertheless defended himself against Macon's remark to protect his reputation and standing in the community. Southern men often responded to this kind of insult with instantaneous violence, especially if the remark had been uttered in the presence of other people. Sometimes, this type of exchange resulted in an affair of honor—a duel. Tyler never fought a duel in his life, but he realized Macon's insult required an appropriate response. His behavior thus needed no justification, and he pointed out that he had given "no insult and repell'd the one given me promptly."[1]

That prompt response indicated that the positive evaluation of his community meant a great deal to Tyler. In fact, his self-worth depended in part on the good opinion of his neighbors. His status as a gentleman depended upon their recognition of that status. He simply could not let Macon's insult pass. The symbolism of the riding crop may also be significant. Typically, only social inferiors were struck with canes or a weapon of this sort. Having endured the blow Macon administered with the riding crop, Tyler may have sought to take the weapon away from him simply to gain the upper hand in the fight. But in the heat of the moment, he may also have given a thought to the implications of allowing Macon to continue the altercation with the riding crop.[2]

More-personal reasons may also have prompted Tyler's aggressive response to what his adversary had said. While Macon's comment had not been meant to demean his health or strength, Tyler may have seen another benefit to reacting as he did. Living in a society in which a robust physical presence and good health served as evidence of a man's worthiness, he was aware that he did not always measure up. Poor health had plagued him his entire life. In fact, a little over one year before his altercation with Macon, Tyler had retired from politics and given up his seat in the US Congress in part to recover from an illness that returned sporadically and often debilitated him. Still suffering from the lingering effects of this affliction in June 1822, Tyler may have knocked Macon in the face and beat him with the riding crop to demonstrate his physical prowess—to prove to bystanders, not to mention himself, that he merited the respect of his community.[3]

That community—the lower Virginia Tidewater—had been home to Tyler's family for generations. Sometime in late 1652 or early 1653, three brothers with that last name fled Shropshire, in western England, and sailed for America. The men were evidently Royalists who had sided with King Charles I in the English Civil Wars of the 1640s. Their support for the Crown and for the established Church of England marked them as enemies of the Puritan leader Oliver Cromwell and the so-called Roundheads, the victors in the conflict. Cromwell had executed the king in January 1649 and seemed intent on persecuting his foes, perhaps with confiscation of their land—or worse. Leaving England, then, was quite possibly a matter of life or death for these three men.

One of the Tyler brothers made his way to Massachusetts. Another sought refuge in Connecticut. The third, forty-nine-year-old Henry, traveling with his wife, Mary, and four others, settled in York County, Virginia, in an area known as Middle Plantation, the site of what would eventually become Williamsburg. Henry was the first of John Tyler's ancestors in Virginia. The future tenth president of the United States, who was born on March 29, 1790, was fifth in descent from this original family settler, making him a sixth-generation Tyler in the Old Dominion.[4]

Henry Tyler was part of an unofficial roster of patricians known later as the First Families of Virginia (FFV), a designation reserved for those whose ancestors had arrived in the colony between the founding of Jamestown in 1607 and the 1660s. Benefiting from the patronage of Royal Governor William Berkeley, who sought to place men from prominent English families into privileged positions in Virginia society and politics, Henry found the Old Dominion a promising place to begin a new life. Taking advantage of the headright system, he secured title to three hundred acres of land and soon established himself as a tobacco planter of some means. He then parlayed his financial success and status as a member of Virginia's emerging gentry into a career in public service at the local level. He won appointment as justice of the peace, a vital position in the colony's county-court system. The post tied Henry Tyler to York County's other prominent families in what historian Charles Sydnor long ago called a system of "county oligarchies."[5]

Successive generations of Tyler men built upon the pattern Henry initiated and established themselves in the Tidewater as leaders and men of substance. For example, the royal governor appointed the future president's grandfather (Henry Tyler's great-grandson) Marshall to the colony's vice-admiralty court. This Tyler helped the English Crown enforce the Navigation Acts that regulated colonial trade. Moreover, his marriage to Anne Contesse, daughter of a Huguenot refugee who came to Virginia when King Louis XIV revoked the Edict of Nantes in 1685, introduced French blood into the Tyler line.[6]

Along with landed estates, slaveholding (eventually), and public service, advantageous marriages to suitable young women marked the Tyler family as members in good standing of the Virginia gentry. Marrying well was one way these men cemented their position in the ruling elite and ensured their children would enjoy the same status. They also sought to hone the characteristics that set them apart from the lower ranks of society. Gentility, demonstrated by the way an elite man carried himself, the way he dressed, and the way he interacted with others, defined the privileged life of the Tidewater, as did the deference a man of this sort usually received from those below him on the social ladder. By the first decades of the eighteenth century, a well-entrenched social order had taken shape in Virginia. Within this hierarchy, the Tyler men occupied increasingly more important and more powerful positions as each generation surpassed the accomplishments of its predecessor. While the family never reached the absolute pinnacle of landholding, wealth, and prestige, the name Tyler nevertheless became synonymous with significant and influential public service in Virginia.[7]

John Tyler's father illustrates this perfectly. Born in 1747 and sharing the name of his father and son (and known historically as John Tyler Sr.), he attended the College of William and Mary in the colonial capital of Williamsburg, where he received a liberal education inside the classroom and a practical one outside it. A studious young man, he often put aside his books for the afternoon and hurried to the House of Burgesses. Sitting in the gallery gave him a crash course on politics and enabled him to see firsthand how government actually worked. He often found it exciting. In 1765 the elder Tyler elbowed his way to a spot near the door of the packed legislative chamber in time to see (and hear) Patrick Henry rail against Britain's passage of the Stamp Act, a warmup for his better-known "Give me liberty, or give me death!" speech of 1775. Henry's performance inspired John Tyler's father and left no doubt in his mind that he, too, wanted a career in politics. More than a decade later, the two men would become political allies. So great was the elder Tyler's esteem for Henry that he named a son *and* daughter after the famed orator.[8]

Determined to pursue a career in the law, which was a virtual prerequisite for winning political office, John Tyler's father prepared for the bar under the direction of Robert Carter Nicholas, perhaps Williamsburg's most esteemed attorney. When the day's lessons at Nicholas's office ended, John Tyler Sr. walked to his lodging in a boardinghouse nearby that he shared with a tall, lanky redhead who was studying law at the same time with another legal powerhouse, George Wythe. The roommate was none other than Thomas Jefferson. The two men eventually became political allies and ideological soulmates, and they remained warm friends for life.[9]

The future president's father solidified his family's status as part of the Tidewater elite through his education, legal apprenticeship, and connections. Determined to carve out a consequential career for himself, he moved roughly thirty-two miles west up the James River from Williamsburg to Charles City County, where he started a legal practice. In 1776, at the age of twenty-nine, he completed the process of establishing himself in society by marrying well. John Tyler's mother, Mary Marot Armistead, all of fifteen years old on the day of her wedding, was the only child of Robert Booth Armistead, a prominent planter from York County, and his second wife, Anne Marot Shields, a woman of French Huguenot descent. The Armisteads, also listed as an FFV, had been in Virginia even longer than the Tylers, their first settler appearing in the colony's land records in 1636. After exchanging marriage vows, the couple moved to a 1,200-acre estate in Charles City County they soon named Greenway, where they would raise their children.[10]

Soon after his marriage, John Tyler's father received the good news from the Virginia legislature that he had been appointed as a judge on the state's admiralty court. Two years later, in the midst of the Revolutionary War, he won election to the newly constituted House of Delegates, the lower house of the Old Dominion's bicameral legislature. He represented Charles City County in that body for eight consecutive years and on four occasions served as Speaker of the House. He had succeeded in outshining his ancestors.[11]

Fully imbued with the patriot's perspective of the American Revolution, Judge Tyler (as he was now called) displayed an intense Anglophobia that lasted for the remainder of his life. Small wonder, then, that his son came of age wielding a deep-seated animus toward the family's ancestral homeland. Indeed, throughout his political career, John Tyler always seemed to operate under the assumption that the British position on *anything* ran counter to the interests of the United States.[12]

John Tyler inherited much more than his father's hostility toward the British. Even more significantly, he mirrored the Judge's steadfast commitment to public service and active participation in the political process. "[G]ood and able Men had better govern than be govern'd," the elder Tyler declared, in a succinct statement of his definition of noblesse oblige. Men of ability should not "withdraw themselves from Society" lest the "venal and ignorant" succeed. Answering the call to a career in politics—and to the bench, a forum with its own set of political expectations—became central to Judge Tyler's conception of what was right and proper. He willingly answered the call, even as he realized that a political career exacted a toll from his family. Often placing service to Virginia and to his country ahead of his wife and children, he became an absentee husband and father. His son would emulate this devotion to public service—and then some.[13]

Judge Tyler's sense of duty and civic responsibility reflected the ideology of republicanism that had inspired and shaped the American Revolution. Of particular concern to him was what his contemporaries called "virtue." His correspondence with Jefferson reveals an almost obsessive preoccupation with it. The classical republicanism of antiquity demanded that virtuous men—those possessing an unselfish commitment to the commonweal—step forward, subvert their own private interests, and accept their roles as public servants. Beholden to no one for political favor, these "disinterested" men had the wisdom to recognize what would benefit society; once voted into office, they could then work to accomplish it. "It has been long a received opinion that republican government can only be supported by virtue," John Tyler's father wrote in his old age. "I concur in this sentiment, that virtue and republicanism are so intimately connected that the neglect of the one will eventually prove destructive to the other."[14]

Historian Gordon Wood has identified a more modern strain of virtue that took shape during the Revolution, which he argues largely supplanted the one associated with classical republicanism. This new version was more realistic in its view of human nature. It prized "affability and sociability," as well as "politeness and decency," and better fit the world of the late eighteenth century because the "social affection" it attempted to foster was necessary for mitigating the selfishness of an increasingly acquisitive, commercially oriented society of men on the make. Put another way, this modern strain of virtue allowed Americans in the early national period to reconcile republicanism and capitalism. Judge Tyler subscribed to this philosophical shift. He lauded the "pure morals" and "good manners" that Wood identifies as "adhesives" of America's newly constructed republican society. What is more, he concurred with many of his countrymen that private virtue—a man's inner character—had become essential to the preservation of republicanism. Judge Tyler believed in a code of conduct from which he could not be shaken and believed that the fate of the republic depended on the willingness of the American people to live by its terms. His son, the future president, expressed the same view while serving in Congress as a young man. "A republican Government can only be supported by virtue," he argued, "and the end of all our legislation should be to encourage our fellow-citizens in its daily practice."[15]

As a republican (and Anglophobe), Judge Tyler also rejoiced in the rejection of an aristocracy of birth and wealth that had followed the American Revolution. He believed instead in what his friend Jefferson called a "natural aristocracy," a constellation of high-minded, genteel, and well-educated men who would offer leadership in the political arena for the betterment of their constituents. The elder Tyler envisioned a world "where every citizen is entitled by a free suffrage to rise to importance in proportion to his wisdom and integrity, without the aid of family connection, wealth, or fictitious grandeur." In short, he dreamed that the United States would become a meritocracy. Education would provide the foundation by nourishing virtue and building a society of well-informed citizens. An educated citizenry would then ensure the survival of the republic. "A proper diffusion of knowledge is the only certain means of accomplishing so glorious a work," Judge Tyler declared, echoing the words Jefferson had used when proposing a plan for public education to the Virginia legislature in 1778. Jefferson failed to persuade his fellow elites of the wisdom of his proposal but found a disciple in his former housemate. When the Judge became governor of Virginia in 1808, he tried to impress upon the legislature the importance of creating a system of public education. He, too, failed to rouse action on the matter. Powerful planters would not hear of anything that might lead to greater social mobility and a diminution of their influence.[16]

We should not read too much into Judge Tyler's progressive views on education. He did not envision females, African American children—enslaved or free—or the very poor being able to use public education to climb the social ladder. There was no place for anyone other than young white males in the vaunted "natural aristocracy." The Judge did not challenge the prevailing orthodoxy on gender and race. Nor was he a social leveler or "democrat." Nevertheless, his appeals to the Virginia legislature were genuine. And by the time his children were old enough to benefit from schooling, he marshalled all of his financial resources to educate them—boys and girls alike. John Tyler would be no less devoted to the education of his own children and would place himself in financial peril so that they could go to school or benefit from the instruction of tutors.[17]

More broadly, John Tyler's father also glimpsed the future and viewed education as a hedge against changes he found deeply troubling. A stagnant overseas market for tobacco after the American Revolution and the exhaustion of their soil had prompted Tidewater planters to shift to the cultivation of wheat. Land values in Virginia, as well as slave prices, consequently fell. Shrinking credit and increased debt had placed Tidewater elites into a precarious position. In addition, less prestigious gentry families and the yeomanry that had been mobilized to fight the British began to demand a greater role in politics. This is not to say that men of the Tidewater elite—men like Judge Tyler—had lost or relinquished their status or that the values undergirding the classical republican tradition had disappeared entirely. But in time, the sons of these men—John Tyler among them—would have to fight to preserve their place atop the social and political hierarchy of their home state. Furthermore, they would witness a decline in the influence of Virginia in national politics. The Old Dominion's proud and once-powerful elites became embittered and over time more socially conservative. Though he would not live to see it, Judge Tyler no doubt worried about such an unhappy outcome. Thus, his hearty support of education can be viewed at least partially as an attempt to stave off decline and place his children in the best position possible to make the most out of their lives.[18]

Despite his forward-looking stance on education, Judge Tyler also exhibited more conservative, even reactionary, views, and he often clung to tradition in the face of worrisome prospects for the future. In at least one area, he framed his loyalty to the past in moral terms. Openly hostile to paper money, in part because of the inflation that had accompanied its widespread printing during the Revolution, he objected mostly because it altered the time-honored relationship between creditors and debtors. Gentry men in the Tidewater, indeed throughout the South, sometimes loaned money to lesser lights in their neighborhoods, and after the Revolution they were often forced to accept repayment in depreciated paper. Judge Tyler found this troubling, for he believed that a solemn promise to pay represented more than a financial transaction: it became a moral bond that cemented the relationship between a patron and his client. Social stability depended on that bond. John Tyler agreed with his father. He took to the floor of the House of Representatives in 1818 to oppose a uniform bankruptcy bill. His speech on the matter indicates that he had taken his father's view of debt—that of a southern planter—as his own. "With the honorable man I should hope," he declared, "that when involved, a desire to meet his engagements, to comply with the principles of integrity, would be found a sufficient stimulus to exertion." Tyler warned his colleagues that efforts to "ameliorate the conditions of the debtor [with the pending legislation] would inculcate dishonorable and unworthy principles." The bill was defeated. Ironically, twenty-three years later, as president, Tyler would sign a bankruptcy bill into law amid tremendous political pressure. Moreover, he struggled all his life with debt and sometimes found living up to the ideals of his father—the ideals he had extolled in the House chamber in 1818—extremely difficult, at times even impossible.[19]

John Tyler clearly absorbed his father's principles, which became the foundation for his own behavior and served as the basic structure of his life. Nowhere was this more evident—or more historically significant—than in his inheritance of the Judge's political principles. Tyler's father distrusted a powerful national government. He became convinced that only a strict construction—or literal reading—of the US Constitution could defend the American people against overreach by the federal government. Such overreach, called "consolidation" by strict constructionists, threatened liberty and fostered tyranny, and Judge Tyler spoke out against it whenever and wherever he could. As an Antifederalist who favored merely amending the Articles of Confederation, the elder Tyler fought in vain alongside men such as Patrick Henry and George Mason to block Virginia's ratification of the Constitution. He never entirely made peace with the Constitution, but he hoped strict construction would ward off potential evils.[20]

Closely related to his belief in strict construction was a belief in the supremacy of the individual states of the Union. The Judge believed in the compact theory of government. According to this idea, the original thirteen states had been the parties to the compact, or contract, that created the Union. In other words, the states had *created* the federal government, and the people of the states had delegated specific and limited powers to it, which were spelled out in Article I of the Constitution. The federal government was thus bound by a solemn compact to exercise only those powers that had been expressly granted to it by the people of the states. The states each retained all other powers.

The fullest expression of Judge Tyler's states' rights views can be found in the Virginia and Kentucky Resolutions, the Jeffersonian Republican response to the Federalist-sponsored Alien and Sedition Acts, which President John Adams signed into law as the country mobilized for possible war with France in 1798. Authored anonymously in that year by James Madison (Virginia) and Jefferson (Kentucky), the resolutions publicly articulated the compact theory of government for the first time. As the original parties to the compact, the states had the right to determine when that agreement had been violated, and the people of the states had the right to judge whether a federal law was unconstitutional. When such a law had been passed, the states could interpose themselves between that law and the people for the purpose of "arresting the progress of the evil." Madison's Virginia Resolutions stopped short of suggesting that individual states could nullify an unconstitutional federal law. Jefferson went further in another set of resolutions the next year and argued for this position. The "Principles of '98," as they soon became known, provided rhetorical ammunition for what one scholar has called the "dissenting tradition" in American politics. Indeed, the Virginia and Kentucky Resolutions charted a way forward for men like Judge Tyler—and for John Tyler himself— to oppose a strong federal government. Thereafter, the "Virginia School," or "Virginia doctrines," lay at the heart of states' rights philosophy. True believers argued that their adherence to the "Principles of '98" reaffirmed the spirit of the American Revolution and represented the logical evolution of republicanism. They saw themselves as the legitimate heirs to the stalwarts of 1776 and took seriously their status as the generation that inherited the Revolution.[21]

John Tyler later saw himself in just that light. Acknowledging the seminal role his father had played in shaping his basic political philosophy, he pointed out proudly that he had "been rear'd in the belief that this gov't was founded on a compact to which sovereign States were the parties." The federal government, he argued, "was created by the States, is amendable by the States, is preserved by the States, and may be destroyed by the States." Tyler championed strict construction and states' rights throughout his political career—at least until he became president—and held fast to what he called the "great and enduring principles of the report and resolutions of 1798–9."[22]

Fealty to strict construction and a belief in states' rights became the twin pillars of Jefferson's Democratic-Republican Party, which John Tyler's father enthusiastically supported and which became the wellspring of the South's political orthodoxy after Jefferson won the presidency in what he called the "Revolution of 1800." As president, however, Jefferson saw fit to loosen the bonds of the political philosophy he had articulated in 1798–99. Indeed, his critics charged that he abandoned the true faith for political expediency. The men who clung to the original Jeffersonian principles of strict construction and states' rights proudly called themselves "Old Republicans." Often playing the role of reactionaries, they have variously been described as "particularists" or "neo-Antifederalists." Today we would call them "conservatives"; indeed, most people in their own day regarded their brand of politics as "conservative," despite their departure at times from the straitjacket of rigid ideology. John Tyler became an Old Republican. There was really no place else for him to go politically. Old Republicanism was the dominant political persuasion in Virginia. Tyler certainly would not have found the nationalist mindset of the Federalist Party congenial to his political beliefs or beneficial to his career. Adopting the views of his father, then, he embraced the prevailing ideology of the Old Republicans and became a neo-Antifederalist himself, even as he maintained reverence for his (and his father's) hero, Jefferson. He demonstrated remarkable ideological consistency throughout his political career. His political values were deeply ingrained and deeply held. But he was not a rigid ideologue. Like Jefferson, Tyler found that the occupant of the White House often had to forego the luxury of ideological purity so that he could better serve the nation's interests. Perhaps the best way to view Tyler's political philosophy is to see it as a guide or compass—his lodestar. When faced with difficult decisions, he usually returned to the Old Republican principles he had inherited from his father.[23]

Tyler's view of slavery reinforced his connection to the Old Republicans— and to Jefferson. He and they regarded their region's peculiar institution as a necessary evil, an unfortunate legacy from America's colonial past that southerners would eliminate if possible. But therein lay the rub—nobody could envision a satisfactory solution to the problem. Despite this conundrum, Tyler and the Old Republicans maintained that slavery was the South's problem alone to address. Lyon Tyler, the tenth president's son, put it this way: "Mr. Tyler, like his father, deplored slavery, but it was here without his fault or that of his contemporaries, and he, like the best patriots of the Revolution, would tolerate no officious interference from without." Lyon thus made an attempt to relieve his father of the responsibility for questioning the morality of slavery—it had been fastened onto the United States before he was born, and, even though he preferred its termination, he was stuck with it. Tyler himself sought to evade that responsibility in an 1857 address commemorating the founding of Jamestown, a speech in which he claimed that the slave trade in early Virginia had primarily made New Englanders—not Virginians—wealthy. Like many of his fellow slaveholders, then, by the late antebellum period, Tyler attempted to "nationalize" slavery by tinkering with historical memory, a strategy that took on more urgency as the abolitionist movement became stronger and more vocal and as the North's "free labor" ideology became more prevalent. The second half of Lyon's statement offers a justification for his father's strident opposition to the abolitionists and his principled stance against northern politicians who sought to stop slavery's expansion into the American West. Tyler never adhered to some of the more extreme aspects of the "proslavery" argument, such as pseudoscientific racism, and he had little time for the intellectual arguments that polemicists made in support of slavery. But he did operate at the edges of the "positive good" defense of the institution, and he certainly shared the racist views toward people of African descent that were commonplace in nineteenth-century America, particularly in the South. Moreover, his anger at what he regarded as meddling and dangerous antislavery northerners placed him fully within the mainstream of southern thought. The Old Republicans took a similar position.[24]

Yet, committed as Tyler was to Old Republicanism, he often found himself at odds with the self-appointed guardians of the brand in Virginia: the Richmond Junto. Led by the jurist Spencer Roane (a colleague and friend of Tyler's father) and Thomas Ritchie, the tireless editor of the *Richmond Enquirer,* this group of some twenty men leveraged family connections and contacts throughout the Old Dominion to become powerbrokers in Virginia politics. Stridently opposed to the nationalism that began to take root in the United States after the War of 1812, they sought to elect candidates to office—especially in the national arena—who would proudly carry the banner of states' rights and strict construction and take the fight to the consolidation they believed imperiled the South and the nation. They monitored Virginia politicians with the vigilance they believed the times demanded and used newspaper editorials and well-placed correspondence to enforce party discipline. John Tyler, however, regularly confounded them. While agreeing with the Junto on the overall goal, he often employed vastly different tactics in an effort to achieve it, throughout his career in national politics adopting positions that ran counter to those of the Junto. His independent streak frustrated them all the more because he deftly avoided the electoral punishment they might have liked to inflict on him. The interplay between Tyler and the men of the Richmond Junto indicates that he was a better politician than history has credited him with being and that these states' rights guardians wielded less power than their vaunted reputation suggests.[25]

Judge Tyler believed a political career was his second son's birthright—especially after his eldest son, Wat, declared an intention to pursue a career in medicine—and he steered him toward the legal profession and groomed him for public life. He undoubtedly recognized that the future president's talent, aptitude, and drive augured well for such a happy outcome. By becoming an attorney and entering politics, young John would continue the pattern Henry Tyler had established generations before when he settled in Virginia. He would fulfill his promise and propel the Tyler name forward into the future. The Judge hoped his son would become a politician of national renown who would leave a legacy for the *next* generation of Tylers.[26]

There is no question that Judge Tyler became the single-most-important influence on his son's life, all the more so because the boy lost his young mother to a fatal stroke in April 1797, when he was seven years old. Eerily, this scene would somewhat repeat itself years later as John Tyler's first wife suffered a pair of strokes before dying at the age of fifty-two while her husband was president.

Tyler's father took the loss of his beloved wife hard but steeled himself with a fatalism that helped him carry on in the face of tragedy. Six years later he did the same after his eldest child, Anne Contesse, died suddenly. The future president actually witnessed his sister's death firsthand; he had begun attending classes in the preparatory division of the College of William and Mary and boarded with Anne and her husband, James Semple, a prominent attorney in Williamsburg. As a young man and later as an adult, he adopted the same fatalistic attitude toward death his father had exhibited. Thus, the Judge passed down more than a framework for pursuing a career in law and politics to his son. The future president inherited his father's basic emotional apparatus as well and dealt with life's difficulties in much the same way.[27]

But this strategy for processing grief took years for John Tyler to develop. His mother's death no doubt shattered his world and affected him profoundly. There appears to be a connection between her passing and the ill health he suffered as a youngster. Slight of build, the sandy-haired, blue-gray-eyed boy was a sickly child prone to regular attacks of diarrhea, which became more frequent after his mother died. His symptoms suggest a high level of anxiety and indicate that he felt his loss deeply—and felt it for years. As John got older, his stomach ailments became more pronounced, and he may have suffered from an ulcer. As a man Tyler wrote and spoke very little about his childhood, perhaps indicating that recalling his mother's death made it too painful to do so.

The sparse evidence indicates that Tyler and his siblings reacted to losing their mother the way the strongest families often do: the children became closer to each other and, along with their father, worked together to fill the void as best they could. Judge Tyler relied on his older daughters to look after the younger children while he was away. Many years later, after he had left the White House, John Tyler praised his sister Martha, eight years his senior, who acted as a surrogate mother, "to whose care and attention I have ever felt myself under the greatest obligations." Help came from outside the family as well. The Judge employed a middle-aged housekeeper whose assistance proved crucial, especially after he became the legal guardian of several other disadvantaged children. Convention may have demanded that John Tyler's father remarry. He chose not to—much like his friend Jefferson—and cobbled together a routine that enabled him to take care of his family. It is a testament to his success at doing so that the future president became confident and self-assured as he approached adulthood.[28]

John Tyler thrived on his father's attention and welcomed every opportunity to prove that his faith in his son was not misplaced. He accepted the Judge's challenges to better himself and sought ways to impress him. And he succeeded. The result was that, by the time the future president was a young man, his carefully nurtured self-esteem fueled his own ambition. With his father's help, he had become confident enough in his own abilities to believe that the career path toward which he had been steered appeared not only possible, but likely.

College nurtured this confidence and self-assurance. There was never any doubt that John Tyler would attend William and Mary. In 1804 the fourteen-year-old entered the baccalaureate program, where he joined Wat, who had started the previous year. Their father's alma mater was in the midst of a resurgence. The college had struggled mightily to attract students after the American Revolution—only eight students were enrolled in 1796—and there was even talk of shutting its doors. James Madison, second cousin of the soon-to-be fourth president of the United States and an Episcopal bishop, became the college's eighth president in 1777. He weathered the most difficult days and began implementing an aggressive approach to turning around the fortunes of the school. By the time the Tyler brothers arrived, more than forty young men were pursuing degrees, including several promising pupils from neighboring states. For example, Tyler's future attorney general, John J. Crittenden, left Kentucky and enrolled at William and Mary the same year Tyler began his studies.[29]

Bishop Madison eliminated the college's rigid classical curriculum that had been modeled on the English system of Oxford and Cambridge. In its place he introduced a freer, more liberal program of study philosophically based on the Enlightenment. Instruction in rhetoric, logic, and philosophy of the human mind as well as moral philosophy, in which students studied the English theologian William Paley's rules of life, became integral components of the new curriculum. So, too, did mathematics, geography, modern languages, ancient history, and instruction in natural law. The study of politics, however, was undoubtedly the hallmark of a William and Mary education. According to one student, there was "probably no College in the United States in which political science [was] studied with so much ardour." Madison himself taught the first course in political economy in the United States, using Adam Smith's *Wealth of Nations* as his primary textbook.[30]

The college president sought to cultivate the Jeffersonian ideals of limited government and free trade in his students. He had enthusiastically supported the Virginia and Kentucky Resolutions of 1798 and rejoiced in Jefferson's Revolution of 1800 that had swept away the "Rubbish" of the Adams administration. Thus, John Tyler's college education reinforced what he had been taught at home. He and many of the young men educated at William and Mary carried the ideals they were exposed to there into the national political arena as they launched careers for themselves.[31]

Yet Bishop Madison made it perfectly clear to his charges that he expected them to think for themselves. Taking the tenets of the Enlightenment to heart, he encouraged them to be skeptical of conventional wisdom, and he practiced what he preached. He was also not afraid to create an intellectual environment at the college that nurtured the antislavery sentiments of his students. His lectures on moral philosophy, for example, highlighted the glaring contradiction of a republican society that cherished the rights of man while holding African Americans in bondage. While he was no abolitionist, Madison clearly held the Jeffersonian view that slavery was a necessary evil and that the slave system had been installed in America by the British long ago, which made it difficult to abolish. This view also reinforced what John Tyler had learned at home.[32]

Tyler distinguished himself academically at William and Mary and became well read. In addition to exposing him to Adam Smith, his coursework required mastery of John Locke's *On Civil Government*, Jean-Jacques Rousseau's *Civil Contract*, Baron de Montesquieu's *The Spirit of the Laws*, and Thomas Paine's *The Rights of Man*. Tyler also discovered a love of Shakespeare and memorized lines from plays that he later used in letters and speeches. Fascinated by ancient history, he committed passages from Livy and Herodotus to memory. College was an intellectual feast for this eager student.

Tyler's time at William and Mary also allowed him to deepen his relationship with his father. Letters dispatched regularly from Williamsburg demonstrated to the Judge that his son was maturing according to plan and that he was preparing to join the "natural aristocracy." Judge Tyler scrutinized each missive his son mailed home, paying careful attention not only to what was written (which delighted him) but also to how it was written. On one occasion John "mortified" his father when he sent a letter home written with sloppy penmanship. "How can you be fit for law business of every description," the Judge demanded in his prompt reply, if there was no "improvement" in your handwriting? "Look at the handwriting of Mr. Jefferson, Wythe, Pendleton, Mercer, Nicholas, and all the old lawyers," he said, "and you will find how much care they took to write handsomely." By invoking the names of men Tyler hoped to emulate, his father hammered home the lesson. The young man got the message; his penmanship improved at once, and he made sure he wrote neatly for the remainder of his life.[33]

In June 1807, after completing course requirements and passing his examinations, seventeen-year-old John Tyler was chosen along with four of his classmates to prepare speeches for William and Mary's commencement exercises. It was customary for exemplary students to address the public as part of the annual Fourth of July festivities in Williamsburg. Bishop Madison invited the community to attend, and the students usually spoke before sizeable audiences.

Tyler chose "Female Education" as the subject of his oration after discussing the matter with his father. The Judge may have even nudged him in this direction. The topic was certainly timely and reflected a trend sweeping American society in the early national period. Indeed, many families had begun educating their daughters more rigorously, seeking to prepare them for the roles they would play as virtuous wives and "republican mothers" who helped safeguard the legacy of the Revolution. Tyler's own household could have served as a case study of this process, and he no doubt drew on the experiences of his sisters to flesh out his speech. His audience seemed suitably impressed. One listener believed that the young orator had made his key point clear: "a liberal and rational education" was essential for "giving perpetuity to republican institutions."[34]

The address capped a highly successful college career. Tyler had distinguished himself as a scholar and had made many friends during his time in Williamsburg. He had received a first-rate education at William and Mary. Just as importantly, he had enjoyed being there. Years later he would declare proudly that his alma mater had "contributed her full share to the public enlightenment" and "made her mark on the tablets of history" by educating numerous "illustrious men." Tyler's active association with the college did not end with his graduation. He would later serve as a visitor on the school's board as well as its rector, and he would play an active role in hiring faculty. His direct involvement lasted virtually his entire life.[35]

Even taking into account that young men tended to graduate from college at an earlier age in the antebellum period than they would in a later time, Tyler's accomplishment is noteworthy. He had spent his formative years in the presence of two extremely influential men—his father and Bishop Madison—who helped him establish his place in the social world of the Virginia Tidewater, who encouraged the development of his intellect, who cultivated a belief in the virtue of public service, who imparted a deep appreciation for and understanding of the republican legacy of the American Revolution, and who shaped his political principles and ideology, all while nurturing an ambition to succeed in politics and win a level of fame that would place him at the top rank of a long line of Tyler men in the Old Dominion. By the time he left college, John Tyler was eager to prepare for the bar and take the next step in what he and his father believed would be a career of renown.

Chapter 2

RESTLESS AMBITION

When a young man prepared for the bar in early nineteenth-century Virginia, he customarily did so by becoming an apprentice and "reading" law under the direction of an established practitioner for a period of from one to three years. John Tyler began his legal apprenticeship under the direction of his father soon after graduating from William and Mary. The Judge also enlisted the help of his nephew, Samuel Tyler, presiding judge of the chancery court of Williamsburg, and between the two of them, they placed their young pupil on a rigorous schedule designed to prepare him well for his chosen profession.[1]

They likely started by having him study St. George Tucker's edition of *Blackstone's Commentaries.* Tucker, a colleague of Tyler's father on the Virginia bench and a man he greatly admired, was a former law professor at William and Mary who had recently published a five-volume annotation of Blackstone's classic text on English common law. Tucker adapted the famed British jurist to American constitutional law and offered a more detailed and practical analysis of common-law topics—property, tenures, estates, titles, and pleadings—that an attorney was expected to master. He did so, moreover, by infusing his analysis with republicanism and states' rights theory. In fact, he devoted a great deal of space in his volumes to what he called the "machine" of dual sovereignty, or the interaction between the federal government and the states. Tucker's adaptation of Blackstone complemented the states' rights principles articulated in the Virginia and Kentucky Resolutions and broadly applied the "Principles of '98" to the law. While there is no direct evidence to confirm that John Tyler began his legal studies by reading Tucker, it seems safe to assume that he did, both in light of his father's regard for the man and because its underlying political philosophy no doubt pleased the Judge. Perhaps the best indication that his father had indeed assigned Tucker for the budding lawyer to read is Tyler's later insistence that his own sons study the work as they prepared for the bar themselves.[2]

The strong likelihood that Tucker's *Blackstone* became the essential text of John Tyler's legal training speaks to the systematic way his father went about molding the ideology and perspective of the future president. Every step Tyler took as he readied himself for the law and politics seems to have been choreographed by the Judge, who sought to instill in his son the values he held dear. The young man apparently never questioned any of what he was being taught, never challenged the Tyler orthodoxy, and fully bought into his father's worldview without ever wondering if perhaps there might have been an acceptable alternative. The unthinking decision Tyler made to always follow his father's lead—grounded above all in an almost overwhelming desire to please him—meant that his views on the law or politics were largely derivative. His thinking lacked originality. He was a true believer in Old Republicanism.

Ironically, however, a Federalist—at least in name—oversaw the completion of Tyler's law studies. The apprenticeship with his father did not see him through to the bar, for in 1808 the Virginia legislature elected the elder Tyler governor. This meant he no longer had time to supervise his son's legal education. He therefore arranged for him to finish his studies under the direction of Edmund Randolph, the son-in-law of Robert Carter Nicholas, the Judge's mentor. Randolph, a fellow graduate of William and Mary, had served as governor of Virginia, delegate to the Constitutional Convention, and attorney general and secretary of state under President George Washington. Aaron Burr had also retained his services when he faced trial for treason in 1807.

Randolph's "massive" intellect challenged Tyler, and the short time he spent under the man's tutelage better prepared him for the bar examination. Many years later the future president remarked that he could "never be too grateful for the instruction he afforded me." Beyond the help it provided in preparing him for the bar exam, Tyler's time with Randolph is significant, demonstrating that the young man was well connected and that his father believed it was important to exploit those connections to help him get ahead. Judge Tyler's relationships with the leading lights of the Old Dominion's legal community offered his son an advantage that undoubtedly made a difference as he established himself in a very crowded and extremely competitive profession. The adage "it's not what you know but *who* you know" applies here. Not only that, by securing Randolph as a mentor, the Judge may have also felt that he was putting his son into the position of having to defend his political perspective against someone who could easily play the devil's advocate—a shrewd move.[3]

Tyler passed the bar exam late in 1809. At the age of only nineteen, he was legally two years too young to be granted a license to practice law. Apparently, however, the board that examined him did not ask him how old he was—his connections may have prompted them to look the other way—and he received his license without difficulty. Perhaps at his father's urging, the newly minted attorney did not immediately set up a practice. Instead, he chose to participate in several moot courts organized in Richmond by Judge Creed Taylor. Taylor, Chancellor of the Richmond High Court of Chancery and another Jeffersonian Republican contact of Tyler's father, welcomed his new charge into a rigorous program designed to improve his debating skills and train him in proper court-room procedure. It was through Taylor that the future president met other young lawyers, including Francis W. Gilmer, Abel P. Upshur, and William C. Preston—men he would later encounter in politics. Competition with his peers ultimately made Tyler more comfortable arguing before a judge and pro-vided a venue for him to apply what he had learned during his apprenticeship.[4]

After honing his skills with Judge Taylor, Tyler was almost ready to embark upon his legal career. A memorable evening with Thomas Jefferson in the fall of 1809 spurred him to make the leap. The Sage of Monticello had returned to Richmond to see his former housemate and shared dinner with the Tylers at the governor's mansion. The aspiring attorney spent the evening listening with rapt attention to Jefferson and his father recall their days as lawyers and politicians in Revolution-era Virginia. Judge Tyler was undoubtedly pleased when the conversation turned to his son's career plans. Jefferson impressed upon the young man that becoming a lawyer was (as he had put it to others before) "the most certain stepping stone to preferment in the political line." The lesson hit its mark. In the early spring of 1810, John Tyler moved back to Greenway and hung out his shingle.[5]

Trying mostly criminal cases in the cramped little county courthouse not far from where he had spent his childhood, he successfully competed with more established attorneys for clients. The Tyler name undoubtedly helped, and it appears the young attorney leveraged his father's reputation and his William and Mary degree to place himself into a favorable position in what one historian has described as the "incestuous" legal community in Richmond. One of his cases landed before the Supreme Court of Appeals in Richmond. Tyler's client retained a prominent attorney named John Wickham, who kept Tyler on as second chair. Wickham, a native New Yorker who had attended William and Mary, was widely regarded as the best of the Richmond bar. His opponent in this case was the formidable William Wirt, soon to be named at-torney general of the United States. Wickham and Wirt had squared off against each other four years earlier, when Wickham (along with Edmund Randolph) defended Aaron Burr against Wirt's prosecution for treason. Tyler knew the history. Barely twenty-one years old, he confided his nervousness to the vet-eran Wickham before their trial began and confessed that he did not feel as if he belonged. Remembering what Tyler's father had told *him* when he was beginning a career many years before, Wickham calmed the frightened novice by saying, "if the law is with you, the court will take care of the balance." He then encouraged his young comrade to make the opening argument. "I did so," Tyler recalled later, "in fear and trembling." He need not have worried, for he overcame his stage fright and made an excellent statement.[6]

Tyler's confidence soared. In subsequent courtroom appearances, he put aside his nervousness and became a highly effective orator on behalf of his clients. In one such instance he matched wits with a lawyer named Andrew Stevenson. Fellow attorneys considered Stevenson, yet another William and Mary graduate, one of the Tidewater's finest litigators. Tyler won the case. Out of this, a rivalry was born—one that would soon extend into politics.[7]

By the time he had reached the age of twenty-five, Tyler was coming into his own and walking out of the long shadow cast by his father. No longer motivated primarily by a desire to please the Judge, he was now intent on proving himself and staking out a career that highlighted his own merit. Before long, he was earning an annual income of nearly two thousand dollars from his efforts at the bar. This relatively lucrative practice meant he was attracting clients and winning cases, all at a time when most young lawyers—indeed, even some established attorneys—struggled to earn a good living. Better still, Tyler's peers recognized him as an able litigator whose oratory in the courtroom often dazzled them. He once said that he believed an attorney should be "bold and fearless" when representing his client, and he relished the opportunity the law gave him to perform in front of an audience. He was clearly in his element.[8]

Yet he was not entirely *happy* practicing law. Even before attaining financial success, Tyler was restless, making it clear to almost everyone that he viewed the practice of law mostly as a means to an end—the end being, of course, a career in politics. Tyler was laying the groundwork for that career and recognized the long-term value in what he was doing as an attorney. Would-be politicians like him realized that their appearances in courtrooms across two or three counties—which might compose an electoral district—could be played for maximum effect. They got to know the influential men who operated as powerbrokers in those counties and could take advantage of the opportunity to establish rapport with the men who sat in jury boxes or who socialized with their neighbors on court day. These men, after all, were the ones who mattered most on election day; they were freeholders who voted.

Tyler had spent little time in front of these men as an attorney, but had apparently made the most of his opportunity. His last name and the connections he enjoyed helped. Barely one year into his law career, Tyler ran for public office for the first time and did so without significant opposition. In April 1811, at just twenty-one years of age, he won a seat representing Charles City County in Virginia's House of Delegates. The legislature met twice every year, with both sessions lasting roughly two to three months. That meant Tyler could still practice law at least six months out of the year. Not surprisingly, he found the other six months more to his liking, despite a disappointing start to his political career.[9]

Tyler's first session in the House began in December 1811. Almost immediately, he thrust himself into the fray. During the previous session, the Virginia legislature had "instructed" its US senators, Richard Brent and William Branch Giles, to vote against the re-charter of the national bank. Alexander Hamilton had secured a twenty-year charter for the bank back in 1791, which would expire in 1811, requiring Congress to vote to renew it (or not). Both Virginia senators disobeyed their instructions. Brent actually voted for re-charter, and Giles, while agreeing with the Virginia legislature's majority that a national bank was unconstitutional, denied the right of instruction itself.

The doctrine of instruction, which originated in Britain as a means to hold members of Parliament accountable to their constituents, had been a key component of the US government under the Articles of Confederation and had been used on several occasions during the Revolutionary War. After ratification of the Constitution, a debate ensued over whether retaining instruction was feasible or even necessary. The matter had never really been settled. Support for the doctrine came primarily from states' righters in the South, who argued that since the state legislatures elected US senators, they could invoke instruction in extraordinary cases. The Virginia legislature believed a vote on re-chartering the national bank qualified as just such an occasion.[10]

The US Senate voted against renewal, and the national bank ceased its operations in March 1811. But that did not prevent the Virginia press and people throughout the state from excoriating Brent and Giles for disobeying instructions. The *Richmond Enquirer* wanted the two senators to publicly account for their behavior. The Society of the Friends of the Revolution called them out at a raucous Fourth of July celebration. Public outcry over the issue continued into the fall. People were still talking about it as the Christmas season approached. Brent and Giles must have wondered if they would ever hear the end of the matter.[11]

John Tyler saw an opportunity to capitalize on the situation and took it. Having been a member of the legislature for all of one month, he boldly introduced resolutions formally censuring Brent and Giles for disobeying instruction. Knowing he stood on the popular side of the issue, he made the case for censure, arguing that the doctrine of instruction was a "great right" essential to "the advancement of the public interests." Brent and Giles, he declared, had "cease[d] to be the true and legitimate representatives of this State" when they disregarded the will of the legislature. This states' rights stance could not have surprised anyone—he was a Tyler, after all.[12]

Tyler sprung the resolutions on the House without warning. He had not sought the opinion or advice of more seasoned colleagues. It showed. Some of the more experienced legislators with whom he served seemed to think the freshman lawmaker had acted a bit rashly and that his resolutions did not go nearly far enough in conveying the seriousness of the state's objection to what Brent and Giles had done. Nor had he expressed in emphatic enough terms Virginia's commitment to the right of instruction. Tyler's brief resolutions sparked no debate and were instead referred to a special committee of the whole House. Benjamin Watkins Leigh, also serving his first term in the legislature (but nine years older than Tyler), chaired that committee. He eventually introduced substitute resolutions that a member of the House praised as "lengthy and superbly elegant." By implication, his versions were superior to what Tyler had introduced. The Virginia legislature adopted Leigh's resolutions—not Tyler's—to formally censure the state's US senators.[13]

Tyler's clumsy effort to make the most of the instruction controversy trumpeted his youth—he was not yet twenty-two—and inexperience, making him appear overeager and a bit foolish. In recounting what had transpired in the House, one of his fellow delegates referred to him as "young Tyler," the rhetorical equivalent of a condescending pat on the head. By seeking to bask in the limelight of what he thought would be an easy political victory, Tyler had instead turned a bright light on himself and found he could not withstand the glare. He had been too keen to make an early mark when he should have been more thoughtful, more measured, and more thorough; at the very least, he should have sought the counsel of a House veteran or two. It was not unusual for the legislature to refer an uncommon motion or resolutions outside the usual range of House business to a special committee, but by ultimately adopting Leigh's substitute resolutions of censure (for which Tyler dutifully voted), the members had sent a message to Tyler that his effort did not measure up. Whether he regarded the ultimate censure of Brent and Giles as validation of his idea is unknown. What seems clear is that he did not present his own resolutions merely to win a partial victory or to have someone else receive credit in the annals of history. It is doubtful he took solace in a moral victory.[14]

For perhaps the first time in his life, John Tyler had been told that something he had done was not good enough to pass muster. As an adolescent and young college student, he had been treated as a special talent by his father and Bishop Madison. By grooming him for a political career, the Judge had bolstered Tyler's self-esteem. The young man had won some early success as a courtroom attorney. He had won state political office at a very young age and no doubt believed his star would rise rapidly. Put simply, he was a bit full of himself. Tyler found actually *being* a politician considerably more challenging than aspiring to be one, however, and he had revealed his immaturity for his colleagues to see. Furthermore, he found that nobody in the legislature much cared who his father was. His fellow lawmakers were not going to genuflect in his presence because of his last name. He would have to earn their respect.

Much later in his life, Tyler reflected on what had happened during the instruction controversy. When corresponding with the Virginia historian Hugh Blair Grigsby in 1855—obviously long after the fact and at an age when he had more searing memories to ponder—Tyler confessed to acting as a lone wolf in bringing his censure resolutions to the floor of the House of Delegates in 1812. He made this disclosure not out of pride, but as an embarrassed admission that he had erred in doing so. His youth and restlessness had gotten the better of him.[15]

Despite the minor blunder, Tyler won reelection to the House of Delegates in April 1812 with no opposition. And the members of the Virginia legislature who made up the Republican majority no doubt appreciated that his heart and his principles were in the right place. On another issue, however, Tyler parted company with many of his fellow Tidewater Republicans. He openly supported a proposal for financing infrastructure projects, what nineteenth-century Americans called "internal improvements." Many Tidewater elites opposed the plan because they feared their taxes would go up to support a system that stood mostly to benefit Virginia's western counties. Tyler, on the other hand, saw its immense potential to benefit the entire state. Moreover, he found the plan ideologically sound because the state—and not the federal government—would earmark appropriations for infrastructure projects. Tyler had heard his father say over and over again that federally sponsored internal improvements represented a dangerous form of consolidation. He had also watched as his father, while governor, failed to spur the House of Delegates to get behind a broad plan of internal improvements.[16]

Passage of this latest internal-improvements proposal would have to wait until after Tyler left the legislature. The United States had recently declared war on Great Britain. The prevailing opinion in the legislature was that Virginia could ill afford to set aside funds for internal improvements when there were budgets to craft and militia companies to raise. In fact, much of the House business during the winter of 1812–13 focused on the War of 1812, with political leaders determined that the Old Dominion would do its part. When President James Madison informed the Virginia governor in February 1813 that the federal government could spare no troops for the defense of the state, the legislature sprang into action.

Amid this heightened tension, John Tyler's father died. Painful bladder stones had prevented him from keeping up with the duties of a federal judgeship, a post to which he had been appointed by President Madison in 1811 after he left the Virginia governor's chair. In December 1812, while in Norfolk, he contracted pleurisy. Dangerously ill and extremely weak, he returned to Charles City a few days before Christmas and died on January 6, 1813, at the age of sixty-five. The family buried him at Greenway beside Tyler's mother.[17]

No letters have come to light that would allow us to gauge the extent of Tyler's grief at having lost the most influential figure in his life. It is impossible to plumb the depths of his emotional world while he was a young man because he apparently did not share regular correspondence with anyone other than the Judge. No doubt his father's passing was a devastating blow. At the time, however, Tyler gave a rather bland statement for public consumption that hid any evidence of just how devastating it was: "Upon me, he conferred the name which he bore, and I shall be well content to reflect but the shadow of his patriotism, intelligence, and worth."[18]

Tyler's formality on the occasion of his father's death allowed him to mask his emotions and keep himself together. His modestly is understandable and even decorous; it is what a son is *supposed* to say when eulogizing a dearly departed father. But we have already seen that Tyler's father groomed him to surpass his own accomplishments in politics. He surely would not have been content to see his son settle for merely "reflect[ing] but the shadow of his patriotism, intelligence, and worth." His father had nurtured his ambition. Upon the Judge's passing, then, Tyler sought to accelerate the trajectory of his career and took steps to fulfill the promise his father had always seen in him.

He started with marriage. On March 29, 1813, his twenty-third birthday, he wed Letitia Christian. The youngest of six daughters of Robert Christian, a wealthy planter and attorney who owned Cedar Grove plantation in nearby New Kent County, Letitia, just months younger than Tyler, was striking, with fair skin, dark hair, and enchanting brown eyes. The couple had met at a party at Greenway in 1809. Tyler was taken with Letitia's shyness, and he enjoyed their initial conversation. He recognized instantly that she would make a suitable wife. "From the first moment of my acquaintance with you," he told the young woman later, "I felt the influence of genuine affection." Tyler received Mr. Christian's blessing to propose to Letitia at some point in 1812. She accepted at once. By this time, Tyler had just started to earn a respectable salary as a lawyer. Moreover, his father's death made setting a wedding date easier. He inherited Mons Sacer—a modest-sized property adjacent to Greenway—and several enslaved people, which made him a man of some means. Yet as executor of the Judge's estate (along with his two brothers), he also inherited some debt, and it is evident that his financial status preoccupied him as he imagined his future with Letitia. The metaphors he used in letters as the wedding day approached provide the clues to his frame of mind. "To ensure to you happiness is now my only object," Tyler told his fiancée, "and whether I float or sink in the stream of fortune, you may be assured of this, that I shall never cease to love you." To a friend, he conveyed his firm belief that, "whether prosperity smil[ed] or adversity frown[ed]," his marriage would be a happy one. Assured of Letitia's love, he nevertheless indicated that the possibility of future financial peril was more than a passing thought in his mind. His adult life would often justify those initial fears.[19]

It also becomes apparent when parsing the words Tyler wrote to Letitia during their courtship that he placed her on a pedestal and had developed an idealized view of her. He was clearly smitten—but certainly not besotted. His use of the word "affection" to describe how he felt about her, for example, rather than using words that conveyed passion, attest to the level of formality that characterized the couple's courtship. Indeed, by the time they wed in March 1813, Tyler had apparently done nothing more passionate than kiss Letitia's hand—once. The formality of their relationship largely reflected the prevailing standards that governed a young man's pursuit of his beloved in the early nineteenth century. Tyler wrote—and spoke—the acceptable language of his time and place, language that kept Letitia on her pedestal and kept him within the proper bounds of behavior. It would be absurd to think he could have done anything else. Custom dictated that he express affection for Letitia rather than passion, because admitting passion meant a man had lost his head, that emotions had overtaken reason, which then called into question his suitability as a husband.[20]

Yet, even taking into account that Tyler courted Letitia according to the terms dictated by propriety, one senses that his words and behavior hewed pretty closely to how he truly felt about her. He put her on a pedestal because he admired her grace, her quiet dignity, and her refinement. More religious than her husband-to-be and baptized in the Episcopal church, Letitia introduced Tyler to the benefits of faith. Though never a deeply religious man and attending church only infrequently, Tyler respected Letitia's devotion to God. In fact, her piety may have been the wellspring of the feminine refinement he admired. He no doubt believed she would make a wonderful mother and keep an efficient home, which was absolutely essential for an up-and-coming politician who would spend a lot of time away from his family. One wonders, too, whether Tyler's choice of a wife reflected an ideal that reminded him of his own mother. Whatever the case, he could not shake that idealized view of Letitia, and it affected the way the couple interacted during their marriage. There was always a level of formality that defined the relationship they shared. The contrast between how Tyler acted around Letitia and how he later acted in the company of his second wife, Julia Gardiner, is striking. Julia was the woman who inspired Tyler's romantic side and flushed him with passion, something Letitia never seemed able to do.

There were other benefits, however, that Tyler enjoyed by virtue of his marriage to Letitia. By marrying into the well-respected and well-heeled Christian family—by "marrying up," frankly—Tyler had solidified his standing in the adjacent county of New Kent and could now count on the support of his in-laws. He could also expect that Letitia's family would introduce him to the powerful men in their circle, men who might make the difference in his pursuit of higher office. Marrying was good for Tyler's career.

After the Episcopal ceremony, the couple traveled to Charles City, ready to begin married life at Mons Sacer. The War of 1812 soon intruded. In the early summer of 1813, not long after the newlyweds had settled into their new home, the British landed a small contingent of troops at Hampton, Virginia, near the coast. The soldiers raided the town, and for a time it appeared that the British might attempt to move up the James River and capture Richmond—or so many residents of Tidewater Virginia, including Tyler, feared. Excited and a little nervous at the prospect of taking up arms against the hated redcoats, Tyler wondered aloud whether the enemy troops in Virginia would "go full gallop" and provoke hostilities with the locals. He joined a Charles City militia company organized to protect the James and repel an attack on Richmond. Drill began not long after the "invasion" of Hampton.[21]

Luckily, the rumor of advancing regulars proved false. The British soon withdrew from the Tidewater, leaving the militiamen—thankfully for the United States—with no enemy to fight. Tyler and Wat, who had also joined the company, saw no action in the War of 1812, though their youngest brother, William, an enlisted soldier serving on the Canadian border, did experience combat. Tyler's political enemies would later mock his service during the War of 1812, disparaging him with the nickname of "Captain Tyler" whenever they sought to put him down. For his part, Tyler gladly accepted the moniker, always pointing out that he had at least served his country.[22]

At war's end, Tyler turned his attention once again to the two things that mattered most: family and politics. He spent a considerable portion of his time after his short-lived military service tending to a new home. After beginning his married life at Mons Sacer, he sold the property in 1815 and moved to a nearby farm called Woodburn. He was also reelected to the House of Delegates for a fifth time in 1815. Shortly after the legislature convened, though, he resigned his seat and accepted an appointment to the Virginia Council of State. The eight-member body, chosen by the House and the state senate, served as the governor's advisory board—a privy council of sorts. The appointment offered Tyler a higher salary and a bit of prestige while attesting to the esteem the young legislator had won during the early part of his career. Most men with ambition did not long remain a member of the council; Tyler was no exception. Fueled by that ambition, he soon eyed a bigger prize.[23]

In September 1816 Virginia congressman John Clopton died after battling a lengthy illness. A special election in November would determine his successor. Excited at the prospect of furthering his career on the national stage, Tyler immediately made himself available for the vacant seat. His opponent was his courtroom adversary Andrew Stevenson, then Speaker of the House of Delegates. By this time, the two men had become friends as well as rivals. They enjoyed success at the bar, shared the same political ideology, and were recognized as loyal Republicans, all essential prerequisites for any chance at winning election to Congress from their district. Clopton's son, John Jr., also threw his hat into the ring, but the more recognizable Tyler and Stevenson quickly outdid him.[24]

The general consensus early in the race was that Tyler would win. "Tyler will be elected," one observer predicted weeks before the ballots were counted, "there is no doubt about it." Sure enough, the prediction held, and Tyler won the election—by a mere thirty votes. He may have benefited from Stevenson's brief unexplained and "unavoidable absence" from the campaign trail in early October. In any case, Tyler was going to Washington to begin his national political career. He offered his formal resignation to the Council of State on December 1, 1816, and prepared to leave Woodburn for the lame-duck session of the Fourteenth Congress.[25]

Chapter 3

THE PERILS OF NATIONAL POLITICS

The Washington City that greeted John Tyler in December 1816 when he arrived to take his seat in Congress still bore the effects of the late war. The British had burned the Capitol and the Executive Mansion in August 1814, leaving charred remains that must have shocked the freshman congressman. The House and Senate conducted business inside a smaller temporary "Brick Capitol" that had been hastily constructed on the spot where the current US Supreme Court Building sits. Tyler did not mind. In fact, he seemed quite pleased with his good fortune and was happy to be there.

Much later in his life—long after he had left the White House—Tyler reflected on his early impressions of the men who made up that Congress. The Speaker of the House, Henry Clay of Kentucky, Tyler said was "one who seemed formed for the station, and the station made for him." No less impressive was Daniel Webster. The New Hampshire congressman, not yet the "Godlike Daniel" he would become as he later represented Massachusetts, nevertheless struck Tyler even then as a marvelous orator. "At the forum, he had but few co-rivals." The penetrating insight of South Carolina's John C. Calhoun, "which was almost as great as that of a lens by which all the rays of light are brought to a focus," inspired awe. All three of these men had achieved a level of national prominence by 1816 that foreshadowed even greater accomplishments in the years ahead as they became America's "Great Triumvirate" in the US Senate.

The man in Washington whom Tyler seemed to find most interesting was a fellow Virginian—John Randolph of Roanoke. Brilliant and eccentric, Randolph had entered Congress in 1799, like Tyler at age twenty-six, and by 1816 led the small contingent of outspoken Old Republicans in the House. Randolph's flair for the dramatic enlivened debate. "How often he ha[d] been seen to enter the House booted and spurred," Tyler recalled, "and with a riding whip in his hand." A man who drank heavily and employed opium to numb both physical and emotional pain, Randolph regularly brought a tumbler of liquor with him to the chamber and, fortified by its effects, often unleashed bitter sarcasm and scathing repartee to wilt foes. Colleagues sometimes found Randolph offensive. Tyler disagreed. He acknowledged that the "weapons of wit and ridicule were often resorted to," but they were used with a "keen and polished edge" so as not to "degrade" the proceedings. The House of Representatives, Tyler averred, was a "model assembly."[1]

As highly esteemed by history as many of the members of the Fourteenth Congress are, by the time John Tyler arrived, their constituents regarded them with considerably less reverence. The House of Representatives had become a house of some ill repute. During the session before Tyler's election, members had passed the Compensation Act, which raised their salary from a per diem of $6 per day to $1,500 for each session, a boost of roughly $600 a year. Supporters of the new law pointed out that the congressional salary had remained the same since 1789 and had not kept pace with the cost of living in Washington City. The American people did not care. Outrage over what was called the "Salary Grab Act" began immediately. In towns large and small, newspapers and angry voters vilified their congressmen. Even members who had voted *against* the bill found themselves facing the fury of the people as guilty of *taking* the new salary. In the fall elections preceding the lame-duck session of the Fourteenth Congress, two-thirds of the House and half the Senate—Federalists and Republicans alike—were ousted from office. Such spirited opposition, and the wrath that went with it, had no precedent in American politics.[2]

John Tyler immediately joined the growing legion of his colleagues who supported repeal of the Compensation Act. Some of them had even been instructed by their state legislatures to vote for abolition of the law. Taking the floor on Saturday, January 18, 1817, for his inaugural speech as a member of the House, Tyler spent a half hour explaining why he was calling for repeal. For him, the question of whether a raise was warranted was beside the point. The issue was whether a representative of the people could rightfully ignore the people's will. "Who was the member of this House that would undertake to set up his opinion in opposition to that of his constituents?" he asked. A congressman should not "adopt the belief that they [the people] might err, but that he could not." Tyler had not been formally instructed to vote for repeal but was certain his constituents wanted him to take that action. He "had had a fair opportunity of knowing their wishes," he said, because he was "fresh from their hands."[3]

Much as he had done by injecting himself into the instruction controversy during his first days in the Virginia legislature, Tyler chose to make his first speech in the House of Representatives on the side of an issue that enjoyed broad popular support. Aware that congressmen who supported the Compensation Act had been roasted in the newspapers during the summer and fall, he saw little risk in arguing for repeal. The *Richmond Enquirer* seemed to speak for the majority of his district when it implored Congress to abolish the salary bill. Tyler could therefore proceed knowing he was in the mainstream of Virginia politics. He also believed that, because the salary bill had passed in the previous session by a margin of only 81 to 67, many of his colleagues were already on his side.

Thomas Grosvenor was not. Tyler's argument in favor of the repeal of the Compensation Act failed to convince the thirty-eight-year-old New Yorker, who afterward asked his freshman colleague if he had mistaken "the importunate clack of a few ephemeral noisy insects of his district, for the voice of the real tenants of the soil." Grosvenor claimed that self-serving hacks throughout the country had demagogued the new law and had succeeded in riling up the voters. In a lengthy speech he defended the salary increase and mocked the doctrine of instruction, scoffing that it would make a representative a "mere agent of a district" who would not be allowed to exercise his own judgment when voting for or against a particular measure. The people's recourse to legislation of which they disapproved, he said, could only come at the ballot box. In an effort to further embarrass Tyler, Grosvenor blamed the young Virginian's immaturity for views that had little merit, condescendingly pointing out that his new colleague had just arrived in Washington and perhaps had "press[ed]" his argument a bit too "earnestly."[4]

On the following Monday morning, Grosvenor sought out Tyler as he entered the Brick Capitol to assure his younger colleague that he had not "intended to utter anything of a personal nature" when responding to his speech on Saturday. Grosvenor's attempt to make amends, however, indicates that he recognized Tyler may have interpreted what he had said in precisely that way—that it *had* been personal—because that had been his intention. Taking time to reflect over the weekend, though, Grosvenor came to regret what he had said, or at least the way he had said it. Pleased that the New Yorker made the effort to clarify what he had meant—or had not meant—during the debate on Saturday, Tyler graciously thanked him, shook his hand, and moved on with no ill feelings.[5]

Tyler could afford to be gracious because he had prepared what he thought was a devastating rejoinder to Grosvenor's remarks. And he was going to enjoy twisting the knife, albeit with all the Virginia courtesy he had at his disposal. Like his colleague from the Empire State, Tyler spent Sunday replaying in his mind what had transpired in the House the day before. His reflection may have sparked questions to himself about whether history was repeating itself. Had he reprised the faux pas of the instruction controversy in the Virginia legislature here in the debate over the Compensation Act? Had his enthusiasm to press an argument and make quick political points gotten the better of him? Was he being put in his place once again for opening his mouth before he had taken the time to really consider his thoughts? Was he being punished for trying to propel himself forward without first paying his dues as a national politician? Had he not learned a lesson from that earlier experience?

Tyler's actions on Monday indicate that the exchange with Grosvenor had had a profound effect on him. He reentered the debate on the Compensation Act, but did so while employing a particular strategy. He started by obliquely flattering his older antagonist, then emphasized that because of his own lack of experience, he had "to combat upon very unequal ground." Just a David throwing stones at Goliath, Tyler compared himself to "a [mere] gunboat opposed to a seventy-four [gun ship of the line]." Despite his "inferiority," however, "he was not disposed to yield without at least exchanging one shot."

He made the most of that shot. Framing his argument in sectional terms, Tyler maintained that he and Grosvenor "differed as widely upon this subject as the north from the south." He presented a robust defense of the doctrine of instruction, as well as a history lesson for his colleagues that placed instruction into the larger context of republican government. "Sir," Tyler intoned, leveling a stare at Congressman Grosvenor, "this right of instruction has been consecrated by the Revolution." Responding to Grosvenor's dismissive comment on Saturday that he had erred in attributing the doctrine of instruction to the English republican theorist Algernon Sidney, he produced a prop. Taking a copy of James Burgh's *Political Disquisitions* out of his bag and brandishing it in the air, he placed the book on his desk, cracked it open, thumbed to page 190, and quoted Sidney directly.

Tyler made clear his belief that the "people of this country are the sovereigns" and confessed that, "although a young man, he had become or was becoming old fashioned in his politics." He further chastised Grosvenor. "The gentleman from New York has acknowledged that with the people resides the sovereign power," Tyler pointed out, "and yet, in the next breath, he advances an argument which goes to show that their sovereignty consists" solely of voting. "If this be all their power," the Virginian declared in a statement that surely elicited nods of approval from his fellow southerners, "they are no better than slaves, and the members of this House are their high-minded masters." Alluding to the compact theory of government, Tyler insisted that the American people had not yielded the right of instruction because they retained all powers not expressly granted to the federal government by the Constitution. Only if they instructed him to violate the Constitution would he ignore the will of the people.[6]

Tyler had presented a spirited defense of the people's right to instruct their representatives and had landed some rhetorical blows on Congressman Grosvenor. Quoting Sidney had been a nice touch, even if the ostentatious show of producing the book containing the relevant passage had been a bit too dramatic. But in the final analysis, Tyler's argument lacked the logical clarity of Grosvenor's. He relied too heavily on abstract allusions to the "will of the people." He failed to explain why he considered himself instructed by his constituents, openly acknowledging that the basis for his judgment was a "supposition." Moreover, he spoke as if the right of instruction had been firmly established in American politics and should have been plain for all to see, when in fact the right itself, as well as its application, remained controversial. Tyler neglected to mention that only four states even allowed the people to instruct their representatives (Virginia not among them). His contention that instruction had been "consecrated by the Revolution" had been particularly dubious. Indeed, neither the records of the debates in the Constitutional Convention nor the Constitution itself mention the right of instruction. Without question, Grosvenor had presented the better argument.[7]

Tyler ultimately recognized this and acknowledged that he had a lot of work to do in order for his speeches to measure up to those of his more seasoned colleagues. Self-doubt crept in and his self-confidence wavered. One year later, for example, as he squared off against Pennsylvania's formidable Joseph Hopkinson, he admitted his shortcomings. "My thoughts," Tyler said at the beginning of a speech, "which are our forces in debate, are undisguised and undisciplined." In this particular speech he also resurrected the naval-battle analogy he had used during the debate over repeal of the Compensation Act and again compared himself to a small boat taking on a much-better-equipped and much-larger ship. "[T]hose [thoughts] of the honorable gentleman [Hopkinson] are well trained and regularly arranged in order of battle," Tyler admitted. "I have ventured my little skiff upon the water, and when it shall sink and be forgotten, his more noble bark will have outlived the storm, and floated in triumph on the waves."[8]

Still, even employing "undisguised and undisciplined" thoughts in his defense of instruction, Tyler affected the overall tenor of the debate on repeal of the Compensation Act. Elijah Mills of Massachusetts proclaimed that he had "been not a little astonished and alarmed" that the doctrine of instruction had been defended so vigorously, seemingly conceding that what the Virginian had said might be enough to sway some of their colleagues in the House. Micah Taul of Kentucky concurred with Tyler that the people had the right to instruct their representatives. By the end of the debate on the Compensation Act, sentiment in the House seemed to favor the right of instruction. Perhaps more importantly, the tide had turned decisively against the salary law. The House repealed it three days after Tyler's speech. One week later the Senate followed suit. The Fifteenth Congress later voted to set congressional salaries at eight dollars per day and eight dollars for every twenty miles of travel, an alternative the American people found much more palatable.[9]

John Tyler thus found himself on the winning side of an issue that one historian has argued established the principle of *Vox Populi, Vox Dei* (the voice of the people is the voice of God) in American politics, heralding an emerging democratic age in the United States in which the common man enjoyed more power and more effectively held public servants accountable. Tyler understood the significance of the outcry over the Compensation Act. Repeal of the law, he maintained, should convince the people "that they are not merely 'hewers of wood and drawers of water,' but that Government is a *trust* proceeding from themselves—an emanation of their strength." The people had *forced* repeal of the odious law. The people mattered. For all of his genuine reverence for the republicanism of the founding era of his father, and while for his entire political career he employed the boilerplate language of disinterestedness and public virtue, Tyler realized that, by the time he got elected to Congress, the transition to democratic politics—to *democracy*—was already well underway.[10]

By participating in the debate on the Compensation Act, Tyler thus demonstrated that he understood the rules of the game. He succeeded in playing to his constituents despite the immaturity of his argument. In fact, the substance of the argument mattered less than the style. Just as significantly, Tyler had benefited from the timing of it all, which would quickly become a recurring theme in his political career. He arrived in Washington just as the Compensation Act became the primary issue in Congress. The voters had laid out his opportunity for him. Furthermore, he recognized the significance of the timing and capitalized on it.

With his condemnation of the Compensation Act and his defense of the doctrine of instruction, John Tyler had announced himself on the national political stage and had done so in a way that would have pleased his father. He had taken the initial step in defining his political identity and crafting his persona as a public servant. Since this was his first extended interaction with men from other states, the stakes were high. First impressions mattered. Disappointed—and angry—at the way he had been treated after his initial speech in the House, Tyler resolved to do better. His competitiveness and almost frantic desire to impress his colleagues spurred him on because he recognized that if he did not respond quickly to Grosvenor's insults with an effective follow-up speech, he would allow the New Yorker to define him. Whatever doubts of himself he may have entertained on that Sunday between his speeches, he quickly got over them and focused on crafting an effective rejoinder. The shortcomings in that second speech were less important than the fact that he had thrown himself back into the debate.[11]

In part, the electoral calendar prompted Tyler's assertiveness. Because he had been elected to replace Clopton at the end of a congressional session, he had to stand for election to the Fifteenth Congress in April 1817, just one month after the Fourteenth Congress adjourned. He thus *had* to make a speech as soon as he could—*had* to establish a national reputation—so that his friends in Virginia could tout his accomplishments to the voters of his district and so that he had a record to run on as he pursued reelection. As an outspoken advocate for the repeal of the salary law, he could virtually ensure his return to Washington.

Tyler also took advantage of a custom with a long history among southern congressmen: the publication of circular letters. A circular letter was a report a national lawmaker addressed to his constituents that summarized his speeches and highlighted his voting record on the major issues of the congressional term. Often, circular letters were printed in newspapers, which enabled congressmen to convey their message to as many voters as possible. Tyler wrote two circular letters during his stint in the House of Representatives, which were published in the *Richmond Enquirer*. He quickly developed a knack for writing subtle appeals for the support of his constituents that balanced a humble and very republican desire to continue to serve them with assurances that he was not directly asking them for their votes. He maintained that his circular letters should not be read as a "low, groveling, mean pursuit of popular favor." But in an acknowledgment of the democratic politics he had seen displayed during the Compensation Act controversy, he just as emphatically made clear that he held himself accountable to the will of the people. Tyler displayed his virtue for his constituents to see and demonstrated that he deserved their votes. It worked. He was reelected to the House in April 1817 and again in April 1819, ultimately serving from the second session of the Four-teenth Congress through the end of the Sixteenth—two and a half terms.[12]

"I wish the great people here knew something more about cooking," Repre-sentative Tyler grumbled to his wife, as he detailed an evening spent in the company of James and Dolley Madison at the Seven Buildings, their tempo-rary quarters while contractors repaired the Executive Mansion. "They have adopted the French style, and I cannot relish anything that they have for din-ner." Tyler savored the champagne that was served at the table but found that the cream-laden "sauces and flum-flummeries" of the meal upset his stomach. He was very likely lactose intolerant. "I had much rather dine at home in our plain way," he told Letitia, "than to dine with them."

Tyler had begged off two previous attempts of the Madisons to get him to break bread with them. Perhaps he knew what was in store for him. Refusing their previous invitations, however, betrayed Tyler's provincialism and a lack of understanding of how crucial the capital's social scene had become to na-tional politics. For all of their vaunted history and boasts of living in the cradle of America, Virginians were largely a parochial lot, and Tyler had initially been shortsighted. Dolley Madison's dinners and weekly drawing rooms, which combined the atmosphere of Old World courts with decidedly American man-ners, brought politicians and diplomats together in an unofficial sphere, apart from the halls of Congress, where they could gossip, trade information, hunt votes, and interact with the president. Under the First Lady's direction, by the time Tyler arrived in Washington, high society neatly complemented high politics. She was creating a capital befitting a republic. The young congress-man had surely heard plenty about Mrs. Madison's social events but initially failed to grasp how attending them might increase his profile in Washington and help him do his job. Despite his lack of sophistication, he found much to admire. The president's wife may not have served the simple boiled greens and bacon that Tyler enjoyed at home in Virginia, but she nevertheless impressed him as a fine hostess who "entertains her company in superb style."[13]

Most of the time, Tyler took his meals at a common table in a boarding-house, or what was called a "mess," which was the customary arrangement for congressmen and senators, most of whom resided in Washington for roughly half the year. Sharing supper with colleagues or enjoying a conversation after a tedious work day brought Tyler further into the unofficial sphere that helped shape national politics during the years he served in Congress. He lodged at Claxton's boardinghouse on Pennsylvania Avenue for the first two years he was in the capital. Thereafter, he took his room and meals at McGowan's Hotel and Tennison's, both also located on Pennsylvania Avenue. Their proximity to the Brick Capitol meant he could easily walk to work every day.[14]

Work energized the young congressman, and he enjoyed being in Washington. But he worried about what was happening at home in Virginia. Tyler's primary concern was ensuring that someone looked after his family while he was gone. Because of frail health—evident even at age twenty-six—and an unwillingness to travel, Letitia did not accompany her husband to Washington. She had no desire to take part in the social life of the nation's capital. There were also two small children in the household now: Mary, the couple's first child, had been born on April 15, 1815; her brother, Robert, had been born on September 9, 1816, around the time that Tyler made known his intention to run for Clopton's seat in Congress. Apparently, both pregnancies had been difficult for Letitia, and Tyler did not want to leave her completely unattended. Fortunately, his sister Maria and her husband, John B. Seawell, lived nearby. Maria and Letitia enjoyed a warm friendship, and Tyler knew he could rely on the Seawells to call on his wife periodically while he was away. Tyler also pressed his youngest sister, Christiana, to come to Woodburn during the winter and keep Letitia company.[15]

Tyler's creation of this support system for his wife reflected the prevalence of kinship networks in the South and demonstrated his awareness that without his extended family pitching in to help matters on the home front, he would have had no national political career. Away from home for half of the year, he sought a way to make Letitia feel better about his absences and ease his conscience for leaving her. Echoing what he had heard from his father as a youngster, he also told her that "nothing but a sense of duty can keep me from you."[16]

Tyler developed his own support system while he was away from home. Christiana, known as Kitty to her family, had married Henry Curtis, in 1813. Two years younger than John Tyler, Curtis was a graduate of the Medical College of Maryland and lived in Hanover County, Virginia. A friendship between the two men began while the young physician courted Kitty. Tyler, in fact, had confided to Curtis his feelings about his own impending marriage to Letitia. As Curtis prepared to lead Kitty to the altar, her older brother felt compelled to offer advice to her fiancé. Playing the role that his late father would have played had he been alive, Tyler told Curtis that he "did not wish [Kitty] to precipitate matters until you were placed in a situation to ensure her a competency." He advised him to obey his head before he "obey[ed] the impulse of affection." Satisfied that Curtis could provide for his sister, Tyler gave his approval to their marriage.

His relationship with Curtis continued to develop and strengthened after he won election to Congress, when the two men further built their friendship through correspondence. The practice was common in the Old South. Letters about politics, family matters, and personal concerns passed regularly between Hanover and Washington. These letters served as an outlet for Tyler, a way for him to candidly express feelings he kept hidden from others, knowing that the information he conveyed would be kept confidential. Tyler usually did not go so far as to divulge his innermost thoughts or his most deeply held secrets, but Curtis became privy to most of the details of his brother-in-law's life. The congressman often sought medical advice from the doctor and returned the favor by offering him legal counsel. He also enlisted his help in printing and distributing circular letters. Curtis became a very important person in Tyler's life—apparently even more important than his own brothers. Their relationship is indispensable for understanding the tenth president, especially before he entered the White House. Since virtually no letters between Tyler and Letitia survive, it is through his correspondence with Dr. Curtis that we learn the most about Congressman Tyler and his initial experience as a national politician.[17]

Tyler had walked onto the stage of national politics at a pivotal moment in his country's history. The United States was amid a transition in which the simpler agrarian society that had characterized the Age of Jefferson was giving way to the market-oriented society of what would soon become the Age of Jackson. Technology was beginning to change the way Americans traveled, the way they shipped their goods, and the way they communicated with one another. A younger generation of nationalists in the Republican Party promoted this transformation, which many historians have called a "market revolution," by seeking to build a strong and energetic federal government. Convinced that a weak national government had nearly led to America's defeat in the War of 1812, they were determined not to court disaster again. In fact, given the precarious state of affairs in Europe, they expected that another war loomed. Consequently, these men pursued what one scholar has called a "statist agenda" in an effort to prepare for that future war and to capitalize on what they believed were the nation's boundless prospects.[18]

These young nationalists were aided by their fellow Republican, President Madison, who in April 1816 signed two laws that would not only have momentous consequences for the American people but also shape the development of their political system for the next few decades. The first of these laws chartered a new national bank; the second established a protective tariff. Both bills had passed in Congress with bipartisan—Federalist and Republican—support as well as with votes from all regions of the country, part of an emerging "Era of Good Feelings" that transcended sectional jealousies and unified the nation.[19]

South Carolina's John C. Calhoun established himself as a key proponent of the expansion of federal power. Capitalizing on the creation of what became the Second Bank of the United States, and with the concurrence of the Kentuckian Henry Clay, another leading light of that younger cohort of nationalist Republicans, Calhoun introduced his Bonus Bill in December 1817. The bill earmarked an extra $1.5 million that the newly constituted bank was required to pay the federal government (as well as the net annual proceeds the government earned in stock dividends from its investment in the bank) for a permanent fund for internal improvements. Calhoun argued that his measure would ultimately "bind the Republic together with a perfect system of roads and canals." His goal was to channel the power of the public sector into stimulating and sustaining economic growth. The national bank would establish a system of credit and a sound currency. The tariff would protect American manufacturing and provide additional funding for internal improvements. Nationalist Republicans aimed to integrate the country's sections by fostering a robust home market, by conquering geographical isolation, and by constructing a national identity of which all Americans could be proud. Clay soon marketed it as the American System.[20]

Spirited debate followed the speech Calhoun gave on February 4, 1817, laying out his argument for the Bonus Bill. The question of constitutionality surfaced quickly. Most congressmen agreed that internal improvements would benefit the Union, but many southerners pointed out that despite those potential benefits, the Constitution had not granted the federal government the power to build roads and canals. Old Republicans like John Randolph were especially outspoken in their attempts to derail the measure. They failed. It passed in the House on February 8 by a vote of 86 to 84; Tyler voted against it. Nearly three weeks later the Senate passed the bill, 20 to 15. President Madison vetoed the measure the day before he left office.[21]

Tyler did not add his voice to the Old Republicans in the House on the Bonus Bill. Chastened a bit by his contentious exchange with Congressman

Grosvenor over the Compensation Act, he gave no speech staking out his position on the matter. He did, however, soon make clear where he stood on federally sponsored internal improvements in a circular letter. Conceding Calhoun's point that a national system of roads and canals would benefit the nation, he explained that he opposed the Bonus Bill because he believed it was unconstitutional. "Congress have no power under the Constitution to interfere with the *police* of the States," he wrote, using the term "police" not in its law-enforcement context, but as an expression of the broad scope of action to make policy for the welfare of their residents given to the states. In Tyler's judgment the states would be well served to assume the responsibility for internal-improvements projects. Not only did his view of the Bonus Bill comport with the position he had taken in the Virginia legislature a few years earlier, but it also provided him with an avenue to establish his strict-construction and states' rights principles in the public mind. He was beginning to plant his flag on terrain occupied by the Old Republicans in national politics, a stance that accorded with the views of the Richmond Junto.[22]

Tyler's tenure in the House, then, was marked more by what he opposed rather than what he supported. He was not the type of legislator who was willing to do the hard work of crafting a bill and then assemble the coalition needed to secure passage. He was not interested in building consensus, unlike his more rightly celebrated colleague Clay. Tyler was an obstructionist, as all of the Old Republicans were—a member of a principled minority who wore their status as a badge of honor. His constituents sent him to Washington because he agreed with them ideologically and because they knew he would fight tooth and nail against consolidation. It did not even matter if he was destined to lose that war. What mattered was that he gave a voice to the Old Republicans in national politics and defended the people of Virginia—and the South—against unconstitutional encroachments on their liberty. This is how he stood out; this is how he made a name for himself as a congressman. In this regard, Tyler was a capable functionary, but not much more.

Beyond his opposition to the Bonus Bill, Tyler also seized opportunities to wage his own war upon the two pillars of the American System that had won passage in Congress before he arrived—the national bank and the tariff. Tyler completely rejected the statist agenda favored by many in Congress. His opportunity to oppose the bank came first. In November 1818 Speaker Clay appointed Tyler to a special committee created to investigate the bank for the alleged misconduct of its directors. He was one of four Republicans (and three southerners) on the committee of five who traveled to Philadelphia, home of the bank, shortly before Christmas. They were responsible for auditing the books, for interrogating bank officials under oath, and for preparing a detailed report assessing whether the bank had violated its charter.[23]

Tyler and the rest of the committee presented their findings to the House in mid-January 1819. The report was devastating. The committee had discovered widespread wrongdoing, concluding that the bank's president, William Jones, had mismanaged the institution and that bank officials in Philadelphia had repeatedly violated the charter. Outright criminal activity also came to light. The investigation revealed that officials at some branches had encouraged speculation in the bank's stock—and had paid themselves dividends on stock they did not own. Tyler found the shady dealings disturbing. "What think you of our Banking gentry?" he asked Dr. Curtis in disgust. While Tyler believed the bank should forfeit its charter, at the very least he wanted Congress to issue what was called a *scire facias*, a judicial writ that would force the bank's directors to appear in federal court to show why the bank should keep its charter. He spoke at length on the House floor in support of this action and put the matter plainly. "If the evils of this system, as disclosed in the report and testimony, be not sufficient to induce us to direct a *scire facias*, in the name of Heaven, I demand to know what would be considered a sufficient inducement?"[24]

Tyler's view put him in agreement with the special committee's chair, John C. Spencer of New York, and with fellow Virginian James Johnson, who moved to repeal the bank's charter outright. But it placed him at odds with the majority of his House colleagues. Support for the bank in Congress was too strong. Many of his colleagues had benefited financially from their association with the bank. Most believed that stripping the bank of its charter would return the United States to the precarious position it had found itself in during the War of 1812. It dawned on Tyler that the special committee had been convened merely for show.

Greatly disappointed, Tyler still felt compelled to put himself on the record. He decided to lay out his argument for holding bank officials to account for their conduct and also wanted to articulate his practical, philosophical, and ideological objections to the national bank. He did so despite having received a petition from some of his constituents that urged him to look for ways to preserve the bank's charter—at least temporarily. The record does not indicate the names of the signatories of this petition, but it is not difficult to imagine that they were some of the most important men of Tyler's district. Spencer Roane, a judge on the Virginia Court of Appeals and the leader of the Richmond Junto, for example, had written privately of "the necessity of supporting the bank" because in his view "a great and general distress would pervade all classes" if the charter were suddenly revoked. Tyler was thus more doctrinaire than even the Junto when it came to the bank. Whoever had signed it, the petition surely reminded the Virginian that the branch of the Bank of the United States located in Richmond had brought benefits to his district and to his state. Therefore, taking to the floor of the House to register his opposition to the bank qualifies as a modest profile in courage.[25]

To no one's surprise, Tyler argued that a national bank was unconstitutional. But he went much further. The entire system established with the creation of the Second Bank of the United States, he declared, departed from the "correct principles of political economy." Directly challenging an argument South Carolina's William Lowndes had made concerning the bank's indispensability, he expressed skepticism "that the Government cannot get on without this bank." Tyler believed an alternative system that relied on responsible state banks would place the nation on sounder financial footing. He maintained that the national banking system left the American people too much at the mercy of the boom-and-bust cycle. He decried the paper money energizing that system. Worse still, "instead of a system abounding in blessings, [the bank] has been converted into an instrument of corruption" that threatened America's republican virtue and invited the nation's decay. Anticipating the argument Andrew Jackson would eventually make in his own war on the bank, Tyler portrayed the institution as a tool of privilege and noted that it had "introduced a spirit of luxury at variance with the simplicity of our institutions."[26]

Tyler's speech against the national bank is significant for a number of reasons. To start, it was a clear statement of his opposition to a key element of economic nationalism and continued to build his reputation as an Old Republican. Second, it clearly illustrates that he had worked hard to grasp the intricacies of the American banking system. A neophyte in such matters when he arrived in Philadelphia to investigate the bank in December 1818, by February 1819, when he spoke in the House, the Virginian understood not only *that* the bank had violated its charter but also *how* it had done so. He had proven himself a quick study. Third, the speech demonstrates that Tyler had matured as a politician. The impatient young man who spoke without fully working through his ideas—whether in the Virginia House of Delegates or the US Congress—had given way to a seasoned legislator who could now debate his colleagues and present his views with confidence and authority. Someone well versed in banking may have quibbled with some of his analysis, but Tyler had showed that he could lay out a methodical argument that was both thorough and persuasive. Finally, by taking a position that did not comport with the pro-bank views of the constituents who had signed the petition he received before making his speech, Tyler had also shown that he would not move in lockstep with the Richmond Junto when he believed preserving his political independence was the right thing to do. "Let my fate be what it may," he declared, "I have discharged my duty, and I am regardless of the consequences."[27]

The House ultimately voted 121 to 30 to allow the bank to keep its charter. No *scire facias* was ever issued. Tyler suffered no adverse political consequences from the stance he had taken on the bank. In fact, his dim view of the institution and the argument he had made in the House challenging the propriety of the entire national-banking system received affirmation in the spring of 1819, when the most devastating depression to date wrecked the nation's economy. Spurred by a collapse in American cotton prices in Britain and falling commodity prices in the United States, the Panic of 1819 ruined countless people and shuttered scores of businesses. Tyler summed it up: "Our wise men flattered us into the adoption of the banking system under the idea that boundless wealth would result." But the exact opposite had happened. "Instead of riches, penury walks the streets of our towns and bankruptcy knocks at every man's door. They promised us blessings, and have given us sorrows."

Tyler and his family seemed to have been spared the worst of the panic. In the final analysis, so had the national bank. Attempting to save the institution before the depression fully settled in, its new president, Langdon Cheves, who replaced the disgraced Jones, called in its loans and initiated an unforgiving policy of deflation. Southerners and westerners were hit hardest. Debtors in the South and West, nearly all of them bankrupt, would neither forgive nor forget what the institution they denounced as the "Monster" had done. Blaming the bank for what twenty-first-century Americans call predatory lending (and largely absolving themselves from their own responsibility for their financial demise), these people would eventually form a sizeable portion of Andrew Jackson's constituency and would revel in their hero's successful effort to destroy the institution they believed had ruined them.[28]

In the meantime, the bank found itself at the center of another controversy in March 1819, when the US Supreme Court unanimously upheld its constitutionality and denied the right of a state to tax one of its branches in the *McCulloch vs. Maryland* case. Chief Justice John Marshall framed the court's argument in support of the bank's constitutionality around the doctrine of implied powers, resurrecting the logic Hamilton had used to defend the original national bank in 1791. Further, invoking the necessary-and-proper clause of the Constitution as well as the document's supremacy clause, the chief justice declared that the "states have no power, by taxation or otherwise, to retard, impede, burden, or in any manner control, the operations of the Federal Government, or its agencies."[29]

The Marshall court's rebuke of the state of Maryland echoed like a thunderclap in Virginia. Old Republicans in Tyler's home state quickly mobilized to sound the tocsin and shape public opinion against the Supreme Court. Throughout the spring and early summer of 1819, the pages of the *Richmond Enquirer* carried numerous editorials and essays denouncing the *McCulloch* decision. Roane labeled *McCulloch* "alarming" and characterized it as "warfare" upon states' rights. Another observer, championing the compact theory of government and the Tenth Amendment, referred to the court's decision as a "bold and dangerous interpretation" of the Constitution—and on and on. Thomas Ritchie solemnly enjoined "those firm Republicans of the Old School" to "rally round" the Constitution and defend "the rights of the states against federal usurpation."[30]

The Old Republicans in Virginia adopted a siege mentality in the wake of the *McCulloch* decision, believing that the hallowed Principles of '98, the foundation of their creed of strict construction and states' rights, had been attacked. They objected not to the bank itself, but to the protection afforded it by the Supreme Court. The *Enquirer* had been critical of the Marshall court since 1816, when its decision in the case of *Martin v. Hunter's Lessee* reversed a judgment of the Virginia supreme court. But the tipping point arrived only with the *McCulloch* decision. The Virginia House of Delegates offered a set of resolutions that inveighed against the court's decision, especially the doctrine of implied powers. The Virginia Senate voted to set the resolutions aside, so they never became the official position of the Old Dominion on the matter, but the point had been made. By 1819, support for the postwar trend toward a robust national government had evaporated in Virginia. The Era of Good Feelings, such as it was, had ended. Many in the state now stood in opposition to the consolidation they believed represented a mortal threat to republicanism. Virginians—and not just those of the old school—invoked the Principles of '98 to guide them through this crisis and prepare them for future battles.[31]

John Tyler had already put on his armor. His effort to thwart the Bonus Bill and call attention to the evils of the national bank demonstrated a steadfast commitment to sound principles. He knew what was at stake, declaring that nationalists in Congress "would establish all the roads asked for, all the

National Banks which can be asked for, and do anything which might, in their belief, promote the general welfare. Let us look well to our rights."[32]

He could soon add the tariff to the list of nationalist goals. On April 21, 1820, as the first session of the Sixteenth Congress neared completion, debate began in the House over a bill (actually three bills that were debated as if only one had been introduced) that called for rate hikes on many imports. The Panic of 1819 had alarmed American manufacturers and convinced them that they needed stout protection for the "security and encouragement" of their livelihoods. They lobbied Congress—mostly through petitions—to provide it. Nationalists like Clay championed their cause. Many southerners in Congress objected. They had interpreted the 1816 tariff as a temporary expedient and had gone along with amendments to the law two years later that provided still more protection to manufacturing. But now, enough was enough.[33]

Part of their objection reflected sectional animosity that had surfaced during congressional debates over the admission of the territory of Missouri to the Union (discussed below). More practically, southerners believed a higher tariff threatened their economic security, which had already been greatly imperiled by the fall of cotton prices that had hastened the panic one year earlier. They began to craft an argument against the tariff with distinctly sectional overtones, pointing out that manufacturers in the North stood to benefit from greater protection, while nothing would be done to aid farmers in the South. Their reasoning here called to mind the contest between Hamilton and Jefferson in the 1790s over whether the United States would become at its core a commercial or agrarian republic. By 1820, southerners had returned to an idea that reconciled these two visions for America in a way they believed would benefit them and the nation as a whole. The answer was free trade.

The *idea* of free trade, with its open access to markets and the pursuit of commerce without government interference, harkened back to the American Revolution. Having thrown off the mercantilist policies of Britain, which they found burdensome and oppressive, Americans had sought the opportunity to trade freely with the nations of the world. Free trade became a component of republican ideology. As a *political* tool, however, it emerged only gradually as a response to the statist agenda nationalists pursued after the War of 1812. Southerners had taken the lead in trying to convert their philosophy into policy.[34]

They found spokesmen in Tyler and three other congressmen from Virginia—Mark Alexander, William Archer, and Philip Pendleton Barbour. Early in the debate over a new tariff, these men took to the floor of the House and laid out cogent arguments against the legislation. Putting aside the question of constitutionality for once, Tyler instead attacked the principle of protectionism. Recalling what he had learned at William and Mary by reading the bible of free-trade philosophy, Smith's *Wealth of Nations,* he pointed out that protectionism actually resulted in negative consequences. Raising the tariff, he argued, would "shut us out from the foreign market" as other nations retaliated against high duties in the United States with prohibitively high taxes on American products. Tyler agreed with Smith's suggestion that the United States should freely participate in the world market, selling those commodities it could cheaply and efficiently produce at home and purchasing those products more cheaply and efficiently produced elsewhere. By keeping prices low, this policy would benefit American consumers. But what was even more important, the South would not find itself at the mercy of northern manufacturing interests, who otherwise would have little incentive to sell supplies and tools at an affordable cost. Free trade was therefore fair trade.[35]

Tyler of course voted against the tariff in 1820. It nevertheless passed in the House by a vote of 91 to 78. The Senate subsequently voted 22 to 21 to postpone the bill until the next session of Congress, which meant, for at least a time, the tariff was dead. Its foes, the shrewdest of whom realized they had likely won only a temporary respite, praised those in Washington who had supported their position. The *Richmond Enquirer* proclaimed, "We have not met with a single citizen, however humble or however high, who does not sincerely thank them [Congress] for their vote." Tyler's speech on the tariff and his vote on the bill may have done little to influence the course of events, but he had at least gone on record favoring the position of Virginia's leading Old Republicans. Later, in November 1820, he won more of their admiration when he defended a group of his Richmond constituents whose petition on the tariff had been attacked in the House by the author of the 1820 bill, Pennsylvania's Henry Baldwin.[36]

Tyler had firmly established himself as a foe of the American System, challenging the constitutionality of federally sponsored internal improvements and the national bank and making the case for a free-trade economic policy that called into question the entire premise behind the tariff and protectionism. Unfortunately, he had found himself on the losing side of each issue. Calhoun's Bonus Bill had failed only because of President Madison's veto. The bank survived the congressional investigation, kept its charter, and became, if anything, even more powerful in the years ahead. Tyler's speech on the tariff bill and his vote against it, moreover, could not prevent its passage in the House. And the Senate's postponement of the 1820 bill only put off the inevitable. Protectionists mobilized; stymied again during the second session of the Sixteenth Congress, they won the day in 1824, when a new tariff became law.

It is little wonder, then, that by 1820, Tyler had begun to question whether being a member of Congress was even worth the effort. His health had suffered during his time in Washington. He was also living dangerously close to financial insolvency, as his congressional salary failed to compensate for the business his law practice lost while he tended to politics. He could only manage his farm haphazardly while he was in Washington. Moreover, the time he spent away from his family took its toll on Letitia and the children, placing enormous pressure on him. Letitia's health was a constant worry. She had given birth to the couple's third child, John Tyler Jr., on April 29, 1819, and it took her weeks to recover her strength.[37]

Letitia had made clear in 1818 that she wanted her husband home all the time. She had pleaded with him to give up his seat in Congress and return to Virginia, where Tyler could pay attention to both his law practice and the family farm. He acknowledged the merit in this. Whenever he left them behind to travel to Washington, the thought that he was shirking his familial responsibility nagged at him. He usually arrived in the capital days or even weeks after sessions began, indicating that he put off his departures from Woodburn as long as he possibly could because he could not bear the scene that inevitably accompanied his goodbyes. In sum, Tyler had found national politics incompatible with a happy personal life, and constantly waging legislative battles on the losing side was sapping his physical and emotional strength.[38]

The person in whom Tyler confided and to whom he shared the details of his health and mindset was, of course, Henry Curtis. If someone had asked the good doctor what national issue troubled Tyler the most during his tenure in the House of Representatives, he undoubtedly would have had a ready reply: Missouri. Indeed, it was the crisis over Missouri's admission to the Union, which took Congress two years to resolve, that finally broke John Tyler.

Missouri Territory applied to Congress for statehood in February 1819, during the second session of the Fifteenth Congress. The House of Representatives drafted an enabling act to bring what would become the nation's twenty-third state into the Union with a constitution permitting slavery. New York congressman James Tallmadge, however, had other ideas. He introduced a two-part amendment that he attached to the enabling act. The amendment stipulated first that no more slaves would be allowed into Missouri once it became a state. Second, all enslaved children born after the territory became a state would be freed at age twenty-five. The Tallmadge Amendment thus provided for gradual emancipation in Missouri; nothing would be done to change the status of the roughly ten thousand slaves already living there in 1819. Tallmadge invoked Article IV, Section 4 of the Constitution, which guarantees a "republican form of government" to each state, to justify such federal intervention.[39]

The Missouri crisis sparked a new and more dangerous debate over whether Congress or the people who lived there retained the authority to determine slavery's fate in a territory. Thomas Jefferson had initiated that debate years earlier when he drafted the Ordinance of 1784, a measure that provided for the gradual abolition of slavery in new states entering the Union after the original thirteen. The antislavery provision of Jefferson's ordinance failed to secure passage in the Articles of Confederation Congress. Three years later the Northwest Ordinance—which did pass—stipulated that slavery would be immediately prohibited in territories in the Old Northwest located north of the Ohio River (Ohio, Indiana, Illinois, and Wisconsin). Furthermore, Congress asserted its authority to oversee the political development of a region at the *territorial* stage—that is, before it became a state. So there existed a precedent whereby Congress dictated slavery policy to residents of a territory. Southerners went along with this in part because the soon-to-be-enacted "Southwest Ordinance" allowed slavery in the territories south of the Ohio River. This demarcation provided a formula of sorts for dealing with the issue of slavery in the territories, which worked well until Missouri—the first would-be-state entirely west of the Mississippi River—applied for statehood.[40]

After Tallmadge introduced his amendment, members of Congress quickly mobilized behind sectional lines. Outnumbering their southern counterparts 105 to 80, northern congressmen secured passage of both parts of the Tallmadge Amendment; Tyler voted against both. Several days later the Senate rejected the amendment. The balance of eleven slave states and eleven free states meant the measure would not become law (some northern states' senators also voted with the South). The Fifteenth Congress adjourned in March 1819 without reaching a decision on Missouri.[41]

As the start of the Sixteenth Congress neared in December 1819, northerners and southerners took to the newspapers to stake out their positions on Missouri and demonize the other side. The question came up again two days into the new Congress and dominated debate throughout the winter of 1820. "'Missouri' is the only word ever repeated here by the politician," Tyler informed Curtis. The stakes had gotten higher, and many southern members of Congress had made their continued support of the Union contingent upon Missouri's admission as a slave state. Tyler wanted Missouri admitted with slavery, if that was what the people who lived there wanted, but he would not stoop to threats against the Union. In fact, he found such a view irresponsible. "Men talk of a dissolution of the Union with perfect non-chalance and indifference," he reported to Curtis with some amazement. Remaining optimistic, Tyler would not allow himself to contemplate such a drastic course. "I for one . . . will not be frightened at false fire," he declared. He looked for Congress to resolve the problem, and in a manner satisfactory to the South. "The storm I trust will burst on the heads of those very wretches who have presumptuously raised it," he predicted.

Unfortunately, it was on Tyler's head that a different type of storm burst early in February, amid the most trying days of the Missouri debate. Sitting at his desk in the House chamber (Congress had returned to the refurbished capitol in 1819), he suddenly felt a "disagreeable sensation" in his head that got so bad he was forced to retreat to his bed at McGowan's Hotel. Before the day was over, he experienced numbness in his hands, feet, tongue, and lips. A physician whose care he sought told him vaguely that he likely had a "diseased stomach." The doctor bled him and administered purgatives, a typically unhelpful remedy common in the early nineteenth century. Knowing the doctor had been out of his depth in diagnosing him and desperately needing to alleviate his symptoms, Tyler eventually sought Curtis's medical opinion through the mail. Whatever it was, the illness differed from anything he had ever experienced, leaving him bedridden for three days and lingering for weeks. Shooting pain in his neck and arms also increased his discomfort. Tyler was extremely shaken by it all.[42]

There was no time for an extended convalescence, as Tyler wanted to throw himself into the fray over Missouri. Still weak on February 17, he rose from his chair to offer his thoughts on the crisis. He knew that Illinois senator Jesse Thomas had devised a compromise during the first week of February that might break the impasse in Congress. The terms of the proposal were straightforward. A line would be drawn at thirty-six degrees, thirty minutes latitude (the southern boundary of Missouri) and slavery would be prohibited north of that line. Slavery would thus be confined in the former Louisiana Purchase territory to the recently created Arkansas Territory. Congress would admit Missouri into the Union as a slave state, while Maine, then part of Massachusetts, would be admitted as a free state. Support for this compromise was slowly building in the House, but northern restrictionists—those congressmen who favored admitting Missouri according to the terms of the Tallmadge Amendment—still held the upper hand.

Tyler largely addressed his remarks to these men and offered full-throated opposition to restricting slavery in Missouri. The speech was far from the best he had ever delivered in the House, and it was clear he had not fully recovered from his illness. Much of what he said, in fact, merely repeated points that many of his southern colleagues had already made during the course of the debate. Tyler weighed in on an issue that had prompted some of the most heated exchanges of the debate: whether Congress had the right to prohibit slavery at the *territorial* stage of a future state's development. When Congress created the territory of Missouri in 1812, it had allowed slavery there. As one historian has argued, Tallmadge's amendment "imposed conditions on Missouri as a territory *and* as a state because it effectively rescinded the right to hold slaves in Missouri and imposed conditions on which it could enter the Union." In Tyler's view Congress had no right to restrict slavery at *any* phase of the process—in Missouri or elsewhere—despite the precedent established in 1787 with the Northwest Ordinance.[43]

Shortly after Tyler's speech, a conference committee of the House and Senate reached an agreement to settle matters according to the terms proposed by Senator Thomas. Tyler voted against what was called the Missouri Compromise, but it passed anyway. President James Monroe signed the measure into law. Another crisis soon erupted after Missouri submitted its constitution for congressional approval. The state had included a clause in the document barring free blacks and mulattoes. Clay engineered a "Second Missouri Compromise" and secured a promise from the legislature of Missouri that the state would never deprive an American citizen of rights guaranteed under the US Constitution. In effect, Missouri's leaders told Congress that the offending clause in their constitution did not mean what it said. It was enough to win congressional sanction, and Missouri entered the Union. Tyler, just wanting the entire ordeal finished, voted for this second compromise.

He believed, however, that the South had made a bad bargain with the first compromise and had given away too much in an effort to prevent disunion. He looked at a map and was struck by how much territory was forever closed to slavery. Years later, when he was asked about the Missouri Compromise, he said, "I would have died in my shoes, suffered any sort of punishment you could have inflicted upon me, before I would have done it." Sentiment throughout Virginia concurred with Tyler's view. Ritchie and the Old Republicans denounced the compromise. The long-term implications seemed clear.

A letter published in the *Richmond Enquirer* warned: "Let us not shut our eyes on the evil that stares us in the face. Let us forecast this thing. The Union is in danger." The author of this letter exaggerated at the time, but his point was well taken, and he correctly predicted the future. By the 1830s, an increasingly polarized North and South would fight to impose their own definition of the Union on each other. In time, northerners sought to marginalize slavery, and a growing abolitionist movement looked for ways to eradicate it. Southerners attempted to nationalize the institution with safeguards designed to ensure its viability and preserve their political power. They also began to defend the institution by portraying it as a positive good rather than a necessary evil. Viewed in its larger context, then, the congressional debate over Missouri from 1819 to 1821, which Jefferson called a "fire bell in the night," augured a period of sectional conflict over slavery that would end only with the Civil War. As president, Tyler would play a role in exacerbating this conflict.

What is strikingly absent from Tyler's speech on Missouri is an outright defense of the institution of slavery. He opposed the Tallmadge Amendment not because it threatened slavery in Missouri per se. What troubled him was the political power northern members of Congress sought to exercise through it and the power they sought for the federal government. His argument against the amendment and his subsequent opposition to the Missouri Compromise must be viewed alongside his efforts to dismantle the American System. Tyler was determined to fight the consolidation that his father warned about long ago in his own battle against the ratification of the Constitution. The statist agenda the nationalists had recently pursued truly alarmed the Virginian. He recognized that it posed a threat to strict construction and states' rights, and he fully believed it threatened liberty. It was unconstitutional. It had to be stopped.

Tyler's obstructionism against internal improvements, the national bank, the tariff, and the Missouri Compromise, then, did not serve as a proxy for the outright defense of slavery, which it did for even more conservative, more doctrinaire Old Republicans such as Virginia's own John Randolph. Taking their cue from Randolph and from North Carolina senator Nathaniel Macon, who declared in 1818 that "if Congress can make canals they can with more propriety emancipate [slaves]," historians have largely refused to accept at face value the constitutional arguments made in opposition to the American System and to the Missouri Compromise. Men such as Tyler, in this view, looked for ways to prevent the federal government from amassing too much power because they sought above all to protect slavery. They hoped to stave off the day when a powerful federal government, with northerners at the helm, would train its sights on their peculiar institution. Thus, they were not saying *exactly* what they meant when they made their stand against consolidation in the years around 1820. This scholarly view mischaracterizes Tyler's career in the House of Representatives.[44]

In fact, the speech Tyler delivered during the Missouri crisis reveals that he envisioned the gradual and "total extinction of slavery" from the United States. Far from exhibiting any original thinking on the matter, however, he merely regurgitated the theory of diffusion that Jefferson and Madison had championed. Tyler maintained that opening Missouri and other western territories to slavery would diffuse America's enslaved population across a wider area, which would eventually result in emancipation. Westward expansion, and the demand for slaves in the newer regions of the country, would spur large slaveholders in states like Virginia to sell their enslaved people in a lucrative market. As more and more slaves were sold west, the number of large slaveholders in the eastern states would dwindle. Moreover, a decrease in the slave population in the older states of the South would make compensated emancipation or deportation—which many saw as essential to ending slavery—less burdensome. Finally, Tyler claimed that opening up Missouri and the West to slavery would "ameliorate the condition of the black man" by providing incentives to the slaveholder to "be more tender in his treatment" so that he could sell a slave for a higher price.[45]

These words demonstrate three things about Tyler's view of slavery. First, he regarded the institution in much the same way as Jefferson did and in the way the Old Republicans did—as a necessary evil that would (hopefully) end one day. His claim that opening the West to slavery would ultimately benefit those held in bondage came close to the "positive good" defense of the peculiar institution but was not fully in line with the proslavery argument that would emerge roughly one decade later. Second, Tyler clearly viewed enslaved people as property to be bought and sold at the whim of their owners. Third, he acknowledged, perhaps inadvertently, the ill treatment many slaves faced at the hand of slaveholders, something many southerners were careful to avoid later in the face of the abolitionist assault on slavery.

Tyler's physical collapse at the height of the ferocious debate over Missouri demonstrated that he had reached his breaking point. Always prone to poor health, his body had failed him. What is more, his mental state revealed a man in crisis. Buffeted by the demands of his office and keenly aware of how much stress his absences from home caused his wife, he looked for a way out.

Tyler wrote Curtis in December 1820 that he would not seek reelection to Congress. He was through with national politics. Privy to the physical and mental strain his brother-in-law had been suffering for some time, Curtis could not have been surprised. He realized this was not a rash decision. "I have become in a great measure tired of my present station," Tyler wrote. He told Curtis that he had devoted "all my exertions" to public service. Dejected at losing the war against consolidation, he concluded in frustration, "I can no longer do good here." Alarmed by the blatantly—as he saw it—antisouthern course the federal government had pursued and angered by the "daring usurpations of this government," he declared that he "stood in a decided minority, and to waste words on an obstinate majority is utterly useless and vain."

Tyler published an open letter in the *Enquirer* informing his constituents of his decision, explaining that poor health was forcing him to exit the national political stage. But there was another, equally compelling consideration he did not make public that influenced his decision to leave Congress. "I owe a duty to my family," he told Curtis. "My children will soon be treading on my heels and it will require no common exertions to enable me to educate them." Indeed, as the father of three small children, with another one on the way, Tyler worried about providing for his growing family. He knew that government service would not provide the lucrative income he might earn by devoting himself fully to a law career. As his experience had made clear, national politics and the practice of law were "almost incompatible with each other." Tyler also knew that he needed to pay more careful attention to his farm. Furthermore, he said he longed for "those enjoyments in the bosom of my family . . . which cannot be found in any other condition of existence."

Accordingly, after Congress adjourned in March 1821, Tyler returned to Woodburn to be with Letitia, to recover his health, and to take an active part in raising his children. At the age of thirty-one, he would have no more of public life.[46]

Chapter 4

A SCHEME TO GO BACK

Tyler's decision to leave Congress seems straightforward on its face: He was ill. He was frustrated by an inability to help win legislative victories for the South. He needed money. He wanted to meet the demands of his family. Acknowledging to a friend that he often felt like an "alien" in his own home because he had been gone so often and for such extended periods of time, Tyler had missed some of the little milestones in the lives of his young children that make fatherhood so rewarding.[1]

But rarely are things so straightforward. If we look below the surface, we see something more complicated. This is particularly true when we examine Tyler's retirement. Southern politicians often used the dramatic gesture of leaving office to demonstrate their independence and to portray themselves as passive, disinterested—and therefore republican—public servants. As one historian has pointed out, it "is almost impossible to find a Southern political leader who did not either resign [or] retire" at some point in his career. So the act of retirement itself was a political act and was often calculated for political effect. Consider what Tyler confided to Henry Curtis shortly before he left the House of Representatives in the spring of 1821: "I think on the whole the chance of future elevation is as great at home as it is here. What can I promise myself on the score of personal ambition, if that is to enter into the estimate, by remaining?—literally nothing." Tyler felt four years as a congressman had been long enough. As a means to further his ambition, the office had outlived its usefulness, or, as he put it, "the honor of the station is already possessed." These private words indicate that Tyler viewed retirement as a way to potentially advance his national career. Not quite certain exactly how a brief retirement might further his prospects, he hoped to return to politics in the future—and he had a loftier office in mind.[2]

Even as he prepared to become a full-time husband and father, then, Tyler made sure his friends knew he would be willing to return to the political battlefield in the future. He assured one of them that if any crisis arose, he would "unhesitatingly overlook all private considerations" and become a politician once again. He did not want his allies to overlook him should some alluring elective office become available. Tyler even went so far as to publicly proclaim his future availability in a circular letter, presumably one he knew he could keep Letitia from seeing. Framing his intentions in terms of honor and portraying himself as a disinterested public servant, he made clear he would not shirk his political duty if called upon. "Should occasion require it," he declared, "and destiny permit, I shall ever be ready to contribute my mite to the advancement of my country's happiness."[3]

Tyler almost acted as if the fate of the republic might depend on his willingness to reenter politics at some point. Even for him, the message conveyed in the circular letter was overdone and demonstrated an inflated sense of his own self-importance. It also makes clear that while his wife and children may have been enjoying his company, they were not enjoying his undivided attention. By laying the groundwork for a second act on the political stage shortly after he had stepped over the threshold at Woodburn, once again Tyler had ensured his family's future unhappiness. He had also ensured that he would be unhappy with his retirement.

Tyler's fourth child, Letitia, had been born on May 11, 1821, and while he could happily report that both mother and baby had recovered from the trauma of childbirth rather quickly, settling in for the long haul as a stay-at-home husband and father seemed unappealing. Right from the start, frustration characterized his life away from politics. For one thing, after recovering somewhat from the poor health of the previous winter, he fell ill again. The sickness lingered. "I get on *but so so*," he complained to Curtis. "For a week at a time I feel as well as ever, but then comes the fit again and I suffer severely." Tyler believed his illness resulted at least in part from chronic stomach problems, and he asked Curtis to recommend a remedy for dyspepsia. But the symptoms he described were similar to those he had suffered in Washington during the Missouri debates and indicate a more serious condition. He told Curtis he felt muscle weakness and tingling in the arms, face, lips and tongue. One physician has speculated that Tyler may have suffered from Guillain-Barre Syndrome, a rare disease that follows viral illness, which is characterized by loss of muscle strength and intermittent paralysis. Tyler may have had an infection that triggered the disease.

Whatever the cause, the malady debilitated him. "The disorder not only affects my body but often my mind," he said. "My ideas become confused and my memory bad while laboring under it." It seemed as if he would never be fully healthy again, and, at one point, Tyler worried that the condition might impair his ability to practice law. "Unless I can remove it [the illness]," he concluded, "it would be idle for me to enter into an active and mentally laborious business."[4]

Tyler sought relief in a trip to the Blue Ridge Mountains during the summer of 1821. Fresh air and an opportunity to bathe in the mineral springs seemed to alleviate his symptoms for a short time. The illness did not disappear completely, however, and he grew increasingly frustrated because the symptoms returned sporadically and were "so variable that [he could not] reduce them to form or order." When friends approached Tyler about running for a seat in the House of Delegates in April 1822, he thought about it briefly but told them he feared putting his health at further risk.[5]

After Tyler set about tending his farm in the fall of 1821, he received an unexpected piece of good news when the owner of his boyhood home, Greenway, put the property up for sale. Tyler's older brother, Wat, had sold the house not long after their father's estate had been settled, and it had been out of the family for several years. The farm had sentimental value for him. Making Greenway additionally attractive, it was much larger than Woodburn, thus a better house for a growing family. Tyler jumped at the chance to purchase it, coming to a complicated agreement with the owner to buy the property for seven thousand dollars.[6]

As he did at Woodburn, Tyler primarily grew wheat at Greenway, seeking to both feed his family and make a profit selling to market. Commercial agricultural production meant that Tyler had to concern himself with another facet of the antebellum southern household: control over slave labor. His bonded labor force, which numbered approximately twenty-four in 1821–22, cultivated enough grain for both farm consumption and sale.[7] Unfortunately, Tyler's retirement from politics coincided with two very poor growing seasons for wheat throughout much of Virginia.[8]

Poor harvests put pressure on Tyler to pursue his law career more vigorously, and he sought out clients once again, though without enthusiasm. At first his chief client was Dr. Curtis. A Tyler relative had given the Dixon estate, a sizeable property in Charles City County, to Curtis and Kitty, Tyler's sister, as a wedding present in 1815. From the start, the estate suffered numerous claims against it and required Tyler's almost constant attention. Many judgments took years to resolve. Eventually, he became executor of the Dixon estate and found himself "greatly harrass'd and much to the *leeward*" as claimant after claimant sought their share of the pie. The situation made what had initially appeared to be a windfall for Curtis a financial nightmare. For Tyler, the problems associated with the estate meant many hours of tedious paperwork as he waded through inquiries and replied to litigants. He had little patience for such work and became unhappy whenever he had to do it. Tyler also had to play the part of bill collector and pursued judgments owed Curtis in an effort to pay off some of the claims against the Dixon estate. To make matters worse, he received little, if anything, in the way of payment and often reached into his own pocket to ward off creditors. Tyler could ill afford to keep this practice up for very long. Thus, while acknowledging Curtis's strained financial situation, he at one point told him bluntly, "I am cashless" and stressed the need for payment. The continuous problems connected with the estate would, in time, lead to a rift between the two men that severely damaged their friendship.[9]

Lingering illness, poor wheat crops, and a trying law practice: little wonder retirement frustrated Tyler. He passed the summer and fall of 1822 at Greenway with his family but was restless—so restless, in fact, that during the winter of 1822–23 he decided to make a run at returning to the Virginia legislature. His addiction to politics had won. Tyler no doubt hoped a successful campaign would become a springboard to a higher national office. The prospects were favorable. Both delegates from Charles City County had chosen not to run for reelection in April 1823, meaning there were two vacant seats available. Fortified by the apparent return of his health—he had suffered no episodes of the recurring illness for several months—he stumped his district. Of the three candidates vying for the two seats, Tyler won the most votes. He eagerly traveled to Richmond for the start of the legislative session in early December 1823. Letitia had given birth to their fifth child—Elizabeth—five months earlier.

Tyler's return to politics coincided with the initial phase of the presidential campaign of 1824. President Monroe had not designated his preferred successor, so the field was wide open. As the campaign unfolded, four men emerged as contenders: Secretary of State John Quincy Adams, Treasury Secretary William Crawford, Speaker of the House Henry Clay, and US senator Andrew Jackson. Adams, Crawford, and Clay were widely known in national political circles and had staked out clearly defined positions to allow their allies to promote their candidacies. Adams and Clay were more nationalist in orientation, while Crawford waved the banner of states' rights and strict construction. Jackson, wildly popular throughout the United States for his heroics at the Battle of New Orleans in January 1815, had sent confusing political signals. Indeed, his record on banks and internal improvements had been inconsistent. No one seemed to know exactly where he stood on these key issues.

Besides his military record, Jackson had one other thing going for him. He had become the preferred candidate of a movement that began in his home state of Tennessee that was designed to dismantle the caucus system of selecting presidential nominees. With the demise of the Federalist Party nationally after the War of 1812, the Republicans had enjoyed what essentially became one-party rule. Every four years, party leaders in Congress came together to choose their nominee in a caucus. Whomever emerged from the caucus as the nominee was then elected president. This had been the case for both Madison and Monroe.

The caucus system had thus allowed for the Virginia "dynasty" of presidents to continue unabated from 1801 to 1820. Crawford, who had been born in Virginia (as had Clay), emerged as the frontrunner in 1824 because most insiders assumed he would win the nomination of the caucus. He was the choice of the Richmond Junto, which favored retaining the caucus. As the campaign season got underway, however, many people outside of Virginia decided that they had had enough and aimed to break the Old Dominion's stranglehold on the Republican Party. The Tennessee legislature passed resolutions denouncing the caucus as undemocratic and a violation of the Constitution. In time, Jackson became the standard bearer of what his supporters were touting as a decidedly more democratic brand of politics.[10]

From his seat in the Virginia House of Delegates, Tyler did all he could to derail Jackson's candidacy. He chaired a legislative committee that defended the caucus system and championed the candidacy of Crawford, the eventual winner of a watered-down caucus. Privately, Tyler referred to Jackson as a "*mere soldier*—one acknowledg'd on all hands to be of little value as a civilian." When Crawford suffered an apparent stroke in September 1823, Tyler threw his support behind Adams, a candidate the Junto and most Old Republicans staunchly opposed. But from Tyler's perspective, the objective was to stop Jackson at all costs.[11]

Tyler's defense of the caucus system merits a close examination. How could a man who had so publicly supported the politics that toppled the Compensation Act and who championed the will of the people while he served in Congress now turn his back on democracy and attempt to prop up a largely discredited method of choosing the president? Since the evidence on this matter is virtually nonexistent, at least as it relates to Tyler, some speculation is called for. Was the caucus system really undemocratic? To start, we must consider how the anticaucus campaign began. Jackson partisans had rhetorically undermined the caucus in the Tennessee legislature and then flayed it in newspapers throughout the country. By doing so, they had launched a movement that played on people's fears of having their will subverted. Caucus opponents had defined the terms of the debate before supporters of the system could mount an effective campaign to save it, fixing the undemocratic aspect of the caucus in people's minds. Furthermore, the premise that the caucus system was undemocratic may have been flawed. Many observers believed that with several candidates vying for the presidency in 1824, the election would most likely be determined in the House of Representatives, where backroom deals could very well scuttle the will of the people. The caucus would prevent the election from being thrown into the House and would therefore actually *protect* the will of the people from conniving politicians.[12] While this point of view is not without its own problems of logic, it is possible that Tyler adopted it as his own as he mounted the campaign in the Virginia legislature to oppose the anticaucus crowd. When the legislature passed a measure (by one vote) postponing action on the formal report Tyler had prepared—which effectively killed it—he took it hard.

Tyler's vote for Adams also deserves attention, in light of how odd it seems on the surface. Tyler had turned to Adams only after Crawford suffered his apparent stroke, believing like many of his former supporters that the Treasury secretary was no longer a viable candidate. The Richmond Junto's decision to back Crawford anyway seemed to Tyler to be a wasted effort that could very well ensure Jackson's election in the House of Representatives. As he put it later, he believed Crawford's "chance of success to have been utterly desperate." Tyler faced later criticism from Thomas Ritchie for backing Adams, but it was misplaced. For one thing, the New Englander's record belied the superficial notion in some quarters that he was hostile to the South. Indeed, as secretary of state, Adams had demanded that the British compensate slaveowners for the enslaved people they had carried off during the War of 1812. He had also concluded that Congress had no power to restrict slavery in Missouri despite his own personal desire to see the institution ended throughout the Union. Moreover, Adams was less strident in his nationalism than Clay, a fact that his contemporaries as well as later historians tended to forget as they focused on the hyper-nationalism he exhibited *after* winning the presidency. As a case in point, Adams had not expressed as much enthusiasm for federally sponsored internal improvements as Clay had. Tyler, no doubt, took all this into account as he weighed his decision very carefully. Finally, widespread support for Adams's candidacy existed in Virginia, which meant that Tyler's decision to vote for him did not occur in a vacuum. Taking into account his distrust for Jackson and his belief that the Old Hero was unfit for the presidency, and a vote for Adams seems not only inevitable but also sensible. There was really no other candidate for Tyler to support.[13]

Ultimately, the House of Representatives decided the 1824 election in Adams's favor after none of the four candidates earned a majority in the Electoral College. Jackson had been stopped, but that did not end matters. When President-elect Adams named Speaker Clay as his secretary of state, the Jackson camp cried foul, alleging that the Kentuckian had used his influence in the House to unfairly tilt the final tally to Adams in exchange for the top job in the State Department. In the quarters of Jackson partisans, Adams's presidency began under a cloud of suspicion, despite his and Clay's denials that a "corrupt bargain" had taken place and despite the opinions of many observers that Clay was the man best qualified for his new post. Despite the outrage in the Jackson camp, no conclusive evidence has ever surfaced to substantiate charges that an actual deal to cheat the senator out of the presidency had taken place. Unfortunately for both Adams and Clay, the corrupt-bargain charge gained traction, especially in the South. As one scholar has argued, the belief in a corrupt bargain gave Jackson's supporters "the ideological cover they needed to justify organizing an opposition party" over the ensuing four years. Moreover, the alleged bargain provided Clay's enemies with enough ammunition to hurt him forever and frustrate his repeated bids for the presidency.[14]

Tyler professed to believe none of the accusations. Dispatching a letter of support to Clay one month after the House election, he flattered the new secretary of state by telling him that he had been "assail'd by unjust reproaches." The Virginian went on to express his approval of Adams's decision to name him secretary of state, making clear that he believed Clay's qualifications for the post were exemplary. Tyler was a shrewd-enough politician to know that holding Clay's esteem would not hurt his own political career, despite the ideological differences that existed between the two men.[15]

After reading Adams's first annual message to Congress, however, Tyler realized he had made a grievous mistake in supporting the former Federalist. The new president announced plans to pursue a strongly nationalistic course. "That message I have ever regarded as a direct insult upon Virginia," Tyler declared later. "It mocked at her principles, and was intended to make her the laughing stock of the rest of the Union." As the reality of Adams's consolidationist agenda sank in, Tyler began to rethink his opposition to Jackson. The buyer's remorse he and others in Virginia felt over their decision to support Adams in 1824 was not unlike the regret Whigs would feel in 1841 after putting Tyler himself on their ticket with William Henry Harrison.[16]

Amid all the excitement of the presidential election of 1824, Tyler was reelected to the House of Delegates. He was also nominated to become Virginia's next US senator. John Taylor of Caroline had died on August 20, 1824. Little-ton W. Tazewell, a Tidewater lawyer known for his formidable intellect, was nominated in opposition to Tyler. Sixteen years older than his opponent, Taze-well had the support of the Richmond Junto, if only because of his experience. Tyler lost to Tazewell by a count of 139 votes to 80, but the discussion in the House that preceded the balloting revealed much about the reputation the for-mer congressman enjoyed among his colleagues. One member praised his "zeal and his talents." Another pointed out that "some politicians . . . leave no trace by which their political principles may be recognized." Tyler, he declared, left no doubt as to his principles. As a result, he inspired the "utmost confidence."[17]

Tyler served for one more year in the House of Delegates. Not surprisingly, his return to politics exacted a cost. His law practice suffered as a consequence of his time in Richmond. He had to refer most of his clients—including Dr. Curtis—to his sister Anne's widower, James Semple, who practiced in Wil-liamsburg. This was a familiar pattern; Tyler became so busy with political matters that his livelihood floundered. He seemed little concerned, however, that he would find himself in the same predicament as before and threw him-self into the business of the legislature. Many of his colleagues soon viewed him as a viable candidate for governor of the state, a reward for his good work and a testament to the status he enjoyed around the capitol in Richmond.[18]

Sure enough, in December 1825 Tyler was elected governor of Virginia by a joint vote of the House of Delegates and the state senate. For a man who consciously sought to emulate the public life of his esteemed father, it must have made him quite proud that he would occupy the same office the Judge had held some fifteen years earlier. In 1826 he was reelected governor.[19]

Tyler pursued an ambitious agenda that reflected his Jeffersonian roots and the influence of his father. He also demonstrated that he was aware of Virgin-ia's declining economic fortunes and its loss of status in the political councils of the nation. To arrest that decline and to regain some prestige for the Old Dominion, Tyler unveiled his own plan to bolster internal improvements in the state and sought legislative approval for a system of public education that built on the idea first championed by Jefferson and resurrected by his father. Tyler thought big. The legislature did not—and these men, not the governor, controlled politics in Virginia. The conservatives in the Tidewater, along with their allies in the Piedmont, sang the same tired refrain that had doomed pre-vious efforts to change the status quo and improve the long-term fortunes of their state: no new taxes and no programs that would cede political power to other areas of Virginia, particularly the Valley and mountain regions. Tyler thus witnessed firsthand the effects of the growing hostility between the reactionary east and the increasingly more aggrieved and clamorous west, a rivalry that would dominate state politics up to the Civil War.

Whether he was fighting for internal improvements, trying to create a system of public education in the state, or publicly eulogizing Thomas Jefferson, which he did after his hero's death on July 4, 1826, Tyler attacked his duties as Virginia governor with great energy. In part, this reflects a dedication to his home state instilled in him by his father. It is safe to say that he had surpassed the standards the Judge set when he had occupied the governor's mansion years earlier. Put simply, Tyler had done credit to Virginia and himself, despite an inability to accomplish his policy objectives. We should also not overlook the effects of Tyler's good health on his job performance. While he was governor, he apparently experienced none of the symptoms that had so troubled him in 1820–21. Tyler worked hard because, physically, he was able to do so. Letitia and the children lived with him year-round as well, which relieved a source of stress.

Perhaps even more importantly, Tyler's ambition played a role in his statesmanlike approach to the governorship. In effect, he was auditioning for higher national office. As he intimated when he left Congress in 1821, he sought the opportunity to return to Washington. Tyler's retirement in 1821 and his return to public life in 1823 had been calculated to put himself in a position to become a US senator. In January 1827 he achieved that goal.

The events that led to Tyler's election to the Senate sullied—ever so slightly—his sterling reputation. To attempt to understand what happened, it is best to begin with the incumbent he replaced—John Randolph. The fifty-three-year-old had been elected to the Senate in 1825. Always outspoken, the volatile Randolph had recently raised the eyebrows of many in the Virginia legislature for his increasingly more erratic and outlandish behavior. For example, on one occasion, Randolph had stripped nearly naked in the Senate chamber; thankfully for all who had to witness that spectacle, he just as quickly put his clothes back on. Randolph's drinking became more excessive, which of course exacerbated the problem. As one member of the House of Delegates put it, "the conduct of Mr. R. had done more, in the last twelve months, to bring disgrace on our country and its institutions, than all the enemies of the country put together."[20]

Still, in January 1827 Randolph retained the support of about half of the

Virginia legislature and remained the choice of the Richmond Junto. His allies may have found his behavior embarrassing, even inexcusable, but they were not willing to abandon him as long as his state's rights, strict-construction orthodoxy remained intact.[21]

In any event, there was more to this story than Randolph's shenanigans. The backdrop for the Senate election of January 1827 was the administration of John Quincy Adams. Supporters of the president in Virginia were determined to see Randolph ousted at all costs. By mid-1827, taking his cue from Ritchie's editorials in the *Enquirer*, Randolph was assailing Adams mercilessly. He had also become an outspoken champion of Jackson's mounting candidacy for the presidency. Indeed, it was no secret that the Junto had been working with Martin Van Buren, the New Yorker responsible for mobilizing the troops of the emerging opposition party, to ensure Jackson carried the Old Dominion—and the nation—in 1828. It was also apparent that many Virginia politicians saw Tyler as someone more sympathetic to Adams. After all, Tyler had supported Adams over Crawford in 1824 and had gone out of his way to soothe Clay's feelings after the "corrupt bargain" charge had been leveled against the so-called Judas of the West. One interested observer of Virginia politics in the winter of 1827, a man calling himself "Virginius," noted that friends of the Adams administration had approached Tyler in an effort to persuade him to throw his hat into the ring against Randolph. "Their personal application to the Governor does not surprise me," Virginius wrote. "They could not have selected a candidate, whose name is more popular, or whose principles are more acceptable to the Legislature of Virginia."[22]

Tyler wrapped himself in his customary garb of disinterestedness and disclaimed any interest in replacing Randolph in the Senate. "I have constantly opposed myself to all solicitations," he declared, in reply to a letter from five prominent members of the legislature who sought to elicit a public statement of his intentions. "I desire most earnestly to be left at peace. There is no motive which could induce me to seek to change my present station for a seat in the Senate at this time." Tyler cited "private interests, intimately connected with the good of my family" as the reason for his desire to remain in the governor's mansion.[23]

But he protested too much in his reply. Tyler disavowed any desire to be elected senator a bit too strongly. He also seemed to go out of his way to say all the right things to maintain his reputation as a principled public servant who would always put Virginia above any selfish personal interests. While the governor claimed he did not want to be elected senator, he conceded that *if* he were to be elected, "I shall then give to the expression of the legislative will such reflection, and pronounce such decision, as my sense of what is due to it may seem to require." By invoking the "legislative will," Tyler framed his position in terms of what would be in the best interests of Virginia. He wanted to be elected to the Senate badly, but he was trying not to show it.[24]

Tyler maintained his public support of Randolph throughout the winter of 1826–27. On the day before the election, Hugh Caperton, a member of the House of Delegates from Monroe County in the western part of the state, approached Tyler outside of the executive chamber. He was there to let the governor know that the western bloc in the House favored Tyler over Randolph and stood in front of him that morning to persuade him to allow the nomination to proceed. Tyler maintained later that he continued to declare "it to be against my decided wishes and that I would not yield my consent to be nominated." But that night the governor allegedly went to Caperton's boardinghouse room in Richmond. What the men said at this meeting is not known, nor is it known whether others were present. Later, however, it became common knowledge that Caperton "manage'd the wires for Tyler" and played a large role in getting him elected. The next morning, the day of the election, Tyler was nominated and afterward defeated Randolph by a vote of 115 to 110. Claiming that his refusal to abide by the legislature's wishes "would be esteemed censurable by all," Tyler accepted the office.[25]

He had gotten his wish. But at what cost? There was no shortage of opinions once the dust had settled. "Tyler was brought forward & elected by the mountain interests," one Virginian declared, in a partially accurate assessment of what had happened. "He is denounced by all the leading men in the lower country [Tidewater] as a designing, electioneering demagogue. With this part of the State he is blown up 'Sky High.' They say he secretly did everything in his power to defeat Randolph, his protestations to the contrary notwithstanding." According to Ritchie's biographer, the *Enquirer* editor was "incensed at the tactics" by which Tyler got elected. More than two months later, anger still bubbled in the Tidewater. Tyler complained that one Randolph supporter had delivered an impromptu address at a tavern in Hanover in which he "assailed me with great asperity, and charged me with having purposely lull'd Mr. Randolph's friends into a state of security, thereby deadening their exertions with the intent of consummating my own election."[26]

The charges stung. Tyler needed to counter them. On March 3, 1827, the day before his term as governor ended, he defended himself at a public dinner held in his honor in Richmond. Before a sizeable number of family, friends, and members of the legislature, he struck back at his critics. He also wanted to make certain everyone understood his position on the Adams administration. This was no small matter. Immediately after the election, Tyler's letter of March 27, 1825, to Clay—written to show his support for the Speaker in the wake of the "corrupt bargain" charges—was made public. Apparently, Clay himself had not so innocently divulged the contents of the letter to a Mr. Clarke of Winchester, Virginia, right before Tyler's Senate election. The substance of what Tyler had written then turned up in a paragraph in a story in the pages of the *Winchester Republican*. Clay's motive in discussing the letter with Clarke is unknown. He of course denied any political chicanery and tried to wash his hands of the mess by saying that the letter "had nothing confidential in it. It was public in its nature, public topics were treated of, and it was addressed to a public man." This explanation certainly must have heartened Clay's other correspondents.[27]

The "Winchester paragraph" embarrassed Tyler. His attempt to curry Clay's favor had backfired on him in ways he could not have foreseen in 1825. Jackson supporters in Virginia, the men who had wanted Randolph reelected, clucked that it revealed Tyler as a Clay and Adams supporter in Old Republican clothing. They entertained hopes that perhaps they could stir things up so that Tyler would be forced to resign the Senate seat he had just won.

Privately, Tyler fumed at Clay. Publicly, he downplayed what the Kentuckian had done. But the situation called for a stronger course of action. Tyler enlisted the help of Robert Douthat, a member of the House of Delegates, to persuade Ritchie to publish a letter he had written explaining that, while he had supported Adams (and Clay) in 1825, he did not presently approve of the administration's course. The *Enquirer* published the letter on February 15, 1827. Tyler's strategy apparently worked, for an editorial in the paper that same day commended his political principles. "They [Tyler's principles] have hitherto been right," the paper acknowledged, "we trust that they *will still* be right,—we believe that they will be right." But the editorial also contained a warning: "Nothing but the boldest and most decided bearing towards the coalition at Washington can suit these times, or can save the nation!" The Richmond Junto would be watching Tyler.[28]

So, what should be made of all this? The circumstantial evidence seems to support the position of Tyler's critics, and it appears that Tyler did scheme to get himself elected. His later claim that he "would do injustice unwittingly to no man" does little to clear up the matter. Politics was politics, however, and was not for the faint of heart. Once the veneer of disinterestedness had been stripped away (assuming *that* could actually be done), Tyler may have felt that political combat justified whatever tactics were necessary to get oneself elected. Whatever the case, he had accomplished a feat of no small significance: he had parlayed the support of roughly thirty Adams men (who must have believed he remained friendlier to their man than he let on), westerners, and Randolph's enemies into a Senate seat. In the process he had tarnished his reputation a bit and damaged his relationship with the Richmond Junto. While that may have bothered Tyler in the short run, he could console himself with the realization that he was headed back to Washington. He would once again enter the national political arena, where he had wanted to be all along.[29]

Chapter 5

A NOT SO DEDICATED JACKSONIAN

"My monied affairs are all out of sorts," an embarrassed and angry John Tyler complained by letter to Henry Curtis, "so much so that I scarcely know how I will reach Washington." Making plans to leave Greenway in the fall of 1827 to take his seat in the US Senate for the start of the Twentieth Congress, Tyler had no cash readily available and realized he needed to raise money so that he could afford his travel expenses.[1]

From the vantage point of the twenty-first century, where aspirants for national office are usually able to tap into personal wealth to finance their campaigns and the victors never worry about having enough money to cover the costs of their travel to Washington, Tyler's financial difficulties seem unfathomable. The sorry state of his finances left him in an even more precarious situation than most of his contemporaries, but it is important to remember that many men from similar backgrounds and experience faced the ever-present possibility of insolvency. Many southern planters found themselves chronically in debt; the owners of valuable assets—land and enslaved people—they nevertheless were cash poor and often unable to meet their financial obligations. No group of men exemplified this situation better than the Virginia gentry class to which Tyler belonged. Collectively, their stories contribute to the larger narrative of an Old Dominion in decline.[2]

By the 1820s, Tyler had become just another Virginia planter wedded to the old ways. He exhibited many of the same self-destructive habits that had characterized his idol Jefferson. Tyler was notoriously poor with money, often spent more than he had, and finagled loans from creditors to pay bills he owed to others. He also placed himself in further peril by lending to family members, a practice emblematic of the old values that was supposed to tie kinship bonds more tightly and enhance his status as a gentleman. In one year, 1820, Tyler loaned several relatives some six thousand dollars, which he borrowed from the many estates he managed in his capacity as legal trustee—itself a morally questionable tactic. He usually stood as personal surety for the loans and issued promissory notes to the borrowers. One default could have ruined him and forced the sale of the estates involved. He also commonly used the promissory notes as collateral for the loans he secured from others or asked family and friends to endorse his notes—in effect, asking them to cosign loans. On several occasions Dr. Curtis endorsed his brother-in-law's promissory notes at the Bank of Virginia. How Tyler kept all of this straight is anybody's guess. He told Curtis at one point that he did not "feel as a freeman should, with these incumberances [sic] hanging over me." Still, his behavior did not change.

Tyler's growing family placed heavy financial burdens on him. His daughter Alice's birth on March 23, 1827, added to a crowded household, now numbering six children: Mary, age eleven; Robert, age ten; John Jr., age seven; Letitia, age five; Elizabeth, age three; and Alice. Another child, Anne Contesse, named for Tyler's sister who had passed away in 1803, died just three months into her young life. Letitia would give birth to their last child, Tazewell, three years later, bringing the total number to eight named children. But Tyler's son Lyon, a child of his second marriage, maintained years later that there was another child born to John and Letitia Tyler who died in infancy. Unfortunately, there is no record of when this child had been born or if he or she had even been given a name.

Tyler faced the prospect of providing for his large family without much in the way of savings. His wheat farm was a modest success, but like any farmer, he was one bad harvest away from a severe blow to his bottom line. Moreover, Tyler's return to the practice of law after his retirement from Congress in 1821 had not been especially lucrative, owing more to his lack of enthusiasm for the profession than an inability to attract clients. He certainly did not push himself. He also apparently did not scrimp when it came to his children, particularly their education. As he fretted over how he would pay for his travel to Washington in the fall of 1827, he sought out a tutor for his children. Knowing he needed money to pay the tutor's salary, and still unsure how to pay for his impending trip to Washington, Tyler resorted to a solution he had used at least once before: he decided to sell one of his slaves.[3]

The person he chose to part with was named Ann Eliza, and she had apparently been a Tyler house servant. "Her sale has become indispensably necessary to meet the demands of my trip to Richmond [the first leg of the journey to Washington]," he informed Curtis. It is not clear why he chose this particular enslaved woman to sell. Perhaps she was a skilled cook or seamstress, which would have made her attractive to buyers and likely a quick sale. Perhaps she had been a discipline problem for the Tyler family. Or worse, perhaps he needed to remove the woman from his household because he had had a sexual relationship with her, and Letitia demanded her exile. All three possibilities may have existed. In any event, Tyler was determined to sell Ann Eliza. At first he hoped Curtis would buy her himself, and he rather aggressively encouraged the transaction. Tyler had sold an enslaved person to Curtis in 1816, so there was reason to expect that the men could reach a similar agreement. When it became apparent that his brother-in-law had no interest in purchasing the slave, Tyler enlisted him to act as his agent and find a buyer. Tyler preferred a sale to someone in Curtis's "neighborhood" in Hanover County, no doubt because he assumed the woman would suffer no mistreatment from an owner who knew his friend. But if no sale came quickly, he instructed Curtis to "hand her over to the Hubbards for public auction."[4]

Tyler was likely referring to James Hubbard (or Hubard), a slave trader from the Yorktown area who profited handsomely by purchasing enslaved people from cash-strapped planters in the Virginia Tidewater. Details about Hubbard are murky, but he likely followed a simple business model: he bought slaves for considerably less than market value and then either sold them to one of the four or five firms conducting slave sales in Richmond or took them himself to the New Orleans auction, where he could fetch top dollar for their sale. Hubbard's activities made him a player in what was known as the domestic, or interstate, slave trade.[5]

His willingness to turn Ann Eliza over to Hubbard is full of significance. Like virtually all southern planters, Tyler adhered as much as possible to the ideology of paternalism, facets of which often did not reflect the reality of life in the antebellum South but that nevertheless stood as an ideal for a slaveholder to seek. Paternalism created a hierarchy in southern society that assigned roles to everyone. Occupying the top spot of this pecking order as a male and a slaveholder, Tyler was responsible for ensuring that his "people" (as slaves were known) had food, clothing, and shelter. The slaveholder—the master—also took an interest in the personal lives of his enslaved people and made them a part of his family. Occupying the bottom rung of the paternalistic ladder, slaves were obligated to show their gratitude to their master by performing the labor required to keep the farm or plantation running. Tyler's effort to see that either Curtis or someone in his "neighborhood" purchased Ann Eliza illustrates the paternalistic ideal because he was doing his best to make sure she ended up in a good home. When that effort failed, he turned to the slave trader Hubbard as a last resort, knowing that she might very well end up on the auction block. Tyler wished to avoid that fate for her if at all possible, but his financial difficulties ultimately meant he had to put aside his scruples for the sake of his bottom line. When faced with the prospect of being unable to afford the cost of his travel to Washington—in short, the potential embarrassment of having to delay the resumption of his national career for want of money—Tyler exhibited no qualms about selling a human being.[6]

Tyler did not wish to dirty his own hands in the matter, however. Nor did he want to deal directly with Hubbard. Slave trading—with its potential to break up slave families and consign people to harsher circumstances as they were moved from Virginia to the Deep South—violated the paternalistic ideal, and most slaveholders wanted no part of it. The slave traders themselves, despised by the master class and treated as outcasts in the Old South, became the scapegoats for the entire system. They were the men who actually engaged in the odious traffic of selling human beings. The mental gymnastics required to frame the issue in this way and construct a useful delusion allowed many a slaveholder to ease his conscience; it appears that Tyler was no different.

He added another layer to it, however, by enlisting Curtis to serve as his agent in Ann Eliza's sale. Doing so afforded him another degree of separation from the sordid details of the slave trade. But it did not make him any less eager to ensure that a sale took place. The aggressiveness with which he goaded his brother-in-law to get on with the business of finding a buyer for Ann Eliza—indeed, his outright insistence that it be done quickly—is quite startling. While his financial circumstances explain his desperation, there was more at work here. Tyler looks the part of a bully. His badgering of Curtis through the mail tells us something about the nature of the relationship the two men shared. Tyler did not treat his brother-in-law as an equal. Rather, he exhibited a sense of entitlement. He *expected* Curtis to get the job done—one way or the other. Perhaps Curtis had already established a relationship with James Hubbard. Possibly he had more experience in selling slaves, and Tyler was therefore taking advantage of his expertise. Or perhaps Tyler believed that it simply would not do for a US senator-elect to have his name publicly connected to the sale of a slave. Curtis, a mere country doctor with no pretensions to national office, could more discreetly—and with less publicity—see to Ann Eliza's sale. Whatever the case, Tyler exhibited no apparent remorse for making Curtis the front man for the sale of *his* slave. Perhaps, then, more than money came between the two men and eventually blew up their relationship. Curtis may have finally tired of acting as a go-between for Tyler in the dirty business of selling slaves.

If that was in fact the case, it did not happen right away. Dr. Curtis continued to serve as Tyler's agent for transactions involving the sale of slaves as late as 1830. Apparently, selling Ann Eliza made it easier for Tyler to reconcile himself to the practice, and he ultimately viewed it as a viable and perfectly acceptable way to raise money to alleviate his financial woes. "I am ready and willing to sell slaves at this moment for this object [debt relief] if I could find a purchaser," he informed Curtis several months after Ann Eliza's sale. Doing so would help him "get clear of the world." This proved to be an elusive goal. Perhaps this was another reason why national politics was so attractive to Tyler. While he was in Washington, he could gratify the part of himself he found most satisfying and fulfilling and could ignore—at least temporarily— the parts of his life he found distasteful. Politics, then, became a form of escape; it nourished his ambition and satisfied his vanity.[7]

There is nothing in the historical record that sheds light on what happened to Ann Eliza once she left the Tyler household. The likelihood of her sale seems certain; the only question is whether she was sold to someone who lived near Curtis or was auctioned at the behest of Hubbard. Whatever the case, Tyler found the funds to finance his trip to Washington and took his seat in the Senate on December 3, 1827.

Tyler's return to the national capital clearly provided him with the ego boost he needed—a jolt to his self-esteem—unavailable to him other than in the arena of national politics. Upon his arrival, he affected an air of triumph to Curtis. "I have been well received in the Senate," he preened in a letter. To another friend, he wrote that his "reception here has been entirely satisfactory." The setting suited him too. He was dazzled by the Capitol building itself, which had been completed in 1825. "It is so large that I have nearly lost myself in it two or three times," he wrote to his daughter Mary. Tyler clearly reveled in his newly won status as a US Senator and was enjoying renewing old acquaintances and meeting new colleagues. He was happy once again. He seemed to also wonder how the nation's capital could have possibly gotten along without him for the past six years.[8]

Tyler was immensely pleased that he would be serving as junior senator to Littleton W. Tazewell. Born in 1774, the tall, well-built native of Williamsburg had spent most of his adult life in the seaport city of Norfolk and owned four plantations in eastern Virginia. Intensely private and usually shunning the limelight, Tazewell was, in Tyler's words, the "most unambitious of men." Nevertheless, when Virginia called, he served, winning election to both houses of Congress and becoming governor of Virginia. He was of course a states' rights man. The pairing of Tyler and Tazewell proved fortuitous for both. Having always been cordial to one another, they became close friends during their tenure in the Senate, a friendship that lasted until Tazewell's death in May

1860. The two men did not always agree, which no doubt explains why Tyler sought his advice on many occasions and why he trusted him. Tyler respected his older colleague as both a man and a politician. So great was his esteem that he even named the eighth and last child he had with Letitia after the senator. Tazewell Tyler was born on December 6, 1830.[9]

Tyler went out of his way to join Tazewell in the mounting opposition to President Adams. As he entered the Senate, this opposition had succeeded in obstructing at least part of Adams's nationalistic agenda. To finish the president off, however, required defeating him at the ballot box in 1828. And to do that, the opposition had to offer a viable alternative. By mid-1827, the anti-administration forces had marshalled an impressive array of support behind the candidacy of Andrew Jackson. Led by a new breed of professional politicians—most notably the New Yorker Martin Van Buren—the Jackson party (as it was known) began to build a national organization that would enable its members to put the Old Hero in the White House. These men attacked the Adams administration at every turn. They created a powerful network of state and local organizations and resurrected the alliance between New York and Virginia that had been instrumental in getting Jefferson elected president in 1801. They made appeals to first-time voters and also took advantage of the revolutions in transportation and communications by starting pro-Jackson newspapers, coordinating their messages, and then using the extraordinary expansion of the US Post Office to deliver these papers to eager constituents. A brash westerner named Duff Green, in fact, exploited the franking privilege of pro-Jackson congressmen to send his *United States Telegraph,* an anti-administration daily in Washington, all over the country free of charge. A brain trust in Nashville known as the "Whitewash committee" also mobilized to respond quickly and forcefully to partisan attacks on Jackson, countering them before they could gain traction in the public mind. In the process, the Democratic Party was slowly beginning to take shape. Indeed, a competitive system of two-party politics was in its early stages, signaling the end of the political experimentation that had drawn people to participate in the democratic process during the so-called Era of Good Feelings. What one scholar has characterized as an "organizational revolution" was transforming American politics. It was fast moving, exciting, and above all, effective. And in Jackson it had the perfect candidate who could generate nationwide appeal.[10]

Even Tyler caught the wave of enthusiasm for Jackson—for the most part. "From having heretofore felt some indifference touching on the matter," he wrote to Curtis in December 1827, "I am now most earnestly solicitous for

Jackson's success. I do believe it to be loudly call'd for by the present state of things." This conversion had not come easily and was, at best, qualified approval. The comment Tyler had made to Speaker Clay back in 1825 that Jackson was a "*mere soldier*" betrayed his distaste for the general as a politician and denigrated how he had won his fame. No doubt Tyler's republican aversion to Caesarism and a military leader who might subvert the popular will was at play here. There were "many, many others whom I would prefer," he said, including New York governor DeWitt Clinton. Once it became obvious that Jackson—and not Clinton—would head the opposition ticket in 1828, Tyler conceded that "we must make the best of our situation." As he discussed the upcoming election with fellow southerners, the Virginian felt better about declaring for Jackson and was no doubt buttressed by the enthusiasm of Ritchie and the Richmond Junto. Rationalizing his support, Tyler maintained that "every day that passes inspires me with the strong hope that his administration will be characteriz'd by simplicity—I mean republican simplicity." He had decided to take the leap of faith for the Old Hero.[11]

Jackson, of course, won a decisive victory in 1828 and captured the prize his supporters believed had been stolen from him four years earlier. Ritchie gloated. "There is no mistake—Jackson is triumphant, and our utmost hopes are realized," he wrote in the *Enquirer*. Having said that, the editor issued a challenge to the victorious Jacksonians, with Jackson himself and Van Buren foremost in his mind. "But it is one thing to *gain* a victory—it is another to *improve* it," he declared. "Now is the time to display the patriotic principles which have actuated the supporters of Jackson. Now is the time to show, that they have fought not for themselves, but their country." Ritchie and the Richmond Junto, indeed all of the Old Republicans, including Tyler, had accepted the Old Hero, warts and all, and trusted the New Yorker Van Buren to lead them to the promised land. They had done so, however, with reservation. Van Buren was to some a "cunning fellow" who had to be watched at all times. Some of the reactionaries in Virginia believed they had allied with the Jackson camp at a cost to their ideological purity. Tyler, for one, obsessed over what the Old Hero had meant when he said during the campaign that he favored a "judicious" tariff. They were all willing to put their misgivings aside, however, and began to look forward to a Jackson administration.[12]

The president-elect left the Hermitage, his home outside of Nashville, on January 18, 1829, and began to make his way to Washington for his March 4 inauguration. His big victory over Adams had been tempered by the death of his wife, Rachel, shortly after the election. Jackson thus donned mourning garb for the trip east. As he made the three-week journey from Tennessee to the nation's capital, he was greeted by enthusiastic crowds and a host of well-wishers, who he gamely and appreciatively thanked for their support. In the meantime, Tyler and his fellow senators went through the motions of the lame-duck session of the Twentieth Congress. It was as if time had stopped and would not resume again until Jackson took the oath of office. Tyler informed a friend that "we have nothing here of the slightest interest other than the numerous speculations which are afloat upon the subject of the next cabinet." Tyler was pleased that Senator Tazewell had emerged as a leading candidate for secretary of state. But until Jackson actually announced his cabinet choices, all Washington society could do was wait. "We are here in a dead calm," Tyler said. "When the General comes we may expect more bustle and stir." He had no idea how much of an understatement this would prove to be.[13]

The bustle and stir began almost from the second Jackson made his cabinet appointments. Tyler and other states' rights men were baffled at some of the choices, quite displeased with others. Tazewell, for example, was offered the head of the War Department, not State, which went to Van Buren. No one should have begrudged the New Yorker his post, however, in light of all he had done to get Jackson elected. But the Old Hero nominated Pennsylvania's Samuel D. Ingham to head the Treasury Department. And after Tazewell turned down the offer of secretary of war, that appointment went to Tennessee senator John Eaton, who had not exactly distinguished himself as an unabashed defender of states' rights principles. Eaton was, however, a Jackson crony and had campaigned for the Hero in both 1824 and 1828. "How sorrowfully all have been disappointed," a friend of Tyler's, soon-to-be Virginia governor John Floyd, later wrote, commenting on Jackson's cabinet decisions. Another Virginian, Francis Brooke, brother-in-law of Thomas Ritchie, called the cabinet a "bitter pill." Jackson had already alienated many of the southerners who had guaranteed his election. Tyler's forebodings seemed prophetic even before the new president had spent his first night in the White House.[14]

Tyler apparently missed the bedlam that ensued after Jackson's inauguration, when the White House doors were thrown open to the crowd that had descended upon Washington to witness the transfer of power to the "people's" president. The crush of people actually forced Jackson to scurry back to the National Hotel, where he had spent the previous three weeks, so he could spend his first night in office in peace. Supreme Court justice Joseph Story noted that "King Mob seemed triumphant," indicating that what had happened on inauguration day signaled the beginning of a change in the way things were done. Indeed, during Jackson's presidency, the Executive Mansion became a place where common citizens seemed just as important as the elite. Harriet Martineau, an Englishwoman visiting the United States at the time, marveled that public officials, diplomats, and wealthy members of Washington society mixed at the White House with "men begrimed with all the sweat and filth accumulated in their days—perhaps their week's labour." Tyler eventually discovered this for himself. Attending a White House party during the worst of the Margaret Eaton scandal, which turned Washington society—and Jackson's cabinet—upside down, he was instantly struck by the president's behavior. Jackson seemed to "have fancied himself at the Hermitage," Tyler reported. "All satisfied me that I stood in the presence of an old fashioned republican, who whenever and in whatever he could, laid aside the affectation of high life." The Tidewater Virginian did not see fit to comment about "Eaton malaria" but was clearly impressed by the man of the people he was able to witness in action that evening. In light of his longstanding negative personal feelings about the president, it is to Tyler's credit that he was open to finding something to like about Jackson.[15]

Tyler's comment puts to the lie a previous biographer's claim that the future tenth president felt uncomfortable around people who did not occupy the same rung on the social ladder as he did. Robert Seager maintained that Tyler "developed no rapport with the masses of people" and suffered from an "ingrained shyness and discomfort in the presence of people with dirty fingernails." Tyler, he argues, was "diffident." Seager conflated the Virginian's desire for social order and a belief that men of his class were best suited to lead with a supposed aversion to interaction with people who were less fortunate. It is true that, like his father, Tyler was no social leveler. He retained the sense of noblesse oblige instilled in him by the Judge his entire life. But his respect for "the people" was genuine, and at various times throughout his political career, he enjoyed taking advantage of opportunities to display his southern charm and graciousness with strangers. There was "nothing of hauteur or condescension in his manner; it is affable, natural, frank, and gentlemanly," one woman who met him remarked. In short, Tyler acted the same around everyone he met—whether their fingernails were clean or not.[16]

The Virginian also understood the broader implications of Jackson's election. The new president's avowed support for the common man meant that the wave of universal white manhood suffrage sweeping over the United States after the War of 1812 would put pressure on the older states in the Union that had thus far resisted the democratizing trend to get on board. Massachusetts changed its constitution in 1820. New York bowed to the pressure a year later. Virginia, on the other hand, held out. Not until 1829 would the voters force the leaders of the Old Dominion to call a convention and write a new state constitution of their own. There was public clamor to expand the suffrage and redress the imbalance of apportionment in the legislature that allowed the Tidewater to hold on to power even as the western portion of the state grew in population.

Tyler knew he would likely be called upon to serve in this convention. He wanted no part of the process. "I am every thing but desirous of being in it," he said. In principle he believed in the right of the people to alter or amend their system of government. While he was governor, he had told Charles Fenton Mercer, an advocate of democratic reform, that "whensoever they [the people of Virginia] shall express their wishes, I shall be ready in good faith to set about with you and others in the work of reformation and amendment." When the day of reckoning arrived, however, Tyler sang a different tune. He feared the political repercussions and recognized that his standing with western Virginia might suffer if he became a member of the convention. He did not want to alienate the men who had helped elect him to the Senate, but his heart was clearly with the eastern conservatives who had resisted change for so long. "Does it become me, representing as I here [in the Senate] do, the interests of the whole state to become a party to this contest," he asked.[17]

For once in his life, Tyler looked for a way to avoid serving—to weasel out of his duty as it were. To that end, he sought out his friend John Rutherfoord. Rutherfoord, a member of the House of Delegates from Richmond, was two years younger than Tyler, a graduate of Princeton, and a talented politician who, eventually, would serve as governor of Virginia. He had a great deal of influence with eastern conservatives. Tyler wanted Rutherfoord to back others for the convention post and do everything in his power to relieve him from the responsibility of serving as a delegate. He also wanted him to be discreet, warning his friend to keep secret the fact that he had approached him for help. The senator realized that if it got out that he was trying to avoid this duty, it would damage his reputation. He did not wish to provide his enemies with an issue they might exploit to drive him from office. If elected to the convention, Tyler would serve, but would not do so happily.

To bolster his argument that he should be exempted from the convention, Tyler showed every trick in his bag. He pleaded ill health, which had returned in the winter of 1828–29. He appealed to Rutherfoord's sense of family, explaining that he had become "literally a stranger to my own household." None of the excuses ended up helping his cause, and Tyler was elected to the convention. Perhaps the only consolation was that Tazewell had also been elected as a delegate.[18]

The convention began on October 5, 1829, and produced a new constitution three months later. Tidewater Conservatives granted some concessions by relaxing suffrage requirements; smaller property owners were given the right to vote. For the most part, however, the apportionment issue had been left unresolved. As one resentful observer noted, the convention succeeded in "giving the people east of the [Blue] Ridge the power in both Houses [of the legislature] forever, or until another Convention, which is pretty near the same thing." Tyler voted for the revised constitution, which voters ratified in April 1830. Eastern conservatives were safe until 1850, when another convention would be called to revise this document.[19]

Tyler had played a minimal role in the proceedings. He felt ill most of the time and preferred to remain away from the action. The senator rarely spoke and did not participate in any of the especially nasty exchanges that arose. When he did address the convention, he took pains to stress that he was a "friend of all Virginia" who wanted his constituents to know that he had the best interests of the entire state at heart. In light of his appeal to Rutherfoord, Tyler's course of action is not surprising. During the convention, when others practiced, or at least attempted to practice, their statesmanship, he played the part of politician. Silence on the most controversial issues demonstrates his concern for his political standing throughout the entire Old Dominion. His vote on the apportionment issue is also revealing. Tyler voted in favor of making the white population the sole basis for representation in the House of Delegates, thus allying himself with the reformers. In other words, he did not favor counting slaves through something like the national 3/5ths formula, which would have benefited the eastern planters. Perhaps he knew that the proposal would fail. But Tyler was certainly no reformer. Voting as he did allowed him to win some political capital from the western regions without having to concede anything of substance that might have alienated his conservative friends.[20]

Because of their participation in Virginia's constitutional convention, Tyler and Tazewell arrived in Washington nearly two months late for the first session of the Twenty-First Congress. They had missed much of the soon-to-be famous rhetorical duel in the Senate between South Carolina's Robert Y. Hayne and Massachusetts senator Daniel Webster on the nature of the Union. When they made it back, they were confronted with the unprecedented number of nominations for government jobs President Jackson had placed before the Senate for confirmation. Jackson was implementing the policy of what he called "rotation in office." The Senate needed to conduct hearings on the appointments as soon as possible, and Tyler and Tazewell had held up the process.[21]

Tyler found most of Jackson's appointments—a fair number of whom were journalists—suspect. Many of them were recess appointments and had already started collecting a government paycheck, a practice that especially riled senators. Tyler sought to block their confirmation and derided what he labeled as Jackson's "purchasing [of] the press." He and Tazewell led the charge against these men.[22]

Tyler's outspokenness against one particular Jackson appointment proved personally troublesome. Virginian Henry Lee IV, son of Revolutionary War hero Light Horse Harry Lee and half-brother of Robert E. Lee, had been nominated as US consul general to Algiers. Lee accepted the post happily; moving abroad would provide him a salary and the means to evade his many creditors. He and his wife, Anne, had sailed for the Barbary Coast in August 1829. But they had jumped the gun, it turned out.[23]

The Senate rejected the nomination of the aptly nicknamed "Black Horse Harry" unanimously in March 1830. He had no qualifications whatsoever to represent the United States in a diplomatic capacity. The debate over his appointment, however, focused not on his fitness for the office, but on a sex scandal he had been involved in some years earlier. Lee had seduced Betsy McCarty, his nineteen-year-old sister-in-law and ward, in 1820. The liaison apparently resulted in a child that had been stillborn, aborted, or murdered. Lee eventually admitted—and reveled in—his adultery (Betsy was beautiful), but he declined to address the circumstances surrounding the baby, whose lifeless body was found in an outbuilding on the Lee estate, Stratford Hall, in Westmoreland County. Making matters worse, Lee had concocted a scheme to have his friend Robert Mayo marry Betsy, undoubtedly hoping to alleviate the minimal guilt he felt for bringing about the downfall of a respectable young woman. Further adding to the scandal, Lee had embezzled Betsy's inheritance while serving as her guardian. A McCarty relative sued him on her behalf in a Richmond court to recover the money. Eventually, Lee was forced to sell Stratford Hall.[24]

Exercising discretion, the Senate discussed Lee's nomination in proceedings closed to the public. According to historian and Lee family chronicler Paul Nagel, Tyler placed himself at the center of this discussion. Somehow, he had obtained documents detailing the whole sordid mess between Henry and Betsy. There were even letters between Lee and Mayo that substantiated the latter's role in the matter. Nagel maintains that Tyler later succeeded in forcing a public discussion of the scandal on the Senate floor.[25]

Unfortunately, Nagel provides no evidence for his claim. There is no record of what was said in the secret session. Nor, for that matter, is there any record in the published *Register of Debates* that indicates the Senate debated Lee's nomination in an open forum. This is not proof that Nagel is wrong—perhaps the discussion of Lee on the Senate floor was brief and not recorded. Nagel is certainly on to something, however, because Lee himself believed Tyler played the leading role in scuttling his nomination.

While living in exile in Paris in 1833, Black Horse Harry enlisted another friend, Richard Brown, a fellow Virginian, to act as an intermediary between himself and the senator. Lee wanted Tyler to answer for what he had apparently done to him in the Senate and hoped his friend could find out as much of the details as possible. Brown wrote to Tyler, informing him that Lee considered him "as having been principally instrumental in causing the rejection of his appointment." According to Brown, Lee did "not complain of this," however, for he believed Tyler had been misinformed about the scandal.[26]

Tyler denied playing such a role and claimed not to have read the letters that passed between Lee and Mayo (but showing that he knew they existed). He was unequivocal that he had not sought to sway his fellow senators to vote against Lee and even maintained that he hated having to cast a negative vote himself. Annoyed and insulted that he had been placed in the position of having to defend himself in this matter, Tyler ended the letter by saying that he had "departed from a rule which I have never in any other instance permitted myself to disregard," namely, explaining any actions taken toward an individual in a "public capacity."[27]

There the matter might have rested. After all, it had been three years since the nomination had been rejected. But Lee could not let it go. He still believed Tyler had led the charge against him in the Senate, claiming to know why he had been deprived of his post at Algiers. The reason was simple, really: "It is then Mr. Tyler's opinion that a man who has committed adultery with his wife's sister is unworthy of an appointment under our government."[28]

In one final letter to Tyler sent through Brown, Lee defended himself in curious fashion. Most troubled by gossips who claimed he had committed not just adultery with Betsy, but incest, Lee argued that Virginia law was ambiguous on whether a man who slept with his wife's sister was guilty of that particular sin. He also tried to cast himself in a better light by comparing his actions with those of fellow Virginians. "In that Commonwealth, which we all so fondly venerate, married Gentlemen have occasionally procreated with their own slaves," he pointed out. He, at least, had not done that. Then, invoking Tyler's "idolatry" of Thomas Jefferson, Lee pressed his point. "Around the shady sides of Monticello, his offspring wander with skins as tawny as their native soil & eyes bright with hereditary lust." Never referring to Sally Hemings by name, Lee nevertheless made his point: Jefferson's illicit affair had brought his wife's mulatto half-sister into his bed. It did not matter that it occurred after his wife had died. If he, Lee, was guilty of incest, then so, too, was Jefferson. The larger implication is that Tyler did not feel Jefferson's rumored sexual indiscretions precluded *him* from holding public office, but Lee was not worthy of the same consideration. There was a double-standard. Lee concluded with bitterness "that a Senator from my native State could cooperate in a course of persecution against me for misconduct, which when more flagrant in another citizen he considered no abatement from perfection, no impediment to promotion, no objection to confidence & no abstraction to eulogy."[29]

There is no evidence that Tyler ever replied to this final missive. It seems probable that he would not have dignified Lee with a response. A reply would have been fascinating, though. Like any elite Virginian, Tyler surely believed that because Lee had had an affair with a white woman—incest or not—his transgression was far more serious than Jefferson's alleged liaison with an enslaved woman. When a white man seduced a white woman, it threatened the patriarchal authority of her husband or father. Such an affair jeopardized the very foundation of southern society. A discreet relationship with a black woman, on the other hand, actually affirmed the control slaveholders enjoyed at the expense of their enslaved people. Patriarchy not just remained intact—it grew stronger. White patriarchal society also held that black women were by nature promiscuous and debased. A sexual relationship with a female slave, then, according to this view, was not as morally repugnant as defiling a supposedly pure white woman. Lee seemed to have forgotten this in writing to Tyler.[30]

In any event, Lee's venom embarrassed his go-between Brown, who must have recoiled at his friend's words. Brown later wrote to Tyler, claiming that Lee had not given him the opportunity to exercise "discretion" in his attempt to find out who or what had derailed the nomination. He told the senator that he regretted "being made the medium of any communication either unpleasant to your feelings, or disrespectful to the memory of one whom I have greatly admired [Jefferson]." And *there* the matter finally rested.[31]

President Jackson may have failed to win the confirmation of Henry Lee— and several others—but Tyler and Tazewell could not prevent confirmation of some of his favorites. Amos Kendall, for example, a Democratic newspaper editor, was nominated as fourth auditor of the Treasury, slipping through after Vice President Calhoun broke a tie vote in the Senate. The president also submitted some of the same names more than once when circumstances appeared more favorable to confirmation. He succeeded in a few instances by using this tactic. Ironically, Tyler would resort to the same method in an effort to win confirmation for some of his own appointments when he occupied the White House.

It was Jackson's appointment of a mission to Turkey, however, that highlighted Tyler's opposition to the president for all to see and gave a strong indication to the Old Republicans in Virginia that he was not a typical party man. Jackson attempted to sneak the members of the mission through on recess appointments in September 1829 and did not submit their names for confirmation when Congress reconvened in December. Many senators wanted to know why and believed that Jackson had circumvented the confirmation process in violation of the Constitution. Tyler and Tazewell were the most outspoken in their opposition to what the president had done.

During the second session of the Twenty-First Congress, more than one year after Jackson had appointed the Turkish mission, an appropriations bill came to the floor of the Senate. One of its provisions called for an allocation of funds to pay the salaries of the men sent to Constantinople. Tazewell wanted to strike out the portion of the bill providing for these salaries because their appointments had been unconstitutional. Tyler had no objection to paying the salaries but wanted an amendment added stating that providing such funds should not be construed as Senate approval for the president's actions. In a speech on the matter, he aimed to send a message to Jackson and to take a jab at the whole principle of rotation in office—what many were calling the "spoils system"—and the baleful effects of partisan politics. Tyler declared that "if we are asked to lay down the constitution upon the shrine of party, our answer is the price demanded is too great." He concluded the speech with a rebuke: "Let us tell the President that he has erred. Let us be true to ourselves, to our constituents, but, above all, to the constitution." These words could very well have summed up John Tyler's political philosophy.[32]

Jackson supporters in the Senate attacked their Virginia colleagues in a war of words. The administration added its two cents as well. Tyler welcomed it, saying that he was content to be "abused, slandered, vilified, as much as my bitterest enemies may please." Bedford Brown of North Carolina opposed Tyler's amendment because he believed it was tantamount to an outright charge that the president had violated the Constitution. Apparently missing the point, Brown also argued that the Virginia senators had made too much of the Turkish mission. "I cannot discover anything in this act of the President, calculated to alarm the fears of those most devoted to a rigid construction of the constitution," he declared. John Forsyth of Georgia was more scathing in his assessment. "But, on this petty appropriation," he taunted, "the grave constitutional question is stirred here by both Senators from Virginia—the one [Tazewell] from despair—the other [Tyler] because an attack ought to be openly made." After debate that lasted for several days, and despite the criticism, Tyler's amendment passed. So, too, did another provision that actually increased the amount of compensation the envoys received.[33]

Back in Richmond and speaking for the Junto, Editor Ritchie criticized the senators, not so much for their opposition to what Jackson had done with the Turkish mission, but for the zealousness with which they had made it known in the Senate. "Our *principles* were right but our *manner* was offensive," Tyler concluded, in assessing the rebuke. He could live with that. The senator still supported Jackson, though he was a bit more wary in 1831 than he had been on the eve of the election of 1828. The Turkish mission, a largely and appropriately forgotten issue in Jacksonian-era politics, nevertheless revealed Tyler's tenuous association with what was becoming the Democratic Party. It also signaled the beginning of a period in which he would continually flirt with an outright break with Jackson. Indeed, he seemed to be searching for an issue that would justify that severing. To some extent, Tyler's position reflected the factionalism that existed in Virginia's Democratic Party, which, despite the Junto's nominal leadership, was never a phalanx of unqualified support for Jackson.[34]

Tyler did find some areas of agreement with the president. He and Tazewell voted for Van Buren's confirmation as minister to England; Vice President Calhoun broke a tie vote in the Senate, however, depriving the New Yorker of his post. Tyler voted against the Maysville Road bill, which appropriated federal dollars to extend the National Road in Kentucky. He spelled out his objections in constitutional terms, very much in line with how he had opposed internal improvements years ago as a member of the House. When the bill passed the Senate anyway (after having already passed the House), Jackson vetoed it. Tyler also voted for the Indian Removal Act of 1830. In fact, it was the one initiative of the president's that he supported without misgivings. "Their removal beyond the Mississippi is called for by consideration not only of great public policy," Tyler maintained, using the same argument as Jackson, "but out of regard to the Indians themselves. Their extinction is inevitable where they are now." Tyler's stance on what ultimately led to the Trail of Tears and the extermination of thousands of Native Americans placed him squarely in the mainstream of southern opinion on the matter. Like many of his fellow southerners in and out of Congress, he also derided the "sympathy and mock-sensibility attempted to be created on behalf of the Southern Indians."[35]

Despite finding some common cause with Jackson, Tyler was far from happy with the direction he saw national politics taking since he had been elected to the Senate. "There is nothing sound in the state of parties here," he complained to Rutherfoord. Tyler pointed to the economic tension between North and South that had emerged again over the tariff and worried that sectionalism was poisoning the nation's political culture. In 1828 Jackson had been able to sidestep the tariff issue by saying that he favored a "judicious" measure. Such wording was deliberately vague. Four years later, to the dismay of southerners, it became evident just what the president believed was judicious. A new tariff bill passed both houses of Congress in July 1832. Tyler, of course, vigorously opposed the measure, to no avail; Jackson signed the bill into law. Tyler noted sarcastically that the president's *"judicious tariff* consists in doing nothing with the Tariff of 1828—except indeed by attempting to guard it by new provisions in relation to the collection of duties."[36]

Tyler's assessment of what ailed national politics was ironic. His arguments on the Senate floor—indeed his entire national career—placed him at the forefront of the sectionalism he lamented. In the previous fifteen years, Tyler had become an outspoken defender of the South. His reputation had been made. He was unmistakably caught up in, and played a leading role in developing, the very situation he now decried. In Tyler's words, however, we see the tension that had existed in his political career since the Missouri crisis of 1819–21. Here was a man who had dedicated himself to safeguarding the interests of his section and state but who also cared deeply for the fate of the Union. Perhaps more than most of his fellow politicians, Tyler understood the potential long-term effects of what was happening in the early 1830s. He recognized the corrosive effect of the fights over internal improvements and the tariff. Indeed, a showdown over the tariff between South Carolina and President Jackson loomed.

Senator Tyler may have found the state of politics worrisome. At this juncture, however, he had no choice but to play the game and remain at least nominally in Jackson's camp. He believed that openly breaking with the president now would leave him politically isolated in Virginia. Nevertheless, he vowed to remain steadfast to his principles and would fight—if need be—to uphold them. In fact, he seemed to recognize that a battle with Jackson and the Democrats was all but inevitable, given his uneasy alliance with them. "Take you this then along with the rest," he promised his friend Governor Floyd, "that if they strike me, I will be apt to strike them a harder blow than they will give."[37]

Chapter 6

ABSENCE AS A WAY OF LIFE

In May 1831 Senator Tyler returned to Virginia from Washington and found an invitation to a political dinner in Richmond waiting for him. After barely setting his bags down, he informed Letitia that he planned to attend the event and told her that he would be leaving shortly. He would likely be gone at least two days.

The very next morning Tyler cancelled his plans. Letitia "was so very ill upon my receiving the invitation," he wrote to Senator Tazewell, who was to meet him in Richmond, "that I was left but one course to pursue, and that was to decline its acceptance."[1]

Letitia spent most of her marriage to John in what he often referred to as her "delicate" health. She was prone to excruciating migraine headaches and, as she got older, debilitating illnesses that frequently confined her to bed. Nine pregnancies and the demands of a large family also took their toll. Women with repeated pregnancies often suffer from chronic hypertension, so it is possible that high blood pressure explains Letitia's headaches. Without access to the modern medicines that can effectively regulate a person's blood pressure and maintain it at an acceptable level, she would have had very little recourse as her condition worsened with age. In fact, she would have had little concrete understanding of the connection between her many pregnancies and her illnesses. Letitia would suffer a stroke in 1839 at the age of forty-nine and another one that took her life at age fifty-one while her husband was president. Her strokes are the best evidence that she did indeed suffer from hypertension.[2]

The trauma of childbirth itself put Letitia's health in peril, as it did all women in the antebellum South. She also may have been subjected to the remedies nineteenth-century physicians employed to mitigate the harmful effects of giving birth. For example, doctors often "bled" a patient, which entailed opening an artery in the temple to reduce blood pressure on the brain. The use of chloroform as an anesthetic did not become common until the late 1840s—after Letitia had given birth to all of her children—so she was likely forced to suffer the ordeals without anything to alleviate her pain. Unfortunately, we do not know any of the details of her pregnancies other than oblique allusions to her lengthy recovery times in her husband's correspondence with Henry Curtis. There can be no doubt, however, that her many pregnancies and deliveries compromised her health. In fact, it is little short of a miracle that she was able to bring eight children to term.[3]

Letitia's problems went beyond her physical health, however. One brief account of her life, composed with the help of her children and daughter-in-law years after she died, mentions her "acute nervous organization" and "sensitive temperament." These are descriptions of her emotional make up, and when read in conjunction with her husband's letter to Tazewell, it becomes apparent that his use of the word "ill" is a code employed to describe something other than a run-of-the-mill physical ailment. Tyler did not reveal his wife's exact symptoms, but his friend no doubt understood what had happened; there was no need for further explanation. John knew why Letitia had become "ill" and knew his behavior was the cause. She could not bear the prospect of yet another of his absences, especially one so soon after he had returned from Washington. That Tyler felt he should not press his luck and leave for Richmond anyway indicates how serious the situation must have been.[4]

Letitia evidently suffered from what physicians of her time called "hysteria," the scientifically imprecise term used to describe the physical symptoms of a woman's poor health that defied a purely medical explanation. These physical symptoms had psychological—as opposed to organic—causes. The term "hysteria" also described what modern healthcare professionals would characterize as depression. Generally uncomfortable discussing the very private, often embarrassing details of their physical health, nineteenth-century Americans—more modest than their counterparts in a later time—were even more circumspect when it came to emotional health. In part, this reflected the lack of a framework for explaining matters pertaining to one's mental state; psychiatry and psychological analysis did not yet exist. People of John Tyler's lifetime did not have the language to explain what they experienced or what they saw in their loved ones.[5]

Men often used code words when alluding to their wives' hysteria, particularly if they were talking or writing to other men about it. They rarely used the term "hysteria" themselves. Men like Tyler instead used the word "illness" to describe what their wives were going through, usually providing enough context to allow the reader of a letter or a visitor in the parlor to infer what they meant. In Tyler's case he may have even discussed Letitia's "illness" with his friend Tazewell in person, perhaps in Washington, sometime before the incident over the political meeting in Richmond. Tazewell would therefore have needed no further context to allow him to understand what had happened.

The proximate cause of Letitia's "illness" that day in 1831, and the source of her hysteria generally, was her husband's absence from home. He spent six months of every year in Washington when he served as a US senator, and when he was home he acted as if he could not wait to get back to the capital. His return to politics after his retirement in 1821 made clear to Letitia that he put ambition before her. "These were the circumstances," John Tyler Jr. said, "that tested my mother's nature and qualities."[6]

Letitia experienced what one historian calls a "marriage trauma" as she realized that her husband neither valued the ideal of the companionate marriage nor shared her expectations for their relationship. In fact, the trauma repeated itself every December as he left for Washington. She may have thought there was a chance to get what she wanted when Tyler retired in 1821 but soon realized she had been waging a losing battle. Ultimately, it was *this* realization that ravaged Letitia's emotional health and prompted her hysteria. Her husband's political career, not emotional intimacy, became the dominant feature of their marriage.[7]

There can be no doubt Letitia found this deeply disturbing. She loved her husband—almost desperately. John Jr. could sense just how much, even as a small boy. "I can see my mother now," he related many years later, "as she would be seated either sewing, or knitting, or reading, when the voice of my father would be heard either approaching or entering the house, instantly a blush would mantle her cheek, a beam of joy would irradiate her countenance, the book or work would fall from her hands, and she would bound forward to meet him." She would instantly catch herself, however. In John Jr.'s words, "such quick, impelling affection, such untutored manifestation of joy," was not what his father wanted to see from his wife because it was "not altogether consistent with proper self-respect" and was unbecoming "the wife of a grave, noble, and lofty Virginia Senator." Letitia "would recover herself" and hurry back to her chair. "Then as he [Tyler] entered the room, she would rise and receive him tenderly yet decorously."[8]

The way Letitia was raised no doubt dictated her behavior when it came to her husband. She had been brought up to keep her emotions in check as much as possible. "Immediately following the first impulsive movement," her son reported, "these reflections would flash through her mind." But there was more to it than that. Recall that when Tyler served in the House of Representatives, particularly in the last two years, he often missed the beginning of the session, sometimes arriving two weeks after the proceedings had started. He may have been forced to remain at home longer than he wished because of his wife's illnesses. At times Tyler could only break away if she was not "unusually unwell," a phrase that clearly indicates the prevalence of the problem. Perhaps she made a scene every time he prepared to leave for Washington. Letitia therefore made a concession by greeting him when he returned home without an abundance of emotion, not wishing to remind him that she often got carried away. Her submission thus became a way for her to compensate for the behavior she exhibited when Tyler prepared to travel back to Washington.[9]

Making the trip with him was not usually an option. Letitia's poor health, her unwillingness to participate in the social life of the capital, and the young children she needed to care for at home precluded her travel to Washington. On one occasion, however, she agreed to go, spending the lame-duck session between December 1828 and March 1829 with her husband. Tyler's only comment on the time they spent together was confined to a brief mention of her presence in a letter to his Norfolk friend Conway Whittle. The fact that Tyler brought his wife to a short session of Congress is suggestive. Perhaps she had only agreed to go because of the relatively limited time she would have to spend in Washington. Perhaps he did not want her there for a longer regular session—for whatever reason—and agreed to bring her on this occasion because they could return to Virginia more quickly than normal. Whatever the case, she never traveled with her husband again.[10]

Complicating an analysis of the separation dynamic of the Tyler marriage is the complete absence of correspondence from Letitia. Apparently, her letters have not survived. It is obvious she wrote to her husband while he was in Washington; the content of his letters makes this clear, and he often responded to concerns she raised in her letters to him. But Letitia lacks her own voice in the sources. We do not get her side of the story and must piece together what little we can from Tyler's responses. What happened to the letters Letitia Tyler wrote to her husband? Perhaps he destroyed them, not wanting to risk anyone finding out about the intimate details of their marriage. If so, did he destroy the letters solely to protect his privacy, or was he embarrassed by their content because they cast him in a negative light as a husband and father?

The fervor of courtship seems to have subsided quickly for Tyler—no doubt more quickly than it had for Letitia. Politics, not his wife, became his consuming passion. Still, the couple had eight children together. Despite their many health problems, the Tylers were an extraordinarily fertile couple. John was a man with a healthy libido, if we can judge by the number of his offspring, and it seems clear that he, not Letitia, set the parameters of their sex life. She seems to have been unable to negotiate with him and win any periods of sustained abstinence while she was in her twenties and thirties, even as her health grew more precarious and the pregnancies more potentially dangerous. The months Tyler spent away from home attending to political matters did not provide Letitia with the true relief her body desperately needed because she was often pregnant during these times. The "rest," therefore, was often not real respite in any meaningful sense of the word.

Letitia may never have broached the subject of abstinence. She may have actually enjoyed sex rather than dreaded it like many wives of her time, though this is difficult to imagine in light of her family's portrayal of her as a prim and excessively shy woman. Regardless of how she viewed intercourse itself, it is entirely possible that Letitia wanted as large a family as Tyler could give her. In light of her poor health, though, this too seems improbable. Many nineteenth-century women positively (and rightfully) dreaded bearing children and were further hampered in any effort to manage their own reproduction by the unavailability and unreliability of birth control. Making matters worse, southern women were even more likely than their northern counterparts to die in childbirth. They knew the risks, often discussing the dangers at length to female friends and relatives who could relate to the fear. It is therefore hard to imagine Letitia reacting to each pregnancy with unbounded joy. But as a southern woman, she grew up with the deeply embedded message that motherhood was expected of her. She had very little room to maneuver when it came to controlling her own destiny. Therefore, she likely resigned herself to her husband's high sex drive and *his* desire for a large family, bearing her trials like most women of her time did—as best as she could. She endured eight (possibly nine) pregnancies; in total, she was pregnant for at least six full years of the seventeen years between the time she and Tyler married in 1813 until their last child was born in 1830.[11]

Should John Tyler be condemned for risking his wife's life through repeated pregnancies? From the perspective of the twenty-first century, yes. Men of Tyler's time, however, were expected to have robust sexual appetites and father children. In fact, fathering *many* children served as proof in the antebellum South that a man had a healthy sex drive—that he was a normal sexual being. Fathering many children also served as evidence that a man directed his sexual impulses toward his marriage and was not seeking pleasure elsewhere; he was exercising self-control and cultivating a public appearance of mastery—over his household, his wife, and his sexual urges. For Tyler, as for any member of the Tidewater elite, how society judged a man was vitally important. His behavior conformed to the accepted—and acceptable—norms of behavior of the Old South. Tyler may also have found having a large family valuable as a way to compensate for his own chronically poor health. His many children allowed him to demonstrate and *confirm* his masculinity, both to himself and to others. This was important for his standing as a planter as well as his stature as a politician.[12]

Letitia no doubt felt that seven children were more than enough. While her husband was in Washington, she faced the burden of maintaining the household and managing the children herself. She relied on one or two house slaves, and at times female relatives assisted her, but it was she who oversaw the day-to-day activities of her large brood. The children also had to adapt to their father's absences. While he was away, Tyler worked hard to cultivate relationships with his offspring, despite the distance between them. He sought to develop a role as their father that he—if not they—found acceptable. He wrote them often, and their letters in reply made him very happy. Tyler especially appreciated those written by Mary. Perhaps because she was the oldest child, he enjoyed a rapport with her not evident in his relationships with the other children, especially the boys. Twelve years old when her father returned to Washington in December 1827, the precocious and always inquisitive Mary pressed Tyler for details about his life away from home. He delighted in his daughter's questions about the capital and explained his responsibilities and told her about the many interesting people he met on a daily basis. He also paid special attention to what she said about her lessons.

Like his own father, Tyler believed an education essential for both boys and girls and wanted Mary to write him as much as possible so he could judge her progress and "bear witness to the expansion of [her] mind." He suggested reading Alexander Pope, Joseph Addison, and Samuel Johnson as well as the newspapers. He advised her to approach her studies with a seriousness of purpose and to take special care not to overly indulge in foolishness and frivolous pursuits—in short, to limit the amount of fun she had. "The highest enjoyments of life pale upon the apetite [*sic*] when indulg'd in for too long a time," he warned. Echoing his own father from years before, Tyler even chided his daughter for poor penmanship, almost to the point of obsession. "A young lady should take particular pains to write well and neatly," he instructed her, "since a female cannot be excused for slovenliness in any respect." The ink blots Mary sometimes left on the page became particularly annoying to her father.[13]

Tyler entertained the idea of sending Mary to school for formal instruction and thought Washington presented a wonderful opportunity for her. "I walked on Saturday last to Georgetown, distant a mile and a half from my residence, on a visit to the monastery and college," he wrote her one winter day, "and was much delighted." Tyler took a tour of both Roman Catholic institutions and came away duly impressed. "The monastery is under the government of young ladies who have devoted their lives to the instruction of young ladies and children," he wrote. "They are nuns, and are entirely secluded from the world. It is an excellent school, and if I bring you on here next winter I think I shall place you there at school." The evidence does not tell us definitively whether these nuns ever taught Mary Tyler. Again, we do know that Letitia traveled to Washington with her husband in December 1828—during the "next winter" that Tyler wrote about. It is entirely plausible that Mary and some of her siblings accompanied their parents to the nation's capital at that time. If they had, Mary may have enrolled in the monastery. There are no extant letters from Tyler to her for this period, perhaps indicating that she was indeed in Washington with her father and the rest of the family. It is also worth pointing out that Tyler's willingness to enroll his daughter in a Catholic school would have horrified many Protestants. At the time he considered the school, the United States was on the cusp of a period of often unrestrained bigotry toward Catholics and the Roman Catholic Church. Tyler, however, exhibited none of the antipopery that characterized the period. His Protestant faith evidently served as no barrier to providing Mary with a fine education.[14]

Even as he articulated to Mary the importance of her education, Tyler did so within the conservative framework of elite southern society. He clearly did not intend that his daughter entertain unrealistic notions of what her education would ultimately mean. He took an active interest in her schooling and sought to direct her studies because he wanted her to seize the opportunity to ensure her own future happiness as a wife and mother. He played a vital role in her character development. "We should rather rely upon ourselves," he told her, "and howsoever the world may deal with us, we shall by having secured our own innocence and virtue, learn to be happy and contented even in poverty and obscurity."

Tyler made it clear that his daughter should look to Letitia for moral guidance. "I could not hold up to you a better pattern for your imitation than is constantly presented you by your dear mother," he said. "You never see her course marked by precipitation, but on the contrary everything is brought before the tribunal of her judgment, and her actions are all founded in prudence." Letting Mary know what he ultimately expected of her, and praising her behavior so far, Tyler proudly stated, "Follow her example my dear daughter, and you will be as you always have been—a great source of comfort to me."[15]

Tyler came to regard Mary as a source of comfort because she dutifully played what was perhaps the most significant role in the household while he was gone. As the oldest child, she often served as messenger to Tyler's other children when he found himself burdened by a busy schedule and unable to write each of them individually. In one letter he told her to inform Robert that he was a "bad fellow for not having written to me." In another he requested that she see to it that her brothers and sisters "sit down and send me messages." Tyler also expressed his hope that his younger girls would emulate their older sister. He teased Letty and Lizzy that if they did not "learn [their] books and be obedient and good girls, I shall not love you." Clearly, Tyler missed his children while he was away. His letters to Mary reveal a marked attempt to keep up with their activities as they grew up without him. Though he joked with them when they did not write, it obviously bothered him when he failed to receive a timely note. Tyler's letters also show an affectionate side to him, even if it was up to Mary to convey that affection to her siblings.[16]

As time passed, Mary also became caretaker of her mother. Tyler relied on her to look after Letitia when she suffered from headaches and to keep him informed of her condition. At one point he purchased a large bathtub for his ailing wife and converted their farm's dairy to a room where she could soak in saltwater for some relief. The family had previously enjoyed two restorative trips to the seashore, and Tyler hoped simulating that environment might help Letitia. Letters dispatched from Washington encouraged Mary to persuade her mother to follow a regimen from which he insisted she would "derive great benefit." Mary was to enjoin a slave to fill the tub with saltwater once or twice per week, whenever her mother appeared to need treatment. Besides illustrating concern for his wife, Tyler's directives also demonstrate that trust in his daughter became a crucial component of the relationship they shared as he directed domestic matters from afar. Tyler trained Mary to act as the primary caregiver—a surrogate for himself—in the household. She attended to the needs of her mother, who could not play that role, as well as to those of her younger siblings. Such an arrangement allowed Tyler to pursue his political career. Indeed, without Mary, his career in the US Senate would have been out of the question.[17]

At times Tyler had to maintain discipline from Washington, which was no easy task. As teenage boys often do, both Robert and John exhibited a penchant for horseplay. They tormented their older sister with pranks and found it amusing to barge in on her in the morning as she was dressing for the day. Letitia's efforts to end this little game failed, and Tyler had to lay down the law through a note dashed off from Washington. "I have been much mortified by your mother's last letter in which she complains of both yourself and John," he wrote to Robert. "She says that neither of you treat her with becoming respect, or obey her wishes after being informed of them." Using admonition and guilt that would have made the most devout Catholic proud, Tyler asked his boys to "carry back your thoughts to the period of your helpless infancy." He wanted them to think about "who nursed you, and watched over you by night and by day?" Making it clear he expected his sons to always mind their mother, he warned, "I hope . . . that I shall never hear of your disobeying her slightest wish, much less her commands." Moreover, he said, "you must teach yourself to regard your sister as a young lady, near and dear to you, and therefore requiring a respectful deportment from you." Above all, he "wish[ed] my children to love each other, and by their conduct to show that love and affection."[18]

Tyler seemed aware that his absences had detrimental effects on his family. After reentering public life, he missed a great deal in his children's lives as they passed from childhood into young adulthood. Despite the time he spent away from them, Tyler hoped to instill the proper values in his children that his father had passed to him. Like his interest in Mary's education, a concern for the scholastic development of his sons is especially evident. He felt "great pleasure" when Robert, following his father and grandfather to William and Mary, performed well in his studies, and he proudly told Dr. Curtis that "Philosophy, Metaphysics, chemistry, Mathematics, all are alike embraced by him and the professors advise me that he has never appeared at lecture unprepared." To his diligent son he wrote, "To witness your advance in knowledge and that of your sisters and brothers will constitute the charm of my future life, and so far I have much reason to be satisfied."[19]

Unlike the recommendations he gave Mary, which reflected a fatherly wish that she prepare herself for marriage, the advice Tyler gave his sons was geared more to making sure they acquired the education necessary for worldly success. In this way he pointedly followed the example of his own father. "Be in haste to prepare yourself for the bar," he instructed Robert while his son was at William and Mary. Though less emphatic than the Judge had been, Tyler passed on the values of noblesse oblige and subtly instilled a sense of honor in both Robert and John as they prepared for adulthood. Perhaps trying to plant the seed and lay the foundation for the political careers he hoped his sons would pursue, he also encouraged Robert to "learn to make yourself popular by accommodating yourself to the feelings nay whims of others." These "others," after all, might someday vote.[20]

For their part, the Tyler boys wrote to their father when he was away about matters they knew concerned him and always made sure to highlight their academic triumphs. Robert found this easy; a consistently high level of achievement marked his teenage years. As a result, he enjoyed the hearty esteem of his father, and the two shared a good—though not especially close—relationship, despite the fact that they saw each other only for brief periods while Tyler served in the Senate. John Jr. was not so lucky. Though he followed his brother at William and Mary and did fairly well, he struggled to measure up to Robert's level of success. Perhaps because of that, there was an emotional distance between him and his father. John shared more of a bond with Letitia, writing most of his letters while at college to her. Curiously, he also referred to his father as "the Old Man." Whether this was a term of affection or, more likely, reflected resentment toward his father, is not exactly clear. What is clear is that John did not enjoy the same relationship with his father that Robert did. More to the point, he did not go out of his way to cultivate a healthy relationship—neither did Tyler.[21]

Prolonged absences also meant Tyler had to manage Greenway from Washington, which he found increasingly more difficult as he pursued his senatorial career. Like most Tidewater planters in the 1830s, Tyler grew wheat and corn on his 1,200-acre farm, choosing to forego tobacco production, which had largely shifted to Virginia's Piedmont. While wheat planters worried about the dangerous Hessian fly that might ravage their crops or despaired over the devastating blight of rust, they found cereal production less troublesome than tobacco. For one thing, it was easier on the soil. Tobacco depleted nutrients very quickly, and cultivation left a field useless after a few growing seasons. Wheat and corn, in contrast, deprived the land of relatively little. Moreover, the production of these staples was not as labor intensive. In cultivating tobacco, an enslaved laborer could only tend two or three acres with any reasonable degree of care. That same slave could easily cultivate twenty acres of wheat, however, and an almost equal acreage of corn. The result was that a planter who grew wheat or other cereals could run an efficient farm and enjoy modest financial success with significantly fewer slaves than his counterparts who chose tobacco as their cash crop. Tyler offers a case in point.[22]

By 1830, twenty-nine enslaved people lived and worked at Greenway. Six were males between the ages of ten and thirty-five and were expected to perform the most arduous tasks. More than half of Tyler's slaves—fifteen, in fact—were children under the age of ten; another was an elderly woman.

Tyler's labor force appears relatively modest when compared with those of wealthier Tidewater planters, who, along with significantly more acreage or more than one farm, might own more than one hundred slaves. Tyler's slave ownership made him comparable to many of his neighbors in Charles City and the surrounding counties. He was a "typical" Tidewater planter of the 1830s.[23]

Tyler was an atypical planter in one important respect, however. Most slaveholders of the nineteenth-century South—and Tidewater Virginia was no exception—exhibited a resident mentality that tied them to their land and slaves. Slaveowners typically felt strong attachments to their home and preferred to stay there if possible. Wealthy Virginia planters from the east sometimes owned land and slaves in the Piedmont or mountain region but ventured to what were essentially secondary holdings only once or twice per year. They usually left their primary residences for specific reasons: either to inspect the operations at other locations or to seek relief from the hot, often malarial summers of the Tidewater. Politicians like Tyler followed a different pattern. Duties either in Washington or their state capitals required these planters to spend several months of every year away from their farms.[24]

Like most slaveholders, Tyler relied on an overseer to manage his labor force and keep his farm running efficiently. Overseers were generally entrusted with the care of slaves, the land, livestock, and farm implements. Absentee planters especially depended upon them for a successful harvest. Unfortunately, the man Tyler had hired for Greenway, an individual named Branton, proved inadequate for his job, and plantation management suffered as a result. In one instance a field at the farm sustained what Tyler's brother-in-law Robert Christian reported to him as an "injury." Though he did not elaborate, it is possible he meant that Branton had directed the slaves to plow the field too soon. Perhaps it had been sown before sufficient time had passed to allow the soil to recover from a previous harvest. Whatever the case, Christian strongly implied that Branton deserved the blame. Tyler had asked his brother-in-law to look in on Greenway periodically and serve as de facto master in his absence but worried that Branton resented the intrusion. "When I was at home I directed him to take as much care of everything as if no change had taken place," Tyler replied, upon hearing this bad news. Upset at what he had been told, the senator declared that he would be "deeply wounded" if his overseer had indeed let him down.[25]

Branton's apparent shortcomings illustrate a general problem that planters often faced when leaving their farms in the care of overseers. Many southerners regarded overseeing as a degrading occupation. Inexplicably, slaveholders themselves often looked with contempt upon the profession. Consequently, as one South Carolina planter put it, only a "limited number" of men, often characterized by "want of education generally," took the job. While some overseers were the sons or close relatives of planters, most were yeomen, who often knew very little about proper agricultural practices. Many were unschooled in the benefits of crop diversification and other aspects of scientific farming that became increasingly popular during the 1830s. In their zeal to generate profits and perhaps increase their own pay, many tried to maximize the size of the crop no matter what it cost in abuse of the land. The planter inevitably paid the price. Making matters worse, overseers often proved temperamentally unsuited to maintaining control over enslaved people. Some also undoubtedly came to resent the authority of the master, which was especially ominous for an absentee planter like Tyler. One contemporary editor summed up the problem: "In the master's absence, the overseer is viceregent; his powers for good or evil are unlimited." That thought could not have made Tyler happy as he left his home for the nation's capital every December.[26]

Why did planters entrust their livelihoods and the care of their enslaved labor to men often intellectually or temperamentally ill equipped to handle the job? Put simply, they had no choice. Men like Tyler needed individuals like Branton. Tyler's political career made it necessary that an overseer assume the day-to-day operations at Greenway. There was no viable alternative. Only under certain circumstances—after the death of a husband, for example—would the woman of the farm exercise authority over a slave force, though few had the necessary training or inclination to attend to business matters. Letitia nominally oversaw Greenway while her husband was away and likely kept the farm's records. Her chronic ill health, however, meant she needed competent help. Tyler relied on Christian to check on Greenway. Asking him to provide oversight allowed the senator to maintain some control over his farm while he was away. The request was not unusual, either. Indeed, it was a practice common in the antebellum South, one born out of both necessity and convention. By imposing upon Christian, Tyler at least implicitly acknowledged the potential danger in placing complete trust in Branton. Accordingly, he dealt with the problem the way most other absentee planters did.[27]

❧

During the spring of 1831, after the second session of the Twenty-First Congress had adjourned, Tyler moved his family to another farm. The new home was a 630-acre expanse of land on the north side of the York River in Gloucester County. He evidently did not think long and hard about a name for his new home, calling the residence Gloucester Place. He had acquired the property from an acquaintance as settlement for a debt, possibly as payment for legal services. Soon after taking control of the farm, he sold Greenway.[28]

Tyler's reasons for abandoning Greenway and moving to Gloucester County are not clear. He easily could have sold the property in Gloucester after acquiring its title and spared his family the aggravation of a move. Surely, selling his boyhood home could not have been easy. He had been overjoyed at the opportunity to purchase the property in 1821, happy it belonged to the Tyler family once again. Letting it again pass to someone outside the family must have been difficult. Perhaps the land no longer yielded a sufficient harvest, or maybe Tyler believed his enslaved labor would be even more efficient on a smaller farm. Whatever the reason, the move proved beneficial from the start. After seeing that Letitia and the children had settled in, Tyler organized the operations of the farm and prepared for the first summer wheat harvest at the new residence. The family enjoyed a banner crop that year. Writing in mid-June to his friend Governor Floyd, Tyler proclaimed proudly that "the sickle is about to go into the best crop of wheat that I have seen in lower Virg[ini]a." The good fortune pleased him immensely and affirmed his decision to move. Understandably, he wanted to show off his new home to Floyd. Inviting him to visit, the senator told the governor, "I will make you an unqualified promise to shew [sic] to you the most beautiful country in Virginia."[29]

The friendship with Floyd grew as Tyler's relationship with Dr. Curtis waned. The tension between Tyler and his brother-in-law first appeared soon after Tyler retired from Congress in 1821. The two men grew irritated with each other over the Dixon estate: Curtis seemed displeased with the way Tyler approached the financial mess of the estate, and Tyler, spurred on by how much he hated dealing with the matter, had gotten angry with Curtis. Harsh words passed between them. The real issue had become Tyler's management of money—or rather, it had become his *mis*management of money. The letters between Tyler and Curtis for the late 1820s provide evidence of several bewildering financial arrangements between the two men and, often, arrangements between them and third parties. Curtis endorsed numerous notes, one instance of which prompted Tyler to thank him for his "willingness to oblige me in regard to my unfortunate bank transactions." Tyler always seemed to owe money to someone. If his annual wheat crop failed to live up to expectations, he saw even more red ink. Because Curtis had endorsed many of Tyler's notes, it meant that he faced losses too. Understandably, he grew tired of putting himself on the hook for his brother-in-law's notes, and the rift between the two men had widened considerably by 1830.[30]

Tyler had better luck dealing with his overseer at Gloucester Place. Before leaving for Washington and the beginning of the Twenty-Second Congress in December 1831, he hired a man named Gregory for the position. Gregory proved more reliable than Branton and appeared more adept at carrying out his duties. Tyler could also rest easier knowing that another brother-in-law, John Seawell, lived just a few miles from Gloucester Place. Much like Christian did at Greenway, Seawell looked in on the farm while Tyler was in Washington. By this time, too, fifteen-year-old Robert had assumed a prominent role in making sure the family's farm ran smoothly. In fact, Tyler often wrote to his oldest son with instructions for Gregory and messages for his Uncle John.[31]

This system, however, was no substitute for seeing to matters himself, and Tyler often expressed frustration at being absent for such long periods of time. If he did not aspire to the life of a farmer, he often acted as if he would have preferred remaining at home so that he could know exactly what occurred at Gloucester Place firsthand. Tyler's attitude toward his farm reflects an ambivalence that characterized him for virtually his entire political career. When he was home in Virginia during recesses of Congress, he longed for the hurly-burly of the nation's capital; he could not wait to return. When he was in Washington, however, he often acted as if he wanted to take the first stage back to Virginia and assume control of his farm. His letters betray a man who felt he was being pulled in two different directions. In short, no matter where he was, Tyler always thought about being someplace else. He was a man burdened by his many responsibilities. Yet national politics remained his chief focus—he was addicted to the political life.

Chapter 7

BECOMING A WHIG

The record of John Tyler's tenure in the US Senate, and the trajectory of a career that ultimately placed him in the White House, depended in large measure on President Jackson. Despite enthusiastic Old Republican support for the Hero in Virginia, Tyler had never entirely trusted the Tennessean, and his membership in the Jacksonian coalition had always made him somewhat uncomfortable. To be sure, there had been nowhere else for him to go in 1828. The consolidationist agenda of John Quincy Adams and the National Republicans repelled him. Furthermore, Tyler had repudiated his support of Adams so that he could get back in the good graces of the Richmond Junto, which of course supported Jackson. The president claimed the mantle of the Jeffersonian Republicans, so, ideologically, Tyler seemed to fit with him and with his supporters in the emerging Democratic Party. For the time being, the senator put aside his misgivings about the man as he pursued his own national political career. But an outright break with Jackson and the Democrats seemed almost inevitable the longer Tyler stayed in the Senate.

The dam burst as a result of Jackson's course of action on the two seminal events of the contentious 1830s: South Carolina's nullification of the tariff and the war on the national bank. As a southerner, Tyler sympathized with the nullifiers and was appalled at the president's response to the crisis. Unsympathetic to the supporters of the bank, he nevertheless regarded Jackson's efforts to kill the institution as a breathtaking abuse of presidential power. Together, these two events, and the political fallout that resulted from them, led Tyler to renounce the Democratic Party and enlist in the opposition that ultimately coalesced around the banner of the Whig Party. His political conversion would have momentous consequences for himself and for the country.

In early January 1832 Henry Clay offered a resolution in the Senate calling for adjustments to the so-called Tariff of Abominations, which had been passed in 1828. South Carolina's robust objection to that law and the state's increasingly louder threats to nullify the tariff as unconstitutional—that is, discriminatory against the South—had forced both the Jackson administration and pro-tariff men in Congress to consider modifications. In his annual message to Congress in December 1831, the president explicitly called for reductions in the rates of the 1828 law. Clay portrayed his proposal as a concession to opponents of the tariff since duties on imports that did not compete with similar articles produced in the United States would be abolished. He also proposed to lower the rates on other selected articles, including wine, tea, coffee, and silk. Clay believed that a majority in the Senate would find his proposed modifications to the tariff appealing. He even expected to enjoy the support of most southerners.[1]

Tyler refused to play along. On February 9 he began an impassioned speech against this latest version of the tariff that lasted for parts of three days. He reiterated much of the argument he had made against the tariff years before in the House of Representatives. Again he attacked as false the premise that protection would make the United States less dependent on other nations for its economic success. He spent most of his time, however, detailing the economic injuries the tariff inflicted on the South—which placed him squarely on the side of the South Carolina nullifiers.

Tyler saw through the rhetoric Clay employed to win support for his resolution, arguing that the principle of protection would remain intact. Furthermore, the "taxes which he proposes to repeal," the Virginian pointed out, "have never been complained of, and have existed from the foundation of the Government." The South would not be fooled by this sleight of hand. Only an adjustment of the tariff undertaken in good faith, he warned, would restore harmony to the Union and quash all talk of nullification in South Carolina. Settlement of the issue, Tyler maintained privately, depended on the individuals he labeled the "tariffite Jackson men and the tariffite Clay men and the reckless latitudinarians" and their willingness to engage in true compromise.[2]

Debate on the tariff continued throughout the winter and early spring of 1832, as President Jackson's reelection campaign heated up. Clay, the National Republican nominee for president, hoped his efforts in behalf of the tariff would burnish his credentials as chief spokesman for the American System and win him votes. Various modifications to the tariff were floated in both the House and Senate, with a bill finally hammered out. On July 14 Jackson signed the Tariff of 1832 into law. In its final form this measure was both lower (most rates falling to 25 percent) and more proportionally protective than the Tariff of Abominations. Jackson was reelected in November.[3]

In October 1832 South Carolina called a special state convention to frame its response to the latest tariff law. At issue was the question of whether the

Tariffs of 1828 and 1832 could be declared unconstitutional—and thus null and void—within the Palmetto State's borders. Deploying the Virginia and Kentucky Resolutions and the compact theory of government, the proponents of nullification maintained that a state could essentially disobey a federal law its citizens deemed unconstitutional; nullifiers adamantly maintained the tariff was one such law. But it was not the tariff alone that had their attention. That issue had called to mind an even larger, more complex problem. If the federal government could assert its authority to implement an unconstitutional tariff and force the South to pay those duties, what was to stop it from passing laws that might lead to the abolition of slavery? In the wake of Nat Turner's bloody slave rebellion in Virginia in August 1831, white South Carolinians had become sensitive to anything they believed might threaten their hegemony over their slave population. Nullification, then, represented an interplay between genuine economic distress and fear of slave rebellion. Standing up to Jackson and the federal government seemed the only course. The South Carolina convention passed the Ordinance of Nullification on November 24 and threatened the state's secession from the Union if Jackson attempted to collect the tariff duties.[4]

Jackson responded with vigor to South Carolina's ordinance. On December 10, just days after sending an annual message to Congress that supported states' rights and called for an end to the protective system of tariffs, he issued a proclamation denouncing the nullifiers, asserting that he believed *their* action was unconstitutional. He denied the very principle of nullification and laid bare his contention that the compact theory of government was ridiculous. Jackson made clear in this strongly nationalistic message that he intended to preserve the Union against a "small majority of voters in a single state."[5]

The leaders of that single state wanted other southern states to stand beside them in defiance of the tariff and the president. They wanted Virginia's support most of all, and at first it appeared the Old Dominion might rally to the nullification standard. On December 13 Governor Floyd sent South Carolina's ordinance to the legislature with instructions to act. Floyd had actually run for president in 1832 as a nullifier and had won South Carolina's electoral votes, so there was no doubt he wanted an official statement from the Old Dominion supporting the Palmetto State's position. Adding to the possibility that Floyd might get what he wanted, Jackson's supporters in Virginia found themselves adrift in the wake of the president's proclamation. Thomas Ritchie, for one, expressed shock at Jackson's utter disregard for states' rights, especially because it had come on the heels of a promising annual message. John

Randolph, too, expressed his displeasure with Jackson. While neither man defended South Carolina's actions, they were shaken by the president's stance. By the end of December, the anti-Jackson forces managed to present a report sharply critical of the president. Virginia seemed ready to jump aboard South Carolina's nullification bandwagon.[6]

Tyler was deeply disturbed by the gauntlet Jackson had laid before South Carolina. Unable to sleep on December 13, he wrote to Governor Floyd, a trusted friend, and admitted his fear. "I tremble for the Union—and equally much for our institutions," he wrote. "That silly proclamation—so unnecessary, so out of place." Tyler believed Jackson had taken a wrongheaded approach to the situation and had left the nullifiers with no way to save face. The president's proclamation had offended Tyler as a states' rights man, for its "ruinous, destructive errors" denied the compact theory of government he held dear. "Not only the Union is in danger," the senator declared, "but all the rights, nay the very existence of the States is greatly threatened by the false doctrines of the proclamation."[7]

Tyler was also losing sleep because his reelection to the Senate appeared very much in jeopardy in December 1832. His opposition to the president on the Turkish mission and his general peevishness when it came to Jackson had antagonized many members of the Virginia legislature. They had just sent Tyler an ominous signal by electing William C. Rives, a vocal Jackson supporter, to the Senate seat recently vacated by Littleton Tazewell. Now they seemed poised to bounce Tyler out of his. Making matters worse, these same pro-Jackson men had succeeded in postponing Tyler's election from early January 1833 to February 16, another portent of doom. Buoyed by the president's annual message to Congress, which had won enthusiastic praise in the Old Dominion, they gambled that the extra time would give them a chance to twist arms and build more opposition that would help remove Tyler. Hedging against his possible rejection by the legislature, Tyler told Tazewell that the "servility of party" disgusted him; he expressed his hope that he might lose the election so that he could give up the political battles and return to Gloucester Place: "Believe me that I am heartily sick of the double dealers and wish myself most sincerely in retirement."[8]

But he did not mean it. Tyler wished to stay exactly where he was. His spirits surely rose in the wake of Jackson's nullification proclamation, whatever he told his friend Tazewell, because it appeared that opposition to the president was building in the Virginia legislature, particularly among representatives of the eastern—Tidewater—portion of the state. Jackson's proclamation had blunted the momentum of his supporters. But Tyler was not out of the woods yet. He knew there was still potent opposition to his reelection.

The tipping point arrived soon, and it was Jackson himself who provided it—who in effect saved John Tyler's political career. On January 16 the president sent a message to Congress seeking permission to use federal troops and an authorization to mobilize South Carolina's militia if the nullifiers responded with force to his efforts to collect the tariff revenue. Rhetoric from South Carolina largely ignored the fact that Jackson had threatened the use of the military only if the nullifiers acted first and portrayed this latest message as a bellicose call to arms. Deriding the proposed Force Bill as the "Bloody Bill," hotheads in South Carolina constructed a narrative of the crisis that they hoped would win them support throughout the South.[9]

No other state officially signed on to nullification, including Virginia, which meant that South Carolina found itself isolated. The Force Bill succeeded, however, in alarming politicians throughout the South—nowhere more so than in the Old Dominion. This was good news for Tyler, who sensed that the tide against him in the legislature had turned. Not content to just sit back and hope for the best, however, he prepared a speech on the entire nullification crisis, which he delivered in the Senate on February 6— that is, in plenty of time to be reported in the *Richmond Enquirer* for the consumption of his constituents and the Virginia legislature before the election on February 16. The speech was ponderous and full of the states' rights ideology for which Tyler was known, but it hit its mark. Tyler ultimately won the election 81 to 62 over Jacksonian candidate James McDowell.[10]

Determined to make clear that principles and not just politics underlay his anti-Jackson stance, Tyler did not rest on the laurels he received from his Senate speech. When the Force Bill came up for a vote on February 20, 1833, fifteen senators, including ten southerners, dramatically walked out of the chamber rather than register their votes. Tyler stayed in his seat, preparing for his own dramatic moment: when the roll call got to his name, he proudly and loudly voted nay, the only dissenting vote in a 32-to-1 tally that passed the Force Bill.[11]

Tyler had become the beneficiary of timing and luck once again. A turn of events, mostly out of his control, had determined his political destiny. He would remain a US senator. Had Jackson not issued his nullification proclamation—nor used the harsh language that so frightened his followers in Virginia—and had he not requested congressional authorization to use force to put down the nullifiers in South Carolina, administration supporters in the

Virginia legislature might have cobbled together enough opposition to Tyler to see their man McDowell squeak by and enter the Senate. Tyler would have been forced to retire.

Yet what is most important in this calculation is the blunder Jackson's supporters in the Virginia legislature unwittingly committed when they insisted on postponing the Senate election. They had made their decision to do so right before Jackson issued his proclamation on December 10, 1832, and several weeks before he requested the Force Bill from Congress on January 16, 1833. The extra time they believed would help them bolster their case against Tyler actually worked in *his* favor because it allowed the nullification crisis to play out. They had gambled and lost. Opposition to Jackson in Virginia, while never taking the shape Governor Floyd had hoped for—outright nullification—built during the second half of January and the first half of February and made Tyler's position as an anti-Jacksonian much more appealing to the majority of those responsible for deciding his political fate. While we will never know if Tyler would have been able to hold on to his Senate seat if the election had occurred in early January as originally planned, it is safe to say that holding the canvass on February 16 contributed, at least in part, to his victory.

The nullification crisis was a turning point in Tyler's political career. Jackson's proclamation and threat to use force in South Carolina justified in Tyler's mind the doubts he entertained since way back in 1824 about the Old Hero's suitability for the presidency. His course of action as he dealt with the nullifiers was "subversive" of all that Tyler had ever considered "dear and sacred." Bitterly, he asked his friend Tazewell, "Were ever men so deceived as we have been, I mean those of the old democratic school, in Jackson?" The president had "swept away all the barriers of the constitution and given us in place of the federal govt. under which we had fondly believ'd we were living, a consolidated military despotism." Tyler's nullification speech and his vote in the Senate on the Force Bill marked the beginning of his public break with Andrew Jackson and the Democratic Party. Tyler and other states' rights southerners began to cast about for an alternative standard to join. Of course, this did not escape the notice of Ritchie, who criticized Tyler for his anti-Jackson position. No matter how disheartened the president's stance on nullification had made him, party loyalty was still everything to Father Ritchie. It remained to be seen how Tyler's disaffection with Jackson would affect his standing with the Richmond Junto and his position in Virginia politics. Perhaps the senator realized that the heyday of the Junto's influence in the Old Dominion had passed.[12]

In the meantime, he encouraged Clay's efforts to craft the compromise tariff that brought an end to the nullification crisis. Signed into law right before Congress adjourned in March 1833, less than two days before Jackson's second inauguration, the bill reduced duties slightly year by year until 1842, when a 20-percent tax on imports across the board would go into effect. Both the House and Senate passed it with minimal opposition. Tyler was credited with helping bring the two sides together. Friends in the Virginia legislature, in fact, acknowledged that his work had helped produce "the most soothing and tranquilising [sic] effect on the public." Ironically, this compromise tariff would become a particularly nettlesome political football when Tyler sat in the White House. The Panic of 1837 and the economic depression that followed drastically depleted the federal government's revenue and prompted Clay and other high-tariff advocates to push for rates above the 20 percent mandated by the compromise of 1833. Tyler would fight them on the matter and defend the compromise as a solemn compact.[13]

After winning reelection in 1832, Jackson sought to kill the institution he despised: the Second Bank of the United States. He ordered the removal of the federal government's deposits and had the funds transferred to specially designated state banks; his enemies called them the "pet banks." Of dubious legality, his transfer of the deposits sparked heated debate in Congress. Jackson supporters defended the removal and the attempt to destroy the bank as necessary to the preservation of republican virtue. To them, the national bank was a tool of privilege and elitism. Moreover, they argued that it was financially unstable and threatened the country's economy. Opponents of Jackson like Tyler maintained that the Constitution did not grant power to the president to meddle with the bank.

On December 26, 1833, Clay offered a resolution in the Senate censuring Jackson for removing the deposits. After months of partisan squabbling, the senators finally passed the resolution on March 28 of the following year. That same day Senator Thomas Hart Benton answered for Jackson, introducing a motion to "expunge" the censure resolution from the Senate *Journal.* Anti-Jackson forces defeated the expunging motion in 1834 and again early in 1835. Benton reintroduced the motion in December 1835, however, knowing he had more support (the Jacksonians had won control of the Senate in the midterm elections), and it passed. The pro-Jackson legislature of Virginia subsequently debated whether to instruct Senators Tyler and Leigh to vote for what was now called the Expunging Resolution.

Tyler recognized that if the Virginia legislature instructed him to vote for expunging the censure, he would face a complex dilemma. Regarded throughout the South as a consistent defender of states' rights, and with his stance on the right of instruction public knowledge, he nevertheless found the "villainous" resolution distasteful and loathed the thought of voting for it. Benton essentially wanted the official record of Senate proceedings mutilated. Tyler declared that he "dare not touch" the *Journal.* "The Constitution forbids it," he argued, alluding to Article I, Section 5. Adding to his dilemma was his conviction that a national bank was unconstitutional. Like many southerners, Tyler would have been happy to see its charter expire. But he found what he considered Jackson's unconstitutional abuse of executive authority appalling. The "advocates of free institutions," he said, must condemn the president's actions.[14]

Tyler's stridency on the expunging question made him a target of Benton, President Jackson's staunchest defender in the Senate. The Missouri senator mocked Tyler's penchant for constitutional arguments and reacted boorishly whenever the courtly Virginian rose to speak on the floor. The feud quickly became personal. Benton's behavior no doubt made Tyler's decision to abandon the Democratic Party a bit easier.

He thus found himself being pushed into the camp of the fledgling Whig Party, which had been founded in 1834 in opposition to "King Andrew." His entry into their ranks was the culmination of a two-step process. The nullification crisis had forced him *out* of the Democratic Party; Jackson's war on the bank and the political consequences of the removal of the deposits led him *into* the new party. The Whigs welcomed Tyler with open arms, some of them even suggesting that he might make an acceptable nominee for vice president in 1836. This enthusiasm for his conversion, however, masked the most problematic aspect of what was an uneasy alliance with the new party. While he certainly wanted to stem the tide of Jacksonianism, particularly in his home state of Virginia, Tyler was no Whig. He disagreed with Clay's American System, which soon became the hallmark of the new party, while his states' rights ideology was at odds with the party's belief in a strong, energetic national government. Tyler had drifted into the Whig camp out of default, solely because of his opposition to Jackson. He thus became a "states' rights Whig," which was almost a contradiction in terms. For their part, the Whigs viewed Tyler as the best possible choice to counter the Democrats in Virginia as he sought reelection to the Senate.[15]

This political marriage of convenience left both Tyler and the Whigs in awkward positions after the Virginia legislature passed resolutions on February 10, 1836, instructing its senators to vote for the Expunging Resolution. Leigh—another Whig by default—made up his mind to disobey the instruction. But Tyler could not do that and remain ideologically consistent. Moreover, having gone on record as opposing the Expunging Resolution, he could not obey instruction either. He leaned toward resigning but delayed making a decision.

Partisan concerns now had to be factored in and assessed, and Tyler received advice from many corners. Whigs like Clay wanted him to vote against the resolution *and* keep his seat because they worried his resignation would hurt the anti-Jackson cause nationally. "Such a course would be against the united judgment of his friends from other States," Clay pointed out.[16] Whig leaders also worried that if Tyler resigned and Leigh did not, the Democrats would capitalize on the apparent dissension in the opposition party. There were Whigs in Virginia, however, who believed his resignation could actually *help* their cause since clinging to principle would highlight the unconstitutionality of Benton's expunging motion.[17]

But more than principles and politics troubled Tyler. Personal reasons also help explain why he took so much time to decide his course of action. Adding to the stress of his perennial financial difficulties, his daughter Mary had recently married Henry Jones; the wedding occurred during the Christmas holidays in 1835, and it had been a costly affair. Tyler confided to his son Robert that his sister's marriage "has drained me pretty well of money" and left him with "large debts to pay." Giving up the senatorial salary of $8 per diem (roughly $1,680 per year; $45,405 in 2019 dollars) would be difficult.[18]

Finally, Tyler derived tremendous personal satisfaction from his position as a US senator. He still enjoyed the "animated discussion" in the chamber. He reveled in the "overflowing galleries," often packed with people who had come to hear important debates. Giving this up would not be easy, notwithstanding the barbs he had endured from Benton's acid tongue.[19]

Handwringing aside, and despite his desire to remain in the Senate, Tyler ultimately concluded that he must resign; it would allow him to remain consistent and preserve the sense of honor he had cultivated during his political career. More importantly, resignation offered a way for him to take the moral high ground regarding the Constitution. *He* would not be a party to a measure merely "calculated to rescue Gen[era]l Jackson's reputation," he assured a friend. Tyler could return home to Virginia and hope the people of the United States vindicated his course with "one general burst of indignation from the Ohio to the Atlantic." By late January 1836, he had made up his mind.[20]

In one last attempt to keep him from resigning, the Virginia Whigs nominated him for the vice presidency of the United States (Tyler ran on Hugh Lawson White's regional ticket, one of four the Whigs organized in 1836 in an effort to throw the election into the House of Representatives and deny Jackson's handpicked successor, Martin Van Buren, the presidency). They hoped he would be grateful enough and consider the good of the party over resignation. Whig senators in Washington also wanted Tyler to reconsider. Once his course became apparent, Clay and Calhoun called on him in an effort to change his mind. Tyler met the two men cordially but quickly put a stop to their pleas. "Gentlemen," he said, "the first act of my political life was a censure on Messrs. Giles and Brent, for opposition to instructions. The chalice presented to their lips is now presented to mine, and I will drink it." Calhoun responded that if he made resignation a "point of honor," there was "nothing more to say." Tyler submitted a formal letter of resignation to the Virginia legislature on February 29, 1836.[21]

Predictably, his resignation prompted responses from both the Whig and Democratic camps. The *Richmond Whig*, by 1836 the leading anti-Jackson newspaper in Virginia, praised Tyler and congratulated him for his "ardent devotion to the Constitution." Though the forced resignation was "shameful," the paper maintained that Tyler could be proud he would have nothing to do with expunging Jackson's censure from the Senate *Journal*. Compared to the moniker "Expunger," the *Whig* declared, the old derisive label "Hartford Conventionist," flung at disloyal Federalists during the War of 1812, seemed like a term of "patriotic worth."[22] In contrast, the Democratic papers were harsh in their condemnation of Tyler. The *Washington Globe* hissed that he wanted to "seduce Virginia into the ranks of the coalition against republicanism." The Virginia senator had been used by Clay to further the Kentuckian's purposes.[23] The *Richmond Enquirer* largely echoed the sentiments of the *Globe*.[24] Tyler's resignation thus became just another weapon in the escalating party warfare between Democrats and Whigs, which only got worse as the 1836 presidential election neared. Ultimately, however, his decision to leave the Senate had little effect on the Whig Party's fortunes.

Out of politics once again, Tyler looked forward to having the time to "put [his] house in order." That house would soon look very different—would in fact, *be* different, and his household was changing. A few months after his return to Virginia, Tyler sold Gloucester Place and moved his family to Williamsburg, where prospects for rebuilding a law practice were more promising. There, he purchased a spacious two-story house from his friend and William and Mary professor Nathaniel Beverley Tucker. John Jr. married Martha "Mattie" Rochelle of Southampton County, Virginia, in December 1838. Seventeen-year-old Letitia wed James A. Semple in February 1839. Robert married Priscilla Cooper, a stage actress and daughter of famed Shakespearian actor Thomas A. Cooper and New York socialite Mary Fairlie, in September 1839. His children's marriages, especially those of John and Robert, pleased Tyler immensely, and he welcomed the new members of his family enthusiastically. After a short honeymoon, Robert and Priscilla returned to Williamsburg to live with the Tylers.[25]

Tyler and Priscilla enjoyed a strong father-daughter bond, and their fondness for each other increased steadily over the years. She treasured the "tenderness and kindness" with which her father-in-law treated her and appreciated his offer to allow her to open an account in every store in Williamsburg. It did not take long, however, for Priscilla to realize that her new family was "extravagant" and lived beyond their means. Because of this realization, she never availed herself of Tyler's generosity. She was also struck by the poor health of her in-laws. "Her health is very bad," she noted, referring to her mother-in-law, "and she cannot bear to be left alone." Priscilla spent countless hours sitting with the elder Letitia, which no doubt endeared her to Tyler even more. She also confessed that she was even "sometimes quite uneasy" about her father-in-law's appearance, for he "look[ed] like a shadow—thin and pale as possible and ha[d] a very bad cough at times." In an effort to help, Priscilla gently suggested that he alter his diet so that the foods he ate did not aggravate his chronically upset stomach.[26]

꙳

While chronic colds and upset stomachs appeared with regularity as he practiced law again, they did not extinguish Tyler's desire to return to public life. It was inevitable that he would do so, starting with a stint as president of the Virginia Colonization Society.

Tyler had quietly advocated for colonization as a solution to the problem of slavery and free blacks for years. He became more committed to the idea as the matter took on more urgency during the early 1830s. Nat Turner's Rebellion as well as a highly publicized debate in the Virginia legislature in 1831–32 over the future of slavery in the state had convinced him that the time had come to address the critical issue of race. Even more importantly, Tyler watched with a growing sense of alarm and a heightening anger as the abolitionist movement gained momentum in the North. Indeed, by 1836, some three hundred antislavery societies, boasting more than 100,000 members, assaulted the South's peculiar institution. As a senator, Tyler had witnessed the unrelenting barrage of incendiary petitions that arrived in Washington through the mails to prod members of Congress toward abolishing slavery in the District of Columbia. He denounced the abolitionists and mocked the spirit of philanthropy that underlay their efforts to free enslaved people from bondage. In August 1835 Tyler delivered a blistering speech on the steps of the Gloucester County courthouse that served as a clarion call to his fellow Tidewater Virginians. His effort was part of a larger antiabolition campaign sweeping the state that year. "The unexpected evil is now upon us," he declared, "it has invaded our firesides, and under our own roofs is sharpening the dagger of midnight assassination, and exciting cruelty and bloodshed." The purpose of the abolitionist movement, he warned, was to "despoil us of our property at the hazard of all and every consequence." Tyler dramatically waved a copy of the *Anti-Slavery Record* for his audience to see and invited them to read for themselves the words supporting the "scourge" of abolitionism. He singled out Arthur Tappan and "Mr. Somebody Garrison" for their roles in the movement and called out the evangelical clergy in the North who worked in behalf of the South's slaves.

Tyler warmed to the subject as he sweated in the hot August sun. As angry as he was, there was something else that struck him as particularly offensive about the abolitionist movement: the participation of women. "Woman is to be made one of the instruments to accomplish their mischievous purposes," he sneered. "Yes, woman is to be made the instrument of destroying our political paradise, the Union of these States; she is to be made the presiding genius over the councils of insurrection and civil discord." Tyler related that he had seen an abolitionist petition signed by 1,500 women the previous winter. He expressed his amazement that so many signatures could be found.

Tyler took the reins as president of the Virginia Colonization Society in January 1838 and, in an address to its members, reiterated the same themes that had animated his Gloucester County speech nearly three years earlier. He proclaimed that the society was the "great African missionary society" and pledged himself to finding the funds to remove free blacks—who a decade earlier, at least, he did not regard as US citizens—from the state and paying for their passage across the Atlantic to new homes in Africa. How seriously he took that pledge, or how realistic he believed the goal, is not entirely clear. What is clear is that Tyler believed colonization was a matter for the southern states to work out. He rejected the national American Colonization Society as an unconstitutional encroachment on the right of those states to decide the fate of slavery. But the Virginia Colonization Society foundered—as did the national society—because of a lack of funding and an impractical plan to persuade free blacks to leave the only land they had ever known. Tyler's stance on the abolitionist movement and the apparent lip service he paid to colonization reflected mainstream opinion in Virginia's planter class. The colonization idea allowed them to delude themselves with the fiction that they were dealing with the problem of slavery and free blacks in a way that promoted gradual emancipation. In this view, these men were eliminating the necessary evil that had vexed them for so long but were not going to suffer the loss of slave property themselves. They also were willfully unaware of the role blacks themselves were beginning to play in the effort to win their own freedom.

Tyler's view of the role of women in the movement is more interesting. While certainly in tune with the way most southern men felt about female participation in political or politicized organizations, it is nevertheless striking for its stridency. Perhaps the willingness of male abolitionists like Tappan and William Lloyd Garrison to deploy women in the movement's behalf came perilously close to threatening his ideal of white southern womanhood, with all the racial overtones that the ideal implied.[27]

In any event, Tyler soon found other outlets for his addiction to politics and public life and left the Colonization Society behind. Much as it had years earlier, the lure of elective office proved too strong. In April 1838, just two years after resigning from the US Senate, he unretired (again) and returned to the Virginia House of Delegates for a third time. Tyler's supporters warmly welcomed him back to Richmond and elected him Speaker of the House.[28]

Tyler enjoyed his return to the political arena and approached his duties as a state legislator with enthusiasm. He devoted much energy to his position as chairman of the Select Committee on Public Lands. The public-lands issue had become a major source of contention in American politics by the late 1830s. Lawmakers in Washington argued over whether lands owned by the federal government in the West should be sold or given away to settlers. Whigs favored the sale of the lands and wanted to distribute the proceeds of such sales to the states for things like public education and internal improvements. Democrats opposed the policy and maintained the land should be given away to settlers. The purpose of the select committee was to formulate Virginia's official position on the matter. Tyler himself favored the Whig policy and believed the individual states were entitled to reap the rewards of the sales. Late in January 1839 he presented a detailed report to the House of Delegates arguing the merits of this position. Largely on the basis of this report, the house passed a series of resolutions that articulated its support of what was called "distribution." The delegates also requested that the Old Dominion's senators and representatives in Washington introduce these resolutions in Congress. The Virginia Senate, however, controlled by Democrats, would have none of it. Determined not to give the supporters of distribution at the national level any satisfaction, the senate tabled the resolutions. Doing so effectively ended the discussion in Virginia and kept support for distribution from becoming the state's official stance.[29]

Despite their success with this maneuver, Virginia Democrats were a weakened lot by 1839. Their party included a significant number—one historian places the number at sixteen—of what were called "Conservative" Democrats. These states' rights men had remained loyal to Jackson during the nullification crisis. Moreover, they had stuck with the president throughout the Bank War, even as the removal of deposits and his subsequent Specie Circular—which mandated that federal-land purchases be made in specie, or hard money— helped spark a widespread financial panic. The Independent Treasury plan President Van Buren soon championed disturbed them, however, and created an ever-widening breach between their ranks and the Democratic stalwarts in Virginia like Ritchie, which weakened the Richmond Junto. Under the Independent Treasury plan, which Van Buren put into practice through an executive order, the national government took the deposits out of the pet banks and placed them in special federal depositories known as "Sub-Treasuries." Conservatives argued that using state banks to house the funds made more sense. Deposit banks could be strengthened by federal regulations, they reasoned, which would provide security for government revenues. What made Van Buren's idea particularly onerous was that it obligated debtors to the national government to pay only in specie. An extension of the Specie Circular, it worsened the financial crisis by reducing the supply of hard currency at a time when a policy of controlled inflation would have been more prudent. The Conservatives ultimately broke with the Democratic Party over this policy.[30]

The break between the Conservatives and Van Buren had a direct influence on the political fortunes of John Tyler. On March 3, 1839, the Senate term of William Cabell Rives expired. Tyler hoped to oust Rives, a Conservative Democrat who had replaced him after his resignation in 1836, and return to Washington. Whig leaders in Congress had other plans. Recognizing the crucial influence the Conservatives would have on advancing their fortunes in Virginia, they shrewdly supported Rives for reelection. The hope was that by championing Rives, the rest of the Old Dominion's Conservatives would follow him foursquare into the Whig fold. The party would then likely carry the spring 1839 elections in the state, which would aid their cause considerably in the presidential election of 1840.

From their vantage point, Whigs in Virginia doubted that Rives was the correct choice and refused to fall into line with what the national party wanted. Many of these Virginians expressed a hope that a "pure Whig" could be found. They caucused in late January 1839 and rejected Rives. Tyler received the most support during the proceedings but, since there were enough Whigs who gave their support to Rives, failed to win the nomination at first. The party eventually voted its support at a second caucus. Tyler would face Rives, the candidate of the Conservatives, as well as the Democratic nominee, John Y. Mason.[31]

Tyler should have been the logical candidate of the national Whigs. His stance on the distribution issue enhanced his standing in the party. More to the point, he had seemingly sacrificed his career three years earlier in support of the opposition to Jackson and the Democrats. Now would have been the time for the Whigs to reward his stance. Partisan considerations necessitated support of Rives, though, and so Tyler stood no chance of returning to the Senate. There were even rumors that Clay had offered him the Whig vice-presidential nomination in 1840 in exchange for his withdrawal from the Senate contest. If Clay had made such an offer, Tyler clearly refused it. The Senate election took place in February 1839. The Virginia legislature voted in joint session, and for the first five ballots, Tyler ran ahead of Rives. Enough Whigs ultimately threw their support behind Rives, however, to force Tyler to realize that he could not win, after which he withdrew from consideration.[32]

But the former senator's part in the election did not end there. Allying himself with a group of Whigs known as the "Impracticables," roughly fifteen members of the Virginia legislature who could not abide a Rives victory, Tyler played a key role in preventing the election of his intraparty opponent. He helped mobilize opposition to Rives and repeatedly voted against his election. By late February, the Conservatives in the legislature had moved entirely into the Whig camp and attempted to seize the election for Rives. But the Impracticables were strong enough in number to prevent this from happening. The result was a deadlock; no man in either of the two factions would budge. Finally, after twenty-eight ballots the House passed a resolution calling for an indefinite postponement of the election. The Virginia Senate concurred, and the Old Dominion's second US Senate seat remained vacant.[33]

Tyler's actions to prevent the election of Rives sparked some bitterness on the part of several Virginia Whigs. It apparently had no consequence on his national standing, however, for in December 1839 the party nominated him for vice president, placing him on the 1840 ticket with William Henry Harrison. Tyler took to the hustings in the fall of 1840 despite a recurrence of his ill health. Not expected to be as prolific on the campaign trail as Harrison, who gave more than two dozen speeches and numerous minor ones, he nevertheless spoke before large audiences in Wheeling, Virginia; Columbus, Ohio; and Pittsburgh, with some appearances at smaller stops along the way. He watched his words carefully and attempted to avoid saying anything that might cause controversy and embarrassment to Harrison and the national Whigs. He was not let off easily. Heckled in Pittsburgh over his position on the tariff, Tyler was forced to offer a bland statement affirming his support for the compromise of 1833. Local Democrats stirred up trouble when Tyler gave a speech in Steubenville, Ohio. There, they demanded to know where he stood on a national bank, which most observers realized would be a Whig priority if they won the election. Boxed in, Tyler mumbled that he agreed with General Harrison's position. In his last speech of the campaign, which he gave a few blocks from his home in Williamsburg, he asserted that he had not yet made up his mind on the bank question but that his supporters could depend upon his adherence to the Constitution and states' rights. This artful dodge foreshadowed the position he adopted when he became president: he would sanction a national bank as long as it comported with his longstanding principles and satisfied his constitutional scruples.[34]

The 1840 "log cabin and hard cider" campaign was one of the most colorful in American history. Whigs attacked President Van Buren with catchy slogans that stuck with the voters, placing blame for the devastating Panic of 1837 squarely on his shoulders and talking up the military exploits of the hero of Tippecanoe. They had learned a lot about how to wage an effective campaign from the Democrats and intended to beat them at their own game. A central committee in Washington, for example, operated in similar fashion to the one Van Buren himself had established to get Jackson elected in 1828, tying the Whigs' national campaign to county-level organizations in many states. They also launched a revolution of sorts by encouraging women to attend rallies and other public events. Perhaps in no other state was this "Whig womanhood" more effectively employed than in Tyler's own Virginia. The spirited campaign led to an unprecedented level of voter turnout, and the contest signaled the vitality of the new Second Party System. More importantly for Tyler, 1840 proved to be the Whigs' year. He was disappointed that the party failed to carry Virginia, which Van Buren won by fewer than 1,400 votes. But Harrison captured the presidency.[35]

In early March 1841 John Tyler left his home in Williamsburg and traveled to Washington, where he took the vice-presidential oath on the fourth, shortly before Harrison's inauguration as the nation's ninth president. As Tyler sat in his room at Brown's Indian Queen Hotel on the evening of March 3, he no doubt thought about what the next four years of his life would entail. He planned to spend most of his time in Virginia, practicing law and seeing to his family. Tyler had wanted the nomination for second place on the Whig ticket in 1840 but realized his new role gave him little chance for national renown. Apparently, it would have to be enough that his career had taken him this far. Leaving Washington amid no fanfare after being sworn in, Tyler returned to his home, unaware that an unprecedented calamity was about to befall the United States and offer him the best opportunity yet to cement his place in history.

Chapter 8

TAKING CHARGE

Just before dawn on the cool spring morning of Monday, April 5, 1841, Vice President John Tyler and his family awoke to sharp knocks on the front door of their Williamsburg home. Startled by the noise, Tyler jumped out of bed and hurried down the stairs, still in a nightshirt. As he made his way through the house, there were more knocks, this time even louder than the ones that had roused him from sleep. Reaching the door, Tyler opened it cautiously. Peering into the early morning darkness, he found two men waiting: Fletcher Webster, chief clerk of the State Department and twenty-three-year-old son of Daniel Webster, and Robert Beale, assistant doorkeeper of the US Senate. After the two men identified themselves, they told the vice president that they had been dispatched from Washington to inform him that President William Henry Harrison was dead. Tyler ushered them inside, where they handed him an official handwritten message signed by the president's cabinet announcing the "melancholy tidings." Harrison had died at 12:30 A.M. on April 4, Palm Sunday. Tyler would have to leave for Washington as soon as possible. He was now president of the United States—and at age fifty-one, the youngest man up to that point to assume the office.[1]

This turn of events did not take Tyler completely by surprise. Though he had received no official notification of Harrison's final illness, his longtime friend James Lyons, a Richmond attorney, had dashed off a letter from Virginia's capital on the evening of Saturday, April 3, informing Tyler that the sixty-eight-year-old Harrison seemed to be near death. Battling a severe cold since being caught in a rainstorm nearly two weeks earlier, the president had sent for a doctor on March 27, complaining of chills and fever. Spending most of the next week in bed, Harrison rallied briefly, only to suffer a relapse that soon developed into pneumonia. Accurately gauging the gravity of the situation, Lyons bluntly told Tyler that he would "not be surprised to hear by tomorrows [sic] mail that Genl Harrison is no more." While it is not altogether clear when exactly he received this letter, it is evident the missive reached its intended destination; it was endorsed by Tyler. Adding further to the likelihood that he knew of Harrison's illness before Webster and Beale pounded on his door, in his letter of April 3, Lyons alluded to another note he had recently sent Tyler, which may very well have provided the news of the president's "violent pleurisy." It seems reasonable to assume, therefore, that Tyler knew Harrison was ill—and gravely so. His friend Lyons likely prepared him for news of the president's death.[2]

Even if he had known of Harrison's illness beforehand, the news Webster and Beale brought with them still must have come as a shock. But there was no time for contemplation. Nor was there time for the tears that one persistent legend falsely maintained Tyler shed upon hearing the momentous news. He discussed the enormity of what had happened with his family, whose lives would change dramatically now, and after a hasty breakfast packed his things for the trip to Washington. Before he left, Tyler sought out his friend and neighbor Nathaniel Beverley Tucker to tell him what had happened. The meeting lasted for only five minutes. Tucker urged Tyler to make a statement as soon as he arrived in Washington "disclaiming irrevocably all pretensions to a second term." Well aware that Tyler's relationship with the majority of the Whig Party was problematic, and recognizing that the Democrats would seek to exploit this difficult relationship, Tucker made clear his position that Tyler could help his case if he pledged only to serve out Harrison's term. The "strife" between the parties, he said, may very well tear Tyler "in pieces as by wild horses" if he appeared overly ambitious. The two men also may have talked policy during their brief meeting. Six days after they spoke, Tucker sent the new president a detailed proposal for a national bank that comported with their states' rights, strict-construction principles. It is likely that Tyler solicited this letter right before he left Williamsburg. He was evidently thinking ahead.[3]

By 7:00 A.M., Tyler was ready to leave. Accompanied by the two messengers as well as by his son John Jr., he traveled from Williamsburg to Richmond by boat, then on to Washington by train. Tyler and his party arrived in the nation's capital around 4:00 A.M. on Tuesday, April 6. The new president immediately took a suite at Brown's Indian Queen Hotel, the same place where he had stayed just one month earlier before he was sworn in as vice president.[4]

As Tyler hurried to Washington, he mulled over Tucker's suggestion about disclaiming a second term. His mind also no doubt returned to a conversation he had had with his friend Littleton Tazewell in the fall of 1840. It may have been the recollection of this very conversation that had prompted Tyler to seek out Tucker before leaving Williamsburg. Tazewell and Tyler had sat in Tyler's home on that autumn day, catching up on family matters and discussing politics. Much of their conversation naturally centered on the "Tippecanoe and Tyler, Too" campaign, and they found themselves hoping for different results as the election neared. Tazewell had remained a Democrat even as his longtime friend had joined the Whigs. The differences in party affiliation did nothing to limit the esteem both men felt for each other, however. In fact, Tazewell's reason for calling on his friend that day was because he was worried about Tyler. Convinced the Whigs would vanquish President Van Buren and win control of Congress—which, of course, gave him no pleasure in asserting—and emphasizing Harrison's advanced age, Tazewell actually predicted that the old general would die in office. He urged Tyler to consider what that "contingency" would mean for him as he took the reins of the government. More specifically, Tazewell pressed him to think about the difficulties that would undoubtedly arise as the states' rights Whig assumed power with a Congress dominated by the nationalist Henry Clay. Tazewell "spoke of violent assaults to be made upon me," Tyler later said, "unless I yielded my conscience, judgment—everything, into the hands of the political managers." Tyler had been drawn "a fearful picture" of what would happen. Tazewell wanted to know how he would respond to the inevitable Whig onslaught. How would he balance his own longstanding principles with the dominant principles of the party to which he tenuously belonged? How would he assert his authority in the face of potentially rabid opposition to his own course of action? These were important questions. Tyler had no ready answers that day but acknowledged that his friend had given him much to think about.[5]

When Tyler arrived in Washington, he learned that four members of President Harrison's cabinet were in the city—Secretary of State Daniel Webster, Treasury Secretary Thomas Ewing, War Secretary John Bell, and Postmaster General Francis Granger (two other cabinet members, Attorney General John J. Crittenden and Navy Secretary George Badger, were away attending to personal matters).[6] Tyler summoned the four men for a noon meeting at Brown's Hotel. They duly complied, anxious to take the measure of their new chief. At noon Tyler took the presidential oath of office in the hotel parlor. William Cranch, chief judge of the Circuit Court of the District of Columbia, administered the oath since Chief Justice of the United States Roger B. Taney was out of the city. Exactly who sent for Cranch is not clear, nor is it known who decided that Tyler should take the oath of office. Tyler himself believed that his succession to the presidency was automatic upon Harrison's death. In the official record of what transpired that day, which is frustratingly sparse, Cranch attested to administering the oath to the vice president. He added a statement acknowledging that Tyler "deem[ed] himself qualified to perform the duties and exercise the powers and office of President on the death of William Henry Harrison, late President of the United States, without any other oath than that which he has taken as Vice-President." But since "doubts may *arise*" over his status "and for greater caution," Tyler took the presidential oath.[7]

Cranch's statement is open to different interpretations. Did *Tyler*, despite his stance that his succession was automatic, worry about the doubts that might arise and thus insist himself that he take what was in his mind a superfluous oath to legitimize his authority? Or was it Webster and the *cabinet* who wanted to eliminate potential doubts by having Tyler take the oath? After all, they had addressed their message to him by referring to him as the "vice president." There had to have been discussion of the issue before Tyler's arrival in Washington. While it will probably never be known with certainty, it is logical to assume that Tyler had insisted on taking the oath of office. In light of how important he later said his conversation with Tazewell had been in preparing him for the moment when he would become president, and in light of his other actions on April 6, perhaps the best interpretation is that Tyler had formulated a strategy while on his way to Washington to solidify his status as president. Worried that both the cabinet and Congress might attempt to undermine his authority, he wanted to assert himself from the very beginning and make clear his intention to be more than a mere figurehead. He would be no placeholder, no "Vice President acting as President," as some would propose.[8]

So what exactly had Tyler done by taking the oath and assuming the office *and* powers of the presidency? According to some scholars, he had misconstrued the original intention of the US Constitution. Article II, Section 1, paragraph 6 states, "In case of the removal of the President from office, or of his death, resignation, or inability to discharge the powers and duties of the said office, the same shall devolve on the Vice President." What is not clear is whether this statement means the "powers and duties" of the presidency devolve on the vice president or "the said office" itself devolves on the vice president, or whether there is even any difference. And there is nothing at all said about the oath. Tyler made no such distinction. His interpretation was that he had inherited the *office* of president once Harrison had died, which, of course, meant that he could now exercise the *powers* and assume the *duties* of the presidency unencumbered. He recognized that taking the oath solidified this position. Historically, the official date of the beginning of Tyler's presidency is April 6, 1841, which is recognition that validates his decision to take the oath. Tyler made history on that day. His assertiveness also staved off a possible constitutional crisis that could have clogged the wheels of government and undermined the authority of the executive branch.

The precedent Tyler established that day—taking the oath and assuming the office of the president—became the commonly accepted practice from that point forward. There would be no more debate on the matter except in academic circles. Subsequent vice presidents who succeeded to the presidency upon the death of the chief executive—Millard Fillmore, Andrew Johnson, Chester Arthur, Theodore Roosevelt, Calvin Coolidge, Harry Truman, and Lyndon Johnson—all followed what Tyler had done by taking the oath of office and assuming the presidency at that moment. To illustrate this point, it is perhaps instructive to remember that the iconic photograph of Lyndon Johnson taking the oath of office aboard Air Force One on November 22, 1963, the day President John F. Kennedy was assassinated in Dallas, was made possible because of the Tyler precedent. Thus, as one presidential historian has put it, such transfers of the office of the presidency became accepted "by virtue of usage rather than by virtue of constitutional provision." Passage and ratification of the Twenty-Fifth Amendment in 1967 settled the issue once and for all. The wording of the amendment—"In case of the removal of the President from office or of his death or resignation, the Vice President shall become President"—codified the precedent Tyler set in the parlor of Brown's Hotel at noon on April 6, 1841.[9]

Not all of Tyler's contemporaries were convinced that his actions actually made him president. John Quincy Adams, the acerbic former president turned congressman, insisted on referring to Tyler as "acting" president and was never willing to acknowledge that taking the oath of office granted the Virginian legitimacy. Adams's view is no doubt best understood as the product of his loathing of Tyler rather than any overly technical reading of the Constitution. Adams, in fact, became one of Tyler's harshest and most outspoken critics in Congress. Brooding on April 4, the day Harrison died, Adams considered what had happened and did what he had done nearly every night for almost fifty years: he vented to his diary. "Tyler is a political sectarian, of the slave-driving, Virginian, Jeffersonian school, principled against all improvement," he fulminated, "with all the interests and passions and vices of slavery in his moral and political constitution—with talents not above mediocrity, and a spirit incapable of expansion to the dimensions of the station upon which he has been cast by the hand of Providence." Hearing that Tyler had taken the oath of office on April 6, Adams contemplated what his presidency would mean for the country. "Slavery, temperance, land-jobbing, bankruptcy, and sundry controversies with Great Britain constitute the materials for the history of John Tyler's administration," he grumbled.[10]

Others were less personally bitter toward Tyler but concurred with Adams that he should be addressed with a title other than "president." Clay, for example, believed that Tyler should continue to view himself as vice president, believing that the new administration "will be in the nature of a regency" and simply carry on the policies of the Harrison administration—a self-serving argument, as Tyler would soon see. The issue of his proper title was a touchy one for Tyler. He made a point of promptly returning unopened any mail he received at the White House, or at his home in Virginia, addressed to the "acting" president or to "Vice President Tyler." He believed he had earned the right to be addressed as "President Tyler" and made sure people knew it.[11]

There was further significance in what Tyler had done on April 6. He had assumed the presidency and had left the vice-presidential office vacant. The Constitution did not mandate that he choose a new vice president to replace himself; that requirement, too, came with ratification of the Twenty-Fifth Amendment. Tyler thus served his entire term as president without a vice president. The Presidential Succession Act of 1792 stipulated that should Tyler die in office, the president pro tempore of the Senate would succeed to the presidency. Should that man die, the Speaker of the House would become president. On April 6, 1841, the president pro tempore was Samuel Southard of New Jersey. He served in that capacity until his resignation on May 31, 1842. North Carolina senator Willie P. Mangum filled Southard's vacancy on that date and held the position until the end of Tyler's term, March 4, 1845.[12]

After administering the oath of office and shaking the new president's hand, Cranch left Brown's Hotel. At some point that day—the record is unclear whether it occurred before or after he took the oath—Tyler told the cabinet members present that he wanted to retain them all. He praised them for their service to Harrison and to the country and told them that he greatly respected their abilities. He also stated that he wanted to get down to the business of his administration immediately and that he would need their help. Harrison's death had thrown official Washington into chaos, and Tyler believed keeping his predecessor's cabinet in place would provide the order and continuity the country needed at this time. He would soon regret his decision.[13]

Taking the lead for the rest of the cabinet, as he customarily did, Secretary of State Webster informed the new president that decisions under Harrison had been made by majority vote—with the president holding but one of the votes. In effect, according to Webster, the executive branch had functioned by committee.

What Webster had told Tyler was literally true, but it was not the full story. Whig ideology called for a weak presidency, with Congress rather than the chief executive assuming more of the robust powers of the federal government. Harrison had also pledged in his inaugural address to serve only one term, which Whigs at the time, and many historians since, have regarded as his acceptance of diminished authority. Many Whigs also tended to view the cabinet as a check on presidential power, and the men of Harrison's cabinet regarded themselves in this way.[14] What Webster had not told Tyler, though, was that Harrison had bristled at the arrangement and, during his short time in office, had not always played the role the party had developed for him.

Nor would Tyler. When Webster brought this up, Tyler shook his head and abruptly cut him off. "I am the President, and I shall be held responsible for my administration," he said sharply. Looking at the men arrayed in front of him, he told them pointedly: "I shall be pleased to avail myself of your counsel and advice. But I can never consent to being dictated to as to what I shall or shall not do." Tyler ended the discussion by telling them that he would accept their resignations if they could not work under this arrangement. The men looked at each other and nodded. Not one of them offered to resign.[15]

Tyler's forceful rejoinder to Webster's attempt to undermine his authority left no doubt as to who was in charge. The new president had forced the cabinet—indeed, its most powerful member—to heel, and he instantly became the commanding presence in the room. Tyler clearly intended to set the right tone for his administration. Webster may have been slightly surprised by Tyler's willingness to assert himself so strongly, but he quickly fell in line and made up his mind that he could work with the new president. The secretary of state still feared, however, that the Old Republican's history might not bode well for the Whig agenda. Expressing unease with Tyler's longstanding principles, Webster nevertheless crossed his fingers and hoped for the best. "My *hope* is," he said, "that he will consider himself *instructed*, not by one single state, but by the *Country*."[16] His fellow cabinet members agreed and decided to give Tyler the benefit of the doubt.

For his part, Tyler recognized that retaining Harrison's cabinet presented its own set of problems; he knew he was swimming in treacherous waters. Each of these men had been carefully chosen for their posts to placate one faction or another in the party. Tyler realized that these factions might tear the Whigs apart. "When I arrived here," he told Tucker some three months later, "I became fully apprised of the angry state of the factions towards each other, and set myself to work in good earnest to reconcile them." He was, as he put it, "surrounded by Clay men, Webster men, anti-Masons, original Harrisonians, old Whigs and new Whigs—each jealous of the others, and all struggling for the offices."[17]

As a longtime politician who had faced intense partisanship and survived many hard-fought battles in the past, Tyler could not have been surprised by the factionalism and jealousies. He had seen all of it on display at the Whig convention in Harrisburg in December 1839 as party stalwarts jostled for advantage. For that matter, he owed his place on the ticket in 1840 to factionalism and jealousy. He realized, however, that these conditions would make his job as president much more difficult. Perhaps still thinking of the conversation with Tazewell, who had warned him of the "violent assaults" to come, he declared an intention to persevere; "in the administration of the government, I shall act upon the principles which I have all along espoused," those learned "from the teachings of Jefferson and Madison, and other of our distinguished countrymen, and my reliance will be placed on the virtue and intelligence of the people." He would act in accordance with the people's will.[18]

Tyler himself knew what course he would pursue. But the rest of the political world was not entirely sure of his intentions, and all of Washington waited impatiently to find out. While they did, something curious occurred. In the days following President Harrison's death, both sides of the partisan divide sought to claim his successor as one of their own. In fact, there developed a fascinating rhetorical back and forth, almost as if both Whigs and Democrats hoped by their words to sway Tyler to their side—as if they could almost guilt him into acting as they wanted. They exhorted him to do the right thing as they defined it.

Many Whigs consoled themselves in tragedy with the thought that Tyler would abide by their principles because of the way he had succeeded to the presidency. A subtle appeal to his patriotism informed this view. The *Washington Daily National Intelligencer,* the Whig paper in the nation's capital, captured this sentiment by declaring that Tyler "ow[ed] his elevation" to "those same principles which put President Harrison in that place before him." Surely he would not go against the will of the people who had brought the Whigs to power in 1840. Others sought to connect Tyler with his predecessor even more directly. Much had been made of the words President Harrison had rasped to one of his physicians as he departed this world: "Sir, I wish you to understand the true principles of the Government. I wish them carried out. I ask nothing more." Supposedly, this dying utterance had been directed at John Tyler. It probably had been. Most certainly these words were not meant for one N. W. Worthington, M.D, the physician who reported hearing them (whether the good doctor was himself a partisan has never been established). The Whigs believed the statement was the equivalent of holy writ. As one put it, "I trust that the last wish of the dying but immortal patriot will be carried out—that

President Tyler and his talented cabinet may fully 'understand and carry out the true principles of the government.'"[19]

Democrats, naturally, sought a different course of action from the new president. Nowhere was this more on display than in the pages of Thomas Ritchie's *Richmond Enquirer*. "Will he carry out the Whig measures," an editorial in the paper asked, "or will he recollect the Virginia State Rights' principles, to which he was formerly devoted?" Whigs like Clay were "beginning to count upon his most active co-operation," the *Enquirer* warned. "It is the street talk of the Whigs, that Mr. Tyler is a Bank man; and the Richmond *Whig* appears certain that he will be swept along with the current of Webster and Co." Another Democratic paper, recognizing that the other side was trying to compel Tyler to take Harrison's dying words to heart, had this to say: "Let him not yield to the dictates of indolence and roll into the bed that others have made for him." In short, Democrats wanted the Old Republican to "eschew the consolidating doctrines" of the Whigs and chart a course for himself that was consistent with his longstanding principles. The Democrats would soon find themselves quite pleased with the new president.[20]

President Tyler discussed the plans for Harrison's funeral with the cabinet during that first meeting. With no established protocol for the funeral of a president who had died in office, Tyler was again in uncharted territory. Mindful of the mood of the city and nation and conscious of the historical significance of Harrison's death, he wanted to make certain that his predecessor received the full honors he deserved.

Tyler saw to it that Harrison's body lie in state in the East Room of the White House. The East Room was (and remains) the largest room in the mansion, so it made sense to use it for this occasion. The bodies of six of the seven other presidents who have died in office—Zachary Taylor, Abraham Lincoln, William McKinley, Warren G. Harding, Franklin D. Roosevelt, and John F. Kennedy—also rested in the East Room as part of their funeral ceremonies.[21] Tyler thus established this precedent as well.

On Wednesday, April 7, Reverend William Hawley, rector of Washington's St. John's Episcopal Church, presided over the funeral rites. At the conclusion of the service, a car drawn by six white horses conveyed Harrison's body to the Congressional Cemetery, where it was placed into a receiving vault. The body would stay there until June 26, 1841, when Harrison's son would accompany it back to North Bend, Ohio, and its final resting place.[22]

Graciously, President Tyler allowed Harrison's family to remain in the Executive Mansion for as long as they wished and "to consider themselves his guests." Several relatives had taken up residence with Harrison on March 4. The dead president's wife, Anna, had not made the trip to Washington in February with her husband; she did not attend the funeral. Tyler sent a personal letter of condolence to her. He also personally made sure that Harrison's funeral train had a military escort when it left Washington for Ohio in June. And finally, he designated May 14, 1841, as a day of national prayer and fasting in Harrison's memory.[23]

꒰ᴥ꒱

The night of Harrison's funeral, President Tyler began taking further steps to establish his administration. Chief among these was preparing what amounted to an inaugural address. This was a matter of great importance to Tyler, for he believed it would further augment his legitimacy as president. He also believed the American people deserved to know the course of action he intended to pursue.[24]

Tyler delivered his brief address before a small audience at the Capitol on April 9. The Washington papers published it that day; the dailies in other major cities and the rags in many small towns had it for their readers within two days. The address focused on three areas—foreign affairs, the patronage system, and financial matters—and also included what could be considered a summary statement of Tyler's political principles. It did not include a promise from the new president that he would refrain from seeking his own term in 1844. That promise, he had apparently already decided, would never come. While he may have composed a statement disavowing a second term in the first draft of his inaugural, it did not survive revisions.[25]

The section that covered foreign affairs was the most cursory of the address. Tyler declared that the "groundwork" of his foreign policy would be "justice on our part to all, submitting to injustice from none." He would "sedulously cultivate the relations of peace and amity with one and all" but would also make certain that "the honor of the country shall sustain no blemish." To that end, he signaled that he intended to seek the appropriation of more money for the army and navy, regarding the protection of America's shores as paramount.[26]

The longest portion of the address focused on patronage, or the "spoils system." The "patronage incident to the Presidential office, already great, is constantly increasing," Tyler pointed out. A "selfishly ambitious" chief executive, he argued, might very well use his "unrestrained power" to appoint and remove federal officials "in order either to perpetuate his authority or to hand it over to some favorite as his successor." This had been the argument Whigs had made against Presidents Jackson and Van Buren, so Tyler's words in this portion of the address coincided fully with party orthodoxy. He declared his desire to put an end to this system, but he did not spell out a precise remedy. "I will at a proper time invoke the action of Congress upon this subject," he announced, "and shall readily acquiesce in the adoption of all proper measures which are calculated to arrest these evils."

Why did Tyler focus so much attention on the spoils system? The short answer to this question came from the president himself. "Numerous removals may become necessary" during his administration, he warned, and he wanted his "countrymen to understand the principle of the Executive action." Tyler declared that he would remove no man from office who had "faithfully and honestly acquitted himself" unless that man "had been guilty of an active partisanship or by secret means" sought to give "his official influence to the purpose of party."[27]

There was a larger political significance to what Tyler said about patronage. What he had done was subtly warn the Whigs that he would not be beholden to the officeholders whom his predecessor had appointed. Many of these men had been foisted on Harrison by influential Whigs throughout the United States, party men who, presumably, would be unsympathetic to Tyler should he oppose the Whig legislative agenda. Tyler would not have appointees to federal jobs scheming against his administration—"guilty of an active partisanship," as he put it—and using their positions to augment a Whig majority in Congress that might seek to undermine his authority. In short, he was putting the Whigs on notice. Tyler even said he was willing to accept limits on the presidential power of appointment—again, a hallmark of Whig ideology that the party had used to denounce Jackson—which he indicated might become permanent under the proper conditions. He also maintained that he would not "neglect to apply the same unbending rule to those of [his] own appointment."[28]

In hindsight, this portion of the inaugural address is an indication that Tyler had already decided to pursue his own election as president in 1844. And it may rightly be said that he was being disingenuous and not a little cynical. Tyler may have paid lip service to the Whig Party's oft-stated goal of taking away some of the president's appointment power, but he never had any intention of invoking "the action of Congress upon this subject." He had to know that party leaders did not want to alter the system because any changes might work against them in later contests with the Democrats. Clay, in fact, had already "deliberately adopted" a "rule of non-interference" with respect to the president's appointment power, and he expected Congress to abide by it. The president no doubt knew this and aimed to use it to his advantage.[29]

Tyler possessed well-honed political instincts that had rarely failed him. On April 9, with the publication of his inaugural address, he signaled his willingness to starve the Whig patronage beast into submission if he thought it necessary to protect his own political interests. Everything he had done since arriving in Washington, then, had been calculated to establish his authority as president. "He seems to *know* that he is *President*," one perceptive Washington insider said of Tyler.[30]

The Old Republican evidently intended to attempt to build his own political base using the presidential power to appoint and remove officeholders. Far from taking Tucker's advice and declaring that he would not seek a term in his own right, Tyler was laying the groundwork for the further advancement of his political career. Had that not been his course of action since he first entered national politics those many years ago? Tyler had always thought two or three steps ahead. In significant ways he was very much the "ambitious man" his inaugural had warned against. His strategy was not without risk, though. One observer proclaimed that a "desire to be again elected President" might be the "rock on which he will split." But as Tyler well knew, there could be no reward without risk. And he was not averse to taking risks. Bold leaders did it all the time.[31]

With respect to the country's finances, the third topic of the inaugural, Tyler declared his intention to uphold the "most rigid economy" in "all public expenditures." Believing that the Whigs might pursue deficit spending to jumpstart the economy, and fully cognizant that such a practice would present a tremendous challenge to his administration and his ideology, he maintained that "a public debt in time of peace [should] be sedulously avoided." With this view, Tyler seemed to be returning to his Democratic roots. Jackson had believed the exact same thing.

The most pressing concern for the Whigs was how the new president intended to respond to the currency issue. Tyler knew that Clay and the Whigs in Congress intended to repeal Van Buren's much-maligned Independent Treasury and replace it with the charter of a real national bank. Clay, in fact, had persuaded President Harrison to call a special session of Congress for the summer of 1841 so the party could do just that. Tyler labeled the Independent Treasury "unwise and impolitic and in a high degree oppressive," and he welcomed its repeal, which no doubt won him some points with Whig stalwarts. So far so good. Then he got to the heart of the matter. "I shall promptly give my sanction to any constitutional measure which, originating in Congress, shall have for its object the restoration of a sound circulating medium, so essentially necessary to give confidence in all the transactions of life, to secure to industry its just and adequate rewards, and to reestablish the public prosperity." In deciding whether to give the presidential imprimatur to what the Whigs devised—that is, in making the judgment as to what was "constitutional"—Tyler proclaimed that he would "resort to the fathers of the great republican school for advice and instruction." Symbolically, and with great portent, he did not use the words "national bank."

Toward the end of the inaugural address, Tyler added a succinct statement of his political principles, which also served as a coda to his words on how he would view the creation of a national bank. National politicians—including himself—"should carefully abstain from all attempts to enlarge the range of powers" of the government unless the people demanded it, "lest by so doing they disturb that balance which the patriots and statesmen who framed the Constitution designed to establish between the Federal Government and the States composing the Union." Such a result would create "a central system which would inevitably end in a bloody scepter and an iron crown."[32]

There it was. Tyler could not have made any clearer his intention to abide by the states' rights, strict-construction, limited-government principles that had guided him for his entire career. But Whigs saw in the inaugural address what they wanted to see. They willfully and perhaps a bit naively read conciliation in Tyler's words. Many were actually reassured by what the Old Republican had said!

Resting at Ashland, his plantation outside Lexington, Kentucky, and recovering from illness, Senator Clay read Tyler's remarks and told an acquaintance: "Mr. Tyler's disposition, I cannot doubt, will be to cooperate in adopting the measures of the Whigs. He has indeed just said as much." To his Senate colleague John M. Berrien of Georgia, he echoed this view, declaring, "we are a good deal relieved by the address of Mr. Tyler to the people of the U. States, the fair interpretation of which is, that he will concur in the leading measures of the Whigs."[33]

Similarly, Secretary of State Webster read the inaugural and was persuaded that "things [would] continue in the expected course." A Maryland Whig concurred, writing to Tyler directly and telling him that he felt certain the president would "faithfully carry out the views with which a great political Revolution has been achieved, under a banner inscribed with the joint names of 'Harrison and Tyler.'" Others believed that by invoking the "fathers of the great republican school," Tyler had signaled his willingness to follow the course of action President Madison had taken in 1816 and sign a bank bill into law should the Whig Congress see fit to pass such legislation. "Does not his address remind you of the days of Madison?" one of these men asked. This particular individual liked Tyler's "intimation about a United States Bank," an intimation he interpreted as *support* for such an institution. One Virginia Whig agreed. If Congress drafted a bill that chartered a new national bank, he wrote, "Tyler *will sign it. I think I see it.*"[34]

Perhaps these Whigs were more outwardly confident in Tyler's course than their private misgivings warranted. Clay, for one, seemed to be sending mixed signals, proclaiming his confidence in Tyler one minute while betraying his doubts the next. "The best and most amicable relations exist between the Vice President and myself; but what his course will be I can only conjecture," the senator admitted to a political associate. "I hope and believe that he will contribute to carrying out the principles and policies of the Whigs." To another, he wrote: "I have known long and intimately the V. President. He has ability quite equal to his predecessor, is amiable, and I think honest and patriotic. His defect is want of moral firmness. I believe—I should rather say, hope that he will interpose no obstacle to the success of the Whig measures, including a Bank of the U.S."[35]

Clay was right about one thing—"amicable relations" had existed between him and Tyler for a long time. By all accounts, they had had a good—though not close—relationship for more than twenty-five years. They had served in Congress together as young men. Recall also that Tyler had defended Clay against the "corrupt bargain" charges in 1825. As US senators, the two men had been allies against Jackson. Finally, Tyler had gone to the Whig convention in Harrisburg in 1839 as a Clay delegate, and while he most certainly did not "shed tears" when Clay lost the nomination to Harrison (always the allegations of Tyler's tears!), there was nevertheless much to bind the two men together politically. Their shared Virginia roots had further cemented the relationship.

The Kentuckian believed that his chance to win the Whig nomination for president in 1844 improved with President Harrison's death and Tyler's elevation. He had antagonized Harrison with his overbearing personality. Moreover, he understood that Webster had strengthened his position with the Whigs by taking the lead in Harrison's cabinet and getting much of he wanted in terms of patronage. Thus, Clay had the sense that he could start afresh with the new president and reassert his dominance of the party. Such a change would be absolutely essential to his larger political goals.[36] But he seriously misunderstood how the political calculus had changed on April 4, 1841. Clay's hopes for the new administration, and his halfhearted assurances to others that Tyler would abide by the Whig agenda, were backward looking, rooted in the past, and did not properly take into account how Tyler's attainment of the presidency—no matter how it came about—rendered all that had come before in the two men's relationship obsolete and irrelevant.

Clay was in the process of misjudging the new president. He was most decidedly wrong in his claim that Tyler lacked "moral firmness." In fact, as he and the Whigs would find out, the president possessed moral firmness in abundance, some would say to a fault. With Tyler, a fine line existed between moral firmness and stubbornness. Once he had settled upon a course of action, it became nearly impossible to force him to change his position. Once he had decided he was right, he could never admit to having been wrong. Tyler's entire career should have told Clay that much. It may not have been evident before the senator returned to Washington in May, but the formerly "amicable" relations between himself and Tyler were about to end. The two men were on a collision course, and the results would not be pretty—for them personally, for the Whig Party, or for the country.

And what of the opposition Democrats? Their leaders did not quite know what to make of Tyler's inaugural address either. They exhibited decidedly schizophrenic interpretations of what he had said as they parsed his words. Some believed the president had chosen to ally himself with the mainstream of the Whig Party. One of these men, Senator Benton of Missouri, Tyler's old nemesis, saw in the address a further Whig attempt to discredit Jackson, calling the Virginian's reproach of a supposedly generic "selfishly ambitious man" who might occupy the presidency "party slang against" the former president. As for the bank, Benton thought he detected Tyler's willingness to support the recharter the Whigs would surely seek in the special session. The address "went into a detail which indicated the establishment of a national bank," Benton said, "or the re-charter of the defunct one." Finally, the fact that Tyler had retained Harrison's cabinet seemed proof that he was committed to giving the Whigs what they wanted most.[37]

From his perch at the Hermitage, the most prominent Democrat of them all, the rapidly aging and pain-wracked Andrew Jackson, interpreted what Tyler had said far differently. Old Hickory seemed unperturbed (for once) that the inaugural address repeated some of the charges that had been leveled against him while he sat in the president's chair. Jackson, too, recalled Tyler's long career but came to the opposite conclusion than the one his loyal ally Benton had drawn. Fully expecting that Clay and the Whigs would attempt a recharter of the national bank as well as raise tariff rates with a disregard for the Compromise of 1833, Jackson maintained confidently that Tyler could not "without abandoning all these professions of republican principles sanction by approval any of these measures." Francis Preston Blair, Jackson's longtime confidant, was not so easily convinced. "I fear that Tyler is such a poor weeping willow of a Creature that he will resign all to the audacious depravity of the political black-leg," he moaned to Jackson. The Old Hero must have smiled when Blair invoked John Randolph's old allusion to Henry Clay, for the years had not softened the general's animus toward his old enemy, the "Judas of the West." He insisted Blair was wrong and that Tyler would abide by his longstanding—and publicly acknowledged—constitutional principles against a national bank. "How then can a President under such a solemn obligation approve a law creating a Bank without wilfull [sic] and corrupt perjury?" Jackson asked his friend. Perhaps the former president enjoyed playing the part of the "Sage of the Hermitage" in his twilight years. Blair would have to wait and see whether Tyler justified the old man's faith in him.[38]

As Whigs and Democrats waited anxiously to find out what Tyler's course of action would be once the special session of Congress began, a small circle of the president's states' rights friends debated among themselves the significance of Harrison's death. "What effect is this unusual event to produce upon the destinies of our country?" one of these men, Abel P. Upshur, rhetorically asked his (and Tyler's) close friend Beverley Tucker. Upshur maintained that he had "no very distressing forebodings on the question." South Carolina senator William Campbell Preston wrote to Tucker and expressed more enthusiasm for the new president than Upshur had shown. "What a change," he said in amazement. "What a destiny for Tyler. I have confidence in him. I do not fear the result." Still another in this group, Edmund Ruffin, dared dream that perhaps Tyler would be able to cobble together enough support for a third party that would champion strict construction and states' rights principles and provide protection for the South. Tucker and Upshur were not nearly as optimistic as Preston or as idealistic as Ruffin. The two men had almost resigned themselves to the reality that politicians would always sacrifice their avowed fealty to the Constitution on the altar of expediency. Would Tyler be any different? "I do not suppose that he [Tyler] will change, either the men or the measures, of Harrison," Upshur concluded.[39]

Tucker and Upshur would become significant actors—for Upshur this was especially true—in the story of Tyler's presidency. They became advisers to Tyler once he assumed the presidency in April 1841. They were most decidedly not typical "politicians," at least insofar as politicians must sometimes make concessions to opponents so that compromise may allow the people's business to get done. The two men were uncompromising reactionaries who considered themselves above party politics and abhorred the partisanship that animated the contests between Whigs and Democrats. Tucker and Upshur instead preferred the intellectual stimulation that came from their friendship with each other and from their writing careers. Both men were sons of Virginia, committed to the Old Dominion and the South, and staunch proponents of the proslavery argument. Together, and to a lesser extent in combination with another William and Mary professor (and president) Thomas R. Dew, they challenged Tyler to hew closely to the theoretical and philosophical states' rights views they espoused. Upshur, in fact, exhibited these principles with a decidedly harder edge than those held by Tyler; he felt John C. Calhoun was the only politician who embodied these principles and often privately chastised Tyler for failing to measure up. The new president's association with these two men, who were portrayed dismissively and with scorn by Whigs and Democrats alike as the "Virginia abstractionists," ultimately led to problems. Perhaps more than anything else, Tyler's connection to Tucker and Upshur would lead his enemies to portray him as a rigid, states' rights ideologue hell-bent on advancing the interests of the South at the expense of the nation as a whole.

If Upshur, who obviously did not wish to raise his hopes too high, believed that Tyler would not change "the men" of Harrison's administration, Tucker was determined to see to it that his friend at least changed "the measures," which were more important anyway. Specifically, Tucker sought to influence Tyler's stance on a national bank. He devised an elaborately complicated plan to alleviate the fiscal crisis of the United States that would pass constitutional muster with the states' rights, strict-construction principles of both himself and Upshur as well as, presumably, Tyler. Tucker penned a lengthy letter to the president on April 11 that spelled out his proposal.

Tyler likely expected this letter; he may have even solicited it on the day he left Williamsburg to go to Washington. He and Tucker may have spoken in general terms—perhaps in Tyler's parlor or over a meal—about the professor's views on a bank in the weeks leading up to Tyler's elevation to the presidency.

Tucker maintained that a bank such as the one the Whigs seemed to want would not square with the interests of the South. His solution for the nation's fiscal crisis called first for a compact between all of the states in the Union. He proposed the creation of a federal banking "association," with each state subscribing to this association an amount of money proportional to the number of its votes in the Electoral College. He then spelled out the further details of a plan that was both unrealistic and unworkable.[40]

President Tyler answered Tucker's letter with a very carefully crafted one of his own two weeks later. He informed his friend that "so far things go on smoothly, and but for the currency question the course would be tranquil. 'There lies the rub.'" Tyler fully recognized that he was experiencing the proverbial calm before the storm, and he knew that when the special session of Congress began on May 31, the bank issue could very well provide him with the first test of his presidency. "My fear now," he said, "is that nothing short of a National Bank, similar in all its features to that which has recently passed out of existence, will meet the views of the prominent men of the Whig party." Left unsaid—for Tucker already knew—was how unacceptable Tyler viewed this prospect.

The president eventually got to the matter at hand and offered his thoughts on Tucker's proposal. He flattered him but made clear that he could commit to nothing his friend had spelled out. "Your plan opens the subject in a strong point of view," he said, "and I have read it with the deepest interest." Tyler instead let him know that he had made a strategic decision. He planned to place the onus for devising a new banking structure for the country entirely on the Whig Congress, an approach he then justified. "Coming so recently into power," he declared, "and having no benefit of previous consultation with Gen. Harrison as to the extra-session, the country will not expect at my hands any matured measure, and my present intention is to devolve the whole subject on Congress, with a reservation of my constitutional powers to *veto*," if necessary. Tyler was gambling that there would be a public outcry against the Whigs should they attempt to charter a new bank. Such a result would insulate him from popular criticism should he be forced to veto such a measure and give him the political cover to come up with his own bank proposal when he deemed it appropriate. Moreover, letting Congress take the lead at the start was in accordance with the Whig perspective that power in the national government emanated from the legislative—and not the executive—branch. Tyler could show an affinity for Whiggery when it suited his purpose.[41]

Politically, Tyler knew that if he presented Congress with a plan such as the one Tucker proposed, it would surely fail and he would look weak. Better to let Whigs in Congress take the lead and craft the bill they wanted so he could then react—that is, veto the bill—and assert his strength and his principles with the stroke of a pen. He seemed to *expect* that he would be forced to use the veto and welcomed the opportunity to do so. One month before the special session of Congress was set to begin, Tyler had decided on a course of action that he believed would enhance his authority as president and set himself up to compete for a second term. By the end of April 1841, the matter had apparently been settled in his mind.

On April 30 Tyler took pen in hand and wrote to Senator Clay, essentially telling the Kentuckian the same thing he had revealed to Tucker. After assuring Clay that he, like the rest of the Whigs, wanted the Independent Treasury repealed, he pointedly stated that he had "no intention to submit any thing to Congress on this subject [the bank] to be acted on." He would instead "leave it [Congress] to its own action—and in the end shall resolve my doubts, by the character of the measure propos'd, should any be entertain[e]d by me." No doubt Clay got the message and interpreted this line to mean that the president reserved the right to use the veto. But Tyler also made clear—and in effect went on the record saying so—that he did not think the timing propitious for congressional action and "would not have it [the bank] urg[e]d prematurely." He argued that the American people still felt "great disquietude" about a bank. Playing for time, the president wanted the bank issue postponed at least until the regular session of Congress began in December 1841. He realized, however, that Clay would not be receptive to postponement no matter how strong he made his case. Should the congressional Whigs sally forth on the matter, Tyler wanted to make sure that a bank bill emanated from Congress—not from the administration—and that it comported with the Constitution.

But this letter did not focus entirely on the bank. Reiterating something he had mentioned in his inaugural address, the president also made clear that "the state of our military defences requires immediate attention" from Congress. He also expressed his support for the distribution of the proceeds from the federal government's sale of the public lands to the states, something near and dear to Clay and most congressional Whigs. But Tyler favored specific conditions for distribution and held reservations about the policy that Clay did not share. Still, he seemed to be offering a chance for the two men to find some common ground that he hoped would mitigate his views on the bank. It also did not hurt that Tyler told Clay he would personally intervene in a patronage matter that would benefit a Kentucky associate as well as sign a naval commission for Clay's son-in-law. At this point the amicable relations that Tyler and Clay had enjoyed remained in force. Tyler was exhibiting the qualities that had made him such a formidable politician for so long.[42]

On the morning of May 8, 1841, a tall, thin man full of nervous energy purposefully and impatiently strode into the White House seeking an audience with President Tyler. Gaining entry from the mansion's doorkeeper, an Irishman named Martin Renehan, he climbed the steps to the second floor. He handed his card to Tyler's usher, a thirty-year-old mulatto named Jim Wilkens, and sat down to wait. The man had "gray-blue eyes, high cheek bones, a large mouth," "low forehead," and hair that curled around his ears. There was a large wad of tobacco in his cheek, and he showed an apparent lack of care for how he was dressed. Indeed, he often walked around town with tobacco-juice stains on his shirt. The visitor might have been mistaken for one of the "eager pack" that Tyler hated dealing with, men who, even one month into his administration, still showed up every day begging for government jobs. This man did not come with the hopes of finding a job, however, for he already had one— and a fairly important one at that. He was Virginia congressman Henry A. Wise, and he had urgent business to discuss with the president.[43]

The thirty-four-year-old Wise was a native of Accomac County, one of two counties located on Virginia's Eastern Shore (Northampton being the other). His family had lived in the county since the mid-seventeenth century. His father, Major John Wise, one of the wealthiest men in the county, had served in the Virginia militia and as a Federalist in the House of Delegates for many years. Thus, the young congressman's outward appearance belied his actual breeding and status in Tidewater society, though it is fair to say that he had never enjoyed the financial or social success of his father.

Wise traveled north to college, leaving Virginia in 1822. He graduated in 1825 from Pennsylvania's Washington College (now Washington and Jefferson College), where he was a prize-winning debater. Returning to the Old Dominion, he read law under the direction of Henry St. George Tucker—Nathaniel Beverley's brother—in Winchester and was admitted to the bar. While in college, Wise fell in love with Anne Jennings, daughter of a local Presbyterian minister. When her family relocated to Nashville, Tennessee, in 1828, Wise followed them, married her, and established a law practice that left him frustrated and unfulfilled. He did, however, benefit from his in-laws' friendship with Andrew Jackson and was a regular guest at the Hermitage. Wise moved back to Accomac County with his wife in 1830. In 1833, when he was twenty-six, he won a close election to Congress as a Democrat. He also later accepted a challenge to his honor from his electoral opponent and fought a duel that left the man shot through the shoulder and permanently incapacitated. Wise, who possessed an uncanny knack for doing so, escaped unharmed.

Wise was an aggressively assertive man. Indeed, his behavior was often at variance with his last name, and he did not always get along well with others. Robert Tyler once wrote that the congressman had "some screw" loose. Though involved in only one duel himself, Wise was an active participant in the duels of several other men over the course of his political career. The most infamous of these affairs of honor left a congressman dead.[44]

By 1841, Wise had become an outspoken, if not entirely dependable, member of the Whig Party. More specifically, he was a states' rights Whig and hoped that he had an ally in Tyler as he sought to prevent the Clay Whigs from chartering a new bank. That in itself was somewhat curious, because earlier in his political career, Wise had voiced support for a national bank, citing President Madison's acceptance of it in 1816 as justification. On the floor of the House of Representatives shortly before Harrison took office, Wise spoke against the "premature agitation" of the bank issue, a view that President Tyler adopted for himself. The congressman also offered his detailed analysis of the financial crisis facing the country and expressed his view that the distribution of the proceeds from the sale of public lands—one of Clay's signature issues—should cease until the Treasury had begun to run a surplus. Like many southerners (including Tyler), Wise feared the depleted coffers of the federal government would lead mainstream Whigs to raise tariff rates. Such were Wise's policy positions when he entered Tyler's office on May 8.[45]

"Wise!" the president exclaimed heartily upon seeing him ushered into his office, addressing the congressman in the informal manner the younger man had come to expect.[46]

While it would be incorrect to characterize the relationship between the two men as close, they were more than mere acquaintances. Tyler had been impressed by Wise's efforts on behalf of the Whig ticket in 1840 and told him after the election that he respected his opinion and would seek his advice should Harrison die and he ascend to the presidency. "In desiring your views I wish to prepare myself for playing my part as may best become me, should it be required of me to play any part," he said, in a statement that clearly indicates Tyler had taken Tazewell's prediction of Harrison's demise seriously. He wanted Wise to proffer his "views then as from friend to friend, and be assured that you have no one in whom you can confide with greater security."[47]

According to Tyler, he and Wise "conversed freely and fully upon the subject of [Tucker's] suggestion as to a financial system." Tucker maintained later that Wise, acting at his behest and playing the role of emissary or political liaison for the intellectuals in Williamsburg, had gone to Washington "on purpose," well before the beginning of the special session, "to talk the matter over." Wise had his own concerns as well. He wanted to speak to Tyler because he had read the inaugural address and feared that the president would side with the Clay Whigs and approve a recharter for a national bank. Tyler told him that he would never accept the kind of bank Clay wanted. Satisfied, the characteristically brash congressman then offered the president some unsolicited advice: he should annex Texas as soon as possible, and he should replace Harrison's cabinet at once with men more sympathetic to states' rights.[48]

Tyler offered little comment on Wise's recommendations. He did not intend to dismiss the cabinet—not yet anyway—and he remained noncommittal regarding the annexation of Texas. But something in the conversation with Wise apparently changed Tyler's mind about the propriety of Tucker's banking-association plan. The next day the president penned a hasty letter to the professor: "Wise left me yesterday . . . and I write now to say, that the more the mind dwells upon it [Tucker's plan], the more I am pleased with it." The chief benefit, Tyler said, was that it left "the question open for each State." He had seemingly come around to Tucker's way of thinking and had apparently changed from his position that Congress should take the lead in the matter, not the administration. Tucker later claimed that both Wise and Tyler had, at that point, given their "unqualified approval" to his plan. The president had even decided that he would introduce a bill to Congress that called for the banking association. But he wanted Tucker and his circle to draft the actual language.[49]

What accounts for this sudden change of heart? Had Wise really been that persuasive? To answer these questions, Tyler's psychological make up must be taken into account, and we must speculate on what his state of mind must have been in the month following his assumption of the presidency.

Tyler had exhibited a remarkable firmness and sense of purpose as he took the reins of power on April 6. He had arrived in Washington determined to assert his authority as president. No doubt having thought about the situation he would find himself in should he actually become president, he approached the first month of his administration almost as if he had been following a carefully constructed script. He made clear he would not settle for merely being an "acting" president. Tyler made certain his cabinet knew that he would be responsible for his administration. He had presented an inaugural address that set out his agenda. Finally, he had made the strategic calculation that Congress should take the lead in crafting a bill for a national bank.

As the start of the special session of Congress drew near, however, Tyler found himself waffling on the bank issue. He certainly did not change his position that a bank bill must satisfy his constitutional scruples. But he did change his mind and come to the conclusion that he should present a bank bill of his own to Congress rather than leave it to the Clay Whigs to present one to him for his signature.

Tyler's states' rights friends—Tucker, Upshur, and Wise—exerted tremendous pressure on him to infuse his presidency with more principle than politics. They wanted him to wave the states' rights banner unabashedly and become a champion of policies—their policies—that they believed would protect the South. Reading his inaugural address (and taking into account his letters to Clay and Tucker), it is clear that Tyler intended to stick to his principles— up to a point. More practical than either the idealistic Tucker or the ideologically cranky Upshur, and a more measured politician than the volatile Wise, Tyler seemed to recognize the danger in abandoning prudence for ideological purity. Yet, as his change of heart on Tucker's banking association plan makes equally clear, Tyler could not easily withstand the entreaties of his friends. His resolve to force the Whig Congress to draft a bank bill disappeared as Tucker and Wise made their appeals. His apparent newfound enthusiasm for presenting Tucker's plan, exhibited in the letter of May 9, reflects a desire to please his friends. It may also be taken as an expression of fear that he would disappoint them if he ignored their proposal. He did not want to alienate the states' rights men—he would need them later as he built a political base for 1844.

Lyon G. Tyler, Tyler's son and biographer, maintains that shortly before the special session of Congress began, his father presented Tucker's banking association plan to his cabinet. They hated it. "It was found too bold and new," Lyon wrote, echoing what his father said two months after that meeting. Tyler then "fell back on" a plan laid out by Hugh Lawson White in the Senate in 1832, a plan he supported at the time and one that satisfied his constitutional scruples since it called for Congress to create a bank in the District of Columbia that could only establish branches in states that had requested them. This proposal received the "reluctant concurrence" of the cabinet, with Secretary of State Webster alone giving "hearty" support to the measure. Webster's approval meant that Clay's supporters in the Whig ranks would likely voice their opposition. So in effect, even the "compromise" Tyler came up with was a nonstarter, though he pressed ahead and asked Treasury Secretary Ewing to draft an administration bill using White's plan as a template. Tyler informed Tucker of these developments later, maintaining that he "preferred" the banking-association plan but that it was simply not feasible for him to mobilize support for it given the time constraints he faced. He explained that White's plan was "the more simple expedient." Here, he was letting Tucker down easy. But whether he used the professor's banking-association plan or White's nearly decade-old proposal, the most important point was that Tyler had decided to shift course and present an administration bank bill to Congress after all.[50]

Unknown to President Tyler, Senator Clay had been in touch with Ewing and had urged the Treasury secretary to prepare a bank bill that could be presented to Congress as soon as the special session began. Clay and Ewing had spoken briefly on the matter before the senator left Washington in March, apparently assuming that President Harrison would be in favor of sending an administration bill to Congress. He now saw no reason why Harrison's death and Tyler's elevation should change things.[51]

Based on his correspondence with Clay, and in light of Tyler's directive to prepare the administration's bank bill, Ewing realized he had been put in the middle of what would likely be a bitter fight between the president and Congress. In an effort to provide himself with political cover, and in keeping with the Whig preference for legislative supremacy, Ewing informed Clay he wanted the Whigs in Congress to formally request an administration bill. "We have attacked the past administration for dictation to the Legislative branches of the Government," he pointed out, and wished to avoid "[a]ny just imputation of this kind." So, while Ewing began to sketch out a Tyler administration bank bill, he worked behind the scenes to ensure that the bill emanated from a directive of Congress and not from the executive branch. As Ewing saw it, a congressional request would accomplish a very important purpose: "when the question shall be presented" to President Tyler, he said, "sanctioned by the representatives of the States & the people, I have no doubt that he will acquiesce in what they may will." Ewing wished to take Tyler at his word that he would be guided by the American people.

Ewing had also paid attention to what Tyler had said about Clay in cabinet meetings since he assumed the presidency. "No man can be better disposed than the President," he told Clay confidently. "His former opinions, some of them unfortunately of record will trouble *him* but *not,* I think, *the country.*" Moreover, Ewing assured Clay, "[h]e speaks of you with the utmost kindness, & you may rely upon it his friendship is strong & unabated."[52]

Had Tyler continued to express these sentiments of friendship toward Clay to convince the cabinet? Or Clay?

Or himself?

Chapter 9

THE POWER STRUGGLE BEGINS

"All things are disjointed. Trade is at a stand; property diminished in value; confidence shaken to the center." So wrote Whig and former New York City mayor Philip Hone in his now-famous diary in April 1841. His succinct analysis perfectly captured the state of things as the Twenty-Seventh Congress convened for its special session on May 31. "Never was there a time when political measures were brought so closely home to men's bosoms," Hone noted grimly. There had been a slight upturn in the economy in 1838, but the benefits had been short lived, and the country plunged into an even deeper depression in 1839. Suffering was widespread. "When or where this will stop, God only knows," one southern newspaper editor wailed. "When, or from whence relief is to come, we know not; but unless relief does come, and come speedily, this country will present a scene of widespread ruin and desolation, such as has never been witnessed before." The effects of the depression placed a tremendous burden on the majority Whig Party to accomplish something—anything—that would relieve the suffering of the American people. The people wanted bold action from the politicians.[1]

By winning control of the White House and both houses of Congress in 1840, Whigs believed they had been given a mandate by the American people to create and implement the strongly nationalistic program the majority of the party championed. Stalwart partisans believed that only this program would remedy the nation's economic ills and place the United States on sound financial footing once again. "The condition of the Country &c &c still requires the adoption of certain great measures," Henry Clay declared. "Let us have hearty & faithful co-operation between the President & his Cabinet, and their friends in Congress, and we cannot fail to redeem all our pledges and fulfill the just expectations of the Country." The senator was eager to begin the work. As he and his adherents would soon find out, though, not everyone in the party interpreted the Whig victory at the polls in 1840 in the same way.[2]

The first, or special, session of the Twenty-Seventh Congress convened at noon on Monday, May 31, 1841. Both the House of Representatives and the Senate mustered a quorum on that first day, and both chambers quickly got down to preliminary business. In the House Henry Wise attempted unsuccessfully to get himself elected speaker. That honor instead went to Clay's fellow Kentuckian John White. The Senate duly chose Samuel Southard of New Jersey as president pro tempore. As Tyler's elevation to the presidency had left the country with no vice president, this meant Southard would preside over the Senate proceedings at all times, which suited Clay.[3]

After these matters had been attended to, both chambers engaged in debate over whether Tyler should rightly be called president of the United States. Democrat William Allen of Ohio raised the issue in the Senate and found support from his fellow Buckeye and Democrat Benjamin Tappan, who argued that Tyler deserved the presidential salary—$25,000—but not the title of president. In the House Democrat John McKeon of New York took the lead in asserting that Tyler should only be regarded as an "acting" president. Ultimately, bipartisan majorities in both houses voted down resolutions that called for referring to the Virginian in this way. Thus, the matter had been settled once and for all, and as Wise declared on the floor of the House, Tyler was "by the Constitution, by election and by the act of God, President of the United States."[4]

By this time, more than his public displays of enthusiasm for Tyler's title had raised Wise's profile in the capital. All of Washington knew that he was advising the president. Most Whigs did not take comfort from this fact. One of them, Ebenezer Pettigrew, a former congressman from North Carolina, came to visit Tyler at the White House. Pettigrew was in Washington on other business but sought out the president seemingly in an effort to gauge his relationship with Wise. "I asked him if Wise was not crazy," he reported in a letter to a friend. Tyler seemed taken aback by the question but assured his visitor "no, that [Wise] was a good whig [sic] & that all was right with him." Pettigrew hoped that this was the case. But he feared the worst about Tyler's association with Wise, owing to both Wise's reputation as a hothead and his record as an atypical Whig. Perceptive Washington insiders also realized that the congressman nursed a grudge against Senator Clay because of lingering hard feelings over a duel to which both men had been a party in 1838. Wise's newfound status as presidential confidant heightened the tension in Washington at the start of the special session.[5]

The gut feelings of Whigs such as Pettigrew were justified. Tyler and Wise had shared a meal alone at the White House on May 29, the Saturday before the special session began. As the two men ate, Wise informed the president that he had had an audience with Clay two days earlier. While there is no evidence that Tyler had prompted his friend to seek out the senator and take his measure, there can be no doubt that he listened intently to what Wise had to say about that meeting and thought about how best to use what he learned. He was in the process of crafting a message to Congress that would be distributed at the start of the special session, and he wanted to speak with Wise before he completed the final draft.

What his fellow Virginian told him could not have surprised Tyler. Clay "is bent upon centralism," Wise declared. Indeed, the senator intended to raise tariff rates and use the proceeds for distribution, "with the avowed reason of relieving the States from public debt." Clay was also determined to have a national bank "with a charter from Congress and a location in Wall Street." Wise had listened to these plans with horror and told the Kentuckian that he disagreed with his agenda "in toto." He could never support such measures. Clay nodded, unconcerned. He was determined to push ahead with his plans. "I never give up," he said firmly. Neither Tyler nor Wise doubted that Clay meant what he said.

The two then discussed what Clay's agenda meant for the Whig Party and for Tyler's presidency. Both men believed the fate of the party would go a long way toward determining whether Tyler could compete for a term in his own right in 1844. As they finished their meal, they dissected the situation. "Clay and Webster are now openly hostile," Wise pointed out. Tyler was already well aware of that fact but wondered how best to use this hostility for their own purposes. Wise suggested letting things between Clay and Webster—and between their supporters—develop naturally. Hopefully, the Democrats would see that it was to their advantage to simply "let the [Whig] factions devour each other, and let the Republicanism left among us thrive by the contest." Tyler had only "to be temperate and firmly neutral between" the warring Whig factions, "and the opposition [Democrats] only to be indulgent a little towards him, and the problem of power will solve itself." At this point Wise believed that Tyler's most promising course of action was to court the Democrats. But the president had to act with nuance—he could not just throw his whole lot with the opposition party. With this advice in mind, Tyler returned to his desk and completed his message.[6]

On June 1 the president submitted the message to both houses of Congress. He intended it as a more specific elaboration of the policy positions he had given in his inaugural address. Having had nearly two months to contemplate the direction he wished the country to take, and having listened to the counsel of his friends Wise and Professor Tucker, he wanted Congress to know where he stood on the important matters to be addressed in the special session. He maintained that he believed the special session was a good idea—at least that was what he said publicly—and offered the extremely politic statement that he looked forward to benefiting from "the combined wisdom" of the House and Senate. The dire times demanded cooperation between the executive and legislative branches, and the president pledged to do his part.

Tyler's message began with brief details on foreign affairs. He mentioned the ongoing trouble with Britain over the fate of Alexander McLeod, a Canadian—and thus a British citizen—who had been indicted for murder and arson by the state of New York for his role in the destruction of the *Caroline*, an American steamer that conveyed men, guns, and supplies to Canadian rebels who were openly defying British authority. If a jury found McLeod guilty of the alleged crimes, he faced possible execution by New York, which could result in war between the United States and Britain. Tyler assured Congress that he and Secretary of State Webster would continue to monitor the situation.

Tyler then detailed the sorry state of the American treasury, reporting that the United States was approaching a national debt of nearly $5 million as well as a sizeable deficit. The "fiscal means, present and accruing, are insufficient to supply the wants of the Government for the current year," he reported. Mindful that the Whig Congress might try to raise tariff rates to alleviate the budget shortfall, he argued that the Compromise Tariff of 1833—which he had helped shepherd into law—"should not be altered except under urgent necessities, which are not believed at this time to exist." He pointed out that the tariff reductions called for in 1833 would finally be completed in the next year, with the compromise itself set to expire on June 30, 1842, and he expressed his hope that rates would "in the future be fixed and permanent." By denying the existence of "urgent necessities" that might lead to a hike in rates, he signaled adherence to the very southern position that rates must be as low as possible. Tyler had evidently taken to heart Wise's information on Clay's plans to adjust tariff schedules upward and wanted to head off the Kentuckian, at least rhetorically.[7]

Tyler also spent considerable time on the bank issue, now knowing for sure the type of institution Clay intended to seek. The president realized that one way or another, a bank bill would emerge out of this special session, despite his efforts to get Clay to postpone it. "To you, then," the president told Congress, "who have come more directly from the body of our common constituents, I submit the entire question, as best qualified to give a full exposition of their wishes and opinions." Thus, with these words Tyler had changed course *yet again* and passed responsibility for a new bank bill back to Clay and congressional Whigs. He detailed some of his misgivings about a bank but offered some concessions—such as giving it the authority to exercise oversight over free-lending state banks—that seemed to indicate he might sign into law whatever Clay and the Whigs devised. But he stated in no uncertain terms that he reserved the power to use the veto if he saw fit, a power, Tyler declared solemnly, "I could not part with even if I would."[8]

Reading Tyler's message to the special session in conjunction with his inaugural address, one begins to appreciate why the Whigs did not know fully what to expect from the president. His words are at once astute and muddled, prudent and bewildering. As one historian has put it, he "displayed that capacity for confusing the minds of others." Some might even say he had a particularly unique talent for doing so. The president raised as many questions as he answered. What accounts for this?[9]

Tyler was not being deliberately opaque. He was not couching his language in such a way as to keep any potential enemies off guard. Rather, his words betray a man who was struggling to fuse his ideology with the need to take bold steps to alleviate the effects of the country's economic crisis. The schizophrenic nature of his public pronouncements and his waffling over whether he wanted to take the lead in drafting a bank bill or have Congress assume responsibility for it reveal a man at odds with himself. Tyler wished to remain true to his political principles, principles with which he had been associated for his entire career, ones that even those who disagreed with him at least respected as earnest and deeply felt. He seemed to recognize, however, that perhaps those long-cherished principles might not see the country through to economic salvation. Indeed, he may have even had a passing thought that they might not be compatible with what needed to be done at this point in the nation's history. Now faced with the most daunting challenge of his political life, Tyler seemed unsure himself as to what course he should pursue. The sure-handedness with which he had taken charge on the first day of his presidency seemed by June 1 to have disappeared, a casualty of his own overthinking and a constant barrage of advice from his friends. His political future was also a consideration. Tyler wanted a second term, wanted to be elected in his own right in 1844. He did not want to settle for being remembered—if indeed he was remembered at all—as merely the man who finished William Henry Harrison's term. The trick for President Tyler over the next three and a half years would be finding a way to reconcile principle, pragmatism, and ambition and come to terms with the world in which he now lived. His success at doing so would determine whether he would become a strong leader with significant accomplishments to his credit. It would not be easy.

The same day Tyler sent his message to Congress, Clay rose in the Senate to begin the process he had been eager to start since the special session had been called back in March. He made a motion that the Senate elect members to the standing committees the next day; this motion carried. Clay also informed his colleagues that the following day he would make a motion to choose a special committee—the Select Committee on the Currency—to discuss the part of President Tyler's message that addressed financial matters "with a view of suggesting such remedy." One senator quickly asked him what the "nature of the remedy" might be. Without hesitation Clay replied, "a National Bank."[10]

The next day, after Clay made his motion, the Senate agreed to form the select committee, which would consist of nine members.[11] Eager to control the process, and acting as Senate majority leader (though this position would not be officially designated until the 1920s), Clay installed himself as chairman and made sure to include southerners as well as northerners, Democrats as well as Whigs. To no one's surprise, though, Whigs outnumbered Democrats six to three. But one of the Democrats—New Yorker Nathaniel Tallmadge—belonged to the "Conservative" faction of the party (a group of six in the Senate, led by Tallmadge and Tyler's former opponent William Cabell Rives, who by this time had become a states' rights Whig)—and could be expected to sympathize with the desire to create a national bank as well as with efforts to bolster a paper-money policy. Clay had also seen to it that Rufus Choate, a friend and political ally of Webster's, had been placed on the committee, perhaps in an effort to keep his enemies within the party close. The chairmanship of this select committee meant that Clay would take the lead in introducing legislation that *he* deemed necessary and proper. When combined with the chairmanship of the Senate Finance Committee, which he had won on June 2 when standing-committee assignments were parceled out, the post enabled him to shape the entire agenda of the special session. He decided the session would deal only with the economic conditions of the country. Clay's goals were the repeal of the Independent Treasury, a higher tariff, a temporary loan to cover the federal debt, and the distribution of the proceeds of the sale of public lands to the states. This was an ambitious agenda, but Clay was confident he could pull it off. He was the most powerful man in Congress. In the eyes of Congressman Wise, he had made himself a "dictator."[12]

Meanwhile, the "dictator" pressed Treasury Secretary Ewing for an administration bill that would charter a new national bank. Tyler had changed his mind once again and was content to let Ewing craft such a bill, but it would have to meet his constitutional requirements. For his part, the secretary submitted a report to Congress on June 2 that called for repeal of the Independent Treasury and expressed support for a national bank. But on actually drafting a bill, he wanted to buy some time and did his best to avoid Clay. At one point he took to his bed with what was apparently a feigned illness—or perhaps the stress was getting to him.[13]

Ewing could not tarry long and had to produce an administration bill. Clay was anxious for the measure and recognized the importance of what would soon happen. "We are in a crisis, as a party," he wrote Kentucky governor Robert Letcher on Friday, June 11. "There is reason to fear that Tyler will throw himself upon Calhoun, Duff Green, etc., etc., and detach himself from the great body of the Whig party. A few days will disclose." The senator even predicted how Tyler would do it: "It is understood that he wants a Bank located in the District [of Columbia], and having no power to branch without the consent of the State where the branch is located. What a Bank would that be!" Clay had little patience for consideration of anything but a national bank. "I am tired of experiments," he wrote one associate.[14]

Clay's ability to predict the branching provision of the administration bill seems to have resulted from a bit of intrigue. In an undated note marked "Confidential," which the editors of his papers assert was sent sometime between June 8 and 11, Clay asked Ewing to provide some of the details of what he had been working on. "If you have matured the branching section suppose you send me a Copy of it either this evening or early tomorrow morning?" he suggested.[15] There is no direct evidence proving that Ewing complied with Clay's wishes, but it is curious that the senator wrote to his friend Letcher on June 11 with the confidence that he knew what the branching provision of the administration's bill would entail. What is interesting is that both President Tyler and Senator Clay appear to have been attempting to secure intelligence on the other in an effort to gain the upper hand as they squared off on the bank. Tyler relied on Wise for his information; Clay received his from Ewing. Both men were trying to place themselves in the best possible political position. They recognized that the resolution of the bank question would go a long way to determining their respective political fates.

A national bank would become the centerpiece of Clay's legislative agenda, but his very first priority was actually the repeal of the hated Independent Treasury. By August, Congress sent a bill to the White House doing just that.

President Tyler happily signed it. At least there was something on which he and the congressional Whigs could agree.[16]

That, however, was the easy part. Ewing went to the White House on the evening of June 8 to discuss his draft of the administration bank bill with the president. Tyler listened to what his Treasury secretary had to say. Ewing's bill would allow the national bank to establish branches in any state, whether the state wanted them or not. Tyler instructed him to strike out the provision, making clear his objection to that provision of the draft. Ewing acceded to the president's wishes and rewrote the section on branching to match the old Hugh Lawson White plan that Tyler favored. The administration bill thus clearly bore Tyler's imprint.[17]

On Saturday, June 12, the wait was over; Ewing's handiwork arrived at the Senate chamber shortly before noon. The measure called for the charter of a fiscal agent in the District of Columbia—with Congress, in its function as the legislature for the nation's capital, chartering the bank—that would be capitalized at $30 million, with the federal government owning one-sixth of the stock. The bill allowed branches, but only in those states that gave explicit permission for their establishment. Clay had been right, exactly right; his letter to Letcher the day before had spelled it out.

Wise knew the details of the bill before Ewing had sent it to Congress. But he realized that what the administration offered was dead on arrival. Clay would now get to work on the bill he wanted after formally referring the administration bill to the select committee. Wise knew what this meant. "Clay is wholly impracticable," he said. "Tyler will veto his full-grown central monster . . . and he is madly jealous enough of T's running for a second term to make it a point now to drive him to a veto if he can." Wise welcomed this. "Let him do it," he sneered. "The veto kills Clay; and Webster and his friends will take shelter under T., and the united opposition forces him back in a war with centralism—Clay for the focus."[18]

Clay was indeed the focus. Determined to get the bank bill he wanted, the Kentuckian mobilized the Whig Senate caucus for a series of meetings in the days immediately following the introduction of the administration bill. He would use the caucus to frame his own bank bill. By doing so, Clay bypassed the Senate select committee, a body that looked more and more like a sham to many Democrats. In fact, Democrats had at first been demoralized—"in a bad temper" as one Whig put it—for they believed the administration bill satisfied Tyler's constitutional objections and would, therefore, pass both houses of Congress. But they quickly realized what Wise had known from the start: Clay would not be satisfied with the bill Ewing had devised. Democrats perked up. Would the hubris of "Harry of the West" force a showdown with the president and give them, the minority party, a new political lease on life?[19]

As the Senate Whigs met to hash out the details of the measure they would introduce, discussion turned to the possibility of a presidential veto. Apparently, someone in the caucus warned Clay about the dangerous effect a veto would have on the party. Clay took the warning to heart. Sometime in June—the evidence suggests it was after the Ewing bill had been introduced but before the Whigs offered their counter bill—the senator made a visit to the White House to see the president. Tyler later told Tucker that the two men had had the "fullest conversation" about the bank and that he had urged Clay "in the strongest manner" to adopt the administration bill. Clay demurred, insisting that the bill was not what he wanted and not what the American people demanded from the Whig majority. Whatever he had hoped to accomplish with this meeting, it did not end well. After listening to him for several minutes, Tyler stood up, looked his adversary straight in the eye, and let him have it. "Then, sir, I wish you to understand this—that you and I were born in the same district; that we have fed upon the same food, and breathed the same natal air. Go you now, then, Mr. Clay, to your end of the avenue, where stands the Capitol, and there perform your duty to the country as you shall think proper. So help me God, I shall do mine at this end of it as I think proper."[20]

Family tradition has it that Tyler's meeting with Clay ended with just this flash of presidential temper. We know the meeting occurred; Tyler referred to it in a letter to Tucker one month later. Whether he ever actually spoke these exact words to Clay is open to question. Historians tend to doubt that the exchange took place in this manner, but it is a good story, and the sentiments Tyler supposedly expressed so forcefully do reflect the hardened view he would take of the senator and the bank as the summer of 1841 and the special session dragged on. What is known for sure is that the battle lines between Tyler and Clay were drawn after Ewing submitted the administration bill to Congress. A showdown loomed.

One very important question remains. Why would Clay have taken pains to ensure that the Tyler administration presented its own bank bill when he knew it would be unacceptable to himself and the majority of the Whigs? Wise thought he knew the answer. "Clay's game, to be plain, was plainly seen," he told Tucker. "One thing which struck us at first was that he wished to play tyrant and dictator, and drive Tyler to *a veto*. A veto, he thought, would kill him." According to Wise, the senator wanted the administration bill presented to Congress so that he could keep it in reserve. He would then work on a bill that created a truly national bank, one that would surely be killed either by the Democrats and states' rights Whigs in the Senate or by the president's veto. Clay "was for playing the 'Great Pacificator' again, instead of the dictator; that he would satisfy Wall-street centralism by offering and pressing his and their plan first, and, after throwing the defeat [of the congressional bill] upon Tyler's friends, then go back to Ewing's scheme in the spirit of *conciliation* and *compromise,*—two terms magical and fortune-making with him."

According to Wise's logic, then, Clay recognized that the bill Ewing had drafted was better than nothing at all, and he would fall back on it as a compromise measure. This would allow him to accomplish three things. First, he would get a fiscal agent, which he could present to the American people as evidence that the Whigs had accomplished what they had set out to do when the special session was called. Second, he would isolate Tyler and states' rights Whigs such as Rives, William C. Preston, William S. Archer, William D. Merrick, and Alexander Barrow, and hopefully drive them from the party. These men could make trouble for Clay's legislative agenda. Third, emerging out of the first two, Clay would consolidate his power and position himself as the Whig nominee for president in 1844. This was the magic and fortune making to which Wise referred.[21]

Wise's conspiracy theory appears plausible—all such theories do to some extent. Certainly, it offers an explanation of why Clay pushed so hard for a truly national bank with vast powers. Unfortunately, there is no real evidence documenting Wise's position. And we must remember that, by the summer of 1841, Wise saw perfidy in just about everything the Whig leader did.

Perhaps the correct answer to why Clay pursued the bank is the simplest: he believed it best for the country and did not believe Tyler had it in him to oppose the measure. Recall that he believed the president lacked "moral firmness." Consider as well Clay's belief that sticking to the Whig program actually gave Tyler the best chance to win the Whig nomination for president in 1844. If Tyler had "further hopes," Clay told an associate at one point, "if, as is quite probable, he may cherish the hope of being elected hereafter to the Presidency, would he not endeavor to retain the confidence of those political friends through whose selection for the second, he has been enabled to reach the first office, in the Nation?" This statement indicates that Clay did not regard Tyler's likely desire for the party's nomination in 1844 as a threat to his own political fortunes. Therefore, he would not have seen the need to isolate the president in the manner that Wise suggested. A further point to consider is that Clay had not fully determined at this point that he would in fact be a candidate for president himself in 1844. While he was the consummate political animal and seemed always to be aware of the potential ramifications of his actions for his presidential ambitions (excepting, of course, the "corrupt bargain"), in June 1841 his focus was on enacting the Whig program.

On the other hand, Wise's charges cannot be wholly dismissed. His claim that Clay intended to isolate Tyler is compelling, especially in light of the senator's assertion that if the president sought election in his own right, "would he not endeavor to retain the confidence of those political friends" who had placed him on the ticket in 1839? What better way to ensure that Tyler *not* retain the confidence of those men than by boxing him in to the position where he would be forced to veto the party's bank bill?[22]

🦎

Clay's version of the bank, which he introduced to the Senate on Monday, June 21, would be capitalized at $30 million, with a congressional option to increase that amount later to $50 million. The bank would be headquartered in Washington and could establish branches wherever it wanted, with no state interference. Clay was confident that the select committee had built in safeguards that would eliminate significant problems that had attended the Second Bank of the United States: there would be a limit on the amount of dividends that could be paid to stockholders, for example, and there would be a ceiling on the total debt the bank could have on its books at any one time. The new institution would also operate with more transparency and allow more congressional oversight than its predecessor. Clay argued that this bank would aid manufacturing, enhance the country's position with respect to foreign trade, and promote the economic recovery of the United States. It all seemed so perfect.[23]

What concessions had the Whigs made to President Tyler? There were a few. For one thing, they located the parent bank in Washington—not on Wall Street or in Philadelphia. This conformed to Tyler's constitutional principle that Congress could establish a bank in the capital because of its power to legislate for the District of Columbia. The parent bank would also be prohibited from making discounts or loans, except for loans to the federal government itself as provided by law. The nine directors of the parent bank, moreover, would be paid a salary and would not receive "the usual form of bank accommodations"—that is, dividends—as compensation. Finally, Clay's national bank would exercise oversight on state and local banks, which the president saw as necessary.

But the major substantive difference between the administration bill and the one that emerged from the Whig caucus concerned the branching provision, and it was this upon which the special session would founder. Tyler snatched up a copy of Clay's report as soon it was made available. What he read merely confirmed what Wise had told him nearly one month earlier. There were no surprises. Now, Clay's goals were part of the official record. Tyler was not fooled by the portions of the report that sounded conciliatory. "Remember always," he wrote Virginia governor John Rutherfoord, "that the power claimed by Mr. Clay and others is a power to create a corporation to operate *per se* over the Union. This from the first has been the contest." There was no way the president could approve of the bill that emerged out of Clay's select committee; he would never sign such a monstrosity into law.[24]

Whig supporters of the administration—and there were several—marshaled their opposition to Clay's bank. Senator Rives introduced an amendment to the Senate bill on July 1 stipulating that the "assent of the Legislature" of a state must be secured before the national bank could establish branches there. To mollify Clay, the amendment also contained a guarantee that once a state had granted its consent to the establishment of a branch, it could not subsequently withdraw consent in the event its legislature changed hands from one party to the other. What Rives had offered, then, was a compromise between the administration and the congressional Whigs. But he had revived the portion of the administration bill that Clay and the majority of the Whigs found most objectionable. The Kentuckian immediately argued against the amendment.[25]

Clay did not know that Rives had offered his amendment at the behest of the president himself. Tyler and Rives had corresponded several times since Tyler assumed the presidency in April and had met at the White House on at least two occasions since May 29 to discuss the bank. They strategized about what course to pursue when (not if) Clay introduced a bill to create a "true" national bank. Rives favored White's bank plan, which meshed nicely with Tyler's preference for that type of fiscal agent.

The relationship between Tyler and Rives had grown more amicable since they had clashed over the Senate seat in 1839, and the two men found that they liked each other. While it may be a stretch to say that they had become personally close, they did begin to see the benefit of acting in concert politically. Rives informed his wife that the president had told him that he was the only member of Congress with whom he communicated confidentially. This may have been Tyler's way of flattering the senator, for surely Wise and Tyler shared confidential communication, but Rives believed—correctly—that he was a vital ally of the president. The two worked together to put their plan of an amendment in place soon after Clay reported his national-bank bill. They put the finishing touches on this plan during the last week of June. Tyler had used Wise's reconnaissance of Clay to prepare himself for the steps he would take to counter him and brought Rives into the fold.[26]

Rives's amendment—and his argument in favor of using the branching provision of the administration bill—yielded dividends. Senator Preston voiced his support. "You need not fear but that we shall have Preston's co-operation," Wise assured Tucker. The South Carolinian, he said, "is trying to be with Tyler. He is already, and wants only to *be trusted.*" Preston "may be relied on with us," the Virginia congressman bluntly said, "because he can do no better." Besides Preston, Wise believed he could count on at least three other states' rights Whig senators to support the president. "Archer is *obliged* to be with us, or perhaps he would not be. He is weak, but not wicked." Further, "Merrick, of Maryland, is with us. Barrow, of Louisiana, may be." Wise's ruminations spoke to a larger truth: despite Clay's stature as undisputed leader of the congressional Whigs, his power was not absolute. Indeed, the very men Wise mentioned, along with a few others as well as the Democrats, mobilized to stymie Clay's attempt to secure passage of his bill in the Senate.[27]

Also working in Tyler's favor was the emergence of the *Daily Madisonian* as the administration organ, which gave the president support in the Washington press. The *Intelligencer* was the Whig paper of record, was highly supportive of Clay, and as such would begin to turn against the president as the bank debate continued. While the *Madisonian* was not, as Wise admitted, "exactly official" in June 1841, its editorial page had gradually begun to tilt in the Tyler administration's direction. Founded in 1838 as a vehicle for Conservative Democrats to oppose President Van Buren's Independent Treasury, the paper's editor, Thomas Allen, found common cause with Rives (a former Conservative Democrat) and favored his amendment to Clay's bank bill. All of this was welcome news to Wise, who understood the importance of having a sympathetic newspaper offering support to the administration. He wished that the paper would come out more boldly in support of Tyler to counter the influence of the *Intelligencer.* "It will and shall, however, insert your arrows in its bow," Wise predicted to Professor Tucker at the end of June, suggesting that it had the potential to coalesce the states' rights men into a base of support for Tyler. By September, the *Madisonian* would be recognized as the proadministration paper and began receiving patronage from the White House. Clearly, Wise was readying himself and the president's allies in Virginia for the battle he hoped was imminent.[28]

When put to a vote on July 6, Rives's amendment was defeated handily, 10 to 38. But it had still served a multilayered purpose. For one thing, it allowed the president to gauge how much Whig support he had in the Senate, which in turn enabled him to speculate on his early prospects of winning the party's nomination for president in 1844. For another, it siphoned off enough Whig votes—8 to be exact—to ensure that, with Democrats voting against it, Clay would not be able to get his bill passed. Finally, by highlighting the branching provision of the administration bill and portraying it as a reasonable solution, Rives cast Tyler in the role of a compromiser willing to do his part to alleviate the country's financial difficulties. Whether it was Tyler and Rives's conscious intention to do so or not, they had also cast Clay as the president's foil, a man whose own actions (they believed) would increasingly undermine his reputation as the Great Compromiser and benefit Tyler.

Chapter 10

BANISHMENT

In the wake of his failure to secure passage of his bank bill, Henry Clay was forced to accept that the optimism he entertained about the president before the special session began had been unfounded. He now saw Tyler for what he was: the major impediment to the creation of a truly national bank and a threat to the entire Whig agenda. "Is it not deplorable that such a cause should be put in jeopardy in such a way!" he shrieked. Clay sensed that Tyler had begun to isolate himself from the prevailing views of both the Whig and Democratic Parties. "He conciliates no body by his particular notions," the senator argued in frustration. "The Loco's [Democrats] are more opposed to the scheme [the administration bill and the Rives amendment] than to an old fashioned bank, and ninety nine out of a hundred of the Whigs are decidedly adverse to it."[1]

Clay's analysis spoke to a developing political situation, the full importance of which he apparently did not yet grasp. Tyler's stance puzzled him. If the president's "notions" pleased neither Democrats nor Whigs, what could he possibly hope to accomplish politically by sticking to his guns? What Clay failed to realize was that Tyler saw the impending fight over the bank as the opening salvo in his campaign for the presidency in 1844 and hoped this fight would allow him to build a political base for that election.

Tyler's friends in Virginia—Beverley Tucker and Abel Upshur—made the urgent case for a states' rights party. Congressman Wise also kept the pressure on the president with regular visits to the White House. To this chorus, Governor Rutherfoord of Virginia added his thoughts as he sought to encourage Tyler for the fight ahead. "It appears to me," he wrote on June 21, "that a bold effort is about to be made to revive the system and principles of [Alexander] Hamilton, and that it becomes all who regard themselves as the disciples of the Jeffersonian school, and would defend State-rights against consolidation, to take a decided stand against the encroachment of Federalism." Rutherfoord expressed his concern about the president's cabinet (this was a constant refrain of Tucker and Upshur too) but acknowledged that "accident" had thrown Tyler and them together. "With *your* principles," he declared, "you could never have called such men around you." Webster and the other members of the

165

cabinet were not to be trusted, nor was Clay. Rutherfoord made clear, however, that there were men Tyler could trust, "none on whom *you* can rely with so much safety as those old State-rights Republicans (whether Democrats or Whigs) who stood by you in times gone by."[2]

Tyler appreciated the support. As president, however, he had the responsibility to see the many layers of the politics of the bank issue and to understand the complexities of what he was tasked to do. While he appreciated the stance that Tucker, Upshur, Wise, and now Rutherfoord had taken on the Whig efforts to recharter a national bank, Tyler did not have the luxury of pursuing the rigid course they favored and hoped from him. He was utterly refusing to play the part of ideologue; it would do him no good. In that sense Upshur's chronic handwringing and his belief that Tyler would disappoint them had merit. Those closer to the situation had an even better idea of what Tyler was attempting to do. John C. Calhoun, for example, argued that the president was "essentially a man for the middle ground." While he questioned the wisdom of an attempt to stake out a position between the Clay Whigs and the Democrats, Calhoun accurately predicted in mid-June that Tyler would "attempt to take a middle position now."[3]

The president sought every opportunity to make common cause with the Whigs. On July 21 he signed a bill into law that allowed the federal government to borrow up to $12 million through the sale of US Treasury bonds, a bill Clay had largely shaped and one both he and Tyler believed essential to the government's ability to conduct its business. The bank bill, of course, was the main attraction, what Clay had decided over the objections of Tyler would be the signature piece of legislation of the special session. The Kentuckian was determined to get it.

Clay sent Virginia congressman John Minor Botts up Pennsylvania Avenue to feel out the president and determine whether he would be amenable to an idea circulating in the Whig caucus that party leaders believed might break the impasse over the bank. Called the "Bison" by his peers for his chronically unshaven face and unruly mop of hair—and described as a "bull-dog, always barking," by one historian—Botts was on friendly terms with Tyler. The proposal he brought with him, however, did not pass muster. The president called it a "contemptible subterfuge, behind which [I] [will] not skulk." Whigs wanted to allow the national bank to establish branches in any state as long as the legislature of that state did not explicitly disapprove at its first session after the bank bill had been signed into law. Further, even if a state refused permission to establish a branch within its borders, Congress could override the legislature and authorize a branch if it was deemed necessary and proper for the public interest.[4]

Why Clay, Botts, or any Whig believed this proposal would receive the president's sanction is difficult to fathom. Tyler later claimed that he let Botts know he would veto a bill that included these provisions. Incredibly, however, Botts informed Clay that the president had accepted the proposal! Perhaps Tyler had not made his intentions entirely clear. Perhaps Botts, for whatever reason, lied. Whatever the case, Clay then offered the proposal as an amendment to the original bank bill and was able to shepherd the revised legislation through both houses of Congress. The White House received the bill on Saturday, August 7, 1841.[5]

So now the matter was in the hands of Tyler. The entire cabinet urged him to sign the bill, but there seemed little doubt as to what he would actually do—most people expected him to use the veto. Nevertheless, suspense hung over Washington. A "commotion" over the issue had taken hold in the city, one observer reported. "The veto anxiety absorbs all thought & attention," said another. Peter Porter, a close political ally of Clay from western New York State, wrote that there was "a most agonizing state of uncertainty in the public mind." Moreover, he saw, as Clay did, that Tyler could potentially snuff out the entire Whig agenda. "It is impossible to foresee the tremendous consequences of a Veto. If the bill should be approved, we shall probably carry all our great measures; if rejected, we may lose most of them." Clay acknowledged the stress on himself and on the party. "We are in painful uncertainty as to the fate of the Bank bill," he acknowledged.[6]

Tyler seemed in no hurry to decide his course of action. The Constitution grants the president ten days before he must either sign a bill into law or send it back to Capitol Hill with a veto message and his objections. If he neither signs a bill nor vetoes it within ten days, it automatically becomes law without his sanction or official disapproval. Tyler apparently intended to take the full constitutional allotment of time to make up his mind. Some, like Upshur, took this as a sign of the president's vacillation and indecision. "I do not believe that he knows what he himself will do," Upshur asserted, growing more anxious and more annoyed with each passing day. Most observers, however, seemed to think that the delay meant a veto for sure.[7]

A portent in the weather added drama to the uncertainty over a potential veto. Amid the heat and humidity of a typical Washington summer, a tornado touched down near Pennsylvania Avenue at about 2:00 P.M. on August 11, tearing the roofs off buildings and scattering debris everywhere. The White House escaped unscathed. People at the Capitol, dumbfounded, were able to watch the entire meteorological event unfold, and "at that place not a breath of air was to be felt, & so everybody said *it was the veto message* coming." The anticipation over the president's decision and the constant prattle of the politicians and other city residents about it made it appear almost as if the veto was "some great beast, like that spoken of [in] Revelation," that would "come raving and tearing along the Avenue."[8]

Tyler finally executed his constitutional duty on August 16, nine days after he had received the bill from Congress. He vetoed the measure. John Tyler Jr., serving as his father's private secretary, was tasked with taking the veto message to the Senate chamber that morning. Dozens of spectators who could not secure seats inside milled about outside in the corridor and at the door, so John had to fight his way through them to hand the message to the sergeant-at-arms. The chamber itself was practically silent, as senators and onlookers craned their necks to see what was going on and readied themselves for what they were about to hear. By the third sentence of the message—"I can not conscientiously give it my approval"—hisses and catcalls cascaded down to the floor from the galleries above. Some of the spectators booed lustily. Thomas Hart Benton, of all people, now suddenly the guardian of decorum, jumped to his feet and shouted above the noise for the "Bank ruffians" and "hooligans" to cease their racket and stop insulting the president of the United States.[9]

The rest of the veto message did little to quiet the Capitol denizens in the Senate chamber galleries, most of whom were apparently Whig in their partisan orientation. Sitting at his desk, Clay stared straight ahead, listening with no apparent emotion, betraying no surprise—but his worst fears had now come true.[10]

So what argument had the president made in defense of his veto? Early in the message, Tyler called the constitutionality of a national bank an "unsettled question." Such a statement obviously revealed that he did not regard the Marshall court's decision in *McCulloch vs. Maryland* as having decided the issue of whether a bank could be chartered. This was a very Jacksonian stance, one that pleased many Senate Democrats. He also maintained that the American people were still "deeply agitated" and divided over the issue. Somewhat defensively, Tyler explained how his own opinion on the bank question had been "unreservedly expressed" for the past twenty-five years. In light of this long-held opinion, and given that his oath demanded that he "preserve, protect, and defend the Constitution," he could not sign the Whig banking measure into law "without surrendering all claim to the respect of honorable men." Jackson had been absolutely right when predicting that Tyler's honor would not permit him to sanction the bank bill.

More substantively, Tyler wholly objected to the part of the bill embodied in the amendment Clay offered to secure its passage in the Senate, the part Congressman Botts claimed had received the president's approval. Tyler also fastened onto a more technical aspect of the bill and opposed granting branches of the national bank the authority to make local loans or discounts of promissory notes. State banks often printed and lent their own notes and commonly "discounted" the interest due on those loans, which meant the borrower would not be required to pay back as much money, an attractive option for someone engaged in commerce. A national bank would almost certainly be able to offer even greater discounts than its state counterparts, which would hamper their ability to offer credit. In effect, this would drive such state banks out of business. As Tyler made clear in his message to Congress before the special session began, he wanted only to rein in the state banks, not to completely destroy them.[11]

The veto drew condemnation from many in Whig quarters, while it energized the Democrats. "This extraordinary step of the President," Peter Porter wrote Clay from Buffalo, "although long threatened, was never realized nor believed until this moment, and has excited universal dissatisfaction and even disgust among the members of the Whig party." Whigs now realized they had a fight on their hands. Tyler had asserted his constitutional prerogative and defended his principles, which left party leaders scrambling to find a way to salvage their legislative agenda. It was shaping up as a battle of wills, and the president had maneuvered to give himself the upper hand.[12]

Still, most Whigs did not lose heart. They thought Tyler's veto message was clear, to the point, and, at least to some in the party, not necessarily a fatal blow to their plans. The congressional caucus had met the night before the veto and discussed whether they should fall back on Ewing's proposal—the administration bill. There was another plan in the works as well. A few short hours after Tyler's message had been read in the Senate, the Whig caucus dispatched Virginia congressman Alexander H. H. Stuart to the White House, anxious to find out whether the president would accept a bank bill if the Whigs deleted the provision allowing branches to offer local discounts on promissory notes. Senator Richard Bayard of Delaware had offered just such a solution during the debate over Rives's amendment on July 6, but nothing had come of it.[13]

Stuart reported that Tyler met him "in the proper temper" and "expressed the belief that a fair ground of compromise might yet be agreed upon." The two men discussed some of the details of the just-vetoed bank bill, including the feature that allowed the bank to offer local discounts on promissory notes. According to Stuart, the president told him that if Congress would send him a bill that removed the authorization for agencies (or branches) of the bank to act in the states as offices of discount and deposit, he would sign it "in twenty-four hours." Tyler would allow the bank to act as the fiscal agent of the government, receive deposits, circulate notes, and deal in bills of exchange, but he would not allow local discounts on promissory notes. Such a practice, again, would threaten the viability of state banks. Tyler also added that he would allow the proposed national bank to establish branches in the states unless they were "forbidden by the laws of the State." Stuart later maintained that the president had grasped his hand as he prepared to leave and exclaimed, "Stuart! If you can be instrumental in passing this bill through Congress, I will esteem you the best friend I have on earth." Tyler instructed him to seek out Secretary of State Webster to frame the new bill but made clear that he did not want to be portrayed as having dictated the terms of the new measure to the congressional leadership. As Stuart made his way out of the White House, he thought he might have succeeded in finding a compromise with the president that the Whigs could use.[14]

At 2:00 A.M. on August 17, the morning after the veto, President Tyler and his family were awakened by a raucous gathering of drunken Whig partisans who beat drums and shouted insults at the tops of their lungs from the lawn of the White House. This bunch had apparently not been privy to the negotiations between Stuart and the president the previous afternoon and had taken to the bottle in the wake of the veto, trying to come to terms with what had just happened. They now took out their wrath on the First Family. The president watched nervously from his window and was shocked to see the mob burn him in effigy. It seemed all of Washington had been turned upside down by the constitutional scruples of John Tyler.[15]

Later that morning, at a more congenial hour, the president received a visit from Whig senator John M. Berrien and Whig congressman John Sergeant, two vocal supporters of the kind of bank Clay wanted. They had come to find out whether what Tyler had tentatively agreed to with Stuart was still in force. Treasury Secretary Ewing called on Tyler while the two men were there. Waved into the office, Ewing took a seat. Tyler told Berrien and Sergeant that he "did not think it became him to draw out a plan of a bank, but he thought it easy to ascertain from the general course of his argument [in the veto message] what he would approve." The president did not even mention the meeting with Stuart (did they ask about it?), leading the new emissaries to wonder how close Tyler and the party really were to working out some sort of an agreement. Ewing interpreted the conversation to mean that Tyler did not object to a national bank located in the District of Columbia, as long as it was not empowered to make local discounts on promissory notes.

Berrien and Sergeant returned the next morning, Wednesday, August 18, for a lengthier meeting with Tyler. He convened a meeting with his cabinet later that morning by telling them that he had refused to get specific with the emissaries over the details of a bank bill he could support. Tyler then asked the men to take seats around his desk and quickly got to the matter at hand. This was the first cabinet meeting since the veto message had been sent to the Senate, and there was a lot to discuss.[16]

Tyler claimed to be surprised by the dissatisfaction his veto had caused. Moreover, he was puzzled as to why the Senate had not yet formally responded. He had apparently expected that it would be taken up on the seventeenth, the day after the message had been read, but thus far Clay had bided his time, perhaps with the intention of finding out whether the Stuart mission or the visits by Senator Berrien and Congressman Sergeant could achieve a breakthrough. The silence from the Senate worried the president. He "expressed anxiety as to the tone and temper which the debate would assume there" once the Whigs formally addressed the veto.

Trying to allay Tyler's fears, George Badger spoke first. "Mr. President," he said, "I am happy to find on inquiry that the best temper in the world prevails generally in the two Houses on this subject." He then informed Tyler that he believed the Whigs were "perfectly ready to take up Mr. Ewing's bill and pass it without alteration except in some unimportant particulars." This assertion provoked a rare outburst of ill temper from Tyler. "Talk not to me of Mr. Ewing's bill," he barked, "it contains that odious feature of local discounts, which I have repudiated in my message."[17]

This was the first indication Tyler had given his cabinet that he no longer supported the administration bill Ewing had sent to the Senate on June 12. It appears that two considerations had changed his mind. First, he had heard grumbling from the Whigs that the administration bill was "declared to have arisen in a spirit of executive dictation." Fear of just that kind of criticism had persuaded Tyler originally that a bank bill should come from Congress. He now regretted allowing Ewing to draft the administration bill and believed without question that a new measure had to at least have the appearance of congressional sponsorship. Tyler bristled that "the war is to be made not only upon my opinions, but my motives." Second, conversations with Wise, in which the congressman had made clear his opinion that Clay would fall back on the Ewing plan in an attempt to play the role of "great pacificator," had turned Tyler against his own administration's effort. The president had said nothing about his objection to local discounts when he read Ewing's draft initially. It appears that he was using this now merely as an excuse to justify killing all chances at reviving the administration bill. Revival would, according to Wise, play directly into Clay's hands and strengthen his position in the party.[18]

There is also evidence that Tyler already knew what the Whigs had planned and that Badger's statement in the cabinet meeting confirmed, rather than allayed, his worst fears. That would certainly explain his anger. According to Lyon G. Tyler, on the day of the veto, August 16, a gentleman of the "strictest veracity" wrote Tyler to explain what was afoot. "The *caucus* last evening," he informed the president, "after much disagreement, came to the resolution to pass a Bank bill on Mr. Ewing's plan. The *object seems to be your destruction and a dissolution of the cabinet*." The letter continued, "They say that you and the cabinet stand pledged to support that scheme, *and that you cannot now assent to it; ergo,* a veto of that would place you fully in the arms of the Locos, and your cabinet would abandon you." The author of the letter claimed that Congressmen William Russell of Ohio and John Taliaferro of Virginia were his informants and that John J. Crittenden was already making plans to resign his position as attorney general.[19]

Ewing, taken aback at both Tyler's repudiation of the administration bill and the vehemence with which he had expressed his feelings, managed to find some words he hoped would placate the president. "I have no doubt, sir," he said, "that the House, having ascertained your views, will pass a bill in conformity to them provided they can be satisfied that it will answer the purposes of the Treasury and relieve the country."

Tyler looked at the men seated before him. "Cannot my Cabinet see that this is brought about?" he asked. Leaning forward in his chair, he told them that he needed their support. "You must stand by me in this emergency," he said pointedly. "Cannot you see that such a bill passes Congress as I can sign without inconsistency?"

Ewing replied that he thought a bill which would satisfy the president may be introduced in the House very soon. "Of the Senate," he admitted, "I am not so certain." The Treasury secretary was unnerved by the way Tyler was conducting the meeting. The president was agitated; he did not seem himself. "If such a bill could pass both bodies speedily and receive your sanction," Ewing continued, trying further to soothe his boss, "it would immediately restore harmony here and confidence throughout the nation."

Tyler paused. "I care nothing about the *Senate*," he stated emphatically, "let the Bill pass the House with the understanding that it meets my approbation and the Senate may reject it on their own responsibility if they think best." The implicit message here was that *Henry Clay* would reject any bill receiving Tyler's sanction and that Clay would suffer the consequences in the court of public opinion.

The president wanted to make certain that his cabinet understood exactly what he could support in a bank bill. He wanted there to be no misunderstanding between them. Tyler put Ewing on the spot and asked his Treasury secretary if he understood the type of bank bill that he could sign into law. "I understand you are of opinion that Congress may charter a Bank in the District of Columbia giving it its location here," he said, no doubt thinking he would dispense with the most obvious point first. Tyler nodded impatiently and motioned for him to continue. "That they may authorize such Bank to establish offices of Discount and Deposit in any of the States with the assent of the States in which they are so established."

Tyler exploded. "Don't name Discounts to me," he shouted angrily, leaping to his feet. "They have been the source of the most abominable corruptions—and they are wholly unnecessary to enable the Bank to discharge its duties to the country and the Government."

Ewing gathered himself and told the president that he was "proposing nothing, but simply endeavoring to recapitulate what I have heretofore understood to be your opinion as to the powers which Congress many constitutionally confer on a Bank. I now understand your opinion to be, that they may not confer the power of local discount even with the assent of the States."

Tyler gave a half-nod, indicating that Ewing now had it correct. The Treasury secretary bravely continued. "And I understand you to be of opinion that Congress may authorize such Bank to establish agencies in the several states with power to receive, disburse or transmit the public monies and to deal in Bills of Exchange without the assent of the States." "Yes," Tyler replied, calming down a bit, "if they be foreign bills or bills drawn in one State and payable in another. That is all the power that is necessary for transmitting the public funds and regulating exchanges and the currency."[20]

Up to this point, the other men in the room had been silent, content to let

Ewing bear the brunt of Tyler's anger, perfectly willing to let him answer the questions the president posed. Webster, nursing the pain of his "rheumatic shoulder" recently aggravated by a carriage accident and a bit out of sorts because of it, did eventually weigh in on the matter. Tyler was interested to hear what he had to say.[21]

"I would like such a bill," Webster began, "with power to deal in Exchanges alone, without authority derived from the States, much better than if it combined the power of Discount with the assent of the States, and the power to deal in exchanges without such assent." He did not "think it necessary to give such Bank the power of local discount, in order to enable [it] to perform all its duties to the country and to the government, unless indeed it be essential to the existence of such institution." Tyler cocked his head back, taking in what his secretary of state had just said. Webster continued, acknowledging that the president's idea to prohibit local discounts was sound. But he asserted that he also believed a bank was necessary for safeguarding the government's money and restoring a sound currency.

When Webster had finished, Tyler "expressed his acquiescence" and told the cabinet that he wanted them to devise a bill that "should assume that form." He also wanted them to tap someone who was a friend of the administration to shepherd the bill through the House of Representatives. "Is Mr. Sergeant agreeable to you?" Ewing asked the president. Tyler indicated that the Pennsylvania congressman was acceptable but curiously (ominously?) added that he did not want the cabinet to commit him—Tyler—"as having agreed to this project." He advised the men that they should, according to Ewing, "say that from the Veto Message and from all that we knew of his opinions we inferred that this would be acceptable." He also instructed them to refrain from calling the proposed fiscal agent a "bank." Some of the members objected to this condition, but they reluctantly agreed to do as the president wished. Tyler then quizzed Webster on the language he would use in providing the bank with branching power. When he was satisfied, he concluded the meeting by telling his cabinet that he found the entire matter bewildering. According to Ewing, the president "had no time to collect his thoughts" and wondered aloud why the bank bill could not be "postponed to the next session" of the Twenty-Seventh Congress.[22]

The answer to that question was simple: Clay and the Whigs in the House and Senate did not want the matter postponed. The senator had decreed at the start of the special session that Congress would address the nation's financial predicament. That, in fact, was the sole reason for convening the special session in the first place. He stood firm in his belief that a robust national bank had to be the centerpiece of those efforts, and he would not allow the president to delay his plans. Politically, Clay realized that since he had set the agenda, he had to follow through or look as if he had lost control of his party.

❧

On Thursday, August 19, Clay finally addressed Tyler's veto in the Senate chamber. He did not have the votes necessary to override it, but he could make absolutely clear where he stood on Tyler's use of executive power. In a methodical speech that lasted nearly ninety minutes, he denounced the president and castigated him for having "not reciprocated the friendly spirit of concession and compromise" with which Congress had passed the bill. Clay characterized the veto message itself as "harsh, if not reproachful." He pointed out that Tyler had stated in his inaugural address that he would support any "constitutional" bank bill that came from Congress. The senator obviously believed his bill passed constitutional muster. Further, the president had promised to "resort to the fathers of the great Republican school for advice and instruction." Clay had taken that to mean that "the president intended to occupy the Madison ground, and to regard the question of the power to establish a national bank as immovably settled."

Clay argued that Tyler's veto had thwarted the wishes of the American people. He exhorted the Whigs to keep up the fight and make good on the 1840 electoral mandate. When Clay finished speaking, Senator Rives took to the floor to defend the veto and the president's character. Clay then eviscerated Rives and took aim at Tyler's other supporters, "a new sort of kitchen Cabinet" he called them, recalling the men President Jackson had surrounded himself with a decade before. The Kentuckian did not doubt that these men sought to "place me in inimical relations with the President" and to "represent me as personally opposed to him." They were "beating up for recruits, and endeavoring to form a third party, with materials so scanty as to be wholly insufficient to compose a decent corporal's guard." Characterizing Tyler as the "unfortunate victim" of his own pride and vanity, Clay maintained that this "corporal's guard" found the president receptive to what they hoped to accomplish because he could not "see beyond the little, petty contemptible circles of his own personal interests."[23]

The "corporal's guard" comment was meant to belittle the amount of support Tyler had for his position on the bank as well as denigrate the quality of the men who supported him. Like most of the Kentuckian's well-placed barbs, it worked. Insult aside, Clay's comment contained some truth. Wise led a coterie of only six Whigs in the House of Representatives who were opposed to their party's banking measures and who favored Tyler's stance: Thomas W. Gilmer, George H. Proffit, W. W. Irwin, Francis Mallory, and Caleb Cushing.[24] In the Senate Rives was solidly in Tyler's corner, at least for the time being, with other Whigs such as William D. Merrick of Maryland, Alexander Barrow of Louisiana, William C. Preston of South Carolina, and John Henderson of Mississippi expressing their support for the president. Wise, as nearly everyone in the capital knew, was trying to portray Clay as personally opposed to Tyler. And he sought to sustain the president and encourage a break with Clay and the majority of the Whigs in Congress. The senator professed to be disturbed by this prospect. "If the President chooses," he said, "which I am sure he cannot, unless falsehood has been whispered into his ears or poison poured into his heart—to detach himself from me, I shall deeply regret it, for the sake of our common friendship and our common country."[25]

But it was not just Tyler's friends who wanted to "detach" him from Clay and the majority of the Whig party. Tyler had made new enemies by wielding the veto pen. Congressman Botts was chief among them. On August 21 the *Madisonian*—a newspaper increasingly taking on the character of the administration's mouthpiece—published a letter Botts had written and addressed to a Richmond coffeehouse on August 16, the day of the veto. "Our Captain Tyler is making a desperate effort to set himself up with the *loco-focos*," the congressman wrote with utter disdain, "but he'll be headed yet, and, I regret to say, it will end badly for him. He will be an object of execration with both parties[—]with the one for vetoing our bill, which was bad enough, with the other for signing a worse one." Tyler was "hardly entitled to sympathy" for the position he found himself in, Botts declared. "He has refused to listen to the admonition and entreaties of his best friends, and looked only to the whisperings of ambitious and designing mischief makers who have collected around him." Botts had proffered the compromise measure he brought to the president "to save him from the alternative of the veto." Tyler, however, "lash[ed] them across the face with the instrument they had thus furnished him, and then attempt[ed] to turn the whole party of friends who placed him in power into ridicule."[26]

Botts had set himself completely against the president. Tyler's refusal to sanction the compromise his fellow Virginian had brought to the White House prior to Senate passage of the bank bill in August played a role in this. Still, he could not have predicted Botts would seek his revenge like this. The coffeehouse letter stung Tyler. He surely did not fail to note the sarcastic reference to his military service during the War of 1812—recall Tyler had attained the rank of captain in a Virginia militia company that saw no action. He also recognized that his enemies were assigning perfidy to his motives for using the veto on the bank bill. It was all too much—Botts had once been a friend!

Tyler had received a copy of the coffeehouse letter the night prior to its publication in the *Madisonian* and, after reading it, hurried over to Webster's office in the State Department. The two men sat talking for an hour, and Tyler, nearly distraught, "complained very much of the ill-treatment" he was receiving at the hands of the Whigs in Congress. Webster wrote later that he "appeared full of suspicion and resentment." The bank issue was clearly taking an emotional toll on the president.[27]

Tyler's state of mind was important because, by August 20, a new bank bill was working its way through the House of Representatives, largely from the efforts of Webster and Congressman Sergeant. Tyler had insisted that his cabinet and the House sponsors not attach his name to the measure, known as the Fiscal Corporation Bill. There would be no official second administration bill. According to Ewing, "the President expressed great sensitiveness lest he should be *committed* by anything that he or we should say to a project which would not be accepted by Congress." In other words, Tyler did not wish to be boxed in by Clay and the Whigs. Nor did he want to look like a fool for vetoing a bill he had sanctioned beforehand. Webster and Ewing complied with his instructions.[28]

Webster brought a copy of the bill to Tyler on the night of August 18, just before debate on the measure began in the House. The two men pored over it together. According to Webster, who would later compose a lengthy memorandum on the bank fight, Tyler "expressed no objection whatever" to the provision that allowed the bank and its branches to use bills of exchange. The president also "made no mention of the necessity of State assent, to a Bank carrying on Exchanges between the States." Tyler did insist on striking the word "bank" from the legislation, preferring "Fiscal Corporation." He also made clear that he wished its capitalization to be reduced from $30 million to $20 million or less and that he wanted the bank to be prevented from selling US stocks. Webster noted these changes on the bill itself and the next day took it to Sergeant.[29]

Tyler asked Webster and Ewing to give him their views of the new bill separately and in writing. Both men supported the measure and composed memoranda explaining their positions. Their support of the bill, however, had no effect on Tyler, who told two New York congressmen calling on him at the

White House on the twenty-third that "he would have his right [arm] cut off, & his left arm too, before he would sign the Bill then pending" in Congress. Webster hinted later that he believed the president had not even read his memorandum, that his mind had been made up to use the veto again ever since he had read Botts's coffeehouse letter. Webster knew how much the letter troubled Tyler from their conversation on the night of August 20, and he rightly characterized that missive as an attempt to "place him [Tyler] in a condition of embarrassment." It worked.[30]

The House passed the Fiscal Corporation Bill—having rebranded it with the name Tyler preferred—by a vote of 125 to 94 on August 23. The next day it went to the Senate. On the twenty-fifth Tyler met with the cabinet for their regular Wednesday morning council and, according to Ewing, "seemed gloomy and depressed." He also "intimated in strong terms that he would not sign the bill and earnestly requested us to get it postponed." When the men informed him that it would not be easy to stop the course of the legislation, which was now in Senate committee, the president replied "that we had got it up easily" so "we might postpone it as easily if we chose to do it."[31]

Webster, who characterized Tyler as "agitated and excited" during the cabinet meeting, agreed to speak to Whig senators to see if they could delay a vote on the bill. He viewed postponement as essential to keeping the Whig Party from falling apart.[32] Ewing also made an effort to bring about a postponement but failed. Tyler, almost unhinged by now, continued to plead for a delay during the last week of August, "not," Ewing said in recounting a comment the president had made, "because of the political but of the personal difficulties which immediate action upon it would involve."[33] Clearly, Tyler dreaded the prospect of having another bank bill before him, and he was putting tremendous pressure on his cabinet to work behind the scenes on his behalf. His behavior demonstrated that he would much rather put off making a difficult and unpopular decision—vetoing the bill—than confront it and get it over with. The John Tyler who had told his cabinet with such force on his first day in office in April that he would be responsible for his administration was nowhere to be found in August. Events had overwhelmed him.

Indeed, Tyler's penchant for waffling and indecision was on full display for all of official Washington to see. By late August, the back and forth between the White House and Congress over the bank bill had become a farce worthy of Shakespeare, with Tyler playing the lead role. "The President is in a wonderful quandary," one congressman wrote. "He is sometimes disposed to approve the new bank bill, and then violently opposed to it." And then there was the matter of the cabinet. "He is sometimes tired of his cabinet & anxious that they should resign, then he is afraid of the storm that would attend their resignation & wishes them to hold on whilst . . . Wise & the locos are urging him to remove them." All most observers could do was shake their heads.[34]

Leading Whigs were convinced that Tyler had decided to veto the latest bank bill should it pass and would welcome the opportunity to overhaul his cabinet. North Carolina senator Willie P. Mangum wrote that it was "believed by many that Tyler will prove a traitor to his party. I think he will be a Loco-foco in three months from this time. His Cabinet will blow up, & Congress be in open war against him." There was also a report that Duff Green was in Kentucky intriguing on behalf of the president, most likely without Tyler's knowledge. In particular, it was said, Green sought to get on the good side of the Wickliffe family—bitter enemies of Henry Clay—and may have dangled a potential cabinet appointment before Charles A. Wickliffe, an anti-bank Whig who was sympathetic to Tyler's predicament.[35]

Supporters of Clay in Washington told everyone who would listen that Tyler intended to dismiss the cabinet and thwart the Whig agenda. Tyler partisans—much smaller in number—maintained that Clay had seen to it that the cabinet would resign should he veto the bill, throwing the government into turmoil and perhaps leading to the resignation of the president himself. None of these rumors could be substantiated. The atmosphere was toxic, much more so than it had been in early August when Tyler was deciding whether to sign the original bank bill. The first veto had heightened tensions and created political theater the likes of which the capital had not seen since the days of Andrew Jackson.[36]

In nearby Baltimore, too, the impending Senate vote on the bank bill had caused a great deal of excitement. Upshur traveled to his in-laws' home there in mid-August and reported to Professor Tucker that people could not stop talking about Tyler and Clay. Speculation was rampant over what the president would do if forced to make a decision on another bank bill. "If I may judge of the state of public opinion, by those expressions of it which I hear in this city," Upshur told his friend, "there is no retreat for Tyler; he must stick or go through." He professed to be "surprised at the strength & *universality* of the condemnation" the Whigs had heaped on Tyler. As usual, he bemoaned the lack of progress in creating a states' rights party. The president and Congressman Wise, he declared, "appear to me to be absolutely odious, & neither of them could command ten votes among all their former admirers in this city." Upshur repeated his criticism that the president "has not been decided enough" and worried that he had "evidently aimed rather to conciliate."[37]

An attempt at conciliation was exactly what was on Attorney General Crittenden's mind on the evening of Saturday, August 28. He and his wife hosted a party at their home in Washington for some one hundred guests that night, having invited the president and Senator Clay. Never one to turn down libations or an opportunity to socialize, Clay eagerly accepted the invitation and arrived in good spirits. Tyler failed to show up. Undeterred, several congressmen left the party and made their way to the White House, where they hoped to persuade the president to accompany them back to the Crittenden home. Surprisingly, given his recent state of mind, Tyler agreed. When he arrived, a nearly drunk Clay answered the door, welcomed the president, and immediately led him to the sideboard and offered to pour him a drink. Clay's beverage of choice was Kentucky whiskey. "Well Mr. President what are you for?" he asked. Tyler looked confused. "Wine, Whiskey, Brandy or Champagne? Come show your hand." According to one witness of the encounter, Tyler replied that he would take a drink of whiskey. After a few minutes of awkward conversation, he seemed to loosen up and told his hosts that he had come "for a frolick [sic]." At least the Crittendens had gotten Clay and Tyler together.[38]

Unfortunately, the party had little effect on the political situation in the capital. Tensions continued to escalate. For some, this was just fine. Wise, for example, could not wait for the Senate to pass the Fiscal Corporation Bill and had no doubt what the final outcome would be. "It will be pushed through, and will be vetoed," he confidently informed Tucker; "Tyler is more firm than ever." Wise also welcomed the dissolution of the cabinet that most observers believed was coming. "We are on the eve of a cabinet rupture," he asserted. "With some of them we want to part friendly. We can part friendly with Webster by sending him to England. Let us, for God's sake, get rid of him on the best terms we can."[39]

Wise's statement is revealing. By using the pronouns "we" and "us," he indicated that he was playing a significant role in the Tyler White House (or at least thought he was). But he had a habit of exaggerating his own importance. At the very least, though, the Virginian had the president's ear, and the two men shared many conversations about what Tyler's course of action should be. No doubt, they had discussed a second veto and what would happen if the cabinet resigned. That Wise wanted to find a soft landing spot for Webster—minister to Britain—reflected his awareness that the secretary of state had done right by Tyler in the fight with the Whigs and was deserving of some loyalty on the part of the president.

To Tyler's chagrin, the Fiscal Corporation Bill passed in the Senate on September 3 by a vote of 27 to 22. Debate over the measure was, to put it mildly, spirited. The Whigs would not back down; Rives was the sole Whig who voted against the bill. Democrats stood united against what the Missourian Benton derisively called the "corporosity." The matter was in the hands of President Tyler yet again.[40]

Senate passage of the bill led each man in the cabinet to agonize over what to do in the likely event of another veto. In an effort to stave off crisis, both Ewing and Webster urged the president to sign the bill. James Lyons, Tyler's friend from Richmond, also weighed in, writing to the president that he "trust[ed], therefore, for your sake and that of the country, that the bill will meet your approbation." On September 4, the day after the Senate passed the measure, Tyler discussed his options with his cabinet. According to Ewing, the president "felt anxious and unhappy." He indicated that he would probably veto the bill and floated the idea of accompanying his veto message with a "solemn declaration" that he would not be a candidate for president in 1844. Tyler "thought such declaration would place his motives fairly before the people and disarm those who were assailing him."[41]

The offer to withdraw from the 1844 race, however, was insincere. Tyler had no intention of squandering an opportunity to be elected president in his own right. When the cabinet advised against including such a statement with his veto message, the idea was "very readily surrendered by the President." In the course of the discussion on this matter, Tyler informed the cabinet that he had deleted a sentence from his inaugural address that disclaimed his desire for a second term. He had done so, he asserted, because he feared that the effect of such a statement "should be to turn the batteries of Mr. Clay and his friends on Mr. Webster."

This was nonsense. Tyler's motives in refusing to disavow a second term were purely personal and reflected his burning ambition to be elected in his own right, regardless of his claims of selflessness and disinterestedness. By framing his decision to delete the statement in the inaugural address as an attempt to shield Webster from political peril, Tyler was perhaps trying to manipulate the secretary of state into staying in the cabinet after he vetoed the Fiscal Corporation Bill. The president acknowledged to his cabinet that day that he "rallied no friends around him and had no party."[42] He would need influential allies as he attempted to build a viable political base for 1844. Evidently, in September 1841 he regarded Daniel Webster as a key component of that base. He most certainly did not view him through the same states' rights prism as Wise, Upshur, and Tucker.

Tyler also informed his cabinet that he intended to issue a much harsher denunciation of the Fiscal Corporation Bill than what he had given Congress in his first veto, saying "he should criticize the bill with much severity." Webster gently told the president that perhaps this was not the proper course to take. For their part, the other cabinet members were not yet ready to concede the veto and expressed their hopes that he might still find a way to sign the measure into law. Ewing, in particular, saw Webster's influence as representing the best chance to persuade Tyler to go along with the bill and save their jobs. These hopes, however, were unrealistic, for all of them were aware of Tyler's stance on local discounts.[43]

As with the veto of the first bank bill, Tyler did not immediately announce his judgment. He again seemed to be in no rush to make his decision public. Upshur, who had made the trip from Baltimore to Washington with the express purpose of persuading Tyler to veto the bill, told Tucker that he had given the president "a chart by which a blind man might have directed his course." Upshur—as well as Wise and Tucker—were anxious for the veto and were frustrated with Tyler for again moving at a glacial pace. As always, Upshur feared the president was going to conciliate. From Richmond, Thomas Ritchie was more optimistic, writing that he hoped that Tyler would "prove himself worthy to the *proud* State to which we belong." But if Tyler "knuckle[d] to aspirants and hotspurs," such as Clay and Botts, "who are attempting to 'head' him then indeed, is his glory eclipsed, the reputation he has just won by his firmness will be gone, and his political days will be numbered."[44]

Whig partisans who favored the Fiscal Corporation Bill were just as certain that Tyler would *not* conciliate. By now, it seemed everyone was watching the White House, waiting for the inevitable veto and wondering what it would mean for the fate of the special session. The toxicity of Washington had even spread to other parts of the country. Kentucky governor Robert Letcher reported to his friend Crittenden that he had "received a letter this morning [September 8], from a man in Russell county, asking me if I thought it would be an unpardonable sin to go to the city and kill him (Tyler)." This potential political vigilante, Letcher said, "wrote as if he thought he had a call to put him to death." Apparently, too, letters arrived at the White House threatening Tyler with assassination. Handbills denouncing him were tacked up on lampposts. All of this, over a veto.[45]

One Sunday evening a messenger brought news of a disturbing rumor to the White House. "They have it through the city that I have been shot!" the president exclaimed to a guest with whom he had eaten dinner. "With paper bullets of the brain, I suppose they mean, Mr. President," his visitor replied. Tyler shook his head. "No," he said, "with leaden bullets from a pistol." He then walked his guest out to the portico, where a crowd had gathered in an effort to determine if the rumor was true. According to one witness, the president seemed indifferent to the report and cared little for where it had originated. One of the men in the crowd made a comment expressing his belief that one could not be too careful with madmen walking the streets. Tyler replied that if someone dared to take a shot at him, "it will be more in malice than in madness." With that, he told the group he needed his daily exercise, took leave of them, and proceeded to walk away, unattended and undaunted.[46]

Matters turned a bit more serious when an unmarked package mysteriously showed up one day in the White House entrance hall. The size of the package was suspicious: it was a good deal larger than most parcels, and the box was made of wood. The servants refused to open it, fearing that what they called an "infernal machine" might be inside. Americans had been shocked in 1835 upon learning of Giuseppe Marco Fieschi's assassination attempt on King Louis-Philippe of France by using what the newspapers referred to as an "infernal machine." Thus, the term and the idea of political murder were on everyone's mind and left the White House in a near-hysterical grip of panic. Alerted by the commotion, President Tyler walked downstairs to where several members of the household had gathered. Nobody—including Tyler—wanted to open the wooden box.

The doorkeeper, Martin Renehan, was summoned. Tyler showed him the package and asked him what he thought. Renehan gave a cursory inspection and told the president that he had an idea. Disappearing, he returned a few moments later with a meat cleaver borrowed from the kitchen. "By the powers," he said calmly, "I'll chop it up in less than no time." Tyler looked on, horrified, as the doorkeeper rolled up his sleeves, picked up the package, placed it on a table, and began hacking away at it. He succeeded in tearing the box apart. Reaching down and pulling its contents out, he held up a model of an iron stove for the president and the frightened servants to see. Everyone breathed a sigh of relief. Crisis averted, Tyler told Renehan that he should not tell anyone about the incident. "If you do," he warned, "they'll have me caricatured." Renehan nodded. Nobody was told, at least not until the doorkeeper related the story in the 1860s.

By the time of this incident, Tyler feared for his own safety and for the safety of his family. He had been unnerved by the drunken mob that had appeared outside the White House in the early morning hours after his veto of the first bank bill. Such public access to his office made him a potential target. Moreover, the strange parcel underscored the very real danger of some harm befalling him or his family.

Renehan kept a gun in his room off the entrance hall, as had been the custom for several years, but Tyler wanted more protection. In early 1842 he would send a bill to Congress calling for an "auxiliary guard" comprising a captain and three men. After some bluster in the Senate that such a guard smacked of Caesarism, both houses passed the bill fairly easily. They thus created the first permanent White House security force—the precursor to the Secret Service, which would begin providing presidential protection after William McKinley's assassination in 1901.[47]

On September 9 the wait was over. He had done it again: Tyler vetoed the Fiscal Corporation Bill. This time Robert Tyler delivered the message up to the Capitol. It was addressed to the House this time, since that body was where the current bill had originated. The House was in session—in the middle of debate, actually—when Robert arrived. He brought with him four bills that his father had signed into law, including one granting lifetime franking privileges for Anna Harrison. These new laws, however, would not lessen the blow of the veto for Whigs. Nor would they spare Robert's father from the torrent of abuse that seemed sure to follow.[48]

Tyler had done his best to follow Webster's advice and resisted the urge to unleash his fury on the Whigs, though the last month had surely tried his patience enough to make him want to vent his anger. In a fit of pique, however, he got a small measure of revenge by sending the message to the *Madisonian* to be printed rather than use the official printers of the House, Gales and Seaton.[49]

Tyler began the message by stating that it was with "extreme regret" that he had sent the veto message to the House, but he felt "constrained" by the duty to "preserve, protect, and defend the Constitution" and thus could not sanction the Fiscal Corporation Bill. He defended the right of a president to use the veto, chastised the Whigs for their sleight of hand in framing the bill so that promissory notes operated like bills of exchange (and thus could be discounted), and defended the South by proclaiming that the bank would primarily benefit the commercial Northeast. To his credit, Tyler concluded the message with praise for the legislative branch, saying that the House and Senate had "distinguished themselves at this extraordinary session by the performance of an immense mass of labor." They had passed several beneficial laws.

It had been Tyler's "good fortune and pleasure to concur with them [Congress] in all measures except this." He hoped for "time for deep and deliberate reflection on this the greatest difficulty of my Administration" and looked forward to the next session, when he hoped they could come together to find a suitable fiscal agent. He had made a commitment to the American people to try again.[50]

The last part of Tyler's message, intended as an olive branch of sorts and designed to soften the blow of yet another bank veto, did little to make the Whigs feel good about the special session. To be sure, they had repealed the Independent Treasury, passed a $12 million bond issue to loan the government money, and won a uniform bankruptcy law that allowed debtors to initiate legal proceedings to relieve them of their financial burdens. They had secured passage of a modest new tariff, which kept duties at the 20-percent level mandated by the Compromise Tariff of 1833, and were able to push a new Land Act through Congress. All of these measures had received President Tyler's signature. But, just as important, all were deeply flawed bills that bore the scars of Democratic amendments, sectional tensions within the Whig Party, and concessions by party leadership. The special session had been successful to some degree, but it had fallen far short of Clay's expectations—and the second bank veto was the hardest blow of all. As it was with the first, the Whigs did not have the votes to override.[51]

"My friends," Clay told the Whig caucus, "we have done our duty. We have maintained the true policy of the Government." The Whigs had pursued their goals in good faith and with the good of the American people in mind. "Our policy has been arrested by an Executive that we brought into power," the senator declared. "[Benedict] Arnold escaped to England, after his treason was detected. [John] Andre was executed. Tyler is on his way to the Democratic camp." After all that had happened, this suited Clay just fine. "They may give him lodgings in some outhouse," he sneered, "but they will never trust him. He will stand here, like Arnold in England, a monument of his own perfidy and disgrace." Clay also scoffed at Tyler's claim that he wanted to work with Congress at the next session to devise a suitable fiscal agency. The "wit of man," he said in exasperation, "and [I] thought [I] had some, but not enough for the purpose—could not devise a plan that would meet the views of the President."[52]

Most Whigs no doubt felt the same as Clay and judged the special session a monumental disappointment. Tyler's second veto; the desire to end the session, which had dragged on for more than three months; and the late-summer Washington heat left many in Congress on edge. They were frazzled and wanted to go home. The toxic political atmosphere and the confrontation be-tween President Tyler and the Whig majority had taken its toll.

Adding to the poison was Congressman Botts, who savagely criticized Tyler after the second veto and called the president's integrity into question. In par-ticular, Botts alleged that on a trip the two men had taken to western Virginia in the summer of 1839, he had heard Tyler say "that he was satisfied a bank of the United States was not only necessary, but *indispensable;* that the country could never get along without one, and that we should be compelled to resort to it." He also claimed that during the 1840 campaign, during a speech in Marshall County, Virginia, Tyler had denounced Jackson for vetoing the bank recharter bill in 1832. Of course, both of these assertions made Tyler out to be a hypocrite. As with most statements Botts uttered, these were of questionable veracity, but they played well to Whigs in Congress.[53]

The president's states' rights friends were, of course, pleased with the veto. "Tyler was right in vetoing the Bank Bill," South Carolinian Waddy Thompson told Tucker, for "he could not have signed it without subjecting himself to the charge of resorting to a subterfuge." Thompson had been mostly outside of Ty-ler's circle up to this point but was making his support of the president known to Tucker and Upshur, who were on the lookout for allies. At Tucker's request, Tyler would soon name Thompson US minister to Mexico. Tyler in-law Major Washington Seawell was "glad to see" that the president "possess[ed] so much moral firmness." Preston offered his support of the president on the floor of the Senate. Upshur applauded the veto message but still found fault. "Tyler *needs* much more counsel than he is willing to take," he sniffed.[54]

Democrats also expressed their approval of Tyler's course. They were downright giddy, in fact. Perhaps the most effusive in his praise in Washing-ton was James Buchanan. He called the veto message "firm and determined in its spirit." More importantly, he gushed, it "precluded all hope of the es-tablishment of any National Bank, or corporation, with private stockholders, as long as John Tyler shall continue to be President of these United States." The country, Buchanan proclaimed, would benefit from the veto. It would be "hailed with pleasure" all over the nation.[55]

Meanwhile, the members of the cabinet found themselves in the very posi-tion they had dreaded for nearly one month. On Saturday, September 11, all of them but Webster resigned. Tyler was pleased to retain his secretary of state, having enjoyed cordial relations with the man and appreciating his steady course of moderation in the cabinet. Tyler also well knew that in a battle with Clay for the supremacy of the Whig Party, it would be better to have Webster in his corner and in his cabinet.[56] For his part, Webster liked the president and felt none of the ill will displayed by congressional Whigs.

Congress announced that it would adjourn on Monday, September 13, at 2:00 P.M. This meant that Tyler had less than forty-eight hours to compose a new cabinet and forward the men's names to the Senate, where they could be confirmed. John Jr. believed this was a deliberate ploy on the part of the Whigs to stymie the Tyler administration. If his father could not receive Senate confirmation on his cabinet nominees before Congress adjourned, the entire government would be thrown into disarray. He feared the president's resignation would follow.[57]

John Jr. was engaging in a bit of melodrama and had assigned motives to the Whig majority based on their treatment of his father over the veto. What seems more likely is that the special session had lasted long enough—too long for some—and the legislators wanted to return to their homes to get some rest before the second session of the Twenty-Seventh Congress began in December. Remember, this had been a *special* session. Usually, Congress did not meet during the summer months, partly a concession to the oppressive heat in the capital. Also, the Whigs believed they had accomplished all they could; staying longer served no purpose. That being said, more than a few Whigs had to have enjoyed the thought of causing trouble for Tyler.

Apparently, the president had been thinking about the men he wanted for at least two weeks and had conversations with Senator Rives on possible cabinet nominees. Tyler sent the names to the Senate on the morning of September 13.[58]

The men who joined Webster in the newly reconstituted cabinet were all Whigs. Tyler took special pleasure in this fact. "I know that it entered into the belief of all the conspirators," he wrote his friend Tazewell, alluding to the Clay wing of the party, "that I could not surround myself with a Whig cabinet." But he had. "I have, in my new organization," Tyler informed him, "thrown myself upon those who were Jackson men in the beginning and who fell off from his administration for very much the same reasons which influenced you and I." They were "men of acknowledged ability," he said, "and conform to my opinions on the subject of a national Bank." The president had stayed within his party, then, albeit with a few states' rights selections, which gave the lie to the assertions of some Whigs that he only wanted to court favor with the Democrats. From Albany, powerbroker Thurlow Weed surveyed the new appointments and remarked, "John Tyler is a good Whig and intends to be hereafter." The *Washington National Intelligencer* concurred with Weed, declaring that "the appointments are upon the whole better than could have been expected."[59]

Tyler named fifty-five-year-old Walter Forward to the Treasury post. A former congressman, Forward was a native of Connecticut but had grown up in Pittsburgh, where he made a name for himself as a lawyer and newspaper editor. An enthusiastic supporter of the Harrison-Tyler ticket in 1840, he had been first comptroller of the Treasury, which made him a logical choice for Tyler's new Treasury secretary. Forward was described by one Whig as "plain and affable." The president no doubt appointed him because of his popularity in the party. He was an uncontroversial selection.[60]

Charles A. Wickliffe received the job of postmaster general. Wickliffe, fifty-three years of age, had recently been governor of Kentucky. A War of 1812 veteran, he and Tyler were friends. In fact, the two men had boarded together in Washington when they were young congressmen. Wickliffe was a sworn enemy of Clay, which must have appealed to Tyler. Also appealing was his friendly relationship with John C. Calhoun, which Tyler may have thought would come in handy at some point in the future.

The president offered John McLean of Illinois the position of secretary of war, which was a rather odd choice since McLean was an associate justice of the US Supreme Court, having been nominated by Jackson in 1829. But Webster wanted McLean. When he turned down the offer, the post went instead to fifty-three-year-old John Canfield Spencer, the secretary of state for New York. A graduate of Union College, Spencer had once served as private secretary to Governor Daniel D. Tompkins and practiced law in Canandaigua, the hometown of Francis Granger. He was a US congressman from 1817 to 1819 and became Speaker of the New York State Assembly in 1820. Spencer had once hosted Alexis de Tocqueville at his home when the famous chronicler of American democracy visited the United States in 1831, later writing the preface to the 1838 American edition of *Democracy in America*. Although now a man whom American historians have largely forgotten, Spencer was well known and well regarded in his day. More importantly, his appointment was Tyler's attempt to court Weed and New York governor William H. Seward, two Whigs decidedly hostile to Clay's ambitions.[61]

Hugh Swinton Legaré was Tyler's choice for attorney general. Forty-four years old in 1841, Legaré was of Huguenot ancestry and a native of Charleston, South Carolina. An odd-looking man—a childhood illness had left him with a fully developed torso but shrunken extremities—he had attended South Carolina College (now the University of South Carolina) and was well known throughout the South for having founded the *Southern Review*. Legaré had opposed his state's nullification stance during Jackson's presidency, had served one term in Congress, and more recently enjoyed a post in Brussels, where he served as US chargé d'affaires. A highly esteemed attorney, by 1841 he was also regarded as one of the South's finest intellectuals, though some questioned his political ability. He believed slavery inhibited the economic development and modernization of his native region but could devise no satisfactory plan of emancipation. Tyler had met Legaré in 1819 when the two men shared a stagecoach trip to Fredericksburg, Virginia. He was instantly impressed with the younger man. "We were strangers to each other," Tyler recalled many years later, "but who waits for an introduction in a stage-coach?" Since that evening Legaré had often spoken of the virtues of Jeffersonian republicanism. It was somewhat surprising that Tyler wanted him in the cabinet, though, because the South Carolinian had supported the national bank in the past. He was also warm friends with Senator Rives and an associate of Senator Preston, which may account for the appointment more than anything else.[62]

Finally, Tyler named Abel Upshur as his new secretary of the navy. He had been rumored to be the president's choice for minister to London but told Tucker that he would have turned down the appointment if it had been offered. He was evidently surprised to be the president's choice for the Navy Department and doubted whether he would have any influence. "You are entirely mistaken that he [Tyler] derives counsel from me," Upshur informed Tucker. A more accurate statement was that Tyler did not derive *all* his counsel from Upshur, who no doubt hoped he could use his new vantage point to press for a new states' rights party. In any case, his appointment meant that one of the Virginia intellectuals now had a direct conduit to President Tyler and a job working for the federal government.[63]

Almost inconceivably, the Whigs in the Senate gave Tyler very little trouble over his new cabinet appointments. Upshur faced the most opposition—five Whig senators voted against his confirmation—but the entire slate was confirmed by one o'clock on the afternoon of September 13. All of the talk about throwing the government into chaos had not come to pass. The new cabinet had now been formed as Congress adjourned. The president could begin preparing for the next session of Congress.[64]

But Tyler himself no longer had a place in the Whig Party. Shortly after Congress adjourned, a group of between fifty and seventy Whigs gathered in

Capitol Square to publicize a manifesto that had been written by the novelist and Baltimore congressman John Pendleton Kennedy. The manifesto roundly criticized Tyler's behavior, especially over the bank issue, and declared that the party could no longer "in any manner or degree" be "held responsible for his actions." The Whigs declared their determination to rid the nation of executive usurpation and, among other remedies, suggested that a constitutional amendment curtail a president's use of the veto. They referred to Tyler as "His Accidency," displaying their resentment over how he had come to the presidency and how he had destroyed their agenda. Then, in ceremonial fashion, Tyler was formally read out of the party. He had been excommunicated. No president had ever been subjected to such ignominy.[65]

Tyler was certainly not happy to have been expelled from the Whig ranks. He may have been particularly disheartened that only three of the fifty-five southern members of the House of Representatives now publicly supported him. But he believed the vetoes that prompted his ouster had allowed him to preserve the integrity of his administration. Ironically, while he may have agonized over the political process of the special session and appeared weak and vacillating to some, in the end, his refusal to go along with the wishes of his cabinet and sign the second bank bill into law allowed him to safeguard the prerogatives of the executive branch. From this point on, Congress might not bend to his authority, but neither would he bend to its wishes. Tyler regained some of the confidence he had displayed on the day he assumed office.

But he was now a president without a party.

Greenway, the house in which John Tyler was born on March 29, 1790, and spent his childhood, was—and still is—located less than two miles from the north bank of the James River in Charles City County, Virginia. After Tyler's father's death in 1813, the house passed out of the family. Tyler bought it back in 1821 and lived there with his growing family until 1831, when he moved them to Gloucester Place. Carnegie Survey of the Architecture of the South, Library of Congress, Prints and Photographs Division, Washington, D.C.

A highly respected attorney and jurist in Tidewater Virginia,
John Tyler, Sr., was without question the single greatest influence on the future tenth president's life. Loving yet firm with his
children, the elder Tyler instilled in his son a devotion to public
service and demonstrated the importance of honor in politics
and domestic life. As an anti-federalist, the judge fought in vain
to block Virginia's ratification of the Constitution. When that
failed, he adopted the ideology of strict construction and states'
rights, which became the guiding political principles of his son.
Virginia Museum of History & Culture.

This engraving shows John Tyler in his mid-thirties, likely in 1826, when he was governor of Virginia. Proud of his service to the Old Dominion—which included three separate stints in the legislature—Tyler found more fulfillment as a national politician. Virginia Museum of History & Culture.

Known for her grace and beauty, Letitia Christian Tyler suffered from chronic ill health for most of her marriage to John Tyler. She gave birth to eight (possibly nine) children, and rarely accompanied her husband to Washington during his national political career in the House and Senate. The separation that defined her marriage to the future president took an immense toll on her both physically and emotionally. Afflicted by a stroke in 1839, she suffered another on September 10, 1842, which killed her, making her the first presidential spouse to die while her husband occupied the White House. Library of Congress, Prints and Photographs Division, Washington, D.C.

Robert Tyler, the oldest of the president's sons (shown here after John Tyler's death in 1862), helped manage the family farm while his father was in Washington serving in the Senate. Like his father and grandfather, Robert graduated from the College of William and Mary. After working for the federal government while his father was president, Robert became an attorney, settling with his family in Pennsylvania before the Civil War. Virginia Museum of History & Culture.

His family believed John, Jr., had all of the gifts that augured well for his success. Unfortunately, his aimlessness and lackluster academic career at William and Mary strained the relationship he shared with his father. Attempting to provide some structure, President Tyler made his son his personal secretary and paid his salary out of his own pocket. Alcoholism poisoned the young man's marriage to Mattie Rochelle and at one point after he left the presidency, John Tyler feared for his son's life. John Tyler, Jr., Papers, Special Collections Research Center, William and Mary Libraries, Williamsburg, Virginia.

Daughter of famed British Shakespearian actor Thomas Abthorpe Cooper, and herself a celebrated stage actress, Priscilla Cooper married Robert Tyler in 1839. Substituting for her ailing mother-in-law, she served as White House hostess from 1841 to 1844. After fainting at her first social event shortly after John Tyler assumed the presidency, Priscilla went on to become a much-admired and important part of her father-in-law's administration. Virginia Museum of History & Culture.

Mercurial and combative, Virginia congressman Henry Wise was a states' rights Whig who became John Tyler's most important confidant and political strategist while he served as president. Relishing the battle with Henry Clay and the majority of the congressional Whigs, Wise defended the embattled chief executive at every turn. Virginia Museum of Fine Arts, Richmond.

Representing Kentucky in the U.S. Senate after a long and distinguished career in national politics, Henry Clay was friendly toward John Tyler before the Virginian became president. During the special session of Congress in the summer of 1841 Clay became Tyler's chief antagonist and political rival. The fight between Tyler and Clay—which both regarded as a matter of principle and which became overtly personal—understandably soured the men on one another, and they never reconciled. Tyler slightly softened his stance on his political enemy after Clay's death. National Portrait Gallery, Smithsonian Institution.

A giant in antebellum American politics and secretary of state in the Tyler administration from 1841–1843, Daniel Webster enjoyed Tyler's company and the two collaborated successfully in the diplomacy that led to the Webster-Ashburton Treaty of 1842. Webster was not afraid to speak frankly to President Tyler and left the administration in large part because he objected to Tyler's pursuit of the annexation of Texas. Brady-Handy Collection, Library of Congress, Prints and Photographs Division, Washington, D.C.

A native of North Carolina and eventually a disciple of Andrew Jackson, Thomas Hart Benton rose to national prominence as a Democratic senator from Missouri. He seemed to take particular delight in antagonizing John Tyler when both men served in the U.S. Senate. Sarcastic and bombastic, Benton leveled especially harsh criticism of President Tyler, and relished the fight between the chief executive and the Whigs. Tyler never forgave Benton for the ill-treatment and denounced his nemesis for the rest of his life.

Undaunted by the thirty-year difference in their ages, John Tyler pursued the dazzling young socialite from Long Island with a vigor that shocked many Washington observers. Devastated by her father's death on board the *Princeton* in February 1844, Julia Gardiner nevertheless agreed to marry Tyler soon after, becoming the first wife of a president to serve as first lady since Louisa Catherine Adams in 1829. She and Tyler had seven children together. White House Collection, White House Historical Association.

Chapter 11

THE ILL-FATED EXCHEQUER PLAN

"The present is the first time under our government that the phenomenon . . . [of a] 'President Without a Party' has been witnessed. Nor is it easy to imagine any possible combination of circumstances which would be likely ever again to reproduce it—at least in a manner as remarkable as exists in the case of Mr. Tyler."[1]

The *Democratic Review* accurately highlighted the unique character of national politics after the Whigs banished John Tyler from their ranks. The journal did not offer its opinion on whether the president or Henry Clay was more responsible for the conflict that had marred the special session, but Washington politicians and ordinary Americans who followed the partisan battles in the capital certainly had their own ideas as to who was to blame.

In assessing the feud between Tyler and Clay, contemporaries as well as later historians tended to blame one man or the other for the political turmoil that left the president without a party and the Whigs deprived of the mandate they believed they had won in 1840. Those sympathetic to Clay portrayed Tyler as a stubborn strict constructionist who misled the congressional Whigs and who could not bear to have the senator's leadership of the party go unchallenged. The president, one Whig newspaper groused, was "a man *destitute of intellect and integrity, whose name is the synonym of nihil*—if so miserable a thing can be called a man!" Tyler supporters viewed Clay as egotistical and unreasonable, a man driven by ambition to put his indelible stamp on the nation's economic recovery and place himself in the best position to win the Whig nomination for president in 1844, no matter the cost. It had been Clay who had "blast[ed] all the fruits of the Whig victory of 1840," a disgruntled observer wrote, and he "would have had the same difficulty with General Harrison had he lived." Both perspectives contain some truth, of course, but they do not tell the whole story. History can seldom be explained with simple either-or propositions.[2]

An explanation of Tyler's behavior during the summer of 1841 must first take into account the circumstances of his elevation to the presidency. The Virginian came to the office under duress. President Harrison's death had thrust him into an unprecedented and extremely difficult situation, one that

he negotiated with admirable skill and decisiveness in the first days of his administration. Tyler arrived in Washington on April 6 determined to establish
his legitimacy as chief executive and set a tone conducive to effective government. He quickly got to work and familiarized himself with the many details
of the office. The start of the special session—which he acquiesced to but did
not fully want—placed Tyler on a collision course with Clay, and he quickly
became mired in self-doubt and exhibited a startling inability to chart a coher-
ent course of action. His decisiveness evaporated quickly. It was as if he had
internalized the "accidental" nature of his presidency and lost the self-confidence that had animated him at the first cabinet meeting. Making matters
worse, Tyler gave confusing signals about his acceptance of a national bank
to his party's leaders—including Clay—as he sought to stake out a position of
leadership for himself from the White House. At the same time, he paid lip
service to the Whig doctrine of legislative supremacy, not wanting to be tarred
with the charge of executive usurpation. Contradictions defined his behavior.

Further complicating the situation for Tyler was the pressure placed on
him by the Virginia "cabal"—Henry Wise, Beverley Tucker, and Abel Upshur.
These men saw in a Tyler presidency the opportunity to push the states' rights
policies they had dreamed of for years and bombarded the president with correspondence and personal visits touting their position. Far from resenting the
intrusion, however, Tyler actively encouraged their counsel, even if he largely
acted according to his own conscience. Oddly, he found himself trying to placate his friends with evasive and half-hearted promises while keeping them
enough at arm's length so that they would not wreck the plans he had begun
to lay for succeeding himself in 1844. He truly was caught in the middle. The
Clay Whigs believed the Virginians unduly influenced Tyler and directed his
actions. The cabal, on the other hand, argued among themselves that Tyler
hewed too closely to Whig orthodoxy and questioned (with good reason) his
sincerity in advancing their goals. The result for the new president was that he
pleased neither group and placed himself in an untenable position.

The events of the special session shattered Tyler's self-confidence. Indeed,
in the buildup to the second veto, he appeared emotionally unbalanced, grop-
ing for something or someone to ease his way and take the pressure off of him.
Tyler also revealed himself to be thin skinned, a dangerous attribute for any
politician, especially the president of the United States. He had fallen prey to
self-righteous bouts of anger and dismay—and at least one outburst of temper—as he followed very closely what a hostile press and adversarial Congress
had to say about him. He seemed to believe that his longstanding political

principles should insulate him from partisan criticism, or at least explain why he acted as he did. He also allowed his hypersensitivity to influence his political behavior. Daniel Webster was surely correct in his view that the Botts coffeehouse letter played at least some role in the president's decision to veto the second bank bill, a decision that, while couched in terms of principle, displayed his insecurity as well as an unbecoming vindictiveness.

In sum, Tyler deserves a large share, though by no means all, of the blame for the situation in which he and Whig leaders found themselves in September 1841. Clay's ambition certainly played a role in what happened, but there is no specific evidence documenting Tyler's assertion that the Kentuckian used the special session as a "favorable opportunity to press [him] to a veto . . . and by exciting the passions of the Whigs to frenzy, to force them into an early committal for himself [Clay] for the succession, and thereby to exclude all other competitors." This was certainly the view of Congressman Wise, who apparently argued the point so much that the president started to believe it. In mentioning "all other competitors," though, Tyler perhaps inadvertently revealed that he considered himself a serious challenger for the presidential nomination in 1844, which would mean that *his* ambition, as well as Clay's, played a role in the disaster of the special session. Whatever the case, neither Tyler nor Clay emerged from the debacle with his reputation entirely intact.[3]

The Whig Party itself must also bear significant blame for the rupture between the president and the senate leader. "Flushed with success," the *Democratic Review* later intoned, the "party anticipated no obstacle to the complete triumph of those favorite schemes" they hoped to enact during the special session. The Whigs were shocked and angry that Tyler had dared to oppose them. Yet the president talked himself hoarse during the summer of 1841, explaining to all who would listen that he had followed the same principles of states' rights and strict construction for his entire public career and that he had always been opposed to the type of bank Clay favored. He saw no need to shed his principles just because he had become president, even though the majority of his party believed he should have adjusted his stance to allow their entire agenda to become law. In fact, as one historian has argued, had Tyler strayed from his longstanding ideals, he would have been "tagged as a hypocrite, a trimmer who tilted with the political winds." He would have risked his honor, a most distasteful prospect for a Virginian from the Old Republican school.[4]

By placing Tyler on their 1840 ticket, the Whigs had made a horrendous decision at the Harrisburg convention. Serious concern about Harrison's advanced age had been disregarded. No Whig asked what a Tyler presidency might look like. No party chieftain was concerned enough with Tyler's tenuous connection to Whiggery to question whether he should even have been their candidate for vice president. To be fair, the contingency of a president's death had no precedent before April 1841. Subsequent national party conventions would at least keep the possibility in mind that the candidate at the top of the ticket might die in office. In fact, today's parties select and nominate their vice-presidential candidates (usually) with care and often think long and hard about the person who will be "a heartbeat away" from the presidency. Had the Whigs considered this, perhaps Willie Mangum or some other suitable southerner would have been placed on the ticket with Harrison in 1840, and the party's agenda would have sailed through at the special session. The Whigs vowed that they would not make this mistake again.

The disastrous decision at Harrisburg, and the seemingly inevitable vetoes and finger pointing between Tyler's allies and Clay's supporters, obscured the very real danger the United States faced in 1841. No one took responsibility for the damage the fracture in the Whig ranks inflicted on the country. The American people suffered most from the break between Tyler and Clay, as promises to improve the economy wilted under the stress of politics. The depression continued. A bank would surely have helped alleviate the nation's economic problems. Clay was correct that such an institution had a demonstrably beneficial effect on credit and capital; for all of the greed and corruption associated in the public mind with the Second Bank of the United States, during its lifetime, it had been integral to America's growing market economy. Clay's bank bills during the special session remedied some of the previous institution's most glaring defects. But the president's two vetoes meant that the senator would never get the type of bank he wanted, at least not while Tyler sat in the White House.

Tyler, of course, believed he had acted in the best interests of the country. And he was still the president even if he had no party. In the wake of the special session, he turned his attention to the promise he had made to devise a suitable fiscal agent that he and Congress could agree on. Upshur and Tyler had discussed the matter, without coming to any agreement over what the administration should offer when the time came. The navy secretary had resurrected Tucker's proposal from April and urged the president to finally get behind it. Evidently, Tyler still could not commit to the plan but could not bring himself to eliminate it from consideration either. This continued waffling, as always, exasperated Upshur, who was not sure at first if he even wanted to be a part of the administration. "I have been at cross-purposes with myself & every body else, ever since I received this Federal appointment," he admitted. He, of course, got over his misgivings and accepted the cabinet position and soon began tackling his duties at the Navy Department with enthusiasm and a singular competence. Modernization would emerge as the theme of his tenure, and a near-total transformation of the naval service resulted, bringing great credit to the Tyler administration and to Upshur personally.[5]

Tyler intended to return to Virginia in the fall of 1841 for a brief vacation before the regular session of Congress began in December, but he promised Upshur he would give a lot of thought to the fiscal agency and put some ideas on paper. He needed the break. The adjournment of the special session did little to relieve what Tyler called the "most oppressive mass of business" he faced as the head of the government. Patronage matters still took up much of his time, and he got tired of seeing the hordes of grimy office seekers who made their way to the White House every day. One visitor was struck by the "persevering and energetic" way these men spat brown tobacco juice and "bestow[ed] their favors so abundantly upon the carpet" of the mansion as they awaited the opportunity to speak with the president for a moment or two. Most of these supplicants for office went away emptyhanded. Tyler usually filled jobs based on the recommendations of men whose judgment he trusted. In doing so, he also sought to maintain his ties to powerful members of the Whig Party. As he told New York governor Seward, who at one point had written on behalf of a loyal party man, a well-timed letter from someone of his stature had "much influence" on him as he made decisions to fill patronage spots throughout the country. Still, the process vexed him, as he admitted to Tucker. "That I should commit many blunders in my appointments," he sighed, "is in no way to be wondered at, with a full understanding of the arts and subtleties to which the eager pack continually resort." Tyler had to sift through a seemingly endless supply of correspondence in an effort to find competent men for government positions. The patronage game was a necessary evil of party politics, particularly in an era in which the spoils system held such sway. Before the Pendleton Civil Service Act of 1883 curtailed the practice somewhat, providing jobs for supporters allowed the president to lubricate the gears of government. Tyler hated it, however. Nor did he believe it was necessarily beneficial to the welfare of the American people. Still, he seemed to recognize that patronage might be a weapon he could use to great effect as a president without a party. Indeed, skillfully utilized, the patronage might even help Tyler build a new party if it came to that.[6]

Before he departed the capital, Tyler wrote two letters to Webster, who had left Washington for his home in Massachusetts in late September. He wanted to make certain that the secretary of state knew he would not be marginalized in the new cabinet and that he had made the prudent decision to stay where he was. "You were right to remain in the cabinet," the president assured him. Tyler also wanted to cement Webster's status as a confidant and political ally and prepare him for the battles ahead. "I pray you to accept the sincere assurances of my confidence and warm regard," he wrote. Though he did not say so directly, the president believed Webster to be the most important member of the cabinet.[7]

Because of his stature and influence, the New Englander's support of the men Tyler had selected for his own cabinet was essential to the administration's sound footing. By writing to Webster, the president sought to lay the groundwork for a productive working relationship between the secretary of state and his new colleagues. "I congratulate you in an especial manner upon having such co-workers," he wrote. "Each man will go steadily to work for the country, and its interests will alone be looked to." Tyler also made clear that he expected a harmonious administration. He wanted each member of the cabinet "to look upon every other in the light of a friend and brother. By encouraging such a spirit," he said, "I shall best consult my own fame and advance the public good."[8]

Tyler's attitude and frame of mind in early October were a far cry from what they had been in the waning days of the special session. In fact, the resignations of Harrison's cabinet members and the reestablishment of his administration—and it was his now, to be sure—energized him. He also seemed to recover at least some of the forcefulness and steady leadership he had shown in the early days of his presidency. He was now free to pursue his goals unencumbered by men who could never be loyal to him or who did not share his objectives. Tyler also took heart from favorable reports he had received from various quarters after Congress adjourned. "My information from all parts of the country is encouraging," he informed Webster, "and although we are to have a furious fire during the coming winter, yet we shall, I doubt not, speedily recover from its effects." Typical of the positive news Tyler had read or heard from other sources was a statement from the Massachusetts Whig State Central Committee, the men to whom Webster himself answered. "We still have a Whig President," the committee declared, "who intends to surround himself with Whig advisers, and to conduct his administration upon Whig principles; and until his acts shall establish the contrary, we hold him to be entitled to the support of the Whig people." Tyler agreed and believed that the course of his administration was "too plainly before us to be mistaken. We must look to the whole country and to the whole people." Indeed, he aimed to rise above partisanship.[9]

Tyler was aware, though, that other members of the party did not concur with the Massachusetts Whigs. Clay supporters schemed for ways to position their man for 1844 and undermine the administration. A New York state convention meeting in Syracuse on October 7, 1841, gave the Kentuckian credit for what had been accomplished during the special session and expressed "deep disappointment and regret" that President Tyler had "not been able to cooperate with the other co-ordinate branches of the Government" in the effort to create a new national bank. The convention also declared its support of the cabinet members who had resigned after the second bank veto.

What had been said publicly, however, was mild compared to what had apparently been said behind closed doors. Tyler received a private letter that detailed some of the more sordid dealings in Syracuse. He found out that Millard Fillmore, a New Yorker and chairman of the House Ways and Means Committee, had pressured Frank Granger to resign from the cabinet. Whether Fillmore's machinations had actually forced Granger to leave was not known, but Tyler had reason to believe he did not leave solely of his own accord. Worse, in a secret session a small cabal of Whigs—again led by Fillmore—had sought a way to force Tyler from office and replace him with Clay. "What a low and contemptible farce," the president sneered by letter to Webster. Clearly, the "furious fire" Tyler expected during the coming winter in Washington had already been lit.[10]

To counteract the intrigue being used against him, Tyler relied on surrogates to frame the events of the special session in a favorable way and to present his actions in a positive light. He needed to build momentum before the regular session of Congress began in December. No surrogate was more enthusiastic than Henry Wise. The congressman traveled throughout Virginia's eastern shore in the fall of 1841 trumpeting the virtues of the president. Speaking late one afternoon in front of a tavern in Accomac County, Wise attracted a sizeable crowd of well-oiled spectators and delivered a blistering denunciation of the Clay Whigs. "He justified Mr. Tyler in the exercise of the veto power, and gave the Whigs a most tremendous run," declared one man who was there. Mocking the efforts of Ewing and Clay to devise a new national bank, Wise "condemned them all decidedly and unequivocally." Tyler appreciated his friend's efforts and expressed his confidence that the congressman's "presence among them [his constituents] will unite them as one man."[11]

But this public-relations campaign would only get Tyler so far. The president believed he needed substantive policy proposals if he was to mobilize support for his administration in Washington and throughout the country. The nation's continuing fiscal difficulties, in particular, demanded attention. As he had indicated to Uphsur, Tyler informed Webster that he planned to devote part of his time in Williamsburg "to meditate in peace over a scheme of finance." He also planned to discuss the matter with Professor Tucker. Tyler seemed determined to come up with a workable solution while he was in Virginia.

The president also took the opportunity at this time to refer to a subject he and Webster had discussed briefly after the special session had ended. "I gave you a hint as to the probability of acquiring Texas by treaty," he reminded the secretary of state. "I verily believe it could be done." The time seemed ripe for making the independent Republic of Texas a part of the United States.

Exactly when Tyler began to think of Texas within the context of his administration's foreign policy is not clear. Although Wise had floated the idea of annexation in a meeting between the two men in May 1841, Tyler had apparently not made his interest in the matter known to anyone before he broached the idea with Webster. What seems likely is that, having become a president without a party, Tyler now sought an issue—a big issue—that would allow him to define his presidency and gather support for a second term. "Could the North be reconciled to it, could anything throw so bright a luster around us?" he asked Webster. Luster was indeed what Tyler craved, what in his view he needed, if he wanted election in his own right to cement his place in history. He recognized the pitfalls. "*Slavery,*—I know that is the objection," he conceded. The objection "would be well founded," Tyler admitted, "if it [slavery] did not already exist among us." But he believed that "a rigid enforcement of the laws against the [international] slave-trade would in time make as many free States south as the acquisition of Texas would add of Slave states, and then the *future* (distant it might be) would present wonderful results." With these words to Webster, the president indicated that he was open to the idea of Texas annexation and wanted to sound out his secretary of state to see if he would be willing to help him accomplish it.[12]

After relaxing for a bit in Williamsburg, Tyler began to brainstorm ideas about the fiscal agent he wished to present to Congress. As he had so many times throughout his political career, he turned to Littleton Tazewell for advice. "I am committed to the country to produce a financial plan to the next session

of Congress," he wrote his friend. "Two have occurred to me, but upon neither have I matured my opinions." Tyler wanted Tazewell to weigh in on the
proposal as it took shape to help the process along. "The naked Sub-Treasury
[Van Buren's Independent Treasury] has been condemned but may not a Treasury arrangement be formed which will not only answer the purposes of the
government, but also furnish a currency for the country?" Tyler hoped so and
used that simple premise to outline a bill.[13]

The proposal the president came up with called for a bank in either Washington or New York City capitalized at $5 million. This institution would be
the "exclusive depository of the public funds" and would be empowered to
"select its own agents [that is, branches] without the grant of the government
of one particle more power than its local charter confers." Government stock
would provide security for bank notes, which would serve as legal tender everywhere and provide a uniform currency. The government would only allow
a limited supply of paper notes to circulate—perhaps $15 million—in the form
of what he called "exchequer bills." The total amount in circulation would be
tied to the par value of specie, that is, gold and silver. The notes, or exchequer
bills, "would not only rest upon specie collected *in advance* of their issue, and
for which they would be the substitute, but the faith of the government would
be pledged for their redemption." For greater security and to prevent price
fluctuation, Tyler proposed that the notes be made redeemable at the place of
issue. So, for example, if the notes were issued in New York City, they would
only be redeemable in New York City.

As for the "machinery" of the bank, Tyler indicated a willingness to depart
from states' rights principles. He envisioned a board of control in Washington,
with up to ten or twelve agencies established throughout the country. The
agencies would act in behalf of the US Treasury and would be empowered to
receive deposits of gold and silver and "issue certificates, which of themselves
would enter into circulation at a decided premium." Furthermore, the amount
these agencies could hold in deposits at any one time would be restricted in
order to prevent the widespread removal of funds from state banks. Tyler again
made clear that he wanted to protect state banks and envisioned them operating "in union with the agencies." Finally, there was the component that had
fueled so much animosity during the special session: discounts and bills of
exchange. The powers of the agencies "might even still further be enlarged,"
Tyler said, by authorizing them "*unless prohibited by the State where located* to
purchase bills of exchange drawn in one State and payable in another."

Such was the plan Tyler developed. All of it seemed feasible, at least to him. Yet one particular obstacle troubled him. "How is the board of control and their subordinates to be placed beyond the reach of executive power?" he asked Tazewell. Mindful of Clay's criticism that, because the country lacked a national bank, the president controlled the "sword" and the "purse"— the military as well as the Treasury—Tyler sought a way out. After all, he had argued in his inaugural address that a "complete separation should take place between the sword and the purse." But was this even possible? He speculated that perhaps the commissioners could be appointed for a specific term instead of serving at the pleasure of the president. Clearly, there were still more details to be worked out.[14]

While Tyler eagerly sought Tazewell's counsel on the matter, by this time, he had decided that he wanted nothing more to do with Tucker's banking scheme. The president spoke with Tucker in Williamsburg and gave him the bad news. When his friend asked for the reason why he would not introduce his measure, the president told him that political considerations made it impossible. "I must have a party," Tyler declared. "Make one," Tucker replied. "I have not time," the president insisted, "I must have one ready made." Tyler then explained the plan he had been working on. Tucker shook his head. Disgusted, he told Tyler that he would "oppose it with tongue and pen, and, in case of need, with sharper weapons." The conversation ended abruptly on that note, and the two men parted, their relationship now strained. In December 1844 Tucker confided in disgust to Clay of all people that he eventually saw that Tyler "would continue to disable himself to effect any good purpose, by making it manifest to all, that in whatever he did, or refused to do, he acted solely with a view to the gratification of his own sordid ambition."[15]

Tyler's insistence that he needed a "ready made" party meant that he would not attempt to build the states' rights party the Virginia cabal wanted—at least not yet. He intended to try to ally himself with one of the two established parties because he evidently believed this was the path to winning election in his own right in 1844. This is not to say that Tyler was intent on abandoning his long-held states' rights principles. As he made clear to Tucker, however, he realized that the reactionary approach to national politics favored by the Virginia "abstractionists" could not succeed. He needed a middle ground and set about refining the plan he had outlined to Tazewell.

The president did so shortly before returning to Washington. On December 7 Tyler sent his first annual message to Congress as required by the Constitution (Congress had convened the day before). The message arrived at the Capitol by courier, possibly John Tyler Jr.; the president did not read it aloud.

In it Tyler addressed the national debt and the debts many states owed to foreign—chiefly British—creditors, which had risen to the staggering sum of $200 million. He urged Congress to consider extending the time for the sale of $12 million in bonds that would compose the loan authorized during the special session, since only $5.4 million had been subscribed so far. He even mentioned the work of a commission that had been organized to determine the boundary between Texas and the United States and indicated that his administration would be watching developments there. "The United States can not but take a deep interest in whatever relates to this young but growing Republic," he declared.[16]

The centerpiece of the message, however, was a general introduction of Tyler's proposal for a fiscal agent, which he soon called the Exchequer. The name is rather curious, for it calls to mind the British treasury—the vilified Charles Townshend had been chancellor of the exchequer before the American Revolution—and Tyler had no love lost for Britain. Largely conforming to the plan he had sketched out for Tazewell in November, and satisfying his constitutional scruples, the Exchequer would be headquartered in Washington and placed under the control of a board composed of five individuals—the treasury secretary, the treasurer of the United States, and three other members the president appointed. Agencies would be established at "prominent commercial points or wherever else Congress shall direct, for the safe-keeping and disbursement of the public moneys." Individual deposits of gold and silver would be accepted by these agencies, and Treasury notes would be issued as currency in exchange for these deposits, with the total value of notes allowed in circulation at one time set at $15 million. This would, Tyler argued, furnish "a sound paper medium of exchange." Furthermore, the agencies would be allowed to conduct interstate financial transactions, provided these were not prohibited by the states in which the agencies were located. The Exchequer would not threaten the business of state banks because it would not be permitted to offer loans. Thus, the hated discounts that had caused Tyler to explode at his cabinet months before would not be an issue. Finally, the president offered a solution to the vexing problem of separating the purse from the sword by informing Congress that his proposal "denie[d] any other control to the President over the agents who may be selected to carry it into execution but what may be indispensably necessary to secure the fidelity of such agents." Tyler "disclaim[ed] all desire to have any control over the public moneys other than what [was] indispensably necessary to execute the laws."[17]

In outlining his plan to Congress, the president alluded to the rancor of the special session and made clear that he had acted in good faith. He professed to believe the Clay Whigs had done the same. Lest there be any misunderstanding, however, he made equally clear that he believed he had done the right thing in vetoing the two bank bills sent to his desk. "Subsequent reflection and events since occurring," he said, "have only served to confirm me in the opinions then entertained and frankly expressed."[18]

Despite his certainty that he had acted appropriately during the special session, and despite what he may have felt was the political necessity of using the message to assert himself and reiterate his position, Tyler took pains to exhibit deference toward Congress. His statement about separating the purse from the sword directly addressed the concern Clay had raised during the special session. Tyler also emphasized that his plan depended upon the willingness of senators and congressmen to support it. It would be, he pointed out, "the creature of the law" and would exist "only at the pleasure of the legislature." Even the approach he took in introducing his proposal was an attempt to soothe members of the legislative branch. Rather than provide every specific detail of his proposal, and determined to avoid the charge of presumptuousness, he informed lawmakers that he would only present the full plan for consideration if he was formally asked to do so. Tyler concluded by assuring Congress that he would seek the Exchequer's repeal "if it be found not to subserve the purposes and objects for which it may be created." He was "wedded" to "no theory."[19]

Tyler was wedded, however, to the idea that he could win election in his own right in 1844. And he was convinced that his Exchequer offered the most beneficial—and constitutional—way to address the nation's currency problems. By exhibiting deference to Congress in his message, the president had accomplished two things. First, he had explicitly paid fealty to the Whig doctrine of legislative supremacy. In this session of the Twenty-Seventh Congress, he would not allow himself to be portrayed as an abuser of executive authority. Rather, he sought to demonstrate to the American people that he was perfectly willing to work with lawmakers to devise a reasonable solution to what ailed the country economically, even though the majority of members and senators had spitefully read him out of the Whig Party in September. Second, Tyler had shrewdly painted the Clay Whigs into a corner. The Exchequer plan would not be "submitted in any overweening confidence in the sufficiency of my own judgment," he declared, "but with much greater reliance on the wisdom and patriotism [emphasis added] of Congress."[20] Clay and the Whigs could either perform their patriotic duty and meet the president halfway, or they could reject his proposal out of hand and risk portraying themselves as unpatriotic and unwilling to do what was best for the country. Thus, there was a bit of political gamesmanship in Tyler's message. The rhetoric mattered. He had crafted the words of his message to make himself appear as a reasonable servant of the people, one who had dedicated his presidency to finding a way out of the economic turmoil of the past nearly five years. This was clearly not a man who sought to antagonize all but the extreme states' rights men, as many in Washington were now claiming. The president wanted the support of moderates.

Here, then, was another example of Tyler combining politics with principles, a recurring theme of his public life. Like nearly all of his state papers, the first annual message contains statements that explain his political philosophy and provides clues as to what motivated him ideologically throughout his career as a politician. Historians have overlooked a portion of this particular document in which Tyler expressed his view of the proper role the federal government should play in the economy. His words anticipated a portion of the free-market conservatism of later presidents such as Calvin Coolidge and Ronald Reagan. Acknowledging that his fellow Americans still suffered from the effects of the panic and recognizing that his Exchequer was not a guaranteed panacea for the country's financial woes, he argued that "no scheme of governmental policy unaided by individual exertions can be available for ameliorating the present condition of things." The American people had to rely largely on the "earnings of industry and the savings of frugality" to succeed economically. Tyler expressed his faith in his nation and in its citizens, proclaiming that the "country is full of resources and the people full of energy, and the great and permanent remedy for present embarrassments must be sought in industry, economy, the observance of good faith, and the favorable influence of time."[21]

In some ways, the concrete ideas that undergirded Tyler's Exchequer plan—especially the notion that a centralized government agency would regulate the circulation of the nation's currency—may be seen as a precursor to the 1913 creation of the Federal Reserve System. Paradoxically, however, his contention that people should not rely on the government for their financial well-being and that instead industry and frugality, not the circulation of paper money, were the keys to prosperity reflects the views of some twenty-first-century opponents of the Fed. The apparent contradiction is perhaps best explained this way: Tyler grudgingly agreed with the Whig Party's fundamental premise, that an adequate supply of paper money in circulation was essential for the country's financial transactions. The complexity of the economy demanded it. But he was himself uncomfortable with a circulating medium that was not solely based on the amount of gold and silver available. What his first annual message reveals, then, and what is evident in his Exchequer plan, is that Tyler was willing to look beyond his own narrow views because doing so was the best for the country. To his credit, he had put aside his strict constitutional scruples and the longstanding aversion to paper money he inherited from his father. Once again, he would not play the part of the stubborn ideologue.[22]

Conceding economic realities was again partly a political calculation. Tyler had devised a fiscal agent that was, in the words of Upshur, "designed as a middle course between the sub-treasury and a national bank." His entire cabinet had supported his proposal, which in itself was undoubtedly gratifying after what had transpired during the special session. "We have *all* agreed, without a single exception," Upshur related soon after the bill was sent to Congress, "that our only course was to administer the government for the best interests of the country, and to trust to the moderates of all parties to sustain us." As the regular session began, the president wanted to see if he could rally enough moderate Whigs and Democrats to the Exchequer to give himself a political base that would bolster his chances of winning election in 1844. The Exchequer would be the vehicle through which he could gauge support for himself and for his administration. The members of the "ready made" party that Tyler had spoken about with Tucker in Virginia were the very moderates Upshur described.[23]

The president sought to straddle the line between the Democratic and Whig Parties, no longer a member in good standing of either but trying to woo elements of both. From Williamsburg, Tucker continued to grumble that a states' rights party was needed. He also believed Tyler had begun to show that he was intent on returning to the Democratic fold. Upshur corrected him. "But you certainly do Tyler some injustice in supposing that he pays any more court to the *locos* than to the other party," he wrote. "His appointments show the reverse; they are made indiscriminately from both parties, but the greater part from the Whigs. He avoids alike Clay-men and Benton-men, for there is nothing to choose between them." Tyler's purpose was to avoid "ultraism on both sides, and ai[m] at the approbation of the temperate and sober minded of both parties." Upshur closed, "Our object was to take what appeared to be good, and reject what appeared to be bad in each."[24]

When the House of Representatives made the formal request—through a resolution of Caleb Cushing, a Tyler ally—for the administration to submit the Exchequer plan for consideration, the president asked his cabinet to draft the bill and an accompanying argument supporting it. "It [was] the work of two or three of us," Upshur informed Tucker, "but chiefly of Webster." Oddly, Treasury Secretary Forward had not been given the primary responsibility of writing the bill, though it did appear under his name in the official presentation to the House. He was already rumored to be on his way out of the administration and was, in the judgment of one Whig senator, "certainly unfit for his place." Chosen largely for his potential help to Tyler in Pennsylvania, Forward was evidently little help at the Treasury Department.[25]

Upshur had apparently tried to persuade Webster to incorporate some of Tucker's ideas into the bill, but the secretary of state "rejected them, probably because they related to, and attempted to, palliate the centralizing tendencies of the scheme." Attorney General Legaré maintained that Webster's handiwork made the Exchequer "plausible." Upshur agreed. "I think the scheme would work well if it were adopted," he declared. But he acknowledged that "there seem[ed] to be but little chance of this, since both parties condemn it. At all events, it is the best that we can do, and we must even be satisfied to trust it to its own fortunes."[26]

Whigs in certain quarters of the country had found themselves impressed and encouraged by Tyler's first annual message. "It is one of the best Papers that has come from Washington for many a long day," one New Yorker gushed to Webster. "I have been all this morning stirring round among the talkers of all parties," this Whig continued, "and have not heard a word but in its praise. Every honest unprejudiced man approves of it & the hope is generally express'd that Mr. Clay will not oppose it." Thurlow Weed very perceptively concluded that President Tyler had "triumphed not only over his enemies but over himself. It is a great message." Weed's *Albany Evening Journal* endorsed the message as did two other Whig papers in New York City, the *Commercial Advertiser* and the *Daily Express*. The *Washington Daily Madisonian* trumpeted Tyler's appeal to the political middle. Upshur was gratified that the message was "well received all over the country." Yet he and many others who lauded Tyler's effort recognized the hurdle awaiting the Exchequer plan in Congress.[27]

For a brief time in late December 1841, that hurdle did not appear insurmountable. The *National Intelligencer*, the Whig paper of record in Washington, counseled that the Exchequer was "entitled to calm and dispassionate consideration." Indeed, some Whigs in the capital believed that since they clearly could not have the type of bank they introduced during the special session, Tyler's version was better than nothing. Horace Greeley's *New York Tribune* even reported that a majority of the Whigs in the House supported the president's plan, a development largely echoed by the probank *United States*

Gazette. Other Whigs, speaking informally, hinted that they might accept the Exchequer with certain alterations.[28]

Ultimately, however, there was never any realistic chance the Exchequer would win the sanction of both houses of Congress so that Tyler could sign it into law. It never received a fair hearing. Senator Clay, of course, loomed large over the Whig majority in both chambers. He wanted a bank—*his* version of a bank—or nothing at all. He certainly would not settle for Tyler's plan, especially if that meant giving the president a political victory. The Exchequer plan, Clay said, "does not stand the least chance of being adopted, in the form proposed." With very little effort expended to take the temperature of the politicians in Washington, he felt assured that the "great body of both parties are opposed to it." According to Clay, the Whigs professed a sense of urgency for taking action to mitigate the effects of the economic depression, but the Exchequer would not see the light of day. For good measure, the senate leader also mocked the president's contention that the Exchequer plan had garnered the support of the American people. Tyler "affects to believe that the People are with him, and the Politicians alone against him," Clay snickered. "Poor deluded man!" To Tyler's and the country's detriment, the Great Compromiser had shown himself as the "Great Uncompromiser."[29]

Clay had returned to Washington in a foul humor because his best-laid plans had been scuttled during the previous session and his party had suffered devastating losses in elections in several states during the fall of 1841, when many Whig partisans simply stayed away from the polls. Voters did not seem to know who spoke for the party—Congress or President Tyler. Clay was also suffering from a bad cold, which confined him to a sickbed for more than one week. In fact, he felt ill for much of the winter and announced that he would be retiring from the Senate during the session. It was therefore left to Mangum to eviscerate the Exchequer on the floor of the Senate and rally Whigs against it, which he did on December 30. The attacks on Tyler resumed as well. With typical bombast, Mangum accused the president of executive usurpation yet again (which makes one wonder if he had read the same message Tyler presented). His speech convinced Whigs who may have entertained the thought of supporting Tyler's proposal to line up behind Clay. It would be a real bank or nothing; no quarter would be given to the president. "There is no prospect of an agreement between Congress and the President on the Currency and Finances," one Whig concluded. Tyler was "so poor an imbecile that there [was] no such thing as keeping terms with him.[30]

Democrats, too, united in opposition to the Exchequer plan, even if they mostly did not exhibit the viciousness of their opponents toward the president. Most Democrats believed a return to the Independent Treasury was the solution to the nation's currency problems. Whigs, of course, would have none of that, and they were, after all, still the majority party in both chambers. Senator Calhoun declared flatly that there was "no chance" the administration bill would pass and explained the reason for Democratic opposition: "We regard it as in fact a government bank, and believe that it would terminate in being a mere paper engine as it stands."[31]

Tyler's earnest attempt to create a middle-of-the-road solution to the country's currency woes had failed. He had pleased no one, and the political base he had hoped for failed to coalesce around the Exchequer. As one historian has put it, "early in 1842 Tyler stood in a no-man's land between the major parties, an untouchable pariah."[32]

There was, however, more to the story. What should not be overlooked in the defeat of Tyler's Exchequer plan was the extent to which the personal rivalry between Clay and Webster played a role. Certainly, any alternative to Clay's bank that Tyler proposed was doomed to irrelevance, but it was not just a matter of putting the president in his place that motivated the Kentuckian. It was not just a struggle between Tyler and Clay. In fact, Tyler became almost a prop in the other drama splitting the Whig Party asunder. By remaining in the cabinet after the vetoes, Webster had sent unmistakably strong signals that he was intent on undermining Clay and wanted to chip away at the senator's stronghold on their party. The fight between Tyler and Clay initiated a schism within the Whig ranks, but the battle beneath the surface between Clay and Webster loomed just as large for determining the future of the Whig Party. "The Clay men are exceedingly bitter against Tyler & his administration, especially Webster," Calhoun observed with some satisfaction. "They hate them much more than their old opponents." The South Carolinian seemed to have forgotten exactly how much Clay and the Whigs had hated President Jackson. Perhaps his memory of *that* battle had dimmed with time, but he did not exaggerate by much in his assessment of what Tyler had brought about. "The whig party is now divided into two hostile sections," Calhoun wrote a political ally, "the whigs proper, as they call themselves, or Clay's division of the party, and the administration whigs, or Tyler's & Webster's division."[33]

Adding to Clay's animus toward the Exchequer plan, then, was Webster's hearty support of it. Many Whigs continued to rail against Webster for having remained in Tyler's cabinet after September 11, when the other members resigned. To some, his seminal role in drafting the administration's bill was too much to take. By offering his outspoken support of the Exchequer plan, Webster was trying to cast himself in the role of statesman and attempting to aid his own political fortunes, with an eye himself to the 1844 presidential campaign. All he succeeded in doing, though, was to further alienate Whigs in his home state of Massachusetts and strengthen his enemies, who over- whelmingly supported Clay's position. His overt support of the Tyler adminis- tration—indeed, his very *place* in the cabinet—sealed Webster's political fate. He stood no chance of receiving the Whig nomination for president in 1844.[34]

Webster had also irritated the thin-skinned Tyler with a speech he deliv- ered at Faneuil Hall defending the Exchequer. After reading it, the president complained to Tazewell that it was "fairly deducible from what he [Webster] says that the exchequer is *his* plan." Tyler wanted the record to reflect what had actually transpired as the administration presented the proposal, and he did not want Webster to claim more ownership than he deserved. "For good or evil," the president declared, "it [was] of my own purposing, it being the best thing which occurred to me. It [was] the cabinet's *by adoption*." Tyler later ex- plained to his son Robert that "the plan itself was my own and was drawn up at my house in Williamsburg" in the autumn of 1841. As always, Tyler remained alert for people who might undermine his authority and his place in history. He wanted it known that he was the one making the decisions in the White House, even if that meant taking the credit for a failed proposal.[35]

Ultimately, that proposal died because of the congressional Whig majori- ty's determination that they—not the president—spoke for the party. By the summer of 1842, they could report with satisfaction that "the exchequer is never mentioned and [it] will soon be forgotten that such a measure ever was proposed." The bill would formally die when it came up for a vote in January 1843, as Democrats who continued to push for a revival of the Independent Treasury joined Whigs who had fallen in line behind Clay to vote it down. Well before that vote, however, knowing that the fate of the Exchequer had already been assured, Tyler began to entertain the thought of doing what Tucker had been urging him to consider for some time: forming a third party.[36]

Chapter 12

PUTTING HIS STAMP ON THE PRESIDENCY

As President Tyler tried to rally support for his doomed Exchequer plan, he also sought to enlist Congress in devising solutions for the other financial difficulties the federal government faced at the beginning of 1842. Chief among these was the deficit. In his annual message, Tyler had alluded to a shortfall of over $627,000. Treasury Secretary Forward prepared a more detailed report that elaborated on just how dire the situation was. Federal spending in 1841 exceeded revenue by nearly 60 percent. The deficit, of course, further ballooned the national debt. The projected deficit for 1842 was $14 million. Quite simply, the federal government was teetering dangerously close to being unable to pay its bills.[1]

By the time he returned to Washington in December 1841, Tyler had concluded that he would have to give a little on his longstanding aversion to higher tariffs. With only $5 million of the proposed $12 million in Treasury bonds subscribed, the government needed to find another way to raise funds. The modest tariff passed during the special session did little to help, raising rates on only a limited number of goods, and then only to 20 percent.

According to the terms of the Compromise Tariff of 1833, rates on most other goods would fall on January 1, 1842, and again on June 30, when they would finally stand at the agreed-upon maximum 20-percent ad valorem rate. Obviously, however, a reduction in tariff *rates* meant a reduction in tariff *revenue* for the federal government.

In his December 1841 message to Congress, Tyler expressed hope that the government could collect the revenue it needed to reduce the deficit with tariff rates no higher than 20 percent. After all, he had been part of the Senate negotiations that settled on that figure eight years earlier and could not now repudiate the hallowed compromise without personal embarrassment and charges of inconsistency. The last thing he wanted now was to offer the *Democrats* a rhetorical club with which to beat him. Already assailed by the Whigs, he could ill afford being buffeted by the majorities of both parties on an issue that had in part defined his career.[2]

Tyler also wanted tariff rates no higher than 20 percent so that the states could still receive the distribution of the proceeds from the sale of public lands. According to the terms of an amendment to the Land Act of September 1841—which Tyler signed into law during the special session—distribution would cease if tariff rates rose above 20 percent after June 30. This provision had been added to the bill as an amendment to placate southern Democrats, some southern Whigs, and northerners who advocated free trade. They all opposed distribution in principle because they believed that, if the revenue from the sale of public lands could not be added to the Treasury, the government would seek an alternative source of revenue and would raise tariff rates. Tyler had long supported distribution but had these same reservations. In fact, he had signed the bill from the special session into law only because it contained the amendment; it had been a condition for his acceptance. Despite the potential salutary effect of distribution, he would not hesitate to abandon it if the Whigs endangered the Compromise of 1833 and pushed for rates higher than 20 percent.[3]

By early 1842, however, the president recognized that keeping tariff rates at 20 percent would do little to address the government's budget shortfall. He began to hint that he might sanction higher tariffs, even pointing out that Congress could subject some goods to a higher variable rate—what was known as "discrimination"—in order to provide the most revenue. He was willing to suspend his longstanding distrust of protection, perhaps in part, as one historian points out, to gain favor with protariff states like Pennsylvania, whose support he would need to win the presidency in 1844. But Tyler made clear that he was amenable to higher rates only because the government needed money and needed it fast. "So long as the duties shall be laid with distinct reference to the wants of the Treasury," he told Congress, "no well-founded objection can exist against them."[4]

Unfortunately, the link between tariff rates and distribution forged during the special session became the raw material for yet another fight between President Tyler and the Whig majority. It took some time before that reality became clear, however, and in the meantime, Congress dithered. Tyler's pleas for lawmakers to revise the tariff were ignored during the entire month of January and early February 1842. The Whigs seemed to want to delay any substantive action on the deficit to place the president in an uncomfortable position and cause the American people to heap blame for the bad economy on the administration. They perhaps also wanted citizens to wonder whether the country would be better off with a national bank. Clay spoke at length in the Senate of the need for a constitutional amendment to allow Congress to override a presidential veto with a simple majority rather than the legally mandated two-thirds and to dispose of the pocket veto. This idea went nowhere. He also sought a constitutional amendment that would formally separate the purse from the sword by mandating that Congress, not the president, appoint the Treasury secretary, as well as one that would impose a one-term limit on the presidency. These ideas, too, went nowhere.

On February 15 Clay presented a series of eleven resolutions designed as a "system of policy" to invigorate the economy. He called for retrenchment in government spending. He denigrated the bond issues and loans with which the government under both Van Buren and Tyler had attempted to raise money and argued instead for the need to raise tariff rates above 20 percent; raising them to 30 percent (with a home valuation) would add between six and seven million dollars. The Whig leader also made clear that he wanted the distribution of the proceeds from the sale of public lands to continue, which meant that the portion of the Land Act of 1841 (passed during the special session) prohibiting it if tariff rates rose would have to be repealed. He knew the president vigorously opposed this course of action.[5]

Yet despite his avowal that confidence in the solvency of the federal government was essential to the nation's economic recovery, Clay seemed in no hurry to spur his Senate charges into action. Nor did House members seem inclined to get moving. Meanwhile, the deficit continued to grow, while the Treasury was running out of money. In early March Tyler sent an urgent message to the House of Representatives informing its members that requisitions from the War and Navy Departments for the months of March, April, and May would create an additional deficit of $3 million. "I can not bring myself, however, to believe," the president wrote, "that it will enter into the view of any department of the Government to arrest works of defense now in progress." He referred to the "unsettled condition of our foreign relations" with Britain—an allusion to the ongoing McLeod Affair—and urged Congress to act. Without saying so explicitly, Tyler clearly believed the intransigent lawmakers were now worsening his negotiating position with the British and threatening his authority as commander in chief.[6]

Navy Secretary Upshur was livid. What he called "our *do nothing* Congress" had been "three months in session and have not matured a single important measure! They seem to look with absolute indifference upon all the high interests of the country," he griped by letter to Beverley Tucker, "and waste their time in trifling partisan maneuvering, or in disgraceful personal squabbles." Upshur, whose department felt the sting of congressional inaction, contended that the administration was being treated unfairly and believed that the American people were the ones who suffered. By March 1842, he had come to appreciate the president and began to defend him against Tucker's persistent charges that he was not moving fast enough on creating a states' rights party. The navy secretary now had his own stake in the administration, and his letters no longer contained exasperated grumblings about Tyler. He was impressed with his chief's devotion to the public good. "I can say with strict and literal truth," Upshur declared, "that I have not heard from him, nor from any one member of his cabinet, any counsel, opinion, or suggestion unbecoming an honest man and a true lover of his country." The administration was also "free from every corrupt and improper design." He was proud to be a part of Tyler's cabinet. "Depend on it, Judge, the men in power are much more to be relied on than those who are seeking to turn them out."[7]

Unfortunately for Upshur and for President Tyler, the Whig members of Congress held all of the cards. They controlled the legislative calendar and still felt no sense of urgency. On March 25 Tyler sent another—lengthier—plea to both chambers requesting action that would stave off financial disaster. The tone of the message conveyed a controlled anger; the president barely kept his simmering resentment under wraps as he charged the members of Congress with having abdicated their responsibilities to the American people.

Tyler now openly acknowledged that raising tariff rates above 20 percent on at least some imports was unavoidable. Gone was the language with which he had attempted to finesse this reality in his early March message to Congress. He pointed out—in a striking departure from a principle that had characterized the entirety of his political career up to this point—that raising the rates would "necessarily affor[d] incidental protection for manufacturing."

John Tyler supported protection! Things *had* gotten bad. While the president had not entirely uprooted his free-trade moorings, and while he wrote that he departed from the Compromise of 1833 with "sincere regret," he nevertheless recognized that fealty to long-cherished ideals would not help the country at this point. He would have to deviate from the principles that had been his since he was a student of Bishop Madison's at William and Mary. Even Upshur had accepted this view. "The free trade men of the South must relax their principles a little," he wrote Tucker. "We shall never maintain our specie payments without the aid of our tariff system." Thus another blow was struck against Tucker's dream of a states' rights party. Yet again, Tyler was playing the part of a moderate and looking for a middle ground, sacrificing his principles for the good of the country.

Staking out a position on that middle ground also meant abiding by the provision of the Land Act of 1841 that had been signed into law during the special session mandating the end of distribution once tariff rates climbed beyond 20 percent. Tyler made clear he intended to honor that law. He called for floating a loan of $15 million to tide over the Treasury until money started flowing in from the more robust tariff schedules. As collateral, he proposed using the proceeds from the sale of public lands, which he argued could be put toward paying the interest on this loan right away. Thus, money that would have been funneled to the states through distribution would be deposited into the federal coffers. He acknowledged, however, that leaders in states that needed these funds for paying their own debts—which is to say most states—would be keenly disappointed.

The president had an answer for their concerns. Defending his support of higher tariffs, Tyler argued that the increased revenue would help shrink the federal deficit and thus place the credit of the national government "on durable foundations." That, in turn, would "produce with the capitalist a feeling of entire confidence." In other words, if the federal government could place itself on firm financial footing, the states would benefit in trickle-down fashion. Investors who had faith in the credit of the US government would be more willing to risk their money in state bonds once again, which would go a long way toward alleviating the harsh effects of the lingering depression and make up for the suspension of distribution. Tyler's argument can best be described as a "glass half full" view, but, quite frankly, it was the only argument he could make.

Fully aware of how this argument would play among Whigs—remember, Clay had already proposed a resolution repealing the 20-percent provision in the Land Act—Tyler framed it in terms of responsibility. "The Executive can do no more," he intoned. "If the credit of the country be exposed to question, if the public defenses be broken down or weakened, if the whole administration of public affairs be embarrassed for want of the necessary means for conducting them with vigor and effect, I trust that this department of the Government will be found to have done all that was in its power to avert such evils, and will be acquitted of all just blame on account of them." Simply put, Tyler was fed up. His patience had evaporated. It was time for Congress to act.[8]

While the president found support from the editorial pages of newspapers in Washington and New York, Clay refused to consider suspending distribution. Two days before Tyler's latest message, Clay addressed from the Senate floor the arguments Democrats had recently made in support of the Compromise Tariff's 20-percent mandate and the Land Act's suspension provision. Specifically, he maintained that while the compromise did set the maximum tariff rate after June 30, 1842, at 20 percent, Congress could raise duties beyond that mark if the administration of the government required it. Moreover, he argued that placing the proceeds from the sale of public lands in the Treasury to pay off the debt instead of distributing them to the states was illegal. He reminded his fellow senators that the original distribution bill of 1833 had earmarked money from such sales to internal improvements, education, and colonization of free blacks in Africa. Therefore, the funds could not be used in the way that President Tyler—and most Democrats—intended to use them. Clay reiterated his position that tariff rates must be set higher than 20 percent and that distribution must continue.[9]

This was Clay's penultimate speech in the Senate, having informed the Kentucky legislature that he intended to retire on March 31. Before leaving, he asked senators to vote on the eleven resolutions he had introduced back in February; two were approved outright, while nine were referred to committee. On the appointed day he bid farewell to his colleagues with a final speech that prompted tears from both the floor and galleries and applause throughout the chamber. Clay claimed that he was resigning to tamp down the conflict between Congress and the Tyler administration and to make it easier for legislation to receive the president's signature; he also pleaded ill health. But everyone knew better: Clay was leaving to ready himself for what would undoubtedly be his last presidential run. Indeed, he seemed at this early date to be the frontrunner for the Whigs' 1844 nomination, and many in the party offered support for his candidacy as soon as he retired.[10]

There is no record of what Tyler had to say about Clay's resignation. Surely it provided at least some small degree of satisfaction. Upshur perhaps spoke for the president and the rest of the cabinet when he wrote: "Clay [was] the great obstacle to wholesome legislation. When he retires something may be done, and not before." The navy secretary was convinced that the Whig majority had clashed with the Tyler administration for a "deliberate purpose to make Henry Clay president of the United States, even at the hazard of revolution." Upshur was glad to be rid of the Kentuckian. It remained to be seen, however, whether the legislation the Whigs would send to Tyler's desk during this session of Congress could be characterized as "wholesome."[11]

President Tyler found a respite from the frustration and anger he experienced over politics in the social life of his administration. Despite the hard feelings between him and congressional opponents, his Thursday and Saturday evening drawing rooms remained popular with official Washington throughout the social season, which began with an open house on New Year's Day and ran through mid-March. "I went yesterday with the multitudes to pay my respects to 'Captain Tyler' and Family," one visitor reported on January 2, 1842. "There was a great deal of confusion, much crowding, and some rudeness, but not more of the first, and not so much of the last as I witnessed on like occasion when Mr. Jackson was our chief."[12]

Tyler recognized that an active social calendar—dinners, drawing rooms, levees—might help him win adherents to a new third party. He invited guests accordingly. "His entertainments embrace both parties," one senator noticed, "and about equal numbers at the same time." Priscilla Tyler, who served as her father-in-law's White House hostess, brought together rivals in Congress and provided the president with a forum to interact with his critics and supporters apart from the pressures of the normal workday. One female observer noted that "Clay Whigs and Van Buren Locofocos, and Tyler Americans" gathered in the lively atmosphere of carefully planned social events. Political differences were put aside—however briefly. Priscilla's social functions, and the cordial mingling they encouraged, allowed Tyler to perform the covert political task of taking the temperature of those "Van Buren Locofocos" and assessing the strength of the "Tyler Americans." The "Clay Whigs" he wrote off, of course, but he nevertheless attempted to lay the groundwork for building a coalition and did his best to gauge his chances for the 1844 election. In the wake of his failure to win support for the Exchequer, this became vitally important.[13]

Perhaps what was most important about the skill Priscilla showed as hostess was that it affected in a positive way the public perception of her father-in-law. Her grace and charm softened the harsh political judgments of the Whig press—ever so slightly. Tyler's association with his beautiful and talented daughter-in-law enabled him to cultivate the good feelings of those who took advantage of the drawing room to make their acquaintance with the administration. Priscilla's preparation for levees and state dinners, not to mention her presence at these affairs, created a favorable impression of the controversial president, one markedly different from what people formulated as he vetoed legislation and drove off his cabinet. "I have never seen a President whose port and manner were so commanding, and at the same time so acceptable to all who approached him," one society woman commented. Comparing Tyler to Andrew Jackson, she continued that the Old Hero was "a man of much dignity of manner, and most imposing presence; but he was capricious, fastidious, irritable, and sometimes overbearing." Not so the current White House resident. "President Tyler is abundantly courteous and graceful in his address." One newspaper correspondent noted with approval that Tyler conducted himself "with a simple elegance which made it seem as though he never could have lived out of the precincts of the most polished court." Indeed, he surprised many visitors to the White House. "It instantly struck me," one commented, "that there was a moral energy in the president of which his enemies little dreamed."[14]

As these accounts make clear, a stark contrast existed between the president without a party portrayed in the partisan newspapers and the actual John Tyler. Ever sensitive, he grew irritated when he was attacked in the press, even more so when these attacks were personal in nature. "The newspaper letter writers have become the curse of the age," he complained in March 1842. "They think to manifest their diligence and talent by catching up every report however ridiculous and false, which is to be found on the Pennsylvania Avenue or elsewhere and forwarding it in a letter from Washington to their employers." Tyler bitterly decried what he called the "retailers of these falsehoods" and resolved to "leave them wholly unheeded."[15]

Unfortunately, he could no more do that than a leopard could change his spots. Being thin skinned was part of who he was. To his credit, though, he seems to have recognized this and soon crafted a strategy of cultivating friendly reporters on whom he could rely to write articles portraying him in a favorable light. For example, he gave Frank Thomas of *Knickerbocker* magazine exclusive access to the White House and allowed him to interview everyone who lived in the mansion, from family members to servants. Thomas took meals with the Tylers and made himself at home. The result was a laudatory article in the magazine that made the president seem down to earth and refreshingly candid, nothing at all like the caricatures found in the partisan press. Tyler also gave an interview to Anne Royall, a middle-aged widow who became the first prominent female journalist in the nation's capital. If one account of the interview is accurate, however, he had little choice. Royall supposedly sat on his clothes while he swam in the Potomac a la John Quincy Adams and refused to leave until he had answered her questions. Tyler complied while standing neck deep in water.[16]

Tyler had clearly learned a valuable lesson during the special session in the summer of 1841 as he was vilified in the press: to change the public percep-tion of him and generate a positive impression among the American people, he had to shape the message. It was a lesson the most skilled and media-savvy presidents—the two Roosevelts, Kennedy, and Reagan—learned to use to their advantage as well.

⁂

The happiest occasion of the 1842 social season occurred on January 31, when President Tyler's daughter, eighteen-year-old Elizabeth, married twenty-one-year-old Williamsburg native William Waller in a small evening ceremony in the East Room of the White House. Reverend Hawley officiated. He had pre-sided over President Harrison's requiem the previous April and was no doubt glad to be back at the Executive Mansion under much happier circumstances. The cabinet secretaries and their wives, as well as a few of the foreign ministers, in addition to Mr. and Mrs. Henry Wise, joined the Tyler family for the nuptials. John Jones, the new owner and editor of the *Daily Madisonian*, was there, as was Dolley Madison, who had become a mentor to Priscilla and a family friend.[17]

Tyler had given two daughters away before Lizzy. Mary had been married in December 1835, and Letitia had wed James Semple in February 1839. A con-templative man, Tyler may have reflected on the marriages of Lizzy's sisters as he watched her join young Waller at the front of the room. Mary's was a suc-cessful union. She and her young family were doing well in Virginia's South-side. The president wished he saw his oldest child more, of course—he always made that clear, sometimes not too gently—but he could rest assured that Henry Jones took good care of his daughter and made her happy. By contrast, Letty's marriage was full of strife. What had seemed like a fortuitous match at first quickly turned sour as Letitia and her husband proved temperamentally unsuited for each other. Before long, the couple would be estranged, and Tyler would be forced to provide a respite for his daughter by finding his difficult son-in-law a job as a navy purser and sending him off to sea.

Tyler's thoughts that night may also have turned to his own marriage. The happiness he felt for Lizzy and William was no doubt tempered when he looked at his own wife. Largely confined to her bedroom on the second floor since she came to the White House the previous spring, Letitia had made it downstairs—for apparently the one and only time—to see Lizzy get married. She usually spent her days quietly reading her prayer book or enjoying visits from her children in the family quarters. Priscilla brought her daughter, one-year-old Mary Fairlie, to see her grandmother nearly every day.

Letitia's health had stabilized for a time after her 1839 stroke, but by early 1842, her condition had worsened. She could no longer speak without difficulty, and partial paralysis hampered her ability to move around freely. Tyler saw his two youngest children—fourteen-year-old Alice and eleven-year-old Tazewell—growing up without the benefit of their mother's nurturing and wise counsel, gifts their older siblings cherished. He did his best to make his wife as comfortable as possible, but the demands of his job and the daily pressure he faced distracted him. Ironically, after spending all those years in national politics as an absentee husband and father, achieving the pinnacle of his political ambition gave him the opportunity to see his wife every night. Now that he could do so, Letitia was not the same woman—nor would she ever recover. Tyler thus bore a heavy emotional burden as he simultaneously dealt with the fractious Clay Whigs and faced the realization that his wife was slowly slipping away. It is also likely that the crisis in confidence he exhibited toward the end of the special session may be partially explained by the anguish he felt in his private life.

Priscilla did her best to provide her father-in-law with some relief from this suffering, and she usually succeeded. One morning she came rushing into his office and breathlessly informed him that Dolley Madison had arrived at the White House and wished to speak to him immediately. Tyler put his pen down, got up from his desk, and followed Priscilla out of the room. They went downstairs and found his granddaughter, little Mary Fairlie, waiting for them. Priscilla had dressed the child to resemble Mrs. Madison, complete with a turban and shawl and a little rouge for her cheeks, and had coached her on an imitation of the venerable woman's accent. Tyler threw his head back and roared laughter.[18]

Priscilla's greatest triumph took place as she and the president hosted the last levee of the 1842 season. On the night of March 15, a reported 3,000 revelers thronged the White House to honor two famous guests: Washington Irving, the celebrated American author, whom Tyler had just named minister to Spain, and Charles Dickens, whom he had met a few days earlier. The rooms of the mansion were "filled to overflowing," with the East Room, in the words of one attendee, a "complete jam." The White House was clearly the place to be that evening. The president and his daughter-in-law had succeeded yet again. And they would continue to do so as their relationship flourished. Priscilla's devotion to him and to his presidency sustained Tyler through some extraordinarily trying times in the spring and summer of 1842, not all of which had to do with politics.[19]

One such difficulty involved John Jr.'s marriage, which was a source of stress for the entire family. Mattie Tyler and the couple's son, two-and-a-half-year-old James Rochelle Tyler, had not followed John Jr. to Washington when his father became president, choosing instead to remain at their home in Southampton County. John had repeatedly begged his wife to join him at the White House but had not been successful in getting her to leave the life she knew in Virginia. Theirs was a seriously strained union.

In April 1842 John Jr. informed Mattie that he intended to seek a divorce. He asked a Williamsburg attorney, George Washington Southall, to handle the suit. "All the facts in the case," he wrote in a letter to Southall, "I will submit to you as soon as I can get to Wmsburg." That proved easier said than done, given John Jr.'s responsibilities as his father's private secretary. Late in May he wrote to Southall again, summarizing the grounds for which he intended to pursue the divorce in court. Mattie was guilty of "*willful & continued* absence," he alleged, despite his "oft repeated prayers & solicitations on his part for her to come to him." According to John, there were no reasons to prevent her from moving to Washington.[20]

Why he chose the spring of 1842 to begin divorce proceedings is unclear. The couple had been separated since shortly after their son's birth in September 1839—a little over one year into their marriage and well before the time John Tyler assumed the presidency and John Jr. moved to Washington. Evidently, John Jr. had lived for some time with his parents and younger siblings at their home in Williamsburg, while Mattie remained at the house the couple shared at the outset of their marriage. John Jr. made several visits to Southampton County with the intention of saving his marriage and persuading his wife to make the move to Washington.

Those visits provided the second grounds for the divorce. John Jr. claimed that whenever he went to see his wife, her brother, James Rochelle, threatened him with "*eminent danger.*" In fact, on one of these visits, James had assaulted him physically. John Jr. claimed that "his life [had] been once attempted" by his brother-in-law. Though he may have exaggerated the seriousness of what had happened on this particular occasion, he nevertheless informed Southall that he could "prove [it] by the best testimony." It may actually have been Rochelle who provided the motivation for John Jr. to seek the divorce. But since he did not specify the date of the violent encounter with his brother-in-law, it is difficult to say with certainty.[21]

For his part, President Tyler tried to mend fences by offering Rochelle a midshipman's commission in the US Navy, which the young man accepted. Perhaps sending troublesome in-laws to sea was the best idea he could think of for his children's difficult marriages—at least this way John Jr. could visit his wife without fearing he would lose life or limb. Tyler also suggested to Mattie's mother that perhaps the two families could purchase an estate near Washington where the estranged couple could live together and work on their marriage. "Can we not by uniting accomplish their settlement in life?" he asked. Tyler confessed that he was "in no condition to make very heavy advances" but assured Mrs. Rochelle that "with a suitable start I have not the slightest fear of John's ultimate success." Mattie's mother, Martha, was not swayed and refused the request.[22]

John Jr. may have begun divorce proceedings, but Mattie seemed to have been the one who had the grounds for dissolution of their marriage. John's claim that she was willfully absent despite his pleas for her to move to Washington is, of course, but one side of the story. Perhaps she had sound reasons for refusing to leave Virginia. John Jr. drank too much and lacked direction and maturity. He had tried intermittently for at least four years to establish a career at the bar but was never able to complete his studies or make the contacts necessary for success in the legal profession, despite his father's best efforts to steer him along the proper course. John Jr. had much going for him—he was strikingly handsome, possessed a bright mind, and enjoyed family connections—but he never seemed interested in putting these qualities to good use for himself and his young family. Tyler had hired his son as his private secretary—and paid him out of his own salary—in part because he was trying to impose some structure on the young man's life. It had done little good.

Mattie's seemingly self-imposed exile in Virginia may have been a way for her to insulate herself from the heartache of her husband's weakness and dissipated habits. No doubt she resented his drinking. Her brother's behavior toward him also may indicate that John Jr. was abusive—perhaps physically— which of course could have been the result of his having had too much to drink. Moreover, her mother's refusal to aid his father in trying to salvage the couple's marriage may speak to her unwillingness to subject her daughter to more difficulty. In any event, John Jr. and Mattie never divorced. They even had two more children together—Letitia Christian, born in 1844, and Martha Rochelle, born in 1846.

While John Jr.'s marital difficulties troubled him greatly, President Tyler found much to be pleased with in his daughter Lizzy's marriage. After their White House wedding, she and William moved to Williamsburg, where he was attempting to carve out a law career for himself as well as become a successful farmer. Tyler missed Lizzy and wanted her to write. "Does Mr. Waller engross all your care and love and attention," he needled his newlywed daughter, "so that fifteen minutes cannot be given to me?" Tyler monitored the Wallers from Washington and was keenly interested in his son-in-law's career. "Has Mr. Waller made a speech at the bar," he asked, "or does he think only of farming?" He complained about his workload and regretted that it kept him from visiting. "I would give much to see you both," he told Lizzy, "but when or how unless you come here, I know not."[23]

Tyler also longed to see his oldest child, Mary. While the pressure of his responsibilities as president had prevented him from writing to her as much as would have liked, he was nevertheless able to maintain the same kind of relationship with her that he had always enjoyed. During the summer of 1842, he sent her a letter responding to her report of an uncomfortable social situation she experienced. Mary was now nearly twenty-seven years old, had been married for more than six years, and was a mother herself, but she was still her father's little girl. He continued to gently dispense advice like he did when she was a teenager. "I write now mostly to say that I regret to perceive that you suffer yourself to be affected by the deportment of the bad people around you," he told her. "Never give a thought to them. They are entirely unworthy of giving you the slightest concern." Tyler soothed his daughter and allayed the fears she had expressed about how unsavory people might affect her reputation. "What can they do or say to change the good opinion of any person towards you? Be perfectly assured that other people, whatever may be outward appearances, know them most thoroughly, and I would, therefore, have you go along as if they did not exist." That way, he concluded, "you obtain the mastery over them."

In this letter Tyler returned to another theme that for so long had characterized his relationship with Mary: the care of Letitia. "Your mother's health is bad," he reported. "Her mind is greatly prostrated by her disease, and she seems quite anxious to have you with her." He had suggested some months before that Mary leave Woodlawn, her plantation in Virginia, and move into the White House, where she could help tend to her mother and make her more comfortable. "I still think," Tyler maintained, "that you would be more happy here than elsewhere." He even suggested that she accompany her brother back to Washington after he had concluded business (perhaps relating to the divorce) in Virginia. "John will be in Charles City on court day," her father informed her, "and then you must come on."[24]

Tyler's letter to Mary indicates that on some level he realized his wife did not have much longer to live. Having relied on his daughter years ago to care for Letitia while he served in the House and Senate, Tyler knew that she was capable—perhaps more so than anyone else—of putting her mother at ease. No doubt he wanted to honor Letitia's wishes and make her as comfortable and as happy as he possibly could. But Tyler also may have wanted his daughter in Washington because he could no longer bear the emotional strain of Letitia's illness while he dealt with the Whigs in Congress. His presidency had exacted such a heavy toll from him that he now found himself almost desperate to find more ballast in his family. Priscilla helped a great deal in this regard. Mary, however, had always been his rock and a source of strength, and the relationship she shared with her mother made her especially well-suited to assume this new burden. Her former role as Letitia's caregiver had allowed her father to pursue his ambitions and build his political career. Now, as he sought a way to win election to the presidency in his own right in 1844, he needed Mary again. As he had as a younger man, Tyler still struggled to reconcile his public and private lives.

We do not know if Mary moved to Washington. She was three months pregnant in July 1842, when her father sent the letter imploring her to come, and may have felt that her health and her family responsibilities in Virginia made such a move impossible. We have no letters explaining her decision or giving an indication of how her mother's worsening condition affected her. There are two pieces of evidence, however, that might indicate she did indeed come to Washington. Laura Holloway, a nineteenth-century chronicler of the First Ladies, mentions that Mary (and her sister Letitia Semple) made "temporary visits." Perhaps one of those visits was in the summer of 1842. Also, Mary's third child, Robert Tyler Jones, was born in the White House on January 24, 1843. It is unclear when she arrived, though. Quite possibly, she hastened to Washington soon after receiving Tyler's letter and stayed through the next winter. By the time Robert was born, however, her mother had died.

Priscilla gave birth to her second child—in the White House—in late spring or early summer 1842. The baby girl was named Letitia in honor of her grandmother. The president arranged for Priscilla's two children, as well as for Alice and Tazewell, to be christened in the mansion on the Fourth of July. The family enjoyed a "splendid" fireworks display on the White House grounds that night, but Tyler was more poignantly affected by the baptisms, which he called the "most interesting matter" of the day. Never a regular churchgoer, he seemed to find peace in the small ceremony. Perhaps the trial of his wife's illness and her now very visible decline had stirred thoughts of the afterlife and Christian salvation. Now more than ever, he needed his religious faith, which he hoped to instill in the children.[25]

President Tyler must have wondered how long it was going to take or what disaster had to befall the country before Congress addressed the dismal state of the nation's finances. His admonition in late March 1842 to both houses to get moving largely failed to yield results in April and May. Congress did augment the loan bill passed during the special session, as Tyler had requested in his first annual message in December 1841, but there was no movement at all on the tariff or distribution. Whigs were determined to have their cake and eat it too—a higher tariff *and* distribution—and were willing to wait out the president, gambling that if they waited long enough, he would be forced to sign whatever they sent to his desk or risk the wrath of the American people.[26]

Back home in Kentucky, Henry Clay wrote letters to leading Whigs in Washington, urging them, cajoling them, to stand firm on what the party wanted and steeling them for the renewed fight with Tyler. He had publicly promised that he would not be an "idle or indifferent spectator" in retirement and pledged that he would maintain his "interest in the welfare of the Union." Throughout the summer of 1842, he made good on that promise.[27]

Instead of addressing the country's financial needs in April and May, the Whigs seemed content to disparage Tyler among themselves, with "imbecile" being the most preferred epithet. They created what later political pundits would call an "echo chamber," writing letters and giving speeches that were long on self-righteous criticism of the president but short on feasible policy ideas. "Of all shallow, ignorant, weak, vain & obstinate fools that ever cursed a free people, Tyler is the worst," proclaimed Kentucky congressman Garrett Davis, with sentiments that captured the attitude of most congressional Whigs toward the president. These ad hominem attacks, even coming (as most did) in private, made it appear as if the Whigs believed they would never be called to account by the voters. They arrogantly assumed that the American people took their side in the fight with Tyler. Some suggested that the president should resign. To make matters worse, many Whigs seemed more interested in highlighting Tyler's apparent inconsistency on distribution than in recognizing that the fragile state of the country's finances had forced him to abandon his longstanding support of the policy. What the *Madisonian* called "the mildew of party spirit" had poisoned the legislative process.[28]

Congressional inactivity could not last forever. As much as the Whigs attempted to portray the president as an obstructionist who foreclosed their earnest efforts to settle the currency question and relieve the nation's financial woes, they eventually realized they could not stand idly by for the entire session while the government ran out of money. Again, the Compromise Tariff of 1833 had stipulated that on July 1, 1842, rates across the board would automatically fall to 20 percent. Whigs found this unacceptable; they wanted rates to stay above 20 percent and did not want June 30 to come and go without ensuring that some other measure replaced the Compromise Tariff. But a new law superseding the 1833 statute would have to be passed before rates could be raised above 20 percent after June 30.

How serious were the Whigs in trying to make this happen? One congressman noted that "not one third of the members stay in the hall during the debate on the tariff bill." When it became obvious that Congress had waited too long to fully debate a new tariff bill, and that there would be no new law before the June 30 deadline, from Kentucky Clay suggested that the House Ways and Means Committee devise a "temporary continuation of the existing law" that could be passed until a new bill had been hammered out. Ways and Means Chairman Millard Fillmore got to work. The result of his committee's effort was the "Little Tariff," which extended the duties in effect on June 1 to August 1. That meant June 30 could pass without a fall in rates to 20 percent; the date on which the rates would fall was now August 1 instead of July 1. The measure also provided for the suspension of the distribution of the land-sale proceeds for one month—that is, until August 1. On June 26 Congress sent the stopgap measure to the president.[29]

With this bill, the Whigs had thrown down the gauntlet. On March 25 the president had made explicit his opposition to continuing distribution if tariff rates remained higher than 20 percent, maintaining that he would honor the Land Act passed in September 1841. It was not likely he would view the temporary suspension of distribution as an acceptable compromise because the Whigs intended to resume the practice after August 1. At least one Whig in the House believed Tyler meant what he said and should probably not be tested. "I believe with truth," James Irvin of Pennsylvania declared, "that he will not approve a revenue and tariff bill that distributes the Land fund." The result, Irvin feared, "will prevent anything from being done . . . that will afford relief to the country."[30]

Senator Mangum of North Carolina expressed his confidence that the bill would receive the president's signature. "I doubt, whether Tyler would dare to Veto," he averred, "yet the extremist rashness often accompany the highest degree of feebleness & imbecility." Mangum had just been elected president pro tempore of the Senate (making him next in the line of succession to the presidency if something should happen to Tyler), which, Clay laughed, "must have given particular satisfaction at the White House." His new position of leadership, however, did not bestow on the North Carolinian any greater understanding of the president.[31]

What, then, accounts for Mangum's confidence that another veto was not in the offing? The answer lay with the Compromise Tariff itself. According to the most commonly accepted interpretation of that law—the one to which Treasury Secretary Forward and most Whigs subscribed—no duties could even be legally collected after June 30 if tariff rates remained above 20 percent and there was not a new law on the books. President Tyler thus faced a potentially knotty problem. He had gone on record acknowledging that shrinking the deficit required tariff rates higher than 20 percent. The "Little Tariff" bill maintained those higher rates. But again Tyler insisted he would support no bill that retained distribution at the same time as the higher tariff duties. Would he really place the Treasury at greater risk by vetoing a bill that would allow the collection of much-needed tariff revenue just so he could abide by his principles? The Whigs had put him into a tight spot, which, Upshur reported, "afforded much disquiet to the President and cabinet."[32]

Attorney General Legaré provided Tyler with a solution. He insisted that the prevailing interpretation of the Compromise Tariff was wrong—duties could indeed be collected after June 30 without passage of a new law. Here he explicitly disagreed with Treasury Secretary Forward and, in effect, overruled him. Furthermore, the president could bypass Congress and suspend distribution on his own if tariff rates remained above 20 percent. It was a clever reading of the law.[33]

With this legal cover, Tyler sent his veto message to the House of Representatives on June 29, 1842. The basis for his rejection of the "Little Tariff" bill was its violation of the principles of the Compromise Tariff of 1833 and its abrogation of the Land Act of 1841. There were no constitutional issues at stake as there had been with the bank bills of the special session. Tyler simply believed it better—given the condition of the Treasury—that both laws remain in force. He again argued that a new tariff law providing for higher duties than 20 percent was needed to restore the credit of the United States and allow the federal government to function. He reiterated his support for the incidental protection of American industry and maintained that, instead of being paid to the states, the proceeds from the sale of public lands would be put to better use by reducing the deficit. In short, the veto message restated the very same arguments the president had made to both houses on March 25. Tyler also expressed his "entire willingness to cooperate in all financial measures, constitutional and proper," that Congress may pass to alleviate the country's financial predicament. He would still work with lawmakers if possible.[34]

Furious Whigs—who should not have been surprised by this latest veto—charged the president with "executive dictation." They did not have the votes to override and were not appeased by Tyler's appeal for them to work together to relieve the poor state of the Treasury. They asserted that his "villainous caprice" had supplanted the legislative authority of Congress. Tyler scoffed at the notion. "The Constitution never designed that the executive should be a mere cipher," he wrote to a group of supporters in Philadelphia, knowing they would publish his letter. "On the contrary, it denies to Congress the right to pass any law without his approval, thereby imparting to it, for wise purposes, an active agency in all legislation." Tyler believed these latest charges were the result of policy differences between the White House and Congress and that the Whigs were angry because they could not force him to heel. They were outraged, he pointed out, because he had upheld a law—the Land Bill—they had passed during the special session. He was right. And the Whigs were beginning to look ridiculous.[35]

Whigs were also angry with Tyler at the end of June for another bill he had actually signed into law. After receiving the final population figures from the 1840 census, Congress passed an apportionment bill that adjusted the ratio of the number of people per representative in the House to 70,680 and reduced the total size of that body. The bill further mandated that each state form districts for the purpose of electing members of Congress. Tyler signed the measure but attached a "special message"—what would later be called a presidential "signing statement"—that made clear he had reservations about the new law. As an advocate of states' rights, Tyler expressed his unease with the districting component of the bill, but because he entertained only "doubts" and was not certain of its unconstitutionality, he yielded to the will of Congress. Nevertheless, he wanted his reservations "left on record." John Quincy Adams led the outcry against what the Whigs believed was another example of executive malfeasance by calling the special message an "amphibious production" that violated the separation of powers. Left out of the discussion was the way in which the apportionment bill threatened the political power of the South in national politics. Ultimately, Virginia lost three seats in the House, Kentucky three, North Carolina four, and Tennessee two.[36]

The controversy over the apportionment bill, however, was but a mere sideshow to the fight over the tariff and distribution. Whig leaders realized that as much as they had tried to place the president into a tight spot with the "Little Tariff" bill, he had now turned the tables on them. They had linked the higher tariff with distribution not just because the two measures were favored components of the party's economic program but because passage of both might not result from separate bills. Many southern and western Whigs who favored distribution opposed a higher tariff. Many northern and eastern congressmen who represented manufacturers wanted higher tariff rates but did not enthusiastically support distribution. Neither bloc in Congress could be counted on beyond doubt to maintain strict party loyalty and vote for both. Tyler's bank vetoes had nurtured party cohesion among the orthodox members of the party and ensured cross-sectional party discipline, but this latest veto called the overall Whig strategy into question. "Shall we pass the Tariff, giving up the lands, or adjourn & let all go together?" John J. Crittenden asked Clay. It was a good question.[37]

Clay most emphatically did not want the party to abandon distribution for the sake of securing higher tariff rates. He wanted both and continued to send letters to Whigs such as Crittenden and Mangum demanding that they stay the course. Clay argued that Tyler's latest veto would continue to aid the party: the president was now even more closely linked to the Democrats, and they to him. This was an idea that gained traction in Washington. "The impression is very strong here," one Whig reported, "that there has been an actual bargain & coalition between Tyler and the leading democrats in Congress. And they are now to support warmly & cordially his administration & election."[38]

Clay had succeeded in getting the members of his party to accept this notion. But he did not stop there. The Kentuckian was also intrigued by an idea first raised by Virginia congressman and vocal Tyler hater John Minor Botts shortly after the president's latest veto. On July 11 Botts took to the floor of the House to call for Tyler's impeachment. When Clay seemed a bit too eager to encourage Botts, Crittenden warned him that pursuing impeachment might very well backfire on the Whigs and damage Clay's presidential prospects. The former senator reluctantly concurred but believed the president would eventually face impeachment anyway. The Whigs would continue to insist on distribution, and Tyler would use the veto again—of this he had no doubt.[39]

The veto of the "Little Tariff" bill had raised the stakes for the Whigs and created an even more poisonous atmosphere in Washington than what had hung like a smoky haze over the special session. Clay was enthusiastic about impeachment because he had personally introduced the resolutions in the

Senate calling for constitutional amendments to curtail the ability of the president to use the veto. He earnestly believed—in accordance with Whig doctrine—that the executive held too much power. He was also driven, of course, by personal reasons. Tyler had vetoed two bills that would have created his precious bank. Now, what Clay called the "pranks of a monkey" not only endangered his beloved distribution but also threatened to sharpen differences within the Whig ranks that he so desperately needed to paper over if the party was to trumpet any legislative success from the Twenty-Seventh Congress. Though he never explicitly used this term, in reading his correspondence, one gets the distinct impression that Clay believed he could just not let the president "win" the battle for supremacy in the federal government. To him, it was a zero-sum game. What is also clear is that his retirement from the Senate meant nothing because he was still directing the members of his party from Kentucky. This still was very much Henry Clay's fight with John Tyler.[40]

For his part, the president was angry that one of the "madcaps"—Botts (he could no longer even refer to him by name)—sought his impeachment. "Did you ever expect to see your old friend under trial for 'high crimes and misdemeanors'?" he asked Williamsburg neighbor Robert McCandlish by letter. "The high crime of sustaining the Constitution of the country I have committed, and to this I plead guilty," he wrote with bitterness. "The high crime of arresting the lavish donation of a source of revenue, at the moment the Treasury is bankrupt, of that also I am guilty; and the high crime of daring to have an opinion of my own, Congress to the contrary notwithstanding, I plead guilty also to that."[41]

Tyler had become the first president to face any kind of formal impeachment action. To place this development into its proper historical perspective, consider the following: John Adams had signed the Alien and Sedition Acts into law in 1798, and though he faced vilification in the ranks of the emergent Democratic-Republican Party for violating the First Amendment, no formal attempt at impeachment had been made. James Madison had waged an unpopular war with the British beginning in 1812, but the opposition Federalists had not moved to impeach him. Andrew Jackson had ordered the removal of the national bank's deposits—for which he faced censure. None of these chief executives were threatened with impeachment. But now John Tyler had been?

He could not quite believe how all of this had transpired. "Did you ever expect that the State-rights men of the Whig party were to surrender all their long cherished opinions at the dictation of the National Republicans?" he asked his friend McCandlish. "Did you expect that Clay would have led off the attack on his own Compromise bill of 1833, and his Distribution act of 1841? And yet, because I will not go with him, I am abused, in Congress and out, as man never was before—assailed as a traitor, and threatened with impeachment."

In contrast to his state of mind during the special session, however—when the stress of the bank fight took its toll and he lost the confidence he had shown when he assumed the presidency—in the summer of 1842, Tyler let his anger breed defiance. "But let it pass," he wrote of the impeachment talk. "Other attempts are to be made to head me, and we shall see how they will succeed. J. Q. Adams leads off a new attack shortly, in what, I suppose, will be a denial to the President of the right to give a reason for what he does,—a privilege which J.Q.A. would readily extend to any free negro in New England."

This defiance, to which he added a bit of self-righteousness, did not mean Tyler remained completely immune from the turmoil swirling around his administration. "Politics," he admitted, "have me in their grip." The "miserable squabbles" with Congress had made his life unpleasant, which he found all the more bothersome because of the daily drudgery of his job. As he related to McCandlish:

> My course of life is to rise with the sun, and to work from that time until three o'clock. The order of dispatching business pretty much is, first, all diplomatic matters; second, all matters connected with the action of Congress; third, matters of general concern falling under the executive control; then the reception of visitors, and dispatch of private petitions. I dine at three-and-a-half o'clock, and in the evening my employments are miscellaneous—directions to Secretaries and endorsement of numerous papers. I take some short time for exercise, and after candle-light again receive visitors, apart from all business, until ten at night, when I retire to bed. Such is the life led by an American President.

"What say you?" Tyler asked his friend. "Would you exchange the peace and quiet of your homestead for such an office?"[42]

The hot and humid month of August 1842 was anything but "peace and quiet" in Washington. On August 6 Congress sent Tyler another bill that linked the tariff with distribution. This measure, optimistically called the Permanent Tariff Bill, called for raising import duties well above 20 percent and continuing distribution unabated. Whigs knew Tyler would veto this one as well. The majority of them welcomed this outcome, convinced, as Clay was, that more vetoes meant political doom for the president and more support for their party from the American people.[43]

Although Webster urged Tyler to hold his nose, swallow his pride, and sign this latest measure, he refused. The president duly sent another veto message to the House on August 9. One observer noted that the Whigs, who still could not override the veto, were now "cross and crabbed" and appeared determined "to let the Government get along as it best can without any further action from them." The party was "now perfectly reckless," and many rank-and-file Whigs "seem[ed] to care not a straw what may be the consequences of their action, provided they can embarrass President Tyler." The Democrat John C. Calhoun again neatly summed up the situation. "The Whigs are now divided into two parties," he wrote, "one preferring the Distribution to the Tariff, and the other the Tariff to Distribution; and neither willing to join in a bill simply for revenue with us." Another Democrat, expressing more glee than the dour Calhoun had, exclaimed that the Whigs had "put themselves so clearly in the wrong that instead of 'heading the Captain,' they are, themselves, *headed!*"[44]

But the Whigs made one final attempt to head "Captain Tyler" before Congress adjourned, and it was an ugly display of spite. Instead of formally receiving the veto message, entering its details into their journal, and reconsidering the bill as the Constitution requires, the House leadership referred it to a select committee of thirteen, which would pronounce judgment on the president. This was unprecedented in the history of the United States. John Quincy Adams, who had made the motion to form the committee, was named its chairman. As Tyler had earlier predicted, Adams set out to satisfy a vendetta.

Henry Wise, Caleb Cushing, and George Proffit loudly protested upon the introduction of the motion to form the committee. They, along with newly emergent Tyler supporter William Cost Johnson of Maryland, engaged in what Adams referred to as "bullying and chicanery" for three hours in an effort to quash the motion. They failed. But their stance probably chastened Adams, for at the first meeting of the committee, he informed its members that he would not draft articles of impeachment. When John Minor Botts—a committee member—sought to introduce a resolution in the House asserting a vote of "no confidence" in the president, Adams killed it. This select committee was designed merely to embarrass John Tyler.[45]

Nine of the thirteen committee members signed the resulting majority report, which highlighted two public letters Tyler had sent to Philadelphia supporters (one quoted above) as well as his veto messages and offered a scathing indictment of his entire presidency up to that point. Adams resurrected the old charge that an "acting president" did not have the same authority as one who had been elected to the office; after sixteen months, these bitter Whigs still could not acknowledge that Tyler was duly sworn in and had taken the oath of office. In addition, Adams pushed for a constitutional amendment that would allow Congress to override a president's veto by a majority of both houses rather than a two-thirds vote, giving new life to Clay's Senate resolution from months before.

It was not the finest hour for Old Man Eloquent (Adams). He had, in the estimation of one Washington insider, "shown more temper, obstinacy, & bad feeling than any other man in the House, & it seems to me as if, in his ungovernable passion, he would rather see his Country sunk into a mobocracy than that *any* Tariff should pass." The *Democratic Review* scolded: "Like bad punch, Mr. Adams's report was at once very hot and very weak. It was a document of the meanest partisan attack and abuse against the President."[46]

Tyler agreed. He was furious at what transpired in the House. In his latest veto message, he had asked Congress to reconsider its effort to link the tariff and distribution, virtually pleading with the Whigs to send him a clean tariff bill, one that he could sign. Adams and his committee, however, had had more pressing matters on which they wanted to focus. The House voted 100 to 80 to accept the majority report and its incendiary content, despite the efforts of Charles J. Ingersoll of Pennsylvania—a somewhat surprising supporter of Tyler in this instance—and James I. Roosevelt of New York, who submitted a minority report, and Thomas Walker Gilmer of Virginia, who submitted a counterreport. Both of these documents supported the president's course of action. The resolution to amend the Constitution to take away presidential power failed 99 to 90, a bit too close.[47]

Tyler took no comfort in the outcome of that vote. He lodged a formal written protest against the House committee, denouncing it as "*ex parte* and extrajudicial." In doing so he followed a precedent set by President Jackson, who in April 1834 delivered a blistering protest to the Senate, which had voted to censure him for removing the deposits from the national bank. Tyler fulminated that Adams's committee had "assailed my whole official conduct without the shadow of a pretext for such an assault, and, stopping short of impeachment, has charged me, nevertheless, with offenses declared to deserve impeachment." Moreover, the report lacked "any particle of testimony to support the charges it contains."

The president argued that he was being subjected to the indignity of this committee's report merely because he had dared to exercise the constitutional authority of the executive branch. He would not shrink from his duties as president unless the Constitution was amended to require him to do so. Furthermore, Tyler complained that he had been "made to feel too sensibly the difficulties of my unprecedented position not to know all that is intended to be conveyed in the reproach cast upon a President without a party." He concluded his protest by "respectfully" asking that it be "entered upon the Journal of the House of Representatives as a solemn and formal declaration for all time to come against the injustice and unconstitutionality of such a proceeding." The House refused to do so—on a motion by Botts. The *Democratic Review,* which had taken Adams to task for issuing the report, now chastised Tyler for "very fairly [bringing] down the laugh upon his own head." The matter had become farcical.[48]

Congress had wasted a lot of time. Finally, its members heeded Tyler's warnings. Two separate bills were passed for him to sign—one that would raise tariff rates, and one that would allow distribution to continue after rates rose beyond 20 percent. He signed the Tariff Act of 1842 into law on August 30 and used the pocket veto on the distribution measure. Congress adjourned on August 31. Tyler had gotten what he wanted for the country—after eight long months. By the following summer, the higher tariff led to a sharp increase in government revenue that eliminated the federal deficit. Of course, Tyler received none of the credit among Whigs in Congress or in the party's newspapers.[49]

On Saturday, August 20, President Tyler and his entire cabinet went to the Washington arsenal. Once they arrived, they boarded a steamboat on the Potomac River and fanned out against the railing of one of the decks. The purpose of their visit was to witness a spectacular demonstration by Samuel Colt. The inventor of the multishot pistol was part of a group that had developed a submarine battery—an underwater mine—that could be detonated from as far as five miles away to blow up enemy ships as they entered or exited a harbor. Colt was hoping to persuade the government to invest in the weapon for the nation's harbor defenses and wanted to impress Navy Secretary Upshur, members of Congress, and the president. Operating from nearby Alexandria and signaled by a twenty-four-gun salute, Colt blew up a vessel—an old clam boat—and sent a "column of smoke, water and fragments . . . several hundred feet in the air." Tyler and what one witness described as "half the city" gasped at the destruction. They were suitably impressed.[50]

Congress appropriated $15,000 for Colt to continue his experiments with the submarine battery, despite the efforts of John Quincy Adams, who believed blowing up ships constituted "not fair and honest warfare." Aided by Samuel F. B. Morse's experiments with copper wire, Colt modified the electrical system upon which his invention depended and offered another demonstration for the president in the spring of 1844. This time he needed to fire his mine three times before only a portion of the ship exploded. Ultimately, the House Committee on Naval Affairs did not recommend adoption of the submarine battery.[51]

Nevertheless, Colt's demonstration in August 1842 was a fitting metaphor for what the Whig Party had done during the second session of the Twenty-Seventh Congress. They had blown up the session and almost completely wasted the summer of 1842 with their insistence that President Tyler accept both a higher tariff and the continued distribution of the proceeds from the sale of the public lands. As historian Michael Holt points out, "Whig efforts to enact a distinctive legislative program . . . proved as abortive as in the special session." While it was true that the Whigs had secured a higher tariff, which pleased northern and eastern constituents, they had alienated many of their southern and western supporters by failing to win passage of a distribution bill. Consequently, states did not receive funds they desperately needed to pay their own debts. Moreover, the Whigs won passage of the tariff only because Democrats in manufacturing states like Pennsylvania had voted with them. Thus they could not take full credit for the measure with the voters.

The party was now in disarray and split more than it ever had been. The factionalism cost Whigs dearly in the state elections held during the summer and fall of 1842, as they lost seats in Congress, in governor's mansions, and in statehouses throughout the country. Democrats would soon win control of the House of Representatives. "A succession of disastrous defeats in the State elections has been the consequence" of efforts to get the better of President Tyler, an Arkansas Whig noted ruefully. "Whether we can recover from this tremendous paralysis by 1844 is questionable."[52]

But Tyler also fared badly. He found himself further weakened politically as the Whigs made their break with him complete and further painted him as a Democrat. They tried to isolate him by tying him more closely to the so-called Corporal's Guard, especially Wise, who was becoming ever more unpopular in Congress. Tyler was "a fool guided by the counsels of a maniac," one House member sputtered. Wise was "like a rattle snake or viper in the fall season, when they become blind by the effects of their own poison—he strikes at everything, and I believe would be happy could he destroy the Govt."[53] For their part, the Democrats were not eager to embrace the renegade president who had spurned their standard years earlier. Tyler was now caught in the middle. His failure to win support for the Exchequer plan also weakened him because it proved that appealing to moderate Whigs and Democrats in order to build a coalition willing to support him in 1844 was going to be more difficult than he had imagined—perhaps impossible.

Within the larger historical context, by the end of the second session of the Twenty-Seventh Congress, Tyler had placed a definite stamp on his presidency, one that has often been overlooked by historians. Like Jackson, he expanded the scope of presidential power, with the veto becoming the means by which he exercised that authority. During his term in office, Tyler vetoed ten bills, including four by pocket veto. This total placed him second to Jackson, who had vetoed twelve. Tyler's rank would last until Andrew Johnson, who vetoed a total of twenty-nine bills. From that point on, presidents resorted to the veto much more regularly.[54]

Like Jackson, Tyler believed legislative overreach required the executive to act to prevent unconstitutional or unwise laws from being foisted on the American people. Old Hickory, however, had always claimed that the president was the direct representative of the people and that his actions—including the veto—were calculated to protect them from threats to their liberty the other branches of government may have posed. Jackson adapted his uniquely republican ideology to the age of universal (white) manhood suffrage and greater political participation; in fact, he had helped build the Democratic Party on it. He was forward looking. Tyler, on the other hand, believed the Constitution sometimes had to be protected against what he had referred to during the special session as "a mere representative majority." For him, the potential tyranny of the majority required—demanded—strict allegiance to the oath of office and the promise to uphold and defend the Constitution. So, while he did invoke "the people" at times to defend his course of action, his view of the presidency and presidential prerogative differed from Jackson's. Tyler's understanding of his role was more reactionary than the Old Hero's had been. But both men found the same result politically. Tyler had been sharply critical of President Jackson for abusing his authority, subverting the Constitution, and expanding the scope of presidential power. He had joined the Whig Party to oppose him. Now the Whigs harried him—Tyler—with the same charges of executive usurpation they once leveled at Jackson. The irony could not have been lost on the president without a party.[55]

Chapter 13

A VICTORY IN RHODE ISLAND

All presidents realize immediately upon taking office that they must multi-task and react to simultaneous events that often develop in ways they cannot fully control. John Tyler was certainly no exception. As he fought for ways to replenish the depleted Treasury and sought to cajole a recalcitrant Congress into passing measures that would better the country's dismal financial prospects, the president worked with Secretary of State Webster to lessen tensions between the United States and Britain. Rumors flew throughout Washington that war with the British was inevitable for various reasons (discussed in the next chapter). Thus, in both the domestic arena and in the realm of foreign policy, Tyler faced enormous pressure.

In the spring and summer of 1842, the president was forced to respond to a unique situation that dealt with the proper relationship between federal and state authority. It also required him to interpret his constitutional authority as commander in chief. The particular problem was an insurrection against the state of Rhode Island, what contemporaries and historians have referred to as the Dorr Rebellion, or the Dorr War.

Rhode Island still operated in 1842 under its unamendable 1663 royal charter and had made absolutely no concessions to the Jacksonian era's call for universal white manhood suffrage. Thus, more than 50 percent of adult white males in the state were denied the franchise. The charter also sharply malapportioned the state legislature in favor of the social upper crust from the seacoast towns who had held power in Rhode Island for generations.[1]

Pressure to replace the charter—which elites steadfastly resisted during the 1820s—grew during the 1830s as reformers monitored the democratizing trend in other states. Thomas Wilson Dorr, a thirty-six-year-old Harvard graduate, Providence lawyer, and former member of the state legislature (as well as an unsuccessful candidate for Congress), assumed leadership of a nascent movement calling for repeal of the charter and replacement with a constitution that greatly expanded suffrage. The Rhode Island legislature pointedly ignored the clamor for change, so in October 1841 Dorr and his followers called a "People's Convention" and drafted their own constitution that gave all white men the vote.[2] They then submitted the document to a referendum of all adult white males; the voters approved the measure overwhelmingly. Spurred on by popular support in early 1842, the so-called Dorrites formed their own government and declared the charter government illegitimate.[3]

Attempting to stave off confrontation with the reformers, which Governor Samuel W. King feared might erupt into violence, the state legislature of the charter government drafted a new constitution of its own. Similar to Virginia's 1830 compact, it granted small concessions to the disfranchised. Ratification failed, however, defeated by disdainful Dorr supporters who could actually vote and conservatives who wanted to preserve the status quo. Unable to entice the Dorrites with the modest democratic reforms of their constitution, King's government subsequently made overt support of the People's Constitution or participation in the shadow government acts of treason, punishable by life imprisonment. Of course, this only served to inflame the Dorrites, who now claimed that what they called the "Algerine law" made the charter government's illegitimacy complete. There matters stood in April 1842.[4]

On April 4 Governor King sent President Tyler an urgent letter asking for military intervention from the federal government to put down what he called an "insurrection" in his state. The emissaries carrying this letter, John Brown Francis, Elisha Reynolds Potter, and John Whipple, called on Tyler and several members of Congress. They particularly sought out slaveholders, who they believed would sympathize with their view that the duly constituted laws of a state must be maintained at all costs and that support for the equal rights of all men—which Dorr claimed to stand for—was potentially inflammatory. Tyler made the connection the gentlemen hoped he would make. According to Potter's memorandum of the men's interview with him, the states' rights president expressed his strong belief that a state's laws must be upheld or there would be nothing "to prevent negroes [from] revolutionizing the south."

Still, Tyler was reluctant to intervene in Rhode Island. He could not imagine that the situation there would deteriorate into "frightful disorder" and responded to the governor in writing on April 11 that what the Dorrites had done thus far did not constitute an insurrection. Article IV, Section 4 of the US Constitution—the guarantee clause—granted the president the authority to protect a state's "Republican Form of government" in the event of an insurrection or some other form of "domestic Violence." Separate laws passed in 1795 and 1807 conferred upon the president the authority to use the militia and federal troops to quash an insurrection. But, Tyler pointed out, he had no power to "anticipate" an insurrection and send troops. He could not order insurgents to disperse if no insurgency yet existed. The president did promise that he would not "shrink" from his constitutional duty of safeguarding the people and government of Rhode Island if the situation degenerated into an insurrection, but he would not interfere short of that contingency. Nor would he comment on whether Dorr and his followers had a legitimate grievance against the charter government. He argued that the president could not be made the "armed arbitrator" between a state and its people. In short, Rhode Island needed to address its difficulties without the aid of the Tyler administration.[5]

While not getting exactly what he wanted, Governor King interpreted Tyler's response as a commitment to uphold the charter government, with force if necessary. Dorr interpreted the guarantee clause as having granted the authority to President Tyler to *remove* the charter government. Worried that King had swayed Tyler, Dorr sent his own representative to Washington to meet with the president and wrote to leading Democrats in Congress, such as Levi Woodbury, Thomas Hart Benton, and Silas Wright, pleading with them to use any influence they could marshal to keep Tyler from intervening on behalf of the charter government. Woodbury replied with understatement that the embattled president had "enough other matters to engross his attention and energies without engaging in new troubles over which in my opinion he has as yet no jurisdiction whatever." Many of these Democrats were sympathetic to Dorr's goals; most counseled him to abandon any thoughts of using violence to get what he wanted, arguing that the president could legally intervene only if he had proper cause to do so. Yet none of these Democrats wanted to be publicly associated with the rebellion. Dorr was disappointed. His envoy, Dr. John A. Brown, accomplished nothing in Washington either and, after meeting with Tyler, wrote to Dorr that the president was "the greatest ass I ever see that had the name of an educated man."[6]

King published Tyler's April 11 letter in the anti-Dorr *Providence Daily Journal* in an effort to bolster his position and tilt popular opinion in the direction of the established government. It was a shrewd move. The charter government and the Dorrites were slated to hold separate elections for governor in a matter of days. By showing that he had the support of the Tyler administration, perhaps King could dampen some of the enthusiasm for the "people's movement."

Dorr was elected under the People's Constitution on April 18. King was reelected to a fourth term two days later. Dorr's supporters had voted in what amounted to an illegal election. Nevertheless, the reformers demanded that Dorr be recognized as governor. Naturally, the charter government refused to sanction the results of this extra-legal balloting. The extent to which the publication of Tyler's letter affected popular sentiment in the elections cannot be fully known, but by the end of April, the rebellion appeared to lose momentum. Governor King took steps to prepare for a possible confrontation just in case, certain that the president and the federal government would sustain him if necessary.[7]

King had also sent Tyler's letter to *Niles' National Register,* which published it in the April 23 edition. The governor now sought to shape national public opinion in his favor, while Dorr traveled throughout New York and New England to rally support to his side. By the end of April, national figures of all stripes expressed their anxiety at what was transpiring in Rhode Island. In the pages of the *New York Tribune,* Horace Greeley criticized the Dorrites for rejecting the charter government's new constitution, which granted at least some of what they wanted. John C. Calhoun acknowledged in the Senate that "the subject was a grave one." Supreme Court justice Joseph Story agreed and wrote to Secretary of State Webster in a state of alarm. "The President's letter to Govr. King is as far as it goes, approved by the Mass of thinking men," he declared. "But it is not sufficient to meet the exigencies which have since arisen." Story wanted Webster to use his influence to press Tyler to send two or three companies of troops to Newport so that they would be ready if violence erupted. The justice feared "open warfare" in Rhode Island and predicted to Webster, "If there should be any such evils, the Administration will be blamed vehemently, even although it may be unjustly and without cause."[8]

The *Madisonian* also weighed in on what was happening in Rhode Island and linked what Dorr and his followers were doing to the abolitionist movement, extending further the argument Francis, Potter, and Whipple had made in their meeting with President Tyler. The rebellion was part of a widespread plot, the paper maintained, to subvert the "Constitutions of the Southern States as well the Federal Constitution." Tyler's public support of the charter government, according to this view, and his avowed willingness to use force to defend Rhode Island against armed insurrection would assure "the perpetuity of our noble institutions." The *Madisonian* called on loyal Americans to support the duly established governments in all of the states and to oppose what the Dorrites sought to do—mobilize the people with calls for equality and overthrow the legal government of Rhode Island.[9]

Dorr did, in fact, oppose slavery, and he did support the growing abolitionist movement. He had traveled in the Deep South and had come to resent both the peculiar institution itself and the power of southern slaveholders to shape national politics.[10] But there was no explicit connection between his movement for constitutional reform and the abolitionists; he was not acting at their behest. In fact, New England abolitionists, as well as Rhode Island's African American population, largely opposed the People's Constitution.[11] John B. Jones, the *Madisonian's* editor, found it expedient to make the link, however. The published rhetoric found in the paper served a two-fold purpose. First, it argued that President Tyler had followed the proper course of action by supporting the state's charter government. One would expect this view, though, coming from the administration's organ. Second, and perhaps more importantly for national politics, by framing the Dorr Rebellion in terms of its dangerous implications for the slaveholding South, the *Madisonian* likely made southern Democrats who might have been inclined to support Dorr think twice about that support. The paper thus added another element to a rift in the Democratic Party that had emerged over events in Rhode Island.

Northern Democrats such as Woodbury of New Hampshire sympathized with Dorr's egalitarian impulses and the rebel leader's belief that the people ruled because those impulses reflected a fundamental tenet of Jacksonian democracy. Indeed, Jackson himself expressed his support for what Dorr was trying to accomplish. New York City's Democratic *Evening Post* proposed a memorial calling on the House of Representatives to impeach Tyler for his stance "against the people of Rhode Island." The memorial was never sent, but it did receive the approval of Tammany Hall. Democrats in the North made it very clear on whose side they stood.

Southern Democrats like Calhoun, on the other hand, more reactionary than their northern counterparts, opposed the reform movement in Rhode Island because they rejected its notion of greater equality and the call for broadened participation in the political process. Calhoun, in fact, released a public letter denying the legitimacy of the Dorrites' conception of popular sovereignty. He also rebuked Dorr personally for his tactics in a meeting between the two men at the South Carolinian's boardinghouse. Whether it was intentional or not—and it probably was not—the *Madisonian's* editor, Jones, had succeeded in complicating the relationship between northern and southern Democrats just as they were beginning to consider who might win the nomination of their party for president in 1844. Whether this internecine conflict would redound to the benefit of Tyler's future presidential prospects remained to be seen.[12]

Back in Washington, Tyler was content to appear presidential by monitoring the situation from the White House and reserving the authority to intervene if necessary. He apparently wrote nothing about his feelings for the philosophical underpinnings of the Dorr Rebellion. Based on his political career, and in light of his position as a southern slaveholder, one might assume he stood closer to Calhoun's position than to Woodbury's. Navy Secretary Upshur, perhaps as reactionary as one could be, argued that what was happening in Rhode Island was "the very madness of democracy." Perhaps Tyler concurred. Certainly, he discussed the matter with Upshur—indeed he had consulted his entire cabinet on the Dorr Rebellion in April—but what his attitude was toward the Dorrites themselves and their conception of government by the people we just cannot know.[13]

Whigs generally opposed the Dorr Rebellion. They viewed its leader as a traitor, even though many of them were willing to acknowledge that Rhode Island's constitution did need revision. Southern Whigs took to heart the *Madisonian*'s argument that the rebellion threatened their cherished way of life. "Dorr is president of an abolition society," North Carolina senator William A. Graham observed, making reference to the Rhode Islander's work for his state's branch of the American Antislavery Society, "and of course goes for the largest liberty. And upon his doctrine a majority without regard to color, or condition, have at any time a right to overturn the existing Government, and set up their will in its stead." With so much opposition to Dorr's efforts in Washington, and with the sectional implications of the rebellion muting northern Democrats' support of it, it is no wonder that the reformer grew frustrated as spring wore on.[14]

Concerned that King and the leaders of the charter government were winning the public-relations war through the newspapers, Dorr decided to travel to the national capital himself to seek an audience with the president. On May 10 he went to the White House; Tyler agreed to a brief meeting. It did not go well for Dorr, who left convinced that the president had made a deal with Governor King and the others to support their position in exchange for their backing when Tyler ran for election in 1844. "The Tories hold out to Mr. Tyler the promise of the state for the next presidential campaign," he sputtered to Woodbury, "in which they have no more power to give to him than Satan had to give the Kingdom of the Earth to the Savior." No such agreement had been made, but Dorr had to explain his failure to receive presidential approval for the rebellion in some way.[15]

Tyler may not have engaged in a quid pro quo with King and the charter government's leaders, but he had recently sent two confidential letters to the governor that restated his position. He hoped these would help bring the conflict in Rhode Island to an end. Responding to a brief letter King wrote on May

4, Tyler made clear that his view of presidential authority in the matter had not changed. He reiterated his promise that the federal government would stand behind the charter government if necessary. He also alluded to reports that the Dorrites had lost support among the people of Rhode Island, writing that "the danger of domestic violence is hourly diminishing, if it has not wholly disappeared." Two days later Tyler sent another message to King, advising the governor to issue a general pardon of amnesty for the Dorrites and suggesting that he call a constitutional convention. If these measures failed, the president reasoned, it would provide more justification for the use of force if it became necessary. King responded quickly, assuring Tyler that the Rhode Island legislature would organize a convention when it met again in June and that he had already decided to pardon any of Dorr's followers who decided to withdraw their support for the rebellion and pledge allegiance to the duly constituted government.[16]

Tyler's cabinet sanctioned the president's course of action. Not surprisingly, it was Webster who played the most important role. He used his contacts in Rhode Island to try to arrange a compromise between the charter government and the Dorrites. With his friend Justice Story's warning ringing in his ears, he worked to avoid bloodshed and hoped the president would not be forced to intervene in the matter. Webster's efforts, combined with Governor King's assurances that he would make accommodations to the rebels, satisfied Tyler by mid-May that matters had been largely settled.[17]

His optimism was premature. In the early morning hours of May 18, Dorr ignored more cautious advice and, with a force of roughly two hundred men, attempted to sack the state arsenal in Providence. Advancing against the post in a heavy fog, Dorr demanded its surrender, which was refused; the men inside were heavily fortified and saw no need to give up their posts. Dorr then brought forward two small cannon commandeered from the Providence military academy and prepared to fire. Luckily, the cannon were so old they failed to light. The farcical siege of the arsenal ended with Dorr's men beating a hasty retreat. Their leader should have recognized that his rebellion was now on its last legs, but he vowed to fight on. He next sought to rally potential troops in neighboring states to his cause. Whether from genuine alarm or from a desire to crush the uprising once and for all, Governor King again appealed to President Tyler for assistance and kept up the pressure, insisting that Dorr had enough men and weapons to threaten the charter government and sustain the rebellion indefinitely.[18]

"I had hoped that we were done with Rhode Island," the president complained to Webster on May 27, "but here comes today, by the hands of a *special messenger,* a call from Govr. King for protection against a supposed plot of Dorr to invade the State with troops from Massachusetts and other States." Tyler had lost patience. "I can not think otherwise of it," he wrote of these latest developments, "than as a continuance of the game of brag, which I had regarded as at an end." The president also believed that Dorr's actions "were meant for effect and for purposes of intimidation merely."[19]

The *Madisonian,* however, saw something more sinister afoot. Extending further the argument it had made one month earlier, the paper maintained that the "wire workers who endeavor to get up a violent and bloody scene in RI, are a band of desperate abolitionists." Indeed, the paper declared, the rabble rousers who spurred Dorr and his men on in their efforts to subvert the charter government were "of the same class that instigated the slaves on board the *Creole* to commit murder and mutiny," a reference to an incident that had rapidly become a sore spot for the Tyler administration (discussed in the next chapter). While the pro-Dorrite *Providence Daily Express* quickly reminded the "wiseacre" *Madisonian* that the People's Constitution had excluded African Americans in Rhode Island from voting and thus was not in league with the abolitionist movement, the Tyler administration's organ had succeeded once again in stirring the sectional pot. Other papers in the South followed suit. The *Charleston Mercury* provided its readers with detailed accounts of Dorr's failed attempt to seize the arsenal in Providence, no doubt stoking fears of slave insurrection. The rebellion in Rhode Island had developed into something much more important nationally, and it was becoming much more than an annoyance for President Tyler.[20]

Some of Tyler's Whig enemies in Washington believed that the news of the attack on the arsenal proved that he should have responded more forcefully to the rebellion and readied troops to confront the rebels. "The President at first manifested proper firmness," Senator Graham allowed, "but I very much apprehend as is his nature, he is vacillating, as usual. Had he acted with the energy of General Washington, in the case of the Wisky [*sic*] insurrection, by sending a sufficient force at once to put down all insurrection, it would have ended without loss of life." According to the North Carolinian, "imminent danger of collision" existed because Tyler had not acted decisively in the first place.[21]

Clearly, Senator Graham viewed the recent events through a partisan lens. The president had not been vacillating; he hoped the trouble in Rhode Island would simply go away. Moreover, Graham's comparison of Tyler's conduct to Washington's during the Whiskey Rebellion of 1794 ignored the fact that the whiskey rebels were flouting a *federal* law. The Dorrites had launched a rebellion against their *state's* constitution. Tyler's prudent response to what was happening in Rhode Island fully comported with his constitutional authority as president. Having condemned President Jackson for his threat to use force to stop the South Carolina nullifiers years earlier, the Virginian also refused to play the part of a hypocrite.

Still, Tyler realized he could not ignore what had happened in Providence on May 18. Nor could he take lightly the intelligence that Dorr was raising troops for the rebellion outside of Rhode Island. Tyler ordered Secretary of War John Spencer to the state to assess the situation. He also quietly reinforced Fort Adams, located in nearby Newport, with several companies of troops and instructed Spencer to place the fort's commanding officer, Colonel James Bankhead, on alert for potential violence. Spencer requested that Brigadier General Abraham Eustis, commander of Fort Independence near Boston, find out how successful the rebels had been in procuring weapons in Massachusetts. The president still would not yet authorize troops to support the charter government and hoped that he would not have to order their deployment, but he understood that doing nothing was no longer a viable option.[22]

Rather than order troops into action as Governor King wanted, Tyler asked Webster to find a "secret agent" who could infiltrate the Dorrites and report their intentions to the federal government. "Now I wish you to select a suitable person to get in among the people who will be able to find out their real designs," he instructed his secretary of state. "He will of course act confidentially, & will be selected for his prudence and sagacity." Webster, seeming to enjoy the clandestine nature of his assignment, duly complied with the request. The man he selected has never been conclusively identified but was probably John Plummer Healy, a thirty-two-year-old former law clerk of Webster's. The evidence is clear that the secretary of state engaged the services of this individual, but his name was kept out of Webster's correspondence and most of the federal government's official records. Healy's name is provided, however, on a document listing the disbursements paid out of what was called the president's "secret contingent fund account." Congress had passed a law creating the fund—also referred to as the "secret service" fund—in 1810 to allow the president to pay for contingent expenses without public knowledge as the United States conducted negotiations with foreign governments. Paying Healy out of this fund stretched the interpretation of the law, to say the least. It would not be the last time Tyler and Webster used the secret-service fund to finance covert activities that furthered their policy goals.[23]

The informant reported in early June that the rebellion had largely fallen apart. While King feared the imminent arrival of a large armed force from other states, and while rumors flew that this force had many weapons at their disposal, the informant believed the supposition of rebel strength "does not seem, to say the least, to be a very reasonable one." Moreover, he maintained that Dorr himself no longer had it "in his power to do any further serious mischief." The rebel leader had been "deserted by his followers at home and disgraced in the estimation of those who sympathized with him abroad."[24]

This assessment contradicted Governor King's written account of the situation, which may have been calculated for effect and led Colonel Bankhead to write to Secretary of War Spencer with reports of a rebellion still very much alive. King saw fit to declare martial law in the state on June 25 in response to the formation of a rebel militia in the little town of Chepachet. But Dorr finally recognized on June 27 that he no longer had the support he needed—any support, really—to continue the rebellion and ordered the dispersal of the few troops who stood with him. The next day the charter government's troops arrived in Chepachet expecting a pitched battle; no rebel was there to confront them. President Tyler, obviously unaware that Dorr had given up and influenced by Bankhead's dire reports, ordered Spencer to ready federal troops and militia in Massachusetts and Connecticut to intervene on June 29 (the same day of Tyler's veto of the "Little Tariff" bill). They never deployed. Such was the anticlimactic end to the Dorr Rebellion.[25]

Dorr himself was arrested in 1843, convicted of treason in 1844, and sentenced to life imprisonment. He served one year; the Rhode Island legislature later voided his conviction. The people of the state legally voted for a new state constitution in November 1842, which went into effect in May 1843 and provided for universal manhood suffrage. In the end, the Dorrites got what they wanted.[26]

President Tyler was subjected to more abuse by Congress for his conduct during the rebellion. Senator William Allen of Ohio introduced a resolution in May 1842 demanding a formal inquiry into the president's actions. Senators Calhoun and Preston succeeded in tabling the motion. Later, in the spring of 1844, responding to a petition from Dorr supporters in Rhode Island, the House of Representatives demanded that Tyler turn over all of the correspondence in his possession that related to the rebellion. A committee chaired by Edmund Burke, a Democrat from New Hampshire, investigated. Nearly two years after the matter had been resolved, many in the House—mostly northern Democrats—sought to embarrass Tyler and further tarnish his reputation. The president responded by forwarding the relevant documents and by writing a spirited and legalistic defense of his conduct. Burke's committee prepared a report of nearly one thousand pages that incredibly charged the president with "usurpation." Another report, written by Maryland Whig John A. Causin and much shorter in length, upheld Tyler's actions. Causin's report actually reflected the general attitude toward the president's response to the crisis. The *National Intelligencer*, for example, saw fit to praise Tyler for his actions during the rebellion. And in 1849 the Supreme Court indirectly upheld what he had done in the case *Luther v. Borden*.[27]

As gratifying as this vindication must have been, Tyler had received affirmation during the rebellion that he was pursuing the proper course of action. His cautious yet firm stance had won "him many friends" in Ohio, one of Webster's contacts reported. "He [was] applauded by all the Whigs, in this region, and temperate Democrats [did] not withhold their praise." For good measure, this correspondent even declared that Allen, "the Jacobin of the Senate," had "completely immolated himself. Even Loco Focoism in Ohio, rabid as it is, dare[d] not justify his unprincipled speeches." Closer to home, Upshur found much to admire in his friend. "Knowing what you think of these things," he wrote to Beverley Tucker, "I calculate upon your approbation of what Tyler has done." Finally, there was Webster. He argued that the president had handled himself with "equal discretion and firmness" and that the result demonstrated the correctness of his actions. Webster further maintained that Tyler's conduct in 1842 and his explanation of that conduct in 1844 "will go far towards establishing just ideas respecting the true relations between the government and State governments in regard to this most important provision [Article IV, Section 4] of the Constitution."[28]

For someone who prided himself on his understanding of and respect for the limits the Constitution placed on the president and on appreciating the proper relationship between the states and the federal government, this was high praise indeed. Webster was right: Tyler *had* followed the proper course of action in addressing the Dorr Rebellion. He had faithfully upheld the Constitution and acquitted himself well as commander in chief. The fact that the rebellion had not led to military confrontation validated Tyler's wise course of restraint.

But there was more to it than that. The president's goal throughout much of 1842 was to push for policies that would cast him as a sensible moderate, as someone who could appeal to the political middle and isolate the "ultraism" of the Clay Whigs and the rabid "locofocoism" of the extreme Democrats. Tyler's response to the Dorr Rebellion, then, must be seen not only in constitutional terms, or within the context of presidential behavior, but also in *political* terms—that is, as an outgrowth of his desire to win the presidency in his own right in 1844. It should be viewed as further evidence that he sought a middle-of-the road approach to national problems and would not be held captive by narrowly conceived, rigidly ideological positions, positions that partisans in both camps had expected him to take and, in fact, maintained he had taken, despite ample evidence to the contrary. Tyler had not given up his hope of assembling a coalition that could carry him back to the White House in two years. Moreover, he had once again demonstrated the confidence and purpose he exhibited in those first heady days of his administration. Far from being weak or vacillating, he was the president of the United States—the *entire* United States.

Chapter 14

AGGRESSIVE FOREIGN POLICY

Shortly after midnight on Monday, October 25, 1841, an American merchant brig, the *Creole,* slipped out of port at Hampton Roads, Virginia, en route to New Orleans. On board were ten crew members, seven passengers, several hogsheads of tobacco, and 135 slaves.

Voyages like this traveled down the Atlantic coast all the time. In fact, the Virginia–New Orleans water route had become a nexus of the interstate slave trade, bringing bondsmen and women who had been sold from the Upper South to the Gulf South. The trip typically took nineteen days. Though the duration of the journey could try the patience and will of the crew and passengers, to say nothing of what the enslaved people themselves had to endure, nobody on board the *Creole* had any reason to believe anything out of the ordinary was in the offing.

What happened on November 7, however, made it clear that the ship's voyage would be anything but ordinary. Shortly after nine o'clock that night, a slave named Madison Washington led an insurrection that resulted in the stabbing death of a passenger, one of the slaveholders. Four crewmembers were wounded in the fracas. The rebellious slaves—nineteen in all—commandeered the ship and forced a white sailor to navigate toward the Bahamas, a British possession. The *Creole* arrived at the port of Nassau on the morning of the ninth.[1]

Washington and the other slaves had chosen the Bahamas as their destination because they believed they would be freed per the British Emancipation Act of 1833. British officials in the Bahamas obliged them by emancipating the slaves who had not taken part in the mutiny and refusing to extradite those who had participated to the United States, where they would stand trial for mutiny and murder.[2]

The report of the incident tempered the happiness Tyler had felt upon learning of Alexander McLeod's acquittal in mid-October 1841. McLeod, the Canadian who stood trial for murder in New York State and who had allegedly been involved in the destruction of the American ship *Caroline,* had faced possible execution if found guilty. The jury's verdict had relieved some of the strain in US-British relations. Outrage in the United States over the *Creole,* however, reignited the tension. Southerners demanded compensation for the owners of the newly freed slaves and argued that British actions in the wake of the mutiny affronted American honor. Many pointed to the recently concluded *Amistad* case to bolster their argument. In that instance, rebelling slaves had been freed without compensation because their Spanish captors had illegally detained them in violation of Spain's 1820 statute outlawing the African slave trade. The illegality of the *Amistad*'s voyage meant that the slaveowners were not entitled to compensation. The *Creole*, on the other hand, had been legally engaged in America's domestic, or interstate, slave trade, so most southerners believed that the slaveholders who lost their property in Nassau were entitled to compensation from the British government.

This was part of the argument that Secretary of State Webster—and thus the Tyler administration—made to the British government, which was relayed through the US minister to London, Edward Everett. The "comity of Nations," Webster argued, should have prompted the British to help the *Creole*'s crew regain control of the ship so it could continue its voyage to New Orleans. Moreover, the nineteen rebellious slaves should have been detained on board the vessel for extradition to the United States to face trial for their crimes. No slave should have been freed. British actions in the case threatened peace, according to the Americans.[3]

The British, of course, saw matters differently. Newly installed in London, the Conservative (or Tory) ministry of Prime Minister Robert Peel and his Foreign Secretary, Lord Aberdeen, backed their officials in the Bahamas and made it clear they would not surrender the nineteen mutineers to the United States. The ministry argued correctly that international law did not compel them to do so. British leaders also rejected Webster's argument for comity because they realized public opinion in England tilted strongly in favor of the *Creole* slaves' freedom, no matter what crimes had been committed on board the ship. Recognizing their poor bargaining position, President Tyler and Secretary Webster never made a formal demand for extradition. In London, Everett gamely continued to press Britain for reparations. Nothing came of that.[4]

While the *Creole* affair was an international dispute, it also led to a political firestorm in the United States. American abolitionists galvanized around the issue of compensation, proclaiming that the British were morally and legally correct in their position that reparations should not be paid to southerners whose slaves had been freed as a result of the mutiny. Southern opinion was just as adamant—and just as loud—that reparations were indeed called for. All of this occurred against the backdrop of recently heightened tension between

North and South in Congress over slavery. The "gag rule"—whereby southern congressmen refused to allow abolitionist petitions to be read on the floor of the House—had been in effect since 1837 and had poisoned debate. John Quincy Adams had made it a personal mission to expose the southern leadership in the House for its unconstitutional assault on the First Amendment. Southerners were just as eager to paint Adams as a radical who deliberately stoked the fires of sectional conflict. The last thing American politics, or President Tyler, needed at this point, then, was the *Creole* affair.

At this time the president also found himself personally at the center of another, quite different, controversy over slavery. The abolitionist editor Joshua Leavitt published an article in the antislavery newspaper *Emancipator* that alleged Tyler had fathered children with one of his slaves. The source of the allegations was apparently a northern Baptist minister, "a man," Leavitt solemnly intoned, "of the highest integrity and scrupulousness of conscience." Some years earlier, the minister had visited the Richmond home of a slave mistress and met one of the woman's servants, a "genteel, slender-built, light complexioned young slave" who claimed to be the son of President Tyler, born on his plantation. Named John Tyler, the young mulatto referred to his father as "Governor Tyler," which obviously reflected the time period in which he had been born, probably sometime in the late 1820s. He also claimed that the president had other children by his mother and that they all had likely been sold.

Leavitt found the claims irresistible and mocked the president in the article. "Now," he declared sarcastically, "we would not express the slightest belief that the man who is now the acting President of the United States ever had children by his slaves, or ever sold his own children; although, from what is known of his pecuniary circumstances, and from the general practice among the slaveholders in lower Virginia, it is altogether probable he has supported his family by selling the increase of his slave stock." Leavitt maintained that he had the "fullest confidence, the certainty," that the conversation the minister related had actually occurred. Whether the slave John Tyler "told the truth or not, Gov. Tyler knows; we do not, and therefore tell the story as it was told to us, for what it is worth."

With this summation, Leavitt betrayed the animosity he felt for President Tyler, apart from what he must have felt upon hearing the minister's story. For one thing, he referred to Tyler as the "acting" president, no doubt relishing an opportunity to rub a sore spot. He also alluded to Tyler's often precarious financial situation, both as a way to embarrass him and to offer a plausible reason for why the president may have sold his slaves. Finally, in reminding his readers that it was the "general practice" of slaveholders in lower Virginia to sell their slaves and break up slave families, Leavitt was expressing his disdain for the entire planter class, a common undertaking for abolitionists. Obviously, he was no unbiased journalist.

We do not know if any of the claims are true. Leavitt did not provide the name of the Baptist minister whose account he relied on for the allegations, so there is no way to find evidence related to that source that could possibly corroborate his story. For that matter, the minister may not have existed at all, though it seems doubtful that Leavitt would have made up the entire story out of whole cloth. It is possible the conversation cited in the article occurred exactly as it was portrayed. The young slave the minister claimed to have spoken to may have indeed believed he was the son of John Tyler—and, in fact, may very well have been—but there is no way to verify his story. Local historians in Charles City County have been working for years to track down leads that may finally settle the question of whether Tyler fathered children with slaves. Indeed, their research has yielded fairly convincing evidence that he did.[5]

Tyler himself never offered a public response to Leavitt's allegations. Nor, as best can be determined, is there anything in his private letters that may offer more insight, either in how he felt about the claims or whether they may have been true. We can imagine that the allegations angered Tyler, for he considered himself a man of upright character who valued personal honor above nearly everything else, and Leavitt had clearly called his honor into question. We might also assume that the charges reminded the president of the allegations James Callender had made about Thomas Jefferson and Sally Hemings many years ago. Whatever the case, Tyler remained silent. Instead, the *Madisonian* spoke for him, denouncing Leavitt's allegations as "Gross Slander" and "wretched fabrications." The paper declined to address the specific charges, deeming them beneath the dignity of the president and not worthy of further comment. And with that, the matter shortly faded from view.[6]

The *Creole* affair, however, did not fade so easily. What happened in the Bahamas threatened to derail negotiations between the United States and Britain over the Maine boundary dispute. Webster had made informal inquiries on that issue during the summer and fall of 1841, but little headway had been made in resolving the border.

That problem had festered for years and had been a longstanding source of contention between the two nations. The Treaty of Paris (1783), which ended the American Revolutionary War, had failed to delineate a feasible boundary between the United States and New Brunswick in Canada. Both Britain and the United States claimed some twelve thousand square miles of disputed territory. Nearly eight thousand miles of it was located in Massachusetts and later, after it became a state in 1820, Maine. This land boasted some of the richest timber in the region, and the coastline provided access to plentiful fisheries and a path to the Atlantic Ocean.

The end of the War of 1812 resurrected the boundary issue, as British and American negotiators tried in vain to come to an agreement on the disputed territory. The Treaty of Ghent stipulated that the King of the Netherlands, William I, would arbitrate a settlement between the two nations. In 1831, frustrated by an inability to locate the "highlands," the king gave up and proposed a compromise: the United States would receive almost eight thousand square miles of the disputed territory, while the British would retain territory necessary for the construction of a military road between Halifax and Quebec. Britain looked past the fact that the king had abdicated his responsibility to decide for either Britain or the United States and expressed a willingness to work out a settlement that followed the "Netherlands award." As a US senator in 1831, Tyler had supported the award, as did his friend and colleague Littleton Tazewell. The majority of the Senate and the state of Maine, however, rejected William's judgment. President Jackson refused to weigh in publicly on what had transpired.[7]

There matters stood eleven years later, with tensions having increased in the meantime. Fights over territory between Maine militia and Canadian lumbermen from New Brunswick had broken out in 1839 along the Aroostook River. Cooler heads in the United States and Britain arranged a truce before any loss of life, but both nations worried the so-called Aroostook War would spread. Moreover, the McLeod trial had highlighted the precarious nature of the relationship between the two countries. Both sides now seemed eager to work harder to arrive at a settlement over the Maine boundary, the *Creole* case notwithstanding. The Peel ministry signaled its intentions in March 1842 by sending a special mission to the United States. The head of the mission was Lord Ashburton, and his appointment pleased Tyler and Secretary of State Webster immensely.

Alexander Baring, Lord Ashburton, was the sixty-seven-year-old retired head of the British banking firm Baring Brothers and Company. He had received his peerage in 1835. Tall, nearly bald, and exhibiting the stoutness common to men his age, Ashburton was dignified and stuffy, commanding instant respect among those who met him. He enjoyed the utmost confidence of Prime Minister Peel, Foreign Secretary Lord Aberdeen, and Queen Victoria herself. He was a most credible emissary, and the British government turned to him rather than the cranky British minister in America, Henry Fox, to negotiate an acceptable settlement with the United States. Ashburton's very appointment thus bypassed the normal diplomatic channels.[8]

Besides enjoying the confidence of the ministry, Ashburton had ties to the United States. In 1795 he purchased more than one million acres of land in Maine (which was then part of Massachusetts) from Federalist senator William Bingham and Revolutionary War hero Henry Knox. None of this land was part of the territory in dispute in 1841, by which time Ashburton had sold most of it anyway. Ashburton married Bingham's daughter, Ann Louisa, with whom he had nine children. In 1803 Baring Brothers helped finance the Louisiana Purchase, with Baring playing a pivotal role in the negotiations. The firm had also aided the Bank of the United States in the 1820s and 1830s. More recently, Baring Brothers had served as banker to the US Navy, a relationship that clearly could not continue if the United States and Britain went to war. Finally, Lord Ashburton enjoyed a warm friendship with Webster.[9]

Financial considerations also played a role in the Peel ministry's decision to send Ashburton to America. The Panic of 1837 had poisoned the financial relationship between the United States and Britain. Many states had borrowed heavily from Baring Brothers—and other European firms—to finance internal-improvement projects that otherwise would have entailed raising taxes. By the time Ashburton accepted his mission, eight states and one territory had defaulted on loans, part of the exorbitant $200 million total debt states owed to creditors mentioned by Tyler in his first annual message. Early in Tyler's presidency, Baring Brothers lobbied the administration to pressure these states to resume making interest payments. The state-debt crisis, while not directly related to the issues Ashburton had been selected to solve, nonetheless added an additional layer to the negotiations. And while Baring Brothers did not hold all of the paper from the state bonds, the firm held enough to make it advantageous to have Ashburton in the United States at work on stabilizing relations between the two countries.[10]

From the perspective of the Tyler administration, Ashburton's clout brought another potential advantage. In October 1841 Webster had asked if the Baring firm would be willing to manage the $12 million loan, or bond issue, Congress had approved during the special session; the American market had proved too weak, evident by how little of the bond had been subscribed by that time. The head of American trade at Barings Bank in London, Joshua Bates, notified the secretary of state that his firm would manage the loan if and when Ashburton's mission met with success.[11]

Unknown to the Peel ministry, President Tyler and his secretary of state had been taking steps to ensure the success of the negotiations long before Ashburton arrived in the United States. A man named Francis O. J. Smith had approached Webster in May 1841 offering his help in selling the people of Maine on the benefits of reaching an agreement with the British on the boundary dispute. A newspaper editor, successful businessman, former politician, and all-around shady character, Smith had dozens of influential contacts throughout Maine. He maintained that the people of his home state had so zealously resisted settlement of the dispute because they could not abide giving up any territory to British Canada. Honor and pride had dictated they hold fast, and up to this point, the federal government had not seized the initiative and asserted its authority so that the dispute could be settled. Smith, in fact, had similarly offered his services to President Van Buren, but he had been rebuffed.

Smith's scheme amounted to a propaganda campaign in Maine. Enlisting the aid of influential politicians—outside of normal political channels—and feeding editorials that supported compromise to the newspapers would gradually sway public opinion. If carried off with nuance, the citizens might even come to believe that they had shaped the compromise themselves.

It was a brilliant plan that Smith had pitched perfectly. Webster loved the idea. But would President Tyler find it appealing? Would he vacillate and delay making up his mind? Would he balk at interfering in the affairs of a sovereign state? There was also the question of how Smith would be paid for his services. While claiming to be "solicitous for the honor" of the Tyler administration, such high-minded idealism by itself would not be enough for Smith to make his plan operational. He wanted money. Ever the enterprising capitalist, he was explicit in detailing what he thought the opportunity was worth. "My own compensation I should expect to be definitively fixed at the rate of $3500 per annum—and my necessary traveling expenses, postage & incidental expenses (all subject to your revision and approval) paid by the government." Moreover, if the United States and Britain negotiated a settlement of the boundary dispute, Smith believed he should receive a "liberal commission" for his efforts. "Success," he emphasized, "would warrant almost any expenditure."[12]

When presented with the details of Smith's proposal, Tyler was intrigued. But he had doubts about the propriety of having the federal government attempt to shape events in one of its states, which seemed all the more questionable because it would be done covertly. Webster, however, reminded the president that the United States stood dangerously close to war with Britain. As the nation's chief executive, he had the responsibility to ensure that the country avoided war if at all possible. Tyler agreed. He put aside his states' rights misgivings, convinced that the greater good of the country required him to act in opposition to longstanding personal principles. Finally, there was probably something in the clandestine nature of Smith's proposal that appealed to Tyler. Webster's enthusiasm for intrigue likely helped get the president on board. In the summer of 1841, Tyler agreed to allow Smith to undertake the propaganda campaign.

Once the decision had been made to let Smith conduct his operation, Tyler and Webster debated over how to compensate him. Because the campaign required secrecy, going to Congress for an appropriation with which to fund it was not an option. It was doubtful that lawmakers, who had been looking for ways to cut costs, would have approved such a measure anyway. The president therefore agreed to use the "secret service" fund to pay Smith and his agents. The evidence does not tell us which man—Tyler or Webster—broached the idea of using the fund. They were in agreement, however, that since the citizens of Maine had obstructed settlement on the boundary issue, waging a propaganda campaign in the state constituted an essential element in negotiations with the British. It was a loose interpretation of the law, much like the one employed to justify paying the secret operative sent to Rhode Island to infiltrate the Dorr camp, but it allowed Webster to hire Smith and others as confidential agents of the State Department. "I placed at his [Webster's] disposal," Tyler said later, "from time to time, ample funds to enable him to employ agents who would be most likely to acquire for the government full and satisfactory information, and aid it in its efforts to secure and advance the general good."[13]

Webster provided Smith with the framework of the boundary settlement the Tyler administration wanted and asked him to publish it in a Maine newspaper. He also drew up some basic conditions he wished the state's citizens to agree to and instructed Smith to make them the basis for the argument of his editorials. Sensitive to the administration's concerns that the call for a settlement should not come from the editorial pages of a partisan newspaper, Smith used the *Portland Christian Mirror*, a politically neutral but widely read weekly, as his vehicle for spreading the propaganda. He published three editorials in the paper in late 1841 and early 1842 under the pseudonym "Agricola" (Farmer) that made the case for compromise. Several other newspapers nationwide reprinted these editorials, which guaranteed that people outside of Maine would be privy to the arguments. Webster himself wrote anonymous editorials for the *Washington National Intelligencer* arguing for the need to settle the dispute. He also asked former Maine senator Peleg Sprague and Maine congressman Albert Smith to make discreet inquiries throughout the state about where the politicians stood on the issue. It was a remarkably well-coordinated and effective campaign and successfully laid the groundwork for the negotiations the administration began with Lord Ashburton in the spring of 1842.[14]

꙼ᵁᵞᵈ

Ashburton—traveling without his wife but with three young aides in tow—arrived in Annapolis aboard the frigate HMS *Warspite* on April 2. He reached Washington two days later. Tyler's cabinet greeted his arrival with optimism and high hopes. Ashburton, on the other hand, was not so enthusiastic about the situation he found in America. It did not take long for him to fully understand just how toxic the political atmosphere in Washington was at the time. President Tyler himself appeared "weak and conceited" and out of his depth. Ashburton, never overly fond of what he felt was the capricious nature of American democracy, marveled at the "singular state of parties" in the United States and worried that both the president and Webster might be "powerless" to accomplish anything. He derided America as a "mass of ungovernable & unmanageable anarchy" and wondered whether the republic would survive another year under the Tyler administration. Yet Ashburton cautioned Aberdeen "not to mistake or undervalue the *power* of this Country." War had to be avoided at all costs. Despite his negative characterization of the United States, Ashburton believed his mission stood a good chance of accomplishing this goal.[15]

Webster composed a checklist of the issues he wished to address with his British counterpart. Foremost on the agenda, of course, was the boundary dispute between Maine and New Brunswick. He also sought British acquiescence to American claims in the area between Lake Superior and the Lake of the Woods in the Old Northwest; an apology for the loss of the *Caroline* (the American ship Alexander McLeod had allegedly helped destroy); indemnity to the slaveholders who had lost slaves in the *Creole* incident; American sovereignty over the Oregon Territory, which had been under joint occupation with the British since 1818; and discussion of the right of search and seizure of ships on the high seas, a particularly nettlesome problem that many Americans believed was a threat to their country's honor.[16]

For its part, the Peel ministry was willing to discuss the *Caroline* affair and the right of visit and search on the high seas, but it recognized that the boundary dispute would occupy much of Ashburton's time while he was in the United States. Lord Aberdeen wanted to maintain British control of the St. John River because the waterway aided the Canadian timber trade. He also believed that the Madawaska settlements along the St. John, which were already under Canadian civil jurisdiction, should be formally granted to the British. Beyond these stipulations, he gave Ashburton no specific orders.[17]

While his emissary was making his way across the Atlantic, however, Aberdeen decided to alter his instructions. He had consulted with Britain's military leadership, which believed the Maine boundary dispute should be settled with an eye toward safeguarding territory for a military road between Halifax and Quebec, a component of the previous Netherlands award. Aberdeen thus instructed Ashburton to negotiate for significantly more territory running northeastward from the St. John River than he had originally planned.

This was easier said than done. Ashburton worried that such a demand would imperil the negotiations entirely. He found still more reason for worry when he and Webster sat down for preliminary discussions soon after he arrived. The secretary of state informed him that on April 11, he had sent letters to the governors of Maine and Massachusetts—John Fairfield and John Davis, respectively—asking them to convene special sessions of their legislatures so that commissioners could be appointed who would come to Washington to consult with the Tyler administration during the negotiations. Webster had promised the governors that no settlement of the boundary would take place unless the commissioners granted their unanimous approval; obviously, he wanted it to appear that the Tyler administration was acting with the concurrence of the states. Taken aback, Ashburton agreed to allow the commissioners to participate but was not happy about it. He thought introducing more actors into the process of negotiation would entail confusion and needless delay, and they might scotch any agreement he and Webster worked out. Ashburton grumpily insisted that the state commissioners deal only with Webster; he wanted no contact with them. The American agreed to this condition but did not share his counterpart's misgivings about allowing state commissioners to play a role in the negotiations. He had already let Governor Fairfield know through backchannels that there was a historical map in the French national archives in Paris, as well as another located in the State Department collections, that supported the British claim to territory in Maine. Providing Fairfield with such evidence of the validity of the British position essentially scared him into submission and served to lower expectations in Maine, which would give the Tyler administration political cover for a final settlement. Moreover, Francis Smith's propaganda campaign through the newspapers was well underway. Webster was confident the commissioners would not dare scuttle the negotiations.[18]

Historian Frederick Merk, a famed scholar of American antebellum politics and diplomacy who made the 1840s his obsession, cautioned against crediting the propaganda campaign waged in Maine with too much influence in pushing residents of the state toward acceptance of a settlement of the boundary dispute. As Merk put it, "Changes in the climate of public opinion are the work ordinarily of basic forces, and this was true in the case of Maine." For example, he points out that the Whig sweep of the state in the 1840 elections had brought to power men who were philosophically more amenable to a compromise with Great Britain that would settle the boundary dispute. Moreover, the long-term economic malaise brought about by the Panic of 1837 stimulated a desire for peace with Britain, which many believed would restore confidence in the transatlantic markets. Merk further argues that the "service of Smith was to turn such forces in Maine towards acceptance of an untried mode of removing an old source of disorder and danger."[19] He is correct in all of this. The fact remains, however, that by the middle of June 1842, as Webster and Ashburton began a concentrated period of negotiation, the Tyler administration found itself in an advantageous position in no small part because of the secret machinations at work in Maine. The *Portland Eastern Argus*, the state's Democratic bellwether and a highly influential paper outside the state, changed its stance from opposing a boundary settlement to offering full support for whatever the administration could accomplish in Maine's behalf.[20] This turn of events, as well as Governor Fairfield's conversion and the legislature's eventual willingness to appoint commissioners to Washington, cannot be explained merely by "basic forces." Rather, it was Webster's agency, complemented by the approval and oversight of President Tyler, that ensured the necessary preconditions for a successful outcome of the negotiations. Shaving the rough edges from his ideology, Tyler had engaged in a bit of realpolitik.

Once negotiations began in earnest, President Tyler displayed remarkable agency himself. In fact, he played a more decisive role in the completion of the treaty that resulted from the negotiations with Ashburton than anyone at the time realized. While Secretary of State Webster received most of the accolades for the treaty, both at the time and historically, Tyler's involvement in every phase of the process charted a new course. His efforts marked a departure from the way diplomacy had been conducted previously in the early republic and represented an attempt to enlarge the authority of the presidency. Yet at the same time he conformed to the role the Constitution prescribes to the chief executive.

Tyler played an active role in the talks with Ashburton. This did not mean he was always in the room with the two men; in fact, he usually was not. But the president offered suggestions to his secretary of state and pored over the correspondence and notes of the proceedings every night so that he could direct the course of the give and take the next day. For example, the president detailed to Webster the changes he wanted made to the record of the negotiations that addressed the *Creole* incident. "The substitution of a few words in some places and addition in others will make it entirely acceptable," he wrote, after reading Lord Ashburton's draft on the matter late in the process.[21]

The evidence clearly shows that the president directed—or micromanaged—the negotiations. As Tyler's second wife put it four years later, Webster "acted under the counsel or after the direction of the P[resident]." Tyler "was the *direct* and Webster only the *passive* agent in every act and every line of correspondence relating" to the resulting treaty. Mrs. Tyler's account no doubt rests too heavily on the pride she felt for her husband. But letters from Webster, both in the immediate aftermath of the negotiations and years later, indicate that Tyler had played a significant role in the process. Once the treaty had been ratified, a grateful and gracious Webster assured Tyler: "I shall never speak of this negotiation, my dear Sir, which I believe is destined to make some figure in the history of the county, without doing you justice. Your steady support and confidence, your anxious and intelligent attention to what was in progress, and your exceedingly and obliging and pleasant intercourse, both with the British minister [Lord Ashburton] and the commissioners of the States, has given every possible facility to my agency in this important transaction."[22]

Part of that "exceedingly and obliging and pleasant intercourse" could be found during a party Priscilla Tyler planned in honor of Lord Ashburton as well as smaller gatherings at the White House. An often overlooked aspect of the Webster-Ashburton negotiations is how these events soothed the elderly British envoy and calmed the frayed nerves of everyone involved as the hot summer of 1842 dragged on. "I contrive to crawl about in these heats by day & pass my nights in a sleepless fever," Ashburton grumbled at one point. "In short," he told Webster, "I shall positively not outlive this affair if it is to be much prolonged." Luckily, Ashburton's White House host knew how to entertain. Priscilla did her part to move the negotiations along; the party honoring

Ashburton was a success, much like the one for Charles Dickens had been some months before.[23]

President Tyler also employed his famed southern charm. At one point Ashburton's patience with the talks ran out. Irritated by the demands of the commissioners from Maine and Massachusetts, whose nitpicking made them a bit more troublesome than Webster had anticipated, he threatened to pack up and sail home to Britain, leaving every issue between the two countries unresolved. "I had hoped that these Gentlemen from the North East would be equally averse to this roasting," Ashburton groused as he suffered through yet another sweltering day in Washington. "Could you not press them to come to the point," he implored Webster, "and say whether we can or can not agree? I do not see why I should be kept waiting while Maine & Massachusetts settle their accounts with the General Government." For a moment, Webster's optimism escaped him. He looked to the president.[24]

"My Lord," Tyler addressed Ashburton as the two men sat down together one morning. "I cannot suppose that a man of your lordship's age and personal position, retired into the bosom of your family after a long and successful life, would have crossed the Atlantic on so arduous a mission, unless you had truly come with the most painful desire to close the unhappy controversies that now threaten the peace of the two countries." Eyeing the president intently, Ashburton nodded. "Your lordship could have felt none of the ordinary diplomatic temptations," Tyler said, "and if you cannot settle them, what man in England can?" Tyler's skill in dealing with people—start with a compliment—was on full display. The flattery continued for a moment or two more, with the president again stressing how important the mission was to the relationship between Britain and the United States. Ashburton had come all this way and should not let the oppressive Washington heat or the churlish state commissioners distract him from the matter at hand. Tyler had won him over. "Well! Well! Mr. President, we must try again," Ashburton exclaimed, willing if not necessarily eager to resume negotiations.[25]

This exchange between the president and Lord Ashburton demonstrates Tyler's facility in negotiation. His agency in the process was not confined to behind-the-scenes wrestling with the treaty's wording, though this he did with vigor. Nor did it involve merely making his wishes known to Webster and placing upon him the responsibility of working out the details, though this occurred as well. Anticipating the actions of several twentieth-century presidents—Franklin Roosevelt, Jimmy Carter, and Ronald Reagan come to mind—Tyler became a diplomat himself and demonstrated a remarkable ability to know just what was called for at the appropriate moment in the negotiations. He was insistent when he needed to be, understated and willing to let Webster take the lead when he believed that course of action was in the best interests of his administration, and perfectly adept at stoking Ashburton's ego when circumstances called for it. No detail was overlooked.

Tyler also recognized that these negotiations required a delicate balancing act. "The President has felt the deepest anxiety for an amicable settlement of the question," Webster explained to the Maine commissioners, "and such as should preserve the rights and interests of the States concerned." Tyler had "sedulously endeavored to pursue a course the most respectful towards the States, and the most useful to their interests, as well as the most becoming to the character and dignity of the Government." He made sure that Webster repeatedly made clear to the state commissioners that the administration sought to defend their interests. But he also wanted these men to know that their interests could not trump the welfare of the entire United States.[26]

Tyler did all of this, of course, amid tremendous political and personal stress. "The President has again vetoed the Tariff this morning," Ashburton informed Lord Aberdeen on August 9, "and parties are in great commotion." The British envoy could also report that the weather had become more "temperate" by this time, but there was nothing temperate about the way the Whigs assailed the president over this latest veto. Trying mightily to compartmentalize and keep domestic politics from intruding on the negotiations with Ashburton, Tyler faced a losing battle. Webster wrote to Everett earlier in the summer that the Whigs in Congress sparked "resentment" in the president and made him irritable. Making matters worse, rumors flew throughout the summer that removals or resignations of cabinet members were imminent. Tyler found little solace in the living quarters of the White House either as Letitia's health worsened. The president could not escape the stress, which was even greater during the summer of 1842 than it had been one year earlier.[27]

Thankfully, by the end of July, the details of a treaty had been hammered out. The United States received more than seven thousand of the twelve thousand square miles of territory in dispute. Webster secured title to southern Madawaska, free navigation of the St. John River, and a boundary line that gave the westernmost land south of the St. John to the United States. The agreement granted American ownership of an area called Rouse's Point, which protected more than two hundred miles of frontage in New York and Vermont along Lake Champlain. Secretary of War Spencer expressed particular pleasure in this part of the treaty, for control of Rouse's Point allowed the United

States to retain the most important invasion route into Canada, should it ever be needed. Finally, Webster and Ashburton worked out a settlement of the boundary between the United States and Canada that ran from Lake Superior to the Lake of the Woods. Unknown to either of the two principal negotiators, the 6,500 square miles of territory granted to the United States contained some of the richest iron ore in North America. Indeed, the Vermilion and Mesabi ranges in what became the state of Minnesota proved a boon to the United States in the last quarter of the nineteenth century.[28]

The British may have conceded more territory to the United States in the treaty, but Ashburton and the Peel ministry believed they had won important concessions as well. They had acquired a buffer zone of territory of some 5,000 square miles between Canada and the United States, out of which they could build their military road connecting Halifax to Quebec. Moreover, while the Netherlands award of 1831 had placed the border of the United States within thirty miles of Quebec, through the treaty, the border was now set at fifty miles from the province. Finally, the British gained valuable timberland along the northern tributaries of the St. John River. In sum, both nations benefited from the pact. It had been a true compromise.[29]

꒰꒱

The boundary issue was, of course, the most important point of contention between the Tyler administration and the Peel ministry, but there were other components of the treaty.[30] Webster had other items on his "checklist" that he wanted to resolve. The easiest to settle concerned the lingering American resentment over the *Caroline* incident. It galled Americans that the British had sanctioned the destruction of the vessel. Ashburton offered an informal apology for what had happened.

Less easily resolved were the issues related to British policy toward American ships on the high seas. Both Tyler and Webster had entered into negotiations with Ashburton determined to win formal British disavowal of the impressment of American sailors. "Would it be possible," Tyler asked his secretary of state, "to induce G. B. to abandon the claim to impress seamen in time of war from American ships[?]" The practice, which violated freedom of the seas and had contributed to the War of 1812, had been curtailed since the Treaty of Ghent in 1815, largely because the British had found it impractical to continue it. Nevertheless, the British government would not officially renounce it. Ashburton called impressment "the most serious cause of animosity and ill will" and worried it would hamper negotiations and prevent settlement of the boundary issue. If it had been up to him, he would have offered the United States the concession Tyler wanted. In the end he agreed to end impressment in a series of diplomatic notes, but not in the formal treaty.[31]

Lastly, and more significant than impressment, was another issue that concerned action on the high seas, the final item on Webster's agenda: the right of "search and visit." Since 1807, when it abolished its own slave trade, Britain had sought to suppress the international trade in enslaved Africans. Beginning in the 1820s, ideas had been floated in both Britain and the United States calling for joint cruising missions that would patrol the waters off the West African coast and prevent ships from carrying slaves to destinations in the Americas. Nothing had come of these ideas. By the late 1830s, Britain had finalized treaties with every maritime nation except the United States that granted the Royal Navy the right to search ships sailing under the flags of those nations on the high seas that they suspected of carrying slaves.

Conceding the right of search would have been tantamount to allowing the Royal Navy to regulate US maritime commerce. Unfortunately, American refusal to allow that right had yielded a particularly repugnant consequence. Slave traders from other nations began flying the US flag to prevent British patrols from boarding their ships. The practice was illegal, but it worked: an estimated 16,000 Africans, in fact, had been brought to the Americas under the Stars and Stripes in 1841 alone.[32]

The British government took a bold step late in 1841 to end this practice and prevent interference with the Royal Navy's efforts to suppress the international slave trade. The Peel ministry organized the London Convention and signed an agreement with four other European powers—Austria, France, Prussia, and Russia—called the Quintuple Treaty. This pact formally renounced the slave trade as piracy and allowed each signatory the mutual right to search their counterparts' ships on the high seas to determine if enslaved Africans were on board. Britain hoped the treaty would pressure other nations—especially the United States—to join the five signatories and allow the right of search.

The implications of the Quintuple Treaty were enormous and potentially troubling for the United States. For one thing, the treaty revised international law. It had long been precedent that no nation could have its ships searched by those of another nation except in times of war (the main reason why impressment so riled Americans) unless a bilateral treaty allowing for the right of search had been signed. Most nations refused to allow a "search" of their vessels as they sailed, though many did recognize a peacetime right of "visit"—a less formal process—that ensured all ships would know the true nationality of the others they encountered. With the Quintuple Treaty, however, Britain aimed to institute a peacetime right of "search," or what it alternatively called "examination," in an effort to stop ships from carrying slaves across the Atlantic Ocean. The treaty stipulated that any ship suspected of involvement in the international slave trade would lose the protection of its flag and would be subject to search. Moreover, the burden of proof of a ship's nationality, which under international law had fallen on the captain and crew of the ship conducting the search, now fell to the captain and crew of the ship being searched. President Tyler grasped the significance of the treaty and did not like it.[33]

Just as troubling, the Quintuple Treaty established an immense area from the Indian Ocean to the Atlantic coast of the United States and the Gulf of Mexico as the zone of search. The coastlines of Georgia and Florida, in addition to those states along the Gulf, were included in the zone, meaning that part of the water route for America's domestic slave trade was subject to the terms of the treaty. It appeared the British government was encroaching on American slavery.[34] Why?

The answer, largely, was economics. For all of its antislavery rhetoric and moral leadership in the worldwide effort to promote abolition, by 1842, leaders in Britain had come to see that they had a distinct financial incentive for weakening the international slave trade and undermining slavery wherever it existed, particularly in Cuba and Brazil but in the American South as well. When Britain abolished slavery throughout its empire in 1833, its colonies in the West Indies converted to an economy based on free labor. Policymakers in London believed at that time that the free-labor system in their colonies might not come close to replicating the profits they had enjoyed under slavery. For this reason, they called abolition in the West Indies the "Great Experiment." By the time John Tyler became president, British leaders realized that the experiment had failed; free labor could not compete economically with slave labor. Their only option, then, was to make the world safe for free labor by undertaking a concerted effort to abolish slavery everywhere. The British would portray their efforts to do so in humanitarian terms and would use the international abolitionist movement as a cover of sorts to further their fundamental economic goal.[35]

Duff Green, traveling in England as an unofficial—that is to say, self-appointed—agent of the Tyler administration, had begun to dissect Britain's true intentions in January 1842. In letters to both Senator Calhoun and President Tyler, he argued that England's "war on slavery and the slave-trade is intended

276 PRESIDENT WITHOUT A PARTY

to increase the cost of producing the raw material [cotton or sugar] in the United States, Brazil, and Cuba, that she can sell to other rival manufacturing, continental powers, the product of her East India possessions cheaper than they can purchase from us." Green also maintained that there was "much more than a work of benevolence in the suppression of the slave-trade." He even went so far as to warn that the United States should be prepared for war with Great Britain.[36]

The Peel ministry, of course, wished to avoid war and hoped the United States could be induced to join the signatories of the Quintuple Treaty. In fact, Lord Ashburton's mission to America had been conceived with that very goal in mind, and he had been given wide latitude to negotiate the boundary issue on terms highly favorable to the United States with the hopes that such generosity would bring the Tyler administration into the international fold. The failure of France to ratify the Quintuple Treaty, however, foreclosed this possibility, and Lord Aberdeen instructed Ashburton to avoid even mentioning the treaty. He was also not to initiate discussions on the right of search or the right of visit. So he was pleasantly surprised when Webster broached the subject of suppression of the African slave trade and volunteered American ships to cooperate with the Royal Navy in a joint-cruising scheme along the West African coast. Again, this idea was not new. Webster was surely aware of the past efforts to bring such a plan to fruition.[37]

The joint-cruising agreement—embodied in Article VIII of the final treaty—committed the United States to sailing an African squadron to quell the slave trade on the high seas. That force would match the British effort. The United States would also join Great Britain in formally denouncing nations that engaged in the trade. Ashburton was elated. "If this arrangement can be brought to execution by Treaty," he wrote Aberdeen, "I shall consider it to be the very best fruit of this mission."[38] Tyler agreed—to a point. When submitting the treaty to the Senate for ratification, he noted that "the treaty obligations subsisting between the two countries for the suppression of the African slave-trade . . . could not but form a delicate and highly important part of the negotiations which have now been held." His view of the success of this particular part of the negotiations, of course, was much different than Ashburton's. The president further added that the treaty "propose[d] no alteration, mitigation, or modification of the rules of the law of nations." In short, the pact upheld the maritime law of freedom of the seas, neutralized the British right of search, effectively killed the Quintuple Treaty, and allowed the United States to take credit for working to eliminate the African slave trade.

The administration had pulled off a remarkable maneuver. Tyler himself had seen to the final wording of Article VIII.[39]

The administration also won a concession from Ashburton relating to the *Creole* incident, though officially this particular settlement did not become part of the treaty itself. While Britain would not surrender the vessel's mutineers to the United States, the Peel ministry would see to it that American ships would receive no "officious interference" should they be diverted into the ports of British colonies "by accident or violence" in the future. Tyler worried about how "officious interference" would be interpreted, belaboring the point in a note to Webster. The secretary of state relayed the president's concerns to Ashburton and told him that Tyler believed it "to be for the interest of both countries that the recurrence of similar cases in future should be prevented as far as possible." Ashburton agreed but thought that Tyler was nitpicking. Calling the president's note "querulous and foolish," he reported to Lord Aberdeen that the "settlement on this point was at last but sulkily received by him [Tyler]."[40]

The actual legal settlement of the *Creole* case did not occur until 1853, some eight years after Tyler left office. Ashburton had agreed to submit the matter to arbitration during negotiations, and an Anglo-American claims commission awarded a sum of $110,330 to indemnify the slaveholders who had lost their bondsmen in the mutiny.

꽃

William Cabell Rives, chair of the Senate Foreign Relations Committee, and still an ally of Tyler, shepherded the Treaty of Washington (it would not be referred to as the Webster-Ashburton Treaty until 1871, when the Grant administration negotiated another Treaty of Washington with the British) through the Senate. The pact was ratified on Saturday, August 20, 1842. The vote of 39 to 9 was 7 votes more than the constitutionally required two-thirds threshold. After the intense turmoil of the past sixteen months, John Tyler finally had a significant accomplishment to his credit. Both nations preserved their honor, and war had been averted.[41]

Abel Upshur wrote that the treaty promised to remove "every possible cause of dispute with England for years to come." His view was shared by many in the capital, and he was largely correct in his prediction. Some Democrats, however, with Senator Benton (of course) leading the charge, found fault with the administration's efforts. Benton gave a longwinded speech in the Senate blasting Tyler and Webster for committing the United States to an "entanglement" with Britain, for not receiving explicit renunciation of impressment, and for capitulating on the right of search and visit. The president was appalled. "He [Benton] stood by with his arms folded during Jackson's and Van Buren's administrations," Tyler angrily wrote to Webster, "and permitted almost a surrender of the principle involved in the *Creole,* and now shows wonderful zeal." Some things never changed.[42]

The criticism did not end with Benton. Lewis Cass, US minister to France, resigned his post in protest of the treaty because it did not specifically renounce in all cases the right of the British to board American vessels on the high seas. While Tyler knew that Cass was playing politics and had been in the process of engineering his resignation so that he could return to the United States and seek the Democratic nomination for president in 1844, the criticism still stung. Tyler sought to address the subject in his second annual message to Congress in December 1842, when he made clear his position that Britain's new so-called right of visit "was regarded as the right of search presented only in a new form and expressed in different words." Furthermore, he maintained that "all pretense is removed for interference with our commerce for any purpose whatever by a foreign government." That statement muted criticism at home but had the effect of angering the British, who read this part of the treaty differently from the president; they maintained the treaty allowed them to retain the right of visit. Tyler and Webster spent the next two months assuring the Peel ministry that nothing had changed since the treaty had been signed. Tyler stood firm, however, on his contention that he had yielded no ground. Many years later, facing renewed criticism from southerners who sought to reopen the African slave trade and who argued that the Tyler administration had bargained away American rights, he vigorously challenged the contention that he had made any concession to the British government.[43]

Looking more closely, it becomes apparent that Tyler was not absolutely correct in his characterization of Article VIII. Perhaps more accurately, the wording of Article VIII lent itself to *both* his interpretation *and* the one the British claimed. The ambiguous passage in the text reads "as exigencies may arise, for the attainment of the true object of this article"—that is, for the suppression of the African slave trade.[44] Read broadly, one can see that there actually was a scenario in which the British might board an American ship, if only inadvertently: for example, if the Royal Navy suspected another nation's vessel of flying the US flag illegally. In that case—in that "exigency"—British sailors might very well demand access to a ship that was, in fact, American. Tyler could not publicly concede the point, however, or he would lose face.

The portion of his December 1842 message to Congress in which he defended his administration on the right of search very deliberately turns on one word, "commerce." Tyler carefully claimed that there would be no interference with American *commerce* from any nation on the high seas. This would, of course, be literally true, though this particular phrase in the message artfully side-stepped the issue of whether the British could *ever* search or visit an American ship—certainly a wise political move given the temper of the times. More-over, by asserting that no nation would interfere with US commerce, Tyler had played to the American people's fear and indignation over what the British had done in the past with impressment. Perhaps he hoped this clever dodge would be enough and that the public would infer or assume that he meant the British had no right to ever search an American ship.

Controversy aside, Tyler had carved out a new role for the president in the treaty-making process, one that previous chief executives had largely delegated to other men. He read the clause of Article II, Section 2 of the US Constitution that gave the president the power to "make treaties" literally, which of course comported with his longstanding affinity for strict construction. His agency in the process was unmistakable. Webster acknowledged that "the negotiations proceeded from step to step and from day to day under the President's own immediate supervision and direction." Tyler "took upon himself," he wrote, "the responsibility for what the treaty contained and what it omitted."[45]

Also vitally important to the successful conclusion of the Webster-Ashbur-ton Treaty—and important to understanding Tyler's agency in the process—was his use of the secret-service fund. Congress had appropriated the money for the president's use expressly "for the contingent expenses of intercourse between the United States and foreign nations." Critics of Tyler in the 1840s, as well as some historians, have charged that the president's disbursal of the money from the fund in this instance was illegal. They argue that because the fund was used to influence sentiment in Maine and not for matters of foreign relations, per se, it should have remained in the federal coffers. One scholar has even gone so far as to declare that Tyler "engage[d] in one of the most bla-tant abuses of presidential covert authority in American history."[46]

Such criticism is unwarranted, though it must be pointed out that with his use of the fund, Tyler interpreted the law broadly and thus moved away from his longstanding belief in strict construction. Moreover, he had willfully exercised federal authority in the affairs of a state, albeit secretly. He pointed out later that his goal was to "induce Maine to unite with the government in an effort to settle the questions in dispute." The position that local politicians had taken—to give no quarter to the British and relinquish no territory—had hardened by 1841, so much so that Tyler could not contemplate beginning serious negotiations with the British over the boundary issue (or anything else, for that matter) unless and until he had laid the groundwork Francis Smith promised when he volunteered his services. Thus, the nature of the "intercourse" between the United States and Britain would have been drastically altered had Tyler *not* used the secret-service fund in the manner in which he did. Tyler's creative use of the fund, and his willingness to allow Webster to take care of the specific details as to how it would be used, were important to removing the most significant obstacle to successful negotiations with Lord Ashburton. Tyler had thought broadly and used all the tools at his disposal to play a leading role in the treaty-making process.

Nearly four years after the ratification of this treaty, Congress investigated Secretary of State Webster for alleged malfeasance in his use of the secret-service fund. Tyler traveled to Washington in June 1846 to appear before two select committees responsible for the investigation, in part to defend Webster of the charges, in part to defend his administration's conduct in the months preceding the Webster-Ashburton negotiations, and in part to justify his use of the fund. The appearance of an ex-president during the proceedings of a congressional hearing was in itself unprecedented. In fact, it marked the first time an incumbent or former president had received a congressional subpoena. Unfazed by the hostility and tension he faced, Tyler calmly and methodically answered the charges. His testimony succeeded in exonerating Webster and quashing further investigation of his administration. The House gave him no more trouble on the use of the fund.[47]

Tyler's testimony affirmed in his mind the correctness of his course during the Webster-Ashburton negotiations. "By night and by day I dreamed and thought only of a fair and honorable adjustment of our difficulties," Tyler wrote later, as he reflected on his role in the treaty, "and contributed all in my power to bring about a happy termination to the negotiation." The treaty eased most of the tension that existed between the United States and Britain until the unresolved Oregon question—the one item on Webster's checklist that did not get addressed—later became an issue. Tyler mentioned Oregon in his second annual message and made clear his position that "every effort should be resorted to by the two Governments to settle their respective claims" there.

Perhaps the only downside to the treaty for the United States was the refusal of Barings to finance the American loan. But Tyler did not dwell on this disappointment. By any measure, the Webster-Ashburton Treaty represented a significant achievement. "So far the administration has been conducted amid earthquake and tornado," Tyler recounted to his friend Tazewell in October 1842, "and yet if it had nothing else to point to but the English treaty as the result of the last eighteen months, I think it would be entitled to some small share of praise."[48]

In the wake of the successful negotiations, President Tyler took steps to further assert himself in the realm of foreign policy. Hawaii's king, Kamehameha III, dispatched emissaries to the United States to press the administration for formal American recognition of Hawaiian sovereignty and independence. More broadly, the king hoped that securing such recognition from the United States would force Great Britain and France to adopt the same policy toward the islands.

On December 30, 1842, Tyler sent a special message to both houses of Congress spelling out what would soon be called the Tyler Doctrine. He asserted America's interest in preserving Hawaii's independence and warned world powers that the United States would not tolerate colonization efforts in the islands. With his brief message, and with Secretary of State Webster's concurrence and aid (Webster had probably written the message), President Tyler had extended the Monroe Doctrine to the Pacific and established an American sphere of influence in Hawaii that guided US policy there until annexation of the islands in 1898. He had also done so with very little financial commitment, recommending that Congress provide funds only for a consulate in Hawaii rather than a full diplomatic contingent.[49]

In the same message that announced his administration's policy toward Hawaii, President Tyler articulated the first US policy toward China in the nation's history. He noted that the recently concluded Opium War between China and Britain terminated with the Treaty of Nanking, which naturally favored the victorious British: among other provisions, including the cession of Hong Kong, China had been forced to open four new ports to English trade. Before the treaty, other nations—including the United States—only had access to Canton. Tyler wanted to ensure an expanded American access to Chinese ports and urged Congress to appropriate money to fund a mission to China. On March 3, 1843, Congress did so. Tyler's friend Caleb Cushing accepted the appointment to head the mission.[50]

The resulting Treaty of Wangxia—ratified by the US Senate—added to the list of Tyler's foreign-policy accomplishments. The administration had proved naysayers in Congress wrong and had added substance to the goal of developing formal American policy in East Asia. Tyler had laid the groundwork for future American interests in China and had oriented the direction of future US foreign policy toward the Pacific. Even better, the United States had muscled its way to parity with the British in China and jumped to the head of the pack in establishing a western presence in the Pacific, which played well with the American people. The opening with China—as well as the policy toward Hawaii—was, in the words of one historian, the "godfather" of Secretary of State John Hay's Open-Door Notes of 1899–1900. The administration's efforts also led directly to Commodore Matthew C. Perry's successful expeditions to Japan in 1853–54. Tyler was proud of his triumphs and predicted in the last months of his presidency that "the influence of our political system is destined to be as actively and as beneficially felt on the distant shores of the Pacific as it is now on those of the Atlantic Ocean." John Tyler was far more successful in the realm of foreign policy than he would ever be in domestic politics.[51]

Chapter 15

A TYLER PARTY?

Monday, September 12, 1842, in the words of one Washington resident, was the "hottest day of this season." Within the last week, a sweltering late-summer heat wave had enveloped the capital. Rain was nowhere to be found. The soaring mercury had made merely walking the dusty streets all but unbearable. Congress had adjourned on August 31, and most of the politicians had fled for their home states a short time later, seeking respite from both the weather and the acrid partisanship that had characterized this session as it had the last.[1]

Ordinarily, a hot spell would not have troubled President Tyler. The climate of his native Tidewater Virginia, after all, was similar to Washington's, especially in the summer. But September 12 was not an ordinary day. In fact, it was likely the most painful day of Tyler's life up to that point. September 12 was the day of Letitia Tyler's funeral.

Letitia had passed away quietly at 8:00 P.M. on the previous Saturday, September 10, the first presidential spouse to die while her husband held the office. She was fifty-two years old. Letitia and John Tyler had been married for twenty-nine years. The next morning, Sunday, church bells tolled throughout Washington earlier and longer than usual as worshipers made their way to services. Clergymen informed their congregations of the melancholy news of the First Lady's death once everyone had been seated. The Tyler family made funeral arrangements, and the president decided that Letitia's remains would lie in state in the East Room of the White House. In the past year and a half, the East Room had been the site of President Harrison's funeral, Lizzy Tyler's wedding, the levee for Charles Dickens and Washington Irving, and now yet another funeral. At four o'clock on Monday afternoon, Reverend Hawley officiated over an Episcopal ceremony before the members of Congress who had remained in the city and the cabinet officials who were able to attend. The next day the entire Tyler family boarded a train to accompany Letitia's remains to Cedar Grove, her family's estate in New Kent County, Virginia, where she would be laid to rest.[2]

Letitia's death sparked an outpouring of admiration from all quarters, more out of respect, it would seem, than anything else, since very few people in Washington had actually met her. The *Washington Globe* as well as the *Madiso-*

nian offered glowing tributes, as did many papers throughout the country. The *Washington Daily National Intelligencer*'s obituary praised her as "loving and confiding to her husband, gentle and affectionate to her children, kind and charitable to the needy and afflicted."[3] This last encomium was recognition of the efforts Letitia had taken in Virginia as a much-younger woman to improve the lives of those less fortunate.

More formal condolences arrived at the White House in the days after Letitia's death. For example, the chaplain of the US Senate, Septimus Tustin, wrote to the president, "How gladly would I bind up your lacerated feelings, and pour the balm of healing into your wounded spirit." Reverend Tustin was also certain that his letter "[gave] utterance to the feelings of the *entire Clergy of this City.*" Indeed, black bunting adorned many of the churches and other buildings in the capital, much as it had done in the wake of President Harrison's death, the event that had, of course, brought Letitia to Washington in the first place back in April 1841.[4]

We can only imagine what Tyler thought of these condolences or how they affected him because he apparently did not share his feelings about his wife's death through letters. Perhaps his silence was a sign of his deep attachment to Letitia, the abiding love he felt for her, and the respect he accorded to her memory. He may have been so grief stricken that he could not bear to vent his feelings for fear they would overwhelm him and force a loss of his composure. What seems more likely is that Tyler employed the stoicism and fatalism commonly exhibited by people of his time to help him navigate his sorrow. His reaction to the loss of another family member years later may provide evidence that he did exactly that. In 1849 a cholera epidemic swept across the United States. The disease killed thousands, including Robert and Priscilla's son, two-year-old Thomas Cooper Tyler—John Tyler's grandson. In consoling Robert on his loss, Tyler wrote that "the decree of Providence cannot be altered" and encouraged him to submit "to an overruling destiny." He wanted Robert to consider the possibility that "what appears a grievous burthen hard to be borne is in truth a blessing" that would make the loss easier to bear. "Cheer up then my son, and placing all your trust and confidence in the Superior Being yield neither to unavailing melancholy or grief." It is not hard to imagine that Tyler had taken this advice himself when he lost Letitia. Never a man given to overtly public displays of his faith, he nevertheless indicated that a belief in God sustained him, especially in difficult times.[5]

Little Thomas's passing occurred suddenly and with scant warning and was therefore a shock to the family. Tyler had had a long time to prepare himself mentally for Letitia's death. He must have also felt some sense of relief that her suffering was finally over. Nevertheless, he was self-aware enough to realize that he needed time away—alone and without any family around—to grieve and recover from the blow. He had decided weeks before Letitia's death that he would escape Washington and seek refuge at the Virginia shore once Congress adjourned. Now that trip seemed more necessary than ever. Soon after the funeral at Cedar Grove, he traveled to the Rip Raps, a presidential retreat at Old Point Comfort, Virginia. Andrew Jackson was the first president to make it a vacation hideaway, and it became rather like a smaller, nineteenth-century version of Camp David. Tyler used it for the first time that September.[6]

While settling in at the Rip Raps, the president wrote a short letter to Jackson. He had received a note from the Old Hero in August and now had the time to reply. Apologizing for having taken so long to write, and alluding to the loss of Jackson's beloved Rachel many years ago, Tyler wrote that he had "repaired to this place for the double purpose of repose and seclusion." He expressed his appreciation for the former president's support of his course of action during the second session of the Twenty-Seventh Congress. Tyler also made clear to Jackson that he would welcome any advice on political matters he might offer in the future.[7]

This was a curious turn of events. Jackson's custom over the course of a long public career had been to write off most enemies forever. He never forgot a slight and seemingly never forgave any man who crossed him. Tyler had left the Democratic Party because he believed Jackson had abused his authority as president during the nullification crisis and violated his oath of office during the bank war. By all accounts, and based on how he treated other Democrats who had done as Tyler had, the Virginian had become an apostate. Jackson had softened toward Tyler, though, and had expressed sympathy for him as he stared down the Whigs in the showdown over the bank in the special session. He had also allowed the *Washington Globe* to publish letters he had written in support of Tyler and congratulated him for maintaining the principles he had espoused for so long, despite the torrent of abuse heaped on him by the Clay Whigs. Their shared opposition to the bank (and Clay) and the kinship the two men shared in the presidency drew them together. Many years earlier Jackson had reached a rapprochement with Thomas Hart Benton, with whom he had once fought a duel and who soon became one of his staunchest supporters in the Senate. Evidently, Jackson was now doing the same with Tyler.[8]

That explanation accounts for Jackson's good feelings. But what explains Tyler's solicitude toward Jackson? Surely, it would have been rude not to reply to Jackson's letter. Perhaps Tyler was merely showing a former occupant of the White House the proper respect he felt he deserved. Again, the shared experience of occupying the presidency is often a strong bond and has very famously brought former political opponents together in a unique solidarity.[9] Or perhaps he was trying to cultivate a relationship with the man many still saw as the head of the Democratic Party. Having Jackson in his corner might buttress Tyler against any looming battles with the Whigs. He might also be able to parlay that support into his drive to succeed himself in 1844. This is not to say that the sentiments Tyler now expressed toward Jackson were anything less than sincere, but it also had to have dawned on him that cordial relations between the two men might help further his political career.

That being said, Tyler was not altogether hopeful about finding a place once again in the Democratic ranks. Indeed, he thought that the party might no longer be amenable to him or he to it. "From portions of the Democratic party," he wrote at one point, "I have received an apparently warm support: but while the *ultras* control in the name of *party*, I fear that no good would arise from either an amalgamation with them, or a too ready assent to their demands for office." Tyler also opposed Martin Van Buren, who still held a sizeable portion of the power within the party.[10]

The Whigs had been saying for some time that Tyler had thrown himself upon the altar of the Democracy and had shown his desire to court the Democrats with his vetoes. These charges were understandable, but overall the Whig rhetoric did not match the reality. The president's course of action thus far had obviously pleased many Democrats. Yet they were apparently in no mood to welcome him back into the fold. Francis P. Blair's *Washington Globe*, the party's most influential newspaper, reminded voters of Tyler's political opportunism years ago. "Mr. Tyler," an editorial pointed out, "at the moment the fortunes of the Democracy were struggling with an accumulation of difficulties, *separated himself from that party,* and became, to a certain extent, the instrument of its overthrow." Now, having "quarreled with his new friends," he "wishes to come back to his old; *or rather to stand where he is while they come to him.* It also appears that he does not expect to be merely tolerated *as a repentant sinner,* but that the Democratic party shall reward him for his desertion by rallying under his banner, and placing him at the head." The *Globe* would not hear of it. "This, we think, is rather asking too much."[11]

Tyler may have feared this was true and realized he had come to a crossroads. Should he ally himself fully and publicly with the Democrats? Should he try to build support among states' rights Whigs? Should he attempt to create a third party, and if so, what would the composition of that party be? He was unsure. The only thing he did feel certain of was his conviction that he should continue to look out for the best interests of the American people and uphold his administration on sound principles. "Is there any other course for me to pursue than to look to the public good irrespective of either faction?" he asked Littleton Tazewell, to whom he turned once again for counsel. Tyler conceded to his friend, however, that "the difficulty in the way of administering the government without a party is undoubtedly great." Something had to give.[12]

Tyler characteristically made no decision at the Rip Raps about what course of action he would pursue; he set no plans in motion. The president returned to Washington late in the fall of 1842 with his political future still very much in doubt. Fortunately, he could take solace in the fact that the lame-duck session of the Twenty-Seventh Congress would have a different feel to it than the two that preceded it due to the Whigs having lost control of the House of Representatives in the 1842 midterm elections; the party retained control of the Senate but had lost seats. Election returns at the state level told a similar story as Democrats made sizeable gains and won control of several legislatures. In Tyler's home state of Virginia, for example, Democrats could gleefully proclaim that "Whiggery is capsized."[13]

Senator Clay's aggressiveness during the special session, and the continued battering of the president the Whig Party employed during the second session, had presented voters with a stark choice: they could either signal their approval of Clay and ratify the party's course, which had resulted in little economic recovery, or they could repudiate the Whigs for playing politics and trying to destroy a president and seek redress by putting the Democrats back in power. The electorate had apparently rendered its verdict. The voters seemingly made no distinction between "Clay Whigs" or "Tyler Whigs"—they wanted them gone.

Historian Michael Holt has shown convincingly, however, that low turnout of their partisans in the 1842 midterms, not a spike in the vote totals of the Democrats, doomed the Whigs at the state and national levels. The same had been true of the off-year elections of 1841. One Democrat in Virginia noted some "apathy amongst the Whigs" in his state, and Clay argued that most of the elections were "lost not by the increased strength of their opponents, but by voters remaining absent from feelings of mortification and disgust, created by the acting President." The Kentuckian overstated his case by solely blaming Tyler for the reversal of the Whig Party's electoral fortunes—his ego certainly did not allow him to acknowledge his own role in demoralizing the partisan ranks and depressing turnout—but he had correctly assessed the primary cause of the party's defeats nationwide. But all was not lost. Clay also found "great confidence prevailing among the Whigs of their success in 1844." He now expected to be the nominee of the party—and the beneficiary of that success. The ever-elusive presidency seemed to be within his grasp.[14]

President Tyler also looked to the 1844 campaign, and he drew a very different lesson from the recent elections than his enemy did. Tyler declared later that the results of the midterms represented the "greatest political victory ever won within my recollection." In terms of the amount of turnover and the percentage of seats that had changed parties, he was absolutely correct. His analysis for the massive electoral shift, however, reflected wishful thinking. Tyler maintained that Democratic success had been "achieved entirely upon the vetoes of the Bank bills presented to me at the extra session." The president believed the voters had sided with him in the fight with the Clay Whigs, and he was pleased with the results. Particularly pleasing was the defeat of his arch-nemesis John Minor Botts. Unfortunately, Tyler also found out that most of his own supporters in the House of Representatives—the men Clay so derisively referred to as the Corporal's Guard—would not return for the Twenty-Eighth Congress. Indeed, George Proffit, Francis Mallory, W. W. Irwin, Caleb Cushing, and James I. Roosevelt had all declined to stand for reelection because they realized they had no chance to win. Only Henry Wise and Thomas Walker Gilmer remained. Wise would be reelected from a different district in Virginia as a "Tyler Democrat" in 1843. Gilmer ran for reelection in 1842 as a Democrat.[15]

The combination of nationwide Whig losses in the midterms, the loss of his supporters in Congress, and the criticism directed toward his administration from newspapers heralding the candidacies of Van Buren and Clay prompted Tyler to finally make up his mind about what course of action he would pursue for 1844. He wrote later that what had transpired in the fall of 1842 convinced him that "it was esteemed every way proper to organize a separate party." His nearly year-long effort to find middle ground between the "ultras" of both major parties and steer a moderate course had clearly failed. He could not use this strategy to build a party. He needed to try something new.[16]

It would be an uphill battle, and Tyler never indicated that he believed it would be anything but a longshot. Previous third-party efforts in American

politics had failed to gain traction nationally. Thus, on one level Tyler's decision to pursue the third-party option must be viewed as an act of desperation.
On the other hand, it might also be viewed as the defiant act of a president
who was unwilling to allow his enemies to dictate his political future.

Tyler's motives for creating this separate party have been the subject of debate and disagreement on the part of historians. Some—most notably Tyler biographer Robert Seager—contend that he sought to build a third party only to
shape the agenda of the 1844 presidential campaign and force the Democratic
Party to pay heed to the issues he cared about most. This view maintains that
by the fall of 1842, Tyler had decided to pursue the annexation of Texas and
wanted to make sure the Democrats made support for annexation part of their
platform. By gathering a sizeable number of his own supporters nationwide in
a separate party, Tyler could release them at the appropriate time, when they
would campaign, vote, and ensure a Democratic victory. In sum, this meant
that Tyler realized he stood no chance of winning the presidency in his own
right but wanted to play the role of kingmaker. Knowing the Democratic Party
favored expansion and aware that the Whigs would likely come out publicly
against the annexation of Texas, Tyler could then have his final revenge on
Clay by preventing him from capturing the White House.[17]

There is some plausibility in this interpretation—the "kingmaker" view—
but it rests upon two assumptions. First, for it to ring true, Tyler had to have
committed fully to the annexation of Texas by November 1842. Certainly, as
we have seen, he was at least thinking about the prospect of annexation one
year earlier, as his letter to Webster in October 1841 makes clear. But as we
have also seen, "thinking about" something for Tyler did not usually translate
into firm action until much time had elapsed. The evidence indicates more
convincingly that at the time he made known his intention to create a third
party, his final decision on whether to pursue annexation had not yet been
made. Second, the kingmaker view assumes that Tyler was petty enough to
want to play the lead role in thwarting Clay's presidential ambitions in 1844.
This was certainly not out of the question, as the tension and bitterness of the
special session had created hard feelings all around. There is no way to know
for sure if this motivated Tyler because he never came right out and said—or
wrote—anything to that effect. What does seem more likely, given how his
presidency had evolved since the special session and in light of his often-over-
weening ambition, is that Tyler believed the ultimate revenge on Clay would
come with winning election in his own right. And in November 1842, Tyler
could still convince himself into thinking this might be a real possibility.

The most compelling evidence for the kingmaker view is a letter Tyler wrote in July 1846, sixteen months after he left the White House, describing his role in the election of 1844. He wrote that he had organized a third party "ostensibly in reference to the presidency in my own person, but in truth for the sole purpose of controlling events, by throwing in the weight of that organization for the public good, in the then approaching election." Tyler maintained that it was with "this purpose, and with this view, and in order to preserve such organization until the proper time should arrive for striking a decisive blow" that he formed his own party.[18]

Historians such as Seager who subscribe to the kingmaker view seem to have accepted this letter at face value and apparently have fastened onto the phrase "ostensibly in reference to the presidency in my own person" to show that Tyler did not *actually* make an effort to build a third party so that he could win election in his own right. The implication of the 1846 letter is that people at the time *assumed* he wanted to use a third party to win the presidency in 1844 but that this perception of his motives was wrong, and he needed to correct the record.

This 1846 letter is self-serving. Having failed in his efforts to create a viable-enough party for him to capture the presidency in 1844, Tyler seemed to have engaged in a bit of revisionist history after he left office. He claimed after the fact that his party was designed only to advance the public good, shape the agenda of the 1844 campaign, and sweep the Democratic nominee into the White House—that it had been created "for the sole purpose of controlling events," as he put it. He had supposedly come to the conclusion after the debacle of the special session of the Twenty-Seventh Congress and his break with the Whig Party that no realistic chance ever existed for him to succeed himself. Declaring that he had never entertained the thought of winning election in his own right and had not been motivated by that thought in his efforts to create a third party allowed Tyler to save face.

Compelling evidence indicates, however, that at least for a while he very much intended his third party to serve as a vehicle to get himself elected president in 1844. The kingmaker view does not seem to have been adopted by any of Tyler's contemporaries. Most politicians assumed he was pursuing the presidency in his own right and that his party—quixotic and unrealistic as it may have been—was designed for that purpose. Daniel Webster certainly adopted this view, and his proximity to the president and the fact that he enjoyed at least some of his confidence would have made him especially attuned to his plans. In March 1843 Webster dispatched a letter marked "Strictly private and confidential" to Nicholas Biddle and instructed him to "burn it" after reading it (an instruction Biddle thankfully ignored). "I may as well tell you, in the strictest confidence," Webster wrote, "the whole truth, respecting the state of things here. The President is still resolved to try the chances of an *Election.*" Tyler's goal of winning the presidency in his own right "enters into every thing." Webster betrayed no small amount of dismay at this situation because Tyler was even "quite disposed to throw himself altogether into the arms of the loco foco party" in order to accomplish his goal. "He will be disappointed," Webster later confided to Edward Everett. "They will certainly cheat him. But he cannot be convinced of this truth." All of this "will lead," he acknowledged, "to movements in which I cannot concur." Though he did not specifically mention the annexation of Texas, the secretary of state no doubt had that particular policy in mind. "But I am expecting, every day, measures, which I cannot stand by, & face the Country," he wrote. As a result, Webster acknowledged that he was preparing to leave the cabinet. The only question would be when.

What most troubled Webster was the way the president had resolved to use the patronage power to build a third party. "He has altogether too high an opinion of the work which can be wrought by giving *offices* to hungry applicants," Webster complained. "And he is surrounded by these, from morning to night. Every appointment, therefore, from the highest to the lowest, raises a question of *political affects* [sic]." Webster believed some of the appointments the president had made to offices in the State Department were unworthy of their new station, and he feared "the interest of the Country, & the dignity of the Govt. may both suffer from it."[19]

Tyler had indeed begun to use the patronage to his advantage. He initiated the process in earnest during the spring of 1842, when he ordered the collector at the Philadelphia custom house, Jonathan Roberts, to fire some thirty Clay partisans and replace them with Tylerites. When Roberts refused, Tyler fired *him.* Early in his presidency, Tyler had appointed many Clay men to government positions as a way of demonstrating good faith to the Whig Party. All of that had changed; the president now sought to give the spoils of office to Democrats or men fully on record as being friendly to him and his administration. "No man suspected of preferring Clay can get an office from him," one congressman reported, "indeed no man who is recommended by a friend of Clay [can get an office]."[20]

Tyler made no apologies for employing the patronage power. This placed him in an interesting position. He had railed against President Jackson's use of the "spoils system" while he served in the Senate. More recently, in his inaugural address he had pointed out that a "selfishly ambitious" chief executive might use his "unrestrained power" to appoint and remove federal officeholders "in order either to perpetuate his authority or hand it over to some favorite as his successor." The use of power in this way made the "will" of the president "absolute and supreme" on patronage matters. Most Whigs held Tyler to account for these words, and they reacted angrily to his aggressive use of the patronage power. "Corruption and Tyler, and Tyler and Corruption, will stick together as long as Cataline and treason," one party member spat. "The name of Tyler will stink in the nostrils of the people; for the history of our Government affords no such palpable example of the prostitution of the executive patronage to the wicked purpose of bribery."[21]

The Whigs forgot, or simply ignored, what else Tyler had said about patronage in his inaugural address. He had warned them that "numerous removals [of federal officeholders] may become necessary" during his term in office if the men who occupied these positions "had been guilty of an active partisanship or by secret means" sought to give "official influence to the purpose of party."[22] What seemed evident in the fall of 1842 is that Tyler had hedged his bets early in his presidency when it came to patronage. He played the part of a good Whig by decrying the baleful effects of the spoils system on the nation's politics. But he had rhetorically given himself enough room so that when he began removing loyal Whigs from federal jobs en masse, he could not be completely tarred with the charge of inconsistency or roundly criticized for having gone against what he had previously said. He had been prescient enough to realize that at some point he might occupy the very situation he now found himself in and knew he would need some means by which to advance his own cause.

Consequently, Tyler embarked on what some Whig newspapers referred to as the "reign of terror," from late 1842 through much of 1843, systematically purging his enemies from the ranks of federal officeholders. He was especially ruthless in wielding the patronage axe in the nation's largest cities, obviously recognizing that the juiciest plums to be had were found either in towns with major ports, in heavily concentrated urban areas, or in those that were both. Tyler removed the collector of the Port of New York, Edward Curtis, and summarily sacked some sixty of his minions. In Boston Tyler used Cushing as an intermediary to grease the skids with newspaper editors and other politicians, most of whom were little more than hacks looking for patronage handouts to alleviate their straitened financial circumstances. The result of this political bloodbath was that any supporters of Tyler now left the Whig Party once and for all. Whigs might have regarded that as good news, but they realized too that the wholesale removal of their own from federal jobs weakened them at all levels of government—national, state, and local—and undermined their efforts to mobilize voters and organize effective opposition to the Democrats.

The tide had turned against the Whigs, Clay's optimism about the party's prospects in 1844 notwithstanding: Tyler's vetoes prevented most of the party's economic agenda from becoming law; the Democratic takeover of many state legislatures in the 1842 midterms meant that, with the recent passage of the reapportionment bill, Democrats could gerrymander congressional districts to benefit their party and deprive the Whigs of many seats in the House of Representatives; and now the federal patronage was slipping away. The party faithful were in a state of shock. The victory of 1840 was but a distant memory. Many Whigs even believed there was actually little use in electing their men to office. Some argued, in the wake of the Democratic takeover of the House, that perhaps it was better for them in the long run if they lost the majority in the Senate, too, so they would not be blamed for the bad economy. Tyler's presidency had indeed wrought havoc on the Whigs—and on the Second Party System itself. Nothing like it had ever been seen before.[23]

Tyler relied on Attorney General Legaré and Secretary of War Spencer for guidance as he reshaped the federal offices. In fact, he ordered Spencer to take the lead in both targeting Whig jobholders for removal and finding suitable replacements. "I am entirely willing to do in regards to the change in office holders whatever you may recommend," Tyler wrote to his war secretary. "We have numberless enemies in office and they should forthwith be made to quit." He made some of his own suggestions for several posts, mercilessly writing that a replacement should be found for one man, "then off with his head. Nor," he went on to assert, "do I care if a like service be done to the Postmaster at Portland." Tyler also sought a clerkship for a "poor O'Bryan," whom he described as "actually starving." Generally, though, the president deferred to Spencer and told him, "unless I have *conclusive reasons* to the contrary will carry out your recommendations." Tyler declared, "action is what we want, prompt and decisive action, but what I say is that we ought to know whom we appoint."[24]

This last directive proved problematic. Because of the rapidity with which the purges were carried out, Tyler and Spencer could not possibly have known or had firsthand knowledge of every single individual who might appear eligible for a patronage position. Turning out Whig loyalists was the easy part; replacing them could be exasperating. Tyler received letters from friends and political allies from around the country who recommended their favorites, including one from Dolley Madison, who sought a consular position in Liverpool for her son John Payne Todd (Tyler declined to appoint him), but many of the positions he filled went to individuals he knew very little about. Mistakes were unavoidable, and some men of questionable loyalty to the president, questionable competence, or both became the beneficiaries of administration largesse. Tyler found this out the hard way in Rhode Island. "We committed a fatal blunder in turning out Littlefield and putting in a Dorrite," he wrote Spencer at one point. Clearly, building a third party through patronage was not going to be easy. The "reign of terror" also provided Congressman Botts with ammunition to bolster his effort to impeach Tyler.[25]

Tyler recognized that patronage alone would not suffice. If he was going to win the presidency in 1844, he needed to construct an organization with leadership nationwide that could mobilize the grassroots. To start, he commissioned a man named Alexander Abell to write a campaign biography. Abell finished the book late in 1843 and released it to coincide with the campaign season. Next, Tyler sought to gather the support of Democrats in the North who opposed the presumptive nominee of the party in 1844, Martin Van Buren. These "Conservative" Democrats—called "Hunkers" in Van Buren's home state of New York—composed a sizeable portion of the party. Finally, Tyler looked to solidify his standing among the states' rights men of both parties in the South. His third-party movement thus took on the character of a hybrid. Tyler sought to co-opt elements of both parties, with Democrats as the most important component. He started in New York, where he believed he enjoyed a following throughout the state and in New York City. Two things nurtured that belief. First, Alexander Hamilton Jr., a friend of the administration, informed him in the spring of 1842 that Democrats in Congress "exhibit[ed] serious alarm at the progress of our course among the people" in New York City. Hamilton wrote that Tyler's position there was "beautiful," though he also advised the president to force Webster and Spencer out of his cabinet. Second, Tyler supported the Democratic candidate for New York governor in 1842, William C. Bouck, who sought to deny Seward another term. Bouck prevailed, and Tyler interpreted his victory as evidence that his endorsement had made the crucial difference.[26]

Efforts to mobilize support in New York City actually predated Tyler's "reign of terror" over the federal patronage and serve as further evidence that he sought a term in his own right in 1844. Recognizing that a viable third party would need a base in the nation's largest city, the president approved Robert Tyler's attempt to buy a stake in James Gordon Bennett's *New York Herald* in June 1841. That attempt failed. So, too, did an effort to secure the loyalty of another city paper, the *Standard*. By July 1842, however, it seemed the nascent Tyler party had found its mouthpiece in New York City: the *Union*, a paper principally owned by smalltime political operative Paul R. George and edited by a lawyer and former diplomat in the Madison administration named Mordecai Manuel Noah. The fifty-seven-year-old Noah, a prominent figure in New York's Jewish community and a member of the Democratic Party organization known as Tammany Hall, also served as chairman of the Tyler General Committee in New York City, which formed late in the spring of 1842.[27]

At one point, Noah served as an operative for Tyler. Mulling over his outsider candidacy and exhibiting his tendency to waffle, the president dispatched Noah to Richmond in January 1843 to visit Thomas Ritchie and ascertain what leading Democrats in Virginia and throughout the South thought of Tyler's chances to become a viable candidate of their party in 1844. The crusty old editor and most of his cronies were committed to Van Buren, while others favored Calhoun. Ritchie still respected Tyler, but like many in the Democratic Party, he could not support the man who had left their ranks to join the Whigs.[28]

On his way back to New York, Noah called on Tyler at the White House. The two men talked at great length about his meeting with Ritchie, then about the political landscape in New York City and what level of support existed for the president throughout the Empire State. During the course of their conversation, Noah bluntly told Tyler that he did not think a third party could be built, at least not one that could get him elected president. "This you cannot do," he said. "You possess patronage, to be sure; and you can use it, without violating any principle; but if it were ten times as extensive as it is it would not enable you to create a party of sufficient consequence to justify you in accepting a nomination even if you could obtain one." At some point in the discussion—the evidence is unclear whether it occurred before Noah's statement against a third party or after—Tyler claimed that he "entertained no hopes of an election himself" but merely hoped his party would be able to influence the Democratic Party's agenda for the 1844 presidential campaign.[29]

What was going on here? As Webster's private and confidential letter to Biddle two months *later* makes clear, on some level Tyler still entertained the hope that he could be elected in his own right *after* his interview with Noah— that is, after he told Noah he did not actually intend to use his third party in an effort to win the presidency in 1844. What appears most plausible in reading the evidence detailing the Tyler-Noah meeting is that the president told his visitor he did not seek election in his own right *after* Noah had taken pains to show him why a third party was not feasible. Tyler seemingly confirmed Noah's view of the situation and denied his actual intentions because he did not wish to defend himself to someone who was obviously not a true believer. He could not abandon his own belief in his candidacy even in the face of Noah's more realistic assessment of his chances.

Tyler's thought process on the 1844 campaign and on a third party reflected the vacillation that drove his friends to distraction and his enemies to ridicule. One moment he seemed determined to build a personal party and pursue his own election. The next moment he thought the more modest goal of influencing the Democratic Party in the 1844 campaign seemed more feasible. Then he wanted to test the waters and find out if the Democrats would seriously consider nominating him for president. His mind was all over the map. He also never clearly defined what he stood for. Tyler spoke often of upholding the Constitution and of administering the government on "sound principles," but these were little more than vague platitudes. He lacked focus. And his conception of a party clearly bore no resemblance to the strictly states' rights variety for which Beverley Tucker and Abel Upshur had for so long hoped.

The president had had an opportunity to attach something substantive to his candidacy and trumpet his middle-ground solution to the fiscal crisis—the Exchequer plan—but despite his private enthusiasm for the proposal, he never fought for it publicly with any kind of conviction. Tyler never took it to the American people and offered it as an idea worthy of support. His support of it in his annual message was too timid; perhaps he did not really believe in it. The policy proposal that would eventually set him apart from the other candidates for president in 1844—Texas annexation—had to be played close to the vest until he was fully ready to present it. In short, Tyler never displayed the will necessary to convince voters that he even deserved to win election in his own right. He did finally come to the conclusion that he stood no chance, but exactly when that realization occurred is difficult to pinpoint.

Tyler's susceptibility to flattery—a character trait his enemies pilloried by publicly calling him the "tool" of a "venal pack of officeholders"—made coming to that realization even more difficult. Democrats who sought patronage often told him what he wanted to hear and found a receptive audience. "There are in this district a great number of voters who are Tyler men," cooed one party hack, who wrote to the president with the aspirations of becoming postmaster at Salem, Massachusetts. "The Administration is growing stronger and stronger here, and it is not uncommon to hear leading Democrats declare, as I heard one yesterday, 'well I believe John Tyler will be the next President in spite of everything.'" With words like these jumping off the page, it is little wonder why Tyler continued to believe in the possibility of his election.[30]

Events in New York City should have given him pause. Early in 1843 the movement to form a third party appeared increasingly unsettled. Most troubling was a rift in the Tyler General Committee. The postmaster of New York City, John Lorimer Graham, a Tyler appointee, and the city's marshal, Silas M. Stillwell, launched an anti-Semitic attack against Noah. They wrote letters to the president arguing that Noah's Jewish religion had put off potential supporters and that his belief in a Tyler candidacy was lukewarm at best. Tyler already knew Noah's enthusiasm for his third party had flagged—their meeting in January had made that clear. Graham and Stillwell forced Noah to resign as editor of the *Union* late in January 1843, apparently persuading him to leave by hinting that they would use their influence with the president to see that he was named surveyor of the Port of New York or US consul to Constantinople. He ultimately received neither position.

Noah blamed Graham and Robert Tyler for his ouster and for his subsequent failure to receive a patronage appointment from the president. He believed the two men had poisoned Tyler against him and had used his religion as ammunition to force him out. Through his newspaper contacts in New York City, Robert undoubtedly became aware of the Tylerites' increasing displeasure with Noah and no doubt counseled his father that he needed to go. There is no evidence, however, that either Robert or the president personally opposed Noah due to his religious orientation. Rather, it seems plain that the decision to force his resignation as editor of the *Union* was solely a political calculation, one based on what the leaders of the Tyler movement in New York City had been telling them would be best for the president's candidacy. It was the anti-Semitism of New York voters, then, that prompted Noah's removal. His face-to-face meeting with Tyler at the White House, however, and the strong argument he made then against using patronage to build a third party had also made him expendable. Finally, the poor circulation figures of the *Union* and the dearth of subscriptions to the rag sealed Noah's fate.[31]

But the problems with Tyler's bid for a third party extended well beyond the newspapers. Very little headway had been made to mobilize the grassroots. In fact, little enthusiasm existed at all for a pro-Tyler party. Turnout at meetings organized during the winter of 1843 to rally the faithful often fell far short of the hoped-for numbers. Noah, who, despite his ouster from the *Union* inexplicably remained head of the Tyler General Committee until March, organized a meeting at New York's Broadway Tabernacle that month and invited Cushing, Wise, and Proffit to give speeches trumpeting the virtues of the president; Cushing was the only one who accepted the invitation. A raucous gathering filled the spacious venue to capacity. Unfortunately, as one newspaper reported, "though the concourse of people was so great, it was abundantly evident that a very small proportion of them attended the meeting as Tyler men." Noah and the officers of the meeting made preliminary remarks "amidst every conceivable variety of noise and slight disturbances which most readily suggest themselves to people who fancy themselves undergoing the operation of being unreasonably bored." After Cushing spoke, partisans of Clay and Van Buren led cheers that drowned out the Tyler supporters. And this was the *best* of the few Tyler meetings held throughout the city.[32]

With paltry support from the grassroots, Tyler continued his purge of federal officeholders. But he soon ran into another problem: the Senate often refused to confirm the men he had nominated to replace the Whig partisans. Clay supporters and Van Buren Democrats there worked together in an unlikely alliance to stymie the president's attempt to reshape the patronage and build a third party. The Senate clearly pursued a vendetta against Tyler and at one point discussed the removals in open debate on the floor in an effort to embarrass him. Whig leaders demanded that the president provide reasons for sacking their loyalists. Tyler ignored them. He found the Senate's ongoing unwillingness to confirm his appointments most frustrating when it came time to reshuffle his cabinet. When the hapless Walter Forward resigned as Treasury secretary on March 1, 1843, Tyler found senators unwilling to accept his nomination of Cushing as the replacement. As a member of Tyler's Corporal's Guard, Cushing had a target on his back, and the president should not have expected his confirmation. As the lame-duck session of the Twenty-Seventh Congress came to an end, the Senate rejected the nomination by a vote of 27 to 19. Stubbornly, Tyler resubmitted Cushing's name two hours later. The Senate again voted him down, this time 27 to 10. Incredibly, Tyler sent Cushing's name to the Senate a third time on the same day! The final vote rejecting the would-be secretary of the Treasury carried at 29 to 2. Tyler then had to scramble and nominate John C. Spencer for the post; the Senate confirmed Spencer by 1 vote. As consolation to Cushing, who had by now become a friend, Tyler eventually appointed him as head of a US mission to China.[33]

Tyler also encountered resistance to his nominations to the US Supreme

Court. Justice Smith Thompson died in December 1843. Tyler nominated Spencer, a man most acknowledged was qualified to wear the robes of the nation's highest court. The Senate rejected him, with Clay supporters providing the decisive votes. Tyler then nominated another New Yorker, Reuben H. Walworth. Before the Senate could take up his nomination, Justice Henry Baldwin died in April 1844. Tyler sought to nominate James Buchanan for Baldwin's seat, but Buchanan declined the offer. Tyler then nominated Edward King. The Senate postponed confirmation votes on both Walworth and King until after the presidential election of 1844. Tyler withdrew both nominations and instead submitted Samuel Nelson, chief justice of New York, calculating that if he could secure the confirmation of a man whom he knew enjoyed bipartisan support, he would have momentum to fill the second vacancy. The Senate did indeed confirm Nelson with very little opposition. Tyler then attempted to fill the remaining opening with John Meredith Read. In a final act of spite, the Senate adjourned before Read received a hearing. The choice of filling this seat would eventually be left to Tyler's successor, James K. Polk. In sum, Tyler was the least successful of all US presidents in winning confirmation of his Supreme Court nominees.[34]

This entire spectacle—the purges and the widespread failure to secure Senate confirmation for his nominees—attested to a presidency in crisis and highlighted the difficulty Tyler faced in trying to govern without a party. The near impossibility of using patronage to build a third party was also laid bare. As one scholar has observed, "Tyler's troubles not only damaged his administration but also proved that political party support is required to ensure nomination" of men he wanted to hold federal offices.[35] Thus, Tyler's status as a president without a party subjected him to a cruel calculus: the patronage process represented perhaps the only way to construct the foundation of a third-party effort, but because he lacked the ballast of partisan support, he could not hope to secure the nominations he needed from the Senate to make patronage work to his advantage. An effort to create a third party, then, was doomed to fail. The strength and vitality of the two-party system of Whigs and Democrats in the early 1840s meant that Tyler never stood a realistic chance of succeeding himself. He had not wanted to admit that early in his presidency, but he certainly came to this realization at some point.

One piece of circumstantial evidence that argues for late summer of 1843 as the transition point when Tyler gave up trying to win election in his own right and dedicated his efforts solely to influencing the 1844 presidential race was the resignation of Daniel Webster as secretary of state. Webster informed the president that he would leave the cabinet on May 8. The New Englander had been contemplating his departure for many months but until this time had not seemed eager to make up his mind to resign. What may have finally pushed him out was Tyler's commitment to pursue the annexation of Texas. Webster had repeatedly told the president he could not be a party to such a policy and had tried to softly dissuade him from making it a focal point of his administration's agenda. Tyler was still hesitating but was now closer to dedicating the remainder of his term to accomplishing what he had told Webster in October 1841 would add "luster" to his presidency.

The two men parted company as friends and assured each other of their mutual respect. Webster told the president that there was "no one who more sincerely or ardently desires the prosperity, success, and honor of your administration."[36] Shortly, he would feel compelled to warn Tyler that this honor was in jeopardy. Troubled by the continuation of the purges and disturbed by the president's apparent desire to woo Democrats by rewarding them with as many patronage plums as possible, Webster wrote a long letter to Tyler in August 1843 in which he spelled out his misgivings. He emphatically told him that his actions had placed his "substantial and permanent fame as President . . . in no small peril."[37]

Tyler apparently took the warning to heart. Less than one week after receiving Webster's letter, he wrote to Spencer and informed him that the reign of terror would be halted. "In fact we have done enough and should pause," he said. "This I am pretty much resolved upon."[38]

Did this change in tactics indicate Tyler had come to the realization he could not build a third party that would allow him to win election in his own right? Perhaps. Patronage appointments would resume in time but would lack the fierce urgency and vindictiveness of the purges that had lasted for well over a year. From this point on, Tyler would exercise more selectivity, using the patronage power more strategically and with a specific purpose in mind, namely to advance the cause of Texas annexation.

Whether he abandoned the thought of third-party glory or not in September 1843, Tyler always seemed to return to the idea that perhaps he could carry the Democratic flag in the presidential campaign a year later. He thought the party might turn to him if the Van Buren and Calhoun factions destroyed each other or if another candidate—Lewis Cass, for example—foundered and they could find no other man to hoist the party's banner. "It is legitimate to argue that I am more available than Mr. V. B. or Mr. C[ass]," Tyler boasted in a "strictly confidential" letter to the editor of a supportive paper in Boston, "and to prove, what the sequel will demonstrate, that the one you advocate is the only person the Democrats can elect." The president now wanted to portray himself as a Democrat who stood above the internecine warfare of faction.[39]

It was a fanciful notion and does not reflect well on Tyler. He could talk sensibly one moment, as he had to Tazewell in October 1842, and seem to accept the political reality of his situation. At other moments he seemed unwilling or unable to come to terms with the predicament he found himself in as a president without a party. Tyler also never seemed to fully grasp that his divorce from the Democratic standard was irreconcilable, as Blair had made clear in the pages of the *Washington Globe.* One should be careful, however, not to judge Tyler too harshly for this or to ascribe his behavior to a defect of character. After all, most first-term presidents are usually given the chance to face reelection and appeal to the people for a second term. Every president up to that time—excepting Harrison, of course—had been afforded that opportunity. Tyler eventually came to the realization that he would have no such prospect. When that realization came, it must have been a bitter pill to swallow, for his whole life had been devoted to accomplishment, to fulfilling ambitions, and to faithfully serving his country. He recognized that his time in public life was approaching its end, whether he liked it or not.

Chapter 16

MISS GARDINER

While the president grieved the loss of his wife at the Rip Raps in September and early October 1842, back at the White House, Priscilla, Robert, and their two daughters, as well as John Jr., attempted to come to terms with Letitia's passing and prepare for life without her. It was a difficult transition. Priscilla noted, "Nothing can exceed the loneliness of this large and gloomy mansion—hung with black—its walls echoing only sighs and groans." Even in ill health, Letitia's gentleness, refinement, and unerring religious faith had made her a model for her children and husband to emulate. Despite her inability to move around as freely as she would have liked, she was the glue that held the family together. "She had everything about her to awaken love," Priscilla remembered warmly.[1]

President Tyler returned to Washington in mid-October. He complained that he had "quitted the Rip-raps most reluctantly" and that his return "was rendered necessary from letters which reached [him] two evenings before [his] departure." Congress was not yet in session, but the press of business—particularly matters at the State Department that concerned British acceptance of the Webster-Ashburton Treaty—demanded his presence in the capital. Though he would have liked to have remained at the Virginia shore for at least a little while longer, Tyler apparently found his time away just what he needed.[2]

When he returned he found things pretty much as he had left them. In the heat of partisan battle, many people seemed to forget that the president had a family and faced issues that any other head of household addressed, only amid pressure that ordinary folks knew nothing about. Tyler tended to micromanage the duties of his office and found that he enjoyed little spare time to devote to his family. But he made the most of that time. He kept abreast of what was happening with his children and corresponded frequently with his married daughters, offering advice on everything from how much they should exercise to the proper way to plant clover seed. A concerned father, he adopted his children's problems as his own and looked for the best possible solutions. He also pressed them to visit in every letter he sent.[3]

One thing Tyler tended not to do when he wrote his children was offer any details about his financial situation. Money was always a source of worry for him—even with a $25,000 annual salary.[4] He complained about how expensive it was to live in the capital. "I am heartily tired of the grocers here who enact extravagant prices for every thing," he griped by letter to one friend, whom he hoped could help him find supplies in New York. "Considering the large amount which I require annually here" at the White House, "I have supposed that I might procure them at wholesale prices—payment to be made in six months." Tyler attached a long list to this letter and asked his friend to purchase the items he requested and ship them "at as early a day as you can." He also hoped he had not made "too great a requisition" on his friendship. When it came to John Tyler and money, this was no idle concern.[5]

Tyler looked for ways to keep money in his pockets. For example, he dismissed the French cooks who had been employed at the White House when he assumed the presidency; he preferred simpler fare anyway. Yet for all of his worry about money and making ends meet, Tyler habitually overextended himself. He continually reenacted the pattern he had established nearly thirty years earlier and tended to live beyond his means. At one point he told his daughter Lizzy that he would pay the cost of finding an enslaved person for work on her farm, an offer that would require a significant outlay of cash. He wrote her, "if I can hear of a servant that would suit you, I will purchase him for you." Tyler even had a particular slave in mind. "I think that Louisa's William would make a good servant and if you choose to try your hand upon him you can do so." His offer did not stop there. "I will willingly my dear daughter pay the hire of a servant maid for you." He suggested that Lizzy find a woman who was a nurse as well as a seamstress, then let him foot the bill.[6]

Tyler seemed to think nothing of taking on added financial burdens if in doing so he could help his children. The problem was keeping up with his obligations. Asking for six months' credit to pay his grocery bill was typical behavior, and, as always, he often robbed Peter to pay Paul. In the fall of 1842, he took on a particularly large expense. Thinking about his retirement from public life, Tyler purchased a farm from his Virginia neighbor Collier Minge for $10,000 called Walnut Grove which he soon renamed Sherwood Forest. Tyler fancied himself a Robin Hood–type figure who enjoyed his outlaw status with the Whig Party. Located just two miles from Greenway, the farm where he had grown up, this new property needed work before Tyler could call it a home worthy of an ex-president. He spent thousands of dollars on renovations over the next two years, which of course taxed his checkbook even further.[7] The stress of keeping up with his accounts must have been almost unbearable at times. Tyler simply did not have the financial resources to live comfortably free from worry, despite his position at the top of the American political ladder.

He put on a good front, however. Certainly, the people who made their way to the White House during the capital's social season every year would have had no reason to think their chief executive often found himself in straitened circumstances. They became accustomed to tasty food—mutton, perch, and oysters, for example—and fine champagne, and Tyler took pride in throwing a good party. But he looked forward to formal dinners and levees with a mixture of anticipation and dread. On the one hand, he usually enjoyed greeting the visitors who came to the mansion; he was a gracious host. On the other hand, it cost money—a lot of money—to entertain in the manner people in Washington expected. Tyler paid for these affairs solely out of his own pocket.[8]

Making matters worse, he was forced to pay for the upkeep of the White House too. Congress had traditionally appropriated money for the purchase of new furniture or for replacing the carpets and drapes when normal wear and tear made it necessary. But the spiteful blackguards in the House of Representatives now withheld these funds from Tyler. People noticed. One reporter called the furniture in the mansion "a disgrace—a contemptible disgrace to the nation. Many of the chairs in the East Room would be kicked out of a brothel." Another newspaper account painted an equally bleak picture: "This building bears the name of the 'White House'; but, alas! how changed since the days of yore: its virgin white sadly sullied—its beautiful pillars disgustingly bespattered with saliva of tobacco—. . . the splendid drapery falling in tatters all around time's rude hand, the fingers of visitors having made sad havoc with their silken folds." Tyler could do little about it except hope that the entertainment he provided compensated for the mansion's frayed interior.[9]

One family that did not seem to mind the threadbare furniture or tattered drapes were the Gardiners of East Hampton, Long Island, New York. David Gardiner and his wife, Juliana, brought their two daughters, Julia and Margaret, to Washington for the social season for the first time in 1840, during Van Buren's presidency, and they became fixtures in capital society during Tyler's administration. The family stayed at Mrs. Peyton's boardinghouse, a fashionable establishment located at the corner of Pennsylvania Avenue and Four-and-a-Half Street, not far from the White House.[10]

President Tyler met the Gardiners—minus Margaret, who, because of a bad cold, remained in her room at Mrs. Peyton's—on January 20, 1842, at a White House reception. New York congressman Fernando Wood introduced them. Twenty-one-year-old Julia, escorted by a young naval midshipman named Richard Waldron, admitted later that "it was with a great deal of interest I, with the rest of our party, had anticipated the interview." She came away suitably impressed. The president "welcomed us with an urbanity which made the deepest impression upon my father, and we could not help commenting, after we left the room, upon the silvery sweetness of his voice, that seemed in just attune with the incomparable grace of his bearing, and the elegant ease of his conversation." Julia thought to herself that the man she had just met bore no resemblance at all to the political outcast vilified by the Whig press.[11]

John Tyler was even more impressed with Julia than she was with him, and he made it obvious that he enjoyed meeting her. Lingering in conversation with her that night, he showered her with so many compliments that the other guests "looked and listened in perfect amazement." For a moment it seemed the president had forgotten that there were even other people in the room.[12]

Tyler seemed to have also forgotten for a moment that his ailing wife remained upstairs in the residence while he and Priscilla hosted the party in the East Room. He had just experienced what most men felt upon first laying eyes on Julia Gardiner: utter fascination. Five feet, three inches tall, with dark hair and large luminous gray eyes, Julia made an indelible first impression. She was "beautiful in both face and form," one newspaper remarked. Her smile tongue-tied men. Dressed in the latest Paris fashions, she was more cosmopolitan than most of the women in Washington. Armed with a rapier wit and a keen intelligence while exuding a buoyant confidence, she was different—a difference that men found irresistible. Numerous congressman as well as Supreme Court justices—fifty-seven-year-old John McLean among them—pursued her publicly, and fierce competition arose over who would spend time with her. The onslaught of potential suitors was overwhelming. So many men called on her and her sister at Mrs. Peyton's, in fact, that the girls' parents were forced to take another room in the boardinghouse so they could receive their guests in a private parlor.[13]

Without question, Julia Gardiner was quite a catch. Her family boasted an impeccable pedigree and had enjoyed a privileged position in New York society for generations. Their first American ancestor, the Englishman Lion Gardiner, arrived in Boston in November 1635 with his Dutch wife and soon settled in Connecticut. In 1639 he made his way south across the Long Island Sound, purchased the island of Manchonake from the Montauk Indians, and planted the first English settlement in what became New York State. Lion quickly established a successful farm on his land, well before the Dutch even relinquished control of the colony they called New Netherland. A 1640 deed from the Earl of Stirling, acting on behalf of King Charles I, granted Lion the island—located near East Hampton and soon to be renamed Gardiners Island—for an annual sum of five pounds. Gardiners Island remains the only seventeenth-century royal land grant in America still in the possession of the descendants of the original settler.[14]

Born in East Hampton in 1784, David Gardiner—Julia's father—graduated in the same class at Yale as John C. Calhoun. He became an attorney, a supporter of DeWitt Clinton, and ultimately a New York state senator. In 1815 David married Juliana McLachlan, the sixteen-year-old daughter of a Scottish immigrant who had settled in New York City by way of the West Indies. When her father died, Juliana inherited real estate worth a considerable fortune. Together, she and David traveled in lofty circles in New York City. At one point the family lived in a townhouse next door to the Astors.

David and Juliana had four children—David Lyon, born in 1816; Alexander in 1818; Julia in 1820; and Margaret in 1822. The boys graduated from Princeton and became attorneys, with Alexander exhibiting more ambition and drive to succeed in the profession than his older brother. Their sister Julia attended Madame N. D. Chagaray's Institute for young ladies in New York City, a school of fine reputation that taught music, mathematics, ancient history, and French. Margaret spent a brief time at a boarding school, where she displayed a quick mind that rivaled those of her siblings. By 1839, both girls had finished their formal education and had settled in again at the family home in East Hampton.

In September 1840 David and Juliana sailed for Europe with their daughters in tow, intent upon taking advantage of the cultural and educational opportunities in London, Paris, and Rome as well as Scotland, Ireland, and Wales. At this time wealthy American parents were just starting to establish a practice that would become commonplace one generation later: crossing the Atlantic in the hopes of marrying their daughters off to European nobility.

The Gardiner girls evidently found agreeable companionship on their European tour wherever they went. Both enjoyed the attention of countless male admirers. Julia, however, stole the show. Lovesick men—including a German nobleman in Rome—found her utterly enchanting and no doubt told themselves they would never forget her. President Tyler would soon come to know exactly what these men had experienced in the presence of Julia Gardiner.

The Gardiners returned to the United States in September 1841, at just about the same time the Whigs were drumming Tyler out of their party. The family stayed in Washington only briefly during the winter of 1842, when they met the president. They returned to the capital in December of that year fully prepared to enjoy the entirety of the social season. When they arrived, they found the White House in mourning: Letitia Tyler had died less than three months earlier. Nevertheless, John Jr.—still estranged from his wife, Mattie—paid a call at Mrs. Peyton's soon after the family's arrival to find out how the Gardiners had fared on their trip from New York. Two days later young Waldron accompanied the girls' father to the White House, where John Jr. greeted them. Official business detained the president that day, but John persuaded Mr. Gardiner to return the next afternoon, telling him he would make sure his father was available. Gardiner did so, and he and the president chatted briefly. As he prepared to go back to his office, Tyler invited Gardiner to share dinner with his family at the White House on Christmas Eve. He happily accepted the invitation and spent a pleasant evening getting to know everyone better—including several Tyler relatives who had made the trip from Virginia. Julia playfully fended off mild flirtations from John Jr. and especially enjoyed Priscilla's company. The two young women became fast friends.

Two days after Christmas, Robert and Priscilla called at Mrs. Peyton's and invited Mr. Gardiner to dine with the president again. By now, it had started to become obvious that Tyler and his family thought very highly of the Gardiners and enjoyed their company. On New Year's Day the president very publicly signaled his esteem when he rose from his seat, bowed, and offered to let the Gardiners sit in his family's pew at St. John's Episcopal Church when they arrived late for services. Julia had remained in her room at the boardinghouse that Sunday with a cold. The first levee of the season was held just days later, and fortunately she had fully recovered. Writing to her brothers, Julia could hardly contain her excitement at having seen the president again that night. "He caught sight of us behind some two or three who were shaking him by the hand and immediately exclaimed Miss Gardiner! at the same instant extending his hand with 'I hope you are very well.'"[15]

Julia was quite well, in fact. She dominated the Washington social season in the winter of 1843. One suitor, South Carolina congressman Francis W. Pickens, boldly proposed marriage. Julia and Margaret made sure family back in New York knew of the latest romantic developments. "You are in the political world," one cousin wrote back, needling Julia. "Pray are you adding a knowledge of Politics to your other various accomplishments?"[16]

The entire Gardiner family became supporters of Tyler's politics, and it did not take long for the president—a widower of just five months—to move to the head of a very aggressive pack of suitors vying for Julia's attention. Robert

Tyler spent many evenings at Mrs. Peyton's, playing whist with the girls and reading his latest efforts at poetry for Margaret's opinion. He also brought messages from his father, a sure sign that a serious courtship was underway. Juliana, who could not help comparing Washington society unfavorably to New York's social scene, had expressed initial reservations, no doubt because of the thirty-year age difference between Tyler and her eldest daughter. The president soon won her over. She wrote to her son David in mid-February 1843: "We all like the Tylers. They are noble in their mien and possess much genius and gallantry. They are superior to political trickery, and I sincerely hope John Tyler will be re-elected President." She told Alexander that Tyler was a "fine man, amiable and agreeable and independent." Her husband and daughters concurred.[17]

A turning point in Tyler's pursuit of Julia occurred on the evening of February 7, 1843. That night he invited the Gardiners and James I. Roosevelt and his wife to the White House for an evening of whist and conversation. Robert, Priscilla, and her father were also there. The Red Room, where tables had been set up for the card games, was so cold the guests could see their breath as they spoke to one another. At nine-thirty the president walked in. After small talk with his guests, and after teasing Margaret a bit about the number of young men who sought her company, he asked Julia to play cards with him.

The two of them moved to a table in the corner of the room where they could talk to each other alone. Ignoring how cold it was, Tyler took advantage of the ambience of the flickering candles. He and Julia made eye contact with one another, establishing a connection that everyone else in the room noticed. "He had quite a flirtation with J[ulia]," Margaret recounted for her brother Alexander, "and played several games of *All fours* [a card game that usually consisted of four players] with her." Thomas Cooper, Priscilla's father, who had not yet seen for himself the chemistry between Tyler and Julia, now had firsthand knowledge of it. "Do you see the President playing *old sledge* [an alternative name for All Fours] with Miss Gardiner?" he whispered in amazement to his daughter. "It will be in the *Globe* tomorrow."

Tyler evidently worried very little about tomorrow; he did not want this night to end. After the Roosevelts said their goodbyes for the evening, the president asked the Gardiners to join him in the family residence on the second floor. They sat around the fire talking for more than two hours. When the Gardiners finally got up to leave, Tyler quickly kissed Margaret on the cheek. "He was proceeding to treat Julia in the same manner," Margaret wrote the next day, "when she snatched away her hand and flew down the stairs with the

President after her around chairs and tables until at last he caught her." The whole scene, Margaret told her brother, was "truly amusing."[18]

Julia may have initiated this scene so that she could continue the flirtation from earlier in the evening. If she had, Tyler certainly took the bait. His effort to give Julia a farewell kiss may have been amusing to Margaret, but it was symbolic of something much more important. Tyler had signaled to the entire Gardiner family that he had made up his mind to win Julia's hand in marriage. It is difficult to imagine a fifty-two-year-old suitor in the mid-nineteenth century feeling comfortable enough in the presence of a young woman's parents to give in to such an impetuous display of playfulness and affection. Tyler, however, thought nothing of it, even though his behavior that night was completely out of character. He was not known for being impulsive. In fact, this may have been the only instance of his entire presidency when an idea popped into his head and he immediately acted on it. Matters of state required ponderous and often agonizing deliberation; matters of the heart did not, at least when it came to Julia Gardiner. This was heady stuff. Julia stirred his imagination and inspired a passion he had never displayed in his work. Tyler's courtship of Letitia thirty years earlier had been marked by an almost painful formality; he had not even dared to kiss her hand until right before their wedding. His pursuit of Julia would be far, far different.

Tyler was not cowed by the thirty-year difference in their ages. In fact, Julia's youth, at least partially, no doubt accounted for his attraction to her. Nor did the many men who also sought her hand intimidate him. In fact, they may have been the catalyst that prompted Tyler to move so quickly in making his intentions known.

He pursued her confidently. So confidently, in fact, that he finally proposed marriage to Julia at the Washington's Birthday Ball at the White House on February 22, 1843. Speaking to a newspaper reporter many years later, Julia recalled that she wore a white ball gown made of a stiff, sheer cotton fabric called tarlatan that night. She also wore a crimson Greek cap with a tassel on her head. Every man—indeed every person—in the room noticed her. "I had been dancing with a young man [Richard Waldron] who was not pleased with the attention the President had been paying me," she remembered. "We had just stopped and were walking about when the President came up, and drawing my arm through his, said to the young man: 'I must claim Miss Gardiner's company for awhile.'" Waldron started to object but quickly realized his commander in chief outranked him. Taking Julia by the arm, Tyler led her out of the room, abruptly stopped, and asked her to marry him.

Julia claimed that she "had never thought of love," so she turned him down, shaking "my head with each word, which flung the tassel of my Greek cap into his face with every move." She admitted, "It was undignified, but it amused me very much to see his expression as he tried to make love to me and the tassel brushed his face." Julia did not tell her parents that Tyler had asked her to marry him, worrying that her father would "blame [her] for allowing the President to reach the proposing point."[19]

David and Juliana may not have known that Tyler had proposed to their daughter that night, but they thought their family's relationship with the president had become close enough to warrant their son Alexander's participation in his efforts to build a third party. Juliana also pledged allegiance to Tyler's politics. "You must be a Tyler man as I believe his measures are wise," she wrote to Alexander. Whether at this point Juliana could even tell what those measures were was almost beside the point. The family liked the president and wanted to do what they could to help him win election in his own right.

Alexander started by publishing an anonymous letter in the New York Post that praised the Tyler administration. The president liked it so much, he asked John Jones to publish the missive in the Madisonian; he was delighted when he found out later that Julia's brother had authored the piece. Heeding a request from his father, Alexander traveled to Washington before the end of the social season. He met Tyler on February 25, when the Gardiners arrived at the White House for tea. Alexander laughed when he saw something along the lines of a repeat performance of the "frolic" that had occurred three weeks earlier. "Julia and I raced from one end of the house to the other," Margaret gleefully reported to her brother David, "upstairs and down, and he [Tyler] after us." The girls "[w]altzed and danced in the famous East Room, played the piano, ransacked every room and in fact made ourselves as much at home as the occupants." Later that evening Tyler escorted the Gardiner family to a concert, the first time he had ventured outside the White House for a social occasion since Letitia had died. Margaret wrote that everyone in the hall took note of the party's arrival and that for the president "to be seen gallanting Julia was a matter of great speculation."[20]

That speculation led to rumors in March 1843 that Tyler and Julia were engaged. Julia herself fed these rumors. Right before the lame-duck session of Congress adjourned, she asked Justice Henry Baldwin to take her autograph book to Capitol Hill and collect as many signatures from prominent officials as he could before they all fled Washington for the recess. Folded inside the autograph book was a poem Tyler had written in Julia's honor. Baldwin and

Justice McLean read the poem and quickly spread the news that the president had taken his pursuit of Julia to another level. By now, McLean had given up the notion that Julia was interested in him as a potential husband, but he still wanted to make the president's romantic life difficult if he could. "The Judges have resolved to put their heads together next winter and try to outdo the P[resident] in writing poetry," Margaret reported. "It is not amusing," she said. Her preference for her sister was clearly Tyler.

The Gardiners remained in Washington until March 27. By the time they left for New York, they knew that Tyler had proposed marriage to Julia. In fact, he had apparently proffered a second proposal and, in the words of Margaret, "began to talk of resigning the Presidential chair or at least sharing it with Julia." While Tyler no doubt thought the latter option preferable, his wishes were unmistakable. Juliana would not allow Julia to formally accept the president's proposal, preferring instead that her daughter use the time away from Washington to clarify her feelings for him and think about whether she really wanted to marry him. This was sound advice, though unnecessary. Julia knew she was not ready to be engaged.[21]

The rumors of her engagement followed Julia home. A Gardiner family friend, J. J. Bailey, teased her shortly after she had settled in again at East Hampton about what he had heard. "John Tyler made an offer of his hand & *fortune!* . . . which was accepted on the following conditions—that the said J. T. should be re-elected for another term—& that Madame should wear the crown at least four years . . . that at Saratoga next summer *she* was to win hearts (her old vocation), gain popularity & electioneer at the North—while Major Noah & Collector Curtis with all the officers of the Customs at their heels, were to drum up recruits here in the South." Bailey further declared that he thought "mischief" would come out of Julia's trip to Washington but that he "did not think it would light on the grey hairs & the venerable brow of republican majesty himself." But it had. And Julia's friend had shrewdly summarized the upside that marriage to the New York heiress would bring with it. Playful banter or not, many in both Washington and New York no doubt thought the same thing.[22]

Chapter 17

A NEW BRIDE AND A NEW STATE

Sam Houston put John Tyler on the spot in the summer of 1843, and he seemed to relish doing it. Now in his second term as president of the Republic of Texas, Houston had been trying for seven years—ever since avenging the loss of the Alamo and ambushing Mexican general Santa Anna at San Jacinto—to persuade the United States to annex his country.

Many Americans had called for the "re-annexation" of Texas in the years after its revolution began in 1836, arguing with some justification that a portion of the territory had been part of the original Louisiana Purchase in 1803 but had been bargained away by Secretary of State John Quincy Adams's Transcontinental Treaty with Spain in 1819. Presidents Jackson and Van Buren had refused to consider annexation, however, fearing it would provoke war with Mexico and ignite a fierce sectional controversy over slavery. President Tyler had acknowledged the problematic issue of slavery when he first broached the idea of annexation with Secretary of State Webster in 1841. He appeared to be content to follow the policy of his predecessors when he rejected two proposals for annexation that Texas officials proffered in the summer and fall of 1842.

Tyler was, however, warming to the idea of annexation and was looking for a way to pull it off. Furthermore, two of his closest advisors—Henry Wise and fellow Virginia congressman Thomas Walker Gilmer—had publicly made the case for the acquisition of Texas, leading to speculation in early 1843 that the president had made up his mind to make annexation an administration goal.[1]

In March 1843 Tyler met privately with Isaac Van Zandt, Texas minister to the United States, and indicated that annexation had become the administration's chief priority, though he could not yet fully commit to it. "Encourage your people to be quiet, and to not grow impatient," he urged Van Zandt. "We are doing all we can to annex you to us, but we must have time." The president informed Van Zandt that his administration would be working to accomplish annexation through a treaty. He also stressed the importance of maintaining absolute secrecy and warned the Texan that "public notoriety" would likely derail administration efforts.[2]

Van Zandt assured Tyler that Texas officials would abide by his wishes. But after another month went by with no movement on annexation, he realized that the admonition to keep administration plans a secret was a way for the

312

president to buy more time—to waste time?—until he could fully reconcile himself to the idea and make the plan operational. Tyler was seemingly frozen by indecision and inaction yet again. He gave the lame excuse that difficulties with the British over the final details of the Webster-Ashburton Treaty had caused the delay. Van Zandt did not buy this explanation but was still inclined to let him off the hook, remaining optimistic. Acknowledging the political challenges Tyler faced as a president without a party and recognizing that the administration had to tread carefully to avoid causing a sectional firestorm in the North, Van Zandt wrote that Tyler was "trying to fix things up to get a good headway—or, as our country boys would say, he is stopping to spit on his hands in order to get better hold." Texans had apparently *always* had a way with words. "He is trying to roll the stones out of his way," Van Zandt continued, "but sometimes he has to roll them up hill, and when he lets go to take another up the last rolls back, so you see he has a hard time of it. He is good pluck, however, and won't easily give up the ship."[3]

During the course of his presidency, Tyler had been compared to Lucifer and to Benedict Arnold. No one as yet, however, had compared him to Sisyphus, the figure from Greek mythology who continually rolled a large boulder up a hill only to watch it roll back down once he got close to the top. The metaphor was apt. Every accomplishment in Tyler's administration resulted from tremendous effort; nothing ever came easily. Whigs and Democrats alike had been rolling stones downhill at Tyler for two years now, and he usually pushed them right back up the hill, determined not to be beaten. His pursuit of Texas would follow a similar pattern. It is not hard to see why Van Zandt expressed both exasperation and admiration for Tyler. The president could be maddeningly indecisive one moment and bravely resolute the next.

Tyler needed a nudge in the right direction, however, and Houston provided it. The Texas president cozied up to the British chargé d'affaires in Texas, Charles Elliott, and played up their relationship to signal to the United States that Britain's influence in Texas was more than incidental. Houston's government also informed President Tyler in February 1843 that the British had designs on Texas and that it was time for the United States to pursue annexation with a sense of urgency. Still Tyler did nothing. Houston ran out of patience with this dithering and believed that, by the summer of 1843, the time was right to press the administration more forcefully. Houston saw an opening. He had received an offer—one he would have regarded as preposterous just a few months earlier—from Santa Anna, now Mexico's ruler. Santa Anna wanted peace between Texas and Mexico, an agreement that would end the revolution. He proposed that Texans accept Mexican sovereignty over them in name only in exchange for a promise from the Mexican government that, in practice, they would be allowed to govern themselves.

At once Houston recognized how he might best use this offer to his advantage. The British wanted an armistice between Texas and Mexico, believing peace would move Texas farther away from the orbit of the United States and would stabilize Mexico itself. The possibility of resuming its war with Texas had also scared British bondholders who had invested heavily in Mexico into thinking they might never see their money again. Britain would no doubt mediate negotiations between Texas and Mexico. Houston could then use London's role in the process to pressure the Anglophobes in the Tyler administration into pursuing annexation, playing the British against the American government to get what he wanted. As the first step, he sent representatives to Mexico City in July 1843 on the pretense of negotiating with Santa Anna. He also ordered Texas officials in Washington—chiefly Van Zandt—to cease discussions with the Tyler administration on annexation. Houston thus conveyed the impression that negotiating a peace settlement with the Mexicans superseded a desire on his part to seek annexation to the United States. Tyler regarded this action as ominous. Hindsight tells us the Texas president was being crafty.[4]

Tyler took the bait—somewhat. On August 28, 1843, he wrote an "Unofficial and Confidential" letter to the American minister in Mexico, Waddy Thompson. It is noteworthy that he designated this as "unofficial" correspondence. The chain of command usually meant the secretary of state was responsible for sending a letter to an American minister abroad. But Tyler was too disturbed about Texas to be concerned with such diplomatic niceties. He demanded answers and believed Thompson was in the best position to provide them. "We feel here the greatest desire to know the precise basis on which the existing negociation [sic] between Mexico and Texas is conducted," the president wrote. He further told Thompson that Britain sought the "total abolition of slavery, and failing in that she proposes to guarantee the sovereignty of Texas and her separate independence."[5]

How had President Tyler so readily made the link between Britain and Texas that Houston hoped he would make? There were two reasons. First, the Peel ministry had approached the administration with a startling proposal to recruit free blacks in the American South for work on the plantations of its West Indian colonies. These plantations desperately needed an influx of laborers. Britain's "Great Experiment" in the Caribbean—the conversion from slave to free labor—had failed. The British had been forced to concede that slavery had been more profitable. The only way for them to compete in the global market was to abolish slavery everywhere.[6]

Second, Duff Green, who was in Britain again as the Tyler administration's unofficial envoy, reported by letter on July 3 that a Texas abolitionist by the name of Stephen Pearl Andrews had visited London with American antislavery leader Lewis Tappan and had secured a solid commitment from Lord Aberdeen, the British foreign secretary, to support abolition in Texas. Moreover, the Peel ministry would pay an indemnity to Texans who emancipated their slaves. Green had been tipped off by Ashbel Smith, Texas minister to Britain, taking what Smith had told him at face value. In fact, no such commitment had been made; Aberdeen had been speaking theoretically. Not one to let the truth stand in the way of his own preconceived notions, however, and recognizing the opportunity to shape history, Green passed the erroneous information on to President Tyler. His letter sounded the alarm about alleged British intrigue in the Texas Republic.[7]

Green no doubt knew he would find a receptive audience in the Tyler administration. Hugh Legaré, who had been serving as both attorney general and secretary of state, died unexpectedly on June 20, 1843, after falling ill during a presidential trip to commemorate the Bunker Hill Monument in Boston. Tyler tapped Maryland Democrat John Nelson for attorney general and named Abel Upshur as his new secretary of state.[8] Upshur wholeheartedly supported the annexation of Texas and saw the British bogeyman lurking around every corner. Having read Green's dispatch from London, he panicked and declared that Texas was ripe for British machinations. "Pressed by an unrelenting enemy on her borders," he wrote breathlessly to William S. Murphy, American chargé d'affaires in Texas, "her treasury exhausted and her credit almost destroyed, Texas is in a condition to need the support of other nations and to obtain it upon terms of great hardship and many sacrifices to herself." If the Lone Star republic received "no countenance and support from the United States, it is not an extravagant supposition" that Britain would fill the void. Now—early August 1843—was the time to persuade President Tyler to pursue annexation.[9]

Despite his "apprehensions and fears" of what was afoot in Texas, Tyler did not favor rash action. True to form, he still played for time. The president recognized that Smith had a vested interest in alarming the administration. "The information which is given me may be intended to awaken a new course of action on the part of this government," he wrote. It "may be designed simply to make this government take strong and decided grounds." Tyler informed Thompson that the intelligence had come from the Texas minister in London, who had confirmed that Lord Aberdeen admitted "the great interest which England took in the abolition of slavery in Texas, and distinctly makes that the basis of interference" in the talks between Mexico and Texas. Tyler wanted Thompson to put his ear to the ground and keep Washington informed as to what was happening in the negotiations. "You have a most important part to play," he encouraged his minister, "and I do not doubt that you will play it well."[10]

Were Upshur's fears justified, or did the circumstances call for President Tyler's hesitation? What exactly *were* British intentions in Texas? Without question, in an ideal world the Peel ministry would have liked to have seen slavery abolished there. The failure of the Great Experiment was real, and Britain and its colonies faced economic challenges that the American South's slave system—and its exports—exacerbated. Emancipation in the Lone Star republic might very well prove salutary to Britain's economic fortunes. Furthermore, enslaved people in states like South Carolina, Georgia, Alabama, Mississippi, and Louisiana might pursue freedom by crafting their own version of "Goin' to Texas," which would destabilize the South and impair its ability to maintain the near monopoly it enjoyed in worldwide cotton. Britain would then become more competitive. Having a nation committed to free labor at the South's doorstep would inevitably undermine slavery there.

Lord Aberdeen seemed to enjoy his government's status as a potential agent provocateur—at least until Tyler began making a habit of publicly demonizing British interests in Texas. In the end the British played up their threat to interfere with slavery in Texas but never made it a specific policy goal. "The subject of domestic slavery," Texas official Anson Jones wrote, "about which so much alarm existed in 1844–'45, was never once so much as mentioned or alluded to by the British Minister to the Government of Texas, except to disclaim in most emphatic terms any intention on the part of England ever to interfere with it here." Jones pointed out that the British government "might be willing to tickle her abolitionists" with the possibility of promoting emancipation in Texas, "but had no idea of going on a crusade with them to abolish slavery in Texas or anywhere else." That being said, London's interest in Texas was not necessarily benign. The Peel government did intend to "build up a power independent of the United States, who could raise cotton enough to supply the world . . . and this not *primarily* to injure the United States, but to benefit herself, not with enmity to brother Jonathan, but love to John Bull."[11]

President Tyler and Secretary of State Upshur, however, had been subjected to Green's dire warnings from London and tended to believe the worst of the British. The US minister to Britain, Edward Everett, whom Green had antagonized while in London, gave little weight to these claims and saw scant cause for alarm. Upshur, however, discounted the Massachusetts-born Everett's assessment because he was unsound on slavery. Green, playing to his audience, upped the ante by constructing what one historian calls a "nineteenth-century domino theory," arguing that Britain intended to spearhead the abolition of slavery in Cuba and Brazil as a precursor to forcing abolition in the United States. According to Green, British machinations in Texas had therefore become part of a hemispheric contest between the United States and Britain over the future of slavery. Tyler never became as convinced of this as either Green or Upshur, and he was personally less ideologically committed to the long-term survival of slavery than either of these two men. With the Monroe Doctrine in mind, he nevertheless exercised due diligence on the matter by alerting the State Department to potential British interference in Cuba as early as December 1841. He also ordered an American naval squadron to Havana at one point.[12]

The president and secretary of state believed they understood the economic motivation of Britain to support abolition and were not fooled by the "impulse of philanthropy" that rhetorically guided London's campaign to end slavery. Recall that Tyler had, in fact, denounced such philanthropy as "no way distinguishable from fanaticism" in a speech he gave as president of the Virginia Colonization Society in 1838, which also served as a brief against the American abolitionist movement. Tyler and Upshur had no way of knowing, however, that the British threat in Texas had been exaggerated and viewed the apparent meddling there with a sense of alarm. No British official, moreover, either in London or Washington, had disabused the administration of this notion. Tyler professed that both he and his fellow Virginian believed the British were just biding their time until they could strike. Clearly, the administration took this threat seriously. That they did so blinded them to what was perhaps the most important question of all: would Texans really consider aligning with the British if it meant they had to give up slavery?[13]

Whether the danger was real or exaggerated, though, misses the point. What was even more important than the perceived threat Britain posed in Texas was the way Texas officials *used* that threat and exploited the Tyler administration's fear of it to force the annexation issue once and for all. Houston knew what he was doing.

For Upshur and, increasingly by the late summer of 1843, President Tyler, the course had become clear. Many Texans resented the inactivity of the United States and made plain that the Tyler administration should take seriously the "friendly offices" of both Britain and France toward their republic. At a meeting with Van Zandt in Washington in mid-August, Upshur broached the subject of British interference in Texas. Van Zandt downplayed it but bluntly told the secretary of state that if Britain "did intend, or was trying to obtain an undue influence over Texas, the better way to counteract her efforts was for the United States to act promptly and efficiently" to make her good intentions known. Upshur responded by assuring the Texan that he would use his power to bring this happy result about.[14]

John Tyler finally fully embraced the annexation project because he believed bringing Texas into the Union would benefit the entire country. He believed the abolitionists had it wrong when they portrayed annexation as a slaveholders' plot. In Tyler's view, acquiring Texas would strengthen the United States and allow America to fulfill its mission as a great power. He firmly believed in what his fellow Americans would soon be calling "Manifest Destiny."

Tyler knew that he needed more than just his own faith that his course of action was the correct one for the United States. He had to take steps to place his Texas project on more secure footing. Doing so required that he somewhat neutralize the British. The president believed a commercial treaty with Britain and a generous settlement of the Oregon boundary dispute, which had festered since the two nations began joint occupation of the territory in 1818, would allow him to augment the good feelings that emerged out of the successful Webster-Ashburton negotiations from the summer before. Tyler also believed that coming to terms over Oregon at the same time he secured the annexation of Texas would allow him to sell both to the American people with maximum effect. Oregon would serve as a "counterpoise in territory" that would offset the addition of more slave territory.[15]

The idea for the commercial treaty went nowhere. Secretary of State Upshur, who believed Tyler had opened the Oregon boundary issue prematurely, dragged his feet, and negotiations with the British on the matter failed to gain traction. Moreover, he was convinced that there was no need for the "counterpoise" Tyler wanted and believed he knew the best way to frame the Texas issue to get northerners on board. "I can make the question so clear that even the Yankees will go for annexation," he wrote. The trick, Upshur thought, was to portray Texas as a major market for northern manufacturing. He had "every reason to hope that they will soon be convinced; no effort will be spared to lay the truth before them."[16]

Aggressive editorials in the *Madisonian* disseminated this truth. Through-

out October and November 1843, the Tyler administration newspaper analyzed annexation from every conceivable angle in an effort to make the case
for bringing Texas into the Union. The editorials hammered home the potential threat of British involvement in the republic.[17] At the same time, President
Tyler authorized Upshur to begin negotiations with Van Zandt that he hoped
would culminate in a treaty he could present to the Senate for ratification.[18]
But he wanted these talks conducted in secret. He wanted to be able to lay the
fait accompli of a treaty before the American people and mute the opposition
that would surely reach a fever pitch if the administration's goal was made
public. The president also realized that making the negotiations known risked
antagonizing Mexico and drawing the United States into war.

Opponents of annexation posed one set of potential problems for Tyler.
Mexico posed another. The Texas government presented yet one more. Houston continued to play coy and was reluctant to engage the administration in
talks that he feared might amount to nothing. He had become accustomed to
getting his hopes up that the United States would follow through on annexation, only to have those hopes dashed repeatedly. Houston continued to pursue a permanent peace with Mexico in the fall of 1843, making a show of his
unwillingness to believe that the time for annexation might finally be at hand.
He also did not want to give up his trump card of British interference unless
he was absolutely certain of Tyler's determination to see annexation through to
the end. Houston knew that if Texas negotiated a treaty with the United States
and the pact failed in the US Senate, it would poison the relationship between
Texas and Britain, to say nothing of what it would do to any progress his government had made with Mexico in the peace talks. Until Houston gave his sanction, the negotiations between Upshur and Van Zandt would be unofficial.[19]

That suited President Tyler, who steadfastly refused to acknowledge for the
record that the administration was laying the groundwork for an annexation
treaty. Hardly anyone doubted what was really going on, however, even if they
had no concrete proof. Abolitionists suspected the worst. The Mexican government also believed annexation might be in the offing. Santa Anna's minister
to the United States even went so far as to warn Secretary of State Upshur in
writing that war would result if Congress moved to bring Texas into the Union.

The president addressed this threat in his third annual message to Congress in December 1843. He was willing to play along with the erroneous
Mexican belief that Congress—and not the administration—might be ready
to pursue annexation because it allowed him to flex American muscle while
keeping the secrecy of Upshur's preliminary negotiations intact. "If designed

to prevent Congress from introducing that question [annexation] as a fit subject for its calm deliberation and final judgment," Tyler declared, referring to Mexico's threat of war, it will fail. At the same time, the president kept open the possibility that the relationship between the United States and Texas might change in the near future and made clear he would brook no interference from Mexico. Tyler declared that the United States would continue to treat Texas as "entirely independent of Mexico" and for good measure urged Mexico to bring an end to the war it had fought on-and-off with the Lone Star republic since the Battle of San Jacinto. No specific mention was made in the message about the negotiations between Texas and the administration.[20]

Tyler's silence on what was transpiring puzzled Texas officials. Van Zandt expected that the president would come right out and urge Congress to act on annexation. When he did not, the grumbling started, and Texans began to feel that they were being had once again. Perhaps Houston was right. Upshur had to reassure them this was not the case. To Murphy, the American chargé in Texas, he acknowledged that Tyler had "created an impression in Texas, either that he is indifferent to that measure or that he despairs of its success. Such an impression does him great injustice." Upshur explained that Tyler wanted to fully work out the details of a treaty before he went public with information about annexation. He further defended the president by pointing out that he was engaged in the delicate process of using the only powers at his disposal—those to make a treaty—to bring about annexation and that the political climate in Washington demanded he proceed in this way.[21]

Upshur buttressed his avowals of good faith on the part of President Tyler with claims that support for annexation continued to grow among the politicians in Washington, a happy result no doubt arising at least in part from the newspaper campaign. He maintained that northerners as well as southerners were warming to the idea of bringing Texas into the Union and that at least two-thirds of US senators favored the treaty. "There is not in my opinion the slightest doubt of the ratification of a treaty of annexation, should Texas agree to make one," he wrote.[22]

Upshur's efforts convinced Houston of the sincerity of the Tyler administration to see annexation through. To strengthen the case, Andrew Jackson was enlisted to write a letter to his old friend and protégé that proclaimed his faith that a treaty was within reach. It also helped that the administration offered Van Zandt verbal assurances that the US military would be ready to defend Texas from Mexico, if necessary, as soon as an annexation treaty had been signed. On February 15, 1844, Houston dispatched General J. P. Henderson to

Washington as the official envoy charged with working out the details of the treaty. "So far as I am concerned or my hearty co[o]peration required," Houston replied to Jackson, "I am determined upon immediate annexation to the United States." The unofficial nature of the process had now come to an end.[23]

As all of this was coming to pass, Tyler's annexation project received a jolt from a Mississippi senator named Robert J. Walker, who published a lengthy open letter in the *Washington Globe* spelling out the benefits of bringing Texas into the Union. Walker's support of Tyler dated to the special session of Congress in the summer of 1841, when he had applauded the president's vetoes of Clay's banking bills. The two men eventually bonded over their mutual desire to secure Texas annexation. Whether Tyler specifically asked Walker to write the open letter on behalf of the project is not clear. Possessed with all the enthusiasm of a true believer, the Mississippi senator would not have needed much in the way of prodding.

Walker's systematic analysis of the relationship between slavery and annexation was the letter's most important feature. He maintained that adding Texas to the Union would not actually expand slave territory, as the abolitionists charged. To the contrary, annexation would allow slaveowners in states where the soil had been exhausted—Delaware, Maryland, Virginia, and Kentucky—to sell their bondsmen and women to Texas, where they would work on land that had not yet been depleted by decades of planting the same crops. Slaves would thus be drained off gradually from the older areas of the South and concentrated in Texas. Eventually, too, Texas slaveholders would exhaust their own soil. At that point they would no longer need their enslaved labor anymore. Facing bankruptcy if they continued to feed, clothe, and shelter their slaves, these planters would ultimately emancipate them. The new free-black population would then flow southward into Mexico, Central America, and South America in search of employment, confident in the knowledge they would find society there more congenial to people of color. "The outlet for our negro race," Walker argued, "through this vast region, can never be opened but by the reannexation of Texas."[24]

This "safety-valve thesis," as it came to be called, gave northerners just as much a stake in annexation as southerners. Walker's letter became the most systematic brief for annexation, as well as the most forcefully argued "solution" to America's twin problems of slavery and race, ever written. One scholar has argued that it was a piece of "cultural fiction capable of both realigning the power structure of the Democratic party and articulating a unified national response" to the challenges the nation faced in the 1840s. Eventually published as a thirty-two-page pamphlet and replete with pseudoscientific racism, it was designed to appeal to moderates—citizens and politicians who occupied the middle ground between the abolitionists, who favored the immediate end of slavery, and southern proslavery zealots, who would not abide the eventual demise of their "peculiar institution." Walker's thesis also comported with the diffusion argument Tyler had made years before as a congressman during the Missouri debates.

The president fully concurred with the overt racism of Walker's letter but said nothing publicly at the time in support of it. In 1847, however, he argued in the pages of *Niles' Register* that Walker's "writings unveiled the true merits of the question, and, aided by the expositions of many editors of the newspaper press, brought the public mind to a just and sound decision." Those connected to the negotiations recognized the important role Walker played in the process. "Senator Walker's letter has given it additional impetus," the secretary of the Texas legation in Washington reported to the Lone Star government, "and in some degree corrected public sentiment in regard to its bearing upon the general interests of the nation. It [annexation] is most decidedly gaining ground."[25]

In February 1844 Tyler could feel confident that his Texas project was in capable hands. He had every reason to believe he and Upshur would succeed in their quest to bring the Lone Star republic into the Union. His spirits had never been higher.

Tyler also had reason to feel good about his personal life. Letitia's last years had been stressful for him, and while nearly everyone who came into contact with him socially found Tyler gracious and accommodating, at times even charmingly friendly, his outward demeanor masked a pervasive sadness. The gloom that had characterized his life for so long, however, began to lift when Julia Gardiner entered his life. It receded further still in the summer of 1843 when he traveled north for the Bunker Hill ceremony and found he could truly enjoy himself for the first time in a long time. Hugh Legaré's sudden death tempered that joy, and Tyler's own brief illness at the conclusion of the trip no doubt made him wonder if he was about to repeat the cycle of poor health that had dogged him since young adulthood. But, overall, Tyler was a happy man again and felt his old, youthful buoyancy return.

His feelings for Julia made him feel young again. Finally freed from the emotional burden of his wife's illness and again a single man, Tyler became flirtatious and almost giddy when he found himself in the presence of women. At times he behaved inappropriately. Visiting Williamsburg shortly before he returned to Washington in August 1843, he called on Dickie and Mary Ann Galt at their home, Tazewell Hall. The couple's adopted daughter, Eliza Fisk Harwood, a young woman of sixteen, thoroughly charmed the president—so much so that he told her that he wished she were ten years older. That comment failed to impress Eliza, who also "refused him a kiss which he thought very strangely of." Sometime later, Tyler replied to a letter from a Mrs. Benson—whom we can hope was a widow and not the wife of his friend Alfred Benson—and told her that he could not "refuse your very friendly request of this morning, although I would have preferred, that my humble name should have been engraved upon your memory—were we both younger I might have said *your heart*."[26]

Despite the attention he paid to these women, it was Miss Gardiner who occupied his daydreams. He looked forward to the coming social season and hoped Julia would again take part. "Are you coming to Washington this winter?" he impatiently asked her by letter. "I am selfish in desiring that you should, as I wish my levees attended by the fairest forms from all parts of the country and who [are] brighter and fairer than you and Margaret?" Tyler got his wish. David Gardiner accompanied his daughters to Washington on February 24. Three nights later they were guests at a White House levee. Julia, of course, commanded the room.[27]

Tyler made sure the Gardiners received an invitation to accompany a presidential party on a cruise of the Potomac on Wednesday, February 28, 1844, the day after the levee. The president and his cabinet, their wives, members of Congress, several foreign ministers, army and naval officers, and other guests, including seventy-five-year-old Dolley Madison—some 350 people in all—sailed on the USS *Princeton*. The magnificent new warship, the first vessel in the American navy to use a steam-powered underwater propeller, measured 164 feet in length and boasted more than 14,000 square feet of canvas rigging. Constructed at a cost of $141,819, the ship was the crown jewel of Upshur's tenure as navy secretary and the culmination of the hard work of its commander, Captain Robert F. Stockton, who had designed its hull and rig. Stockton was anxious to show the *Princeton* off; in fact, the floating party had been his idea. He also wished to demonstrate the sheer power of the ship's new 27,000-pound cannon, wryly christened the "Peacemaker," which had been built with wrought iron rather than the bronze or cast iron that composed the typical naval gun. The captain was justifiably proud of the innovativeness of the ship and its largest weapon.

With blue skies and unseasonably warm temperatures, the weather could not have been more perfect for the occasion. The day ended in spectacular tragedy, however. During the third demonstration of the Peacemaker, the cannon exploded, killing Upshur, Navy Secretary Thomas Walker Gilmer, US diplomat Virgil Maxcy, Commodore Beverley Kennon, and David Gardiner. President Tyler's valet and two of the ship's crewmen also died in the explosion. Senator Thomas Hart Benton, who had been nearby when the cannon exploded, was knocked unconscious and suffered a punctured eardrum.[28]

The third state funeral in as many years took place at 11:00 A.M. in the East Room on Saturday, March 2, 1844. Black bunting adorned the White House. Reverend Hawley was again pressed into service as the presiding clergyman; on this occasion he was assisted by two other ministers. Four open caskets were lined up across the floor; Maxcy's body had been removed by his family for a private burial in Maryland, perhaps owing to his having lost both arms and a leg in the accident. Tyler sat with Julia and Margaret in front of their father's casket. The saddest moment of a very sad day occurred when Gilmer's young son was taken up to his father's casket. "There's my pa!" he exclaimed, as if he expected to be able to talk to him again. There was not a dry eye in the room.[29]

After the service, a large procession of nearly one mile in length accompanied the bodies to the Congressional Cemetery, where they would be entombed until the families made arrangements to have them moved to plots in their hometowns. Members of Congress, military officers, and other dignitaries served as pallbearers for all of the victims. Minute guns were fired as the hearses made their way through the streets of Washington, the clop-clop of horses' hooves the only other noise. One witness felt the day's weather perfectly matched the somber occasion. "It was dark & lowering as if the very heavens were hung in mourning, and a few drops, like Angels' tears, fell at times from the murky canopy above."[30]

Unfortunately, the dark day had more in store for President Tyler. As he, John Jr., and daughter Letitia made their way back by carriage to the White House from the Congressional Cemetery, the coachman, Pat Burrell, lost control of the reins. The horses galloped pell-mell down Pennsylvania Avenue at breakneck speed, with all three men utterly helpless and unable to stop them. People were forced to jump out of the way of the runaway coach. Thankfully, an alert pedestrian—reportedly a free black man—heard the shouts coming from the carriage and decided to help. He walked out into the street as the racing carriage approached. Bravely, the man jumped in front of the horses, reached for the reins, and somehow succeeded in finally bringing the animals to a stop. In light of the tragedy of the last few days, Tyler could hardly believe what had just happened. He had been extraordinarily lucky to escape the mishap unscathed.

After the shock of the terrible accident had subsided, Tyler was distraught. "You have heard no doubt of the terrible occurrences on board the *Princeton* together with all the particulars," he wrote his daughter Mary two days after the state funeral. "A more heart rending scene scarcely ever occur[e]d. What a loss I have suffered in Upshur and Gilmer. They were truly my friends and would have aided me for the next twelve months with great effect." The stress of the tragedy had brought back Tyler's ill health, "I hope however to be restored in a day or two." To David Henshaw, briefly Tyler's navy secretary, he wrote: "I have braced myself up to the utmost to endure the sad and almost irreparable privation which I have experienced. Sometimes I almost despond." Alluding to the Senate rejections of his cabinet nominees, including Henshaw himself, who had been replaced by Gilmer, the president wrote, "The embarrassments thrown recently in my way by the action of the Senate, and now followed up by an act of Providence would seem directed to my undoing, but I will not despond." On the contrary, he declared that he would "rouse myself to further action" and throw "myself into the hands of the great father of all, [and] implore unceasingly his support of me in my efforts for the common good of my beloved country." Tyler's fatalism would guide him through.[31]

He also found succor in the many condolences that poured into the White House in the wake of the tragedy. Well-wishers knew how lucky Tyler himself had been to escape serious injury or death. Indeed, the United States had come perilously close to having two presidents from the same election die while in office. And since Tyler had no vice president, had he been killed aboard the *Princeton*, Senate president pro tempore and Whig nemesis Willie P. Mangum would have become the nation's eleventh president. That this was prevented likely made Tyler ever more grateful that the divine hand of Providence had spared his life.[32]

The president sent his own condolences to the families of the men who were killed.[33] He also reportedly made one extraordinary gesture: he sent the mother of his valet a check for two hundred dollars. Referred to variously in primary and secondary sources as either Armistead, Henry, or I. More, the valet had dressed Tyler every day and had become a valued part of the president's life. It is unclear whether he had been a free man, though Tyler's gesture certainly indicates he may have been. Whatever the case, the valet apparently provided a measure of financial support to his mother, and Tyler wished to compensate her in a tangible way for a loss she would certainly never get over.[34]

Tyler himself could not afford to wait until he had gotten over the tragedy. The *Princeton* explosion meant that—yet again—he would have to reconstitute his cabinet. He knew he needed to act quickly and hoped the Senate would react with magnanimity and confirm his nominations without engaging in the petty partisanship that had characterized the process thus far in his presidency. Tyler wanted a Virginian to replace Gilmer as navy secretary and was sure the man he had in mind would find favor on both sides of the Senate aisle. On March 5, 1844, he dispatched a letter to forty-four-year-old Democrat John Young Mason, a federal judge, formally offering him the navy post.[35]

Initially, Mason turned him down. An offer of the post then went out to Tennessee Democrat James K. Polk. Polk briefly, but probably not seriously, considered accepting. In the meantime Mason changed his mind. Tyler quietly saw to it that Theophilus Fisk, a Virginia newspaper editor, congressional clerk, and confidant of Polk, delivered the news that the offer was being rescinded. The Senate confirmed Mason with no debate on March 14. Perhaps the nomination sailed through because no senator wanted to oppose Mason and give President Tyler added sympathy in the wake of the tragedy. Perhaps the Senate simply judged Mason on his merits and recognized that no legitimate opposition to his nomination could be raised. Whatever the case, the Virginia judge was a sound addition to the administration and a far cry from some of the president's recent cabinet choices.[36]

That left the crucial post of secretary of state. The Senate wasted little time in confirming none other than sixty-one-year-old John C. Calhoun as the seventeenth man in American history to hold the job. How the legendary Cast Iron Man had come to be Tyler's nominee to head the State Department has been a matter of scholarly dispute. Calhoun biographers Charles Wiltse and John Niven argue that the president specifically wanted the South Carolinian in the most important position in the cabinet because he believed Calhoun offered the best opportunity to finish what Upshur had started regarding the Texas treaty. Calhoun had long been on record as an enthusiastic proponent of Texas annexation. Furthermore, his southern loyalties were indisputable, and no man on the public stage at this time enjoyed more stature for both his service and intellect. This argument also claims that Tyler had tried on at least two other occasions to bring Calhoun into the cabinet but had been unable to persuade him.[37]

Other evidence suggests, however, that Tyler had Calhoun forced on him because of a self-described "spirit of rashness" by Henry Wise. Wise, who had just resigned from Congress, claimed that early on the morning of February 29, the day after the *Princeton* explosion, he went to the Washington home of South Carolina senator George McDuffie, a Calhoun confidant, to ask whether he thought Calhoun would come out of retirement and accept the position of secretary of state. Calhoun's supporters had just withdrawn his name as a candidate for president in 1844, making him available (and acceptable). Wise offered his opinion that Calhoun represented the best chance for the administration to secure annexation. McDuffie did not ask if the offer had come directly from President Tyler—he just assumed it had. Wise urged McDuffie to write to Calhoun at once (Calhoun was at home in South Carolina) and inform his friend that his name would be sent to the Senate for confirmation as secretary of state and advise him to accept the appointment. McDuffie agreed to do so.

Later that morning Wise told Tyler what he had done, which prompted an angry outburst from the president. According to Wise, Tyler then softened and instructed him to send a letter to Calhoun that contained a formal offer of the cabinet post. The congressman replied that he could not write to Calhoun, explaining to the president that the South Carolinian's name had to be submitted to the Senate and his nomination confirmed—and quickly. Only a fait accompli would prevent Calhoun from refusing the post. He believed the Senate would not dare reject the nomination.[38]

Wise recounted the events of the morning of February 29 some twenty-seven years later in what he called a "memoir" of John Tyler's life. What he claimed to do on that day was perfectly consistent with his character. Indeed, Wise often seemed to live by the maxim that it is better to beg forgiveness than to ask for permission. Some historians—Wiltse and Niven chiefly—have discounted his story because they do not believe Tyler would have allowed himself to be manipulated in this way. But Tyler biographer Oliver P. Chitwood accepts Wise's version of events, as does later biographer Robert Seager, primarily because John Tyler Jr. corroborated it in an interview many years later. Wise's biographer agrees that his subject's account offers a persuasive telling of what happened. Nevertheless, we will probably never know for sure exactly how Calhoun came to be Tyler's secretary of state.[39]

In any event, Tyler dispatched a letter to Calhoun on March 6 that spelled out the precarious position his administration found itself in as a result of Upshur's death. "The annexation of Texas to the Union, and the settlement of the Oregon question on a satisfactory basis, are the great ends to be accomplished," he wrote. "The first is in the act of completion and will admit of no delay. The last had but barely opened, when death snatched from me my lamented friend." Tyler left Calhoun no choice. "Do I expect too much of you when I, along with others, anticipate at your hands, a ready acquiescence in meeting my wishes, by coming to the aid of the Country at this important period?" Later that day Tyler informed the South Carolinian that the Senate had confirmed his nomination. It was a fait accompli.[40]

The new secretary of state left his home in South Carolina and arrived in Washington on Friday, March 29, 1844, President Tyler's fifty-fourth birthday. J. P. Henderson, Sam Houston's choice to work out the final details of a treaty with the United States, arrived the following day. Upshur and Van Zandt had already completed most of the hard work, and it did not take long to reach an agreement. On Friday, April 12, Calhoun, Henderson, and Van Zandt signed a treaty of annexation. President Tyler could at last announce that his administration had been at work on the Texas project and that he would submit the resulting treaty to the Senate on April 15, the following Monday.[41]

That weekend Tyler and Calhoun learned that the Democratic Party's organ in Washington, the *Globe*, would publish an editorial in its Monday edition endorsing annexation. On its face, that would have seemed to work in the administration's favor. But the president did not send the treaty to the Senate on April 15 after all. Why not? The answer is politics. The *Globe* supported Van Buren for president in 1844. If the paper came out for annexation, it would appear that Van Buren supported it. Tyler—and for that matter Calhoun, who wanted to stymie the New Yorker too—would not allow Van Buren to upstage the administration and use the treaty to his advantage on the presidential campaign trail. The *Madisonian* issued a stern warning on April 16: "If the *Globe*, or any other organ of Mr. Van Buren, shall attempt to appropriate the measure in a manner to operate on the Baltimore Convention, or at the polls, we shall denounce such a proceeding."[42] By alluding to the Democratic National Convention, which was slated to convene in Baltimore on May 27, the Tyler paper indicated that the president still believed he had a chance to win the party's nomination by trumpeting the Texas-annexation treaty. He made a political calculation to withhold the treaty from the Senate, both to mute the effectiveness of a potential *Globe* editorial and to give the administration time to come up with a strategy that would prevent Van Buren from capitalizing on his expansionist efforts.

Tyler and Calhoun conflated the *Globe*'s apparent support for the annexation treaty with Van Buren's support for the measure, an understandable assumption but one far from reality, as the entire country would soon find out. By withholding the treaty from the Senate, Tyler gave his new secretary of state the opportunity to strike a blow against Van Buren that would ultimately destroy the New Yorker's quest to win the Democratic Party's nomination for president in 1844. Unfortunately, Calhoun's actions also politicized the annexation treaty and injected into the debate the sectionalism that Tyler had wished to avoid when he began his pursuit of Texas.

While Calhoun was getting settled at the State Department, he found a recent letter from British minister Richard Pakenham in Upshur's files, a letter the president apparently knew nothing about. In it Pakenham explained that Lord Aberdeen had requested he address the American charges that the British intended to interfere in Texas as a way to undermine slavery in the United States. The letter acknowledged that Britain sought the abolition of slavery across the globe and confirmed that Aberdeen had encouraged Mexico to negotiate an armistice and recognition of Texas on the condition that the Lone Star republic emancipate its slaves. But it explicitly denied any British desire to act as a catalyst to end slavery in the American South.[43] Calhoun decided to draft a formal response to the Pakenham letter. The result, Senator Benton proclaimed, was a "bombshell."

Calhoun's reply pointed out that, despite Britain's disavowal of any intention to interfere with slavery in the United States, its policy of pursuing abolition throughout the world meant that the South's "safety and prosperity" were in jeopardy. He noted that President Tyler expressed "still deeper concern" that Britain sought to broker Mexico's recognition of Texas upon the condition that the republic abolish slavery. A Texas agreement to free its slaves would have grave repercussions for the United States, given the "geographical position" of the Lone Star republic. The treaty of annexation between Texas and the United States, therefore, had become the "most effectual, if not the only, means of guarding against the threatened danger" Britain posed—US security was at stake.

Calhoun was not content to stop there, however. In the second half of the Pakenham letter, he asserted that while Britain had the right to end slavery in its own possessions, which "may be humane and wise," the US Constitution protected the institution. Furthermore, he presented a proslavery, or "positive good," defense of the South's "peculiar institution" and unmistakably tied the annexation of Texas to its protection. He dispensed with the pretense of diffusion, making the case that Texas would not serve as a "safety-valve," as Senator Walker had imagined, but as a bulwark to defend slavery. Calhoun's letter to Pakenham thus made the Texas treaty a sectional document.[44]

Calhoun, however, quite possibly saw his Pakenham letter as something that would actually *unite* the country. He wanted to make Americans in the

North see that the threat to slavery inherent in Britain's Texas policy imperiled the entire Union. He hoped to arouse indignation against the British and rally all Americans to the South's aid. More broadly, he wanted to legitimize slavery's status in the nation's mainstream. In effect, Calhoun had laid down the gauntlet to the North, especially northern senators. The Pakenham letter became a litmus test: either you were with the South or you were with the British. He hoped framing the debate in this way would allow the Tyler administration to tap into a potent wellspring of anti-British sentiment in the United States and secure passage of the treaty.[45]

Historians have called Calhoun's thinking into question. Did he really believe making the Texas treaty a sectional document would allow it to win ratification in the Senate? The answer is yes, he probably did. No contemporary of John C. Calhoun, nor any scholar, ever accused him of being a shrewd politician. He had made a career of sacrificing pragmatism and expediency on the altar of principle.

The more compelling question is whether Tyler sanctioned his secretary of state's reply to Pakenham. The evidence indicates that Calhoun had not acted alone, as some historians have seemed to think. The response to Pakenham had been written at the behest of the president. Tyler later claimed, however, that this had not been the case, maintaining that Calhoun—and Upshur before him—had injected the slavery question into the debate and made annexation a purely sectional question, which he had not wanted. "My view of that subject [annexation] was not narrow, local or bigoted," Tyler wrote to his son Robert and to Daniel Webster on the same day in 1850, defending himself. "It embraced the whole country and all its interests." Tyler portrayed his view of annexation in economic terms. "The monopoly of the cotton plant was the great and important concern," he declared. "That monopoly, now secured, places all other nations at our feet." Yet "with these results before him, Mr. Calhoun unceasingly talked of slavery and its abolition in connection with the subject. That idea seemed to possess him and Upshur *as a single idea.*" Tyler pointed out in this later account that both Calhoun and Upshur had "gone to their long homes," Calhoun having died less than three weeks before the Virginian wrote these letters. In death, neither Calhoun nor Upshur could contradict him, nor could they offer any evidence that Tyler himself had advocated the very view that Calhoun had presented in the Pakenham letter.[46]

Two pieces of evidence contradict this later account by Tyler. The first is Calhoun's Pakenham letter itself. The secretary of state wrote that he was "directed by the President" to convey the displeasure of the administration toward Britain's Texas policy. The second is a letter Tyler wrote to Andrew Jackson on April 18, 1844, the same day Calhoun composed the Pakenham letter. Tyler told Jackson that he had delayed sending the Texas treaty to the Senate because he wanted Calhoun to address Pakenham's original letter to Upshur, the one found in the State Department files. These documents—the Pakenham letter and Tyler's letter to Jackson—indicate that Tyler and Calhoun had worked in tandem to formulate an answer to the official British position on Texas. It is inconceivable that Calhoun would have sent his response to Pakenham without having shown it to the president first. Both men knew the letter would soon be made public anyway.[47]

The possibility exists that Calhoun had not shown Tyler the *entire* letter he sent to Pakenham. Perhaps the secretary of state added the "positive good" portion of the letter after he had shown the president the part that addressed British involvement in Texas. In other words, perhaps Tyler only knew about the first half of the letter, the half that spelled out official administration policy toward Britain and Texas; perhaps Calhoun added the other portion on his own initiative. This seems unlikely, however, especially since Tyler expressed no outrage or even surprise at what his secretary of state had written once the Pakenham letter became public. His complaints—expressed in the letters in 1850—were only voiced well after the fact.

Had Tyler become a proponent of the proslavery argument? The evidence from his early career reveals a slaveholder who tended to view the institution as a "necessary evil," as something that he wished would quietly go away. That had been the underpinning of his diffusion argument; he saw diffusion as the way to eventually rid the nation of slavery. But now his secretary of state had justified Texas annexation in part on the "positive good" defense of slavery. Tyler never wrote or said publicly anything along the lines of what Calhoun had written. Perhaps the only safe assertion to make in the absence of any definitive evidence on this matter is that Tyler willingly signed on to Calhoun's Pakenham letter because it served him politically; he was again operating at the edges of the proslavery argument. He could use the letter to isolate Van Buren and place himself in a better position to receive the Democratic nomination for president (still thinking he had a chance, however remote). Tyler could reap the benefits while also remaining silent on the more unsavory aspects of Calhoun's argument. And if the treaty failed in the Senate because of Calhoun' sectional bombshell, the president had a backup plan.

The administration sent the treaty and its supporting documents to the Senate on April 22, 1844, hoping that details from the Pakenham letter would remain confined to the chamber until a vote for ratification had occurred. A leak to the press soon changed the political calculus. One Van Buren ally summed it up well when he wrote, "the Texas treaty is made upon a record which is sure to destroy any man from a free state who will go for it." The *Washington Globe* had endorsed annexation on April 15, as Tyler and Calhoun had expected. The paper had to alter its stance on April 27, when Van Buren came out publicly against the immediate annexation of Texas. He added qual- ifications—chiefly that he would support annexation if Mexico formally rec- ognized Texas independence—but it quickly became clear he had almost in- stantly lost the support of Democrats in the South.[48]

Pushing annexation and highlighting the importance of the treaty to the protection of slavery thus had the effect both Tyler and Calhoun wanted: to put Van Buren on the ropes, fighting for his political life. Nearly as significant was what the two men had done to the Whigs. The treaty forced their pre- sumptive nominee for president, Henry Clay, to confront the Texas question. On the same day Van Buren made his stance on Texas public, the *Washington Daily National Intelligencer* published a letter from Clay opposing immediate annexation. This had been expected. The Whigs were generally hostile to an- nexation both because they believed expansion bad for the Union and because they saw it as a cynical political ploy on the part of the Democrats. As a result, Whigs largely enjoyed intersectional unity on the issue. But by forcing Clay to address Texas at all, which he and the Whigs had wanted to avoid, Tyler had gained a small measure of revenge on his bitter enemy.[49]

Tyler had also "hoisted his [own] flag for the Presidency," one member of the Texas legation in Washington reported. His slogan was simple: "Tyler and Texas." Not quite as catchy as "Tippecanoe and Tyler, Too," it nevertheless conveyed all the American people needed to know. It also served notice that Tyler—and Calhoun—had made Texas annexation the single-most-important (though not the only) issue in the 1844 presidential campaign. As one poli- tician later put it, "who could have thought a few years ago—that *John Tyler could kick up such a fuss in this great nation*."[50]

His supporters went through the motions of convening a Tyler party nom- inating convention in Baltimore on May 27 at nearly the same time the Dem- ocrats were meeting several blocks away to nominate their own candidate for president. Tyler received the perfunctory nomination from what he claimed were "a thousand delegates, and from every State in the Union"; the conven- tion did not name a candidate for vice president. He called for the immediate annexation of Texas. He also maintained that he would rather step aside and see Texas become part of the Union than win the presidency without it. Annexation had become his signature issue—and he sought to make it his legacy.[51]

"The Democratic convention felt the move," Tyler later gloated to Henry Wise. "A Texan man or defeat was the choice left,—and they took a Texas man." The Democrats adopted his Texas annexation project and made it the most significant plank of their platform in the 1844 campaign. The party faithful spurned Van Buren "because," Tyler wrote later, "of his having thrown himself on the drawn sword of the administration on the Texas question." James K. Polk of Tennessee was nominated instead. He promised the "re-annexation" of Texas and the "reoccupation" of Oregon. The Whigs duly nominated Henry Clay.[52]

Unfortunately for Tyler, the call he had made for immediate annexation when he accepted the nomination for president went unheeded. According to one Democratic senator, the "great majority" of the party, including those in the North, would have supported annexation but for Calhoun's "ill-advised, unfortunate correspondence." The Senate rejected the treaty 16 to 35 on June 8. In light of such a decisive defeat, and since the Whigs controlled the Senate, the treaty stood absolutely no chance of securing the necessary two-thirds vote it needed for ratification. Tyler had been prepared for this outcome, though, and sent a message to the House on June 10 suggesting that Texas could be brought into the Union through other means.[53]

Though the president declined to state specifically what those other means might be, he was thinking of a joint resolution of Congress. The idea of a joint resolution had first been broached in administration circles in January 1843, though it is not clear whether the idea originated with Tyler himself. Even as Upshur optimistically assured Texas officials they could rely on the support of at least two-thirds of the senators when the treaty came up for a vote, the contingency of failure had been forefront in Tyler's mind. Perhaps he had given Calhoun support for the Pakenham letter because he assumed he could pull the joint-resolution rabbit out of his hat if sectionalism scuttled the annexation treaty. Whatever the case, the time had come to pursue the fallback option. A joint resolution required only a bare majority of both houses of Congress to approve annexation, and at first glance it seemed to offer a more promising route to finalizing the process of bringing Texas into the Union. Tyler would have to wait, however, since Congress adjourned on June 17 and would not convene for the second session of the Twenty-Eighth Congress until December. He needed the time to lobby potential supporters.

President Tyler had not spent all of his time on Texas, as time consuming as the annexation project had been. He continued to supervise the work on Sherwood Forest from afar, offering his daughter Mary, who lived there with her husband during renovations, advice on how to deal with painters and carpenters. He wanted details: "I wish to know the precise state of things." He also regularly sent checks—for $120, for $50—to pay for the work. By April 1844, Tyler had clearly come to think of his retirement from public life more and more.[54]

He also thought more and more of Julia Gardiner. She had returned to New York on March 5, just days after the *Princeton* accident had claimed the life of her father, and had spent the remainder of the winter and spring in mourning with her family. Tyler missed her greatly and resolved to propose marriage to her again after a suitable period of time had passed. He apparently had other options, though. "I have received a proposition to address a lady worth 300,000 in cash besides houses," he confided to Mary. This lady, presumably a very rich widow, did not interest him: "if I get married at all it will be to J.G. or no one—she is the greatest thing now living and it is better to give you a young step-mother than an old one." Tyler reassured his daughter that he had room in his heart for a young wife and for her, somewhat strangely writing about Mary in the third person to convey his feelings. "My dear daughter I know will be satisfied with any course I may take," he wrote, "as in advancing my own happiness I shall in no degree be unmindful of her."[55]

Tyler needed to prepare Mary for the possibility that she and her siblings would soon have a young stepmother (indeed, one younger than three of them); a day earlier he had written to Juliana Gardiner asking for her blessing to marry Julia. The letter was brief and to the point. Informing her that Julia had given him permission to write, he expressed his hope "that you will confer upon me the high privilege of substituting yourself in all that care and attention which you have so affectionately bestowed upon her." Tyler said nothing directly about his finances in the letter but instead drew upon the esteem he knew the Gardiner family had developed for him during the past two years to make his case that he was a suitable match for Julia. "My position in society will I trust serve as a guarantee for the assurance which I give, that it will be the study of my life to advance her happiness by all and every means in my power." He said nothing of the thirty-year age difference between him and his intended bride, though it no doubt dawned on him that his prospective mother-in-law was younger than he was—by nine years![56]

Julia had agreed to marry him, having accepted his third proposal, because she too believed he would advance her happiness. She had grown up quickly in the wake of her father's death and was now ready for marriage. The *Princeton* tragedy had been a major turning point in her life. "After I lost my father I felt differently towards the President," she related years later. "He seemed to fill the place and to be more agreeable in every way than any younger man ever was or could be." She saw no impediment in the age difference. In fact, as she indicated, it made Tyler even more attractive.[57]

Her mother was apparently little troubled by the age difference as well. Juliana consented to Tyler's wish to marry Julia, though not without other misgivings. Skirting a direct reference to his financial prospects in a letter of her own, Juliana still made her position clear. Her daughter's "comfortable settlement in life," she pointed out, "a subject often disregarded in youth but thought of & felt in maturity, claims our mutual consideration." Juliana wanted to make sure Tyler had no illusions. "Julia in her tastes & inclinations is neither extravagant nor unreasonable," she maintained, "tho' she has been accustomed to all the necessary comforts & elegancies of life." She hoped this would not change upon her daughter's marriage to the president.[58]

Having received Juliana's blessing, the newly engaged couple settled on June 26, 1844, as the day they would marry. Because the Gardiner family was still in mourning, the wedding would be a small affair, with only Julia's immediate family, a small number of friends, John Jr., and a couple of the president's associates in attendance. The ceremony would also be conducted in private, with no fanfare and no press.

On Tuesday evening, June 25, President Tyler boarded a train in Washington with John Jr.; John Lorimer Graham, postmaster of New York City; Robert Rantoul, a Boston Tylerite; and naval officer Robert Stockton, Tyler's friend, and settled into his seat for the journey to New York. The men arrived at 10:30 P.M. and hastily made their way to Howard's Hotel. Luckily, no one except the hotel's proprietor, D. D. Howard, recognized the president, and they were able to proceed to their rooms right away.

The following day was sunny and hot. Shortly after 1:00 P.M., Tyler and his party made their way to the Church of the Ascension on Fifth Avenue at Tenth Street. They were met there by the Right Reverend Benjamin Treadwell Onderdonk, fourth Bishop of the Episcopal Diocese of New York, and the

Reverend Dr. Gregory Thurston Bedell, rector of the church and friend of the Gardiner family. The two men explained the details of the ceremony, which was set to begin at two o'clock. It began promptly at that time. Thirty minutes later, President John Tyler and Julia Gardiner were man and wife.

After the ceremony, the wedding party returned briefly to the Gardiner home at Lafayette Place. The carriages made a commotion in front of the townhouse, and it did not take long for neighbors to hurry to their windows to find out what was going on outside. They quickly realized what had just happened. One onlooker later told Juliana that Julia was a beautiful bride and that the president "looked younger than he expected to see him." The heat of the day apparently did not bother Tyler, though he did take advantage of the food and cold drinks the Gardiner servants had set out for the guests. Julia changed into more appropriate traveling clothes, and the newlyweds and Margaret then made their way to the pier at Courtland Street, where they boarded the ferryboat *Essex* for a triumphant trip around New York harbor. Cannon from nearby ships saluted them, likely tipped off beforehand by Stockton. Finally, the couple arrived at Jersey City and caught the train for Philadelphia, where they stayed on their wedding night.[59]

From Philadelphia, the president, Julia, and Margaret, as well as a maidservant, traveled to Baltimore and then on to Washington. They arrived at the White House on the evening of June 27 and were greeted by Tyler's daughter Letitia. She had recently taken over the hostess duties of the mansion from Priscilla, who, along with Robert and the children, had moved to Philadelphia in March. After several days in Washington, Margaret returned home to New York City, and Tyler and Julia made their way to a newly completed government cottage at Old Point Comfort, Virginia, for their honeymoon. There they were feted by the officers of the military companies stationed in and around Norfolk. The couple traveled up the James River to Sherwood Forest for a few days so that Julia could see the home over which she would preside after they left the White House. They returned to Old Point Comfort and made their way back to Washington in early August.[60]

Tyler had become the first president to marry while in office. It is almost impossible to imagine how the president of the United States and a family of such stature in New York could have pulled off such a remarkable feat without the knowledge of the public. "The whole affair is considered one of the most brilliant *coups* or [illegible] ever enacted," Julia's brother Alexander declared, "and I cannot but wonder myself, that we succeeded so well, in preserving at once the President's dignity, and our own feelings, from all avoidable sacrifices." Once word got out, the marriage was all anyone could talk about—in New York and Washington. People marveled at the secrecy of the wedding, and most observers seemed to think Tyler had done quite well for himself. The *Brooklyn Daily Eagle* described Julia as "accomplished, beautiful, interesting, an heiress, and 22." The president, on the other hand, was "known to be as homely as a brush fence, and 55 [sic] years of age." There were other opinions. "He is most desperately in love," one woman in the capital who saw the couple reported, "and she is a fine looking woman." George Templeton Strong, a young New York lawyer Julia's age, was less impressed. "Poor, unfortunate, deluded old jackass," he sniffed to his diary. "It's positively painful to think of his situation, and the trials that lie before him."[61]

Tyler certainly may have worried that further political trials awaited him as he pursued the annexation of Texas, but in the first heady days of his second marriage, he basked in the glow of his young wife's popularity. At a White House party on the Fourth of July, the guests demanded she come downstairs to greet them, even though she had slept until nearly noon and was unprepared for visitors.[62]

The public's clamor for Julia is understandable. For nearly two years, Letitia Tyler's death had cast a pall over White House social occasions. Priscilla had been a popular hostess, and Tyler's daughter Letitia had filled in admirably once her sister-in-law and brother left Washington, but throughout the combined presidency of William Henry Harrison and John Tyler, the wife of the president had never served as First Lady. For that matter, since the two immediate predecessors of Harrison and Tyler—Van Buren and Jackson—had been widowers, the last wife of the president to perform the duties of White House hostess had been Louisa Catherine Adams in 1829, more than fifteen years earlier. Thus, Tyler's marriage was welcome indeed. And Julia brought all the gaiety and fun of a young woman who clearly reveled in her new role.

At first Julia had to rein in some of her clear delight in being married so that the president could attend to his duties. She willingly displayed her affection for her husband publicly, so much so that her mother—tipped off by Margaret—felt compelled to write and admonish her that "business should take the precedence of *caressing*—reserve your caressing for private leisure hours & be *sure* you let no one see it unless you wish to be laughed at." Margaret also chided Julia. "You spend *so much* time in kissing," she wrote, "things of more importance are left undone." Juliana claimed that the "President complains [Julia] won't go to bed nor get up, nor let him work," but Tyler hardly acted as if he minded.[63]

Margaret also reminded her sister that marrying the president of the United States ought to bring benefits beyond hugging and kissing. "Recollect that A[l-exander] too would like to have you make hay for him while the sun shines," she wrote. Indeed, Alexander had already been brought into the Tyler political fold, writing pro-Texas articles for the newspapers in support of the third-party effort. He had made some recommendations on patronage matters in New York City too. But despite Julia's lobbying, Tyler was reluctant to do much more than cheer his brother-in-law on as Alexander sought election to the New York State Assembly on the Democratic ticket. The president had been stung by political opponents who leveled charges of nepotism against him for the posts he had secured for members of his family. If Alexander wanted a political career, he would have to stake his claim without a nudge from the White House. The young man won the nomination on his own, but he lost the election.[64]

The 1844 presidential election interested Tyler far more than his brother-in-law's campaign for the New York legislature. The president announced his withdrawal from the race on August 21, having been promised by leading Democrats that his supporters would be welcomed back into the party's fold as members in good standing. He wrote to Alexander Gardiner that these men called on him and told him that he "held the fate of the Democratic party" in his hands and that "upon my course depended its success or defeat," a view echoed by the party's newspapers. A letter from Andrew Jackson exhorting Tyler to abandon the canvass so that he and his supporters could now work for Polk's election sealed his decision.[65]

Polk won the presidency in a close election, the beneficiary of a surge in new Democratic voters, many of whom were immigrants, and, of course, the enthusiasm for Texas annexation in the South. The president's supporters played some role in Polk's victory, but it is difficult to gauge how much they mattered. By injecting the Texas issue into the campaign, Tyler himself had bedeviled Clay and the Whigs one final time. The irony, however, is that had he continued with his third-party bid for the White House, Tyler might have split the Democratic vote and helped his arch-nemesis finally win the presidency.[66]

The president interpreted Polk's election as a mandate to proceed with his plans to annex Texas. In his final annual message to Congress in December 1844, Tyler maintained that "the decision of the people and the States on this great and interesting subject has been decisively manifested." There was no doubt in his mind, even though Polk had barely won. "It is the will of both the people and the States that Texas shall be annexed to the Union promptly and immediately." For the first time in a public forum, the president called for annexation through a joint resolution of Congress.[67]

⚜

As Tyler made plans to secure the annexation of Texas before he left office, the First Lady made plans to host the final ball of her husband's presidency. Wednesday night, February 18, 1845, promised to be a magnificent evening in the nation's capital. Two thousand invitations went out. Every detail received the utmost attention. Washington society was abuzz with anticipation.[68]

When the night arrived, chilly but clear, "the heart of many a *demoiselle* and many a chevalier leaped with delight as the appointed hour drew near." The clop-clop of horse-drawn carriages and the muffled laughter of partygoers could be heard on the streets surrounding the White House around 9:00 P.M. Shortly after nine, people began making their way inside. "From the ante rooms to the reception room," Julia's brother Alexander reported, a "constant stream of beauty and elegance" waited to be announced to the president and First Lady, who met their guests in the Blue Room. In the East Room the chandeliers sparkled brilliantly, while hundreds of candles (which cost Tyler $350) illuminated four other rooms opened for the occasion and accentuated the jewels worn by the ladies.[69]

Of course, Julia was the evening's main attraction, and she did not disappoint. Her adoring husband did not seem to mind the fuss made over her. In fact, he had grown quite accustomed to "los[ing] all the presidential honors, as all eyes . . . seem[ed] directed to Julia." Indeed, on this night, as on so many before, she found herself the center of attention, and "with her sister, cousins, and [seventeen-year-old] Miss Alice Tyler, contributed a galaxy of beauty" the likes of which no court of Europe could equal."[70]

Partygoers danced polkas, waltzes, and cotillions to the music of the Marine Band. They ate a sumptuous buffet supper and enjoyed eight dozen bottles of champagne and wine that "flowed like water." According to Margaret Gardiner, everyone present "acknowledge[d] that nothing half so grand has been seen at the White House during any Administration, and fear nothing so tasteful would be again."[71]

Toward the end of the evening, well after midnight, exhausted revelers congratulated President Tyler for throwing such a grand ball. Smiling broadly and pleased that his guests had enjoyed themselves, he joked, "Yes, they cannot say *now* that I am a President *without a party*."[72]

꒰ꞏꞏ꒱

This final White House ball was an emphatic capstone to Julia Tyler's eight-month tenure as First Lady. The capstone to Tyler's presidency occurred during his final week in office. On January 25, 1845, the House of Representatives had voted 120 to 98 in favor of the joint resolution to annex Texas. On February 27 the Senate met at 6:00 P.M.—an unusual night session—to vote on the measure. Though Senator Robert J. Walker had ably led the proannexation members of the upper chamber and had lobbied wavering colleagues, potent opposition remained. John J. Crittenden, in particular, sought to stymie President Tyler. The joint resolution was very much in doubt as all fifty-two senators made their way to their desks. The galleries were filled. For some three hours, both sides gave final speeches touting their positions. Finally, shortly before nine o'clock, rollcall voting began. When it was over, the Senate had voted 27 to 25 to pass the joint resolution.[73]

But there was a catch. Senators had amended the original House resolution by calling for the president to begin new negotiations with the Texans to devise another treaty. Senator Walker offered a compromise that gave Tyler the option to choose whichever version—House or Senate—he preferred. The 27-to-25 vote, in fact, had approved Walker's compromise. The House now had to vote on the amended resolution. It did so the next day, February 28, voting to pass it by an even larger margin than before—132 to 75. Tyler signed the joint resolution on March 1, three days before he left office, on the terms offered by the House. He presented the pen with which he signed the document to Julia.[74]

The razor-thin margin by which the joint resolution passed in the Senate raises an intriguing constitutional question. All fifty-two senators voted on the resolution. Had one who voted "yea" changed his vote, the final tally would have stood at 26 to 26. According to the Constitution (Article I, Section 3), the vice president votes in the case of a tie in the Senate. But there was no vice president under Tyler. The president pro tempore of the Senate—Willie Mangum in this case—presides over the Senate in lieu of the vice president, but Mangum surely could not have been allowed to vote twice—he had already voted against the joint resolution. How would this situation have been resolved? There is no constitutional provision for deciding what happens if a tie vote occurs under these conditions—and this was one of the most momentous votes in the history of the US Senate. His administration already hounded by bad luck, it appears the gods decided to bestow good luck on Tyler in this instance. Yet it would have seemed fitting for his administration to have ended on the same note with which it began: a constitutional crisis.

Thin margin or not, Tyler had secured the annexation of Texas. He claimed that he had hesitated to sign the joint resolution into law because of a "feeling of delicacy" toward President-elect Polk, worried that doing so would "imply a want of confidence in him [he] did not feel." According to Tyler, his cabinet advised him to take "immediate action" on the resolution, so he did. Charles Wickliffe later remembered in a letter to Tyler, "The Cabinet was unanimous in their opinion that it was not only your right but your imperative duty to act and to act promptly."[75]

It is hard to believe that Tyler hesitated at all, though his habitual tendency toward delay and deliberation make his account somewhat plausible. But as he acknowledged later, "Texas was the great theme that occupied me." He had made clear to his trusted advisors—and to Julia—that accomplishing the annexation of Texas was important to securing his legacy and would compensate for his inability to win election in his own right in 1844. As he signed the joint resolution, he realized it would take time for Texas to officially join the Union. The Lone Star government had to formally accept what was essentially an invitation to become part of the United States. Tyler understood that his successor would put the finishing touches on what he had started, with details that remained to be worked out. But make no mistake—John Tyler wanted the credit for Texas.[76]

John Quincy Adams, the most vocal and outspoken opponent of annexation in the House of Representatives, did give Tyler the credit, to be sure, but the former president considered it "the heaviest calamity that ever befell myself and my country," not something for which to be proud. Nor did Adams approve of the means by which Tyler had accomplished his goal. "I regard the joint resolution as the apoplexy of the Constitution," he wrote in his diary.[77]

Adams was not alone in this judgment. Other Tyler critics decried the joint resolution as illegal or as an affront to the Constitution or charged the president with betraying the principles of strict construction that had guided him for most of his political career. Tyler was portrayed as a hypocrite who had succumbed to expediency because he could not accomplish annexation through the constitutionally sanctioned means of a treaty. The joint resolution had creatively allowed him to overcome the failure of the accords to pass in the Senate, and his opponents were angry about it.

The truth is President Tyler had acted in accordance with the Constitution. Adams's assessment of the joint resolution was wrong and had no basis in fact. He ignored Article IV, Section 3 of the Constitution, which reads: "New States may be admitted by the Congress into this Union." Congress had the constitutional authority to bring Texas into the Union, and the joint resolution was a "necessary and proper" way to do it. As scholars Gary Lawson and Guy Seidman point out, a treaty—like the one the Jefferson administration and France signed in 1803 that ceded Louisiana to the United States—exists to enforce an obligation upon a sovereign nation in the international community of nations. Because Texas was a sovereign nation that had willingly acceded to its acquisition by the United States, no treaty was necessary. Once annexation occurred, Texas as an independent nation ceased to exist; therefore, there would have been nothing for the treaty to operate upon, no nation to enforce an obligation upon.[78]

In the final analysis, Tyler had abided by his longstanding constitutional principles after all, no matter what his critics said. He had also framed his pursuit of annexation in terms of the benefits it could bring to the entire nation and did his best to forestall the notion that he acted solely to advance the cause of the South. That argument suffered a blow with Calhoun's Pakenham letter, however, and ultimately, the sectional aspect of annexation became its most important historical legacy.

Texas did add to the number of slave states, though it was just one, not the four or five many antislavery northerners had feared. With the addition of Florida, which also joined the Union in 1845, the slave states held a 28–26 advantage, an advantage most useful in the US Senate, where legislative attempts to stop the spread of slavery in the territories met with defeat. Furthermore, the annexation of Texas played a significant part in getting Polk elected to the presidency. The Tennessean would pursue his own version of territorial aggrandizement in the form of a war with Mexico, which in part resulted from the annexation of Texas. That war, and the resulting acquisition of California and New Mexico, sharpened the sectional debate over slavery's extension and exacerbated tensions between North and South. While it would be a mistake to argue that all of this made the Civil War inevitable, it is clear that what John Tyler accomplished in March 1845 put the United States on the path to that cataclysmic struggle.

Chapter 18

YOU CAN TAKE THE MAN OUT OF POLITICS . . .

Early on Monday, March 3, 1845, John and Julia Tyler awoke for their last morning in the White House. They concluded their packing and sent their belongings to nearby Fuller's Hotel, where they would spend the next two nights. Shortly after noon, the president opened the doors of the mansion, and he and Julia welcomed a steady stream of well-wishers who had come to say good-bye. General John Peter Van Ness, one-time mayor of Washington, delivered a brief speech in the Blue Room praising Tyler, saying that he was sure he spoke for everyone there when he expressed his regret that the Tylers were leaving. Humbled by Van Ness's words, the president gave an impromptu speech of his own. "His voice was more musical than ever," Julia proudly told her mother by letter, "it rose, and fell, and trembled, and rose again. The effect was irresistible, and the deep admiration and respect it elicited was told truly in the sobs and exclamations of all around." The Tylers would be missed.

That night a throng of people descended on Fuller's to pay their respects to the outgoing president and First Lady. The revelry lasted well into the night. The next morning, March 4, amid cheers and a steady rain, Tyler walked out of the hotel and climbed into an open carriage. He was on his way to pick up President-elect Polk at Coleman's Hotel. The two men would drive together to the Capitol at the head of a large procession, and Tyler would watch Chief Justice Taney administer the oath of office to inaugurate his successor as the nation's eleventh president. Tyler's term was now over.

The Tylers did not attend the inauguration ball that night. Tired and knowing they had a long journey ahead of them the next day, they went to bed early. The couple hurried to a wharf on the Potomac at nine o'clock the following morning for their trip to their home in Virginia. To their dismay, they found that the boat had departed without them. They were forced to return to Fuller's until nine o'clock in the evening, when they finally departed Washington. After stopping off in Richmond the next night, at noon on Friday, March 7, they reached Sherwood Forest.[1]

Tyler wrote that with retirement from the presidency, he felt like "the mariner who has reached the haven of repose, after having been for years tempest tossed on angry seas." Now, instead of fighting Clay and the Whigs, he tackled a new challenge: becoming a full-time farmer. How would he handle the transition? How would he fare in this new phase of his life?[2]

It certainly helped that his new estate offered promises of success. Located roughly two miles north of the James River, with a clear view of the water from its perch above a sloping hill, Sherwood Forest consisted of sixteen hundred acres of land, with several hundred acres cleared and suitable for farming. Tall pine and oak trees shaded much of the property. The house measured ninety feet by forty-two feet, and there was ample room for expansion. Julia saw the potential in her new home immediately. "I found the situation to be a very beautiful one and though now in its partial wilderness very fine in appearance, capable of being made truly magnificent," she wrote upon seeing the estate for the first time on her honeymoon some eight months earlier. The house was still unfinished when the Tylers arrived for good in March 1845. In fact, work would not conclude until after Christmas. "I do not fear so much the noise of the hammers as the scent of the paint," Tyler wrote to his daughter Mary, but he resolved to be patient until the house was exactly as he and Julia wanted it. He gave his wife free rein to instruct the workmen and enslaved people as she saw fit and relied on her to decide, for example, whether to wallpaper the sitting room or have it painted. He also left the decorating to her. She told her mother that "in everything the President appeals to me. In the world, as here, wherever he goes and whatever is done it is *me* in all situations he only seems to consider."[3]

Deferring to his capable young wife on household matters showed wisdom that every married man ought to possess. It also allowed Tyler to focus his attention on the farming operations of Sherwood Forest and to consider the best strategy for making the plantation productive. Wheat would be the staple crop, and much of the improved land on the property would be devoted to producing it for market. Tyler chose to grow what was commonly known as winter wheat. Sowed in the fall, the plants typically remain in the dormant stage throughout the winter, germinate and grow during the spring, and are ready for harvest in June. Tyler likely settled on winter wheat because it generally produced a higher yield compared to wheat seeded in the spring. Planting in late fall, moreover, usually helped ward off the dreaded Hessian fly, which could ravage a wheat crop to nearly nothing.[4]

Tyler would also plant corn at Sherwood Forest, some of which he sold. The corn was planted in April and harvested in the fall. He raised livestock and grew various other fruits and vegetables, such as peaches, figs, peas, and asparagus, that would enable the farm to be self-sufficient as well, providing enough food for the family as well as for the farm's enslaved labor.[5]

Between sixty and seventy slaves lived and worked at Sherwood Forest in 1845. That number would fluctuate somewhat over time but would not significantly rise or fall over the remainder of Tyler's life. By most definitions, then, he was a large "planter," though not one of the largest in Virginia's Tidewater. His bonded-labor force was sizeable enough and his estate and surrounding grounds spacious enough that he needed an overseer to supervise the fields. Tyler also relied on some specially appointed slaves to ensure that the household routine stayed on course. Using a political metaphor, he explained that his "whole cabinet council consists of my overseer and a few trusty domestics." And within the household, Julia took on a crucial role.[6]

Like all planters who owned a large number of enslaved people, Tyler established strict rules at Sherwood Forest to make the plantation operate smoothly and eliminate potential problems. These rules established a system to maintain order and enhance efficiency, holding everyone—including Tyler himself—accountable on a day-to-day basis. Of course, he occupied the top rung of the estate's hierarchy and possessed the ultimate authority. He was the one who had to make sure the system worked. If he thought it necessary, Tyler meted out punishment.

Referring to "my negroes" or "my people" and treating them as part of an extended family, Tyler embodied the paternalism of the antebellum South's slave system and indicated that he took a personal interest in the lives of his slaves. He had done this to some extent during his days as a young planter, though his political career made his total involvement impossible. The stakes were higher now, though, because farming had become his chief means of earning a living and supporting his family. As an older man, he possessed the wisdom of experience and could take comfort in understanding what had worked before and what had not.[7]

The first responsibility of a slaveholder was to make sure the African Americans who lived and worked on his farm were sufficiently fed, adequately clothed, and properly housed. The historical evidence does not demonstrate with any specificity how well slaves at Sherwood Forest were fed or whether they had passable clothing, clean cabins, and dry roofs over their heads. The manuscript record—admittedly from white, mostly family, sources—does indicate that Tyler took his responsibility to provide for "his people" very seriously and paid close attention to their most basic needs. The health and wellbeing of his labor force remained a constant concern throughout his life as head of Sherwood Forest. More than just a capital investment, his slaves were the most important component of Tyler's farming operations, and he depended on them to be able to perform their assigned tasks.

Tyler shaped the lives of his slaves in other ways. For example, he sometimes hired them out to neighbors whose wheat-production schedules differed from those at Sherwood Forest; they were allowed to keep the pay they earned. He apparently further allowed them the opportunity to tend to their own small plots of land on which they could grow vegetables and raise chickens for sale, keeping the proceeds of those sales. Tyler also encouraged the spiritual development of his slaves. On Sunday mornings many of them could be found at a small Baptist church some four miles from Sherwood Forest. Notably, a white minister officiated at these services. Since Nat Turner's Rebellion in 1831, Virginia planters largely forbid slaves from attending churches with black preachers. Turner, a self-proclaimed preacher and prophet, served as a reminder to white Virginians of what might happen without proper vigilance. The lesson lingered long after his demise.

From what we are able to glean from correspondence of the family and visitors to the plantation, it appears that Tyler succeeded in setting up a system that not only maximized efficiency but maintained order as well. Eben Horsford, a Harvard professor and husband of Julia's cousin Mary Gardiner, visited Sherwood Forest in 1852. As a northerner, he was curious to see the slave system firsthand and spent a few days with the Tylers, paying close attention to how the plantation operated as well as to the interactions between the family and their slaves. Horsford recorded his observations in a letter to his mother. "The slaves are treated like children—punished when they deserve it, rewarded when they should be," he wrote. "All of them permitted to earn *extra* pay—cared for when sick, and I should think uniform, cheerful and happy & by no means hard worked."[8]

The enslaved of Sherwood Forest might have taken issue with Horsford's comment that they were not "hard worked." Their labor was most heavily concentrated during four months of the year—October (planting) and June (harvest) for the wheat, April (planting) and September (harvest) for the corn—but they worked year-round on a variety of tasks. They removed stones from fields, cut trees, hauled wood to sawmills or down to the river to be loaded onto boats, constructed and maintained log and stone fences to keep livestock out of the fields, threshed the wheat grown on the farm, cut the clover that grew in the fields after a wheat harvest, and performed a variety of other tasks essential to Sherwood Forest's successful operation. Growing wheat and corn may not have been as labor intensive as cultivating tobacco, the crop that dominated the Virginia landscape in an earlier era. Nor did it require the backbreaking labor characteristic of a Mississippi cotton plantation or Louisiana sugar plantation. But it still required extremely arduous work—work that Horsford seemingly failed to appreciate.[9]

Furthermore, Horsford's remark that Tyler's slaves were cheerful and happy denotes the superficial justification of slavery found among southern planters and common to many northerners sympathetic to the institution. His observations also underscore that the central tenet of paternalism was at work on Tyler's plantation. As historians Eugene Genovese and Elizabeth Fox-Genovese made clear throughout their long careers studying southern slavery, the master-slave relationship was constructed on an understanding of duties, responsibilities, and certain privileges that were all dictated by the slaveholder. At any time, the slaveholder could become more demanding and revoke privileges. Discipline had to be maintained at all costs. Tyler saw himself—understood himself—as a benevolent master, and comparatively speaking, he may have been. His benevolence, however, was always tempered by firmness and the constant threat, if not necessarily the use, of violence. Worse was the underlying threat that a slave might be sold away from his or her spouse or children at Tyler's whim. Maximizing profits required this dynamic. Framing the entire arrangement in terms of family and viewing his slaves as part of his extended family allowed Tyler to justify the system of exploitation that undergirded his life as a planter.[10]

❦

As a busy plantation owner, Tyler concerned himself most of all with what went on at Sherwood Forest. But he also kept one eye on the nation's political developments. You could take the man out of politics, but you could not take the politics out of the man. Indeed, for all of his proclamations about how much he looked forward to repose and retirement, and for all the happiness he had found in his marriage to Julia, it becomes clear reading his correspondence that he missed being president. He also still had a stake in what was going on in Washington.

The matter that most interested him in the several months following his return to Virginia was the progress of Texas annexation. He eagerly read the

Richmond Enquirer for news on this score and waited anxiously for Texas to officially join the Union so his legacy would be secure. Andrew Jackson Donelson, whom Tyler had appointed US chargé d'affaires to Texas, assured him in late May 1845 that the Texans regarded annexation as "a certain calculation." The news pleased Tyler. "If we had done nothing else than unite Texas with us," he wrote to Charles Wickliffe, his postmaster general, "we could not be looked upon as wholly unprofitable servants." Tyler professed confidence in his successor, who had largely allowed events to take the course he had charted with the joint resolution. "Mr. Polk in that matter has faithfully fulfilled his pledges," he continued, "and I am now delighted with the energy displayed by him in guarding the rights of the U. States." In Tyler's view Mexican saber rattling and an apparent willingness to go to war threatened those rights. He worried that Santa Anna would lash out after the Texas government voted to accept the joint resolution and become part of the United States on July 4, 1845. Mexico would still not accept reality and officially recognize Texas independence. "What I have chiefly feared was that in her impotent rage, she might strike a blow at some weak point and obtain an ephemeral triumph," Tyler confided to John Young Mason, his former navy secretary whom Polk had retained as attorney general. Eerily foreshadowing Polk's future plans, he further declared, "The truth is that if war is to take place, it should much rather have proceeded from us, since she has continually offered us insult and inflicted upon us injury." Tyler would ultimately find much to criticize in Polk's conduct leading up to the Mexican War (1846–48). For the time being, though, he was pleased that the president had taken steps to safeguard the United States from a Mexican attack and "consider[ed] him entitled to the support of the whole country for his course on the Texas question."[11]

Tyler may have found much to praise in Polk's efforts to keep Mexico at bay and put the finishing touches on the annexation of Texas, but he found much to dislike about the way his successor wielded the patronage. When Tyler conceded to the Democratic Party and bowed out of the 1844 presidential canvass, he received assurances that his supporters would be viewed as party members in good standing. He took that as a promise that many of the men he had placed into government jobs during his term would be allowed to remain. Polk had, in effect, broken that promise (in Tyler's eyes) by turning out nearly all Tylerites in his effort to reshape the federal bureaucracy. "I left some two hundred personal friends in office," Tyler grumbled, "who were also the warm, active, and determined friends of Mr. Polk in the late contest—a small number in comparison to the 40,000 office holders. They have been for the most part removed or superseded. Some half dozen remain." He bitterly deplored the removals but would not criticize Polk publicly, choosing to forego the political strife that might have ensued.[12]

At home Tyler worried about a different kind of strife—the potential conflict between his four daughters and their new stepmother. He tried to put one possible source of discord to rest by addressing the matter of money head on. "My affection for you will in no degree be diminished," he assured his daughters, "nor shall I leave you unprovided for. Before the year [1844] closes I will make arrangements that will be satisfactory to you." He highlighted the fact that Julia brought her own wealth into the marriage. "Her property will be, I have no doubt, large enough for herself, and mine will remain for my children. It [the marriage] will interfere with no one and cannot seriously affect my arrangements." Whether these assurances mollified the girls is unknown. These were odd promises for Tyler to make, though, because they indicate he did not expect to have children with Julia. Given the straitened financial circumstances in which he usually found himself, it is also fair to wonder how he could make good on his pledge to provide for his daughters. Finally, if by "making arrangements" Tyler meant he would prepare his will by the end of the year, he failed to fulfill that promise.[13]

Besides the matter of money, two other potential problems remained. First, all four daughters had been very close to their mother and were taken aback when their father married so soon after her death. Second, Julia's comparative youth made her an unconventional stepmother. Mary was actually five years older than Julia but accepted her father's remarriage with grace, suppressing her misgivings with the solace that he was truly happy. Lizzy, just three years younger than Julia, struggled with the change. "For weeks after your marriage," she wrote to Julia, "I could not realize the fact and even now it is with difficulty that I can convince myself that another fills the place which was once occupied by my beloved mother." Lizzy felt no ill will toward her personally but asserted that no woman could ever replace her mother. She also maintained that because Julia was so close to her in age, she would find loving her like a mother "impossible." But, she assured her, "I shall endeavour to love you with the affection of a sister and trust it may be reciprocated on your part." Their relationship flourished, in part, because Lizzy and her husband lived in Williamsburg and could visit often—for brief stays.[14]

Mary's and Lizzy's graciousness when it came to accepting Julia reflected their personalities. It was hard to find anyone who could not get along with either woman. Lizzy, Julia wrote, was "gentle and conciliating in manner." The other two Tyler daughters—Letitia and Alice—were prone to being headstrong and opinionated and were sometimes difficult. As a result, their relationships with Julia were far more complicated and contentious. Letitia was initially cordial toward her but soon exhibited a frostiness that ultimately developed into deep animosity. Julia eventually returned the favor in spades, with a contempt she could never completely conceal. She called Letitia a "bitter piece" and eventually came to dread the woman's visits to Sherwood Forest. Their slight difference in age—Julia was only one year older—certainly accounts for some of this. There was more to it, however. Growing up, Letitia always seemed to be competing with Mary and Lizzy for her father's affections. Perhaps adding still more competition into the mix was too much for her to bear. Perhaps, too, her unhappy marriage to James Semple soured her on her father's happy marriage and the woman who had brought him that happiness. Alice, seven years younger than Julia, tended to treat her stepmother as a nuisance. Already rebellious, she became more so after her father's remarriage. For the most part, Tyler put a stop to the bad behavior. "Whenever Alice has been fractious her Father has not failed to show severely his displeasure," Julia informed her sister, Margaret. Ultimately, Alice and Julia came to a rapprochement, but tension still characterized their relationship.[15]

The Tyler sons got along well with Julia and supported their father's remarriage wholeheartedly. Robert had liked Julia upon meeting her in Washington and grew to accept her and love her unconditionally. It helped that she and Priscilla had grown close. Similarly, John Jr. accepted Julia without question. Tazewell, the furthest removed in age from Julia at ten years, was the one sibling who could actually treat her as a stepmother, and that dynamic continued for the duration of his father's life. "I have no difficulty with him at all and he does not interfere with me in the least," Julia reported. Tazewell's residence at a boarding school no doubt helped their relationship most of all.[16]

Tyler appreciated his sons' willingness to welcome Julia into the family. But if their relationships with his new wife were far less stressful to him than those of his daughters, he still found a lot to worry about when it came to their prospects. Robert felt pressure from both his father and his wife to establish a law career that would allow him to earn a respectable living. Priscilla recognized that he needed to move out of his father's shadow to do that and longed for the day when Robert would acquire a "name and subsistence." That meant leaving Washington. In March 1844 she and Robert packed up their belongings and two small daughters and moved to Philadelphia. This was not without risk, as Robert gave up steady employment in the US Land Office and his family left the comforts of the White House. But he and Priscilla had determined to make it on their own. Soon after moving into their new home, Robert began a rigorous course of self-directed study to prepare for the bar.

To Priscilla's dismay, however, he hastily returned to Washington—without her and the girls and leaving her seven months pregnant—in late May to aid his father's campaign for the presidency. Tyler needed the help, and Robert, who found studying the law tedious, jumped at the chance to do something more exciting. Priscilla protested, arguing to no avail that he should stay in Philadelphia and press on with his studies. She felt her twenty-seven-year-old husband was refusing to grow up. John Tyler bore some of the blame for this by enabling his son's behavior. He finally realized it when Robert allowed him to read a letter Priscilla sent to him shortly after his return to Washington. "My dear husband you must return to Philadelphia," she wrote, "give up the life of political care and excitement in which you live, find your dearest happiness in your wife and children . . . , and have the pleasure of moulding your own fortunes." Priscilla exhibited no anger toward her husband but firmly told him what she expected. "Come back soon, determined 'to do or die' at the law, and give happiness to your own devoted wife." Tyler sheepishly wrote a note to Priscilla, telling her that "the advice you give Robert is excellent." Robert returned to Philadelphia within a month and was on hand for the birth of his son, John Tyler IV, in July.

With Priscilla's constant encouragement, Robert studied hard for the bar. His work was interrupted in February 1845, when Mary Fairlie became seriously ill. The child died in June and was buried next to her grandmother, Letitia Tyler, in New Kent County, Virginia. Devastated, Robert and Priscilla knew they had to remain strong for their two other children. They rented a small house in Bristol, the town where they had gotten married, determined to pay their bills and pick up the pieces. After he accompanied Priscilla on a trip to Alabama to visit her sister, Robert returned home to make one final push to prepare for the bar. By the fall of 1845, he reported to his father that he was nearly ready. Pleased with the news, Tyler encouraged his son to keep moving forward. It took a while for him to establish himself, but he eventually secured a job as solicitor to the sheriff of Philadelphia. That position, coupled with a modest private practice, finally allowed Robert and Priscilla a steady income. With his wife's steadfast help, and through his own talents, Robert had made something of his life.[17]

It remained to be seen whether John Jr. would follow suit. Alcohol had already poisoned his marriage to Mattie and had been a continuing source of tension between John and his father. Late in the last year of his presidency, Tyler relieved his son of his duties as private secretary. The reasons for his dismissal are murky, but it is possible that John had failed to perform his tasks to his father's satisfaction and that alcohol abuse had been the cause. "He has many talents," Julia acknowledged, "that is certain—indeed in many respects he is gifted—and is it not a cruel shame he should regard them so improperly?" Twenty-six in the summer of 1845, John at last showed some initiative. He swore off liquor and moved back to Southampton County to work on his marriage and immerse himself in the study of law. He declared that he would "keep out of debt if he ha[d] to dress in Virginia cloth and eat nothing else than corn bread." John Jr. was trying to turn his life around at the same time his brother Robert pledged to establish himself in the legal profession.[18]

John's commitment to clean living appears to have been prompted by two incidents—one that occurred shortly after his father married Julia, and another that took place soon after they left the White House. The first incident could have ended tragically. The *Richmond Whig* had published a derogatory article about Tyler's course as president that angered John Jr. He and Hugh Rose Pleasants, the author of the article and brother of the paper's editor, John Hampden Pleasants, agreed to meet each other on the dueling grounds in Northampton, North Carolina, on July 4, 1844. John arrived at the appointed place with his second at two o'clock in the afternoon, the agreed-upon time, but Pleasants was nowhere to be found. Quickly growing impatient, John waited for at least a half hour for his adversary to show up and was preparing to leave when a messenger rode up on horseback. Pleasants was at the home of a woman some twelve miles away, rip-roaring drunk. His second would stand in his place, the messenger reported, and would arrive shortly. Satisfied that he fulfilled his obligation under the dueling code of honor, John refused to wait and left for Old Point Comfort, where he joined his father and Julia.[19]

The second incident occurred in Washington in April 1845. John Jr. had stayed in the city after his father left office because he hoped to secure a patronage job from President Polk. No such job was forthcoming, but he did find ample opportunity to drink and carouse with friends. One evening he and two of these friends stumbled out of a tavern and "fell foul of a young Cuban Creole" who was passing by. They beat the man up pretty severely. The *New York Herald* reported the incident and embarrassed John Jr. and his family. Now the paper's readers found out what Mattie Tyler already knew: John Jr. became verbally and physically abusive when drunk.[20]

John and Julia Tyler waited to see if John Jr. had been chastened and could indeed turn his life around. In the meantime, they settled in as a married couple at Sherwood Forest. Tyler worried that his wife would quickly grow bored of life on the James River, a rather provincial and remote area when compared to the New York City or Washington she was used to. He knew she missed her family. He was also sensitive to the fact that she had not gotten over the tragic death of her father. Julia sometimes dreamed of her father, and it was clear that she harbored a deep sense of loss. Tyler did his best to make her happy, showering her with affection and almost undivided attention. He brought her wildflowers from his walks around the plantation. He nursed her when she felt ill. They would sit out on the back piazza of the house many evenings, reading or talking and watching the traffic on the river. "The President is puzzling his wits constantly to prevent my feeling *lonely*," Julia wrote Margaret, "and if a long breath happens to escape me he springs up and says 'What will you have?' and 'What *shall* I do? for I am afraid you are going to feel lonely.'"[21]

Tyler's vigilance betrayed his insecurity and attested to doubts he kept close to the vest that he could keep his much-younger wife happy. He went out of his way to make sure Julia enjoyed her new life in Virginia. He purchased a mare for her—Emily Booker—which she rode sidesaddle around the property. He bought a mate for her beloved canary Johnny Ty. He also indulged her when she sought to outfit the slaves who served as oarsmen on the family's bright blue boat *Pocahontas* in uniforms of fancy livery. The couple used the boat often as they made trips downriver to the plantations of neighbors. This was new for Tyler. He had not visited the homes of the prominent families in the area with any regularity while he was married to Letitia; her health or his preoccupation with politics had usually prevented it. In his life as a retired newlywed, however, he found his social card filled quite frequently. He could now allow himself the luxury of making calls and found he enjoyed the added benefit of showing off his beautiful and cultured—and young—wife.[22]

The couple returned to Old Point Comfort in late June 1845 to celebrate their one-year anniversary. They enjoyed the area, and Julia delighted in her husband's fondness for splashing around in the ocean. The trip was not all pleasant, however. While they were there, a severe thunderstorm—Julia referred to it as a "hurricane"—ripped off part of the tin roof of their hotel and damaged the piazza. Their room flooded with rain. Thankfully, no one suffered any injuries, but some of the female guests fainted, and there was a mad rush to take cover. Tyler calmly took it upon himself to oversee the evacuation of the guests from the top floor of the hotel.[23]

More travel followed later in the summer. Toward the end of August, Tyler escorted Julia and Alice to the resort at White Sulphur Springs, in Greenbrier County, Virginia. People from all over the South had been coming here since 1810, when the original proprietor, James Caldwell, saw to the construction of several rows of some sixty cottages. Thousands—Julia called them the "wealthiest and best Southerners"—flocked to the mountain retreat every summer to escape the oppressive humidity and mosquitoes of their plantations, bathe in the soothing mineral waters, and take part in the activities of fashionable society.[24]

The Tylers found lodgings in a charming cottage in what was known as "Baltimore Row." The proprietor had initially reserved the "President's House" for them, but an "immensely fat" lady had arrived from New Orleans shortly before they did and insisted that she be allowed to stay there because it was the closest residence to the dining room, and she "declared she could not occupy any other and *go to her meals* without a railroad was contrived." No tracks having been laid from the cottages to the dining room, the woman was allowed to settle in where she wanted. Baltimore Row suited John and Julia just fine. Their cottage was spacious enough to allow Alice some privacy and for William Short and Fanny Hall, two of the ex-president's enslaved people, to lodge with them. The Tylers stayed for two weeks.[25]

An embarrassing incident occurred shortly before supper one evening that somewhat marred their stay. The couple had called on a Mr. Singleton and were sitting with him and his wife on the portico of their cottage waiting for the meal to be served. Andrew Stevenson, Tyler's political opponent from long ago, was also there, and the five of them chatted amiably as dusk settled. All of a sudden, the party heard footsteps and realized someone was coming up the stairs. Because it had gotten dark, no one could tell who this person was until he was on the portico right in front of them. It turned out to be Henry Clay. Clay shook hands with Singleton and turned to greet the others. He stopped instantly when he realized Tyler was sitting there. An awkward silence ensued. Stevenson reported later that the "whole party, including Mr. Clay, were considerably flushed." After a "short and embarrassing conversation, interrupted by occasional and distressing pauses," Singleton announced that supper was ready. He led Julia inside while Tyler and Clay stood up. One of them—probably Clay—apologized to Singleton and said he had another engagement. The other—probably Tyler—excused himself by saying he had a letter to write.[26]

Tyler was put off by having to see his old nemesis. "What has brought him here I leave you to infer," he all but spat in a letter to John Young Mason. He thought Clay was "much changed" in appearance since he had seen him last. "He is as old as his gait indicates," Tyler noted with some pleasure, happy that *he* was the one with the much younger wife. As always when it came to Clay, Tyler believed an ulterior motive was at work. Was the Kentuckian at White Sulphur Springs to press the flesh and kiss babies? "Can it be that he looks to '48—is the fire of ambition never to be extinguished?" Tyler marveled.[27]

Former Virginia governor John Rutherfoord, who also made an appearance at the Springs at this time, conceded that perhaps Clay did entertain thoughts of the next presidential election. He wondered about his friend Tyler's ambition too. Rutherfoord informed Thomas Ritchie by letter that he had heard "many surmises about the motives of the ex-President" and that Tyler might have come to White Sulphur Springs because he wanted to get elected senator again.[28]

This talk was not merely idle chatter. Rutherfoord had no way of knowing for sure, but the speculation that Tyler might be seeking public office once again had come close to the mark. Perhaps politics beckoned after all. Shortly after Polk's election, a Tyler supporter from Boston named Holbrook wrote the soon-to-be-ex-president telling him of the "general desire" among some members of the Democratic Party to see him elected to the US Senate, where he "would be able to meet and confront and *annihilate*" Clay supporters.[29]

Tyler may or may not have considered running for the Senate again. Likely he did not. Any reply to Holbrook's letter—if indeed there had actually been one—has been lost to history. The chance to annihilate his enemies, however, no doubt appealed to him. He had sought vindication for his conduct as president ever since the Whigs read him out of their party in September 1841. It also troubled him that he had been vilified by his political opponents in Virginia and that their invective had damaged his standing in the Old Dominion. Perhaps, then, a run for statewide office would enable him to repair his reputation. But the Senate might not be the appropriate venue. Perhaps an alternative existed. "I frankly admit that an election to the governorship would be acceptable in one point only," Tyler confided to Robert in November 1845, "and that as an offset to the numerous attacks which have been made upon me, and as evidence that my native State still retained its confidence in me."

He would not commit to a concrete plan of action but vowed that "if anything further transpires, I shall take steps accordingly."[30]

Eight months removed from the White House and Tyler was again considering a run for office. Apparently, nothing further transpired that would have forced him to make good on his promise to seek the Old Dominion's governorship, which was probably a good thing. But the fact that he even entertained the idea at all is remarkable—and revealing. Tyler simply could not accept criticism and could not come to terms with the unpopularity of his presidency. He regarded it as a slap in the face and an insult to his long record of public service that a sizeable portion of his fellow Virginians disagreed with him and no longer held him in high regard. Convinced of the correctness of his course of action while president, he could not refrain from self-righteousness. He still seemed to believe that he should be exempt from partisan attacks, when a simple history lesson would have told him that no president of the eight that preceded him (excepting Harrison) left office as popular as they were when they entered the White House. He needed to let go and allow his record to speak for itself. More broadly, toying with the idea of getting back into politics was remarkably similar to the way Tyler had acted when he "retired" from public life twice before. Even after reaching the pinnacle of American politics, he still seemed to be plotting a way to get back in the game. Was *his* fire of ambition ever going to be truly extinguished?

🙟

After leaving White Sulphur Springs in late August 1845, Tyler, Julia, and Alice spent a short time at another resort nearby, the "Sweet Springs." From there they traveled to New York to spend time with the Gardiners at both the house at 43 Lafayette Place and at East Hampton. It was Tyler's first visit to Long Island. They left New York in early October because he needed to return to Sherwood Forest to supervise the seeding of the wheat crop. "He is too good a planter to rely entirely on the judgment of the overseer," Julia remarked to her brother.[31]

Tyler spent three to four hours every day on horseback out in the fields, exhorting his enslaved laborers to complete their tasks and inspecting their work. Julia was correct in her assessment: he wanted to know what was going on at Sherwood Forest at all times. The overseer and slaves got used to seeing him. And Tyler was easy to spot from far away, having started wearing a large Panama hat, an accoutrement that became his trademark. Julia laughed when she saw him wear it for the first time because the brim was so wide that it swallowed up his face. In fact, Tyler's whole daily ensemble amused her. "He will never observe that anything is *worn out* until you tell him of it," she sighed. Tyler had too much else on his mind to worry about fashion or to concern himself with frayed cuffs and well-worn trousers. Besides, he thought he looked just fine. "I do cut the d . . . dest figure in this hat," he mischievously told Julia as he strutted in front of a mirror.[32]

When Tyler returned to Sherwood Forest from New York, he found some disorder in the ranks of his slaves. One small boy had died while he was gone, victim, Tyler supposed, of his habit of eating dirt. He had spoken to the child several times in a futile effort to get him to stop the practice. The youngster's death is significant. The disease beriberi, caused by a vitamin B-1 deficiency, often stimulates a nearly irresistible urge to eat dirt. Such behavior usually indicates that a person has been chronically malnourished or that they lack variety in their diet. If that was the case here, it raises the disturbing question of whether the enslaved at Sherwood Forest were being given enough to eat. In light of Tyler's chronic money problems, it is entirely possible he scrimped when it came to providing food for the slaves on his farm. Perhaps his professions that he was attentive to the care of "his people" sometimes did not match his actions. The boy's death was not the only problem Tyler found when he returned to Virginia. Other slaves were suffering from the ague, a typical summertime affliction in the Tidewater that caused high fevers and shivering. Most commonly associated with malaria, these symptoms could become serious enough to inhibit the normal work routine. Tyler apparently did not summon a physician to Sherwood Forest—his brother Wat Tyler would have been available—suggesting that the illness in the slave quarters was not widespread enough to warrant his alarm.[33]

The death of one young slave and the illnesses of some of the others did not hinder Tyler's plans for his first post-presidential wheat crop. Three hundred sixty bushels of winter wheat were seeded at Sherwood Forest in the fall of 1845. Tyler was pleased with how the planting had proceeded. He could not resist a little boasting some six weeks before the harvest. "Tell W[illia]m Waller that if he wants to see a crop of wheat he must come up" to Sherwood Forest in the summertime, Tyler wrote to his daughter Lizzy.[34]

His focus necessarily remained outside. Julia's centered on what happened inside the house. While she and Tyler had been in New York, Julia mentioned to her mother that she wanted help finding a young white woman who could help her manage the household at Sherwood Forest. The matter took on more urgency soon after they returned to Virginia when Tyler sent Fanny Hall, the slave woman he called Julia's "right hand in all that relates to her chamber," down to Williamsburg to assist Lizzy with her children. Fanny would return, but it appeared she would be gone for at least several weeks, if not longer. Julia repeated her request for a housekeeper by letter to her sister and mother.[35]

The Gardiners answered her plea in early November when they dispatched a young Irish woman named Catherine Wing to Sherwood Forest. Catherine came highly recommended by Julia's mother, who presumably conducted an interview with the housekeeper to determine her suitability for a Virginia plantation. Arriving by boat at the landing near the home, Wing quickly readied herself for duty. Well organized and a stickler for detail, particularly when it came to the preparation of meals, she became a highly valued member of the Tyler household. Before long, she was supervising the domestic slaves in their daily routine. Catherine thrived, even when Tyler unexpectedly brought back several hungry men from a fox-hunting outing, all of whom expected a feast.[36]

Traveling with Catherine Wing from New York was another soon-to-be member of the Tyler family, this one of the four-legged variety. Tyler had purchased an Italian greyhound for Julia directly from Naples. She had owned a dog of this breed before her marriage and was fond of them. Tyler had asked the head of the US legation in Naples, William Boulware, to procure the dog while he and Julia still resided in the White House. Boulware, however, worried that the weather would be too cold to permit the dog's safe travel—Tyler had made the request in the fall of 1844—so he waited until a more opportune time to put him on a ship crossing the Atlantic. The dog finally arrived in New York in the fall of 1845 and was immediately taken to her mother's home at Lafayette Place. Julia christened him Le Beau.

She eagerly anticipated the arrival of her new pet, the Italian greyhound with the French name. The Gardiners had kept him for several weeks in an effort to train him before sending him to his new home in Virginia. Apparently, the "training" did not go well. Le Beau ripped up carpets, chewed on furniture, and generally behaved badly. In other words, he acted just like a puppy. At one point an exasperated Margaret resorted to putting him in a dark closet in an effort to punish him, a measure for which she earned a sharp rebuke from Julia. Apparently, no one in the Gardiner family was sorry to see the dog crated and put on the ship for the one-way passage to Sherwood Forest.

Le Beau was cute, despite being a handful. Julia loved him instantly. Tyler, whose fondness for just about every kind of animal matched his wife's, enjoyed Le Beau as well. In fact, Julia wrote her mother that he "is more attached to it even than I." Tyler often chuckled at the dog's antics and was particularly amused that Le Beau commanded the house, a big presence in a small package. He indulged the pet. Julia walked into the parlor one evening and found her husband swaddling Le Beau in blankets on the sofa, trying to keep him warm in a cold house, laughing while he did it. Another time, Tyler placed one of his nightcaps on the dog and wrapped a shawl around his little body, setting him down for a night's sleep on the sofa, which by this time had become a dog bed. "It has become perfectly cultivated by the attention paid to it," Julia reported to her mother. Still, she thought it all a bit much. "Did you ever know such nonsense as we practice," she laughed.[37]

Her own spirits, however, seemed to change from day to day. But there was a good reason. Julia found out in November 1845 that she was pregnant. Tyler doted on her and did everything he could to make her comfortable. The couple curtailed their social calls along the James River and spent Christmas at home. Tyler happily welcomed daughters Mary and Lizzy and their families to Sherwood Forest for the holidays. He missed his other children. "We should have been rendered still happier by having you and yours," he wrote to Robert on New Year's Day.[38]

Not long after the holidays, the Tylers received some news that upset Julia a great deal. A newspaper in New York City published a story that alleged the couple had separated and that she had returned to her family home at East Hampton. Julia's brother Alexander had heard a similar rumor while he was in Washington on business. David Gardiner, Julia's other brother, immediately went to the offices of the paper and demanded an explanation. The editor apologized and told him the story had landed in the paper without his knowledge. David assured the man that the rumor was ludicrous and that his sister was living happily with the ex-president in Virginia. The next day the paper printed a retraction. Apparently, Tyler's last attorney general, John Nelson, had heard something from a third party about John Jr.'s marital difficulties and assumed the person meant John Tyler, his former boss. "The whole matter I hope will afford the President and yourself as hearty a laugh as it has me," David wrote to Julia, "although at first I must confess I was somewhat *riled*."[39]

John and Julia Tyler's marriage was on firm footing. It became even more so on July 12, 1846, when David Gardiner Tyler was born. Tyler had accompanied his wife to East Hampton for the latter stages of her pregnancy; she wanted to be spared the heat and humidity of the Tidewater and also felt more secure knowing that her mother and sister could attend to her. Juliana acquitted herself well as a midwife, and both baby and mother handled the rigors of childbirth with aplomb. Tyler, a father for what was now the ninth time, could not have been more pleased with his new son. There never was any doubt that the baby would be named after Julia's late father and oldest brother. The family called the child Gardie.

Another reason Julia preferred to give birth in East Hampton was her husband's busy schedule, which took him away from her for parts of the summer. He spent a few days in Washington testifying before the congressional committees that investigated Secretary of State Webster's conduct during the Webster-Ashburton negotiations. While in the capital, he shared dinner at the White House with President Polk and the US minister to Mexico, John Slidell, who had been recalled in May 1846 when the Mexican War began. In recounting the details of the evening to Robert, Tyler did not indicate that he and the president discussed the patronage matters that had so angered him right after he left office. Tyler likely thought things were better left unsaid. They did, however, discuss some of what had transpired thus far in the war. Tyler did not quite know what to make of Polk's course so far. Nor did he have a sense of how long the conflict might last. In any event, he believed "few laurels more will be won."

Tyler found reason to be personally concerned about the Mexican War because both Robert and John Jr. sought to join the military. Robert organized a company in Philadelphia, which did not go over well with his father, who feared it would derail his budding law career. "I care but little about your entering into it," Tyler wrote in reference to the war, "as it is so important that your office should be attended to. I almost regret that you have thrown yourself at the head of a company. These people might be well inclined to push your company off to get rid of you." Tyler indulged John Jr.'s martial spirit, perhaps because he thought the regimentation of military life would be good for him. He wrote directly to President Polk to secure for him a captain's commission. Robert's company never got past the planning stages, while John Jr. resigned his commission before his regiment saw action. As a father, Tyler must have breathed a sigh of relief.[40]

Financial matters, as always, also troubled Tyler at this time. His most pressing concern, of course, was the success of his farm. But in the year or so after he and Julia settled in at Sherwood Forest, he also focused his attention on a 1,400-acre expanse of land he owned in Caseyville, Union County, Kentucky, on the Ohio River in the western portion of the state. He had bought the property in the 1830s but had made no improvements on the land. Traveling west to inspect his purchase in July 1839, he found much more rugged terrain than he had anticipated; a heavy forest also dominated the land. In an effort to make some money from his investment, Tyler leased some 50 acres to two farmers for an annual rent of $100. He tried to sell the parcel in 1839 but attracted no takers.[41]

When Tyler left the White House, he resolved to sell the land once again. "I have lost a fortune in your State by neglect," he lamented to his friend, Kentuckian Charles Wickliffe. He just wanted to be rid of the headache and would seemingly take any reasonably fair offer he could get. Two things shortly changed Tyler's mind, however. First, his brother-in-law Alexander saw value in developing the land. "I have a strong conviction that it might by proper management be made to yield a handsome income," Alexander told him. Tyler admired the younger man's shrewd business instincts and took seriously what he had to say. Second, it appeared that Tyler's land held rich deposits of coal. Excited by this prospect, Tyler agreed to pay $200 for a proper survey of the land. He still preferred to sell it but now entertained the possibility of pursuing a coal mining venture that might end his financial woes forever.[42]

But, alas, it was not to be. Tyler and Alexander eventually formed a partnership in an effort to get rich in Caseyville, either by mining coal or, later, by harvesting the timber on the property to sell to steamboat companies whose boats plied the Ohio. Neither venture succeeded. Both men lost significant sums of money on the land despite Tyler's outrageous claim that he "solemnly [thought] that it can be made to yield $20,000 per annum." Part of the problem was the property's distance from either Sherwood Forest or New York City. It was difficult to keep abreast of what was happening in Kentucky, and the agents hired to oversee operations proved untrustworthy or incompetent. Tyler and Alexander took one trip out to Caseyville together in November 1847. Alexander made a return trip seven months later and found insurmountable problems. In 1850 Tyler appealed to Wickliffe to ask him to use his influence with members of the Kentucky legislature to stop a subsidiary of the Kentucky Coal Company from using its might to exploit the coal veins near the property, some of which may actually have been on his land. Tyler had clung to hope for as long as possible, but by the spring of 1848, he wanted no more part of owning the property. "I am ready to approve whatsoever you may do in regard to the Kentucky land," he wrote Alexander in near despair. They finally put the land up for sale. Not until September 1853 did they finally attract a buyer willing to pay the $20,000 asking price. Sadly, Alexander had died in January 1851. His half share of the sale proceeds went to Julia.[43]

Tyler was keenly disappointed by his failure to reap a windfall from his land in Kentucky. His bad experience served as yet another sobering reminder that he seemed destined to live forever precariously close to financial ruin. This state of affairs had become a recurring theme in his life that he could not shake. Julia had brought money to the marriage, but her brothers largely managed her funds from New York. Tyler found himself short of ready cash all the time. Repeating a pattern from earlier in his life, he borrowed money from multiple banks—usually in Richmond or Norfolk—and struggled to make the payments. It troubled him a great deal. "I so horribly dislike a state of indebtedness," he confessed to Alexander, disclosing that his money problems "terrified" him.[44]

Thankfully, the Gardiner brothers thought enough of him—and their sister—to help out whenever possible. In fact, both David and Alexander went above and beyond the call of duty in efforts to keep their brother-in-law solvent. They repeatedly secured loans for him in New York or endorsed loans he had worked out elsewhere, in effect acting as his cosigners. They sometimes made interest payments on loans for him and became his creditors themselves. To read through the correspondence between Tyler and Julia's brothers, particularly from 1846 to 1851, when he struggled most to sustain his wheat crops, is to come away with the appalling realization that he could not have survived without them. Letter after letter, sometimes one per week, contains details of this note or that bond, all requiring some sort of action from Alexander or David. The amount of money in question ranged from $25 to over $1,000. It is a wonder Tyler could even keep his different accounts straight. Debt and being short of cash were common among planters in the antebellum South. Tyler's situation, however, represented an extreme that most of these men were able to avoid.[45]

Tyler was very lucky his brothers-in-law were willing to help him with his bills, but their assistance was a double-edged sword. By involving them in his financial transactions, he made them privy to the most embarrassing component of his life. He was forced to lay bare the circumstances of his finances in order to receive their help. Tyler was mortified on one occasion when one of his New York creditors boldly knocked on the door of the Gardiner family home at Lafayette Place and demanded settlement of an account. Tyler promised David that he would "take care to guard against such annoyance in future," but with all of the financial juggling he was forced to do, he could not have been absolutely certain such a dreadful episode would never happen again.[46]

It is also worth considering how much of this Julia knew about. It appears her brothers kept the minute details of their transactions with her husband from her, not because they were necessarily trying to hide something so important, but because they believed these matters were best left between men—

this was the mid-nineteenth century, after all. Tyler, too, did not wish to worry his wife. Still, she had a pretty good idea of what was going on, especially since her husband traveled to Richmond and Norfolk several times a year to take care of his banking concerns and told her where and why he was going. Moreover, Juliana had a very good idea of the state of the family's finances. At one point she wrote to Julia expressing "great uneasiness" about the predicaments her daughter and son-in-law often found themselves in and admitted "on that score I feel great regret." After Alexander died, and with her brother David in California pursuing business opportunities, Julia asked her mother to be the one who signed the Gardiner name to endorse Tyler's promissory notes. Juliana no doubt recalled his pledge before marrying Julia that he would provide for her daughter in the manner to which she had grown accustomed.[47]

In the early 1850s, Tyler began to receive financial assistance from two other men: his former navy secretary and old friend Mason and Norfolk attorney Conway Whittle. Mason's involvement was not nearly as extensive as the Gardiner brothers' had been, and he apparently did not loan Tyler money, but he was still asked to endorse drafts drawn on an account at the Farmer's Bank in Richmond and to renew notes in order to postpone payments. Tyler always seemed to have an excuse for why he needed Mason's intervention with his creditors. At one point he had a sizeable portion of his wheat crop stolen right out of his barn while he and Julia were away, which, of course, cut into his profit margin. Tazewell graduated from Jefferson Medical College in Philadelphia in 1853. The tuition, as well as room and board, Tyler told Mason, "drained my purse." Their friendship had to have suffered, especially when Tyler had the gall to write, "I am sure no apology is necessary for my continued requisition upon you[,] which subjects you to no loss and to me is a great convenience." Whittle played much the same role for him that Mason did. Tyler sometimes tempered his requests for Whittle's endorsements on notes by acknowledging he was imposing on him. Still, he wrote at one point, "I rely on your known friendship to excuse" me.[48]

That an ex-president of the United States could find himself in so much financial distress and be subjected to economic peril underscores one of the many differences between the individuals who served in the White House in the nineteenth-century and those who came later. In the twenty-first century, former presidents make millions every year on public-speaking fees alone. Indeed, tenure in the Executive Mansion is a virtual guarantee of financial security for the remainder of a chief executive's life, no matter how much—or how little—personal wealth he may have enjoyed before entering office.

Tyler had no opportunities to cash in on his status as an ex-president. He did occasionally give public addresses, but asked only that his travel expenses be paid; there were usually no honoraria given. He believed strongly that as a former president, he was almost obligated to lecture for the public benefit. Over the course of his retirement, Tyler traveled to Richmond, Baltimore, the University of Virginia in Charlottesville, and to Jamestown, Virginia, to speak before audiences. These venues were never far from Sherwood Forest, but travel being what it was in the 1850s, he did incur some hardship in making these trips, so he was always happy to receive reimbursement.[49]

Tyler also made regular trips to Williamsburg to perform another "public duty" he believed was important. In the late 1840s he served on the Board of Visitors at the College of William and Mary, a post he had held for a time while he lived in Williamsburg before becoming president of the United States. One year before becoming a board member again, Tyler helped renowned scholar George Frederick Holmes from Richmond College (later the University of Richmond) secure a professorship in history and political economy. "I have had to endorse you strongly, but most cheerfully and confidently," he wrote Holmes shortly after the decision to appoint him to the faculty had been announced. When the professor left one year later to become president of the University of Mississippi, Tyler used his influence to help Henry Augustine Washington, a descendant of George Washington and son-in-law of Beverley Tucker, become professor and chair of history, political economy, and international law, a position once held by the venerable Thomas Dew. In the 1850s Tyler became rector at the college, a post that gave him oversight over the Board of Visitors and placed him squarely at the forefront of decisions over hiring faculty. In 1860 he was named chancellor of the college, "an honor of which I am quite proud," he told a friend, "as of any other ever confer'd upon me." His affection for his alma mater had not dimmed with time. He still believed the school played a vital role in educating young Virginia men, and he wished to do his part to ensure the institution thrived. Populating the faculty with well-known stars was the best way to accomplish that goal.[50]

To hear Tyler tell it, he himself had thrived in the five years or so since he left the White House. Notwithstanding his chronic indebtedness and constant worry about his wheat crops, he tackled the problems of running Sherwood Forest with fortitude and good spirits, nurturing optimism about the future. He seemed to be adjusting to retirement quite well. "For myself," he wrote a friend in the winter of 1850, "I am no longer in any way connected with the busy world, but devote all my energies to the improvement of my lands which although originally of good quality had by a course of injudicious husbandry continuing for 200 years, been worn down to a condition of barrenness." With hard work, however, Tyler claimed that he "already [had] the happiness to see a fresher and a brighter smile enlivening the landscape" of Sherwood Forest.[51]

Tyler was no longer in any substantive way connected to the busy political world. But he always remained alert to efforts to alter the historical record regarding the annexation of Texas. It absolutely drove him to distraction when anybody tried to minimize the role he had played in bringing Texas into the Union. For the remainder of his life, he jealously guarded his agency in that process as his legacy to the American republic. He might have been deprived of a legitimate chance to win the presidency in his own right in 1844, but he would not let anyone deprive him of his rightful place in history.

Calhoun, his former secretary of state, attempted to do just that in February 1847 amid the Mexican War. Back in the Senate by this time, Calhoun had come under attack from Thomas Hart Benton, who claimed that the South Carolinian had personally brought about the war by pushing the House version of the joint resolution that invited Texas into the Union—that is, he had rejected the Senate version, which Benton had written. Mexican rage had been the result, and the war soon followed.

Calhoun responded to this charge by noting that there had been others willing to take credit for Texas in the twelve months or so after passage of the joint resolution, including President Polk. But now that the Mexican War had become unpopular, it was fashionable to tar him with the responsibility for annexation. That was fine with Calhoun. "I will not put the honor aside," he declared defiantly on the Senate floor. "I may now rightfully and indisputably claim to be the author of that great event—an event which has so much extended the domains of the Union, which has added so largely to its productive powers, which promises so greatly to extend its commerce, which has stimulated its industry, and given security to our most exposed frontier." To hear Calhoun's answer to Benton, one would think *he* had been president in March 1845 and that it had been the ink from *his* pen that signed the joint resolution. Modesty had never been his strong suit.[52]

Tyler was livid when he read Calhoun's remarks. He wanted to give his former secretary of state a "severe rebuke" but settled for venting to his brother-in-law Alexander. "Was there ever anything to surpass in selfishness the assumption of Mr. Calhoun?" he railed. "He assumes everything to himself,—

overlooks his associates in the cabinet, and takes the reins of the government into his own hands." Tyler scoffed that Calhoun could not be content with his role as an advisor in the annexation process. That, he sneered, "would be too small game. He is the great 'I am,' and myself and cabinet have no voice in the matter."[53]

For good measure, Tyler also found fault with his old enemy Senator Benton and the contention that the joint resolution for annexation had brought about the Mexican War. "The man is the most raving political maniac I ever knew," he wrote.[54] But Calhoun had committed the real sin. "The idea that Calhoun had anything to do with originating the measure is as absurd as it is designed to be wicked," Tyler declared. He thought he might write his memoirs, which would settle the matter once and for all. Nine years later—and six years after Calhoun's death—what the South Carolinian had said to Benton still rankled Tyler. He spoke of the "fancied connection" to Texas that Calhoun had created to tie himself more closely to annexation. "If Mr. Van Zandt, the Texas minister, had possessed full power to negotiate the treaty at the time of its inception by me," Tyler groused to one friend, "the work would have been done by Mr. Upshur before Mr. Calhoun, who was then in retirement at Fort Hill, would have ever heard of it." Calhoun had come to the process after it had been nearly completed. Moreover, he had never tried to tamp down the sectionalism the Pakenham letter brought to annexation. This "chafed" Tyler, who argued that "it substantially converted the executive into a mere Southern agency in place of being what it truly was—the representative of American interests, whether those interests were North, South, East or West; and if ever there was an American question, the Texas was that very question."[55]

Tyler later lashed out publicly at Sam Houston, who claimed that his friend Andrew Jackson had played a more substantial role in the annexation of Texas than most people knew. Tyler set the record straight in the *Richmond Enquirer.* Worse was an article in the *Washington Daily National Intelligencer* that claimed Tyler had been compelled to pursue the annexation of Texas by members of his cabinet who had speculated in Lone Star land. The editors of the paper had apparently found out that Thomas Walker Gilmer, Mason, and Duff Green stood to profit from annexation. The article also insinuated that perhaps Tyler himself had benefited financially. In response, the former president wrote a letter to the editor of the *Enquirer* that explicitly denied the charge. "Certain it is," he made clear, "that I never owned a foot of Texas land or a dollar of Texas stock in my life, nor do I understand the editors of the *Intelligencer* as intending to intimate such a thing." Financial considerations had played absolutely no role in the Texas project. "Nor was it until I received *authentic* information that other nations were exerting all their efforts to induce a course of action on the part of Texas, at war, as I firmly believed, with the permanent interests of the United States," he declared, "that I gave directions to my lamented friend, Abel P. Upshur . . . to break up and scatter to the winds the web of their intrigues by a direct proposition for annexation." National security, then, had dictated Tyler's course of action. There is absolutely no evidence suggesting that Tyler had gained financially by the course he pursued as president.[56]

The final controversy over the particulars of the annexation process began in the summer of 1848, when Senator Benjamin Tappan of Ohio and Democratic newspaper editor Frank Blair published letters claiming that, as president-elect, Polk had favored the Senate version of the joint resolution—the one championed by Senator Benton—in which negotiations would resume with Texas officials with the goal of producing a treaty acceptable to both republics. Tappan and Blair alleged that Polk had persuaded senators to vote for the House version with the understanding that, after he took the oath of office, he would countermand Tyler's orders and revoke the joint resolution his predecessor had signed into law.

Tyler called the Tappan and Blair letters "extraordinary." He was angered by the implication that he had behaved dishonestly and somehow undercut Polk's wishes by signing the House version of the resolution. He also seemed to think the letters credited Polk with more than he deserved. Tyler was so upset that he immediately fired off letters to Calhoun, Wickliffe, and Mason, asking them to commit to writing their recollections of how the administration had arrived at its decision to pursue the House version. Mason did his best to calm down Tyler, assuring him that he had not acted dishonorably and that Polk had, in fact, concurred with his course of action after having been told by Calhoun that he—Tyler—would sign the House version of the resolution.[57]

It is almost inexplicable why Tyler got so unhinged by the Tappan and Blair letters, particularly in light of the fact that Polk dismissed them and ascribed political motives to the two men, at least one of whom—Tappan— was attempting to puff up Van Buren's candidacy for the 1848 presidential campaign by undermining the Polk record. That meant almost by definition that Polk's course in finishing the Texas annexation process had to be cast in a negative light. The matter did not directly involve Tyler, and nothing much was made publicly about his connection to what Tappan and Blair had written. Therefore, he need not have concerned himself with the controversy over the letters; he was not the one under attack. But he could not help himself. Tyler wanted every little detail of the process verified by the historical record. He wanted people to acknowledge that he had acted with integrity and with the best interests of the country at heart. He had not undermined his successor. Most importantly, he wanted the *credit*. Any claim that challenged what had really happened was, ultimately, a challenge to him personally and a threat to his standing in history. Perhaps the best evidence that this last point was exactly what motivated Tyler comes from a note he wrote to Alexander Gardiner immediately after learning of the Tappan and Blair letters. "Have you seen Blair and Tappan's disclosures as to Polk and Texas?" he asked. "Texas was lost but for my prompt action," he declared.[58]

Tyler sidestepped the real issue that drove the Calhoun-Benton exchange on the Senate floor and the Tappan and Blair letters: the Mexican War. He never seemed to ask himself if the manner in which he pursued Texas and his prompt action in signing the House version of the joint resolution might have lit the spark that led to the conflict. He got angry with Calhoun for not defending his administration when Senator Benton suggested that very connection. In defending himself, Tyler repeatedly made the point that Texas had augmented the South's cotton monopoly and strengthened the US economy relative to the rest of the world. He hammered home the idea that he had pursued annexation as a matter of national security.[59] In sum, Tyler saw only positives when it came to Texas. He seemed not to notice that the role he had played in the process, which he defended with such zeal, also cast him in the larger drama of sectional tension that was beginning to dominate national politics.

Chapter 19

FATHERHOOD, PART TWO

On April 7, 1848, John and Julia Tyler welcomed their second child—John Alexander—into the world. Unlike his brother, Gardie, little Alexander (or, Aleck as he would be called) had been born in Virginia, a circumstance that pleased his father immeasurably. Julia's mother, Juliana, had made the trip from New York in March so that she could be at Sherwood Forest to assist her daughter with the birth of the twelve-pound baby. Everything went so well that within three days Julia had recovered enough to laugh heartily while she and her mother regaled Tyler with stories of the Gardiner family's trip to Europe in 1840.[1]

For a man steeped in fatalism and possessing an abiding belief in the will of Providence, the joyous event that spring surely represented a perfect example of the biblical maxim in Job 1:22, "The Lord Giveth, the Lord taketh Away." Aleck's birth came ten months after the death of Tyler's eldest child, his beloved daughter Mary; she had died eleven months after Gardie had been born. Mary and her husband, Henry Jones, had moved to a farm not far from Sherwood Forest. She had given birth to a baby boy herself in mid-June 1847. Tyler had traveled to see his new grandson and had returned home when a messenger brought word that Mary had suddenly become ill. By the time Tyler made it back to the Jones farm, it was too late. Mary died on June 17, likely from a postpartum infection; her new baby died as well. The news stunned the Tyler family. "I have felt it most deeply," Priscilla Tyler wrote to her sister's family in Alabama. "She died after the birth of a little boy, who has since been mercifully taken to his mother again." Mary left behind her husband and three sons. She was all of thirty-two years of age.[2]

Tyler had not dwelled on his loss. Instead, he focused his attention on the children he had left from his marriage to Letitia, dispensing advice to all of them, corresponding about politics with Robert, worrying about John, seeing Letty and Lizzy whenever possible, meeting young men who courted Alice, and prodding Tazewell to think about a possible career. He also became a doting father to the children of his second marriage. He never got tired of talking about them. In April 1849 he could report to Julia's sister, Margaret, now married and with a son of her own, that the nearly three-year-old Gardie, a child the enslaved people at Sherwood Forest called a *"buster,"* both for his sturdy build and his assertiveness, had "improve[d] in his manners somewhat." One-year-old Alexander, less buoyant than his brother had been as a toddler, already exhibited a willfulness that perhaps boded ill for the future. "If he is requested to do what is disagreeable to him," his father wrote to Margaret, "he plainly says, *I won't,* and if solicitation is resorted to he shows his perfect determination by sucking his thumb." Julia expressed concern when Aleck continued to suck his thumb at three years of age, but Tyler did not worry.[3]

Alexander did not long remain the baby of the family. On Christmas Day 1849 Julia gave birth to Julia Gardiner Tyler. Again, Juliana attended to her. Her husband was elated. He informed Alexander Gardiner of the happy event, writing, "Our beloved Julia is delighted with the little stranger and pronounces her, with an eye beaming with unspeakable delight, most beautiful." There was a potential caveat, however. "I fear *my nose* may after all be more in the way than may be desirable," Tyler joked.[4]

A new father again at the age of fifty-nine, Tyler could hardly believe his good fortune. He had almost forgotten what it was like to have young children under foot and clearly delighted in being able to relive the experience. "My youth or the recollection of it," he wrote to a friend, "is in the mean time restored to me in the birth since I left Washington of two of the finest boys in creation and *now a girl* who engrosses the care of its mother and has the heart of the Household." Tyler joked suggestively that he had "been no idle drone since [he] parted with politics and the politicians."[5]

The theme of alternating joy and sorrow continued on June 1, 1850, however, when Lizzy Waller, three weeks shy of her twenty-seventh birthday, died from complications of childbirth. She left four children behind. Her sudden death came on the heels of the tragic passing of Margaret's husband, John Beeckman, who died of an accidental gunshot wound in California in April 1850. Beeckman had gone west to pursue his fortune with the other forty-niners, including David Gardiner. Margaret had stayed at Sherwood Forest while he was away so that her young son, Harry, could play with his cousins and she could be with Julia. She was now a twenty-eight-year-old widow. "Death follows death in endless succession," Tyler wrote to his brother-in-law Alexander in near disbelief. "We were bending over the grave of my beloved Daughter when we were startled by the communication of Mr. Beeckman's death."[6]

Julia's beloved brother Alexander would himself be dead seven months after receiving this letter from Tyler. Then, on December 2, 1851, Julia gave birth to Lachlan Tyler, her fourth child and the former president's twelfth.

Lyon Gardiner Tyler followed less than two years later on August 24, 1853. Juliana had guided her daughter through two more births. If only Mary and Lizzy had been able to take advantage of her skills as a midwife.

As always, Tyler chose to focus on the good in his life. Despite the heart-breaking loss of his two daughters, he maintained, "I have much cause also for gratitude." Writing to his sister Martha Waggaman shortly before Lyon's birth, he took stock of his family and surveyed the lives of his children. "Robert has already won high distinction in the community in which he lives," he wrote, alluding to his eldest son's growing stature in the Pennsylvania Democratic Party, "and John is daily developing talents of no common order. Tazewell has entered upon his profession with correct habits, and Letty and Alice are hap-pily situated."[7]

Tyler's comment about John Jr. papered over the difficulties the family con-tinued to face as a result of his alcohol abuse and reflected a father's need to see the good in his children no matter the evidence to the contrary. John's promise to rid himself of the evils of strong drink and devote himself to pre-paring for a legal career had amounted to nothing. Julia noted with disgust "the utter impossibility of [John Jr.] abstaining from liquor" and decried his "easy conscience." By the summer of 1847, she had had enough and wished he would no longer return to Sherwood Forest. "It is a wonder that he is this mo-ment alive," Julia wrote her mother. "He has neglected any advantage and has thrown aside any means of distinction." At one point Tyler professed to have given up on him and said that he expected to hear his troubled son had been committed to a "mad house."[8]

John Jr. was clearly an alcoholic. His behavior exhibited the classic signs of an addict. After disappearing on spectacular binges—what Julia referred to as his "frolics"—John would sober up, return to Sherwood Forest, tearfully apolo-gize, and resolve to do better. He usually renewed his pledge to become a law-yer and do right by Mattie and his children. He would succeed in warding off his demons for several days or even weeks at a time, only to repeat the familiar pattern. It happened over and over again. After one especially long bender, he joined a temperance society in an effort to persuade his father that he wanted to attack his alcoholism head on. Each time John made promises he could not keep, Tyler forgave him and hoped that this time it would be different. He did not have the heart to banish his namesake from the family home. To placate Julia, he placed all of the liquor bottles in a locked cabinet whenever his son was in the house.[9]

In the spring of 1849, John Jr. expressed a desire to go back to Washington, saying that he wanted to find government employment again. Tyler knew the real reason for his interest in returning and forbade him to go, arguing in what had become a tiring and tiresome refrain that he should instead return to his wife and prepare for the bar. John ignored the entreaties and traveled to the capital anyway. While he was in the city, he met up with friends, all of whom were as dissolute as he was. They made their rounds of the taverns and bars and drew attention to themselves as they staggered throughout the streets harassing passersby. At least nobody was beat up this time. News of John's embarrassing drunken escapades eventually made its way back to Sherwood Forest. Tyler was "obliged to hear from all quarters of the new fall of John," Julia reported to her mother, "who is in Washington, violated his pledge and the *devil is to pay with him.*" The news distressed Tyler so much he became ill. He and Julia expected to hear news of John's death before long. But his father never gave up hope—no matter how angry he got—that his son would turn his life around.[10]

The election of Franklin Pierce to the presidency in 1852 gave John Jr. the chance to do just that. President Pierce named old Tyler ally Caleb Cushing as his attorney general. Cushing then did Tyler a favor by hiring John Jr. as his assistant. "I am grateful that he has placed you along side of himself in your office," Tyler told his son. "The only fear is that his successor, if successor he is to have, may prefer some other associate and thus cut you adrift." Unfortunately, that was exactly what happened when James Buchanan became president. There was no more room for John Jr., a rather ironic situation in light of how important Robert Tyler had been to securing Buchanan's election. "What is he to do?" his father groaned. "The people in Washington seem to be resolv'd to give him nothing and I am much concern'd about him. That a man of his fine talents and accomplishments should not be able to earn his daily bread, or should fail to set about the task of doing so, is to me incomprehensible." Tyler worried that idleness would lead John Jr. back to the bottle. "I had rather see him following the plough than doing nothing," he confided to Robert, "and yet I feel persuaded that all the honors and emoluments of the profession [of law] are before him, if he would but pursue it steadily." And therein lay the rub—John Jr. did not pursue anything steadily. "His course is an enigma which I cannot solve," Tyler admitted.[11]

John Jr. remained the child he worried most about. The comment Tyler made to his sister about Letty, however, also reflected some wishful thinking, for she remained trapped in her unhappy marriage to James Semple. Alice, on the other hand, seemed relatively well settled. She had married Henry Denison, an Episcopal minister from Williamsburg and Bruton Parish Church, at Sherwood Forest on July 11, 1850. The couple moved to Brooklyn, where he became assistant rector of a parish church. After a falling out with his superiors, Reverend Denison found another parish—St. Paul's—in Louisville, Kentucky. He and Alice moved there and welcomed a daughter, Elizabeth Russel Denison, called Bessie, in March 1852, a joyous event that partially compensated for the loss of their first baby in April 1851. They seemed to enjoy a happy marriage, though Tyler admitted to Robert that, while he liked Reverend Denison, he would have "preferred to see [Alice] in more secure circumstances, in anticipation of those contingencies to which all are subject." Tazewell had just embarked on a medical career. His future appeared bright.[12]

While the children from his first marriage made their way in the world as adults—with varying degrees of success—Tyler shifted his focus a bit. "My attention is now to be given to Julia's children," he told his sister. And with this statement, he perhaps unconsciously framed a new conception of fatherhood for himself.[13]

🙣

Absence defined the relationships Tyler shared with the children from his marriage to Letitia. As we have seen, his political career made him largely an absentee father. For Mary and Robert, this arrangement seemed to work fine. John Jr., on the other hand, did not react as well to his father's frequent absences. Letty and Lizzy coped rather well but at times still expressed their unhappiness with the circumstances of their family life. With the exception of Alice and Tazewell, who were younger and benefited most from their father's retirement from the Senate in 1836, the children Letitia bore Tyler came of age without his presence.

The dynamic of Tyler's second family differed significantly from that of the first. With his political career now over, he was able to become a fulltime father and devote a great deal of attention to his young children. He was no longer forced to reconcile his responsibilities inside the family with his political career. Tyler did become overseer of one of the roads in Charles City County, a position bestowed on him as a joke by the still-bitter Whigs who lived in the area. He took his duties seriously, however, and, according to his son Lyon, confounded the planters who had played the joke on him by commandeering their slaves for work on the road at exactly the time their wheat crop needed harvesting. (This was another advantage of growing *winter* wheat.) His chores in this minor political "office," however, did not require him to travel out of town, so he was home with his family every evening. On those occasions when he did leave Sherwood Forest—for Richmond or Norfolk—he was usually gone for only one night, and Julia often accompanied him. Tyler thus inverted the pattern that had characterized the roles he had played as husband and father while he was married to Letitia. Attentive to Julia's every need, and serving as a true partner in childrearing simply by being there and taking on day-to-day responsibilities, Tyler embodied the companionate ideal to which he could not bring himself to conform during his first marriage.[14]

The most obvious difference between the behavior Tyler exhibited toward his second family and the behavior he displayed toward his first was his ability to spend what later generations of Americans would call "quality time" with his children. For example, he often hoisted Gardie up on the seat of a small carriage and spent the morning with him as he rode around the Sherwood Forest property. The young boy loved being with his father. Tyler would also take all of the children fishing, the little ones trailing behind him with their poles as he led the way to the perfect spot. He looked for any opportunity to "give them some fun" and enjoyed it immensely himself.[15]

Sherwood Forest was a happy place for the Tyler children to grow up. Unless it was very cold or oppressively hot, or they were attending a grammar school in the neighborhood, they played outside all day long. Margaret, Julia's sister, noted that the farm had so much land, they could run to their hearts' content. The boys learned to shoot at an early age and enjoyed outdoor pursuits. No wayward hare or squirrel could tempt fate for long with Gardie or Aleck on the loose before ending up on the family dinner table. Tyler, who was himself a good shot, encouraged the development of the masculine attributes associated with outdoor activity in his sons, as did most elite fathers in the South. This did not differ from what he had instilled in Robert, John Jr., and Tazewell. The difference now, with his second set of sons, was that Tyler could witness their development as young southern men firsthand instead of having to read about it in a letter or find out about it in a conversation when he returned home from Washington.[16]

The boys preferred being outside, where they could run barefoot and capture bugs and snakes. But there was fun indoors, as well. Tyler loved to play the fiddle for his children, as his father had done before him, and the family spent many evenings dancing to the rhythm of the music. Margaret, who brought Harry to Sherwood for long stays after the death of her husband, delighted in seeing the children "endeavor[ing] to outvie each other in curious antics." Harry and Gardie kept "perfect time to the President's music," stamping their feet and clapping their hands until they were both out of breath and had collapsed on the floor. Little Julia also got in on the fun and, by the age of three, had begun to display her own musical talent. One day Tyler found her sitting by herself at the piano, banging away on the keys. She was no prodigy, but her father enjoyed her effort just the same.[17]

Tyler also enjoyed Christmas at Sherwood Forest. As a US congressman and senator, he had often been away during the holidays, so the children from his first marriage usually opened their presents without him. His second family, on the other hand, got to see just how much the season animated him. He acted like a big kid himself. Julia loved Christmas, too, so the house was always festive. Tyler delighted in seeing his wife "up to her knuckles in mince meats, plumb puddings, and all the preparations." He enjoyed a little eggnog. He also solemnly told his children that they needed to go to bed early on Christmas Eve or Santa Claus would not come. One year Tyler heard commotion coming from Gardie and Aleck's room around eleven o'clock. He came upstairs and found the two boys sitting on their beds—wide awake. "They were watching for Santa Claus," Tyler related to Margaret with a laugh, "and complained of his tardiness." Tyler ordered them back into bed. "Being told that Santa Claus objected to being seen, and did not like boys to watch for him, they finally went to sleep; but the day had not fairly dawned when their exclamations filled the whole house."[18]

The noise was music to Tyler's ears, and he loved seeing his children rip open wrapping paper on Christmas morning and playing with their new toys. He appeared content as he watched his second batch of children grow up. With the first set, he always seemed to be on borrowed time, trying to fulfill the role of father they expected of him as the day drew near when he would once again leave them for Washington. Public life did not deprive Tyler's second family of his presence, and he no longer viewed fatherhood with ambivalence. He was no longer torn between family and politics. Family had become the priority.

Despite giving some thought to the idea of running for governor of Virginia again soon after he left the White House, Tyler assumed his days as a politician were over. There would never be another early morning knock on the door summoning him to Washington to take his place in history. All of that was in the past now. For the first time in his adult life, he was emotionally free to enjoy family life and give his wife and children his undivided attention. His ambition had been sated; his vanity had been satisfied. He seemed eager to make the most of it.

Tyler enjoyed indulging his children, perhaps a little too much. While their grandmother called them "as fresh and ruddy as cherubs," Margaret referred to her sister's children as Harry's "wild cousins" and marveled at their seemingly endless capacity for roughhousing. They were loud and boisterous. Another visitor to Sherwood Forest remarked that "the children seem to me to have grown up without very much religious influences about them." Perhaps this was a polite way of saying they behaved like little hellions. Whatever the case, that observation was literally true since Tyler still did not regularly attend church. In fact, Julia often attended Sunday services without him and the children. But more broadly, Tyler seemed unwilling to discipline his young children. He had been no stern taskmaster when forced to correct the behavior of the children from his first marriage. He often took a didactic approach to disciplining them, sparing the rod and choosing to impart his moral authority and wisdom, a strategy made necessary because his long absences meant he counseled them through letters. Similarly, the evidence indicates Tyler never raised his hand to the children of his second marriage. He preferred to sit them on his knee and gently explain why he wished them to behave in a certain way. Sternness was not his method of discipline.[19]

One other very important similarity existed between the experiences of Tyler's first and second families. The irony of fatherhood for Tyler was that his children with Julia also largely came of age without his presence, even though politics did not tear him away from them. The absence in their case resulted from their father's death while they were all still very young. In fact, when Tyler died, the oldest child, Gardie, was not quite sixteen years of age. The age difference between Tyler and Julia—thirty years—ensured that the children they had together would not enjoy the benefit of having their father around as they grew to adulthood. As a result, despite very different circumstances, they came to understand some of what their half-brothers and sisters had experienced. A father's death is, of course, far different than his absence for several months at a time, so the children of Tyler's second marriage may have felt his absence more acutely.

As significant as the age difference between their parents ultimately became for the children, it did not appear to have had a negative effect on the marriage itself. By all accounts, John and Julia Tyler bridged the age gap between them well. They were happy together and enjoyed each other's company. They respected each other. Tyler was a genuinely thoughtful man who took great pleasure in bringing back small presents for Julia when he returned from trips. He got up in the middle of the night to tend to teething babies so that she could sleep. He composed poetry to her. For her part, Julia often secretly wrote to her family in New York, asking them to use her funds to buy things for her husband—a new pair of gold-rimmed spectacles to replace the two pairs of glasses he had lost, for example, and a new carriage for him to ride around the Sherwood Forest property in—so that she could surprise him with gifts. They obviously loved each other very much. Edmund Ruffin, the famed agriculturalist and ardent states' rights Virginian, visited Sherwood Forest on two occasions during the 1850s and came away impressed with the Tylers' relationship. He praised Julia in the pages of his diary. "But I must do Mrs. Tyler justice to say that she, & her marriage to an old man, seem to offer an exception to the rule I have thought to be universal," he wrote, "that such marriages could produce nothing but unhappiness to both parties—if not disgust on one side, & hatred on one or both." Having spent several days in the fall of 1857 at the Tyler home, Ruffin could declare with certainty, "If ever a young wife truly loved an old husband, (which I have deemed impossible) she does."[20]

Julia did not dwell on whether having a large family with a much older man would come back to haunt her after he had died and she was left with young children to raise. She naturally expressed some anxiety over the dangers of childbirth itself, however, as any woman of her time did. She needed to look no further than the tragic deaths of Mary and Lizzy for the risks to hit home. There are references in Julia's letters to Margaret that offer hints of her fears, but she generally accepted her pregnancies with fortitude and looked forward to the births of her children.

She really had little choice. Tyler apparently lost no sleep worrying about leaving Julia with the responsibility for caring for a sizeable brood of children after he died. In fact, he reveled in his large second family. "So you see I am not likely to let the name become extinct," he rather blithely wrote his sister a few weeks before Lyon was born. Julia never complained, at least not to her mother or sister, but Tyler's lack of concern for what she had in store for her after he was gone betrays a selfishness and irresponsibility that do not comport with how he treated her otherwise throughout their marriage. His precarious finances should have given him pause. Perhaps this was exactly what Julia's mother had in mind when she expressed misgivings about how often her daughter was pregnant. At one point she even offered the opinion that having so many children was unseemly. After Lyon—her fifth—had been born, Julia looked for ways to break the news of her two subsequent pregnancies to Juliana in the most delicate way possible. She knew her mother would not be happy.[21]

It is not clear whether John and Julia Tyler ever discussed birth control with each other. Julia considered ways to prevent pregnancy and indicated she would have preferred to try to do so. Three months before Lyon was born, she wrote her sister, seemingly with some regret, "it seems I have not found the French secret yet," a reference to the mid-nineteenth-century version of a condom. We cannot know whether her oblique statement meant that she had been unable to procure one, whether she and Tyler had unsuccessfully tried one, or that he had refused to use one. The fact that she bore two more children seems to indicate the French secret remained just that—a secret.[22]

Tyler's virility—with fifteen, he is the American president who fathered the most children—belies how utterly unhealthy he was throughout the 1850s. Julia dispatched countless letters to her family in New York detailing her husband's ailments. "The Pres. is an invalid, alternating between better & not so well much of the time," she wrote on one occasion. Tyler was "under a severe attack," she reported in another. Still another informed the Gardiners, "The family are generally well, except the P[resident], who has been very much out of order recently and last night he had an attack of flatulent colic." Tyler himself complained of catarrh—a buildup of mucus in the nose and throat—as well as debilitating headaches, stomach aches, and arthritis. Some of this may be attributed to advancing age—aches and pains "will attend upon a sexagenarian," he said—but it is clear other, more serious, health issues plagued him. At one point he complained of lithic acid, what twenty-first-century doctors call uric acid, a condition characterized by crystals forming in the urine that may lead to kidney stones or gout. Digestive troubles also plagued him. "I find that I cannot indulge in sweets or acids," he informed Robert, "and avoiding them I get on very well." This comment indicates Tyler may have suffered from acid reflux, a condition that must have been nearly unbearable at times, or possibly had developed an ulcer. He attempted to alleviate his symptoms by eating an even-blander diet than usual—tea and bread and butter for breakfast, then rice and bread at dinner, with no meat or vegetables. That regimen made his stomach feel better, but his numerous illnesses often kept him confined to the home, particularly during the cold winter months, and he sometimes spent days at a time in bed or sitting quietly in a chair. He became quite adept at playing solitaire.[23]

After 1853 or so, poor health also forced Tyler to turn down most of the numerous invitations he received to lecture before public audiences. This was particularly unfortunate because he had begun to enjoy a post-presidential rise in popularity and esteem. Enthusiastic spectators greeted him at the venues where he did accept invitations. In March 1855 he traveled to Baltimore to deliver an address at the Maryland Mechanics Institute. His effort that night even contained some kind words for his old enemy, the late Henry Clay, who had died in June 1852. Perhaps indicating how gaunt and drawn he looked, a rumor spread the next night that Tyler himself had died in his room at Barnum's Hotel. One year later, on April 24, 1856, he addressed an audience in Petersburg, Virginia, and spoke eloquently and with great emotion on "The Dead of the Cabinet," a paean to Hugh Legaré, Abel P. Upshur, Daniel Webster, John C. Calhoun, and John C. Spencer. In 1857 the organizers of a celebration marking the 250-year anniversary of the settlement of Jamestown contacted Tyler and asked him if he would be willing to prepare a speech detailing the history of the Old Dominion from the founding of the Virginia Company of London through the American Revolution. He complained that "they have not given me time enough" but agreed to throw himself into the task. The Jamestown address, delivered on May 13 before a reported eight thousand spectators, lasted more than two and a half hours. Some in the audience complained of its length. Even Tyler himself thought it too long. Henry Wise, governor of Virginia by this time and a true friend of Tyler, declared the address "the best composition I have heard or seen from him." The effort thoroughly wore out the former president, something he feared would happen if he ascended the public stage too much. He accepted an invitation in February 1859 from William and Mary to speak on the occasion of the college's 166th anniversary—an event that took on even more significance because of a recent fire that destroyed the main library on campus—but increasingly Tyler just did not have the energy for these appearances. Invitations from Cincinnati, Saint Louis, and Poughkeepsie, New York, among other places, were politely refused.[24]

Tyler did muster enough energy to make annual trips to White Sulphur Springs with Julia and the children throughout the early to middle 1850s; he even met President Pierce on one of these vacations. Bathing in the waters and breathing in the fresh air undoubtedly did him some good, and he usually returned to Sherwood Forest ready to tackle the many duties of the farm. Similarly, he found travels to New York City and Saratoga with the Gardiners a welcome respite from the plantation.[25]

The renewed vigor these vacations brought, however, usually only lasted for short periods of time. Tyler's ill health returned in due course and became a customary part of life at Sherwood Forest. There was no shortage of medical advice for him as he battled chronic sickness. Tazewell attended to his father when he was able to return to Virginia. Dr. Wat Tyler, the ex-president's brother, sometimes stayed at the house. Finally, Tyler's brother-in-law Dr. Henry Curtis, Christiana's widower, also visited frequently; two of his sons had died young. These tragedies provided an opening for Tyler to mend fences with Curtis and get past some of the ill will over money that had developed when the two men were younger. Some financial entanglements between them were opened anew in the late 1850s, but they had successfully rebuilt their friendship. Julia's letters indicate Curtis almost always examined Tyler when he came to Sherwood Forest. He often prescribed and dispensed medicine.[26]

It was Julia, however, who provided the most in the way of medical care for her husband. She believed strongly in the benefits of fresh air and threw open the doors and windows of the house whenever possible, even in the wintertime. Cold, bracing air did wonders for a person's health, she claimed.

Most of her remedies were not nearly as benign. Always willing to try the newest fad in medicine, Julia administered dozens of pharmaceutical concoctions to her husband and children whenever they complained of being ill. Castor oil, chamomile, and calomel were staples in the Tyler medicine cabinet. She also tried rhubarb and magnesium pills to combat upset stomachs and experimented with something known as the Haynes pill, an emetic that "initiate[d]" the bowels, and another formula called Perry Davis's Vegetable Pain Killer. The label on the bottle of this last medication showed six little angels flying high in the sky ready to deliver a dose of the elixir to a sick patient. Made of opiates and ethyl alcohol, too much of this drug would surely cause patients to either see little angels themselves or know the feeling of flying high above the earth.[27]

The entire family believed a pill, powder, or liquid could cure anything that ailed them. Julia placed her faith in quack medicines, and her husband and children placed their faith in her. Tyler once drove up to the front of the house in his little carriage and ran inside, calling to Julia that he had been stung on the face by a bee. He wanted to know where the "painkiller" was and wanted to take it immediately. For the episode of what Julia called flatulent colic (mentioned earlier), she gave Tyler a dose of morphine, "which with a hot iron when the pain was greatest, had the effect to relieve him entirely." But she acknowledged that the next morning he felt the "consequences very much . . . in the shape of headaches and [heart] palpitations." Another time, suffering from an excruciating headache, Tyler decided to try a drug that had recently arrived by mail—laudanum and hartshorn. Laudanum was a popular opium-based wonder drug; hartshorn was another name for baker's ammonia, a leavening agent harmful if ingested unless it has been fully baked. Tyler went to the medicine cabinet, took out the bottles, and mingled several drops of both drugs. He promptly swallowed it down, failing to follow the directions, which called for diluting the ingredients with water. Julia described what happened next to her mother: "It took his breath away for a minute and I believe really liked to have killed him and the consequence was it *skinned* his tongue in such a degree you never saw. He was punished for his thoughtlessness by not being able to *chew his tobacco* for several days or indeed to eat much of anything or drink hot tea." The cure in this case was decidedly worse than the disease. Most appallingly, the Tyler children were not spared the bad effects from their mother's medicines. Eight-year-old Gardie, for example, once started foaming at the mouth after Julia administered "5 grains of Calomel."[28]

The drug in which Julia placed the most faith was something known as the "blue pill." She swore by it and encouraged everybody—her husband, her mother, her sister, her friends—to take it for their most severe illnesses. "The P[resident]'s better since taking a blue pill," she would report to her family in New York. Julia was not alone in believing the blue pill the most effective medicine available. Most of her contemporaries in nineteenth-century America had taken it at one time or another. Physicians prescribed it often; many people took it regularly.[29]

The blue pill, what was also sometimes called the "blue mass," was actually a round gray pellet roughly the size of a peppercorn. But within that small package came a large dose of danger, for it consisted of finely dispersed elemental mercury. Mercury is toxic to humans and, if ingested over a long period of time, may result in neurobehavioral disorders or renal failure. Because it is excreted from the body only slowly, over months or years, small doses of mercury would be enough to cause a person to suffer chronic poisoning. This is apparently what happened to John Tyler.[30]

It is extremely difficult to say with any certainty how far along Tyler's mercury poisoning had gotten before he died. Surely some of the symptoms he complained about in letters to family and friends may be traced to side effects of the blue pill. But he was not prone to the mood swings and sometimes violent behavior that are symptoms of advanced mercury poisoning. Nor did he appear to suffer from depression or memory loss, two other symptoms attributed to the long-term ingestion of mercury. One must remember, however, that sometimes these changes occur so gradually a person might not notice them right away. What is known in Tyler's case is that he took the blue pill often, though perhaps not regularly and certainly not all of the time. Julia, who acknowledged that taking too many would "weaken the system almost without you knowing it," sometimes gave him another variant of the blue pill, what was called "Mercury with chalk," or Hydrangyrum Cum Creta, a moist gray powder made of three parts mercury and five parts chalk. He also took calomel—mercury chloride—as did the children, so the poison entered his body in different forms. Tyler once wrote to Letty after taking calomel that he was "recovering from its prostrating effects," an acknowledgement of the drawbacks of using the drug. Yet he, like his contemporaries in nineteenth-century America, did not fully understand the long-term havoc they wreaked on their bodies every time they took medicine.[31]

On June 14, 1854, Tazewell Tyler rushed to Sherwood Forest from Richmond with awful news. Just by chance, he had run into an acquaintance the night before who informed him of his sister Alice's sudden death in Louisville. The telegraph wires had relayed the news to Virginia's capital, and the item had been published in a newspaper, but this was the first Tazewell had heard of it.

According to a letter from Alice's husband, Reverend Denison, to the Tyler family, she had taken ill with what the physicians called bilious colic, a nineteenth-century catchall for an acute stomach pain. The evidence suggests Alice suffered from gallstones or obstruction of the bile duct. She had been sick for several days and suffered a great deal. Doctors finally resorted to opiates to make her more comfortable but had no success in alleviating the cause of her illness. She died on June 8.

The news shocked the family. Alice had been twenty-seven, very nearly the same age as her sister Lizzy had been when she died almost exactly four years earlier. Tyler was dumbfounded, forced to confront the loss of yet another daughter at a very young age.

The question arose over what to do with Alice's remains. She was the first Tyler child to die outside of Virginia. Getting her body back to the state entailed a difficult journey via the Ohio River; a long, bumpy coach ride through the mountains of Virginia; and finally another boat down the James River from Richmond. The decision of where Alice would be buried became contentious. Apparently, she had been interred at a cemetery in Louisville shortly after she died. Someone in the family—likely her sister Letty—decided to bring her home and bury her alongside her mother and sister Mary in the Christian family plot at the Cedar Grove Cemetery in New Kent County.

Alice's body, accompanied by her husband and daughter, Bessie, arrived at the boat landing on the James near Sherwood Forest on a bitterly cold and dreary December day in 1854. John and Julia Tyler along with Tazewell, all three bundled up to ward off the cold, were there to greet the somber party. Julia wrote her sister that Letty and James Semple had also accompanied Alice's body, but it is unclear whether she meant they had traveled to Louisville or had waited in Richmond for Reverend Denison to arrive so that they could all take the steamer to Charles City County together.

Arrangements had been made for the body to be placed into a carriage for the trip to New Kent; another carriage would convey the family to the gravesite. Tyler decided not to accompany his children to lay Alice to rest. He even wondered aloud whether it would not have been better for Alice to have remained in Louisville, where she could have been buried at her husband's church. He and Julia would return to their house.

Letty would have none of this and caused a scene. She could not believe her father intended to forego the burial and pleaded with him to change his mind. Tyler refused. Letty cast an angry look at Julia, suspecting that she was the reason her father would not make the trip to New Kent. In truth, Tyler did not need his wife to persuade him to stay home. His health, the poor weather, and what Julia called the "reviving of melancholy things" after the months had passed since Alice's death made his decision for him. He would mourn his daughter's death all over again sitting quietly in his chair by the fire.[32]

By the time of Alice's death, the relationship between Julia and Letitia had become so acrimonious that nobody in the family believed it could ever be repaired. Julia had given up any pretense of civility, in large part because Letitia had already done the same. She dreaded visits from the Semples but, recognizing that Letitia was her husband's sole remaining daughter from his first marriage, did her best to give him the opportunity to spend time with her. James Semple acted as a buffer of sorts between his wife and Julia. Despite his attempts to keep the peace, Julia could not wait to get them out of her house. For his part, Tyler acted as he always had with Letitia and seemed to ignore the tension that arose whenever she and Julia were forced together.[33]

Tyler came close to losing Letty, too, in June 1855. She had been traveling with her husband in New York and "was taken suddenly very ill, with inflammation of the stomach." Her symptoms sounded eerily similar to those that had led to Alice's death one year earlier. James wrote to Tyler explaining what had happened, telling his father-in-law that Letitia had "suffered very much" and that "for two days her life hung by a very slender thread indeed." Thankfully, two capable physicians had seen to her care, and she emerged from her illness "restored to her *usual health*." She recovered fully and a year later, in the fall of 1856, traveled to Europe with her husband, a trip that pleased Tyler. He was happy the couple were together. He was also thrilled that Letitia would be able to do something he had never been able to accomplish: leave the United States and travel to distant shores. "Advancing as I am in years," he wrote her, "I feel as if my schoolday boyhood would be restored to me by looking on scenes and standing on the very spots which are hallowed by the memories of the past ages." He could be forgiven if he was just a little envious of his daughter.[34]

Closer to home, Tyler faced another crisis at the same time Letitia was on her tour of Europe and while Julia was at her mother's new home on Staten Island. Ten-year-old Gardie "fell alarmingly ill" with what his father described as a "bilious attack." Tyler reported to Robert that his young son was "frantic and wild beyond anything I ever knew, and opiates had to be freely administered." The physician Tyler summoned, Dr. Gay, "cupped [Gardie] freely in the temples." Gardie rallied but then suffered a relapse in the form of a high fever. After several days the danger passed, and the boy was able to sit up and read the newspapers and entertain himself with a deck of cards. Tyler breathed a huge sigh of relief and declared, "my heart was filled with gratitude to my Maker for the rescue of my noble boy . . . from an untimely grave." He expressed this gratitude in no small part because Julia had left Gardie and Aleck "behind under my guardianship, so as to enable them to go to school." Any father who has ever watched his children while his wife is away appreciates full well the panic Tyler experienced when Gardie became ill. He frankly admitted to Margaret, "it will be a relief to me to have her here" once again.[35]

Julia had gone to New York as an escort for her mother, who was returning to her home after staying at Sherwood Forest for several months, primarily to see her daughter through another pregnancy. Robert Fitzwalter Tyler had been born on March 12, 1856, less than three weeks before his father's sixty-sixth birthday. The little boy was Tyler's fourteenth child and the sixth he had had with Julia. "I am happy to say that Mrs. Tyler passed through her trial on the 12th inst[ant] presenting me a fine boy under favorable prospects," Tyler proudly reported to Henry Wise.[36]

By the time Fitzwalter (as he was known) had been born, Tyler had begun to think of his own mortality. His age, about which he had become obsessed, certainly had a lot to do with where his thoughts took him, as did his declining health. The artist George P. A. Healy had come to Sherwood Forest to paint his portrait, a sign, perhaps, that people thought Tyler might not be alive much longer to sit for it. Healy completed two portraits in two different sittings; one hung in the parlor at Sherwood Forest and was, Tyler thought, the "one good likeness of me"; the other now hangs in the White House.[37]

The alternating joy and sorrow that had characterized the experience of his family throughout the late 1840s and 1850s also provided fodder for Tyler's thoughts of mortality. The pattern continued in 1857, as twenty-seven-year-old Tazewell married Nannie Bridges and Julia's sister Margaret died at Sherwood Forest in May. Margaret had suffered from migraine headaches for years and frequently used laudanum to alleviate her symptoms and bring some relief. She had apparently taken some of the drug at this time and gone to sleep. When Julia went to rouse her later, she had stopped breathing. The death of his thirty-five-year-old sister-in-law hit Tyler especially hard. He immediately suffered "an attack of illness" that laid him low for several days. "She was very dear to me and I loved her as a sister, and my affection was fully returned by her," he wrote sadly. Margaret was buried at Sherwood Forest and reinterred later at South End Cemetery in East Hampton.[38]

Tyler found that other things reminded him that his time on earth was nearing an end. Like many elderly people, he faced the reality that many friends his own age were dying. His brother-in-law, Judge John B. Christian, for example, died in February 1856. News of his passing did not shock Tyler, but it was a blow nonetheless. "So pass away the friends of my early days," he lamented.[39]

Christian's death prompted Tyler to reminisce about his youth. He also thought a great deal about his political career. "It but now occurs to me that this is leap year," he wrote to the Virginia historian Hugh Blair Grigsby on February 29, 1856, "and this day twenty years ago, I resigned my seat in the U.S. Senate sooner than expunge the records of that body—a la Benton." During his illnesses, Tyler repeatedly wondered—in fact, often seemed tormented by—how posterity would judge him as president. "My thoughts during my confinement have seen very much upon the picture which might follow my departure from the world and especially upon the history of my life, and particularly on the incidents of my four years in Washington [as president]," he wrote to John Jr. in January 1857.[40]

Tyler had decided to turn all of his papers over to his adult sons and sons-in-law so that they could oversee the completion of a biography that would provide "a fair history of my administration." Originally, Alexander Gardiner had indicated a willingness to write that history. After Alexander's death, Tyler's friend Caleb Cushing expressed an interest in undertaking the task once he finished his political career. "I hope most sincerely that this may be so,"

Tyler wrote, certain that one of the stalwarts of the "Corporal's Guard" who had supported his presidency would set the record straight and leave the American people with a positive impression of John Tyler. He preferred that the work be completed while he still lived but acknowledged that this might not be possible. Cushing never got around to beginning the project, and it was ultimately left to Tyler's son Lyon to complete the biography of his father in the 1880s.[41]

When his thoughts turned to his days as president, Tyler naturally remembered Henry Clay, his principal antagonist and the man who had perhaps done more than anyone else to tarnish his reputation and make a project like the one Cushing contemplated necessary. His view of Clay remained complicated. "He did me great wrong," Tyler noted shortly after the Kentuckian's death, "and caused thousands to entertain opinions of me which had no foundation in truth." Tyler ascribed Clay's actions during the special session of Congress in 1841 to an all-consuming ambition to be president and argued that "while injuring me, he did more serious and lasting injury to himself and his fame. History is the impartial arbiter to decide between us, and to her decision I fearlessly submit myself." He professed to have gotten over some of what had happened between the two men. "My feelings of anger towards him are all buried in his grave," the former president claimed. The gracious comments Tyler made about Clay during his address at the Maryland Mechanics Institute in 1855 seem to bear this out, though one might imagine they were proffered somewhat grudgingly.[42]

In contrast to what he had to say about Clay, Tyler's harsh view of another enemy, Thomas Hart Benton, neither softened with age nor receded with the man's death. The longtime Missouri senator died on April 10, 1858. Tyler said nothing publicly but was unsparing in private. "I do not believe that any man who had play'd a prominent part in the politics of his own time ever had less of the public sympathy in life, or was less lamented in death" than Benton, he charged in a letter to Robert. "Of what consequence his opinions may be to his blood relatives I know not, but they undoubtedly have no influence over the public mind." Still smarting years later from Benton's insults and from the senator's attempts to undermine his presidency, Tyler recalled his former adversary's "excessive egotism and ill-regulated antipathies." Benton's two-volume memoir, *Thirty Years' View*, had been published a couple of years earlier. Tyler had not read it. "I would as soon undertake a journey through the dismal swamp as to wade through his ponderous folios," he said. A friend had once showed Tyler the second volume, however, and he thumbed through it enough to know that Benton had devoted more than half of the book to the Tyler administration. Tyler handed the tome back to his friend with the sarcastic retort that he appreciated the "very high compliment" Benton had paid him by focusing so much attention on him. He would take his hatred of Thomas Hart Benton to his own grave.[43]

The same year Benton died—1858—Tyler feared his family would soon be digging that grave. He passed the winter in "sickness and pain" and spent more than two months as a prisoner in his own home, unable to go outside—unable to do much of anything at all, really—and largely confined to his bed. "Most of those around me considered my case as likely to terminate fatally," he reported to Conway Whittle, "and I confess that I myself regarded it as every way doubtful." Tyler confided to Julia's brother David that he was "at a loss to know how I have survived." He still felt "quite feeble" in late April and, even after passing through the worst of it, noted that he "labor[ed] under one of my old attacks."[44]

Nearly all of the letters Tyler addressed to friends and family from roughly 1853 on at least mention that he felt ill or had been sick recently. He referred to his "old attacks" many times in these letters, implying that the people to whom he wrote had some idea of what he meant. So what did he mean? While the available evidence does not permit certainty, it is possible he was referring to the same illness that had afflicted him in 1820 while he served in Congress and again a year later after he had retired. As noted earlier, one physician has raised the possibility that Tyler suffered from Guillain-Barre Syndrome. Perhaps the symptoms of this condition appeared intermittently throughout his life and became increasingly more regular as he aged. Whatever the disease, Tyler clearly suffered from its recurrence and experienced the same symptoms that had characterized it earlier in his life. He recognized the telltale signs of the illness all too well and dreaded its onset. Julia referred to the condition as her husband's "besetting complaint," clearly signaling that she was aware that it recurred, even if she chose to be no more specific in her description.[45]

In light of how frequently he suffered from serious illnesses, it is surprising Tyler waited until October 10, 1859, to draft a will that made provisions for Julia and their children. The opening paragraph "revoke[d] and cancel[ed] all other wills and testaments heretofore made by [him]." This statement strongly suggests that he had drawn up a will on at least one other occasion, yet no such document or documents have been found in the records pertaining to his life. Presumably, an earlier version of his will would have provided for Letitia and the children they had together. Whatever the case, it did not matter. The will drawn up in 1859 left his entire estate to Julia, as long as she remained unmarried, and it made her the sole executor. He noted the "great responsibility" of raising their children and wanted his wife to enjoy any income she could derive from his estate "as the means of starting them in life and of perfecting their education." His children with Letitia received nothing, a fact not surprising considering that his sons were all adults and his sole surviving daughter was married. He wrote that he wished the children of his first family to view this condition as resulting from a "limited" estate and that it was "nothing more than an attempt and desire on my part, to place these children on a footing of equality with themselves as far as I am able." The terms of his will should not imply, Tyler assured the children of his first marriage, "any want of devoted affection for them or the descendants of any of them."

Perhaps the most interesting feature of the will concerns the manner in which Tyler dealt with his enslaved people. He freed none of them upon his death. In fact, he stipulated that when his daughter Julia married, she was to receive her choice of a female slave under her own age as a maidservant. Tyler also expressed his "hope" that his wife would select a bondsman for each of his sons when they turned twenty-one. With respect to his favorite slaves, head butler William Short and Fanny Hall, he wished his wife to "take good care" of them "so that their old age may be rendered comfortable." Finally, a codicil to the will written on March 13, 1860, granted Julia the "authority to sell and dispose of any slave or slaves who may prove refractory, either reinvesting in other or after such manner as she may deem most conclusive to the interest of my estate."[46]

This codicil naturally raises the question of how often Tyler himself sold slaves who lived and worked at Sherwood Forest. The evidence is sparse, but on at least one occasion, on February 28, 1857, he transferred title to a slave named Ned to a William L. Day in Spotsylvania County, Virginia. A receipt from Tyler shows that Day paid $1,200 for Ned, a figure indicating that he considered the enslaved man valuable, perhaps because he was of an age and possessed the physical strength to make him what was known as a "prime field hand" or because he possessed certain skills.[47]

The receipt for the sale of Ned does not indicate *why* Tyler decided to sell him. Perhaps he needed the money. Recall that Tyler had sold Ann Eliza in 1827 because he needed funds to pay for his trip to Washington after his election to the US Senate. Perhaps Ned was a "refractory" slave that Tyler felt he needed to banish from Sherwood Forest. Whatever the case, his sale clearly shows Tyler would sell an enslaved person if necessary, whatever the underlying reason may have been, as he had been willing to do earlier in his life.

For several years, Tyler experienced enough episodic trouble with his enslaved laborers to indicate that Ned may have indeed been sold for behavior
his owner found intolerable. In 1854 a newspaper in New York State reported
that one of Tyler's slaves ran away while he and Julia were at Saratoga Springs.
Two years later, during the Christmas holidays, William Short's son Roscius
came to blows with John Jr. after John reprimanded him for some infraction.
Roscius, who may have been drunk, ran away and found himself imprisoned in
a jail in Richmond. Tyler, angry at John Jr. for instigating the fight, demanded
that he make his way in the snow to retrieve Roscius; he intended to teach his
son a lesson. Finally, in the summer of 1860, Tyler grew exasperated when it
became apparent slaves were stealing cornmeal from the cellar. He wanted the
cellar locked and the key removed from the door. "Every possible economy is
necessary in our expenditures," he told Julia, "and in order to ensure that, the
greatest vigilance is requir'd."[48]

The theft of the cornmeal was more than a trifling concern for Tyler. He
had carefully allocated portions of it to feed his labor force. With several bushels missing, it meant he had to purchase additional bags more quickly than he
had planned. The entire episode underscored the extremely small margins
Tyler faced as he worked his farm at Sherwood Forest. Every penny counted.
When he needed to make repairs to the milldam or purchase additional farm
implements, it affected his bottom line. Maintaining livestock was expensive.
He could ill afford to lose money as a result of slave resistance that depleted
his food supply. Such episodes also placed far-greater pressure on him to bring
in a bountiful harvest.

Tyler enjoyed mixed success as a Tidewater wheat farmer. Some years his
crop did well, and its sale brought in the money he had anticipated when he
began planting. More often, however, Tyler complained that his wheat gave
him "infinite trouble." Several times his crop suffered a rust blight. He experimented with different varieties of wheat—Pennsylvania Blue Stem and a
strain called Zimmerman—and always sought ways to increase his yield. He
had particular success with South African wheat one year, telling the man
who had procured the seeds for him that "the result has more than realiz'd my
expectations." Tyler also became a convert to the use of guano as fertilizer and
apparently used marl, a calcium-carbonate mud that reduced acidity in the
soil. The use of these techniques indicates he had been influenced by Edmund
Ruffin's work on agricultural reform, popularized in Virginia and elsewhere
throughout the 1850s by articles in the leading farm journals.[49]

For the most part, Tyler kept his head above water financially throughout the 1850s, despite some years of dismal wheat crops. That changed in 1860. "My wheat crop of the year failed," he informed Conway Whittle, "and I am made dependent on future crops to make all things smooth." To tide him over, Tyler reverted to his old course of action, asking Whittle to help him secure a loan for $600. "Will you grant me your endorsement for that sum?" he pointedly asked. "Be assured that you will have no cause to regret it." The records do not indicate whether Whittle came to Tyler's aid once again. Whatever the case, his request exemplified his life at Sherwood Forest: the stress of worrying about whether his crop would bring in enough money and a reliance on the good offices of friends to see him through when straitened finances left him teetering on the edge of ruin. It was an all-too-familiar pattern.[50]

In June 1860 Julia Tyler gave birth to her seventy-year-old husband's fifteenth and last child, a little girl they named Pearl.[51] The family had traveled to Hampton, Virginia, so that Pearl could be born at Villa Margaret, a summer home named in honor of Julia's late sister they purchased in 1858. Julia, in fact, had bought the property with her brother Alexander's share of the proceeds from the sale of the Kentucky lands that she had inherited from his estate when he died. Again, Juliana was on hand to assist her daughter with the delivery of the baby.[52]

The proud father was overjoyed. In the fall of 1860, he wrote Grigsby, "I gaze upon the dimples and smiles of our dear little *Pearl* now but three months old with indescribable satisfaction." The historian's wife had also just delivered a daughter. Tyler teased him that perhaps the happy occasion "may require a large addition to your tobacco crop." Finances, as always, concerned Tyler. "I cannot add, as you do," he told Grigsby, "the one hundred thousand hills of Tobacco every time the new crib is set to rocking, but I do invoke the Father of all Mercies to place around it all good angels to watch over and guard it."[53]

Pearl's birth coincided with the heightened sectionalism brought about by the 1860 presidential election campaign. Grigsby would have understood if Tyler had told him he wished to invoke the Father of all Mercies to watch over and guard the Union, which most political observers acknowledged was in real peril. "The country is undoubtedly in an alarming condition," Tyler noted to Robert. Indeed, men talked openly of secession and civil war, and many southern politicians warned that the Union would dissolve if Republican Abraham Lincoln won the presidency in November. Tyler steeled himself for that possibility as he held his newborn daughter in his arms. The political world as he knew it had changed rapidly in just a few short months. Littleton Tazewell, his mentor and friend, had died on May 6. The Democratic Party, the standard he had returned to after his presidency, had split. Tyler had no way of knowing it in the summer of 1860, but he was about to compose a final, dramatic chapter in his political career, one that he hoped would bring him glory. Instead, it would ultimately color forever the way his fellow Americans viewed him.[54]

Chapter 20

RENOUNCING THE UNION

As an ex-president, John Tyler had a unique perspective on the political battles his successors waged after he left office in March 1845. As a fellow American, he felt he had a stake in how those battles turned out. As a southerner, he increasingly came to view those battles through a sectional lens.

Throughout the late 1840s and 1850s, the question of whether slavery would be allowed to expand into the western territories dominated national politics. To some extent, this question began again with Tyler's pursuit of the annexation of Texas, after remaining dormant since the Missouri Crisis of 1820–21. The issue consumed not only the occupants of the White House but also the men serving in both chambers of Congress. It caused a rift in the Democratic Party, helped destroy the Whig Party, and led directly to the creation of a new party, the Republican, which adopted an uncompromising platform opposing the expansion of slavery. Tyler watched these developments with no small amount of dismay. "I fear a great and permanent alienation of feeling between the sections," he wrote.[1]

Tyler believed this alienation had come about largely because of antislavery northerners who kept injecting themselves into southern affairs. The Wilmot Proviso—an unsuccessful attempt by northern congressmen to prohibit slavery in territory the United States won during the Mexican War—angered him. Furthermore, in his view, the Compromise of 1850, a series of laws that defused the sectional crisis arising out of the admission of California to the Union, had been the best deal the South could get. But its antislavery provisions made him uncomfortable. In fact, he deplored abolitionism from any quarter and feared it would rip the Union apart. When Julia published a sharp rebuke to Britain's Duchesss of Sutherland, whose name appeared at the top of an address designed as a step toward the end of slavery in the American South, Tyler applauded it. "Rely upon it," he wrote a friend, "that the golden rule of life . . . is for each person to attend to his own business, and to let his neighbor's alone." Tyler had harsh words for people—whether his fellow countrymen or the British—who violated this precept. "Woe, woe unto those who shall violate this rule of life. Better for them that they had never been born."[2]

But if Tyler sometimes despaired about the fate of the republic, he believed

393   RENOUNCING THE UNION

the Democratic Party gave the nation its best chance of staving off disunion, despite the growing assertiveness of northern members inclined toward anti-slavery. His faith in the Democratic standard afforded Tyler the opportunity to return to his political roots. He spoke and wrote often during the 1850s about how important he believed it was for the country to look to the hallmarks of the ideology he had largely followed since his days as a young politician—those Old Republican, states' rights fundamentals embodied in the Virginia and Kentucky Resolutions and the ideology of Thomas Jefferson. They represented the true faith for Tyler, and as he told his son Robert, he believed "that the preservation of our institutions depends on the maintenance of sound Jeffersonian principles."

After the Compromise of 1850 had been settled, Tyler assessed the party he had returned to at the end of his presidency. He liked what he saw. "The purification of the Democratic party has been effected by throwing over Van Buren and his train attendants," he declared with satisfaction, "and my hope is that it will not hereafter run into its former errors and excesses." He had no doubt the party was up to the task. "The great conservative Democratic party, under the inspiration of her example, will heal these discontents and with the principles of '98–99 inscribed unmistakably upon their banner will march to renewed triumphs. So may it be, for the sake of a Union which bestows incalculable benefits on all who live under it."[3]

Tyler's characterization of the Democratic Party of the early 1850s as "conservative" indicates that he had no use for or little understanding of the generational shift brought about by the Young America Movement, which was attempting to remake the party by advocating for more aggressive and progressive government at the state and national levels. These "New Democrats," excited by the spirit of Manifest Destiny, attempted to infuse the old party with new ideas, meeting with varying degrees of success. Tyler clung to the old Jeffersonian-Jacksonian standard and was firm in his belief that it alone could weather the storms brought about by the slavery question and provide ballast as sectionalism buffeted the country. The Free-Soil Party that ran Van Buren in 1848, as well as the Whigs, had shown an inability to offer solutions capable of sustaining the Union. Tyler called the Democrats the "constitutional party of the country" and enthusiastically supported New Hampshire native Franklin Pierce for president in 1852, a man who enjoyed the support of southern Democrats because he was a "doughface"—a northerner with southern principles. "If, upon being elected," Tyler wrote, "he brings along with him the fixed purpose of reuniting the old Jackson party of 1828, which was the sound

Republican party, and shall accomplish that purpose, he will have given a new lease to the Union, and a still brighter day to the Constitution."[4]

Scholars have judged Pierce a failed president. Beset by alcoholism and demonstrating weak leadership, he consistently ranks near the bottom in polls that assess executive performance. In Tyler's assessment, however, Pierce deserved high marks. His support of Illinois senator Stephen Douglas's Kansas-Nebraska Act, which repealed the Missouri Compromise line and established two territories in the Great Plains according to the dictates of popular sovereignty, pleased Tyler immensely. Potentially, one of these territories might become a slave state. Tyler saw in the law a way to "prevent the busy intermeddling of Congress" embodied in the detestable Wilmot Proviso. He applauded popular sovereignty as "a rule of universal application to all the Territories" that would allow the country to surmount difficulties over slavery.[5]

By 1855, however, one year before he would seek reelection, President Pierce had lost the support of many in the Democratic Party. Popular sovereignty had resulted in violence and bloodshed in Kansas, as proslavery settlers clashed with free-soilers in the battle to organize the territorial government and prepare for statehood. "Bleeding Kansas" outraged northerners, even northern Democrats who had supported Pierce, and the president took much of the blame. His status as a doughface also worked against him in the North, with many people in that section of the country turning increasingly hostile to what they saw was a slave-power conspiracy in the federal government. Northern voters made clear their hostility to the slave power in the midterm elections of 1854–55 by bouncing many Democrats out of office. For their part, southerners lost their zeal for the president because Kansas had not been established as a slave state. Pierce's renomination seemed unlikely.[6]

The Kansas-Nebraska Act devastated the northern wing of the Democratic Party and finished the Whigs as a national party. The sectional strains over slavery were just too much for the Whigs to bear. Many of the northern members of the party joined the ranks of what was called the Know-Nothing Party or found themselves drawn to the newly emerging Republican Party. Some northern Democrats also migrated to one of these new standards. Many southern Whigs joined the Know-Nothings. Southern Democrats held fast, but, by 1855, it was clear there had been a realignment of the political parties.[7]

Tyler watched these political developments with a great deal of interest. The Know-Nothings troubled him. Formally known as the American Party, its members cohered around the single issue of hostility to immigrants. Tyler told Robert that he was "sorry" that their anti-immigrant stance had gained wide currency. As disturbing as he found the Know-Nothings, however, Tyler expressed even more alarm over the rise of the Republican Party, which seemed to possess more staying power, especially after many northern Know-Nothings joined their ranks. These men rallied to the Republican banner after South Carolina congressman Preston Brooks beat Senator Charles Sumner with a cane on the Senate floor in May 1856, loudly protesting the brutality of the slave power as they did so. The Republicans nominated their first-ever candidate for president in 1856, John C. Frémont, who ran on a platform of stopping the extension of slavery in the territories. The Republicans also proclaimed slavery itself a "relic of barbarism."[8]

Tyler hoped the Democrats would renominate Pierce for the presidency in 1856, and when it became apparent they would not, he mused about a possible Henry Wise candidacy. His friend and political ally had been elected governor of Virginia in 1855, and Tyler proclaimed that he would "truly rejoice if one so correct in opinion, and so honorable in action, can be elevated to the presidency." Something had to be done to prevent the election of Frémont. Tyler pulled no punches in his assessment of the stakes. "It is quite sensibly felt by all that the success of the Black Republicans would be the knell of the Union," he wrote.[9]

Tyler maintained his faith in the Democratic Party to prevent that unhappy circumstance and supported the party's nominee for president in 1856, James Buchanan, despite nursing a grudge over how shabbily the Pennsylvanian had treated him during his presidency. It mattered little to Tyler that Robert had actually been instrumental in securing the nomination for Buchanan or that his son had become a close confidant of the candidate. Tyler also wondered whether the Pennsylvanian's "former associations" might seal his doom. Personal feelings aside, he genuinely wished to see Buchanan win the White House, arguing that "it will go further towards settling the distractions of the country than all else combined."[10]

Frémont and the Republicans made a strong showing by winning eleven of the sixteen free states. Nevertheless, Buchanan won the election. Trouble marked his administration from the start, as the Taney Supreme Court announced its controversial opinion on the *Dred Scott* case, and Kansas again became a political battleground over slavery. In fact, it was Buchanan's policy on Kansas that proved most detrimental to his future political prospects. He supported the fraudulent proslavery Lecompton Constitution, which had been drawn up by a minority of Kansans in an effort to make their territory a slave state. The president made matters worse by refusing to demand that the constitution face a referendum of Kansas voters. Tyler supported this position, arguing that "it was best to admit Kansas under the Lecompton constitution, and, if she afterwards deemed change to be necessary, leave her to work out her own redemption at some other day." Senator Douglas and other northern Democrats disagreed and openly broke with the president. By the summer of 1859, Tyler acknowledged that his party was in disarray and conceded that Buchanan was a lame duck. For a fleeting moment, Tyler thought *he* could be the savior of the Democracy. "I have daily assurances from plain men of an anxious desire on their part to restore me to the presidency; but I receive them as nothing more than the expressions of good will, and so let it pass. I could not improve upon my past career."[11]

Instead of attempting to improve upon his own career, Tyler looked for ways to improve that of his son Robert. Still hoping for a Wise presidential campaign, Tyler believed Robert would be a fine choice for second place on the Democratic ticket. "If the South is to furnish the nominee of 1860," he argued, "I incline to think that Wise will be the man." Tyler acknowledged that Virginia senator Robert M. T. Hunter enjoyed a following in parts of the South and might attempt to win the Democratic nomination himself, but he believed Wise the better candidate. The "idea prevails and that extensively that there is wanting for the times a bold, impulsive and fearless man and that Wise is of that description," he told Robert. "I think that with Wise as President and *yourself* as V.P.," he continued, "the Democracy would be triumphant. Why cannot this be brought about? Why should not *your* leading friends start the idea, or some such, and press it for *your* benefit?" Tyler recommended that his son write articles articulating his positions on the issues of the day and place them in newspapers throughout the nation.[12]

The idea of a Wise nomination, at least, was not as farfetched as it might seem. The Virginia governor had gained traction throughout the South as Buchanan faltered, and he consciously strategized for ways to attract northern Democrats to his candidacy. Then, as so often happens in politics, fate intervened to derail Wise's presidential ambitions. On October 16, 1859, John Brown and eighteen others seized the federal arsenal at Harpers Ferry, Virginia. Two days later, after an exchange of gunfire, US troops under the command of Brevet Colonel Robert E. Lee apprehended Brown and took him into custody. On November 2 a Virginia court convicted Brown of treason for attempting to incite servile insurrection and sentenced him to death.

As governor of Virginia, Wise had the authority to commute Brown's death sentence to life imprisonment. He refused to do so, maintaining that he needed to allow the execution to proceed if he hoped to retain the support of the slave states for the presidency in 1860. Tyler believed that this was a mistake. In a letter to his friend written in November 1859, the former president argued that commutation of Brown's sentence would demonstrate the "magnanimity of Virginia" and redound to Wise's political prospects, resulting in "the wisdom of her Governor extolled, the enemy disarmed, and the triumph of the Democracy secured." Wise got angry at the unsolicited advice, forcing Tyler to clarify his position in a subsequent letter. "Do not misinterpret my last note," he pleaded. "I merely suggested a point of political policy as cold as marble. Brown deserves to die a thousand deaths upon the Rack to end in fire & terminate in Hell. But still policy should be consulted—the profoundest policy." Tyler did not want to see Brown hailed as a martyr to the antislavery cause. Brown went to the gallows on December 2. Wise retained a sizeable following in the South for this but failed in his effort to win the Democratic nomination for president. Needless to say, Tyler's hopes for his son Robert amounted to nothing.[13]

Tyler had predicted a highly contentious Democratic nominating convention, scheduled to meet in Charleston in April 1860, and he worried about what that would ultimately mean. "I fear very much that the Charleston convention is destined to prove the grave of the Democratic party," he confided to Robert. Still, he did not lose all faith. "If there is a rally through the North around the Democratic flag, I can not doubt its success.[14]

Tyler should have expressed more concern about whether the *South* would rally around the Democratic banner. Stephen Douglas appeared to be the frontrunner for the party's nomination for president. But he did not have widespread support in the southern states. The fire-eaters, who openly sought to break up the Union, were downright hostile to his presidential aspirations.[15] Tyler suspected the Charleston convention would founder on sectionalism. Incredibly, he once again entertained the thought the Democrats might turn to him as a compromise candidate, claiming that friends had given him "daily assurances" of their desire to return him to the White House. Tyler shrugged off such flattery. Privately, however, he seemed to believe he could be a viable candidate again, despite his poor health, his old age, and his young family. His ambition had never been completely extinguished. He was like a past-his-prime athlete who believes he could come out of retirement and still perform at a high level. If he had intended to pursue the presidency again, he would have portrayed himself as a moderate, much as he had done with his attempt to win support for his Exchequer plan and similar to how he had sought support for the annexation of Texas. A Tyler candidacy, he believed, would have appeal in both the North and South.

The former president had again situated himself in the political middle and argued that his record demonstrated a commitment to the entire Union. His position had merit. Clearly, as a slaveholding southerner, he could not be tied to the abolitionists or to the Republican Party. More importantly, he was no southern fire-eater who desired the breakup of the Union. He opposed reopening the African slave trade, which by the late 1850s had become a hobby-horse for southern disunionists. "The fire-eaters agitate it for the sole purpose of reviving the agitations of the slave question in and out of Congress," he asserted. Indeed, the radicals had apparently seized on the issue as a way to alienate northern Democrats and divide the national party. Tyler wanted nothing to do with the proposal. In fact, he had returned to the idea of colonizing newly freed slaves in Liberia. The last thing he seemed to want was an *addition* to America's slave population.

More than just political and practical reasons convinced him that reopening the African slave trade was a bad idea. The very thought of it appalled him because it would undermine one of the most significant accomplishments of his presidency—the Webster-Ashburton Treaty. Article IX of the pact pledged the United States and Britain to a joint effort to suppress the international market in African slaves. Moreover, Tyler and Webster had faced harsh criticism in both Washington and London for the treaty's wording on a ship's right of visit. They had won the day, but it had been a hard-fought victory. Now the fire-eaters threatened to blow it all up. "Repeal the provision in the Treaty and the American flag will fly at the mast-head of every slaver on the coast of Africa," Tyler predicted. "G[reat] B[ritain] will revive the question of her right of visit as she claimed it and the consequences may end in war. This claim will go far towards the annihilation of the U. States trade on that coast and the engrossment of that trade by G. B."[16]

Tyler tended to see the developing crisis of the Union in a transatlantic context and partially through the prism of his longstanding dislike of the British. He was no doubt correct that Britain would seek to abrogate the relevant sections of the Webster-Ashburton Treaty should the United States—or part of the United States—reopen the African slave trade. That was bad enough. He also surmised that London would attempt to capitalize on the sectional crisis in the United States, particularly if the dissolution of the Union resulted. "Those rascals across the water are gloating over the idea of our destruction,"

Tyler complained. In the weeks leading up to the 1856 presidential election, he noted that a leading British newspaper "chaunt[ed] the praises of the Fremont party, and hail[ed] his election as the first step to dissolution." Buchanan's election had put the British in their place.[17]

Tyler clearly thought a great deal about the big picture and recognized the national and international implications of the turmoil roiling the United States as the 1860 presidential election neared. His thinking demonstrated a statesmanlike approach to the problems the country faced. It is unclear how much he actually believed that he stood a chance to win the Democratic nomination in Charleston. In any event, it was a moot point. Eight southern states bolted the Charleston convention rather than support Senator Douglas or the party platform. Ultimately, the Democrats split. Douglas won the nomination of what was left of the party—essentially, he became the northern Democratic candidate—and Buchanan's vice president, John C. Breckinridge of Kentucky, received the nomination of southern Democrats.

What Tyler had feared had come to pass. "The Country is undoubtedly in an alarming condition," he wrote to Robert. He maintained that the "bolters" (as they were called) should have kept their seats in the convention and used their clout to wrest the nomination away from Douglas. Tyler apparently failed to realize or acknowledge that the bolters had deliberately sabotaged the convention to further their own aim of bringing about the dissolution of the Union. With four candidates in the race in 1860—the Republicans nominated Abraham Lincoln and another group calling itself the Constitutional Union Party had nominated Tyler's former secretary of war, John Bell—that prospect seemed increasingly likely. Tyler thought so. "Let things result as they may, I fear the great Republic has seen its best days," he gloomily predicted.[18]

Still, all was not necessarily lost. "The consequences of Lincoln's election I cannot foretell," Tyler wrote. "Neither Virginia, nor North Carolina, nor Maryland (to which you may add Kentucky, Tennessee and Missouri) will secede for that." That was the good news. "My apprehension, however, is that South Carolina and others of the cotton States will do so, and any attempt to coerce such seceding States will most probably be resisted by all the South. When such an issue comes, then comes also the end of the Confederacy." Letting matters take their course seemed the only sensible policy. He imparted this wisdom to his family, not only while sitting at the dinner table with Julia and the children but also through the mail. On October 30 he received a letter from his grandson William Waller, his late daughter Lizzy's son, who was a cadet at the US Military Academy at West Point. William had written to his grandfather seeking advice on what to do if Lincoln won the presidential election. The young man apparently wanted to resign his commission at once if that occurred. Tyler counseled against it in a return letter. "I would not think or resigning my place of cadet until Virginia had distinctly and plainly marked out her course after the election," he wrote. Tyler argued that it would be "injurious to the interests of the South" if all southern cadets left school prematurely. Their departure would diminish their standing at West Point; he instead wanted his grandson to "think only of [his] studies." Tyler admitted he did not know if William's father would concur with the advice he had given him, but he nevertheless hoped his letter would prevent "any rash step." He believed William was getting ahead of himself, as young men often do. "If Lincoln is elected, and appearances all point strongly that way," he wrote, "disunion may not necessarily follow."[19]

The suspense soon ended. "So all is over," Tyler wrote grimly on November 10, 1860, "and Lincoln elected. South Carolina will secede. What other States will do remains to be seen." His primary initial concern was with Virginia's reaction. He expressed confidence that his home state would "abide developments" and take a wait-and-see approach on the matter of secession. Tyler expected the leaders of the Old Dominion to choose their course wisely and offer sage counsel to the politicians in other southern states as they attempted to stifle the "miserable demagogues" who now happily pushed for disunion. "Always conservative, she will be ready to intervene with conservative views," he assured a friend.

But Tyler offered a caveat as well. He noted President-elect Lincoln's intention to prevent the extension of slavery in the territories, which was the part of the Republican Party platform that had actually driven the secession talk in the months leading up to the election. "On one thing I think you may rely," Tyler declared, "that [Virginia] will never consent to have her blacks cribbed and confined within proscribed and specified limits—and thus be involved in all the consequences of a war of the races in some 20 or 30 years. She must have expansion, and if she cannot obtain it for herself and sisters that expansion in the Union, she may sooner or later be driven out of it."

Tyler saw the question of slavery's expansion as he always had—within the context of the diffusion argument. He hoped for slavery's end, albeit at some distant point in the future—two to three decades apparently—but argued that it could only come about if slaves were gradually diffused over a large portion of territory. He had said as much during the Missouri crisis many years ago, and it explains why he had found Senator Walker's "safety-valve" thesis so compelling as he pursued the annexation of Texas. Tyler recognized the difficulty he and other supporters of diffusion faced with Lincoln's election: "no more slave States has apparently become the shibboleth of Northern political faith." He "fear[ed] the end will not prove to be propitious to the Union."

Lincoln's election had almost become, in Tyler's view, a point of no return. "I am not prepared to say that harmony can ever be restored," he asserted, "and sometimes I think that it would be better for all peaceably to separate. The North would have its wish for a Republic homogenous in its population and so would the South." He believed that "commercial relations would soon spring up between them, and all things be restored to peace." It seemed Tyler had reconciled himself to disunion.

On the other hand, the idea of the Union, which his father had had a small part in creating, retained an almost irresistible pull for him. "And then again when I look to the grandeur of our institutions and their ultimate glory," he wrote, "I sigh over the degeneracy of the times which will not let well enough alone, and the enthusiasm of bygone days is awakened for the Union as it was of yore." Tyler believed both sides—the fire-eaters and the so-called Black Republicans—were to blame for threatening the Union he loved. "Madness rules the hour," he complained, "and statesmanship in all its grand and massive proportions gives place to a miserable demagogism which leads to inevitable destruction." Statesmanship was indeed what the country needed at this time, what was necessary to save the Union, but Tyler could not foresee anyone rising to the occasion to provide it. He certainly did not expect that he would play a role. "In the midst of all this I remain quiescent," he wrote. "No longer an actor on the stage of public affairs, I leave to others younger than myself the settlement of existing disputes." Having said that, however, Tyler left the door partially open to his participation. To Robert, he privately acknowledged that he would remain quiet "unless I see that my poor opinions have due weight."[20]

South Carolina seceded from the Union on December 20, 1860. Six Deep South states—Georgia, Florida, Alabama, Mississippi, Louisiana, and Texas—soon followed suit. By mid-February 1861, they had established the Confederate States of America. Jefferson Davis of Mississippi was elected president.

Tyler attempted to find out if his "poor opinions" held weight even before the secession crisis began. In mid-December 1860 he began circulating an idea in Richmond to gather representatives from the border states together at a convention in Washington. He envisioned a contingent of commissioners from six free states—New Jersey, Pennsylvania, Ohio, Indiana, Illinois, and Michigan—meeting with counterparts from the six slave states of Virginia, Delaware, Maryland, Kentucky, Tennessee, and Missouri. Tyler thought the border-states convention "might lead to adjustment" of the current difficulties. These states, he maintained, "are most interested in keeping the peace, and, if they cannot come to an understanding, then the political union is gone, as is already, to a great extent, the union of fraternal feeling."[21]

Tyler believed even more strongly in his idea once the secession dominoes began falling. He credited President Buchanan with a "wise and statesman-like course" in the early stages of the crisis. "A blow struck" by the Buchanan administration against the seceded states, Tyler argued, "would be the signal for united action with all the slave States, whereas the grain States of the border are sincerely desirous of reconciling matters and thereby preserving the Union." Tyler noted that a similar idea to his had circulated in Washington. Indeed, Kentucky senator John J. Crittenden, still active in politics after all these years, had convened an ad hoc gathering of congressmen from border states. That body had temporarily disbanded after the late-December announcement that Major Robert Anderson had moved his garrison from Fort Moultrie, on Sullivan's Island off the coast of South Carolina, to the more formidable Fort Sumter in Charleston harbor. When the group came together again, it faced stiff opposition, especially from Republicans in Congress. Ultimately, nothing came of Crittenden's gathering. Tyler hoped a better fate awaited his.[22]

To his dismay, however, the Virginia General Assembly mangled his proposal. While the legislature agreed with the former president that a convention seemed prudent, it passed a series of resolutions on January 15, 1861, calling for a gathering of representatives from *all* thirty-three states to convene in Washington on February 4. Tyler had most emphatically not wanted the convention to include individuals from states that had already seceded. Nor did he want men from northern states such as Massachusetts and New York present. He reasoned that a convention of all the states would include too many of what he regarded as extremists on both sides. Again, employing his measured approach to political problems, Tyler argued for the moderate course. Only representatives from the geographic middle of the country could be counted on to provide a way out of the predicament the country found itself in, something the Virginia legislature failed to grasp. His convention proposal had been "so trammeled" that he feared "we shall have a doubtful result."[23]

Frantic and determined to salvage the plan, Tyler penned a lengthy response to the Virginia legislature's resolutions that appeared in the *Richmond*

Enquirer on January 18. He again urged a convention of border states only, reiterating in stronger terms his reasons for excluding the other states. He believed the border states retained sufficient influence with those of both the North and South. As long as the men attending a convention could reach an agreement on a course of action, Tyler maintained, "their recommendation will be followed by the other States and incorporated into the Constitution." The cooler heads of his twelve states were better equipped to reach a compromise.[24]

But the wishes of the Virginia legislature carried the day—the call went out for delegates from all the states. The general assembly chose Tyler as a delegate, along with four other men, and instructed them to work toward a compromise similar to the one Crittenden had proposed. The senator advocated a series of six constitutional amendments that he believed would put to rest the issues that had prompted the secession crisis. Chief among them was an extension of the Missouri Compromise line to the Pacific coast and a stipulation that the line would apply to any territory the United States acquired in the future.[25]

In addition to selecting him as a representative to the peace convention, the general assembly appointed Tyler the Old Dominion's special emissary to President Buchanan. The legislature clearly hoped to capitalize on Tyler's status as an ex-president and no doubt believed Robert Tyler's relationship with Buchanan would provide an opening for talks. Tyler was to take a series of resolutions to Buchanan from the general assembly that impressed upon him the need to avoid "any and all acts calculated to produce a collision between the States and the Government of the United States," at least until the peace convention had deliberated. Virginia wanted a firm commitment. Tyler agreed to call on the president and present the resolutions, but he had been ill for much of the month of January. By the twenty-second, he was ready to travel to Washington. Fortified by a hefty dose of Julia's mercury with chalk, and with fourteen-year-old Gardie in tow, he left Sherwood Forest and made his way to the national capital.

Father and son arrived there the next day. Tyler immediately sent word to the White House that he wished to meet with Buchanan. The two men sat down at ten o'clock on the morning of January 24. Buchanan greeted Tyler cordially. After quickly perusing the resolutions Tyler handed him, he expressed his agreement that rash action must be avoided at all costs. The president agreed to include the Virginia legislature's resolutions in a special message to Congress. Tyler asked if he might see the message after Buchanan had prepared it. Buchanan agreed, and Tyler returned to the White House the following morning. Satisfied that the message clearly represented his state's resolutions, he took leave of the president and prepared to return to Virginia. He would have a little over one week at home before the peace convention convened.[26]

Despite Buchanan's willingness to incorporate the Virginia resolutions into a special message to Congress, Tyler expected little of substance from the lame-duck president. He sensed that Buchanan merely wanted to finish his term and retire to his estate in Pennsylvania. "His policy obviously is to throw all responsibility off his shoulders," Tyler told a friend. Though he never directly said so, there was some frustration on Tyler's part in dealing with Buchanan, especially since "Virginia [was] making every possible effort to redeem and save the Union." Buchanan had told him he could offer no firm commitment to prevent a collision of arms between the federal government and the states and that only Congress, under its power to declare war, could do so. Unfortunately, Congress sent a very clear message to Tyler, and to Virginia and the other border states, when both houses refused to refer the resolutions to a committee. Instead, they were allowed to lie on the table indefinitely without debate. Moreover, in what many Virginians rightly interpreted as an insult, neither house saw fit to print the resolutions so that the public could read them, a courtesy afforded even the most perfunctory messages Congress received.[27]

When Tyler returned to Washington for the start of the peace convention on February 4, 1861, he was accompanied by Julia, twelve-year-old Aleck, seven-month-old Pearl, and Fanny Hall. The family checked into Brown's Hotel—the same establishment where Tyler had stayed after arriving in the capital to assume the presidency in April 1841. Julia could hardly contain her excitement at being in Washington again. Proud of her husband, she marveled at the way everyone "deferentially" gathered around him. "There seems to be a general looking to him by those anxious to save the Union," she reported to her mother. "They all say if through him it cannot be accomplished, it could not be through any one else." Tyler harbored no such illusions. Instead, he threw himself into his duties as he always had, working long hours, meeting fellow delegates, and making himself sick in the process. His stomach bothered him constantly; mercury with chalk—administered in ever greater doses—offered little relief. The conference, meeting at Willard Hall adjacent to Willard's Hotel, unanimously elected him president. To some of the delegates, Tyler seemed a "tottering ashen ruin." He looked and felt every bit of his nearly seventy-one years.[28]

Twenty-one states sent delegates to the convention. One historian has called the gathering an "Old Gentlemen's Convention." Indeed, most of the men had spent long years in public life and had achieved a significant degree of success and fame. Only one had served as president of the United States.[29]

These men hoped they could display their political skills once more and hammer out a compromise that would save the Union and bring them ever-lasting fame. They failed utterly. The convention accomplished nothing. Debate on the floor often turned rancorous; shouting became the norm, and a few times Tyler even lost control of the proceedings as delegates nearly came to blows. As he had predicted, too many extremists from both sides, North and South, prevented compromise. Tyler complained later that he "had to address 'stocks and stones,' who had neither ears nor hearts to understand." He confessed that he had "aspired to the glory of aiding to settle this controversy," wanting to find a compromise that would restore the Union. Were it not for circumstances beyond his control, the convention could have afforded him the "proud crowning act of my life."[30]

Tyler's characterization of the peace convention is curious since he had a hand in ensuring its failure. He fought the proposed constitutional amendment drawn up by the convention committee responsible for that task. This proposal—which represented the views of a majority of the delegates—resembled the Crittenden Compromise: it permitted slavery south of the Missouri Compromise line of thirty-six degrees, thirty minutes; prohibited the institution north of the line; and allowed slaveholders to take their bondspeople into any territory south of the line until the residents of a territory drafted a state constitution that specifically forbade slavery. For most moderates, including two of the five Virginia delegates, the proposal was a sound one. Tyler, however, had other ideas.

He favored another plan, one the pro-secession Virginia delegate James A. Seddon had devised. Seddon submitted a minority report on the same day the committee presented its compromise amendment to the entire convention. The minority report advocated a constitutional amendment that would give the South a veto on legislative and executive appointments south of the compromise line. More significantly, Seddon's proposal stipulated that a state had the constitutional right to secede from the Union whenever and for whatever reason it wished. When the time came to vote, Tyler shunned the neutrality that delegates probably expected from the convention president and took to the floor in an effort to win support for Seddon's amendment. After bitter debate and several votes, the moderates defeated the minority report. The convention forced Tyler to forward the majority compromise proposal to Congress. He sent it along, but with the qualification that he did it because he had been instructed to do so. Whether his support for the majority amendment would have made any difference is difficult to say; it probably would have mattered little. Whatever the case, Congress refused to submit the proposal to the states and let the amendment die with little discussion. The peace convention ultimately faded into oblivion.[31]

Tyler's behavior obviously signaled that he had come to the conclusion that the Union could not be saved. Two factors may account for the shift in attitude. For one thing, by late February, he had become convinced that President-elect Lincoln was indeed a threat to slavery and the South. Tyler and several other delegates of the peace convention had called on Lincoln in his suite at Willard's Hotel on February 23, two days before Tyler spoke in favor of Seddon's minority report. The slim available evidence indicates that Lincoln reiterated his pledge to stop the extension of slavery in the territories. Moreover, echoing a theme similar to what he had argued in his "House Divided" speech from 1858, he apparently hinted to his visitors that war might be preferable to relentless political strife over slavery. One thing is certain: Lincoln did nothing to reassure Tyler or any of the southerners, and they did not have to wait until he delivered his inaugural address on March 4 to find out his position on secession and the future of slavery. If Tyler had thought Lincoln would change his position, he was mistaken.[32]

Tyler also realized the dangerous potential of Lincoln's use of the patronage, which explains why he supported Seddon's proposed amendment giving the South a veto over legislative and executive appointments in the territory below thirty-six degrees, thirty minutes. "I knew that the man who was in the presidential office would appoint his own friends to office. It was natural that Mr. Lincoln should do so, and I took for granted that the Chicago platform would be the constitution of every man of them." In other words, Tyler knew all of Lincoln's appointees would abide by the Republican Party platform of 1860 that promised to prohibit the extension of slavery.[33]

The second factor that may explain Tyler's shift directly concerns his experience as president of the convention. As the proceedings wore on, it became increasingly apparent to him that the northerners present would not budge; they were in no way amenable to compromise. "I found that many had come with no olive branch in their hands," Tyler later said. "They had nothing to give—nothing to yield." Furthermore, he realized the constitutional amendment favored by the majority of delegates stood no chance of securing approval from three-fourths of the states, especially since the seven seceded states would not cast votes. "We worked together, and we tried every possible expedient to overrule this state of things," Tyler maintained, all to no avail.[34]

࿓

At the conclusion of the convention, the Tyler family left Washington. They arrived in Richmond on February 28. Tyler addressed a crowd gathered in front of the Exchange Hotel with an impromptu speech that made the case for Virginia's secession. The next day he went to the Mechanics' Institute, where a special state convention to debate secession had convened a few weeks earlier. He had been chosen as a delegate to that body, as well, this time by the voters of Charles City County and Williamsburg. Though Tyler believed that "a majority of the Convention and of the people are against secession," he stuck to his decision to abandon the Union. He was pleased to find out other members of his family agreed with him. His nineteen-year-old granddaughter, Letitia Tyler, Robert and Priscilla's eldest child, had just raised the Confederate flag to the top of the capitol building in Montgomery, Alabama, where the provisional government of the Confederacy conducted its business. On March 13 Tyler addressed the convention for the first time with a three-and-a-half-hour speech that let his fellow Virginians know where he stood.[35]

Despite his own desire for secession, Tyler had correctly gauged the mood and sentiments of the majority of his state. Unionism, or more precisely antisecessionism, still held sway in the Virginia convention in late March. Old-line Whigs generally clung to the Union; states' rights Democrats such as Tyler tended to support secession. The split led to highly contentious proceedings. As late as April 3 the convention voted against a secession resolution by a count of 90 to 45.

Unionists held strong even after news of the firing on Fort Sumter reached Richmond on April 12. Their efforts to hold back the secessionist tide soon failed, however. President Lincoln provided the catalyst that finally turned Virginia against the Union and prompted the convention to vote in favor of secession. On April 15, three days after Sumter, Lincoln called for the southern states that remained in the Union—North Carolina, Tennessee, Arkansas, and Virginia—to raise 75,000 troops to put down what he called the rebellion in South Carolina. Lincoln's action affronted the most basic tenet of Tyler's states' rights principles. He believed the states had created the federal government and could, therefore, leave the Union if they chose to do so. He had earlier said he did not believe the federal government had the right to coerce seceded states back into the Union. In fact, that belief had animated his discussions with President Buchanan back in January. Now he argued that Lincoln had taken coercion a step further, and by asking southerners to take up arms against their sister state, he had demanded what Tyler bitterly called "submission." Tyler believed honor demanded secession.

The call for troops galvanized the secessionists in the Virginia convention. "All party feelings have faded away," Tyler wrote Julia. That was not entirely true. A "good many other old line Whigs" had moved into the secessionist camp. But, the final vote tally of 103 to 46 in favor of secession hid some remaining partisanship and obviously reflected lingering sentiment for remaining in the Union. Some members of the convention, for example, wished to wait for the secession of the three other states that had received the call for troops. The result, however, was unmistakable. "Virginia is no longer a state of the Old Union," Tyler informed Robert by mail. The voters of Virginia ratified the convention's secession ordinance on May 23, and the Old Dominion soon became an official member of the Confederate States of America.[36]

Tyler immediately left the Mechanics' Hall after the convention voted for secession. He and Wise walked a few blocks to Richmond's Metropolitan Hall, where a meeting called the Spontaneous Southern Rights Assembly had gathered to put pressure on the unionists in the official convention. The two men strode into the hall moments after it had been announced that Virginia would be leaving the Union. One witness described the scene: "President Tyler and Gov. Wise were conducted arm-in-arm, and bare-headed, down the center aisle amid a din of cheers, while every member rose to his feet. They were led to the platform, and called upon to address the Convention."

Physically exhausted and overcome with emotion, Tyler told the audience he was unable to express what he thought and felt. "Nevertheless," one observer related, "he seemed to acquire supernatural strength as he proceeded, and he spoke most effectively" for fifteen minutes. "He gave a brief history of all the struggles of our race for freedom, from *Magna Charta* to the present day; and he concluded with a solemn declaration that at no period of our history were we engaged in a more just and holy effort for the maintenance of liberty and independence than at the present moment." Tyler spoke of the "aggressions" of the Republican Party, "which fully warranted the steps we were taking for resistance and eternal separation." He maintained that "if we performed our whole duty as Christians and patriots, the same benign Providence which favored the cause of our forefathers in the Revolution of 1776, would again crown our efforts with similar success." Nearing the close of his remarks, Tyler expressed doubt that he would "survive to witness the consummation of the work begun [this] day; but generations yet unborn would bless those who had the high privilege of being participators in it."[37]

❧

"The prospects now are that we shall have war, and a trying one," Tyler wrote to Julia from Richmond on April 16, one day before the convention passed the secession ordinance. "The battle at Charleston [Fort Sumter] has aroused the whole North. I fear that division no longer exists in their ranks, and that they will break upon the South with an immense force." He was, of course, correct. Just two weeks after Virginia seceded, Tyler observed that a Union naval squadron had blockaded the mouth of the James River. "The river no longer runs to Norfolk," he noted, a particularly alarming situation given the location of Sherwood Forest. Tyler immediately contacted an officer in the newly constituted Virginia navy to request help. "Pardon me for suggesting that it might be wise to put cannon and crew on board one of the steamers lying at Rockets [in Richmond] and under a faithful officer, to ply up and down the river," he wrote. The reality of civil war was beginning to sink in.[38]

Worrying about water access to Norfolk was not Tyler's only concern in the early days of the war. He feared for the safety of Robert and Priscilla in Philadelphia. "Poor Robert is threatened with mob violence," an alarmed Tyler wrote to Julia. Pro-Union mobs had harassed Robert because he was a southerner and had even hanged him in effigy. "I wish most sincerely he was away from there," his father declared. "I attempted to telegraph him to-day [April 18], but no dispatch is permitted northward." Robert and Priscilla eventually made their way to Virginia, arriving at Sherwood Forest after a harrowing trip.[39]

During the summer of 1861, Tyler found himself more directly affected by the war. In June he had allowed the Confederate army to impress half of his enslaved men into service for manual labor, as had several of his Charles City County neighbors. When they had not been returned to him six weeks later, he complained directly to Confederate war secretary Leroy P. Walker, emphatically noting that the reduction in his slave-labor force had made threshing his wheat crop more difficult. Tyler also questioned the legality of the measure. The entire matter had "engendered some little feeling of discontent" in the county.[40]

Still, Tyler acknowledged the importance of every southerner doing his duty—for both their state and their new country. "It becomes one and all to contribute all in our power to give success to our good old mother," he declared. For Tyler, that meant public service, and he again resolved to take part in the political battles, convinced that, with his stature and experience, he had much to offer the Confederate States of America.[41]

Tyler won election to the provisional Confederate Congress and allowed his name to be placed into nomination for the permanent Congress as a candidate from the Old Dominion's Richmond and Charles City County district. He framed his candidacy in terms of duty, as he had so often in the past, and portrayed himself as a disinterested statesman, as had the heroes of the Revolutionary generation. Tyler would yield to the voters' wishes. He had first entered politics in 1811 at the age of twenty-one. The lure of public life had never diminished—of course he wished to serve![42]

Tyler won the election. After the Christmas holidays, he made the trip to Richmond to take care of political business and meet with other newly minted members of the Confederate government. He took a room at the Exchange Hotel. The opening session of Congress was slated to begin in early February. Julia would make the post-holiday rounds at Brandon and Shirley, homes on the James River, and then she and Pearl would travel to Richmond to join him.

꙳

On the morning Julia was set to leave for Brandon, she awoke with a start. She told Nancy, her maidservant, that she had just had a dream in which she saw her husband "looking pale and ill." In the dream Tyler had asked Julia to hold his head. Deeply troubled, she made the decision to travel directly to Richmond without making her planned stops, wanting to be with her husband as soon as she could. She, Fanny, and baby Pearl arrived at the Exchange on the evening of January 10. When Pearl saw her father, she clapped her little hands. "I really believe she knows me," Tyler laughed, as he took her from Fanny. Not expecting them so soon, he of course wanted to know why Julia had changed her plans. She told him of her dream, which he shrugged off with a chuckle.

The next night, a Saturday, Julia awoke with a terrible headache. Tyler got up and prepared a dose of morphine for her. She refused a call to the doctor, but Tyler noted her forehead was cold. "You see your dream is out," he said, "it is *your* head that *I* am holding, and not you mine."

The following morning, with the sun barely up, Julia woke to the sight of Tyler, fully dressed, standing in front of the fireplace in their room. He told her that perhaps there had been something to her dream after all because he felt chilled and had a cough. He decided to make his way downstairs to the hotel restaurant for a cup of tea. "I begged he would have it sent for," Julia recalled later, "and lie down again; but he preferred to go for it, and so I, not thinking his illness was serious, remained where I was, to sleep off the effects of the morphine."

Julia awoke again to the sound of the door opening. She sat bolt upright in bed when she saw her husband staggering into the room toward her with his collar open and his cravat in his hand. Tyler told her he had fainted at the breakfast table and had to be revived by some of the staff and other guests. He insisted upon returning to his room alone so that he would not alarm Julia. Shortly after his return, there was a knock on the door; several of the people who had seen what had happened had come by to make sure he had recovered. Tyler assured them he felt better but decided to summon his doctor anyway.

Dr. Peachy arrived, examined Tyler, and told him he had suffered a bilious attack. Concerned about his patient's cough, which he suspected was bronchitis, the physician prepared a morphine mixture and instructed him to make plans to return home to Sherwood Forest, where he could rest more peacefully. Tyler refused the advice at first and even began seeing colleagues—including William Cabell Rives—in his suite. Continuing to feel ill after a few more days, Tyler asked Rives if he would see to it that the Confederate Congress excused him for a short time so that he could return home. Rives agreed, and Tyler made plans to leave on Saturday, January 18.

He never made it. On the night of Friday, January 17, Tyler awoke coughing and frightened, convinced he was suffocating. Robert had joined the family in the suite to help look after his father and was sleeping on the sofa when he heard the commotion. He immediately went down the hall to rouse a Dr. Brown, who came at once. In the meantime, Tyler had tried to get up and had bumped the cot next to the bed where Pearl had been sleeping. The child whimpered, prompting Tyler to say, "Poor little thing, how I disturb her." He insisted on having Fanny bring his daughter to him so he could kiss her. Dr. Brown entered the bedroom and ordered mustard plasters and brandy for Tyler. "Doctor, I think you are mistaken," he replied, delirious with fever. Julia pressed a glass of brandy to his lips, which he took gratefully. Dr. Peachy, who had also been alerted to Tyler's condition, walked into the room. By now it was early morning on Saturday, January 18, 1862.

"Doctor," Tyler said when he saw him, "I am going."

"I hope not, sir," Peachy replied.

"Perhaps it is best," Tyler said softly.

Julia again held the glass to her husband's lips. His teeth chattered on its rim, but he could take no more. He "looked forward with a radiant expression," she related later, "as if he saw something to surprise and please, and then, as if falling asleep, was gone." Julia noted that the "bedstead on which he died was exactly like the one [she] saw him upon in [her] dream" and was "unlike any of our own."[43]

Tyler's body lay in state in the Confederate Capitol on Monday, January 20. Members of the Virginia legislature and Confederate Congress delivered eulogies. The following day at noon, amid a chilling rain, the casket was taken to St. Paul's Church for the funeral mass, officiated by Bishop Johns. Once what one attendee called a "beautiful and chaste production" had concluded, a procession that included President Davis and the entire Confederate government, in addition to many Virginia state politicians and the Tyler family, accompanied John Tyler to his final resting place at Richmond's Hollywood Cemetery overlooking the James River. He was buried in a tomb adjacent to that of President James Monroe.[44]

EPILOGUE

History's Judgment

William McFarland was the man assigned the task of preparing the resolutions of the Confederate Congress that would honor John Tyler. "Any announcement of the decease of the Hon. John Tyler is imperfect and inadequate," he declared, "[or it] fails of giving utterance to the nation's lamentation, if it do not present him as a statesman and patriot in whom his countrymen delighted to repose their confidence, and who failed not to derive fresh incentives to honor and revere him from the faithfulness and ability with which he administered every trust." Tyler's fame was "indissolubly blended with the history of his times, and shall survive the most enduring memorials of personal affection, or of public esteem." McFarland continued with a sketch of Tyler's tenure as president and praised him for being "ever intrepid in avowing his opinions, and resolute in defending them." Tyler, he stated, "will be gratefully remembered," and "admiring memories will fondly revert to, and recall him."[1]

History has largely proven McFarland wrong in his assessment of how people remembered Tyler. While flags throughout the Confederacy flew at half-mast in solemn recognition of the contributions he had made over a long career in public life, the other half of the country for whom he had served as president refused to acknowledge his passing. President Lincoln did not order the lowering of flags. No church bells tolled in Washington or in cities throughout the North. Most northern newspapers did not even take note of his death; where they did, it was only in the most perfunctory fashion.

Northern silence reflected what amounted to a disavowal of the life and political career of John Tyler. And it continued long after January 1862. Tyler's reputation suffered a great deal in the years following the Civil War. The northern public remembered him as the very embodiment of the states' rights ideology and system of slavery the war had succeeded in toppling. He represented an anachronism not worth calling to mind. Southerners, too, seemingly preferred to forget the man and banish him from their collective memory, not wanting reminders of what had really brought on the Civil War, choosing instead the comfort of the Lost Cause mythology.

The only American president to have been read out of his own party is also the only chief executive of this country to have repudiated his oath of office and turned his back on the nation he once led. In effect, he renounced his American citizenship, which many people regarded—correctly—as traitorous. And that action, much more than anything he did as a young politician, US senator, or any course he pursued as president, has shaped the way Americans view him today.

Thomas Bragg, a North Carolinian who served as his state's governor and later as senator and who became Jefferson Davis's first attorney general, appreciated the fact that Tyler had served in the US government for so many years, then pledged his allegiance to a country at war with that government. Bragg had done the same thing, albeit on a smaller scale, since he had never been president of the United States. Watching Tyler's funeral from a pew in St. Paul's Church, he entertained a thought that might serve as the most appropriate way to frame the tenth president's life and career. Bragg believed that "time alone can shew [sic] whether [Tyler] died too soon or too late."[2]

In terms of his private family life, Tyler had died too soon. He was not there to help Julia raise their seven children. He was not there to help her pass through the trauma of war. In large measure this reflects his age—and hers. But the fact remains that she faced the twenty-seven years she had left on earth without her husband. Her children grew to adulthood without their father's guidance. Little Pearl hardly remembered him at all.

In terms of his historical reputation, Tyler died too late. Had he passed away before Lincoln's election to the presidency—indeed, he was at death's door at least once during the 1850s—he never would have been able to give his sanction to secession and would not have had the opportunity to join the Confederate government. Tyler would have been remembered as a traitor to the Whig Party but not viewed as a traitor to his country. And over the remainder of his lifetime, his fellow Americans had grown to appreciate the principles for which Tyler stood in his fight with Henry Clay, so he likely would have been judged more charitably on that score.

Tyler's overweening commitment to stand on principle led him to embrace secession. His inveterate inability to sit out political battles led him to seek a seat in the Confederate Congress. Both actions came at tremendous cost. His role in helping Virginia out of the Union ruined his national reputation. His decision to then actively join the government of the Confederacy showed an indefensible lack of concern for the future of his wife and children. Tyler's choices no doubt emboldened Union troops to loot Sherwood Forest when they came upon the house during the war. They saw no reason to respect the home of the ex-president because, in joining the Confederacy, he had shown disrespect for the Union for which they now fought. Tyler's association with the Confederacy also made Julia's later efforts to win a pension from the US government as a former president's wife much more difficult. She was punished for her husband's sins. Newspapers delighted in calling attention to her marriage to the traitor president.

Ultimately, Tyler's decision to join the Confederate government is best understood as the product of what may properly be described as his tragic flaw: an all-consuming ambition and a desire for political fame. An obsessive concern for his standing among his contemporaries, as well as his pursuit of a legacy of historical significance, drove him. As a result, his finances, his health, and most of all his relationships with the people he loved all suffered. Yet he could see no alternative to the life he seemed almost destined to pursue, a life he had inherited from the father he revered.

There is an anecdote from a later president—John F. Kennedy—that captures the mindset of ambitious politicians such as Tyler. In the run up to Kennedy's reelection campaign for 1964, New York governor Nelson Rockefeller wavered in his pursuit of the Republican nomination and seemed willing to forego the opportunity to square off against the Democratic incumbent. Amid controversy, the governor had recently married his much-younger second wife, and it seemed at times that he would rather devote his attention to her rather than pursue the highest office in the land. In fact, the highly publicized divorce he engineered so that he could be with the woman he loved all but destroyed his presidential prospects. Rockefeller's behavior baffled Kennedy. "No man would ever love love more than politics," he declared.

John Tyler would have agreed.

Notes

ABBREVIATIONS USED IN NOTES

People

AG	Alexander Gardiner (Julia's brother)
APU	Abel Parker Upshur
CW	Conway Whittle
DLG	David Lyon Gardiner (Julia's brother)
DW	Daniel Webster
HC	Henry Clay
HW	Henry Wise
JCC	John C. Calhoun
JG/JGT	Julia Gardiner; Julia Gardiner Tyler
JT	John Tyler
JT Jr.	John Tyler Jr.
LCT	Letitia Christian Tyler (wife)
LGT	Lyon Gardiner Tyler
LT/LTS	Letitia Tyler (daughter); Letitia Tyler Semple
LWT	Littleton W. Tazewell
MG/MGB	Margaret Gardiner; Margaret Gardiner Beeckman
MT/MTJ	Mary Tyler; Mary Tyler Jones
NBT	Nathaniel Beverley Tucker
PCT	Priscilla Cooper Tyler
RT	Robert Tyler
TR	Thomas Ritchie
WCR	William Cabell Rives
WPM	Willie P. Mangum

Archives

DU	David M. Rubenstein Rare Book and Manuscript Library, Duke University, Durham, NC
LC	Division of Manuscripts, Library of Congress, Washington, DC
LVA	Library of Virginia, Richmond, VA
SHC	Southern Historical Collection, Wilson Library, University of North Carolina, Chapel Hill
UA	W. S. Hoole Special Collections Library, University of Alabama, Tuscaloosa
UNC	Louis Round Wilson Library Special Collections, University of North Carolina, Chapel Hill
UVA	Albert and Shirley Small Special Collections Library, University of Virginia, Charlottesville

VHS   Virginia Historical Society, Richmond, VA

WM   Earl Gregg Swem Library, College of William and Mary, Williamsburg, VA

Primary Sources

AC   *Annals of Congress*

CG   *Congressional Globe*

GTFP   Gardiner-Tyler Family Papers, Sterling Memorial Library, Yale University, New Haven, CT

LTT   Lyon G. Tyler, *Letters and Times of the Tylers,* 3 vols. (Richmond: Whittet and Shepperson, 1884–85, 1896)

MPP   James D. Richardson, *A Compilation of the Messages and Papers of the Presidents, 1789–1902,* 10 vols. (Washington, DC: Government Printing Office, 1896–99)

PDW-C   Charles M. Wiltse, Harold D. Moser, et al., eds., *The Papers of Daniel Webster,* ser. 1, *Correspondence,* 7 vols. (Hanover, NH: University Press of New England, 1974–88)

PDW-D   Kenneth E. Shewmaker et al., eds., *The Papers of Daniel Webster,* ser. 3, *Diplomatic Papers,* 2 vols. (Hanover, NH: University Press of New England, 1983)

PHC   James F. Hopkins, Mary W. M. Hargreaves, et al., eds., *The Papers of Henry Clay,* 11 vols. (Lexington: University Press of Kentucky, 1959–92)

PJCC   Robert L. Meriwether, W. Edwin Hemphill, Clyde N. Wilson, et al., eds., *The Papers of John C. Calhoun,* 28 vols. (Columbia: University of South Carolina Press, 1959–2003)

PWAG   J. G. de Roulhac Hamilton and Max R. Williams, eds. *The Papers of William A. Graham,* 8 vols. (Raleigh: North Carolina State Department of Archives and History, 1957–96)

PWPM   Henry Thomas Shanks, ed. *The Papers of Willie Person Mangum,* 5 vols. (Raleigh: North Carolina State Department of Archives and History, 1950–56)

ROD   *Register of Debates* (of Congress)

Periodicals

JER   *Journal of the Early Republic*

JSH   *Journal of Southern History*

TQ   *Tyler's Quarterly Historical and Genealogical Magazine*

VMHB   *Virginia Magazine of History and Biography*

WMQ   *William and Mary Quarterly*

Newspapers

DM   *Washington Daily Madisonian*

NI   *Washington Daily National Intelligencer*

RE   *Richmond Enquirer*

PROLOGUE: DECISION AT HARRISBURG

1. Nathan Sargent, *Public Men and Events,* 2 vols. (Philadelphia: J. B. Lippincott, 1875), 2:93; Robert V. Remini, *Daniel Webster: The Man and His Time* (New York: W. W. Norton, 1997), 500–501; Michael F. Holt, *The Rise and Fall of the American Whig Party: Jacksonian Politics and the Onset of the Civil War* (New York: Oxford University Press, 1999), 26–105.

2. JT to George E. Belcher, July 10, 1840, Tyler Family Papers, WM; JT to RT, December 14, 1857, in *LTT,* 2:13–14; *Proceedings of the Democratic Whig National Convention* (Harrisburg, PA: R. S. Elliott, 1839), 7, 11, 20–21; Lyon G. Tyler, ed., "John Tyler and the Vice-Presidency," *TQ* 9 (1927): 89–95.

3. Horace Greeley, *Recollections of a Busy Life* (New York: J. B. Ford, 1869), 131.

4. *NI,* December 10, 1839.

5. Allan Nevins, ed., *The Diary of Philip Hone,* 2 vols. (New York: Dodd, Mead, 1927), 2:553.

INTRODUCTION

1. Bertram Wyatt-Brown, *Southern Honor: Ethics and Behavior in the Old South* (New York: Oxford University Press, 1982), 34.

CHAPTER 1

1. JT to Henry Curtis, June 21, 1822, JT Papers, LC. The classic work on the culture of honor is Wyatt-Brown, *Southern Honor,* esp. 43–48. See also William J. Cooper Jr., *Liberty and Slavery: Southern Politics to 1860* (1983; repr., Columbia: University of South Carolina Press, 2000), 180. For a discussion of what it meant to be a "gentleman," see Tom Cutterham, *Gentlemen Revolutionaries: Power and Justice in the New American Republic* (Princeton, NJ: Princeton University Press, 2017), 1–6.

2. Joanne B. Freeman, *Affairs of Honor: National Politics in the New Republic* (New Haven, CT: Yale University Press, 2001), xv–xxi.

3. JT to Henry Curtis, October 9, 1820, JT Papers, LC; JT to Curtis, September 30, 1821, ibid.; Dickson D. Bruce Jr., *Violence and Culture in the Antebellum South* (Austin: University of Texas Press, 1979), 29, 64–65, 70–71; Wyatt-Brown, *Southern Honor,* 14.

4. *LTT,* 1:41–42; George C. Greer, comp., *Early Virginia Immigrants, 1623–1666* (Baltimore: Genealogical Publishing, 1973), 335; JT to William Seymour Tyler, October 14, 1845, Tyler Family Papers, VHS; JT Jr. to LGT, November 29, 1884, ibid.; JT to George M. Dallas, March 23, 1857, in *The History of America in Documents: Original Autograph Letters, Manuscripts, and Source Materials,* pt. 3 (New York: Rosenbach, 1951), 9; Nell M. Nugent, abstracter and indexer, *Cavaliers and Pioneers: Abstracts of Virginia Land Patents and Grants, 1623–1666* (Baltimore: Genealogical Publishing, 1963), 25.

5. David Hackett Fischer, *Albion's Seed: Four British Folkways in America* (New York: Oxford University Press, 1989), 210–13, 224–25, 837–38; Warren M. Billings, *Sir William Berkeley and*

the *Forging of Colonial Virginia* (Baton Rouge: LSU Press, 2004); Nugent, *Cavaliers and Pioneers,* xxiv–xxv, 272; Charles S. Sydnor, *American Revolutionaries in the Making: Political Practices in Washington's Virginia* (New York: Free Press, 1952), chap. 6; Richard R. Beeman, *The Varieties of Political Experience in Eighteenth-Century America* (Philadelphia: University of Pennsylvania Press, 2004), 48–52; A. G. Roeber, *Faithful Magistrates and Republican Lawyers: Creators of Virginia Legal Culture, 1680–1810* (Chapel Hill: University of North Carolina Press, 1981), 42–43.

6. JT to William Seymour Tyler, October 14, 1845, Tyler Family Papers, VHS; Edward Pessen, *The Log Cabin Myth: The Social Backgrounds of the Presidents* (New Haven, CT: Yale University Press, 1984), 21; *LTT,* 1:51–53.

7. Rhys Isaac, *The Transformation of Virginia, 1740–1790* (New York: W. W. Norton, 1982), 131–36; Allan Kulikoff, *Tobacco and Slaves: The Development of Southern Cultures in the Chesapeake, 1680–1800* (Chapel Hill: University of North Carolina Press, 1986), 263–300; Wyatt-Brown, *Southern Honor,* chap. 4. Richard L. Bushman describes the process by which gentlemen of successive generations in rural Delaware solidified the status of their forebears. See *The Refinement of America: Persons, Houses, Cities* (New York: Vintage Books, 1992), 10–12.

8. *LTT,* 1:55–56, 194–95. Pres. John Tyler's older sister, Maria Henry Tyler, was born in 1785; his older brother, Wat Henry Tyler, named for both the famed English rebel Wat Tyler (whom the family claimed as an ancestor) and Patrick Henry, was born in 1788.

9. *LTT,* 1:55–56, 63–64, 205–8.

10. Greer, *Early Virginia Immigrants,* 12; Nugent, *Cavaliers and Pioneers,* 45; *LTT,* 1:61–63.

11. Earl G. Swem and John W. Williams, *A Register of the General Assembly of Virginia, 1776–1918, and of the Constitutional Conventions* (Richmond: Davis Bottom, 1918), 5–6, 8, 11, 13–21, 243.

12. T. H. Breen, *Tobacco Culture: The Mentality of the Great Tidewater Planters on the Eve of Revolution* (Princeton, NJ: Princeton University Press, 1985); John Tyler Sr. to Joseph Prentiss, January 26, 1809, Webb-Prentiss Family Papers, UVA. Anti-British sentiment gained wide currency in the United States during the antebellum years. See Sam W. Haynes, *Unfinished Revolution: The Early American Republic in a British World* (Charlottesville: University of Virginia Press, 2010).

13. John Tyler Sr. to Thomas Jefferson, May 16, 1782, in *The Papers of Thomas Jefferson,* ed. Julian P. Boyd et al., 42 vols. to date (Princeton, NJ: Princeton University Press, 1950–), 6:183–84; John Tyler Sr. to JT, March 1, 1807, JT Papers, LC; John Tyler Sr. to Thomas Jefferson, June 10, 1804, in *LTT,* 1:208.

14. "Governor [John Tyler Sr.]'s Message," 1810, in *LTT,* 1:239. The classic explication of the republicanism of the American founding period is Gordon S. Wood, *The Creation of the American Republic, 1776–1787* (Chapel Hill: University of North Carolina Press, 1969), chap. 2. See also Drew R. McCoy, *The Elusive Republic: Political Economy in Jeffersonian America* (New York: W. W. Norton, 1980), chap. 2.

15. Gordon S. Wood, *The Radicalism of the American Revolution* (New York: Random House, 1991), 216–18; John Tyler Sr. to Thomas Jefferson, May 12, 1810, in *LTT,* 1:244; *AC,* 15th Cong., 1st sess., 911. Drew McCoy asserts that republicanism in the early national United States was "an ideology in flux, caught precariously between traditional concerns anchored in classical antiquity and the new and unstable conditions of an expansive commercial society." *Elusive Republic,* 48. Judge Tyler's blend of the old and the new manifestations of virtue offers a perfect illustration of the tension McCoy describes.

16. Gov. John Tyler Sr., "Message," December 4, 1809, in *LTT*, 1:238–39. For a brief discussion of what Jefferson meant by "natural aristocracy" and how it differed from the "artificial" aristocracy of birth and titles found in Britain, see Merrill D. Peterson, *Thomas Jefferson and the New Nation: A Biography* (New York: Oxford University Press, 1970), 954–55. For the connection between education and the "natural aristocracy," see Jennings L. Wagoner Jr., *Jefferson and Education* (Charlottesville: Thomas Jefferson Foundation, 2004), 130–31. For the importance of an informed citizenry to the success of America's republican "experiment," see Richard D. Brown, *The Strength of a People: The Idea of an Informed Citizenry in America, 1650–1870* (Chapel Hill: University of North Carolina Press, 1997).

17. *RE*, July 9, 1800.

18. Robert G. Parkinson, *The Common Cause: Creating Race and Nation in the American Revolution* (Chapel Hill: University of North Carolina Press, 2016), shows how the gentry and other leaders of the Revolution mobilized popular support for the fight against the British. Susan Dunn analyzes the process of decline in *Dominion of Memories: Jefferson, Madison, & the Decline of Virginia* (New York: Basic Books, 2007). For one family's response to the changes, see Philip Hamilton, *The Making and Unmaking of a Revolutionary Family: The Tuckers of Virginia, 1752–1830* (Charlottesville: University of Virginia Press, 2003).

19. John Tyler Sr. to Joseph Prentiss Sr., March 31, 1809, Webb-Prentiss Family Papers, UVA; *LTT*, 1:76–77; Norman K. Risjord, *The Old Republicans: Southern Conservatism in the Age of Jefferson* (New York: Columbia University Press, 1965), 212; *AC*, 15th Cong., 1st sess., 907–18. For the moral dimension of the paper-money issue, see Gordon S. Wood, "Interests and Disinterestedness in the Making of the Constitution," in *Beyond Confederation: Origins of the Constitution and American National Identity*, ed. Richard Beeman, Stephen Botein, and Edward C. Carter II (Chapel Hill: University of North Carolina Press, 1987), 106–7.

20. Dan Monroe, *The Republican Vision of John Tyler* (College Station: Texas A&M University Press, 2003), 12–13.

21. John Tyler Sr. to William Wirt, [n.d.], in *LTT*, 1:183; William J. Watkins Jr., *Reclaiming the American Revolution: The Kentucky and Virginia Resolutions and Their Legacy* (New York: Palgrave Macmillan, 2004), 1, 66–78; H. Jefferson Powell, "The Principles of '98: An Essay in Historical Retrieval," *Virginia Law Review* 80 (April 1994): 703–27. Cooper places the Resolutions into the broader context of southern political history, arguing that they should be viewed as both political and ideological documents that shaped opposition to the federal government in the antebellum period. See *Liberty and Slavery*, 90. For the connection between the "Principles of '98" and republicanism, see Kathryn R. Malone, "The Fate of Revolutionary Republicanism in Early National Virginia," *JER* 7 (Spring 1987): 27–51. Saul Cornell, *The Other Founders: Anti-Federalism and the Dissenting Tradition in America, 1788–1828* (Chapel Hill: University of North Carolina Press, 1999), defines the "dissenting tradition."

22. JT to William F. Pendleton, January 19, 1833, JT Papers, LC; *ROD*, 22nd Cong., 2nd sess., 363.

23. Lance Banning, *The Jeffersonian Persuasion: Evolution of a Party Ideology* (Ithaca, NY: Cornell University Press, 1980), 283–90. John Lauritz Larson uses the term "neo-Antifederalist" and employs it to explain the opposition of the Old Republicans to a national program of public works after the War of 1812. See *Internal Improvement: National Public Works and the Promise of Popular Government in the Early United States* (Chapel Hill: University of North Carolina Press, 2001), esp. 110–19. See also Risjord, *Old Republicans*, 1–10; and William G. Shade, *Democratizing*

the Old Dominion: Virginia and the Second Party System (Charlottesville: University Press of Virginia, 1996), 84–85, 313n31.

24. *LTT*, 1:313. For slaveholders attempting to use historical memory to "nationalize" slavery, see Robert E. Bonner, *Mastering America: Southern Slaveholders and the Crisis of American Nationhood* (Cambridge: Cambridge University Press, 2009), chap. 5. For a discussion of the components of the "proslavery argument," see Peter Kolchin, *American Slavery, 1619–1877* (New York: Hill and Wang, 1993), 179–99. For the Old Republicans' stance on slavery and the issue of expansion, see Christopher Childers, "The Old Republican Constitutional Primer: States Rights after the Missouri Controversy and the Onset of the Politics of Slavery," in *The Enigmatic South: Toward Civil War and Its Legacies*, ed. Samuel C. Hyde Jr. (Baton Rouge: LSU Press, 2014), 3–23.

25. Risjord, *Old Republicans*, 177–82; Rex Beach, "Spencer Roane and the Richmond Junto," *WMQ*, 2nd ser., 22 (January 1942): 1–17; F. Thornton Miller, "The Richmond Junto: The Secret, All-Powerful Club, or Myth," *VMHB* 99 (January 1991): 63–80.

26. John Tyler Sr. to Thomas Jefferson, June 10, 1804, in *LTT*, 1:208.

27. For Judge Tyler's fatalism, see John Tyler Sr. to Thomas Jefferson, June 10, 1804, in *LTT*, 1:207.

28. JT to DLG, January 7, 1854, Tyler Family Papers, WM; *LTT*, 1:188, 192. For a general discussion of how planter families reacted to death, and for how a young Tyler may have viewed the loss of his mother, see Daniel Blake Smith, *Inside the Great House: Planter Family Life in Eighteenth-Century Chesapeake Society* (Ithaca, NY: Cornell University Press, 1980), 271–73, 279–80.

29. *LTT*, 1:200; Susan H. Godson and Ludwell H. Johnson, *The College of William and Mary: A History*, 2 vols. (Williamsburg, VA: King and Queen Press, 1994), 1:126–41. Tyler was one of three US presidents to attend William and Mary; Thomas Jefferson and James Monroe were the others.

30. John Hartwell Cocke's lecture notes, 1798–1801, College of William and Mary, Cocke Family Papers, UVA; David W. Robson, *Educating Republicans: The College in the Era of the American Revolution, 1750–1800* (Westport, CT: Greenwood, 1985), 16; Joseph Shelton Watson to David Watson, January 17, 1801, in "Letters from William and Mary College, 1798–1801," *VMHB* 29 (April 1921): 159–60; Michael O'Brien, *Conjectures of Order: Intellectual Life and the American South, 1810–1860*, 2 vols. (Chapel Hill: University of North Carolina Press, 2004): 2:878.

31. Ruby O. Osborne, "The College of William and Mary in Virginia, 1800–1827" (Ph.D. diss., College of William and Mary, 1981), chap 1; Robson, *Educating Republicans*, 169–71; [Bishop] James Madison to Thomas Jefferson, April 15, 1802, "Letters to Jefferson," *TQ* 9 (October 1927): 88; *LTT*, 1:204; Charles Crowe, "Bishop James Madison and the Republic of Virtue," *JSH* 30 (February 1964): 62.

32. For a discussion of the connection between Bishop Madison's lectures and antislavery sentiment at William and Mary, see Suzanne Cooper Guasco, *Confronting Slavery: Edward Coles and the Rise of Antislavery Politics in Nineteenth-Century America* (DeKalb: Northern Illinois University Press, 2013), 30–31.

33. John Tyler Sr. to JT, February 7, 1807, JT Papers, LC; Lorri Glover, *Southern Sons: Becoming Men in the New Nation* (Baltimore: Johns Hopkins University Press, 2007), 57–59; Steven M. Stowe, *Intimacy and Power in the Old South: Ritual in the Lives of the Planters* (Baltimore: Johns Hopkins University Press, 1987), 142–43; Jon L. Wakelyn, "Antebellum College Life and the Relations between Fathers and Sons," in *The Web of Southern Social Relations: Women, Family, and*

Education, ed. Walter J. Fraser Jr., R. Frank Saunders Jr., and Jon L. Wakelyn (Athens: University of Georgia Press, 1985), 107–26.

34. John Tyler Sr. to JT, March 1, 1807, in *LTT*, 1:203; *RE*, June 23, July 7, 1807. For the importance of female education in the years following the American Revolution, see Mary Beth Norton, *Liberty's Daughters: The Revolutionary Experience of American Women, 1750–1800* (Ithaca, NY: Cornell University Press, 1996), chap. 9. For "republican motherhood," see Linda K. Kerber, *Women of the Republic: Intellect and Ideology in Revolutionary America* (New York: W. W. Norton, 1980), 199–201.

35. *The Address Delivered by His Exc'y John Tyler, and the Poem Recited by St. George Tucker, Esq. On the 166th Anniversary of the College of William and Mary in Virginia* (1859). This address is reprinted in John Tyler, "Early Times of Virginia—William and Mary College," *DeBow's Review* 27 (August 1859): 136–49.

CHAPTER 2

1. E. Lee Shepard, "Breaking into the Profession: Establishing a Law Practice in Antebellum Virginia," *JSH* 48 (August 1982): 394–96; *LTT*, 1:204.

2. St. George Tucker to John Page, February 27, 1801, Tracy W. McGregor Autograph Collection, UVA; Charles T. Cullen, "St. George Tucker and Law in Virginia, 1772–1804" (Ph.D. diss., University of Virginia, 1971), chap. 7; F. Thornton Miller, *Juries and Judges Versus the Law: Virginia's Provincial Legal Perspective, 1783–1828* (Charlottesville: University Press of Virginia, 1994), ix–xiv.

3. *RE*, December 10, 1808; John Tyler Sr. to Joseph Prentis Sr., January 26, 1809, Webb-Prentis Papers, UVA; JT, "Richmond and Its Memories," November 1858, in *LTT*, 1:221; JT quoted in Alexander Gordon Abell, *Life of John Tyler, President of the United States, Up to the Close of the Second Session of the Twenty-Seventh Congress* (New York: Harper and Brothers, 1844), 136. Tyler's statement praising Randolph was made during a debate in the US Senate. See *ROD*, 22nd Cong., 2nd sess., 361–62.

4. *LTT*, 1:272; JT, "The Dead of the Cabinet," ibid., 2:388; Richard B. Davis, *Intellectual Life in Jefferson's Virginia, 1790–1830* (Chapel Hill: University of North Carolina Press, 1964), 356; Risjord, *Old Republicans*, 72; Claude H. Hall, *Abel Parker Upshur: Conservative Virginian, 1790–1844* (Madison: State Historical Society of Wisconsin, 1964), 14–16.

5. Daniel P. Jordan, *Political Leadership in Jefferson's Virginia* (Charlottesville: University Press of Virginia, 1983), 55–56; Anthony F. Upton, "The Road to Power in Virginia in the Early Nineteenth Century," *VMHB* 62 (July 1954): 271–72.

6. This story is recounted in JT, "Richmond and Its Memories," November 1858, in *LTT*, 1:222. On the Wickham-Burr connection, see Nancy Isenberg, *Fallen Founder: The Life of Aaron Burr* (New York: Viking, 2007), 329–37, 359–61; and Peter Charles Hoffer, *The Treason Trials of Aaron Burr* (Lawrence: University Press of Kansas, 2008), 125–28.

7. *LTT*, 1:281.

8. JT to Dr. Henry Curtis, December 8, 1820, in *LTT*, 1:336; JT to Curtis, April 13, 1819, JT Papers, LC.

9. *LTT*, 273.

10. C. Edward Skeen, "An Uncertain 'Right': State Legislatures and the Doctrine of Instruction," *Mid-America* 73 (January 1991): 29–47.

11. *RE,* January 3, 15, 17, 19, 24, February 9, July 9, 12, 1811.

12. *Journal of the House of Delegates,* January 17, 1812, 70; *LTT,* 1:274–75.

13. JT to Hugh Blair Grigsby, January 16, 1855, JT Papers, LC; John Campbell to David Campbell, December 29, 1812, Campbell Family Papers, DU; *Journal of the House of Delegates,* February 19, 1812, 155–60.

14. John Campbell to David Campbell, December 29, 1812, Campbell Family Papers, DU.

15. JT to Hugh Blair Grigsby, January 16, 1855, JT Papers, LC.

16. Douglas R. Egerton, *Charles Fenton Mercer and the Trial of National Conservatism* (Jackson: University Press of Mississippi, 1989), 87–88, 100–102; Philip M. Rice, "Internal Improvements in Virginia, 1775–1860" (Ph.D. diss., University of North Carolina, 1950), 122–24, 127–44.

17. John Tyler Sr. to Thomas Jefferson, May 17, 1812, in *LTT,* 1:264; *RE,* January 12, 1813.

18. *LTT,* 1:269.

19. JT to Letitia Christian, December 5, 1812, in Laura C. Holloway, *The Ladies of the White House; or In the Home of the Presidents* (Philadelphia: Bradley, 1882), 369–72; JT to Henry Curtis, March 23, 1813, in *LTT,* 1:276.

20. Ellen K. Rothman, *Hands and Hearts: A History of Courtship in America* (New York: Basic Books, 1984), 38–39.

21. Armistead Thomson Mason to John Thomson Mason, June 29, 1813, in Kate Mason Rowland, "Letters of Armistead Thomson Mason: 1813–1818," *WMQ,* 1st ser., 23 (April 1915): 230; JT to Henry Curtis, March 23, 1813, JT Papers, LC.

22. JT to John K. Martin, February 27, September 26, 1851, Tyler Family Papers, WM; Julia Gardiner Tyler Pension Application, February 18, 1881, GTFP; *Muster Rolls of the Virginia Militia in the War of 1812* (Richmond: William F. Ritchie, 1852), microfilm; *LTT,* 1:278–79.

23. *LTT,* 1:281–82, 307–8; Oliver Perry Chitwood, *John Tyler: Champion of the Old South* (1939; repr., Newtown, CT: American Political Biography Press, 2000), 30.

24. *RE,* September 28, 1816; Upton, "Road to Power in Virginia," 262.

25. Claiborne W. Gooch to David Campbell, October 24, 1816, Campbell Family Papers, DU; *RE,* October 2, November 30, 1816.

CHAPTER 3

1. JT, "Lecture at the Maryland Mechanics' Institute, 1855," in *LTT,* 1:289–91. On Randolph, see David Johnson, *John Randolph of Roanoke* (Baton Rouge: LSU Press, 2012).

2. C. Edward Skeen, *1816: America Rising* (Lexington: University Press of Kentucky, 2003), chap. 5.

3. *AC,* 14th Cong., 2nd sess., 619–20.

4. *AC,* 14th Cong., 2nd sess., 624–37.

5. *AC,* 14th Cong., 2nd sess., 649–50.

6. *AC,* 14th Cong., 2nd sess., 649–52.

7. Skeen, "Uncertain 'Right,'" 30–31; Skeen, *1816,* 90.

8. *AC,* 15th Cong., 1st sess., 907.

9. *AC*, 14th Cong., 2nd sess., 662, 673; Skeen, *1816*, 93.

10. Skeen, *1816*, 94–95; JT to "Freeholders of the Congressional District," February 25, 1817, in *Circular Letters of Congressmen to Their Constituents, 1789–1829*, ed. Noble E. Cunningham Jr., 3 vols. (Chapel Hill: University of North Carolina Press, 1978), 1:998–99; JT to Col. Robert McCandlish, February 22, 1851, in *LTT*, 1:403; Sean Wilentz, *The Rise of American Democracy: Jefferson to Lincoln* (New York: W. W. Norton, 2005), 201–2. The theme of democracy replacing republicanism animates Donald B. Cole, *A Jackson Man: Amos Kendall and the Rise of American Democracy* (Baton Rouge: LSU Press, 2004). Recent scholarship has demonstrated that the rise of "democracy" occurred earlier than had been previously thought, though not evenly or in all geographic areas of the country equally. Furthermore, historians have expanded the definition of what "democratic politics" and partisanship entailed, thus broadening our perspective beyond voting. See, for example, Donald J. Ratcliffe, *Party Spirit in a Frontier Republic: Democratic Politics in Ohio, 1793–1821* (Columbus: Ohio State University Press, 1998); Jeffrey L. Pasley, "The Cheese and the Words: Popular Political Culture and Participatory Democracy in the Early American Republic," in *Beyond the Founders: New Approaches to the Political History of the Early American Republic*, ed. Jeffrey L. Pasley, Andrew W. Robertson, and David Waldstreicher (Chapel Hill: University of North Carolina Press, 2004), 31–56; and David Waldstreicher, *In the Midst of Perpetual Fetes: The Making of American Nationalism, 1776–1820* (Chapel Hill: University of North Carolina Press, 1997).

11. For the importance of a southern politician's first speech, see Kenneth S. Greenberg, *Masters and Statesmen: The Political Culture of American Slavery* (Baltimore: Johns Hopkins University Press, 1985), 13.

12. JT to "Freeholders of the Congressional District," February 25, 1817, in Cunningham, *Circular Letters*, 2:998–1001. For a national politician's need to establish a reputation and for maintaining accountability to his constituents, see Freeman, *Affairs of Honor*, 31–38; and Andrew W. Robertson, *The Language of Democracy: Political Rhetoric in the United States and Britain, 1790–1900* (Charlottesville: University of Virginia Press, 2005), 23.

13. JT to LCT, February 1, 1817, in *LTT*, 1:288–89; Catherine Allgor, *Parlor Politics: In Which the Ladies of Washington Help Build a City and a Government* (Charlottesville: University Press of Virginia, 2000), chap. 2. See also Catherine Allgor, *A Perfect Union: Dolley Madison and the Creation of the American Nation* (New York: Henry Holt, 2006), 186–201; and Constance M. Green, *Washington: Village and Capital, 1800–1878* (Princeton, NJ: Princeton University Press, 1962), 63–78. Susan Dunn, in *Dominion of Memories*, sees Virginians' provincialism as one of the factors leading to the state's decline.

14. Cynthia D. Earman, "Messing Around: Entertaining and Accommodating Congress, 1800–1830," in *Establishing Congress: The Removal to Washington, D.C. and the Election of 1800*, ed. Kenneth R. Bowling and Donald R. Kennon (Athens: Ohio University Press, 2005), 128–47; Cynthia D. Earman, "Boardinghouses, Parties, and the Creation of a Political Society: Washington City, 1800–1830" (M.A. thesis, LSU, 1992), 204, 238, 261; James Sterling Young, *The Washington Community, 1800–1828* (New York: Harcourt, Brace, and World, 1966), 98–100. Rachel A. Shelden, *Washington Brotherhood: Politics, Social Life, and the Coming of the Civil War* (Chapel Hill: University of North Carolina Press, 2013), examines the personal relationships forged in unofficial spheres in the later antebellum period. Alice Elizabeth Malavasic, *The F Street Mess: How Southern Senators Rewrote the Kansas-Nebraska Act* (Chapel Hill: University of North Carolina

Press, 2017), demonstrates how one group of national politicians employed their membership in a mess to influence legislation.

15. Maria Henry Seawell to LCT, [unknown month] 23, 1816, JT Papers, LC; Maria Henry Seawell to LCT, July 3, October 5, 1816, Tyler Scrapbook, Tyler Family Papers, WM; JT to Henry Curtis, November 19, 1817, JT Papers, LC.

16. JT to LCT, December 20, 1818, Tyler Family Papers, WM.

17. *LTT*, 1:194; JT to Henry Curtis, May 18, 1813, November 19, 1817, JT Papers, LC; Anya Jabour, "Male Friendship and Masculinity in the Early National South: William Wirt and His Friends," *JER* 20 (Spring 2000): 91.

18. Charles Sellers, *The Market Revolution: Jacksonian America, 1815–1846* (New York: Oxford University Press, 1991); Daniel Walker Howe, *What Hath God Wrought: The Transformation of America, 1815–1848* (New York: Oxford University Press, 2007); Richard E. Ellis, "The Market Revolution and the Transformation of American Politics, 1801–1837," in *The Market Revolution in America: Social, Political, and Religious Expressions, 1800–1880*, ed. Melvyn Stokes and Stephen Conway (Charlottesville: University Press of Virginia, 1996), 149–56; Ronald P. Formisano, "State Development in the Early Republic: Substance and Structure, 1780–1840," in *Contesting Democracy: Substance and Structure in American Political History, 1775–2000*, ed. Byron E. Shafer and Anthony J. Badger (Lawrence: University Press of Kansas, 2001), 19; Daniel Feller, *The Jacksonian Promise: America, 1815–1840* (Baltimore: Johns Hopkins University Press, 1995), 53–54; Nicholas Onuf and Peter Onuf, *Nations, Markets, and Wars: Modern History and the American Civil War* (Charlottesville: University of Virginia Press, 2006), 241–50.

19. William K. Bolt, *Tariff Wars and the Politics of Jacksonian America* (Nashville: Vanderbilt University Press, 2017), 14–17.

20. *AC*, 14th Cong., 2nd sess., 296; Larson, *Internal Improvement*, 64–67; Brian Balogh, *A Government Out of Sight: The Mystery of National Authority in Nineteenth-Century America* (Cambridge: Cambridge University Press, 2009), 129–33; Sellers, *Market Revolution*, 71–75.

21. Larson, *Internal Improvement*, 67; *AC*, 14th Cong., 2nd sess., 934. For an analysis of Madison's veto, see Drew R. McCoy, *The Last of the Fathers: James Madison and the Republican Legacy* (Cambridge: Cambridge University Press, 1989), 92–99.

22. JT to "Freeholders of the Congressional District," in Cunningham, *Circular Letters*, 1:1001; Monroe, *Republican Vision of John Tyler*, 22. For Tyler's connection to the Junto, see Trenton E. Hizer, "'Virginia Is Now Divided': Politics in the Old Dominion, 1820–1833" (Ph.D. diss., University of South Carolina, 1997), chap. 3. On the states' "police power," see Gary Gerstle, *Liberty and Coercion: The Paradox of American Government* (Princeton, NJ: Princeton University Press, 2015), 3–4, chap. 2.

23. *AC*, 15th Cong., 2nd sess., 335.

24. JT to Henry Curtis, January 18, 1819, JT Papers, LC. For the committee's report, see *AC*, 15th Cong., 2nd sess., 552–80. For JT's speech, see ibid., 1309–28.

25. Roane quoted in Richard E. Ellis, *Aggressive Nationalism: McCulloch v. Maryland and the Foundation of Federal Authority in the Young Republic* (New York: Oxford University Press, 2007), 116. Ellis also provides a trenchant analysis of the Junto's often misunderstood appraisal of the national bank. See ibid., 112–16.

26. *AC*, 15th Cong., 2nd sess., 552–80, 1309–28; Monroe, *Republican Vision of John Tyler*, 32–33.

27. *AC*, 15th Cong., 2nd sess., 1328. Kenneth Greenberg argues that demonstrating indepen-

dent behavior at times was a way for a southern politician to solidify his standing as a disinterested public servant. See *Masters and Statesmen*, 7.

28. *AC*, 15th Cong., 2nd sess., 1411–15; *RE*, May 18, June 1, 1819; JT to Henry Curtis, December 18, 1818, JT Papers, LC; Harry L. Watson, *Liberty and Power: The Politics of Jacksonian America* (New York: Hill and Wang, 1990), 38–39.

29. Marshall quoted in Howe, *What Hath God Wrought*, 145. See also Mark Killenbeck, *M'Culloch v. Maryland: Securing a Nation* (Lawrence: University Press of Kansas, 2006). Killenbeck points out that most historians, taking their cue from the spelling the Supreme Court employed, have misspelled the name of James M'Culloh. Charles F. Hobson details Marshall's use of the necessary-and-proper clause and supremacy clause in his decision in the case. See *The Great Chief Justice: John Marshall and the Rule of Law* (Lawrence: University Press of Kansas, 1996), chap. 5.

30. *RE*, April 2, 13, June 11, 1819; TR quoted in Killenbeck, *McCulloch v. Maryland*, 124.

31. Ellis, *Aggressive Nationalism*, 116–31; Shade, *Democratizing the Old Dominion*, 228.

32. JT to Henry Curtis, January 19, 1819, JT Papers, LC.

33. *AC*, 16th Cong., 1st sess., 737.

34. Bolt, *Tariff Wars*, 27–34. For the connection between free trade and Revolutionary republicanism, see McCoy, *Elusive Republic*, chap. 3.

35. For a discussion of the concerted and coordinated effort on the part of the four Virginians to influence the tariff debate, see William S. Belko, *Philip Pendleton Barbour in Jacksonian America: An Old Republican in King Andrew's Court* (Tuscaloosa: University of Alabama Press, 2016), 59.

36. Tyler's sparring with Baldwin and the broader question of the role of petitions in the tariff debate is analyzed in Daniel Peart, *Era of Experimentation: American Political Practices in the Early Republic* (Charlottesville: University of Virginia Press, 2014), 90–92.

37. Technically, the baby was John Tyler IV, but the family called him John Jr.

38. JT to CW, December 18, 1828, CW Papers, WM; JT to LCT, December 20, 1818, Tyler Family Papers, WM.

39. There is a vast literature addressing the Missouri crisis. The discussion that follows relies on William W. Freehling, *The Road to Disunion*, vol. 1, *Secessionists at Bay, 1776–1854* (New York: Oxford University Press, 1990), chap. 8; Cooper, *Liberty and Slavery*,134–42; Matthew Mason, *Slavery and Politics in the Early Republic* (Chapel Hill: University of North Carolina Press, 2006); Robert Pierce Forbes, *The Missouri Compromise and Its Aftermath* (Chapel Hill: University of North Carolina Press, 2007); Christopher Childers, *The Failure of Popular Sovereignty: Slavery, Manifest Destiny, and the Radicalization of Southern Politics* (Lawrence: University Press of Kansas, 2012); and John R. Van Atta, *Wolf by the Ears: The Missouri Crisis, 1819–1821* (Baltimore: Johns Hopkins University Press, 2015).

40. Christopher Childers analyzes the early debate and its practical consequences. See *Failure of Popular Sovereignty*, chap. 1.

41. *AC*, 15th Cong., 2nd sess., 1170–1204; John Craig Hammond, "'Uncontrollable Necessity': The Local Politics, Geopolitics, and Sectional Politics of Slavery Expansion," in *Contesting Slavery: The Politics of Bondage and Freedom in the New American Nation*, ed. John Craig Hammond and Matthew Mason (Charlottesville: University of Virginia Press, 2011), 138–39; Mason, *Slavery and Politics in the Early American Republic*, 135–36.

42. JT to Henry Curtis, February 5, 1820, JT Papers, LC.

43. *AC*, 16th Cong., 1st sess., 1382–88; Childers, *Failure of Popular Sovereignty*, 44–65. See also Monroe, *Republican Vision of John Tyler*, 40–41.

44. Macon quoted in Larson, *Internal Improvement*, 105. William Belko takes apart the historiography that has usually prevailed about the Old Republicans. See *Philip Pendleton Barbour*, chap. 7.

45. *AC*, 16th Cong., 1st sess., 1391. On diffusion, see Freehling, *Road to Disunion*, vol. 1, *Secessionists at Bay*, 150–57; and John Chester Miller, *The Wolf by the Ears: Thomas Jefferson and Slavery* (Charlottesville: University Press of Virginia, 1991), chap. 25.

46. JT to Henry Curtis, December 8, 1820, in *LTT*, 1:335–36; *RE*, January 15, 1821.

CHAPTER 4

1. JT to Howard Shields, November 2, 1821, Tyler Family Papers, WM. For analysis of Tyler as father, see Christopher Leahy, "Torn between Family and Politics: John Tyler's Struggle for Balance," *VMHB* 114 (September 2006): 323–55.

2. JT to Henry Curtis, December 8, 1820, in *LTT*, 1:336–37; Greenberg, *Masters and Statesmen*, 17.

3. JT to Howard Shields, November 2, 1821, Tyler Family Papers, WM; JT, "To the Freeholders . . . ," in *LTT*, 1:337.

4. JT to Henry Curtis, July 20, 1821, JT Papers, LC ; John R. Bumgarner, *The Health of the Presidents: The 41 United States Presidents through 1993 from a Physician's Point of View* (Jefferson, NC: McFarland, 1994), 65.

5. JT to Henry Curtis, October 9, 1820, JT Papers, LC; JT to Henry Curtis, September 30, 1821, ibid.; JT to Howard Shields, November 2, 1821, Tyler Family Papers, WM.

6. *LTT*, 1:339–40.

7. US Census Bureau, *Fourth Census of the United States*, 1820, Charles City County, VA.

8. *RE*, May 31, 1822.

9. William T. Banks to Henry Curtis, June 19, 1818, Henry Curtis Papers, VHS; JT to Henry Curtis, July 20, September 30, 1821, JT Papers, LC; JT to Henry Curtis, May 19, 1830, Tyler Family Papers, VHS.

10. On the 1824 campaign, see Donald Ratcliffe, *The One-Party Presidential Contest: Adams, Jackson, and 1824's Five-Horse Race* (Lawrence: University Press of Kansas, 2015); Peart, *Era of Experimentation*, chap. 4. On the Virginia Dynasty and presidential politics, see Richard P. McCormick, *The Presidential Game: The Origins of American Presidential Politics* (New York: Oxford University Press, 1982), 77–80. On the Junto's support for Crawford, see Lynwood M. Dent Jr., "The Virginia Democratic Party, 1824–1847," 2 vols. (Ph.D. diss., Louisiana State University, 1974), 1:39–40.

11. *Journal of the Virginia House of Delegates*, 1823–24 sess., 55; JT to HC, March 27, 1825, in *PHC*, 4:189–90; Shade, *Democratizing the Old Dominion*, 85.

12. Ratcliffe effectively examines this point of view in *One-Party Presidential Contest*, 82.

13. JT to HC, March 27, 1825, in *PHC*, 4:189. Ratcliffe, *One-Party Presidential Contest*, 58; Shade, *Democratizing the Old Dominion*, 85; Dent, "Virginia Democratic Party," 1:41–42.

14. Ratcliffe, *One-Party Presidential Contest*, 253–57; William J. Cooper, *The Lost Founding Father: John Quincy Adams and the Transformation of American Politics* (New York: Liveright, 2017),

217–22; James C. Klotter, *Henry Clay: The Man Who Would Be President* (New York: Oxford University Press, 2018), 123–37.

15. JT to HC, March 27, 1825, in *PHC*, 4:189–90.

16. JT to Henry Curtis, March 18, 1828, in *LTT*, 1:384–85.

17. Robert E. Shalhope, *John Taylor of Caroline: Pastoral Republican* (Columbia: University of South Carolina Press, 1980), 212; *RE*, December 9, 1824. On Tazewell, see Norma Lois Peterson, *Littleton Waller Tazewell* (Charlottesville: University Press of Virginia, 1983).

18. JT to Henry Curtis, November 11, 182[4?], JT Papers, LC; *RE*, February 3, 10, 17, 19, December 8, 1825.

19. *RE*, December 13, 1825.

20. *RE*, January 16, 1827.

21. Hizer, "'Virginia Is Now Divided,'" 48–50; Johnson, *John Randolph of Roanoke*, 212–15.

22. Dent, "Virginia Democratic Party," 1:63; *RE*, January 4, 9, 1827.

23. JT to "Gentlemen," January 13, 1827, in Abell, *Life of John Tyler*, 88–89.

24. JT to "Gentlemen," January 13, 1827, in Abell, *Life of John Tyler*, 88–89.

25. JT to Henry Curtis, April 13, 1827, JT Papers, LC; John Campbell to David Campbell, January 18, 1827, Campbell Family Papers, DU; JT to "Gentlemen," January 18, 1827, Gooch Family Papers, VHS; Abell, *Life of John Tyler*, 89.

26. John Campbell to David Campbell, January 18, 1827, Campbell Family Papers, DU; Charles Henry Ambler, *Thomas Ritchie: A Study in Virginia Politics* (Richmond: Bell, Book, and Stationery, 1913), 107; JT to Henry Curtis, April 13, 1827, JT Papers, LC.

27. Abell, *Life of John Tyler*, 91–92; HC to Francis T. Brooke, February 16, 1827, in *PHC*, 6:204.

28. C. W. Gooch to JT, n.d., 1827; JT to Robert Douthat, February 13, 1827; and Robert Douthat to the Editors of the *RE*, February 14, 1827, in *LTT*, 1:366–70; John H. Pleasants to HC, February 14, 1827, in *PHC*, 6:199–200; *RE*, February 15, 1827.

29. JT to Henry Curtis, April 13, 1827, JT Papers, LC; Dent, "Virginia Democratic Party," 1:64.

CHAPTER 5

1. JT to Henry Curtis, September 4, 1827, JT Papers, LC.

2. Herbert E. Sloan, *Principle and Interest: Thomas Jefferson and the Problem of Debt* (Charlottesville: University Press of Virginia, 1995), 23–32; Dunn, *Dominion of Memories*, 27–29.

3. JT to Henry Curtis, November 23, 1827, JT Papers, LC.

4. JT to Henry Curtis, November 16, October 26, 1827, JT Papers, LC; Bill of Sale, January 1, 1816, Henry Curtis Papers, VHS. For a discussion of the significance of selling an enslaved person in the "neighborhood," see Steven Deyle, *Carry Me Back: The Domestic Slave Trade in American Life* (New York: Oxford University Press, 2005), 219–23.

5. *Norfolk Virginian*, February 2, 1896; Deyle, *Carry Me Back*, 116–23. See also Robert H. Gudmestad, *A Troublesome Commerce: The Transformation of the Interstate Slave Trade* (Baton Rouge: LSU Press, 2003).

6. On paternalism, see Eugene D. Genovese, *Roll, Jordan, Roll: The World the Slaves Made* (New York: Vintage, 1974); and Kolchin, *American Slavery*, chap. 4. See also James Oakes, *The Ruling Race: A History of American Slaveholders* (New York: Vintage Books, 1983). It is important

to point out that, more recently, historians have questioned whether Genovese's conception of paternalism accurately characterizes the slaveholders' worldview and whether the term accounts for what Jeffrey Robert Young calls an "individualistic component of southern proslavery thought" that acknowledged an enslaved person's human potential for growth occurring outside of a patriarchal framework. Young, *Domesticating Slavery: The Master Class in Georgia and South Carolina, 1670–1837* (Chapel Hill: University of North Carolina Press, 1999), 9–10. Young prefers the phrase "corporate individualism" to "paternalism" and stresses the bourgeois aspect of a slaveholder's worldview. David Brion Davis points out that "today it is highly unfashionable to discuss the effects of paternalism in either the antebellum or post-Reconstruction period," in large part because doing so implies a passivity on the part of the enslaved that historians writing about slave resistance argue has been overstated. Davis, *Inhuman Bondage: The Rise and Fall of Slavery in the New World* (New York: Oxford University Press, 2006), 228. Lacy K. Ford, *Deliver Us from Evil: The Slavery Question in the Old South* (New York: Oxford University Press, 2009), 147, builds on the concept of paternalism Genovese wrote about, pointing out that negotiations characterized the master-slave relationship, "negotiations [that] created room for maneuver on the part of slaves and the need for some measure of accommodation on the part of masters." While the documentary record of Tyler as a slaveholder is not overly abundant, in light of the available evidence, the paternalist "paradigm" Ford defines still seems to me the best way to characterize how John Tyler saw himself and how he operated within the South's slave system.

7. There is a document that indicates Henry Curtis continued to serve as Tyler's agent for transactions involving slaves as late as 1830. See Folder 3, Box 8, Conway Whittle Papers, WM.

8. JT to Dr. Henry Curtis, December 16, 1827, JT Papers, LC; JT to John Rutherfoord, December 8, 1827, John Rutherfoord Papers, DU; JT to MT, December 26, 1827, in *LTT*, 1:389.

9. Robert Allen to JT, February 10, 1834, JT Papers, LC; JT to RT, May 18, 1859, in *LTT*, 2:550; Peterson, *Littleton Waller Tazewell*, x, 91, 113–15, 135–39.

10. Mark R. Cheathem, *Andrew Jackson and the Rise of the Democratic Party* (Knoxville: University of Tennessee Press, 2018), 83–91; Donald B. Cole, *Vindicating Andrew Jackson: The 1828 Election and the Rise of the Two-Party System* (Lawrence: University Press of Kansas, 2009), 13–15, 50, 79; Lynn Hudson Parsons, *The Birth of Modern Politics: Andrew Jackson, John Quincy Adams, and the Election of 1828* (New York: Oxford University Press, 2009); David S. Heidler and Jeanne T. Heidler, *The Rise of Andrew Jackson: Myth, Manipulation, and the Making of Modern Politics* (New York: Basic Books, 2018); Howe, *What Hath God Wrought*, 282; Richard R. John, *Spreading the News: The American Postal System from Franklin to Morse* (Cambridge, MA: Harvard University Press, 1995); Peart, *Era of Experimentation*, 6–13; Reeve Huston, "Rethinking the Origins of Partisan Democracy in the United States, 1795–1840," in *Practicing Democracy: Popular Politics in the United States from the Constitution to the Civil War*, ed. Daniel Peart and Adam I. P. Smith (Charlottesville: University of Virginia Press, 2015), 59.

11. JT to Henry Curtis, December 16, 1827, in *LTT*, 1:379; JT to Henry Curtis, September 4, 1827, ibid., 375; JT to Henry Clay, March 27, 1825, in *PHC*, 4:189–90.

12. *RE*, November 25, 1828; William W. Norvell to Jesse Burton Harrison, January 12, 1830, Burton Harrison Family Papers, LC; JT to John Rutherfoord, December 8, 1827, in *LTT*, 1:377–78; Shade, *Democratizing the Old Dominion*, 89; Jon Meacham, *American Lion: Andrew Jackson in the White House* (New York: Random House, 2008), effectively chronicles the administration and captures the indomitable will of President Jackson.

13. Robert V. Remini, *Andrew Jackson: The Course of American Freedom* (New York: Harper and Row, 1981), 157–58; JT to CW, December 18, 1828, Conway Whittle Papers, WM; JT quoted in Robert Seager II, *And Tyler Too: A Biography of John and Julia Gardiner Tyler* (New York: Mc-Graw-Hill, 1963), 82.

14. Remini, *Andrew Jackson*, 151–55, 158–65; "Diary of John Floyd," *John P. Branch Historical Papers of Randolph-Macon College* 5 (June 1918), 120; Francis T. Brooke to HC, March 3, 1829, in *PHC*, 7:634.

15. Harriet Martineau quoted in Jack Larkin, *The Reshaping of Everyday Life, 1790–1840* (New York: Harper and Row, 1988), 162–63; JT to John Rutherfoord, March 14, 1830, John Rutherfoord Papers, DU. On the Eaton scandal, see John F. Marszalek, *The Petticoat Affair: Manners, Mutiny, and Sex in Andrew Jackson's White House* (Baton Rouge: LSU Press, 1997); and Allgor, *Parlor Politics*, chap. 5.

16. Seager, *And Tyler Too*, 61–62; Mrs. E. F. Ellet, *The Court Circles of the Republic; or the Beauties and Celebrities of the Nation* (Hartford, CT: Hartford Publishing, 1869), 298.

17. JT to John Rutherfoord, February 23, 1829, John Rutherfoord Papers, DU; JT to Charles Fenton Mercer, December 5, 1826, Tracy W. McGregor Autograph Collection, UVA; Hizer, "'Virginia Is Now Divided,'" 190.

18. JT to John Rutherfoord, February 23, 1829, John Rutherfoord Papers, DU.

19. Robert P. Sutton, *Revolution to Secession: Constitution Making in the Old Dominion* (Charlottesville: University Press of Virginia, 1989), 84–94; William W. Norvell to Jesse Burton Harrison, March 23, 1830, Burton Harrison Family Papers, LC; *RE*, January 21, 1830; Shade, *Democratizing the Old Dominion*, 76–77.

20. *RE*, December 5, 25, 1829; JT to William Morgan, April 24, 1830, Tyler Family Papers, WM; JT to Col. Robert McCandlish, February 22, 1851, in *LTT*, 1:402–3; Hugh Blair Grigsby, "Sketches of Members of the Constitutional Convention of 1829–1830," *VMHB* 61 (July 1953): 323–24.

21. On Webster-Hayne, see Christopher Childers, *The Webster-Hayne Debate: Defining Nationhood in the Early American Republic* (Baltimore: Johns Hopkins University Press, 2018).

22. JT to John Floyd, May 4, 1830, Johnston Family Letters and Papers, 1779–1891, LVA.

23. Paul C. Nagel, *The Lees of Virginia: Seven Generations of an American Family* (New York: Oxford University Press, 1990), 216.

24. Elizabeth Brown Pryor, *Reading the Man: A Portrait of Robert E. Lee through His Private Letters* (New York: Penguin, 2007), 36–37. Cynthia A. Kierner, *Scandal at Bizarre: Rumor and Reputation in Jefferson's Virginia* (New York: Palgrave Macmillan, 2004), details a similar tale.

25. Nagel, *Lees of Virginia*, 218–19.

26. Richard T. Brown to JT, April 27, 1833, Tyler Scrapbook, Tyler Family Papers, WM.

27. JT to Richard T. Brown, May 5, 1833, in *LTT*, 1:409–10.

28. Henry Lee to Richard T. Brown, August 24, 1833, JT Papers, LC.

29. Henry Lee to Richard T. Brown, August 24, 1833, JT Papers, LC. Lee's vitriol against Jefferson actually began a year earlier than his letters to Tyler. In 1832, while living abroad, he published *Observations on the Writings of Thomas Jefferson*. In the words of Merrill Peterson, "no work in the literature [about Jefferson] takes higher rank for sheer malice" than *Observations*. See Peterson, *The Jefferson Image in the American Mind* (1960; repr., Charlottesville: University Press of Virginia, 1998), 115–16.

30. Kierner, *Scandal at Bizarre*, 74–76. On white southern womanhood, the classic is Anne Firor Scott, *The Southern Lady: From Pedestal to Politics, 1830–1930* (Chicago: University of Chicago Press, 1970).

31. Richard T. Brown to JT, November 17, 1833, JT Papers, LC.

32. JT to Robert Christian, May 13, 1830, JT Papers, LC; *ROD*, 21st Cong., 2nd sess., 215–17, 261–67.

33. *ROD*, 21st Cong., 2nd sess., 266, 271, 295, 310–11, 328.

34. *RE*, March 10, 1831; JT to LWT, May 8, 1831, in *LTT*, 1:422; Dent, "Virginia Democratic Party," 1:81–93.

35. *ROD*, 21st Cong., 1st sess., 433–34; ibid., 2nd sess., 347–48; JT to William Morgan, April 24, 1830, Tyler Family Papers, WM; JT to John Rutherfoord, March 14, 1830, John Rutherfoord Papers, DU.

36. JT to John Rutherfoord, March 14, 1830, Johnston Family Letters and Papers, 1779–1891, LVA; JT to John Floyd, May 4,1830, ibid.

37. JT to John Floyd, May 4, 1830, Johnston Family Letters and Papers, 1779–1891, LVA; JT to General Hayne, June 20, 1831, JT Papers, LC.

CHAPTER 6

1. JT to LWT, May 8, 1831, in *LTT*, 1:422.

2. JT to Henry Curtis, May 1, 1828, JT Papers, LC; Ludwig M. Deppisch, *The Health of the First Ladies: Medical Histories from Martha Washington to Michelle Obama* (Jefferson, NC: McFarland, 2015), 33–34.

3. Sally G. McMillen, *Motherhood in the Old South: Pregnancy, Childbirth, and Infant Rearing* (Baton Rouge: LSU Press, 1990), 45.

4. Holloway, *Ladies of the White House*, 383–84.

5. Carroll Smith-Rosenberg, "The Hysterical Woman: Sex Roles and Role Conflict in Nineteenth-Century America," in *Our Selves, Our Past: Psychological Approaches to American History*, ed. Robert J. Brugger (Baltimore: Johns Hopkins University Press, 1981), 205–27; Ann Douglas Wood, "'The Fashionable Diseases': Women's Complaints and Their Treatment in Nineteenth Century America," in *Clio's Consciousness Raised: New Perspectives on the History of Women*, ed. Mary Hartman and Lois W. Banner (New York: Harper and Row, 1974), 1.

6. Holloway, *Ladies of the White House*, 400.

7. Anya Jabour, *Marriage in the Early Republic: Elizabeth and William Wirt and the Companionate Ideal* (Baltimore: Johns Hopkins University Press, 1998), 53.

8. Holloway, *Ladies of the White House*, 401–2.

9. Holloway, *Ladies of the White House*, 401–2; JT to Henry Curtis, April 13, 1819, JT Papers, LC.

10. JT to CW, December 18, 1828, CW Papers, WM. After the lame-duck session, which ended on March 3, 1829, the day before Jackson's inauguration as president, a special session of the new Twenty-First Congress met, but it adjourned on March 17. The total time Letitia spent in Washington before her husband's presidency was three months.

11. V. Lynn Kennedy, *Born Southern: Childbirth, Motherhood, and Social Networks in the Old South* (Baltimore: Johns Hopkins University Press, 2010), chap. 2; Anya Jabour, *Scarlett's Sisters:*

Young Women in the Old South (Chapel Hill: University of North Carolina Press, 2007), 220–27; McMillen, *Motherhood in the Old South*, 107.

12. Glover, *Southern Sons*, 126; Craig Thompson Friend, "Sex, Self, and the Performance of Patriarchal Manhood in the Old South," in *The Old South's Modern Worlds: Slavery, Region, and Nation in the Age of Progress*, ed. L. Diane Barnes, Brian Schoen, and Frank Towers (New York: Oxford University Press, 2011), 251–57.

13. JT to Henry Curtis, October 26, November 23, 1827, JT Papers, LC; JT to MT, December 26, 1827, in *LTT*, 1:389; JT to MT, May 13, 1830, ibid.; JT to MT, March 4, 1830, JT Papers, ser. 4, LC; JT to MT, June 15, 1832, ibid.

14. JT to MT, February 24, 1828, in *LTT*, 1:390–91.

15. Catherine Clinton, "Equally Their Due: The Education of the Planter Daughter in the Early Republic," *JER* 2 (Spring 1982): 39–60; Stowe, *Intimacy and Power in the Old South*, 131; Philip Greven, *The Protestant Temperament: Patterns of Child-Rearing, Religious Experience, and the Self in Early America* (New York: Alfred A. Knopf, 1977), 265–95; JT to MT, March 4, 1830, JT Papers, ser. 4, LC.

16. JT to MT, February 24, 1828, in *LTT*, 1:390; JT to MT, April 30, 1828, ibid., 392; JT to MT, December 28, 1831, ibid., 429.

17. JT to Henry Curtis, May 1, 1828, JT Papers, LC; JT to MT, June 15, 1832, JT Papers, ser. 4, LC.

18. JT to RT, March 15, 1832, Elizabeth Tyler Coleman Papers, UA.

19. JT to Henry Curtis, March 28, 1834, JT Papers, LC; JT to RT, February 2, 1832, ibid.

20. JT to RT, February 15, 1836, JT Papers, LC.

21. JT Jr. to LCT, January 6, October 12, 1836, JT Papers, LC; JT Jr. to LCT, January 15, 1837, Tyler Family Papers, VHS.

22. Clement Eaton, *The Growth of Southern Civilization, 1790–1860* (New York: Harper and Row, 1961), 5, 182–83; Avery O. Craven, *Soil Exhaustion as a Factor in the Agricultural History of Virginia and Maryland, 1606–1860* (Urbana: University of Illinois Press, 1926).

23. US Census Bureau, *Fifth Census of the United States, 1830*, Population Schedules: Charles City County, VA.

24. Kolchin, *American Slavery*, 101–2.

25. William Kauffman Scarborough, *The Overseer: Plantation Management in the Old South* (Baton Rouge: LSU Press, 1966), xi, 5–6; JT to Robert W. Christian, May 13, 1830, JT Papers, LC.

26. Drew G. Faust, *James Henry Hammond and the Antebellum South: A Design for Mastery* (Baton Rouge: LSU Press, 1983), 124–26; H. N. McTyeire, "Plantation Life—Duties and Responsibilities," *DeBow's Review* 29 (September 1860): 363; Scarborough, *Overseer*, 44–45, 102–12; Oakes, *The Ruling Race*, 156, 174–75.

27. Scarborough, *Overseer*, 119–20; Elizabeth Fox-Genovese, *Within the Plantation Household: Black and White Women of the Old South* (Chapel Hill: University of North Carolina Press, 1988), 205–6.

28. *LTT*, 1:415; JT to LWT, May 8, 1831, JT Papers, LC; Seager, *And Tyler Too*, 103.

29. JT to General Hayne, June 20, 1831, JT Papers, LC; JT to Gov. John Floyd, June 16, 1831, John Floyd Papers, Miscellaneous Manuscript Collection, LC.

30. JT to Henry Curtis, May 1, 1828, JT Papers, LC; JT to Henry Curtis, April 23, 1828, ibid.

31. JT to RT, February 2, 1832, JT Papers, LC.

CHAPTER 7

1. *MPP*, 2:556; *ROD*, 22nd Cong., 1st sess., 67; Bolt, *Tariff Wars*, 110.

2. *ROD*, 22nd Cong., 1st sess., 338–40, 359, 367; JT to General Hayne, June 20, 1831, JT Papers, LC.

3. Bolt, *Tariff Wars*, 112–15.

4. William W. Freehling, *Prelude to Civil War: The Nullification Controversy in South Carolina, 1816–1836* (New York: Harper and Row, 1965), 258–64.

5. *MPP*, 2:650; Richard E. Ellis, *The Union at Risk: Jacksonian Democracy, States' Rights and the Nullification Crisis* (New York: Oxford University Press, 1987), 83–84; Donald B. Cole, *The Presidency of Andrew Jackson* (Lawrence: University Press of Kansas, 1993), 160–68.

6. Ellis, *Union at Risk*, 133–35.

7. JT to Gov. John Floyd, December 13, 1832, Tyler Family Papers, VHS.

8. JT to LWT, February 2, 1833, JT Papers, LC.

9. Cole, *Presidency of Andrew Jackson*, 167.

10. *ROD*, 22nd Cong., 2nd sess., 360–77.

11. *ROD*, 22nd Cong., 2nd sess., 688–89.

12. JT to William F. Pendleton, January 19, 1833, JT Papers, LC; JT to LWT, February 2, 1833, ibid.; *RE*, February 12, 1833.

13. John M. Patton to LWT, April 1833, Tazewell Family Papers, LVA; Merrill D. Peterson, *Olive Branch and Sword: The Compromise of 1833* (Baton Rouge: LSU Press, 1982), 33, 53, 66–84; Donald J. Ratcliffe, "The Nullification Crisis, Southern Discontents, and the American Political Process," *American Nineteenth Century History* 1 (Summer 2000): 21.

14. James Campbell to David Campbell, March 4, 1827, Campbell Family Papers, DU; JT to RT, February 15, 1836, JT Papers, LC; *LTT*, 1:536; JT to William Patterson Smith, March 31, 1834, William Patterson Smith Papers, DU. On the Bank War, see Stephen W. Campbell, *The Bank War and the Partisan Press: Newspapers, Financial Institutions, and the Post Office in Jacksonian America* (Lawrence: University Press of Kansas, 2019).

15. HC to Charles J. Faulkner, January 26, 1833, in *PHC*, 8:616.

16. HC to Thomas W. Gilmer, January 1836, in *PHC*, 8:820.

17. William Crump to JT, February 14, 1836, Tyler Scrapbook, Tyler Family Papers, WM; *Richmond Whig*, February 13, 1836.

18. JT to RT, January 16, 1836, in *LTT*, 1:529–30; Seager, *And Tyler Too*, 103, 112–13. For the conversion of Tyler's Senate salary to 2019 dollars, see davemanuel.com.

19. JT to MTJ, January 20, 1836, in *LTT*, 1:531.

20. JT Jr. to LCT, January 6, 1836, Tyler Family Papers, VHS; JT to William F. Gordon, January 8, 1836, James M. Rochelle Papers, DU; JT to MTJ, January 20, 1836, in *LTT*, 1:531.

21. JT to RT, February 15, 1836, JT Papers, LC; JT to Hugh Blair Grigsby, January 16, 1855, copy, Hugh Blair Grigsby Letterbook, Hugh Blair Grigsby Papers, VHS; Seager, *And Tyler Too*, 114.

22. *Richmond Whig*, March 4, 1836.

23. *Washington Globe*, March 1, 1836.

24. *RE*, February 16, March 3, 1836.

25. JT to William F. Pendleton, October 27, 1836, JT Papers, LC; JT to NBT, October 29, 1837, Tucker-Coleman Papers, WM.

26. PCT to her sisters, October 1839, Elizabeth Tyler Coleman Papers, UA; PCT to Mary Grace Raoul, August 1840, in Elizabeth Tyler Coleman, *Priscilla Cooper Tyler and the American Scene, 1816–1889* (Tuscaloosa: University of Alabama Press, 1955), 82.

27. JT, speech in Gloucester County, n.d., in *LTT*, 1:574–79; JT, speech as president of Virginia Colonization Society, ibid., 567–70. On Nat Turner's Rebellion, see David Allmendinger Jr., *Nat Turner and the Rising in Southampton County* (Baltimore: Johns Hopkins University Press, 2014). On the Virginia slavery debates, see Alison G. Freehling, *Drift towards Dissolution: The Virginia Slavery Debate of 1831–1832* (Baton Rouge: LSU Press, 1982). On the anti-abolitionist campaign in Virginia, see Shade, *Democratizing the Old Dominion*, 212–13. On the national campaign, see Leonard L. Richards, *"Gentlemen of Property and Standing": Anti-Abolition Mobs in Jacksonian America* (New York: Oxford University Press, 1970). On the controversy the petitions to Congress generated, which led to the Gag Rule in the House, see Freehling, *Road to Disunion*, vol. 1, *Secessionists at Bay*, chap. 17. On the American Colonization Society, see Eric Burin, *Slavery and the Peculiar Solution: A History of the American Colonization Society* (Gainesville: University Press of Florida, 2008); and Ford, *Deliver Us from Evil*, chap. 10. On the connection between Virginia states' rights beliefs and colonization, see Eva Sheppard Wolf, *Race and Liberty in the New Nation: Emancipation in Virginia from the Revolution to Nat Turner's Rebellion* (Baton Rouge: LSU Press, 2006), 176. On women in the abolitionist movement, see Ronald G. Walters, *The Antislavery Appeal: American Abolitionism after 1830* (New York: W. W. Norton, 1978), 10–12. For the role of African Americans in the movement, see Manisha Sinha, *The Slaves' Cause: A History of Abolition* (New Haven, CT: Yale University Press, 2017). Tyler expressed his view that free blacks should not be considered citizens of the United States in a letter to LWT, May 2, 1826, in *LTT*, 1:331.

28. Chitwood, *John Tyler*, 153.

29. Daniel Feller, *The Public Lands in Jacksonian Politics* (Madison: University of Wisconsin Press, 1984).

30. JT to Thomas R. Dew, January 16, 1839, in *LTT*, 1:588, *RE*, January 29, 30, 31, February 2, 1839; Chitwood, *John Tyler*, 157; Shade, *Democratizing the Old Dominion*, 94–96; Dent, "Virginia Democratic Party," vol. 1, chap. 6; Major L. Wilson, *The Presidency of Martin Van Buren* (Lawrence: University Press of Kansas, 1984), 63–78; Jean E. Friedman, *The Revolt of the Conservative Democrats: An Essay on American Political Culture and Political Development, 1837–1844* (Ann Arbor, MI: UMI Research, 1979).

31. HC to Francis T. Brooke, January 7, 1839, in *PHC*, 8:266–67; Shade, *Democratizing the Old Dominion*, 95–96; Dent, "Virginia Democratic Party," 1:259–60.

32. *RE*, February 16, 17, 23, 1839. There is no conclusive evidence to prove whether Clay actually offered Tyler the vice-presidential nomination in exchange for his withdrawal from the Senate contest. Clay preferred Rives, but *PHC*, volume 8, contains no letter that indicates he made the offer. The source of the controversy appears to have been Henry Wise, who asserts that Clay approached Tyler with the proposal. See *Seven Decades of the Union: The Humanities and Materialism Illustrated by a Memoir of John Tyler* (Philadelphia: J. B. Lippincott, 1872), 165–66. Lyon G. Tyler, Tyler's son and family chronicler, accepted Wise's account.

33. Dent, "Virginia Democratic Party," 1:260–61.

34. Chitwood, *John Tyler*, 184–91.

35. Mark R. Cheathem, *The Coming of Democracy: Presidential Campaigning in the Age of Jackson* (Baltimore: Johns Hopkins University Press, 2018), chap. 12; Elizabeth R. Varon, *We Mean*

to Be Counted: White Women and Politics in Antebellum Virginia (Chapel Hill: University of North Carolina Press, 1998), 3; Michael F. Holt, "The Election of 1840, Voter Mobilization, and the Emergence of the Second American Party System: A Reappraisal of Jacksonian Voting Behavior," in *A Master's Due: Essays in Honor of David Herbert Donald*, ed. William J. Cooper Jr. et al. (Baton Rouge: LSU Press, 1985), 16–58; Holt, *Rise and Fall of the American Whig Party*, 105–13; Robert Gray Gunderson, *The Log Cabin Campaign* (Lexington: University of Kentucky Press, 1957); Shade, *Democratizing the Old Dominion*, 97–98; William Nisbet Chambers, "Election of 1840," in *History of American Presidential Elections, 1789–1968*, ed. Arthur M. Schlesinger Jr. (New York: Chelsea House, 1971), 665–90; JT to Henry Wise, November 25, 1840, in *LTT*, 3:84.

CHAPTER 8

1. Chitwood, *John Tyler*, 202. *Niles' National Register*, April 10, 1841, published the message Webster and Beale brought Tyler.

2. Fred Shelley, ed., "The Vice President Receives Bad News in Williamsburg: A Letter of James Lyons to John Tyler," *VMHB* 76 (July 1968): 337–39; James Lyons to JT, April 3, 1841, JT Papers, ser. 4, LC.

3. NBT to TR, July 12, 1845, Tyler Scrapbook, Tyler Family Papers, WM.

4. *LTT*, 2:11–12; Benjamin Perley Poore, *Perley's Reminiscences of Sixty Years in the National Metropolis*, 2 vols. (Philadelphia: Hubbard Brothers, 1886), 1:269; *NI*, April 7, 1841.

5. JT to LWT, October 11, 1841, in *LTT*, 2:127; JT to LWT, November 2, 1841, ibid., 131; JT, "Extract from a Letter Addressed by President Tyler to the Norfolk Democratic Association, dated September 1844," ibid., 95–96; Peterson, *Littleton Waller Tazewell*, 256.

6. Albert D. Kirwan, *John J. Crittenden: The Struggle for the Union* (Lexington: University Press of Kentucky, 1962), is silent on whether Crittenden was in Washington on April 6. Most historians have assumed he was there and that he attended the first Tyler cabinet meeting. But evidence indicates that he was out of the city. See HC to Waddy Thompson Jr., April 23,1841, in *PHC*, 9:522; HC to Thomas Ewing, April 30,1841, ibid., 524; and William H. Seward to John J. Crittenden, May 31, 1841, in *The Works of William H. Seward*, ed. George E. Baker, 5 vols. (Boston: Houghton, Mifflin, 1888), 2:586–88.

7. *MPP*, 4:31–32.

8. Stephen W. Stathis, "John Tyler's Presidential Succession: A Reappraisal," *Prologue* 8 (Winter 1976): 227; Robert J. Morgan, *A Whig Embattled: The Presidency under John Tyler* (Lincoln: University of Nebraska Press, 1954), 9.

9. Edward S. Corwin, *The President: Office and Powers, 1787–1957* (New York: New York University Press, 1957), 54; Norma Lois Peterson, The *Presidencies of William Henry Harrison and John Tyler* (Lawrence: University Press of Kansas, 1989), 49; Leonard Dinnerstein, "The Accession of John Tyler to the Presidency," *VMHB* 70 (October 1962): 447–58; John D. Feerick, *The Twenty-Fifth Amendment: Its Complete History and Applications* (New York: Fordham University Press, 1992), 5–7, 111–13.

10. Charles Francis Adams, ed., *Memoirs of John Quincy Adams, Comprising Portions of His Diary from 1795–1848*, 12 vols. (Philadelphia: J. B. Lippincott, 1876), 10:456–57, 459.

11. HC to NBT, April 15, 1841, in *PHC*, 9:520.

12. The Presidential Succession Act of 1792 was never invoked. In 1886, Congress passed another Presidential Succession Act that replaced the 1792 law. This measure placed the cabinet secretaries into the line of succession, thus replacing the president pro tempore of the Senate and the Speaker of the House. This law, like its 1792 counterpart, was never invoked. In 1947, spurred on by heavy lobbying from Pres. Harry Truman, Congress passed another Presidential Succession Act. This measure—still on the books today—placed the president pro tempore of the Senate and the Speaker of the House back into the immediate line of succession after the vice president but switched their order from what the 1792 act had stipulated. Thus, the order of succession is now vice president, Speaker of the House, president pro tempore of the Senate, and then the cabinet positions in the order in which their departments were created. Incidentally, there was no Speaker of the House in place when Tyler assumed the presidency because the second session of the Twenty-Sixth Congress had adjourned on March 15, 1841. The Whig majority in Congress chose Kentuckian John White as Speaker when the Twenty-Seventh Congress convened for its special session on May 31.

13. Seager, *And Tyler Too,* 149.

14. George Rawlings Poage, *Henry Clay and the Whig Party* (1936; repr., Gloucester, MA: Peter Smith, 1965), 37.

15. Frank G. Carpenter, "A Talk with a President's Son," *Lippincott's Monthly Magazine* 41 (May 1888): 417–18.

16. DW to John Davis, April 16, 1841, in *PDW-C,* 5:108.

17. JT to NBT, July 28, 1841, in *LTT,* 2:53.

18. JT to WCR, April 9, 1841, in *LTT,* 2:20.

19. *NI,* April 7, 1841; *MPP,* 4:31; S. W. Pearson to Caleb Cushing, April 10, 1841, Caleb Cushing Papers, LC.

20. *RE,* April 6, 9 1841; *Washington Globe,* April 7, 1841.

21. The lone exception was James A. Garfield.

22. "President William Henry Harrison: The Funeral Ceremonies," Historic Congressional Cemetery, http://www.congressionalcemetery.org/president-william-henry-harrison, accessed 20 June 2014 (page removed); *CG,* 27th Cong., 1st sess., 93–94.

23. JT to Mrs. [William Henry] Harrison, June 13, 1841, Tyler Family Papers, WM; Howe, *What Hath God Wrought,* 589.

24. *MPP,* 4:36–37.

25. Duff Green claimed later that he had visited Tyler at the White House on the morning after he had taken the oath of office and persuaded him to strike out a paragraph in the inaugural address that declared he would not be a candidate for president in 1844. In Green's account of this meeting, Tyler told him "that his desire was, if possible, to withdraw the question of the currency from the vortex of party, and that he had been persuaded that such a declaration would conciliate the co-operation of the several aspirants." Green replied that such a declaration would have the exact opposite result of what Tyler intended. Green further claimed that he came back to the White House the next day, when Tyler showed him on his draft of the address that he had crossed out the paragraph disclaiming a second term. See Duff Green to APU, December 29, 1842, in *LTT,* 2:25–26. Also, Tyler's Treasury secretary, Thomas Ewing, later claimed that the president had alluded to the deletion of the statement in a cabinet meeting on September 4, 1841. See Ewing, "Diary of Thomas Ewing, August and September, 1841," *American Historical Review* 18 (October 1912): 109.

26. *MPP*, 4:37.

27. *MPP*, 4:38.

28. *MPP*, 4:38; C. S. Todd to JT, May 25, 1841, JT Papers, LC.

29. HC to James F. Conover, April 9, 1841, in *PHC*, 9:518.

30. Arthur Campbell to David Campbell, April 24, 1841, Campbell Family Papers, DU.

31. Arthur Campbell to David Campbell, April 24, 1841, Campbell Family Papers, DU.

32. *MPP*, 4:38–39.

33. HC to Henry B. Bascom, April 17, 1841, in *PHC*, 9:520; HC to John M. Berrien, April 20, 1841, ibid., 521.

34. DW to Leverett Saltonstall, April 12, 1841, in *PDW-C*, 5:108; John L. Kerr to JT, April 20, 1841, JT Papers, ser. 4, LC; Thomas S. Dabney to Thomas Smith, April 25, 1841, William Patterson Smith Papers, DU; Philip Rainey to John Bennett, May 5, 1841, John Bennett Papers, VHS.

35. HC to James F. Conover, April 9, 1841, in *PHC*, 9:518; HC to John L. Lawrence, April 13, 1841, ibid., 519.

36. Sydney Nathans, *Daniel Webster and Jacksonian Democracy* (Baltimore: Johns Hopkins University Press, 1973), 152–53.

37. Thomas Hart Benton, *Thirty Years' View; or, A History of the Working of the American Government for Thirty Years, from 1820 to 1850*, 2 vols. (New York: D. Appleton, 1854–56), 2:212–13.

38. Jackson and Blair quoted in Robert V. Remini, *Andrew Jackson and the Course of American Democracy, 1833–1845* (New York: Harper and Row, 1984), 473.

39. APU to NBT, April 10, 1841, Tucker-Coleman Papers, WM; Preston quoted in Robert J. Brugger, *Beverley Tucker: Heart over Head in the Old South* (Baltimore: John Hopkins University Press, 1978), 139. The source for Ruffin's view is ibid.

40. Brugger, *Beverley Tucker*, 140–41.

41. JT to NBT, April 25, 1841, JT Papers, LC.

42. JT to HC, April 30, 1841, in *PHC*, 9:527–29.

43. On Renehan, see William Seale, *The President's House: A History*, 2 vols. (Washington, DC: White House Historical Association, 2008),1:210. On Wilkens, see *Washington Capital*, May 11, 1884, Tyler Family Papers, sec. 3, VHS; and PCT to JT, June 26 [28], 1844, "Letters from Tyler Trunks, 'Sherwood Forest,' VA," *TQ* 18 (July 1936): 24. For Wise's physical description, see Poore, *Perley's Reminiscences*, 1:278. For Tyler's nickname for the office seekers, see JT to NBT, July 28, 1841, in *LTT*, 2:53.

44. RT quoted in William A. Link, *Roots of Secession: Slavery and Politics in Antebellum Virginia* (Chapel Hill: University of North Carolina Press, 2003), 16; Craig M. Simpson, *A Good Southerner: The Life of Henry A. Wise of Virginia* (Chapel Hill: University of North Carolina Press, 1985), 3–4, 9–15, 37–41. See also Joanne B. Freeman, *The Field of Blood: Violence in Congress and the Road to Civil War* (New York: Farrar, Straus, and Giroux, 2018), 80–83.

45. Simpson, *Good Southerner*, 47–50.

46. John S. Wise, *Recollections of Thirteen Presidents* (New York: Doubleday, Page, 1906), 21.

47. JT to HW, November 25, 1840, in *LTT*, 3:85.

48. JT to NBT, May 9, 1841, *LTT*, 2:33; NBT to TR, July 12, 1845, Tyler Scrapbook, Tyler Family Papers, WM; Simpson, *Good Southerner*, 23; Brugger, *Beverley Tucker*, 141.

49. JT to NBT, May 9, 1841, in *LTT*, 2:33; NBT to TR, July 12, 1845, Tyler Scrapbook, Tyler Family Papers, WM.

50. *LTT*, 2:33; JT to NBT, July 28, 1841, ibid., 54.

51. HC to Thomas Ewing, April 30, 1841, in *PHC*, 9:524–25.

52. Thomas Ewing to HC, May 8, 1841, in *PHC*, 9:530.

CHAPTER 9

1. Nevins, *Diary of Philip Hone*, 2:537; Holt, *Rise and Fall of the American Whig Party*, 130–31; *Vicksburg (MS) Whig* quoted in Alasdair Roberts, *America's First Great Depression: Economic Crisis and Political Disorder after the Panic of 1837* (Ithaca, NY: Cornell University Press, 2012), 21. See also Jessica M. Lepler, *The Many Panics of 1837: People, Politics, and the Creation of a Transatlantic Financial Crisis* (Cambridge: Cambridge University Press, 2013).

2. HC to Thomas Ewing, April 30, 1841, in *PHC*, 9:526.

3. *CG*, 27th Cong., 1st sess., 1.

4. *CG*, 27th Cong., 1st sess., 1–5; Morgan, *A Whig Embattled*, 14–16.

5. Ebenezer Pettigrew to James Cathcart Johnston, May 17, 1841, in *The Pettigrew Papers*, ed. Sarah McCulloh Lemmon, 2 vols. (Raleigh: North Carolina Division of Archives and History, 1988), 2:467; Simpson, *Good Southerner*, 42, 46.

6. HW to NBT, May 29, 1841, in *LTT*, 2:34.

7. *MPP*, 4:40–43. Tyler's estimate of the national debt was actually low. By June, Treasury Secretary Ewing estimated that the probable debt was closer to $9.5 million, with the strong possibility that maturing Treasury notes could balloon the figure to $19.5 million. See *PHC*, 9:567.

8. *MPP*, 4:45–46.

9. William R. Brock, *Parties and Political Conscience: American Dilemmas, 1840–1850* (Millwood, NY: KTO, 1979), 90.

10. *PHC*, 9:534; *CG*, 27th Cong., 1st sess., 8.

11. *CG*, 27th Cong., 1st sess., 11.

12. HW to NBT, June 27, 1841, in *LTT*, 2:47; *PHC*, 9:539; *CG*, 27th Cong., 1st sess., 22; Friedman, *Revolt of the Conservative Democrats*, 25.

13. *CG*, 27th Cong., 1st sess., 13, 18–21; HC to Thomas Ewing, June 2, 1841, in *PHC*, 9:535; WPM to Duncan Cameron, June 26, 1841, in *PWPM*, 3:182.

14. HC to Robert P. Letcher, June 11, 1841, in *PHC*, 9:543; HC to Henry C. Carey, June 11, 1841, ibid.

15. *PHC*, 9:546. The undated message is actually located in the Thomas Ewing Papers at the LC.

16. Merrill D. Peterson, *The Great Triumvirate: Webster, Clay, and Calhoun* (New York: Oxford University Press, 1987), 305–6.

17. Richard A. Gantz, "Henry Clay and the Harvest of Bitter Fruit: The Struggle with John Tyler, 1841–1842" (Ph.D. diss., Indiana University, 1986), 100–101; JT to NBT, July 28, 1841, in *LTT*, 2:54; "President Tyler's Statement (1842)," ibid., 69; Monroe, *Republican Vision of John Tyler*, 208n44.

18. *CG*, 27th Cong., 1st sess., 48–49; HW to NBT, June 5, 1841, in *LTT*, 2:37–38.

19. William A. Graham to James W. Bryan, June 13, 1841, in *PWAG*, 2:198.

20. JT to NBT, July 28, 1841, in *LTT*, 2:54.

21. HW to NBT, June 27, 1841, in *LTT*, 2:47.

22. HC to Waddy Thompson Jr., April 23, 1841, in *PHC*, 9:522.

23. *CG*, 27th Cong., 1st sess, 79–80; Gantz, "Clay and the Harvest of Bitter Fruit," 109.

24. JT to John Rutherfoord, June 28, 1841, in *LTT*, 2:50–51.

25. *CG*, 27th Cong. 1st sess., 133, app., 354; Peterson, *Presidencies of William Henry Harrison and John Tyler*, 68.

26. Raymond C. Dingledine Jr., "The Political Career of William Cabell Rives" (Ph.D. diss., University of Virginia, 1947), 387, 390n39.

27. HW to NBT, June 18, 27, 1841, in *LTT*, 2:46–47; Holt, *Rise and Fall of the American Whig Party*, 132. Barrow, like Tyler a former Democrat who turned against Andrew Jackson, also opposed the orthodox Whig stance on the tariff, so it was not only the patronage he sought but also the affinity for states' rights that brought him into the administration's orbit. See John M. Sacher, *A Perfect War of Politics: Parties, Politicians, and Democracy in Louisiana, 1824–1861* (Baton Rouge: LSU Press, 2003), 55–56, 107.

28. *The United States Magazine and Democratic Review* 4 (Washington, DC: Langtree and O'Sullivan, 1838), 11; HW to NBT, June 27,1841, in *LTT*, 2:47–48; JT to HW, September 27, 1841, *WMQ*, 1st ser., 20 (October 1911): 7.

CHAPTER 10

1. HC to Francis T. Brooke, July 4, 1841, in *PHC*, 9:557. "Loco focos" was the pejorative nickname probank Conservative Democrats gave to so-called radical Democrats, who were stridently opposed to banks. The radicals wore the epithet proudly.

2. John Rutherfoord to JT, June 21, 1841, in *LTT*, 2:48–49.

3. JCC to Thomas G. Clemson, June 13, 1841, in *Annual Report of the American Historical Association for the Year 1899*, vol. 2, *Calhoun Correspondence* (Washington, DC: Government Printing Office, 1900), 478.

4. Link, *Roots of Secession*, 15, 259n7; *LTT*, 2:55–56.

5. *CG*, 27th Cong., 1st sess., 260.

6. Benjamin Brown French, *Witness to the Young Republic: A Yankee's Journal, 1828–1870*, ed. Donald B. Cole and John J. McDonough (Hanover, NH: University Press of New England, 1989), 120; Richard Milford Blatchford to William H. Seward, August 9, 1841, Papers of William H. Seward, Department of Rare Books, Manuscripts, and Archives, Rush Rhees Library, University of Rochester, microfilm; Peter B. Porter to HC, August 9, 1841, in *PHC*, 9:581; HC to Benjamin O. Tayloe, August 11, 1841, ibid., 583.

7. APU to NBT, August 7, 1841, Tucker-Coleman Papers, WM.

8. French, *Witness to the Young Republic*, 121.

9. David S. Heidler and Jeanne T. Heidler, *Henry Clay: The Essential American* (New York: Random House, 2010), 348; *MPP*, 4:63.

10. Robert V. Remini, *Henry Clay: Statesman for the Union* (New York: W. W. Norton, 1991), 590.

11. *MPP*, 4:63–68; Peter Temin, *The Jacksonian Economy* (New York: W. W. Norton, 1969), 33; Sharon Ann Murphy, *Other People's Money: How Banking Worked in the Early American Republic* (Baltimore: Johns Hopkins University Press, 2017), 47–49.

12. Peter B. Porter to HC, August 20, 1841, in *PHC*, 9:592.

13. Peterson, *Presidencies of William Henry Harrison and John Tyler*, 71.

14. "Stuart's Statement," in *LTT*, 2:78–79.

15. Seager, *And Tyler Too*, 156.

16. DW, "Memorandum on the Banking Bills and the Vetoes, 1841," in *PDW-C*, 5:177.

17. Ewing, "Diary of Thomas Ewing," 100–101.

18. JT to NBT, July 28, 1841, in *LTT*, 2:54; HW to NBT, July 11, 1841, ibid., 52.

19. *LTT*, 2:81.

20. Ewing, "Diary," 101.

21. DW to Caroline Le Roy Webster, August 16, 1841, in *PDW-C*, 5:141.

22. Ewing, "Diary," 102–3.

23. HC, "Speech in the Senate," August 19, 1841, in *PHC*, 9:587–91; Peterson, *Presidencies of William Henry Harrison and John Tyler*, 78–79.

24. Remini, *Henry Clay*, 593; Garrett Davis to Gen. John Payne, August 30, 1841, John Payne Papers, LC.

25. HC's "Speech in Senate," August 19, 1841, in *PHC*, 9:587–91.

26. *LTT*, 2:65, 112; *DM*, August 21, 1841.

27. DW, "Memorandum," 176.

28. Ewing, "Diary," 103; DW to JT, August 20, 1841, in *LTT*, 2:86.

29. DW, "Memorandum," 178; Nathans, *Daniel Webster and Jacksonian Democracy*, 176–77; Peterson, *Presidencies of William Henry Harrison and John Tyler*, 80.

30. DW, "Memorandum," 178–79; DW to Isaac Chapman Bates and Rufus Choate, August 25, 1841, in *PDW-C*, 5:147.

31. Ewing, "Diary," 104.

32. DW to Bates and Choate, August 25, 1841, in *PDW-C*, 5:147.

33. Ewing, "Diary," 104–5.

34. Garrett Davis to Gen. John Payne, August 30, 1841, John Payne Papers, LC.

35. WPM to Charity A. Mangum, August 24, 1841, in *PWPM*, 3:220; Peterson, *Presidencies of William Henry Harrison and John Tyler*, 82–83.

36. Peterson, *Presidencies of William Henry Harrison and John Tyler*, 83.

37. APU to NBT, August 28, 1841, Tucker-Coleman Papers, WM.

38. William A. Graham to Susan Washington Graham, August 29, 1841, in *PWAG*, 2:236. Clay's most recent biographers, David S. Heidler and Jeanne T. Heidler, write that Tyler asked for champagne. See *Henry Clay*, 350. Robert V. Remini, in his *Henry Clay*, also asserts that the president drank a glass of champagne. Both books rely on the memoir of John Quincy Adams for their information. I have relied on William A. Graham's account and maintain that, given the political situation and the state of Tyler's mind in late August 1841, he probably felt the stronger drink was more appropriate.

39. HW to NBT, August 29, 1841, in *LTT*, 2:90–91.

40. *CG*, 27th Cong., 1st sess., 380; Peterson, *Presidencies of William Henry Harrison and John Tyler*, 80; Ewing, "Diary," 107.

41. James Lyons to JT, August 28, 1841, in *LTT*, 2:118; Ewing, "Diary," 109.

42. Ewing, "Diary," 109–10.

43. Ewing, "Diary," 110–11; *LTT*, 2:117.

44. APU quoted in Hall, *Abel Parker Upshur*, 116; TR to unknown, August 30, 1841, in "Un-

published Letters of Thomas Ritchie," *John P. Branch Historical Papers of Randolph-Macon College* 3 (June 1911): 246.

45. *LTT*, 2:92.

46. Quotes taken from Frank Thomas, "Our Public Men: Personal Traits of President Tyler and His Family," *Knickerbocker* 22 (July 1843): 56.

47. Seale, *President's House*, 1:235–36.

48. *CG*, 27th Cong., 1st sess., 444.

49. Poage, *Henry Clay and the Whig Party*, 101.

50. *MPP*, 4:68–72.

51. Holt, *Rise and Fall of the American Whig Party*, 135–36; *CG*, 27th Cong., 1st sess., 449.

52. HC to the Whig Caucus, September 13, 1841, in *PHC*, 9:608; HC, "Remark in Senate," September 11, 1841, ibid., 607.

53. Chitwood, *John Tyler*, apps. B and C, 471–77.

54. Waddy Thompson to NBT, September 13, 1841, Tyler Scrapbook, Tyler Family Papers, WM; Maj. Washington Seawell to Maria H. Seawell, September 18, 1841, in "Removal of the Florida Indians: Letter of Major Washington Seawell," *TQ* 2 (October 1929): 112; *CG*, 27th Cong., 1st sess., 446; APU to NBT, September 10, 1841, Tucker-Coleman Papers, WM; JT to NBT, n.d., [1841], JT Papers, LC.

55. *CG*, 27th Cong., 1st sess., 446.

56. Oliver P. Chitwood argues that there was evidence to suggest that, at one point, Tyler wanted the entire cabinet—Webster included—to resign, citing APU to NBT, September 10, 1841, Tucker-Coleman Papers, WM. In this letter Upshur informed Tucker that the solution for getting Webster out of the cabinet was to appoint him minister to Britain. My reading of this letter, however, differs from Chitwood's. In keeping with the give and take between Tyler and his Virginia advisors that occurred throughout the special session, I think the evidence points even more strongly to the possibility that Upshur and Tucker (and Wise) made the suggestion to Tyler to appoint Webster to the London mission. Tyler probably at some point agreed with them that this would be a beneficial course of action—*if* he decided that Webster had to go. I contend that Webster was too important to Tyler, both domestically and as the nation's chief diplomat, for the president to seek his removal and that this was another case of Tyler attempting to placate his friends while intending to ignore their advice. See Chitwood, *John Tyler*, 279–80.

57. Chitwood, *John Tyler*, 279–80.

58. Dingledine, "Political Career of William Cabell Rives," 402.

59. JT to LWT, October 11, 1841, JT Papers, LC; Weed quoted in Nathans, *Daniel Webster and Jacksonian Democracy*, 183; *NI*, September 16, 1841.

60. David Lambert to WPM, October 14, 1841, in *PWPM*, 3:245.

61. Peterson, *Presidencies of William Henry Harrison and John Tyler*, 88; DW to John McLean, September 11, 1841, in *PDW-C*, 5:151; Leo Damrosch, *Tocqueville's Discovery of America* (New York: Farrar, Straus and Giroux, 2010), 59.

62. Michael O'Brien, *A Character of Hugh Legare* (Knoxville: University of Tennessee Press, 1985); Marvin R. Cain, "Return of Republicanism: A Reappraisal of Hugh Swinton Legare and the Tyler Presidency," *South Carolina Historical Magazine* 79 (October 1978): 266–67; JT, "The Dead of the Cabinet," in *LTT*, 2:384–85.

63. APU to NBT, September 7, 1841, in *LTT*, 2:122.

64. Peterson, *Presidencies of William Henry Harrison and John Tyler*, 89.

65. Peterson, *Presidencies of William Henry Harrison and John Tyler*, 89–90; *DM*, September 16, 1841. On Kennedy, see Andrew R. Black, *John Pendleton Kennedy: Early American Novelist, Whig Statesman, & Ardent Nationalist* (Baton Rouge: LSU Press, 2016).

CHAPTER 11

1. "Passages from a Politician's Note-Book," *United States Democratic Review* 11 (October 1842): 428.

2. Chitwood, *John Tyler*, 318; extracts of the diary of Henry Jarvis Raymond, *Scribner's*, November 1879, Tyler Family Papers, VHS.

3. JT to LWT, October 11, 1841, in *LTT*, 2:127–28. For a sympathetic view of Clay's fight with Tyler, see Thomas Brown, *Politics and Statesmanship: Essays on the American Whig Party* (New York: Columbia University Press, 1985), chap. 5. For another, see Daniel Walker Howe, *The Political Culture of the American Whigs* (Chicago: University of Chicago Press, 1979), 142–44.

4. "Political Portraits with Pen and Pencil, No. XXXIV: John Tyler," *United States Democratic Review* 11 (November 1842): 503–4; Monroe, *Republican Vision of John Tyler*, 183.

5. APU to NBT, September 29, 1841, Tucker-Coleman Papers, WM; APU to NBT, September 16, 1841, in "Correspondence of Judge N. B. Tucker," *WMQ*, 1st ser., 12 (January 1904): 148. For Upshur's tenure as navy secretary and an explanation of how this staunch states' righter advocated for enlarged federal powers to advance his proslavery ideological agenda, see Matthew Karp, *This Vast Southern Empire: Slaveholders at the Helm of American Foreign Policy* (Cambridge. MA: Harvard University Press, 2016), chap. 2.

6. JT to Thomas A. Cooper, October 8, 1841, in *LTT*, 2:125; Charles Dickens, *American Notes: A Journey* (1842; repr., New York: Fromm, 1985), 124; JT to William H. Seward, July 5, 1841, Papers of William H. Seward, University of Rochester, microfilm; JT to NBT, July 28, 1841, in *LTT*, 2:53.

7. JT to DW, October 11, 1841, in *LTT*, 2:126.

8. JT to DW, October 11, 1841, in *LTT*, 2:126.

9. JT to DW, October 11, 1841, in *LTT*, 2:126; *Boston Semi-Weekly Atlas*, October 2, 1841, quoted in *PDW-C*, 5:164.

10. *The Schenectady Cabinet; or Freedom's Sentinel*, October 19, 1841; JT to DW, October 11, 1841, in *LTT*, 2:126–27; Millard Fillmore to Thurlow Weed, September 23, 1841, in *Publications of the Buffalo Historical Society*, vol. 11, *Millard Fillmore Papers*, vol. 2, ed. Frank H. Severance (1907; repr., New York: Kraus, 1970), 225–26.

11. J. Milton Emerson Journal, 1841–42, October 9, 1841, DU, 35; JT to HW, November 2, 1841, in Forbes Collection of American Historical Documents, Sale 1032, March 27, 2002.

12. JT to DW, October 11, 1841, in *LTT*, 2:126.

13. JT to LWT, October 11, 1841, in *LTT*, 2:128.

14. JT to LWT, November 2, 1841, in *LTT*, 2:129–31; JT, "Inaugural Address," in *MPP*, 4:37.

15. NBT to TR, July 12, 1845, Tyler Scrapbook, Tyler Family Papers, WM; NBT to HC, December 25, 1844, in *PHC*, 10:183.

16. *MPP*, 4:79.

17. *MPP*, 4:84–87; Peterson, *Presidencies of William Henry Harrison and John Tyler*, 96.

18. *MPP*, 4:84.

19. *MPP*, 4:84–87.

20. *MPP*, 4:86.

21. *MPP*, 4:84.

22. Monroe, *Republican Vision of John Tyler*, 118.

23. APU to NBT, December 23, 1841, in *LTT*, 2:153–54.

24. APU to NBT, December 23, 1841, in *LTT*, 2:153–54; APU to NBT, December 12, 1841, ibid.; APU to NBT, January 12, 1842, ibid.

25. APU to NBT, December 23, 1841, in *LTT*, 2:154; William A. Graham to James W. Bryan, February 10, 1842, in *PWAG*, 2:256.

26. APU to NBT, January 12, 1842, in *LTT*, 2:154–55.

27. DW to Edward Curtis, December 4, 1841, in *PDW-C*, 5:174–75n3; Charles Augustus Davis to DW, December 8, 1841, ibid.; Thurlow Weed to DW, December 18, 1841, ibid.; APU to NBT, December 12, 1841, in *LTT*, 2:153; *DM*, December 15, 16, 1841.

28. Gantz, "Clay and the Harvest of Bitter Fruit," 269–70.

29. HC to HC Jr., December 26, 1841, in *PHC*, 9:625.

30. Remini, *Henry Clay*, 600–601; Gantz, "Clay and the Harvest of Bitter Fruit," 273–74; William A. Graham to James W. Bryan, February 10, 1842, in *PWAG*, 2:255–56.

31. JCC to Wilson Lumpkin, December 26, 1841, in *PJCC*, 16:20.

32. Gantz, "Clay and the Harvest of Bitter Fruit," 274.

33. JCC to John R. Mathew[e]s, January 2, 1842, in *PJCC*, 16:31; JCC to V[irgil] Maxcy, December 26, 1841, ibid., 21.

34. Remini, *Daniel Webster*, 572.

35. JT to LWT, October 24, 1842, in *LTT*, 2:249; JT to RT, n.d., Forbes Collection of American Historical Documents, pt. 4, 2006.

36. Peterson, *Presidencies of William Henry Harrison and John Tyler*, 97–98; William B. Campbell to David Campbell, July 10, 1842, Campbell Family Papers, DU.

CHAPTER 12

1. Roberts, *America's First Great Depression*, 104.

2. Monroe, *Republican Vision of John Tyler*, 127.

3. *MPP*, 4:82; Peterson, *Presidencies of William Henry Harrison and John Tyler*, 99; *LTT*, 2:145–46, 149–50.

4. *MPP*, 4:81–82; Monroe, *Republican Vision of John Tyler*, 117–19.

5. Heidler and Heidler, *Henry Clay*, 360–62; Remini, *Henry Clay*, 602; HC, "Speech in Senate," March 1, 1842, in *PHC*, 9:665; Peterson, *Olive Branch and Sword*, 117.

6. *MPP*, 4:102.

7. APU to NBT, March 6, 1842, in *LTT*, 157–58.

8. *MPP*, 4:107–11; APU to NBT, March 28, 1842, in *LTT*, 2:165.

9. HC, "Speech in Senate," March 23, 1842, in *PHC*, 9:683.

10. HC, "Remark in Senate," March 30, 1842, in *PHC*, 9:689–90; Heidler and Heidler, *Henry Clay*, 362–65; HC to Richard Hines et al., March 21, 1842, in *PHC*, 9:681.

11. APU to NBT, March 13, 1842; APU to NBT, March 6, 1842, in *LTT*, 2:157–58.

12. S. Johnston to Abraham Robinson Johnston, January 2, 1842, Abraham Robinson Johnston Papers, Cincinnati Historical Society.

13. William A. Graham to David L. Swain, January 6, 1842, in *PWAG*, 2:249; Ellet, *Court Circles of the Republic*, 334. For the construction of this "unofficial" space at White House parties, see Allgor, *Parlor Politics*. For Priscilla Cooper Tyler's role, see Christopher J. Leahy, "Playing Her Greatest Role: Priscilla Cooper Tyler and the Politics of the White House Social Scene, 1841–1844," *VMHB* 120 (September 2012): 236–69.

14. Ellet, *Court Circles of the Republic*, 297–98; *New York Herald*, March 8, 1842, in *The Dolley Madison Digital Edition*, ed. Holly C. Shulman (Charlottesville: University of Virginia Press, Rotunda, 2004), http://rotunda.upress.virginia.edu/dmde/DPM5124, subscription required, accessed 30 January 2013; Frank Thomas, "Personal Traits of President Tyler and His Family," *Knickerbocker* 22 (July 1843): 49–50.

15. JT to Colonel Ware, March 15, 1842, Sang Autograph Collection, Seymour Library, Knox College, Galesburg, IL.

16. *Lexington (VA) Gazette*, January 13, 1904. On Royall, see Elizabeth J. Clapp, *A Notorious Woman: Anne Royall in Jacksonian America* (Charlottesville: University of Virginia Press, 2016).

17. *The Experiment* (Norwalk, OH), March 8, 1842; PCT journal, n.d., Elizabeth Tyler Coleman Papers, UA.

18. Coleman, *Priscilla Cooper Tyler and the American Scene*, 99.

19. *DM*, March 17, 1842; Nevins, *Diary of Philip Hone*, 2:591; JT to MTJ, July 6, 1842, in *LTT*, 2:172.

20. JT Jr. to George W. Southall, April 21, May 22, 1842, George Washington Southall Papers, WM.

21. JT Jr. to George W. Southall, May 22, 1842, George Washington Southall Papers, WM.

22. JT to Mrs. Martha Rochelle, September 4, 1841, James H. Rochelle Papers, DU; George B. Cary to James H. Rochelle, January 5, 1842, ibid.; JT to Mrs. Martha Rochelle, October 22, 1843, ibid.

23. JT to Elizabeth Waller, May 27, 1842, JT Papers, LC.

24. JT to MTJ, July 6, 1842, in *LTT*, 2:172.

25. Holloway, *Ladies of the White House*, 388.

26. Holt, *Rise and Fall of the American Whig Party*, 146.

27. HC to Richard Hines et al., March 21, 1842, in *PHC*, 9:681; HC to John J. Crittenden, June 3, 1842, ibid, 706.

28. Garrett Davis to John Payne, February 2, 1842, John Payne Papers, LC; Priestley H. Mangum to William A. Graham, May 12, 1842, in *PWAG*, 2:308–11; *DM*, July 6, 1842.

29. William B. Campbell to Gov. David Campbell, June 22, 1842, Campbell Family Papers, DU; HC to Leverett Saltonstall, June 7, 1842, in *PHC*, 9:708; Peterson, *Presidencies of William Henry Harrison and John Tyler*, 101.

30. James Irvin to James M. Bell, June 18, 1842, James M. Bell Papers, DU.

31. WPM to HC, June 15, 1842, in *PWPM*, 3:358–59; HC to WPM, June 7, 1842, in *PHC*, 9:707.

32. APU to NBT, n.d., in *LTT*, 2:167.

33. C[aleb] Cushing to HW, September 24, 1842, in *LTT*, 3:105; Cain, "Return of Republicanism," 272–73.

34. *MPP*, 4:180–83.

35. JT to Messrs. Harris, Graves, Mears, Connell, English, and Taylor, Committee, etc., July 2, 1842, in *LTT*, 2:171; William B. Campbell to Gov. David Campbell, June 30, 1842, Campbell Family Papers, DU.

36. Johanna Nicol Shields, "Whigs Reform the 'Bear Garden': Representation and the Apportionment Act of 1842," *JER* 5 (Fall 1985): 367; JT, "Special Message," June 25, 1842, Gerhard Peters and John T. Woolley, *The American Presidency Project*, https://www.presidency.ucsb.edu /documents/special-message-4212, accessed 24 July 2014; Leonard L. Richards, *The Slave Power: The Free North and Southern Domination, 1780–1860* (Baton Rouge: LSU Press, 2000), 102.

37. John J. Crittenden to HC, July 2, 1842, in *PHC*, 9:722.

38. William B. Campbell to Gov. David Campbell, June 30, 1842, Campbell Family Papers, DU; Peterson, *Presidencies of William Henry Harrison and John Tyler*, 102–3.

39. CG, 27th Cong., 2nd sess., 742–43; HC to John J. Crittenden, July 16, 1842, in *LTT*, 2:185–86.

40. Peterson, *Presidencies of William Henry Harrison and John Tyler*, 103.

41. JT to Robert McCandlish, July 10, 1842, in *LTT*, 2:173.

42. JT to Robert McCandlish, July 10, 1842, in *LTT*, 2:173.

43. William B. Campbell to David Campbell, July 10, 1842, Campbell Family Papers, DU.

44. DW to JT, August 8, 1842, in *PDW-C* 5:235–36; French, *Witness to the Young Republic*, 141; JCC quoted in Holt, *Rise and Fall of the American Whig Party*, 147.

45. John Quincy Adams diary 43, "1 January 1842–8 July 1843," August 10, 12, 15, 1842, pp. 232, 234, 237 (electronic edition), *The Diaries of John Quincy Adams: A Digital Collection* (Boston: Massachusetts Historical Society, 2005), http://www.masshist.org/jqadiaries, accessed July 12, 2019.

46. Peterson, *Presidencies of William Henry Harrison and John Tyler*, 104–5; French, *Witness to the Young Republic*, 142; *United States Democratic Review* 11 (October 1842): 425.

47. Peterson, *Presidencies of William Henry Harrison and John Tyler*, 105.

48. *MPP*, 4:190–93; *United States Democratic Review* 11 (October 1842): 427.

49. A pocket veto occurs when a president refuses to either sign a bill into law or send a veto message to Congress within the Constitution's mandated timeframe of ten days and Congress adjourns before the ten-day period expires. Holt, *Rise and Fall of the American Whig Party*, 166–67.

50. French, *Witness to the Young Republic*, 142–43.

51. Michael Brian Schiffer, *Power Struggles: Scientific Authority and the Creation of Practical Electricity before Edison* (Cambridge, MA: MIT Press, 2008), 124–27.

52. Holt, *Rise and Fall of the American Whig Party*, 148–49; Jesse Turner to William A. Graham, June 15, 1842, in *PWAG*, 2:343.

53. William B. Campbell to David Campbell, July 10, 24, 1842, Campbell Family Papers, DU.

54. Robert J. Spitzer, *The Presidential Veto: Touchstone of the American Presidency* (Albany: State University of New York Press, 1988), 72. Tyler was the first president to have a veto overridden by Congress.

55. Monroe, *Republican Vision of John Tyler*, 106; Marc Landy and Sidney M. Milkis, *Presidential Greatness* (Lawrence: University Press of Kansas, 2000), 98–99; *MPP*, 4:68.

CHAPTER 13

1. Erik J. Chaput, *The People's Martyr: Thomas Wilson Dorr and His 1842 Rhode Island Rebellion* (Lawrence: University Press of Kansas, 2013), 2–3; Ronald P. Formisano, "The Role of Women in the Dorr Rebellion," *Rhode Island History* 61 (1993): 91.

2. A debate occurred in the convention over whether to allow black suffrage. Dorr himself favored it and pushed for it strongly. But the delegates ultimately voted 46 to 18 against it. See Chaput, *People's Martyr*, 57–59.

3. Wilentz, *Rise of American Democracy*, 539–40.

4. George M. Dennison, *The Dorr War: Republicanism on Trial, 1831–1861* (Lexington: University Press of Kentucky, 1976), chaps. 1–3.

5. JT quoted in Dennison, *Dorr War*, 72; JT to "his Excellency the Governor of Rhode Island," April 11, 1842, in *LTT*, 2:194–96; Morgan, *A Whig Embattled*, 99.

6. Chaput, *People's Martyr*, 9; Dennison, *Dorr War*, 72–74; Levi Woodbury to Thomas Dorr, April 15, 1842, in John B. Rae, "Democrats and the Dorr Rebellion," *New England Quarterly* 9 (September 1936): 477; Brown quoted in David Grimsted, *American Mobbing, 1828–1861: Toward Civil War* (New York: Oxford University Press, 1998), 215.

7. Dennison, *Dorr War*, 75–76.

8. *Niles' National Register*, April 23, 1842; Glyndon G. Van Deusen, *Horace Greeley: Nineteenth-Century Crusader* (Philadelphia: University of Pennsylvania Press, 1953), 75; JCC quoted in *PJCC*, 16:239; Joseph Story to DW, April 26, 1842, in *PDW-C*, 5:202–3.

9. Dennison, *Dorr War*, 115–16.

10. Chaput, *People's Martyr*, 22–23.

11. Erik J. Chaput, "Proslavery and Antislavery Politics in Rhode Island's 1842 Dorr Rebellion," *New England Quarterly* 85 (December 2012): 683.

12. Chaput, *People's Martyr*, 129–30; Arthur May Mowry, "Tammany Hall and the Dorr Rebellion," *American Historical Review* 3 (January 1898): 294; Chaput, "Proslavery and Antislavery Politics," 659–61; John Ashworth, *Commerce and Compromise, 1820–1850*, vol. 1 of *Slavery, Capitalism, and Politics in the Antebellum Republic* (Cambridge: Cambridge University Press, 1995), 207; Wilentz, *Rise of American Democracy*, 545.

13. APU to NBT, April 20, 1842, in *LTT*, 2:198.

14. Ashworth, *Commerce and Compromise*, 207; William A. Graham to Paul C. Cameron, May 20, 1842, in *PWAG*, 2:313; Chaput, *People's Martyr*, 42–43.

15. Dennison, *Dorr War*, 79–80; Dorr quoted in Chaput, *People's Martyr*, 88.

16. JT to the Governor of the State of Rhode Island, May 7, 9, 1842; and Samuel W. King to JT, May 12, 1842, both in *MPP*, 4:293–95.

17. Rae, "Democrats and the Dorr Rebellion," 481n11.

18. Dennison, *Dorr War*, 85–87; Samuel W. King to JT, May 25, 1842, in *MPP*, 4:298.

19. JT to DW, May 27, 1842, in *PDW-C*, 5:213–14; JT to Elisha R. Porter, May 20, 1842, in *MPP*, 4:296.

20. Chaput, "Proslavery and Antislavery Politics," 683–84.

21. William A. Graham to Paul C. Cameron, May 20, 1842, in *PWAG*, 2:313.

22. J. C. Spencer to Brigadier General Eustis, May 29, 1842, in *MPP*, 4:300.

23. JT to DW, May 27, 1842, in *PDW-C*, 5:214; "Secret Contingent Fund Account," July 19, 1842, in *PDW-D*, 1:637.

24. Unknown to DW, June 3, 1842, in *MPP*, 4:300–301.

25. Dennison, *Dorr War*, 95–96; JT to Secretary of War, June 29, 1842, *MPP*, 4:307.

26. Dennison, *Dorr War*, 103, 195–96.

27. Dennison, *Dorr War*, 128–36; Peterson, *Presidencies of William Henry Harrison and John Tyler*, 111–12. JT's statement in his own defense is in *MPP*, 4:283–86. *Luther v. Borden* held that whether a state government is a legitimate "republican" form of government (as guaranteed by Article IV, Section 4 of the Constitution) is a political question to be decided by the president and Congress. DW argued the case before the Taney court.

28. Ambrose Dudley Mann to DW, May 25, 1842, in *PDW-C*, 5:213; APU to NBT, April 20, 1842, in *LTT*, 2:198; DW to JT, April 18, 1844, ibid., 199.

CHAPTER 14

1. Eric Robert Taylor, *If We Must Die: Shipboard Insurrections in the Era of the Atlantic Slave Trade* (Baton Rouge: LSU Press, 2006), 156–58.

2. Phillip Troutman, "Grapevine in the Slave Market: African American Geopolitical Literacy and the 1841 *Creole* Revolt," in *The Chattel Principle: Internal Slave Trades in the Americas*, ed. Walter Johnson (New Haven, CT: Yale University Press, 2004), 209–10; Howard Jones and Donald A. Rakestraw, *Prologue to Manifest Destiny: Anglo-American Relations in the 1840s* (Wilmington, DE: Scholarly Resources, 1997), 86–90.

3. DW to Edward Everett, January 29, 1842, in *PDW-D*,1:179–80; Matthew Mason, *Apostle of Union: A Political Biography of Edward Everett* (Chapel Hill: University of North Carolina Press, 2016), 140–44.

4. Jones and Rakestraw, *Prologue to Manifest Destiny*, 96.

5. *Emancipator*, December 10, 1841, quoted in *The Liberator* (Boston), December 17, 1841.

6. *DM*, December 28, 30, 1841.

7. Howard Jones, *To the Webster-Ashburton Treaty: A Study in Anglo-American Relations, 1783–1843* (Chapel Hill: University of North Carolina Press, 1977), 3–6, 10–16; Jones and Rakestraw, *Prologue to Manifest Destiny*, 7; *LTT*, 3:205–6.

8. Jones, *To the Webster-Ashburton Treaty*, 96.

9. Ralph W. Hidy, *The House of Baring in American Trade and Finance: English Merchant Bankers at Work, 1763–1861* (Cambridge, MA: Harvard University Press, 1949), 28–52; Edward Everett to DW, January 3, 1842, in *PDW-D*, 1:488.

10. Jones, *To the Webster-Ashburton Treaty*, 95–96; Scott Reynolds Nelson, *A Nation of Deadbeats: An Uncommon History of America's Financial Disasters* (New York: Alfred A. Knopf, 2012), 124; Jay Sexton, *Debtor Diplomacy: Finance and American Foreign Relations in the Civil War Era, 1837–1873* (Oxford: Clarendon, 2005), 28–29.

11. Sexton, *Debtor Diplomacy*, 35–36.

12. Francis Ormand Jonathan Smith to DW, [June 7, 1841], in *PDW-D*, 1:94–96.

13. House of Representatives, "Official Misconduct of the Late Secretary of State," *House Documents*, 29th Cong., 1st sess., no. 684, 1846.

14. Frederick Merk, *Fruits of Propaganda in the Tyler Administration*, with the collaboration of Lois Bannister Merk (Cambridge, MA: Harvard University Press, 1971), 62–64.

15. Ashburton quoted in Jones, *To the Webster-Ashburton Treaty*, 118; Lord Ashburton to Lord Aberdeen, April 26, 1842, in *PDW-D*, 1:544–45, 145n2; Ashburton to Aberdeen, May 29, 1842, ibid., 571.

16. Remini, *Daniel Webster*, 544.

17. Remini, *Daniel Webster*, 550.

18. Lord Ashburton to Lord Aberdeen, April 26, 1842, in *PDW-D*, 1:545–46; DW to John Fairfield and John Davis, April 11, 1842, ibid., 534–37; Jared Sparks to DW, February 15, 1842, ibid., 513–16; DW to Jared Sparks, May 14, 1842, ibid., 556–57; Jones, *To the Webster-Ashburton Treaty*, 120–21; Remini, *Daniel Webster*, 550.

19. Merk, *Fruits of Propaganda*, 68–69.

20. Jones, *To the Webster-Ashburton Treaty*, 93–94.

21. JT to DW, May 8, 1842, in *PDW-D*, 1:550; JT to DW, August 7, 1842, ibid., 671.

22. JGT to Juliana Gardiner, April 14, 1846, GTFP; JGT to MG, April 16, 1846, ibid.; DW to JT, August 24, 1842, in *PDW-D*, 1:695.

23. Lord Ashburton to DW, July 1, 1842, in *PDW-D*, 1:604.

24. Lord Ashburton to DW, July 1, 1842, in *PDW-D*, 1:604; Webster quoted in *LTT*, 2:217.

25. *LTT*, 2:217–18.

26. DW to William Pitt Preble, Edward Kavanagh, Edward Kent, and John Otis, July 15, 1842, in *PDW-D*, 1:622; William Pitt Preble, Edward Kavanagh, Edward Kent, and John Otis to DW, June 29, 1842, ibid., 592–603; DW to Lord Ashburton, July 8, 1842, ibid., 605–13.

27. Lord Ashburton to Lord Aberdeen, August 9, 1842, in *PDW-D*, 1:680–81.

28. Thomas LeDuc, "The Webster-Ashburton Treaty and the Minnesota Iron Ranges," *Journal of American History* 51 (December 1964): 476–81.

29. Jones, *To the Webster-Ashburton Treaty*, 134–37.

30. At one point in the negotiations, Webster and Ashburton believed separating the components into different treaties would ensure passage of the boundary settlement and eliminate the chance that southerners in the US Senate would vote it down because they objected to the provisions dealing with slavery. Tyler understood and to some extent shared the concerns of the two men but ultimately persuaded Webster to abandon the idea and link each component into one document. See JT to DW, August 8, 1842, in *PDW-D*, 1:679–80.

31. JT to DW, May 8, 1842, in *PDW-D*, 1:550; JT to DW, August 1, 1842, Tyler Family Papers, WM; Jones, *To the Webster-Ashburton Treaty*, 141.

32. Steven Heath Mitton, "The Free World Confronted: The Problem of Slavery and Progress in American Foreign Relations, 1833–1844" (Ph.D. diss., Louisiana State University, 2005), 60.

33. JT to DW, n.d., [1842], in *LTT*, 2:233.

34. Mitton, "Free World Confronted," 57–62.

35. Mitton, "Free World Confronted," xi.

36. Duff Green to JCC, January 24, 1842, in *PJCC*, 16:84; Green to JT, January 24, 1842, Duff Green Papers, SHC.

37. Mitton, "Free World Confronted," 90–95.

38. Ashburton quoted in Mitton, "Free World Confronted," 95.

39. *MPP,* 4:166–68.

40. Jones, *To the Webster-Ashburton Treaty,* 148–49; JT to DW, August 7, 1842, in *LTT,* 2:221–22; DW to Lord Ashburton, August 1, 1842, in *PDW-D* 1:658; Lord Ashburton to Lord Aberdeen, August 9, 1842, ibid., 680.

41. DW to WCR, August 10, 1842, WCR Papers, LC; JT to WCR, August 12, 1842, ibid.

42. APU to NBT, August 11, 1842, in *LTT,* 2:179; Benton, *Thirty Years' View,* 2:430–32, 449; JT to DW, n.d., [1842], in *LTT,* 2:235; DW to Edward Everett, December 29, 1842, in *PDW-D,* 1:871–72.

43. Lewis Cass to DW, September 17, 1842, copy, WCR Papers, LC; *MPP,* 4:196; JT to RT, August 29, 1858, in *LTT,* 2:240–41; "Ex-President Tyler's Letter, Of Mr. Barbee's Sheaf," *TQ* 32 (October 1950): 103–9; Don E. Fehrenbacher, *The Slaveholding Republic: An Account of the United States Government's Relations to Slavery,* completed and edited by Ward M. McAfee (New York: Oxford University Press, 2001), 169–70.

44. The entire text of the treaty is found in Jones, *To the Webster-Ashburton Treaty,* app., 181–87.

45. *LTT,* 3:205–6.

46. Stephen F. Knott, *Secret and Sanctioned: Covert Operations and the American Presidency* (New York: Oxford University Press, 1996), 120.

47. Stephen W. Stathis, "Former Presidents as Congressional Witnesses," *Presidential Studies Quarterly* 13 (Summer 1983): 458–59.

48. JT to DW, November 6, 1851, in *The History of America in Documents: Original Autograph Letters, Manuscripts, and Source Materials,* pt. 3 (New York: Rosenbach, 1951), 3; JT to DW, March 12, 1846, in *PDW-C,* 6:130; JT, "Second Annual Message," in *MPP,* 4:194–95; JT to LWT, October 24, 1842, JT Papers, LC; Sexton, *Debtor Diplomacy,* 38–39.

49. *MPP,* 4:211–13.

50. *MPP,* 4:213–14; John M. Belohlavek, *Broken Glass: Caleb Cushing and the Shattering of the Union* (Kent, OH: Kent State University Press, 2005), chap. 6.

51. Kenneth E. Shewmaker, "Forging the 'Great Chain': Daniel Webster and the Origins of American Foreign Policy toward East Asia and the Pacific, 1841–1852," *Proceedings of the American Philosophical Society* 129 (1985): 236; JT, "Fourth Annual Message," in *MPP,* 4:336; Edward P. Crapol, "John Tyler and the Pursuit of National Destiny," *JER* 17 (Fall 1997): 486.

CHAPTER 15

1. French, *Witness to the Young Republic,* 143.

2. *The Press* (Philadelphia), April 2, 1877.

3. Seager, *And Tyler Too,* 179.

4. Septimus Tustin to JT, September 1842, JT Papers, ser. 4, LC.

5. JT to RT, July 19, 1849, in *Forbes Collection of American Historical Documents,* pt. 5, Sale 1720, November 2, 2006.

6. RT to WCR, September 20, 1842, WCR Papers, LC; HW to JT, September 15, 1842, JT Papers, LC; *Hampton Roads (VA) Daily Press*, April 8, 1990.

7. JT to Andrew Jackson, September 20, 1842, in Lyon G. Tyler, ed., "Some Letters of Tyler, Calhoun, Polk, Murphy, Houston and Donelson," *TQ* 6 (April 1925): 225.

8. Monroe, *Republican Vision of John Tyler*, 153–54.

9. This is the theme of a book on more recent presidents. See Nancy Gibbs and Michael Duffy, *The Presidents Club: Inside the World's Most Exclusive Fraternity* (New York: Simon and Schuster, 2012).

10. JT to LWT, October 24, 1842, in *LTT*, 2:248–49.

11. *Washington Globe* quoted in *LTT*, 2:304.

12. JT to LWT, October 24, 1842, in *LTT*, 2:248–49.

13. C. W. Hunton to C. W. Gooch, June 19, 1842, Gooch Family Papers, UVA.

14. C. Campbell to Richard B. Gooch, May 30, 1842, Gooch Family Papers, UVA; Holt, *Rise and Fall of the American Whig Party*, 151–55.

15. JT to Alexander Gardiner, July 11, 1846, in *LTT*, 2:341–42; W. W. Irwin to Caleb Cushing, March 24, 1843; and DW to Caleb Cushing, March 29, 1843, ibid., 3:108–10.

16. JT to Alexander Gardiner, July 11, 1846, in *LTT*, 2:341–42.

17. Seager, *And Tyler Too*, 170–71, 224–25.

18. JT to Alexander Gardiner, July 11, 1846, in *LTT*, 2:341–42.

19. DW to Nicholas Biddle, March 11, 1843, in *The Correspondence of Nicholas Biddle Dealing with National Affairs, 1807–1844*, ed. Reginald C. McGrane (Boston: Houghton Mifflin, 1919), 345–46; DW to Edward Everett, April 23, 1843, in *PDW-D*, 1:916.

20. Garrett Davis to John Payne, February 2, 1842, John Payne Papers, LC.

21. *MPP*, 4:37–39; Holt, *Rise and Fall of the American Whig Party*, 150.

22. *MPP*, 4:37–39.

23. JT to HW, September 13, 1843, JT Papers, LC; William Hogan to Caleb Cushing, February 18, 1843; W. H. Fortin to B. H. Cheever, February 17, 1843; William Brigham to Caleb Cushing, February 17, 1843; George Story to Caleb Cushing, February 18, 1843; Linus Child to Caleb Cushing, February 18, 1843; Charles Paine to Caleb Cushing, April 19, 1843; N. F. Williams to Caleb Cushing, April 19, 1843; William H. Montague to Caleb Cushing, April 21, 1843; Samuel Bridge to Caleb Cushing, June 1, 1843; and Samuel Bridge to Caleb Cushing, June 3, 1843, Caleb Cushing Papers, LC; Silas Reed to D[avid] L. Ogden, February 25, 1843, Ogden Family Papers, DU; Holt, *Rise and Fall of the American Whig Party*, 150; *New York Tribune*, November 14, 1842; Seager, *And Tyler Too*, 232–33.

24. JT to John C. Spencer, May 12, 1843, JT Papers, LC; JT to George Roberts, June 1, 1843, ibid.; Silas Reed to JT, October 1, 1842, ibid.; JT to Spencer, December 18, 1843, ibid.; JT to Spencer, May 15, 1843, in Steven S. Raab Autographs, *Catalog No. 45* (September 2003); JT to Spencer, April 12, 1843, in *The History of America in Documents: Original Autograph Letters, Manuscripts, and Source Materials*, pt. 2 (New York: Rosenbach, 1950), 122; Cain, "Return of Republicanism," 277–78.

25. JT to John C. Spencer, September 2, 1843, JT Papers, LC; William C. Preston to JT, October 26, 1843, ibid.; Bailie Peyton to JT, December 17, 1843, ibid.; JT to Dolley Madison, September 26, 1844, in *Forbes Collection of American Historical Documents*, pt. 2, Sale 1139, Christie's, October 9, 2002; *CG*, 27th Cong., 3rd sess., 134, 144–45.

26. Alexander Hamilton Jr. to JT, April 23, 1842, JT Papers, LC; Seager, *And Tyler Too*, 220.

27. Seager, *And Tyler Too*, 221–22; Jonathan D. Sarna, *Jacksonian Jew: The Two Worlds of Mordecai Noah* (New York: Holmes and Meier, 1981), 146.

28. Chitwood, *John Tyler*, 373.

29. Seager, *And Tyler Too*, 223–24.

30. Walter Jones to Gales and Seaton, [*Washington National Intelligencer* office], June 18, 1843, Loose Letter, VHS; C. V. Woodbury to JT, January 13, 1843, Caleb Cushing Papers, LC.

31. Seager, *And Tyler Too*, 222–23; Sarna, *Jacksonian Jew*, 147.

32. *New York Evening Post*, March 16, 1843.

33. JT to unknown, June 14, 1842, JT Papers, LC; Peterson, *Presidencies of William Henry Harrison and John Tyler*, 182–83.

34. Kermit Hall, ed., *The Oxford Companion to the Supreme Court* (New York: Oxford University Press, 1992), 884–85.

35. Mitchel A. Sollenberger, *The President Shall Nominate: How Congress Trumps Executive Power* (Lawrence: University Press of Kansas, 2008), 66.

36. DW to JT, May 8, 1843, in "Webster-Tyler Letters," *TQ* 8 (1927): 23; JT to DW, May 8, 1843, ibid.

37. DW to JT, August 29, 1843, in "Webster-Tyler Letters," 24–26.

38. JT to John C. Spencer, September 2, 1843, JT Papers, LC.

39. JT to George Roberts, September 28, 1843, in "Letter of President Tyler," *WMQ*, 1st ser., 19 (January 1911): 216.

CHAPTER 16

1. PCT to her sister, October 1842, Priscilla Cooper Tyler's Journal, Elizabeth Tyler Coleman Papers, UA.

2. JT to LWT, October 24, 1842, in *LTT*, 2:248.

3. JT to Elizabeth Waller, January 16, 1843, JT Papers, DU; JT to MTJ, December 20, 1843, JT Papers, LC.

4. The salary of $25,000 in 1842 would be worth $757,575 in 2019 dollars. See the inflation calculator at davemanuel.com.

5. JT to Alfred Benson, November 5, 1842, JT Papers, LC.

6. JT to Elizabeth Waller, January 16, 1843, JT Papers, DU.

7. Seager, *And Tyler Too*, 179–80; JT to MTJ, May 2, 1842, Elizabeth Tyler Coleman Papers, UA; JT to MTJ, December 20, 1843, JT Papers, LC.

8. "Expenses of House from the 26th of February up to March 4, 1844," Bills and List of Tyler's Expenses, 1844, Correspondence of JT, Huntington Library, San Marino, CA.

9. Seager, *And Tyler Too*, 177.

10. "Reminiscences of Mrs. Julia G. Tyler," app. B, in *LTT*, 3:195.

11. "Reminiscences of Mrs. Julia G. Tyler," app. B, in *LTT*, 3:196–97.

12. MG to Alexander Gardiner, January 21, 1842, GTFP.

13. *Baltimore Sun*, July 3, 1844.

14. JT to RT, December 23, 1859, JT Papers, LC.

15. JG to Alexander and David Lyon Gardiner, January 6, 1843, quoted in "Julia Gardiner

Tyler: A Nineteenth-Century Woman," by Theodore Delaney (Ph.D. diss., College of William and Mary, 1995), 59.

16. Marie Gardiner to JG, January 4, 1843, "Letters from Tyler Trunks," *TQ* 18 (July 1936): 13.

17. Juliana Gardiner to Alexander Gardiner, January 27, 1843, GTFP.

18. Seager, *And Tyler Too*, 194–95.

19. "Mrs. John Tyler," *Louisville (KY) Courier-Journal*, July 14, 1889.

20. Seager, *And Tyler Too*, 196–97.

21. Seager, *And Tyler Too*, 198–99.

22. J. J. Bailey to JG, May 13, 1843, "Letters from Tyler Trunks," *TQ* 18 (July 1936): 17–18.

CHAPTER 17

1. Joel H. Silbey, *Storm over Texas: The Annexation Controversy and the Road to Civil War* (New York: Oxford University Press, 2005), chap. 1; John H. Schroeder, "Annexation or Independence: The Texas Issue in American Politics, 1836–1845," *Southwestern Historical Quarterly* 90 (1985), 137–47; Frederick Merk, *Slavery and the Annexation of Texas* (New York: Alfred A. Knopf, 1972), 192–204.

2. Isaac Van Zandt to Anson Jones, March 15, 1842 [*sic*, 1843], in Anson Jones, *Memoranda and Official Correspondence Relating to the Republic of Texas, Its History and Annexation* (New York: D. Appleton, 1859), 213; Van Zandt to Jones, March 16, 1843, ibid., 218.

3. Van Zandt to Jones et al., April 5, 1843; and Van Zandt to Jones, April 19, 1843, in Jones, *Memoranda and Official Correspondence*, 221–22.

4. Haynes, *Unfinished Revolution*, 234–35; Freehling, *Road to Disunion*, vol. 1, *Secessionists at Bay*, 369–71; Leila M. Roeckell, "Bonds over Bondage: British Opposition to the Annexation of Texas," *JER* 19 (Summer 1999): 265–66; Charles Elliott to Anson Jones, July 7, 1843, in Jones, *Memoranda and Official Correspondence*, 226; Sam Houston to Anson Jones, July 30, 1843, ibid., 233; Jesse S. Reeves, *American Diplomacy under Tyler and Polk* (1907; repr., Gloucester, MA: Peter Smith, 1967), 122–23.

5. JT to Waddy Thompson, August 28, 1843, in "Correspondence of President Tyler," *WMQ*, 1st ser., 12 (January 1904): 140–41.

6. Mitton, "Free World Confronted," 115–16, 122; Seymour Drescher, *The Mighty Experiment: Free Labor versus Slavery in British Emancipation* (New York: Oxford University Press, 2002), chaps. 8–12.

7. JT to Edward Everett, April 27, 1843, in Merk, *Slavery and the Annexation of Texas*, 211–12; Duff Green to JT, May 31, 1843, ibid., 217–21; Duff Green to JT, July 3, 1843, ibid., 221–24; Ashbel Smith to Anson Jones, August 2, 1843, in Jones, *Memoranda and Official Correspondence*, 236–37; W. Stephen Belko, *The Invincible Duff Green: Whig of the West* (Columbia: University of Missouri Press, 2006), 359–67; Freehling, *Road to Disunion*, vol. 1, *Secessionists at Bay*, 385.

8. To replace Upshur as navy secretary, Tyler wanted his friend Capt. Robert Stockton, a naval officer of distinction. Stockton turned him down, so Tyler named Massachusetts Democrat David Henshaw to the post.

9. APU to William S. Murphy, August 8, 1843, in *Diplomatic Correspondence of the United States: Inter-American Affairs, 1831–1860*, ed. William R. Manning, 12 vols. (Washington, DC: Car-

negie Endowment for International Peace, 1939), 12:45–46; Mitton, "Free World Confronted," 120–23; Edward Bartlett Rugemer, *The Problem of Emancipation: The Caribbean Roots of the American Civil War* (Baton Rouge: LSU Press, 2008), 212–13.

10. JT to Waddy Thompson, August 28, 1843, in "Correspondence of President Tyler," 140–41.

11. Jones, *Memoranda and Official Correspondence,* 82.

12. Jay Sexton, *The Monroe Doctrine: Empire and Nation in Nineteenth-Century America* (New York: Hill and Wang, 2011), 90–91; Mason, *Apostle of Union,* 144–47; Karp, *This Vast Southern Empire,* chap. 3. Matthew Karp presents impressive evidence to support his argument that southern foreign-policy elites like Upshur and, later, Calhoun, egged on by Green, framed their response to the British threat to slavery in Cuba and Brazil as a hemispheric contest that required a strong US response. But I think he conflates the zeal of Green, Upshur, and Calhoun, who were largely outliers, with the attitude of Tyler, who, in my reading of the evidence, was much less *ideologically* committed to saving slavery in Cuba and Brazil. This is not to say that Tyler wished to see slavery end there. He chose to show American strength when it was necessary. But he did not hold the staunch "proslavery" views shared by Upshur and Calhoun, which Karp argues sustained their course of action on the matter. See also Joseph A. Fry, *Dixie Looks Abroad: The South and U.S. Foreign Relations, 1789–1973* (Baton Rouge: LSU Press, 2002), 54–57.

13. *LTT,* 1:568; APU to JCC, August 14, 1843, in *PJCC,* 17:355.

14. William S. Murphy to Hugh S. Legaré, July 8, 1843, in Manning, *Diplomatic Correspondence,* 12:295; Isaac Van Zandt to Anson Jones, August 12, 1843, in Jones, *Memoranda and Official Correspondence,* 243–44.

15. JT to Edward Everett, April 27, 1843, in Merk, *Slavery and the Annexation of Texas,* 212.

16. APU to NBT, October 10, 1843, Tucker-Coleman Papers, WM (also partially reprinted in Merk, *Slavery and the Annexation of Texas,* 234); APU to William S. Murphy, September 22, 1843, in Manning, *Diplomatic Correspondence,* 12:51–52.

17. *DM,* October 30, 31, November 15, 16, 27, 1843, reprinted in Merk, *Slavery and the Annexation of Texas,* 245–57.

18. APU to Isaac Van Zandt, October 16, 1843, in Manning, *Diplomatic Correspondence,* 12:53–54.

19. Com. John G. Tod to Anson Jones, October 25, 1843, in Jones, *Memoranda and Official Correspondence,* 262; *LTT,* 2:281.

20. *MPP,* 4:262.

21. Gen. J. P. Henderson to Anson Jones, December 20, 1843, in Jones, *Memoranda and Official Correspondence,* 279; APU to William S. Murphy, January 16, 1844, in Manning, *Diplomatic Correspondence,* 12:61.

22. APU to William S. Murphy, January 16, 1844, in Manning, *Diplomatic Correspondence,* 12:64.

23. William S. Murphy to APU, February 15, 1844 (two letters); Anson Jones to William S. Murphy, February 15, 1844; and William S. Murphy to APU, February 19, 1844, in Manning, *Diplomatic Correspondence,* 12:329–32; Sam Houston to Andrew Jackson, February 16, 1844, in *Correspondence of Andrew Jackson,* ed. John Spencer Bassett, 7 vols. (Washington, DC: Carnegie Institution of Washington, 1927–1928), 4:262; Edward P. Crapol, *John Tyler: The Accidental President* (Chapel Hill: University of North Carolina Press, 2006), 202–3.

24. *Letter of Mr. Walker, of Mississippi, Relative to the Annexation of Texas* (Washington, DC: Printed at the *Globe* Office, 1844), reprinted in Merk, *Fruits of Propaganda,* 221–52. See also ibid., 95–128.

25. Thomas R. Hietala, *Manifest Design: Anxious Aggrandizement in Late Jacksonian America* (Ithaca, NY: Cornell University Press, 1985), 26–35; Stephen John Hartnett, *Democratic Dissent and the Cultural Fictions of Antebellum America* (Urbana: University of Illinois Press, 2002), 107; JT in *Niles' Register*, September 11, 1847, quoted in Merk, *Fruits of Propaganda*, 27; C. H. Raymond to Anson Jones, February 17, 1844, in Jones, *Memoranda and Official Correspondence*, 314–15.

26. Mary Ann Galt and Eliza Fisk Harwood to Tristrim Lowther Skinner, August 4, 1843, Skinner Family Papers, SHC; JT to Mrs. Benson, November 23, 1843, Sale 7881, Christie's, New York City, 12 June 1996. I am grateful to Mary Maillard, editor of the Skinner Family Papers and publisher of four e-books on the collection, who allowed me to see her transcription of the Galt and Harwood letter before publication.

27. Seager, *And Tyler Too*, 203.

28. A. H. Miles, "The 'Princeton' Explosion," *Proceedings of the United States Naval Institute* 52 (November 1926): 2225–45.

29. John M. McCalla to Maria McCalla, March 2, 1844, John Moore McCalla Papers, DU; French, *Witness to the Young Republic*, 159–61; *Baltimore Sun*, March 4, 1844.

30. *Brooklyn Daily Eagle*, March 4, 1844; *Gettysburg Compiler*, March 11, 1844; French, *Witness to the Young Republic*, 161.

31. JT to MTJ, March 4, 1844, in *LTT*, 2:289; JT to David Henshaw, March 5, 1844, *Forbes Collection of American Historical Documents*, pt. 3, Sale 1685, Rockefeller Plaza, New York City, November 15, 2005.

32. E. Brooks to JT, March 12, 1844, GTFP.

33. JT to Mrs. [Anne] Gilmer, March 4, 1844, JT Papers, LC.

34. *Utica (NY) Daily Gazette*, March 13, 1844; *New Orleans Times-Picayune*, March 17, 1844.

35. JT to John Young Mason, March 5, 1844, Mason Family Papers, VHS.

36. Theophilus Fisk to James K. Polk, March 9, 1844; Aaron V. Brown to Polk, March 10, 1844; Cave Johnson to Polk, March 10, 1844; and Theophilus Fisk to Polk, March 13, 1844, in *Correspondence of James K. Polk*, ed. Wayne Cutler, 9 vols. (Nashville: Vanderbilt University Press, 1969–96), 7:82–89; James K. Polk to Theophilus Fisk, March 20, 1844, in *LTT*, 3:133–34; JT to John Young Mason, March 14, 1844, Mason Family Papers, VHS.

37. Charles M. Wiltse, *John C. Calhoun: Sectionalist, 1840–1850* (Indianapolis: Bobbs-Merrill, 1951), 161–63; John Niven, *John C. Calhoun and the Price of Union* (Baton Rouge: LSU Press, 1988), 272–73; JCC to Thomas Walker Gilmer, December 25, 1843, in *LTT*, 2:296. In a letter to Duff Green, Calhoun wrote what may be interpreted as a refutation of the claim made in Wiltse's book: "There was no foundation for the rumor of my going into Mr. [John] Tyler's Cabinet. I have given him a fair support, whenever I could, but without the least understanding between us." See JCC to Green, August 31, 1842, in *PJCC*, 16:437.

38. Wise, *Seven Decades of the Union*, 222–25.

39. Chitwood, *John Tyler*, 286–87; Seager, *And Tyler Too*, 217; Simpson, *Good Southerner* 57–58, 332–33n42.

40. JT to JCC, March 6, 1844 (two letters), in *PJCC*, 17:828.

41. Freehling, *Road to Disunion*, vol. 1, *Secessionists at Bay*, 407–8. The treaty is reprinted in *PJCC*, 18:215–19.

42. Charles Sellers, *James K. Polk: Continentalist, 1843–1846* (Princeton, NJ: Princeton University Press, 1966), 57–58.

43. Edward Everett to JCC, April 17, 1844, in *PJCC*, 18:263.

44. JCC to Richard Pakenham, April 18, 1844, in *PJCC*, 18:273-78.

45. William J. Cooper Jr., *The South and the Politics of Slavery, 1828–1856* (Baton Rouge: LSU Press, 1978), 191–92, app. A, 375–76; Haynes, *Unfinished Revolution*, 243–44.

46. JT to RT, April 17, 1850, in *LTT*, 2:483; JT to DW, April 17, 1850, JT Papers, LC. For the economic effects of the "monopoly of the cotton plant" around which Tyler explained his pursuit of Texas, see Brian Schoen, *The Fragile Fabric of Union: Cotton, Federal Politics, and the Global Origins of the Civil War* (Baltimore: Johns Hopkins University Press, 2009), 183–95. For the global importance of cotton and America's role in the international market, see Sven Beckert, *Empire of Cotton: A Global History* (New York: Vintage, 2014).

47. JT to Andrew Jackson, April 18, 1844, in Bassett, *Correspondence of Andrew Jackson*, 6:279.

48. Silas Wright quoted in Silbey, *Storm over Texas*, 45; James McDowell to members of Central Democratic Committee [of Richmond], May 6, 1844, Ritchie-Harrison Papers, WM.

49. Michael A. Morrison, *Slavery and the American West: The Eclipse of Manifest Destiny and the Coming of the Civil War* (Chapel Hill: University of North Carolina Press, 1997), chap. 1; Rachel A. Shelden, "Not So Strange Bedfellows: Northern and Southern Whigs and the Texas Annexation Controversy, 1844–1845," in *A Political Nation: New Directions in Mid-Nineteenth-Century American Political History,* ed. Gary W. Gallagher and Rachel A. Shelden (Charlottesville: University of Virginia Press, 2012), 11–35.

50. C. H. Raymond to Anson Jones, April 24, 1844, in Jones, *Memoranda and Official Correspondence*, 344; Arthur Campbell to Gov. David Campbell, February 23, 1845, Campbell Family Papers, DU.

51. JT to HW, [n.d.], in *LTT*, 2:317; "President Tyler's Letter of Acceptance," May 30, 1844, ibid., 320–21.

52. JT to HW, [n.d.], in *LTT*, 2:317; JT to RT, June 3, 1858, JT Papers, LC.

53. William King quoted in Hietala, *Manifest Design*, 40; *MPP*, 4:323–27.

54. MTJ to JT, [n.d.; 1844?], GTFP; JT to MTJ, June 18, 1844, Presidential Autograph Collection, Collection of the Albany Institute of History and Art Library, Albany, NY.

55. JT to MTJ, April 21, 1844, Heritage Auctions, February 2006, Dallas Books, Autographs and Manuscripts Auction, New York City, Lot 26128.

56. JT to Juliana Gardiner, April 20, 1844, GTFP.

57. Seager, *And Tyler Too*, 207.

58. Juliana Gardiner to JT, April 22, 1844, Tyler Family Papers, WM, typescript.

59. *Brooklyn Daily Eagle*, June 27, 1844; Juliana Gardiner to JGT, July 9, 1844, "Letters from Tyler Trunks," *TQ* 18 (January 1937): 142.

60. JGT to Juliana Gardiner, June 30, 1844, "Letters from Tyler Trunks," *TQ* 18 (July 1936): 29; JGT to Juliana Gardiner, July 11, 1844, "Letters from Tyler Trunks," *TQ* 18 (January 1937): 143–46; JT to MTJ, June 18, 1844, Presidential Autograph Collection, Collection of the Albany Institute of History and Art Library, Albany, NY.

61. AG to JGT, June 28, 1844, "Letters from Tyler Trunks," *TQ* 18 (July 1936): 2; *Brooklyn Daily Eagle*, June 27, 1844; Jane Tayloe (Lomax) to Eleanor Worthington, July 7, 1844, Lomax Family Papers, VHS; Allan Nevins and Milton Halsey Thomas, eds., *The Diary of George Templeton Strong: Young Man in New York, 1835–1849* (New York: Macmillan, 1952), 238.

62. JGT to Juliana Gardiner, July 1844, "Letters from Tyler Trunks," *TQ* 18 (October 1936): 93.

63. Juliana Gardiner to JGT, July 1844, "Letters from Tyler Trunks," *TQ* 18 (October 1936): 94–95; MG to JGT, July 8, 1844, ibid., 141.

64. MG to JGT, July 8, 1844, "Letters from Tyler Trunks," *TQ* 18 (October 1936): 141; AG to JGT, October 11, 1844, GTFP; MG to JGT, October 23, 1844, ibid.; JT to AG, October 18, 1844, Tyler Family Papers, WM.

65. *DM*, August 21, 1844; Calvin Blythe to JT, August 27, 1844, Correspondence of John Tyler, Huntington Library, San Marino, CA; JT to AG, July 11, 1846, in *LTT*, 2:341–42; Andrew Jackson to J. B. Sutherland, September 2, 1844, ibid., 341.

66. Holt, *Rise and Fall of the American Whig Party*, 198–99; Cooper, *South and the Politics of Slavery*, 224.

67. *MPP*, 4:342–45.

68. F. W. Thomas to JGT, February [12], 1845, Tyler Family Papers, WM, typescript; Seager, *And Tyler Too*, 262–65.

69. AG, "Mrs. Tyler's Final Ball," GTFP.

70. Seager, *And Tyler Too*, 263; MG to Juliana Gardiner, July 2, 1844, Tyler Family Papers, WM, typescript; AG, "Mrs. Tyler's Final Ball."

71. MG quoted in Seager, *And Tyler Too*, 263.

72. "Reminiscences of Julia G. Tyler," in *LTT*, 3:200.

73. *CG*, 28th Cong., 2nd sess., 359–63.

74. Silbey, *Storm over Texas*, 1–5; *LTT*, 2:364–65. Julia made a necklace out of the pen and wore it from time to time until it was misplaced sometime after her husband's death. See "Reminiscences of Mrs. Julia G. Tyler," ibid., 3:200.

75. *LTT*, 2:364–65; JT to Charles A. Wickliffe, November 20, 1848, Preston Davie Papers, VHS, typescript; Charles A. Wickliffe to JT, December 20, 1848, ibid.

76. JT to HW, April 20, 1852, in *LTT*, 3:170. Texas became part of the United States on December 29, 1845.

77. John Quincy Adams diary 45, "1 January 1845–10 August 1846," February 28, 1845, p. 59 (electronic edition), *The Diaries of John Quincy Adams: A Digital Collection* (Boston: Massachusetts Historical Society, 2005), http://www.masshist.org/jqadiaries, accessed July 13, 2019.

78. Gary Lawson and Guy Seidman, *The Constitution of Empire: Territorial Expansion & American Legal History* (New Haven, CT: Yale University Press, 2004), 92–93.

CHAPTER 18

1. JGT to Mrs. [Juliana] Gardiner, March 6, 1845; and AG to MG, March 4, 1845, in *LTT*, 2:367–70; "Retirement of Ex-President Tyler and Family," *Journal of Commerce*, March 3, 1845, ibid., 366–68.

2. JT to N. P. Tallmadge, November 7, 1844, in "Letters of Tyler, Calhoun, Polk, Murphy, Houston and Donelson," *TQ* 7 (July 1925): 9.

3. JGT to Juliana Gardiner, July 11, 1844, "Letters from Tyler Trunks," *TQ* 18 (January 1937): 145; JGT to Juliana Gardiner, July 22, 1844, ibid., 159; JT to MTJ, April 21, 1844, Heritage Auctions, February 2006, Dallas Books, Autographs and Manuscripts Auction, New York City, Lot 26128.

4. Belko, *Philip Pendleton Barbour*, 48.

5. JGT to AG, April 1845, Tyler Family Papers, WM, typescript.

6. JGT to Juliana Gardiner, July 11, 1844, "Letters from Tyler Trunks," *TQ* 18 (January 1937): 145; JT to Philip R. Fendall, April 9, 1845, Philip Fendall Papers, DU.

7. On paternalism, see Kolchin, *American Slavery*, 111–32; Genovese, *Roll, Jordan, Roll*; and Oakes, *The Ruling Race*. See also chapter 5, note 6 above.

8. Eben Horsford to Charity [Norton] Horsford, February 14, 1852, Eben Norton Horsford Papers, Archives and Special Collections, Rensselaer Polytechnic Institute, Troy, NY.

9. JT to DG, April 10, 1848, Tyler Family Papers, WM; Ralph V. Anderson and Robert E. Gallman, "Slaves as Fixed Capital: Slave Labor and Southern Economic Development," *Journal of American History* 64 (June 1977): 28; Gavin Wright, "Slavery and American Agricultural History," *Agricultural History* 77 (Fall 2003): 543.

10. Oakes, *Ruling Race*, 156; Kolchin, *American Slavery*, 109; Eugene D. Genovese and Elizabeth Fox-Genovese, *Fatal Self-Deception: Slaveholding Paternalism in the Old South* (Cambridge: Cambridge University Press, 2011), 1–5.

11. JGT to MG, May 29, 1845, GTFP; JT to Charles A. Wickliffe, August 24, 1845, Preston Davie Papers, VHS, typescript; JT to John Young Mason, August 23, 1845, Mason Family Papers, VHS; JT to Dr. William Collins, September 17, 1845, "Some Letters of Tyler, Calhoun, Polk, Murphy, Houston and Donelson," *TQ* 7 (July 1925): 11. In the summer of 1845, President Polk sent 3,500 US troops, under the command of Brig. Gen. Zachary Taylor, to the Nueces River, citing a possible Mexican invasion.

12. JT to Dr. William Collins, September 17, 1845, "Some Letters of Tyler, Calhoun, Polk, Murphy, Houston and Donelson," 10; Sellers, *James K. Polk: Continentalist, 1843–1846*, 268–69.

13. JT to MTJ, June 18, 1844, Presidential Autograph Collection, Albany Institute of History and Art Library, Albany, NY.

14. Lizzy [Elizabeth] T. Waller to JGT, September 11, 1844, GTFP; JGT to Juliana Gardiner, December 28, 1846, ibid.; JT to Elizabeth Waller, March 1, 1845, JT Papers, DU.

15. JGT to Juliana Gardiner, April 3, 1845, May 21, 1855, GTFP; JGT to MG, April 16, 1845, May 18, 1855, ibid.; Alice Tyler to JGT, November 6, 1844, May 29, 1845, ibid. For Julia's attitude toward Alice, see JGT to Juliana Gardiner, February 18, April 2, 30, 1851, ibid.

16. JGT to MG, April 16, 1845, GTFP.

17. Coleman, *Priscilla Cooper Tyler and the American Scene*, 109–21; JT to RT, November 20, 1845, in *LTT*, 2:447; JGT to My dear Brother [AG], July 22, 1845, GTFP; JT to RT, July 16, 1849, Tyler Family Papers, WM, typescript.

18. JGT to Juliana Gardiner, October 21, 1845, GTFP; JGT to My dear Brother [AG], July 22, 1845, ibid.

19. *Baltimore Sun*, July 6, 1844; *New Orleans Times-Picayune*, July 16, 1844; JGT to Juliana Gardiner, July 11, 1844, "Letters from Tyler Trunks," *TQ* 18 (January 1937): 144.

20. *New York Herald*, April 30, 1845.

21. JGT to MG, April 10, 1845, Tyler Family Papers, WM, typescript; JGT to MG, March 18, 1845, ibid., typescript; JGT to MG, April 16, 1845, GTFP.

22. JGT to Juliana Gardiner, April 3, 1845, GTFP; JGT to AG, April 1845, Tyler Family Papers, WM, typescript; JGT to Juliana Gardiner, September 1845, ibid., typescript.

23. JGT to My dear Brother [likely AG], June 17, 1845, Tyler Family Papers, WM, typescript; JGT to MG, June 29, 1845, GTFP; Juliana Gardiner to MG, July 7, 1845, ibid.

24. JGT to My dear Brother [likely AG], June 17, 1845, Tyler Family Papers, WM, typescript; Charlene M. Boyer Lewis, *Ladies and Gentlemen on Display: Planter Society at the Virginia Springs, 1790–1860* (Charlottesville: University Press of Virginia, 2001), 18–20.

25. JGT to Juliana Gardiner, August 10, 1845, Tyler Family Papers, WM, typescript.

26. John C. Rutherfoord to TR, September 1, 1845, *John P. Branch Historical Papers of Randolph-Macon College* 4 (June 1916): 385–86.

27. JT to John Young Mason, August 23, 1845, Mason Family Papers, VHS; JT to Charles A. Wickliffe, August 24, 1845, Preston Davie Papers, VHS, typescript.

28. John C. Rutherfoord to TR, September 1, 1845, *John P. Branch Historical Papers of Randolph-Macon College* 4 (June 1916): 386.

29. J. Holbrook to JT, November 9, 1844, Tyler Family Papers, WM.

30. JT to RT, November 20, 1845, in *LTT*, 2:446–47.

31. JGT to My dear Brother [AG], July 22, 1845, GTFP; JT to RT, July 16, 1849, Tyler Family Papers, WM, typescript; JT to RT, November 20, 1845, in *LTT*, 2:447.

32. JGT to My dear Brother [likely AG], June 17, 1845, Tyler Family Papers, WM, typescript.

33. JGT to MG, October 9, 1845, GTFP. T.H.Breen and Timothy Hall, *Colonial America in an Atlantic World* (New York: Pearson/Longman, 2004), 157, briefly discuss the effects of beriberi on enslaved Africans during the so-called "seasoning" process in the Caribbean.

34. JT to RT, November 20, 1845, in *LTT*, 2:447; JT to Elizabeth Waller, April 21, 1846, JT Papers, DU.

35. JGT to MG, October 9, 1845, GTFP; JT to Elizabeth Waller, October 18, 1845, JT Papers, DU.

36. DLG to JGT, November 10, 1845, GTFP; JGT to Juliana Gardiner, December 28, 1846, ibid.

37. William Boulware to JT, October 30, 1844, Tyler Family Papers, WM, typescript; DLG to JGT, November 10, 1845, GTFP; JGT to Juliana Gardiner, February 10, 1846, ibid.

38. JT to RT, January 1, 1846, in *LTT*, 2:450.

39. DLG to JGT, February 22, 1846, GTFP.

40. JT to RT, June 1, 1846, in *LTT*, 2:457; James K. Polk to JT, March 8, 1847, in *Correspondence of James K. Polk*, ed. Tom Chaffin and Michael David Cohen, 12 vols. (Knoxville: University of Tennessee Press, 2013), 12:117; JT Jr. to James K. Polk, March 16, 1847, ibid., 128.

41. Seager, *And Tyler Too*, 362.

42. JT to Charles A. Wickliffe, August 24, 1845, Preston Davie Papers, VHS, typescript; AG to JGT, November 28, 1846, GTFP; AG to JGT, November 29, 1845, ibid.

43. JT to AG, November 9, 1846, Tyler Family Papers, WM; JT to Messrs. Tilford and Samuel, March 2, 1847, ibid.; JT to AG, February 14, 21, March 16, April 16, May 21, 1848, March 27, April 24, 1849, January 7, 24, May 30, June 15, 1850, ibid.; AG to JGT, December 5, 1846, GTFP; JT to Charles A. Wickliffe, August 12, 1850, Preston Davie Papers, VHS, typescript; AG to JT, November 15, 1849, Correspondence of JT, Huntington Library, San Marino, CA.

44. JT to AG, March 20, 1850, Tyler Family Papers, WM.

45. For example, see JT to DLG, May 4, 1847, Tyler Family Papers, WM; JT to AG, April 4,

October 21, November 7, 1848, March 6, 15, 1850, ibid. See also AG to DLG, September 15, 1846, GTFP; and DLG's Account Book, 1851–52, ibid.

46. JT to DLG, May 4, 1847, Tyler Family Papers, WM.

47. AG to JGT, November 28, 1846, GTFP; David Hedges to Juliana Gardiner, February 22, 1851, ibid.; JGT to Juliana Gardiner, February 1, 8, March 7, 15, 24, 1851, ibid.; JGT to MGB, April 21, 1851, ibid.; JT to DLG, June 23, 1854, Tyler Family Papers, WM.

48. JT to John Young Mason, November 24, 1850, October 30, 1851, July 2, 1852, March 5, 1853, Mason Family Papers, VHS; JT to CW, October 25, 1852, March 2, 1854, CW Papers, WM.

49. JT to Mr. Wheaton, June 9, 1856, Tyler Family Papers, WM; MGB to Juliana Gardiner, March 20, 1855, Gardiner Papers, Tyler Family Papers, WM, typescript.

50. JT to John Young Mason, July 2, 1852, Mason Family Papers, VHS; JT to George Frederick Holmes, February 23, 1847 (copy), George Frederick Holmes Letterbook, George Frederick Holmes Papers, DU; Harvey Wish, "George Frederick Holmes and Southern Periodical Literature of the Mid-Nineteenth Century," *JSH* 7 (August 1941): 347; JGT to Juliana Gardiner, July 11, 1848, April 12, 1858, GTFP; John Rutherfoord to JT, November 18, 1848, Letter 99, Tucker-Ewell Papers, LVA; George M. Dallas to JT, June 29, 1855, JT Papers, LC; HW to JT, August 7, 1855, ibid.; Lucian Minor to JT, August 30, 1855, ibid.; John C. Rutherfoord to JT, September 15, 1855, ibid.; Benjamin Stoddart Ewell to JT, September 6, 1855, GTFP; JT to Hugh Blair Grigsby, November 23, 1859, JT Papers, ser. 4, LC, typescript; JT to Dr. Sprague, October 22, 1860, in *LTT*, 2:382–83; O'Brien, *Conjectures of Order*, 1:144–45, 316, 327.

51. JT to J. M. Porter, February 19, 1850, Tyler Family Papers, WM.

52. JCC, "Speech in Reply to Thomas H. Benton on the Mexican War," February 24, 1847, in *PJCC*, 24:196.

53. JT to AG, March 11, 1847, in *LTT*, 2:420.

54. JT to AG, March 11, 1847, in *LTT*, 2:420.

55. JT to RT, May 9, 1856, Personal Papers Collection, LVA; JT to RT, March 11, 1847, in *LTT*, 2:421; JT to John S. Cunningham, May 8, 1856, ibid., 415; JT to AG, June 17, 1847, ibid., 426.

56. JT, "To the Editors of the 'Enquirer,'" September 1, 1847, in *LTT*, 2:428–31; JT, "To the Editors of the *Richmond Enquirer*," in *LTT*, 2:425.

57. John Young Mason to JT, September 18, 1848, Mason Family Papers, VHS; JT to Mason, September 22, 1848, ibid.; Mason to JT, November 1, 1848, ibid.; JT to Mason, November 13, 27, December 11, 1848, ibid.; JT to AG, November 24, 1848, Tyler Family Papers, WM.

58. JT to AG, August 7, 1848, Tyler Family Papers, WM; Paul H. Bergeron, *The Presidency of James K. Polk* (Lawrence: University Press of Kansas, 1987), 55–56.

59. JT, "To the Editors of the 'Enquirer,'" September 1, 1847, in *LTT*, 2:428.

CHAPTER 19

1. JT to DLG, April 10, 1848, Tyler Family Papers, WM.

2. PCT to Frederic Raoul, July 14, 1847, Elizabeth Tyler Coleman Papers, UA; JGT to Juliana Gardiner, June 21, 1847, GTFP.

3. JGT to AG, January 20, 1847, GTFP; JT to MGB, April 3, 1849, in "Letters of John Tyler, 1849," *Massachusetts Historical Society Proceedings* 61 (June 1928): 220; JGT to MGB, May 1851, GTFP.

4. JT to AG, January 7, 1850, Tyler Family Papers, WM.

5. JT to J. M. Porter, February 19, 1850, Tyler Family Papers, WM.

6. JT to AG, June 15, 1850, Tyler Family Papers, WM; John H. Beeckman to MGB, September 23, 1849, GTFP; Henry Beeckman Livingston Freemont to Gilbert Beeckman, April 27, 1850, Gardiner Papers, Tyler Family Papers, WM, typescript.

7. JT to Dear Sister [Martha Waggaman], June 8, 1853, Tyler Family Papers, VHS.

8. JGT to Juliana Gardiner, June 1, July 6, 1847, GTFP.

9. JGT to Juliana Gardiner, July 6, October 18, 1847, GTFP.

10. JGT to Juliana Gardiner, April 13, 1849, GTFP.

11. JT to JT Jr., January 5, 1857, JT Papers, LC; JT to RT, June 3, 1858, ibid.

12. JT to RT, April 17, 1850, in *LTT*, 2:483; JGT to Juliana Gardiner, February 18, April 2, 23, 1851, GTFP.

13. JT to Dear Sister [Martha Waggaman], June 8, 1853, Tyler Family Papers, VHS.

14. *LTT*, 2:465; JGT to Juliana Gardiner, March 28, 1851, GTFP.

15. JGT to Juliana Gardiner, April 4, 1851, March 31, 1855, GTFP; JGT to MGB, May 12, 1855, ibid.

16. JGT to Juliana Gardiner, December 1848, GTFP; MGB to Juliana Gardiner, November 22, 1854, March 2, 1855, Gardiner Papers, Tyler Family Papers, WM, typescript; Glover, *Southern Sons*, 103.

17. MGB to Juliana Gardiner, March 2, 1855, Gardiner Papers, Tyler Family Papers, WM, typescript; MGB to Juliana Gardiner, February 23, 1853, ibid., typescript.

18. JT to MGB, December 25, [n.d.], JT Papers, ser. 4, LC; JT to MGB, December 25, 1855, in *LTT*, 2:523.

19. Juliana Gardiner to AG, January 22, 1851, GTFP; MGB to Juliana Gardiner, March 2, 1855, Gardiner Papers, Tyler Family Papers, WM, typescript; Eben Horsford to Charity [Norton] Horsford, February 14, 1852, Eben Norton Horsford Papers, Archives and Special Collections, Rensselaer Polytechnic Institute, Troy, NY.

20. JGT to MGB, June 4, 1851, [n.d.], 1855, GTFP; William Kauffman Scarborough, ed., *The Diary of Edmund Ruffin*, 3 vols. (Baton Rouge: LSU Press, 1972–89), 1:124. There is a bit of irony in Ruffin's views on marriages between old men and young women. In 1923 his great-granddaughter, Sue Ruffin, married Tyler's son Lyon. Thirty-six years in age separated the two.

21. JT to Dear Sister [Martha Waggaman], June 8, 1853, Tyler Family Papers, VHS; JGT to Juliana Gardiner, November 28, 1859, GTFP.

22. JGT to MGB, May 3, 4, 1853, GTFP; John D'Emilio and Estelle B. Freedman, *Intimate Matters: A History of Sexuality in America*, 2nd ed. (Chicago: University of Chicago Press, 1997), 58–60.

23. JGT to MGB, May 3, 4, 1853, GTFP; JGT to Juliana Gardiner, July 29, 1856, November 10, 1859, ibid.; JT to MGB, June 23, 1855, February 17, 1856, JT Papers, LC; JT to RT, December 23, 1845, in *LTT*, 2:449; JT to RT, November 24, 1854, Tyler Family Papers, WM; JT to RT, January 6, 1855, JT Papers, ser. 4, LC; JGT to Juliana Gardiner, March 24, 1851, GTFP; JT to John Young Mason, July 2, 1852, Mason Family Papers, VHS; JT to Col. J. S. Cunningham, April 20, 1852, Alfred W. Van Sinderen Collection, Yale University, New Haven, CT.

24. JGT to Juliana Gardiner, March 22, 1855, GTFP; JT to CW, [n.d.], 1857, CW Papers, WM; JT to DLG, April 6, 1857, JT Papers, LC; JT to LTS, October 29, 1856, ibid.; JT to Mr. [Benjamin] Ewell, February 11, 1859, ibid.; JT to NBT, April 13, 1859, ibid.; JT to Mr. Wheaton, June 9, 1856,

Tyler Family Papers, WM; JT to RT, October 22, 1856, in *LTT*, 2:534; JT to unknown, May 20, 1857, in *LTT*, 2:538; Mrs. Cynthia B. T. Washington to Lawrence Washington, February 9, 1859, in "Miscellaneous Letters," *WMQ*, 1st ser., 23 (April 1915): 286–88; Ralph Hardee Rives, "The Jamestown Celebration of 1857," *VMHB* 66 (July 1958): 259–71.

25. *LTT*, 2:505.

26. JGT to Juliana Gardiner, April 30, 1849, February 21, 1850, GTFP; JT to Dr. Henry Curtis, January 25, 1844, December 1858, JT Papers, LC.

27. JGT to MGB, February 5, 1846, March 19, 1851, GTFP; JGT to Juliana Gardiner, April 4, 30, 1851, ibid.; JGT to MGB, April 10, 1854, ibid.

28. JGT to MGB, May 15, 1851, GTFP; JGT to Juliana Gardiner, February 3, 1846, November 10, 1859, ibid.; JGT to MGB, April 10, 1854, ibid.

29. JGT to AG, December 13, 1850, GTFP.

30. Norbert Hirschhorn, Robert G. Feldman, and Ian A. Greaves, "Abraham Lincoln's Blue Pills," *Perspectives in Biology and Medicine* 44 (Summer 2001): 315–32.

31. JGT to Juliana Gardiner, March 7, 1851, GTFP; JT to LTS, December 8, 1857, JT Papers, LC; JT to RT, July 14, 1858, Tyler Family Papers, WM.

32. JGT to MGB, June 15, 1854, GTFP; JGT to Juliana Gardiner, December 11, 1854, ibid.

33. JGT to MGB, May 12, 1855, GTFP.

34. James Semple to JT, June 24, 1855, JT Papers, LC; JT to LTS, October 29, 1856, ibid.

35. JT to LTS, October 29, 1856, JT Papers, LC; JT to MGB, October 21, 1856, ibid.; JT to RT, October 22, 1856, in *LTT*, 2:534.

36. JT to HW, March 17, 1856, JT Papers, LC.

37. JT to JT Jr., May 7, 1854, Tyler Family Papers, VHS; JT to Mr. [Benjamin] Ewell, February 11, 1859, JT Papers, LC.

38. JT to Samuel S. Gardiner, June 26, 1857, Sylvester Manor Archive, Record Group 3, Fales Library and Special Collections, Elmer Holmes Bobst Library, New York University; JT to unknown, n.d., [June 1857?], CW Papers, WM.

39. JT to MGB, February 25, 1856, JT Papers, LC.

40. JT to Hugh Blair Grigsby, February 29, 1856 (copy), Hugh Blair Grigsby Letterbook, Hugh Blair Grigsby Papers, VHS; JT to JT Jr., January 5, 1857, JT Papers, LC.

41. JT to Samuel S. Gardiner, July 3, 1851, Sylvester Manor Archive, Record Group 3, Fales Library and Special Collections, Elmer Holmes Bobst Library, New York University; JT to Hugh Blair Grigsby, February 29, 1856 (copy), Hugh Blair Grigsby Letterbook, Hugh Blair Grigsby Papers, VHS; JT to JT Jr., January 5, 1857, JT Papers, LC.

42. JT to John S. Cunningham, July 15, 1852, in *LTT*, 2:499.

43. JT to RT, June 3, 1858, JT Papers, LC.

44. JT to CW, April 26, 1858, CW Papers, WM; JT to DLG, March 29, 1858, JT Papers, LC.

45. JGT to Juliana Gardiner, July 29, 1856, GTFP; JT to RT, May 7, 1855, Tyler Family Papers, WM; JT to RT, December 23, 1859, JT Papers, LC.

46. Will of John Tyler, October 29, 1860, Oversize Papers Collection, 22546, LVA.

47. William L. Day, receipt from John Tyler for slave sale, February 28, 1857, Personal Papers Collection, LVA.

48. *Syracuse Evening Chronicle*, August 21, 1854; JGT to Juliana Gardiner, January 23, 1856, GTFP; JT to JGT, June 27, 1860, JT Papers, ser. 4, LC.

Note on Sources

The following essay highlights the sources I have found essential to a biography of John Tyler. Not all of the sources I used in my research and writing appear here. For a complete accounting of the sources, please refer to the book's notes.

Any serious study of John Tyler's life and presidency must begin with Lyon G. Tyler's *Letters and Times of the Tylers* (3 vols., Richmond: Whittet and Shepperson, 1884–85, 1896). Lyon Tyler, the fifth child of the marriage of John Tyler and his second wife, Julia Gardiner Tyler, and eventually president of the College of William and Mary, set out to rehabilitate his father's image in the wake of the Civil War and Reconstruction. The three volumes he produced therefore contain a biased narrative account of the Tyler family and the life and political career of the tenth president. What makes the work valuable—indeed indispensable—is the collection of letters Lyon Tyler amassed during the course of his research, which compose the bulk of his volumes. These include letters sent and received by President Tyler's father, Judge John Tyler, as well as hundreds sent and received throughout his life by the president himself. Many Tyler letters were destroyed by Union troops who ransacked Sherwood Forest during the Civil War; others that Julia Tyler had placed in the Farmers' Bank of Richmond for safekeeping were lost as Richmond burned in 1865.

Much of the president's correspondence included in *Letters and Times* is found in the Library of Congress collection of John Tyler Papers, 1,410 documents that can be accessed on three reels of microfilm, and in an additional document series (series 4) located in the LOC itself. Several of the letters reproduced in *Letters and Times* are missing a small portion of their text, so checking them against the ones found in the LOC is essential. The LOC has undertaken a project to digitize the John Tyler Papers; consequently, many of the documents in the microfilm collection are now available to scholars online, though it should be pointed out that the quality of the reproductions on microfilm is often superior to that of the digital versions. The John Tyler Papers, when combined with *Letters and Times*, provide the best documentary record of the president's political career as well as his first marriage and the relationships he shared with the children of his union with Letitia Christian. More recently, the LOC has digitized letters to and from Tyler's second wife, in addition to correspondence from members of the Gardiner family.

The Tyler Family Papers Collection at the College of William and Mary's Swem Library is also indispensable for research into John Tyler's life and political career. William and Mary is in the process of digitizing at least a portion of this massive collection. The Virginia Historical Society in Richmond is home to another collection of Tyler Family Papers. The museum's collections also contain papers of various Virginia families and politicians that include letters to and from John Tyler. There is a smaller John Tyler Papers collection at the David M. Rubenstein Rare Book and Manuscript Library at Duke University. The prodigious Gardiner-Tyler Family Papers in Sterling Memorial Library at Yale University cover the last eighteen years of John Tyler's life, when he was married to Julia Gardiner and living at Sherwood Forest, their home in Charles City County, Virginia. An account of that portion of his life, in fact, cannot be crafted without reliance on this collection of papers. Scattered throughout the United States are collections in archives that contain from a few to a dozen or more letters by and from John Tyler, including the University of Virginia, the Library of Virginia in Richmond, Knox College, and the Huntington Library. In the early twentieth century, two journals, *William and Mary Quarterly* and *Tyler's Quarterly Historical and Genealogical Magazine,* also regularly published important Tyler correspondence.

The first scholarly treatment of John Tyler's life, Oliver Perry Chitwood's *John Tyler: Champion of the Old South* (1939; repr., Newtown, CT: American Political Biography Press, 2000), contains the essential facts of the tenth president's life and career but is dated, overly sympathetic, and lacking in critical analysis. Robert Seager II's *And Tyler Too: A Biography of John and Julia Gardiner Tyler* (New York: McGraw-Hill, 1963) is comprehensive but saves most of its analysis for Julia's life. Edward P. Crapol's *John Tyler: The Accidental President* (Chapel Hill: University of North Carolina Press, 2006), while providing biographical detail, is more concerned with President Tyler's foreign policy and his belief in (what Crapol calls) America's "national destiny." Gary May, *John Tyler* (New York: Times Books, 2008), part of the American Presidents Series (edited by Arthur M. Schlesinger Jr. and Sean Wilentz), is a succinct look at Tyler's life and career. Alexander Gordon Abell, *Life of John Tyler* (New York: Harper and Brothers, 1843), is an 1844 campaign biography that is still useful because it contains letters and speeches that may be difficult to access elsewhere.

Situating John Tyler and his family (especially his father, Judge Tyler) within the context of Tidewater Virginia and, more broadly, within the context of the South is important since a devotion to the place of his birth animated the tenth president's life and helps explain the progression of his political career. Rhys Isaac, *The Transformation of Virginia, 1740–1790* (New York: W. W. Norton, 1982); Allan Kulikoff, *Tobacco and Slaves: The Development of Southern Cultures in the Chesapeake, 1680–1800* (Chapel Hill: University of North Carolina Press, 1986); T. H. Breen, *Tobacco Culture: The Mentality of the Great Tidewater Planters on the Eve of Revolution* (Princeton, NJ: Princeton University Press, 1985); and Charles S. Sydnor, *American Revolutionaries in the Making: Political Practices in Washington's Virginia* (New York: Free Press, 1952) are essential to understanding Tyler's social world. Bertram Wyatt-Brown's highly influential classic *Southern Honor: Ethics and Behavior in the Old South* (New York: Oxford University Press, 1982) and Dickson D. Bruce Jr., *Violence and Culture in the Antebellum South* (Austin: University of Texas Press, 1979), analyze the honor culture that undergirded this social world and shed light on the values that shaped Tyler's life as a southern planter. Lorri Glover's *Southern Sons: Becoming Men in the New Nation* (Baltimore: Johns Hopkins University Press, 2007) examines the characteristics of masculinity found in and expected of young southern men of John Tyler's generation and makes a persuasive case that the values these young men developed transformed them into southern nationalists who ultimately helped destroy the Union. Her book is essential to understanding the relationship between John Tyler and his father, and it provides the context for Tyler's maturation as a southern "gentleman." Three older books that still hold enormous value for explaining the social world of Tidewater Virginia and the Old South are Daniel Blake Smith, *Inside the Great House: Planter Family Life in Eighteenth-Century Chesapeake Society* (Ithaca, NY: Cornell University Press, 1980); Jan Lewis, *The Pursuit of Happiness: Family and Values in Jefferson's Virginia* (Cambridge: Cambridge University Press, 1985); and Steven M. Stowe, *Intimacy and Power in the Old South: Ritual in the Lives of the Planters* (Baltimore: Johns Hopkins University Press, 1987). Susan Dunn, *Dominion of Memories: Jefferson, Madison & the Decline of Virginia* (New York: Basic Books, 2007) adds further to our understanding of Tyler's social world by charting Virginia's economic stagnation and its declining influence in the civic affairs of the nation by 1850. Dunn argues that Old Dominion planters like Tyler remained wedded to slavery and the values of plantation society to the detriment of their state.

Tyler inherited a respect for and devotion to the republicanism of the American Revolution from his father. The scholarly literature on republicanism is vast, with much of it published in the 1970s and 1980s, when the debate over whether the Revolution could best be explained by republicanism or liberalism was at its height. Gordon S. Wood, *The Creation of the American Republic, 1776–1787* (Chapel Hill: University of North Carolina Press, 1969), is the classic explication of revolutionary republicanism. Wood expands on his argument, and offers a more nuanced reading of republicanism's concept of "virtue," in *The Radicalism of the American Revolution* (New York: Random House, 1991). Both books yield insight into why Judge Tyler found republicanism so compelling. Drew R. McCoy, *The Elusive Republic: Political Economy in Jefferson's America* (New York: W. W. Norton, 1980), describes an "ideology in flux" and demonstrates how revolutionaries such as Judge Tyler adapted republicanism to the realities of the emerging commercial society of the early nineteenth century. More recently, Dan Monroe, *The Republican Vision of John Tyler* (College Station: Texas A&M University Press, 2003), examines Tyler's political principles and political philosophy framed around his devotion to the republicanism of the American Revolution.

An Antifederalist who fought against ratification of the US Constitution, John Tyler's father feared the consolidation of power by the national government. When James Madison and Thomas Jefferson authored the Virginia and Kentucky Resolutions in 1798, Judge Tyler found the best explication of his political ideology. He passed this ideology down to his son, and the resolutions—the "Principles of '98"—became the wellspring of the future president's steadfast belief in states' rights and strict construction. Saul Cornell, *The Other Founders: Anti-Federalism and the Dissenting Tradition in America, 1788–1828* (Chapel Hill: University of North Carolina Press, 1999), examines the "dissenting tradition" to which Judge Tyler and his son belonged. William J. Watkins Jr., *Reclaiming the American Revolution: The Kentucky and Virginia Resolutions and their Legacy* (New York: Palgrave MacMillan, 2004), is a good introduction that places the resolutions into a broader context.

Politically, John Tyler found a home in the "Old" Republican camp, a small group of southerners who adopted Jefferson's original ideals of states' rights and strict construction. Norman Risjord, *The Old Republicans: Southern Conservatism in the Age of Jefferson* (New York: Columbia University Press, 1965), traces the development of this group chronologically. Christopher Childers, "The Old Republican Constitutional Primer: States' Rights after the Missouri Controversy and the Onset of the Politics of Slavery," in *The Enigmatic South: Toward Civil War and Its Legacies*, edited by Samuel C. Hyde (Baton Rouge: LSU Press, 2014), 3–21, expands the scope of Risjord's work by connecting the Old Republicans to what historian William J. Cooper Jr. calls the "politics of slavery." Childers also alludes to the relationship between the Old Republicans and the debate over slavery in the territories, a theme that receives fuller treatment in his outstanding *The Failure of Popular Sovereignty: Slavery, Manifest Destiny, and the Radicalization of Southern Politics* (Lawrence: University Press of Kansas, 2012). Still useful in explaining the Old Republicans and their place in the Jeffersonian coalition is Lance Banning, *The Jeffersonian Persuasion: Evolution of a Party Ideology* (Ithaca, NY: Cornell University Press, 1980). The best biography of the Old Republicans' leader is David Johnson, *John Randolph of Roanoke* (Baton Rouge: LSU Press, 2012).

John Tyler's college experience at William and Mary played a significant role in shaping his political philosophy. Susan H. Godson and Ludwell H. Johnson, *The College of William and Mary: A History*, 2 vols. (Williamsburg: King and Queen Press, 1994), provides the context for the future president's years as an undergraduate. See also David W. Robson, *Educating Republicans: The College in the Era of the American Revolution, 1750–1800* (Westport, CT: Greenwood, 1985), and the Glover volume detailed above. On Tyler's mentor, Bishop James Madison, see Charles Crowe, "Bishop James Madison and the Republic of Virtue," *Journal of Southern History* 30 (February 1964): 58–70. Suzanne Cooper Guasco, *Confronting Slavery: Edward Coles and the Rise of Antislavery Politics in Nineteenth-Century America* (Dekalb: Northern Illinois University Press, 2013), contains a brief analysis of Bishop Madison.

Tyler's first forays into politics, both at the state level and nationally, conformed to established practices that are expertly examined in Daniel P. Jordan, *Political Leadership in Jefferson's Virginia* (Charlottesville: University Press of Virginia, 1985). Also useful for explaining Tyler's political milieu is Anthony F. Upton, "The Road to Power in Virginia in the Early Nineteenth Century," *Virginia Magazine of History and Biography* 62 (July 1954): 259–80. Virginia's *Journal of the House of Delegates*, available on microfilm from the Library of Virginia, contains records of Tyler's activity in the state legislature, including his resolutions censuring Senators Brent and Giles in 1812.

Part of understanding John Tyler's pre-presidential career means assessing his relationship to the Richmond Junto, a problematic task exacerbated by the ambiguous historiography of its leader, *Richmond Enquirer* editor Thomas Ritchie, and the other men who made up this group of self-proclaimed guardians of Old Republicanism. F. Thornton Miller, "The Richmond Junto: The Secret, All Powerful Club, or Myth," *Virginia Magazine of History and Biography* 99 (January 1991): 63–80, questions the very existence of the Junto. Rex Beach, "Spencer Roane and the Richmond Junto," *William and Mary Quarterly*, 2nd ser., 22 (January 1942): 1–17; and Charles H. Ambler, *Thomas Ritchie: A Study in Virginia Politics* (Richmond:

Bell, Book, and Stationery, 1913), seem to take for granted the Junto existed, though they provide no definitive evidence. Moreover, both of these works are extremely dated and are of limited value. A modern biography of Thomas Ritchie is desperately needed. William G. Shade, *Democratizing the Old Dominion: Virginia and the Second Party System, 1824–1861* (Charlottesville: University Press of Virginia, 1996), has little time for the question of whether the Richmond Junto existed. He maintains that it did and situates it at the core of Republican (and, therefore, Virginia) politics in the early national period. Agreeing with Shade on that point, my view is that the Junto did indeed exist but that John Tyler's political career shows that its power in Virginia politics was far from absolute; it was perhaps weaker than historians have previously thought.

National politics between the post–War of 1812 period, when Tyler entered Congress, and the era some scholars still refer to as the "Age of Jackson," when the Virginian served in the US Senate, have received a great deal of scholarly attention. C. Edward Skeen, *1816: America Rising* (Lexington: University of Kentucky Press, 2003), takes a topical approach and places the events of that year into their broader historical context. The book is a good place to begin for understanding the currents of political change sweeping the United States in these years. Skeen is especially strong in his analysis of the Compensation Act controversy that Tyler used to establish his national profile. Three ambitious synthetic works offer competing interpretations of the years 1815–48. Charles Sellers, *The Market Revolution: Jacksonian America, 1815–1846* (New York: Oxford University Press, 1991), launched a historiographical revolution that is only now beginning to recede. Sellers views the events of this period through the lens of a transformation in capitalist market relations that had wide-ranging implications for America's economic, social, cultural, and political development. Sean Wilentz, who covers much of the same ground as Sellers in *The Rise of American Democracy: Jefferson to Lincoln* (New York: W. W. Norton, 2005), champions the Jacksonians and the emerging Democratic Party and takes seriously their rhetoric of expanding political opportunity for all white Americans. Daniel Walker Howe, *What Hath God Wrought: The Transformation of America, 1815–1848* (New York: Oxford University Press, 2007), on the other hand, writes from a perspective sympathetic to the Whig Party. A briefer, and in my view underrated, synthesis of these years is Daniel Feller, *The Jacksonian Promise: America, 1815–1840* (Baltimore: Johns Hopkins University Press, 1995).

The essays in Melvyn Stokes and Stephen Conway, eds., *The Market Revolution in America: Social, Political, and Religious Expressions, 1800–1880* (Charlottesville: University Press of Virginia, 1996), use Sellers's concept of the market revolution to (in part) reframe the traditional political narrative of these years. Ronald P. Formisano, "State Development in the Early Republic: Substance and Structure, 1780–1840," in *Contesting Democracy: Substance and Structure in American Political History, 1775–2000*, edited by Byron E. Shafer and Anthony Badger (Lawrence: University Press of Kansas, 2001), 7–35, highlights the "statist agenda" of congressional Republicans after the War of 1812 and points out that southern Old Republicans like Tyler fought that agenda, which they viewed as the first step toward dangerous consolidation by the federal government. Formisano's essay allows us to place

Tyler's vehement opposition to the presidency of John Quincy Adams into its proper context. John Lauritz Larson, *Internal Improvement: National Public Works and the Promise of Popular Government in the Early United States* (Chapel Hill: University of North Carolina Press, 2001), addresses one aspect of the statist agenda Formisano lays out. Congruent with Formisano's argument, Brian Balogh, *A Government Out of Sight: The Mystery of National Authority in Nineteenth-Century America* (Cambridge: Cambridge University Press, 2009), argues that the national government intervened significantly in the lives of Americans during a period that has traditionally been considered an age of laissez-faire. Tyler's rhetoric certainly substantiates Balogh's main point. Richard E. Ellis, *Aggressive Nationalism: McCulloch v. Maryland and the Foundation of Federal Authority in the Young Republic* (New York: Oxford University Press, 2007), is an important book because it explains how the US Supreme Court expanded federal power in a way that particularly alarmed Tyler and the Old Republicans. For more on the McCulloch case, see Mark Killenbeck, *M'Culloch v. Maryland: Securing a Nation* (Lawrence: University Press of Kansas, 2006).

An expanded role for the federal government in the early national period corresponded with political behavior that was moving away from deference and toward greater participation in the process. The transition often proved messy, as recent scholarship has shown. In the early twenty-first century, a historiographical trend emerged that expanded the definition of "political" behavior beyond voting and electoral campaigns. The prototype for this approach is a collection of essays: Jeffrey L. Pasley, Andrew W. Robertson, and David Waldstreicher, eds., *Beyond the Founders: New Approaches to the Political History of the Early American Republic* (Chapel Hill: University of North Carolina Press, 2004). Daniel Peart, *Era of Experimentation: American Political Practices in the Early Republic* (Charlottesville: University of Virginia Press, 2014), adopts an approach consistent with this larger trend and examines the often-neglected years of the early 1820s. He argues that Americans experimented at this time with alternative forms of political organization because they found political parties inhibiting, rather than promoting, democracy. Peart's chapter on federal tariff policy is especially applicable to John Tyler's early national political career. For the transition to democracy, Donald B. Cole, *A Jackson Man: Amos Kendall and the Rise of American Democracy* (Baton Rouge: LSU Press, 2004), is excellent. Cole's work is especially illuminating on how republicanism gave way to democracy, using Kendall as the vehicle to explain the process. It was a process Tyler came to understand as he carved out a national political career for himself.

More specialized studies have also enhanced our understanding of national politics in these years. Joanne B. Freeman, *Affairs of Honor: National Politics in the New Republic* (New Haven, CT: Yale University Press, 2001), while chronologically stopping before the period of John Tyler's congressional years, is nevertheless extremely helpful in explaining how the culture of honor set the parameters of a national politician's behavior—even in the later period. Moreover, Freeman's insightful work analyzes how a politician like Tyler crafted a national persona and why that was important. Her recent work, *The Field of Blood: Violence in Congress and the Road to Civil War* (New York: Farrar, Straus, and Giroux, 2018), extends the chronological reach of *Affairs of Honor* and is especially illuminating on Tyler's political ally Henry Wise. Kenneth S. Greenberg's *Master and Statesman: The Political Culture of American Slavery* (Baltimore: Johns Hopkins University Press, 1985) argues persuasively that southern politicians acted in ways that set them and their section apart from their northern counterparts.

Catherine Allgor's *Parlor Politics: In Which the Ladies of Washington Help Build a City and a Government* (Charlottesville: University Press of Virginia, 2000) examines the social world of the nation's capital in the early national period, a realm John Tyler found confusing at first, but one he ultimately navigated successfully. Tyler's experience lodging at Claxton's boardinghouse on Pennsylvania Avenue, where he took his meals in what was called a "mess," was typical for national politicians who were usually away from their families while they served in Congress. Cynthia D. Earman's work was the first to examine the place of the mess within the larger context of national politics; see her essay "Messing Around: Entertaining and Accommodating Congress, 1800–1830," in *Establishing Congress: The Removal to Washington, D.C. and the Election of 1800*, edited by Kenneth R. Bowling and Donald Kennon (Athens: Ohio University Press, 2005), 128–47. Rachel Shelden, *Washington Brotherhood: Politics, Social Life, and the Coming of the Civil War* (Chapel Hill: University of North Carolina Press, 2013), and Alice Elizabeth Malavasic, *The F Street Mess: How Southern Senators Rewrote the Kansas-Nebraska Act* (Chapel Hill: University of North Carolina Press, 2017), delve more deeply into the significance of Washington's male-oriented social life and argue for its importance in shaping politics.

Fully understanding Tyler's career in both houses of Congress requires an examination of four key primary sources. The *Annals of Congress* contains the day-to-day proceedings of the House of Representatives (and the Senate) and includes most of Tyler's speeches on matters such as the Compensation Act and the tariff while he served in the House. The *Register of Debates* chronicles his later speeches in the Senate. The *Richmond Enquirer* newspaper is absolutely essential for assessing reaction in Virginia to Tyler's course of action in Washington. Finally, Tyler's circular letters to his constituents while in the House are reprinted in Noble E. Cunningham, *Circular Letters of Congressmen to Their Constituents 1789–1829*, 3 vols. (Chapel Hill: University of North Carolina Press, 1978).

Scholarship on the central issues of Tyler's congressional career makes clear why those issues were so important—to him personally, to the South, and to the nation. William K. Bolt, *Tariff Wars and the Politics of Jacksonian America* (Nashville: Vanderbilt University Press, 2017), is the first full account of the antebellum tariff controversies in over a century. William S. Belko, *Philip Pendleton Barbour in Jacksonian America: An Old Republican in King Andrew's Court* (Tuscaloosa: University of Alabama Press, 2016), assesses one of Tyler's Virginia allies in the fight against the tariff and argues convincingly that opposition to the tariff did not necessarily mean the issue served as a proxy for the defense of slavery. On the crisis over Missouri's admission to the Union, which ultimately forced Tyler out of the national political arena, see William W. Freehling, *The Road to Disunion*, vol. 1, *Secessionists at Bay, 1776–1854* (New York: Oxford University Press, 1990); William J. Cooper Jr., *Liberty and Slavery: Southern Politics to 1860* (1983; repr., Columbia: University of South Carolina Press, 2000); Matthew Mason, *Slavery and Politics in the Early Republic* (Chapel Hill: University of North Carolina Press, 2006); Robert Pierce Forbes, *The Missouri Compromise and Its Aftermath* (Chapel Hill: University of North Carolina Press, 2007); John Craig Hammond, "'Uncontrollable Necessity': The Local Politics, Geopolitics, and Sectional Politics of Slavery Expansion," in *Contesting Slavery: The Politics of Bondage and Freedom in the New American Nation,* edited by John Craig Hammond and Matthew Mason (Charlottesville: University of Virginia Press, 2011), 138–60; Christopher Childers, *The Failure of Popular Sovereignty: Slavery, Manifest Destiny, and the Radicalization of Southern Politics* (Lawrence: University Press of Kansas, 2012); and John R. Van Atta, *Wolf by the Ears: The Missouri Crisis, 1819–1821* (Baltimore: Johns Hopkins University Press, 2015). On the diffusion argument, to which Tyler subscribed, see the Freehling volume above as well as John Chester Miller, *The Wolf by the Ears: Thomas Jefferson and Slavery* (Charlottesville: University Press of Virginia, 1991). The Freehling and Cooper books are also important for their analysis of the southern perspective on the many other pertinent issues that ultimately led to the Civil War.

John Tyler's reentry into politics in 1823 coincided with the rise of Andrew Jackson as a presidential contender. The controversial 1824 election—which Jackson lost—set the agenda for an emerging Jacksonian coalition that solidified years later as the Democratic Party. Donald Ratcliffe's *The One-Party Presidential Contest: Adams, Jackson, and 1824's Five-Horse Race* (Lawrence: University Press of Kansas, 2015) analyzes the contest and convincingly overturns many aspects of the standard interpretation. Most notably, Ratcliffe argues that Adams enjoyed more popular support than previously thought and that the "corrupt bargain" was a myth embellished to enhance Jackson's stature for the ensuing election in 1828. His point about Adams's support is crucial because it demonstrates that Tyler's vote for Adams in 1824 was not as incomprehensible as it may seem on the surface. The election vanquished the caucus system for choosing presidential nominees, finally undid the so-called "Virginia dynasty" of presidents, and reshaped presidential politics. Richard P. McCormick, *The Presidential Game: The Origins of American Presidential Politics* (New York: Oxford University Press, 1982), charts these developments and is particularly strong in analyzing how the Jacksonians played the presidential game.

Jackson's success at attaining the presidency has received a lot of scholarly attention. Mark R. Cheathem, *Andrew Jackson and the Rise of the Democratic Party* (Knoxville: University of Tennessee Press, 2018), analyzes the American political system as a whole from the early national period to the eve of the Civil War and argues for the transformative effect of Jackson's populism on the Democratic Party and on partisanship in general. Two other books by Cheathem should be essential reading: *Andrew Jackson, Southerner* (Baton Rouge: LSU Press, 2013) challenges the prevailing view that Old Hickory was more westerner than southerner, while *The Coming of Democracy: Presidential Campaigning in the Age of Jackson* (Baltimore: Johns Hopkins University Press, 2018) looks at the evolution of presidential campaigning from 1824 to 1840 and is especially helpful for understanding the campaign most important to John Tyler's career—that of 1840. Donald B. Cole, *Vindicating Andrew*

Jackson: The 1828 Election and the Rise of the Two-Party System (Lawrence: University Press of Kansas, 2009), explains Jackson's election to the presidency and shows how his winning coalition emerged in several of the states. Also useful on the 1828 election is Lynn Hudson Parsons, *The Birth of Modern Politics: Andrew Jackson, John Quincy Adams, and the Election of 1828* (New York: Oxford University Press, 2009). David S. Heidler and Jeanne T. Heidler, *The Rise of Andrew Jackson: Myth, Manipulation, and the Making of Modern Politics* (New York: Basic Books, 2018), exposes the seamier side of Jackson's election in 1828, shunting aside the interpretation that greater democracy paved the way for the Hero of New Orleans, and instead focusing on how friendly newspaper editors and other operatives crafted an image of Jackson they could sell to the American people. The result was the first "modern" campaign in presidential politics, the ramifications of which are still felt today.

Since John Tyler served in the US Senate while Andrew Jackson occupied the White House, the central issues and controversies of the seventh president's administration necessarily influenced his career. A good overview of the period is Harry L. Watson, *Liberty and Power: The Politics of Jacksonian America* (New York: Hill and Wang, 1990). Donald B. Cole, *The Presidency of Andrew Jackson* (Lawrence: University Press of Kansas, 1993), is a balanced and judicious study of the administration. More-specific issues have also received scholarly attention. William W. Freehling, *Prelude to Civil War: The Nullification Controversy in South Carolina, 1816–1836* (1965; repr., New York: Oxford University Press, 1992), argues that South Carolina nullifiers reacted so strongly against the tariff in part because of anxieties over slavery. Richard E. Ellis, *The Union at Risk: Jacksonian Democracy, States' Rights, and the Nullification Crisis* (New York: Oxford University Press, 1987), is more comprehensive than Freehling's volume and includes an entire chapter on Virginia's response to the crisis; Tyler becomes a key figure in Ellis's interpretation. Merrill D. Peterson, *Olive Branch and Sword: The Compromise of 1833* (Baton Rouge: LSU Press, 1982), provides a brief analysis of the resolution of the nullification crisis. Daniel Feller, *The Public Lands in Jacksonian Politics* (Madison: University of Wisconsin Press, 1984), is the only full study of that important issue. Stephen W. Campbell, *The Bank War and the Partisan Press: Newspapers, Financial Institutions, and the Post Office in Jacksonian America* (Lawrence: University Press of Kansas, 2019), is a much-needed modern study of President Jackson's war on the Second Bank of the United States, the fallout from which forced Tyler's resignation from the Senate. Unfortunately, the expunging-resolution controversy, which directly prompted him to resign, has received short shrift in the scholarly literature.

Two doctoral dissertations have shaped my understanding of Virginia politics in the Jacksonian period and help explain the pressures placed on John Tyler by the Richmond Junto. Lynwood M. Dent Jr., "The Virginia Democratic Party, 1824–1847," 2 vols. (Ph.D. diss., Louisiana State University, 1974), and Trenton E. Hizer, "'Virginia Is Now Divided': Politics in the Old Dominion, 1820–1833" (Ph.D. diss., University of South Carolina, 1997), both highlight Tyler's significance to what was transpiring in Virginia politics while he served in Washington. Moreover, they augment Shade's *Democratizing the Old Dominion*, mentioned above.

Biographies of Tyler's contemporaries in national politics have contributed to my understanding of Tyler's pre-presidential and presidential careers. For example, see William J. Cooper Jr., *The Lost Founding Father: John Quincy Adams and the Transformation of American Politics* (New York: Liveright, 2017); Robert V. Remini, *Daniel Webster: The Man and His Time* (New York: W. W. Norton, 1997); Remini, *Henry Clay: Statesman for the Union* (New York: W. W. Norton, 1991); David S. Heidler and Jeanne T. Heidler, *Henry Clay: The Essential American* (New York: Random House, 2010); James C. Klotter, *Henry Clay: The Man Who Would Be President* (New York: Oxford University Press, 2018); John Niven, *John C. Calhoun and the Price of Union* (Baton Rouge: LSU Press, 1988); W. Stephen Belko, *The Invincible Duff Green: Whig of the West* (Columbia: University of Missouri Press, 2006); and Norma Lois Peterson, *Littleton Waller Tazewell* (Charlottesville: University Press of Virginia, 1983).

The place to start an examination of John Tyler's presidency is Norma Lois Peterson, *The Presidencies of William Henry Harrison and John Tyler* (Lawrence: University Press of Kansas, 1989). An older study is Robert J. Morgan, *A Whig Embattled: The Presidency under John Tyler* (Lincoln: University of Nebraska Press, 1954). Michael F. Holt, *The Rise and Fall of the American Whig Party: Jacksonian Politics and the Onset of the Civil War* (New York: Oxford University Press, 1999), is a comprehensive study that will likely never be surpassed. Its value for my work is immense. Holt devotes significant attention to Tyler and how his presidency—chiefly his fight with Henry Clay—prevented the Whigs from fully capitalizing on their historic electoral victory in 1840; in fact, the clash between the president and the Whig leader in the Senate shattered the party.

That clash began during the special session of Congress that convened in the summer of 1841 to address the nation's dismal economic circumstances resulting from the Panic of 1837. On the panic, see Alasdair Roberts, *America's First Great Depression: Economic Crisis and Political Disorder after the Panic of 1837* (Ithaca, NY: Cornell University Press, 2012), and Jessica M. Lepler, *The Many Panics of 1837: People, Politics, and the Creation of a Transatlantic Financial Crisis* (Cambridge: Cambridge University Press, 2013). Merrill D. Peterson, *The Great Triumvirate: Webster, Clay, and Calhoun* (New York: Oxford University Press, 1987), examines the fight between Tyler and Clay with an eye toward how it affected the political fortunes of his three subjects. Richard A. Gantz, "Henry Clay and the Harvest of Bitter Fruit: The Struggle with John Tyler, 1841–1842" (Ph.D. diss., Indiana University, 1986), is balanced and relatively comprehensive. Still useful is George Rawlings Poage, *Henry Clay and the Whig Party* (1936; repr., Gloucester, MA: Peter Smith, 1965).

The so-called Virginia cabal that allied with Tyler as soon as he became president should be approached first through two excellent biographies. Craig M. Simpson, *A Good Southerner: The Life of Henry Wise of Virginia* (Chapel Hill: University of North Carolina Press, 1985), captures Wise's eccentricities but argues for his political significance, particularly during the years Tyler occupied the White House. Robert J. Brugger, *Beverley Tucker: Heart over Head in the Old South* (Baltimore: Johns Hopkins University Press, 1978), shows the complexities that underlay the thoughts and actions of Professor Tucker, whose friendship with Tyler suffered as a result of Tyler's unwillingness to build a states' rights party. Claude Hall's *Abel Parker Upshur: Conservative Virginian, 1790–1844* (Madison: State Historical Society of Wisconsin, 1964) is the only full-length biography of the other essential member of the cabal. Hall adequately accounts for Upshur's significance as President Tyler's navy secretary but fails to convey his subject's importance to Tyler personally. Moreover, the section in the book that covers Upshur's time as secretary of state is superficial and lacks sufficient analysis.

The essential primary sources for Tyler's presidency—besides *Letters and Times* and the manuscript collections detailed at the beginning of this essay—are the published volumes of the correspondence of the era's major protagonists. Henry Clay's papers are found in James F. Hopkins, Mary W. M. Hargreaves, et al., eds. *The Papers of Henry Clay,* 11 vols. (Lexington: University Press of Kentucky, 1959–92); volume 9 covers the Tyler presidency. For Daniel Webster, see Charles M. Wiltse, Harold D. Moser, et al., eds., *The Papers of Daniel Webster,* ser. 1, *Correspondence,* 7 vols. (Hanover, NH: University Press of New England, 1974–88), vols. 5–6; and Kenneth E. Shewmaker et al., eds., *The Papers of Daniel Webster,* ser. 3, *Diplomatic Papers,* 2 vols. (Hanover, NH: University Press of New England, 1983), vol. 1. John C. Calhoun's correspondence is found in Robert L. Meriwether, W. Edwin Hemphill, Clyde N. Wilson, et al., eds., *The Papers of John C. Calhoun,* 28 vols. (Columbia: University of South Carolina Press, 1959–2003); volumes 15–21 cover the Tyler years. The correspondence of two lesser-known Whigs is also important. Henry Thomas Shanks, ed., *The Papers of Willie Person Mangum,* 5 vols. (Raleigh: State Department of Archives and History, 1950–56), vols. 3–4, deal with this particularly vocal Tyler enemy. J. G. de Roulhac Hamilton and Max R. Williams, eds. *The Papers of William A. Graham,* 8 vols. (Raleigh: State Department of Archives and History, 1957–96), vols. 2–3, offer more detail about the Whig caucus that opposed President Tyler.

Other key primary materials include James D. Richardson, comp., *A Compilation of the Messages and Papers of the Presidents, 1789–1897,* 10 vols. (Washington, DC: Government Printing Office, 1896–99), vol. 4, which contains all of Tyler's annual messages to Congress as well as various other public documents that came out of the White House during his term in office. Newspaper sources include the *Washington Daily National Intelligencer,* the Whig paper of record, and the *Washington Daily Madisonian,* the Tyler administration organ. The *United States Democratic Review* and *Niles' National Register* also contain useful articles that provide commentary on the Tyler presidency.

Apart from the fight with Henry Clay and the congressional Whigs, the domestic realm of John Tyler's presidency has received scant attention, even from more recent scholarship on Tyler. An exception is the Dorr Rebellion. Erik J. Chaput's *The People's Martyr: Thomas Wilson Dorr and His 1842 Rhode Island Rebellion* (Lawrence: University Press of Kansas, 2013) is outstanding. His book supplants older works on this subject, but its focus is not on the Tyler administration per se. Nevertheless, it has shaped my thinking on the larger significance of the rebellion and its place in the history of antebellum America. Historians have largely judged Tyler a failure in domestic politics, so it is perhaps understandable that more attention has not been paid to the Dorr Rebellion, his response to which I argue was a major success for the embattled president.

Scholars have paid attention to Tyler's record in foreign affairs. Howard Jones and Donald A. Rakestraw, *Prologue to Manifest Destiny: Anglo-American Relations in the 1840s* (Wilmington, DE: Scholarly Resources, 1997), provides an overview of the context surrounding the negotiations between the United States and Britain over (among other things) a boundary dispute concerning the state of Maine, resulting in the Webster-Ashburton Treaty of 1842. Howard Jones, *To the Webster-Ashburton Treaty: A Study in Anglo-American Relations, 1783–1843* (Chapel Hill: University of North Carolina Press, 1977) is the standard work on the treaty, but it overemphasizes how much the Tyler administration sought to preserve American honor as the negotiations proceeded. Other factors were more significant to the process. Jay Sexton, *Debtor Diplomacy: Finance and American Foreign Relations in the Civil War Era, 1837–1873* (Oxford: Clarendon, 2005), rightly emphasizes the role financial concerns played, which is particularly appropriate since the Tyler administration wanted the British banking house of Baring Brothers (Lord Ashburton was the retired head of the firm) to underwrite a loan to the federal government. Don E. Fehrenbacher, *The Slaveholding Republic: An Account of the United States Government's Relations to Slavery,* completed and edited by Ward M. McAfee (New York: Oxford University Press, 2001), explains how Tyler's foreign policy augmented slavery.

President Tyler's aggression in foreign policy—aided and abetted by Secretary of State Daniel Webster—is the subject of Frederick Merk, with the collaboration of Lois Bannister Merk, *Fruits of Propaganda in the Tyler Administration* (Cambridge, MA: Harvard University Press, 1971). The Merks demonstrate that the Tyler administration undertook a propaganda campaign in Maine to win support for its efforts to reach a settlement on the boundary issue. Tyler paid individuals carrying out this campaign from the president's "secret service fund" that Congress had appropriated for use in diplomacy. Congressional critics at the time, and some historians, sharply criticized him for using the fund in this way. Stephen F. Knott, *Secret and Sanctioned: Covert Operations and the American Presidency* (New York: Oxford University Press, 1996), is especially harsh in his denunciation.

There is scholarly consensus on the significance of the Tyler Doctrine, which asserted America's interest in preserving Hawaii's independence and warned world powers that the United States would not tolerate colonization efforts in the islands. Similarly, Tyler receives credit for articulating the first US policy toward China in the nation's history and for sending Caleb Cushing to negotiate the Treaty of Wangxia, which ensured an expanded American access to Chinese ports. Crapol's *John Tyler: The Accidental President* (mentioned above) deals at length with these two foreign-policy accomplishments. For an excellent account of Cushing's life, which is particularly strong in explaining the China mission as well as his support for President Tyler, see John M. Belohlavek, *Broken Glass: Caleb Cushing and the Shattering of the Union* (Kent, OH: Kent State University Press, 2005).

The aspect of Tyler's presidency that has received the most attention from historians is the annexation of Texas. It is appropriate to view Tyler's pursuit of Texas as part of his foreign policy. Yet it also became a controversial domestic political issue once his effort to secure annexation became public. The scholarly literature on the topic is extensive. A good overview of the annexation process, and one that is sound on its domestic political implications, is Joel H. Silbey, *Storm over Texas: The Annexation Controversy and the Road to Civil War* (New York: Oxford University Press, 2005). Freehling, in *Road to Disunion*, vol. 1, *Secessionists at Bay* (detailed above), provides a lively account and is especially strong on the individual actors who played roles in the process. Duff Green, Abel Upshur, and some figures who have been largely lost to history animate his chapters on Texas. Freehling is at his interpretive best when he emphasizes the contingent nature of the events leading to annexation. In *The South and the Politics of Slavery, 1828–1856* (Baton Rouge: LSU Press, 1978), William J. Cooper Jr. places Texas into its larger context of sectional politics, arguing that the issue once and for all (in the antebellum period) relegated economic matters to at best a secondary importance. Moreover, he rightly emphasizes that President Tyler himself was actively engaged in the process of bringing Texas into the Union. Frederick Merk, *Slavery and the Annexation of Texas* (New York: Alfred A. Knopf, 1972), still holds value, though largely because the book reprints several important documents that shed light on annexation.

The documents in Anson Jones, *Memoranda and Official Correspondence Relating to the Republic of Texas, Its History, and Annexation* (New York: D. Appleton, 1859), which have sometimes been overlooked by historians, are essential to understanding the perspective of Texans on the annexation process. William R. Manning, ed., *Diplomatic Correspondence of the United States: Inter-American Affairs, 1831–1860*, 12 vols. (Washington: Carnegie Endowment for International Peace, 1939), contains crucial documents.

Several scholars have highlighted the connection between British antislavery efforts and Texas annexation. Stephen Heath Mitton, "The Free World Confronted: The Problem of Slavery and Progress in American Foreign Relations, 1833–1844" (Ph.D. diss., Louisiana State University, 2005), examines the transition the British made from slave labor to free in the Caribbean—what they called the "Great Experiment"—and analyzes the implications for President Tyler's pursuit of Texas. In Mitton's view the push for annexation was a reaction to fears that the British sought to emancipate Texas slaves. Mitton's work complements that of Seymour Drescher, *The Mighty Experiment: Free Labor versus Slavery in British Emancipation* (New York: Oxford University Press, 2002). See also Edward Bartlett Rugemer, *The Problem of Emancipation: The Caribbean Roots of the American Civil War* (Baton Rouge: LSU Press, 2008). More recently, Matthew Karp, *This Vast Southern Empire: Slaveholders at the Helm of American Foreign Policy* (Cambridge, MA: Harvard University Press, 2016), argues that southern slaveholders pursued an aggressive foreign policy—including the annexation of Texas—not because they feared losing the battle against the champions of worldwide emancipation, but because they were confident that they could keep slavery firmly entrenched in the Western Hemisphere.

At the same time John Tyler was pursuing the annexation of Texas, he also married his second wife, Julia Gardiner. The fullest account of their courtship and marriage, including Julia's stint as First Lady, is found in Seager's *And Tyler Too* (mentioned above). When the couple retired to Sherwood Forest plantation in Charles City County, Virginia, in March 1845, John Tyler took on the responsibilities of his wheat farm full time. That also meant he became a fulltime slaveholder. My analysis of his years at Sherwood Forest has been informed by the literature on slavery in the antebellum South. In particular, I have relied on Peter Kolchin, *American Slavery, 1619–1877* (New York: Hill and Wang, 1993), which offers a trenchant discussion of paternalism. The classic work on paternalism is Eugene Genovese, *Roll, Jordan, Roll: The World the Slaves Made* (New York: Pantheon, 1974). I also found James Oakes, *The Ruling Race: A History of American Slaveholders* (New York: Alfred A. Knopf, 1982), and Eugene D. Genovese and Elizabeth Fox-Genovese, *Fatal Self-Deception: Slaveholding Paternalism in the Old South* (Cambridge: Cambridge University Press, 2011), helpful in framing my discussion of Tyler as slaveholder. For works that challenge the paternalism "paradigm," see Jeffrey Robert Young, *Domesticating Slavery: The Master Class in Georgia and South Carolina, 1670–1837* (Chapel Hill: University of North Carolina Press, 1999); and David Brion Davis, *Inhuman Bondage: The Rise and Fall of Slavery in the New World* (New York: Oxford University Press, 2006). Lacy K. Ford, *Deliver Us from Evil: The Slavery Question in the Old South* (New York: Oxford University Press, 2009) is a fuller explication of paternalism.

Of course, Tyler did not completely cut himself off from national politics in his retirement years. He watched the growing rift between North and South with increasing alarm during the 1850s and was especially apprehensive over the issue of slavery in the territories. For the territorial issue in American politics after Tyler's presidency, see Michael A. Morrison, *Slavery and the American West: The Eclipse of Manifest Destiny and the Coming of the Civil War* (Chapel Hill: University of North Carolina Press, 1997), chaps. 2–8; and Michael F. Holt, *The Fate of Their Country: Politicians, Slavery Extension, and the Coming of the Civil War* (New York: Hill and Wang, 2004). Tyler believed the Democratic Party represented the best hope for preserving the Union. But the party was not as stable as he perceived it to be, as Yonatan Eyal, *The Young America Movement and the Transformation of the Democratic Party, 1828–1861* (Cambridge: Cambridge University Press, 2007); Wallace Hettle, *The Peculiar Democracy: Southern Democrats in Peace and Civil War* (Athens: University of Georgia Press, 2001); and Michael Todd Landis, *Northern Men with Southern Loyalties: The Democratic Party and the Sectional Crisis* (Ithaca, NY: Cornell University Press, 2014) make clear. Jonathan H. Earle, *Jacksonian Antislavery and the Politics of Free Soil, 1824–1854* (Chapel Hill: University of North Carolina Press, 2004), and Joshua A. Lynn, *Preserving the White Man's Republic: Jacksonian Democracy, Race, and the Transformation of American Conservatism* (Charlottesville: University of Virginia Press, 2019), assess the changing nature of the Democratic Party after Tyler left the presidency. Elizabeth R. Varon's *Disunion! The Coming of the American Civil War, 1789–1859* (Chapel Hill: University of North Carolina Press, 2008) is a compelling and persuasive look at the way Americans—northerners as well as southerners—employed the word and concept of "disunion" during the antebellum period. The work blends political and cultural history to explain the coming of the Civil War, providing an overview of the world in which Tyler found himself (and that he helped create) during his retirement years.

In an effort to stave off civil war, Tyler returned to politics once again. Robert Gray Gunderson, *Old Gentlemen's Convention: The Washington Peace Conference of 1861* (Madison: University of Wisconsin Press, 1961), is a dated look at the ill-fated peace conference Tyler led during the secession winter. William J. Cooper, *We Have the War upon Us: The Onset of the Civil War, November 1860–April 1861* (New York: Alfred A. Knopf, 2012), is more thorough and offers much better analysis. On secession, Henry T. Shanks, *The Secession Movement in Virginia, 1847–1861* (Richmond: Garret and Massie, 1934), retains some of its explanatory value. A modern interpretation of Virginia's decision to cast its lot with the Confederacy, one that emphasizes the role enslaved Virginians played in the political dynamic that resulted in secession, is William A. Link, *Roots of Secession: Slavery and Politics in Antebellum Virginia* (Chapel Hill: University of North Carolina Press, 2003). In his epilogue Link details the consequences of secession on Virginia's fortunes. The consequences for John Tyler were just as profound as they were for his beloved Old Dominion.

Index